ADOGANguides

PARIS

DANA FACAROS & MICHAEL PAULS

About the authors

Dana Facaros and **Michael Pauls** have written over 40 books for Cadogan Guides, including several in the France series. They have lived all over Europe but have recently moved to a farmhouse surrounded by vineyards in the Lot valley.

About the updater

Lily Delancey Pauls moved to France aged six and is currently studying for a degree in marine biology in Swansea, Wales. A seasoned traveller, Lily has also updated the Cadogan Guide to Crete.

Cadogan Guides
Highlands House, 165 The Broadway, London SW19 1NE
info@cadoganguides.co.uk
www.cadoganguides.com

The Globe Pequot Press
246 Goose Lane, PO Box 480, Guilford,
Connecticut 06437–0480

Copyright © Dana Facaros and Michael Pauls 1999, 2002, 2004
Updated by Lily Delancey Pauls 2004

Series design: Andrew Barker
Series cover design: Sheridan Wall
Art Director: Sarah Rianhard-Gardner
Photography: OLIVIA, © Olivia Rutherford
Maps created by the XYZ Digital Map Company and customized by Map Creation Ltd
Additional mapping: Angie Watts

Series Editor: Christine Stroyan
Editor: James Alexander
Proofreading: Rosalind Neely
Indexing: Isobel McLean
Production: Navigator Guides Ltd
Printed in Italy by Legoprint
A catalogue record for this book is available from the British Library
ISBN 1-86011-117-3

Contents

Introduction

Paris has always been a special case – culture-mad, precocious and exasperating, a shining light and a showcase to the rest of the world. Into the City of Light are squeezed the brains, government, finances and most of the art and treasures of a wealthy and talented nation for all to see. French *savoir faire* has made Paris a by-word for elegance and style, for the finest in food, fashion, perfume and luxury goods. The Paris basin – the Île de France – is the top economic region in Europe and has a sixth of the country's population. The rest of France is merely *province*.

Never destroyed by enemies or by an act of God, Paris has been perpetually devouring and re-creating itself for hundreds of years in its restless metamorphosis. This comes in spurts; the current one has been going since the late 1960s and can only be compared to Baron Haussmann's boulevard-building a century before. Paris still has its perfect setting on the Seine, its splendid landmarks, stately prospects and all the familiar things that make it Paris – the boulevards, elegant squares and gardens, cosy cafés and bars, markets, Art Nouveau métro entrances, Wallace fountains and poster-coated Morriss columns. Successive presidents have given all that a good polishing, and added pricey *grands projets* across the city in a bid to make it the 'culture pole of the 21st century'. The result is a new, improved Paris, with more to offer and entertain its 12 million annual visitors than ever before. Even the plonk in the cafés is better.

Side by side with all these gains, however, is a tangible nostalgia for the gritty, earthy, spirited Paris of the past, and a sense that the technocrats may finally have gone too far. On so many occasions in the past, the Parisians have imposed their will on the nation, and now that the national government has turned the tables on them they feel a keen lack. But even as you read this, things could be changing. 'Paris is bored,' they'd murmur in the 19th century, always right before a revolution in art or politics, or both.

The Neighbourhoods

The Grand Axe

Opéra and Palais Roya

Musée d'Orsay and the Invalides

Eiffel Tower and Trocadéro

St-Germain

Montparnasse

Montmartre
nd the North

8 Sacré-Cœur and
Montmartre, p.192

In this guide, the city is divided into
the 12 neighbourhoods outlined on
the map below, each with its own
sightseeing chapter. This map also
shows our suggestions for the Top
Ten activities and places to visit in
Paris. The following colour pages
introduce the neighbourhoods in
more detail, explaining the distinctive character and highlights
of each.

Beaubourg
and Les Halles

6 Pompidou
Centre, p.162

The Islands

Marais and
Bastille

The Latin
Quarter

Jardin des Plantes

1 Louvre, p.98

2 Notre-Dame,
3 Sainte-Chapelle, p.82
p.90

The Islands

Paris was born in the Seine, on the ship-shaped Île de la Cité, which to this day harbours key institutions of Church and State. Where the first temple of Jupiter stood, the cathedral of Notre-Dame soars gracefully over the rooftops; where Clovis and the kings of France had their first palace you'll find the Palais de Justice, the infamous Conciergerie and the incomparable jewel box of Sainte-Chapelle. Delightful shady squares, intimate restaurants and a flower market offer relief from the monumentality, while Île St-Louis, swimming just behind the Cité, is all Grand Siècle swish.

Clockwise from top: Marché aux Fleurs, Sainte-Chapelle, Notre-Dame, Pont Neuf, early-morning café.

The Islands
The Islands chapter p.79
Hotels p.300 Restaurants p.316 Bars p.342

The Grand Axe

For 450 years, kings, emperors and presidents have been studiously perfecting the city's most glittering prospect, from the crystal Pyramid through the chestnut alleys of the Tuileries, across the magnificent Place de la Concorde and up the fabled Champs-Elysées to the Arc de Triomphe, with monuments strung along it like diamonds on a necklace. The Grand Axe is Paris at its most elegant, the scene of France's great moments, from the Liberation parade to the annual finale of the Tour de France. And at its eastern end waits the Louvre, the greatest treasure trove of all.

Clockwise from top left: Petit Palais, Arc de Triomphe, Louvre Pyramid, café on the Champs-Elysées, Place de la Concorde.

The Grand Axe
The Grand Axe chapter p.95
Hotels p.300 Restaurants p.317 Bars p.344

From top: Musée d'Orsay façade, Hôtel des Invalides, garden of Musée Rodin.

Musée d'Orsay and the Invalides

Over on the Left Bank, this is the quarter of Paris that runs France, where the Assemblée Nationale and ministry buildings stand shoulder to shoulder. The Musée d'Orsay, a former train station, holds a dazzling collection of 19th-century art, its top floor filled with the glowing colours of the Impressionists and postimpressionists. To the west, the grand Esplanade culminates in the Invalides, the sprawling, golden-domed home built by Louis XIV for his disabled veterans. Napoleon's tomb and a military museum lie within, but if time is short you may prefer the far more intimate Musée Rodin, arranged in the sculptor's home and garden. By the river you can also explore the city's smelliest attraction – its sewers.

Musée d'Orsay and the Invalides
Musée d'Orsay and the Invalides chapter p.119
Hotels p.304 Restaurants p.319 Bars p.342

Clockwise from top left: Palais de Chaillot, Eiffel Tower, view over the Champ de Mars to Ecole Militaire and Tour Montparnasse, view from Eiffel Tower.

Eiffel Tower and Trocadéro

Paris was a World Fair addict, putting on nine exhibitions in 80 years before the fad died out in 1937. One of these gave the city its symbol, the ineffable Eiffel Tower, which casts its lanky shadow across the old fairgrounds of the Champ de Mars and Jardins du Trocadéro, and the former fair pavilions, which now house an array of museums. In this neighbourhood you'll find one of the world's top collections of Asian art, in the atmospheric Musée Guimet.

Opéra and Palais Royal

Paris keeps some magnificent set pieces in this high-rent district: Garnier's over-the-top Opéra, the elegant Place Vendôme, the Greek temple of the Madeleine, the 17th-century Palais Royal, and the reading room of the old Bibliothèque Nationale. But the main emphasis here is on shopping – truly grand department stores, famous couturiers in Faubourg St-Honoré, quaint old shops in the 19th-century arcades and the most regal food shops on this planet. And when you're ready to drop, collapse in a smart café along the boulevards and indulge in Paris' favourite pastime – watching the world go by.

Clockwise from top: La Madeleine, Opéra, arcades in the Palais Royal, caviar for sale.

Beaubourg and Les Halles

This jumping, seedy-shiny neighbourhood was the city's business centre for centuries, the part of its urban anatomy known as the 'Belly of Paris', at least until the wholesale market of Les Halles was relocated in 1969. At the same time, a surprising new focus for the district seemingly landed from Mars, with the arrival of the inside-out Pompidou Centre, the first of the *grands projets* that have transformed the face of Paris. A great collection of 20th-century art, a public library, cinemas and more make it as popular as the Eiffel Tower. The rest of the neighbourhood is still predominantly commercial; Le Sentier, just north, is Paris' bustling garment district.

Clockwise from top: Forum des Halles, *bouquiniste* stall, Sentier district, Pompidou Centre.

Expositions

Clockwise from top left: Old shop sign, Colonne de Juillet, the Bastille at night.

Marais and Bastille

Made fashionable after the building of Henri IV's delightful Place des Vosges, the Marais for centuries saw the nobility rivalling one another to build the most exquisite *hôtels particuliers*. After decades of decline, the district has been beautifully restored. A few of the mansions are museums (on Picasso, Paris, hunting and locks, for example), allowing a look into their splendid interiors. The Marais also has the city's Jewish neighbourhood, with the best delis in Paris, while its trendy bars have become the headquarters of Gay Paree.

To the east, where the Bastille once stood, sopranos warble arias in Mitterand's controversial Opéra; this has sprouted a fashionably arty district along Rue du Faubourg-St-Antoine, which bustles with workshops, galleries and cafés.

Montmartre and the North

The Naughty Nineties birthed much of Paris' mystique, and its cradle was up in Montmartre, impossible to miss under the white cream cake of Sacré-Cœur. An independent village until 1860, Montmartre's picturesque streets may already be familiar thanks to the scores of artists who worked and starved here when rents were low; some, like Picasso, went on to change art history.

There's no better place to watch the sun go down, while Pigalle, at the foot of the hill, remains the heart of Paris clubland, where fashionable night spots buzz next to old favourites like the Moulin Rouge and Elysée Montmartre.

Clockwise from above: Local bakery, Algerian restaurant, Sacré-Cœur, Montmartre nightlife.

St-Germain

In the heart of the Left Bank, once-independent St-Germain has been the citadel of the intelligentsia and the arty since the Middle Ages, and in the 18th century it naturally became the seat of the academies of language and art. Now increasingly chic, with designer boutiques opening around the bookshops, art galleries and cafés once favoured by Voltaire, Danton and Sartre, St-Germain has yet to lose its old cosiness. Just south is the city's best-loved park, the Jardin du Luxembourg, laid out for a Medici queen.

Anticlockwise from top: St-Germain by night, restaurant in St-Germain, boutique window display, *pâtisserie*, street sign.

St-Germain

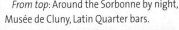

From top: Around the Sorbonne by night, Musée de Cluny, Latin Quarter bars.

The Latin Quarter

Since the 11th century, millions of students have studied and quarrelled and drunk their way through the medieval streets of the Latin Quarter. Although the University of Paris is now spread out across the metropolis, the old core of the Sorbonne is still one of the city's liveliest neighbourhoods, crowded night and day with young people. The exquisite *Lady and the Unicorn* tapestries and hundreds of other medieval treasures wait in the Musée de Cluny, the most popular of several museums in the area. When they die, the best and brightest students remain in the Latin Quarter – interred on the top of the hill with the other 'immortals' in the Panthéon.

Jardin des Plantes

This informal, slightly gritty neighbourhood grew up just east of the
Latin Quarter, outside the medieval
city walls. Piquant Rue Mouffetard,
with its colourful local market and
spillover of student hangouts, offers
a tasty slice of old Paris. A 17th-
century botanical garden grew into
the verdant Jardin des Plantes, a park
with a small zoo and natural science
museums, including the sleek new
Grande Galerie de l'Evolution. Two
important monuments for Paris'
large Muslim community are here as
well: the Grande Mosquée and the
Institut du Monde Arabe, the most
elegant of the city's new buildings.

From top: Scenes in the Jardin des Plantes,
the Grande Mosquée.

Montparnasse

Montparnasse, the highest point of
the Left Bank, became fashionable
between the wars, when its low rents
and abundant studio space stole the
young artists and writers from
Montmartre, who were joined by
Eastern European émigrés and a
noisy band of 'Lost Generation'
Americans escaping Prohibition.
Many of their favourite watering
holes are still in business, thanks to
the media and advertising types who
now live here. The sights are a mixed
bag: a Grand Siècle observatory, the
Tour Montparnasse (the city's tallest
skyscraper), a surviving royal abbey,
museums dedicated to the post
office and sculptors and, under Place
Denfert-Rochereau, the Catacombs.

Jardin des Plantes
Jardin des Plantes chapter p.231
Hotels p.311 Restaurants p.335 Bars p.343
Montparnasse
Montparnasse chapter p.241
Hotels p.311 Restaurants p.336 Bars p.346

Days Out in Paris

Couples' City p.16

Parisian's City p.18

Paris des Artistes p.22

Madame LAMBOUKAS
dite EDITH PIAF
1915 – 1963

Peace and Quiet p.20

Grand Siècle Paris p.24

Gritty City p.26

COUPLES' CITY

'We'll always have Paris,' as Humphrey Bogart told Ingrid Bergman in *Casablanca*, Hollywood's confirmation of Paris' age-old reputation as the City of Lovers. Strolling along the quays of the Seine, lingering in the leafy squares and parks, sharing an intimate table in a sidewalk café, and dinner in a candle-lit restaurant after watching the sun set over the city: these are classic romantic idylls real-life couples will always have as long as there is a Paris.

One

Start: Métro Invalides.
Breakfast: A pastry at the intimate **Pâtisserie Jean Millet**.
Morning: **Musée Rodin**, to see *The Kiss* and other works by the sculptor in the beautiful setting of his house and garden (*photo above*).
Lunch: Cross over to the Right Bank and walk through the Tuileries for lunch in the chic **Café Marly**, in the Louvre's courtyard.
Afternoon: Discover an unexpected intimate side to Paris in our **walking tour** of the *passages* (*photo top*).
Dinner: **Drouant**, in a sumptuous Art Deco setting.
Evening: A night of music in the 19th-century surroundings of the **Opéra Comique**.

Two

Start: Métro Cité.

Breakfast: A cup of tea overlooking
    Notre-Dame at **Le Flore en l'Ile**.

Morning: Visit the monsters on the
    roof of **Notre-Dame** and the
    glorious stained glass of the
    Sainte-Chapelle (*photo below*).

Lunch: **Caveau du Palais**, in romantic
    Place Dauphine.

Afternoon: Lounge around **Square du
    Vert-Galant**, then take a walk along
    the quays and bridges around the
    islands. In late afternoon take the
    métro to Anvers and the funicular
    up to **Sacré-Cœur** for the sunset.

Dinner: A sumptuous (and extravagant) meal in the lavish surround-
    ings of **A Beauvilliers**.

Evening: Walk off some of your meal
    on our **Montmartre by Night**
    walking tour (*photo below*).

PARISIAN'S CITY

Although many Parisians put a premium on the parts of their city as yet untouched by the planners and gentrifiers, as fashion victims *par excellence* they still swarm to the latest trendy bar, restaurant or club, only to leave it high and dry when a newer venue surfaces. On Friday and Saturday nights friends get together for dinner and a night out, and on Sunday mornings everyone heads for the street markets to buy the ingredients for a big Sunday lunch with the family, followed by a post-prandial stroll in the nearest park.

Three

Start: Métro St-Paul.
Breakfast: **Jo Goldenberg**, the city's best deli.
Morning: Visit Paris' attic, the **Musée Carnavalet**, with everything from Proust's bedchamber to the keys to the Bastille, then wander over to the **Place des Vosges**, the city's favourite square (*photo on p.19*).

Lunch: At the old-fashioned bistrot **Le Temps des Cerises**.
Afternoon: Get to know Paris from a different angle, on a **city bike tour**.
Dinner: **Chez Paul**, for a slice of old Paris.
Evening: Unpack your designer gear ready for **Les Bains**, where you can pose and dance the night away – if you get past the bouncers.

Four

Start: Métro Place Monge.

Breakfast: If you're not quite awake yet you can sink into a comfy chair at **Café Delmas**.

Morning: Shop for food or just take in the colours and smells at the **Rue Mouffetard market**, then take the métro a couple of stops for a cup of mint tea at the **Institut du Monde Arabe**, Paris' favourite new building.

Lunch: Cross the Pont de Sully over the tip of Ile St-Louis and walk up to **La Galoche d'Aurillac**, an authentic Auvergant bistrot.

Afternoon: Stroll along the Promenade Plantée and check out the craft shops below in the **Viaduc des Arts**.

Dinner: It's worth making the trip out to the lovely **Pavillon Montsouris**, far from tourist Paris.

Evening: See some cutting-edge theatre or modern dance at the nearby **Théâtre de la Cité Internationale**.

Madame LAMBOUKAS
dite EDITH PIAF
1915 - 1963

PEACE AND QUIET

In spite of being more densely populated than Manhattan, Paris has its share of places where you can enjoy the double advantage of being in Paris and hearing yourself think. Besides the larger parks and gardens, the search for peace and quiet may lead to a score of unusual little museums, dedicated to locks, counterfeiting, spectacles, magic tricks and so on, where the odds are fairly good that you'll have the place all to yourself.

Five

Start: Métro Jussieu.
Breakfast: A refreshing glass of mint tea in the café of the **Grande Mosquée** (*photo above*).
Morning: Look around the mosque, then take a stroll around the flower gardens and greenhouse in the **Jardin des Plantes** (*photo above*).
Lunch: **La Tour d'Argent**, dating from 1582 and with peaceful views of Notre-Dame.
Afternoon: Visit Jim Morrison, Oscar Wilde and Edith Piaf on our walking tour of **Père-Lachaise cemetery** (*photo top*).
Dinner: A bowl of *moules* at laid-back **Café Divan**.
Evening: Have a few drinks while browsing through the books at **La Belle Horthense**.

Six

Start: Métro Jean-Jaurès.

Breakfast: Pick up a croissant in La Villette to munch on the boat.

Morning: Admire the Géode (*photo above*) in **Parc de la Villette**, then cruise down the **Canal St-Martin** to Port de l'Arsenal, passing through old locks and under footbridges.

Lunch: From Quai de la Rapée, walk to Gare de Lyon and pick up the métro to Palais Royal for lunch at **Palais Royal**, in the former palace gardens.

Afternoon: Visit the reading room of the old **Bibliothèque Nationale** and the treasure of the kings of France in the **Cabinet des Médailles et Antiques**.

Dinner: **Le Domaine de Lintillac**, where each table has a toaster for making fresh toast to go with your foie gras.

Evening: Catch a vintage silent film at the **Cinémathèque**.

PARIS DES ARTISTES

Modern art was invented in Paris. For a hundred years, up until the last world war, manifestos flew and ism chased ism in rapid succession as artists flocked here from all over, drawn by the seething cultural ferment. Paris may no longer be the art capital of the planet, but it still has more than its share of galleries (Bastille, the Marais and Beaubourg are places to go in search of the next Picasso), while a host of museums enshrine the realists, Impressionists, postimpressionists, Symbolists, Fauvists, Cubists, Surrealists, and so on.

Seven

Start: RER Musée d'Orsay.

Morning: Take a crash course in Impressionism at the **Musée d'Orsay**, the city's fabulous shrine to 19th-century art, housed in the romantic setting of a former train station. Manet, Monet, Renoir, Degas, Van Gogh, Cézanne...the most famous names are all here, along with works from other schools of painting and sculpture, furniture, decorative arts and photography (*photo top left*).

Lunch: You'll probably be too tired and hungry to walk far after all that art – the **museum restaurant** makes an ideal place to reflect on what you've seen.

Afternoon: Do the Trail of the Artists in **Montmartre**, favoured quarter of the Impressionists and Cubists among others, and still a haunt of artists, these days mostly of the pavement variety. If you have room to take in a few more paintings, there's the **Espace Montmartre Salvador Dalí** or the **Musée d'Art Naïf Max Fourny**.

Dinner: **Chez Claude et Claudine**, a cosy Montmartre classic serving up onion soup.

Evening: Champagne and cancan dancers at the **Moulin Rouge**.

Eight

Start: Métro Bastille or Chemin-Vert.
Breakfast: **Ma Bourgogne**, in the beautiful Place des Vosges.
Morning: Immerse yourself in the work of one of the city's most famous artistic residents at the **Musée Picasso**, with representative works from each of his 'periods'.
Lunch: Soak in the atmosphere at **Le Loir dans la Théière**.
Afternoon: Bring your knowledge of modern art right up to date at the **Musée National d'Art Moderne**, in the Pompidou Centre (*photo right*), which takes up where the Musée d'Orsay left off.

Dinner: Head down to another arty quarter of Paris and dine in the bohemian atmosphere of **Aux Artistes**, in Montparnasse.
Evening: Jazz at **Le Petit Journal Montparnasse**.

GRAND SIÈCLE PARIS

The 17th-century reigns of Louis XIII and Louis XIV have gone down in history as the Grand Siècle, when France stood centre-stage in Europe. Although the Sun King himself vamoosed to Versailles, he and his contemporaries lavished money and elegant buildings on Paris, in a unique French synthesis of High Renaissance and Baroque, leaving Paris entire neighbourhoods of lavish *hôtels particuliers* in the Marais and Ile St-Louis, as well as a slew of grand monuments and prospects that set the scale for the city of today.

Nine

Start: Métro Palais Royal-Musée du Louvre.

Breakfast: Take your pick from a wide range of breads and pastries at **Paul**, in the Galerie de Carrousel du Louvre.

Morning: A visit to the **Louvre**, the building itself (as well as much of the contents) a perfect introduction to the Grand Siècle. Seek out the Sun King's crown jewels.

Lunch: Chic **Café Marly** in the Palais du Louvre, where you can get everything from burgers to caviar.

Afternoon: Walk through the **Jardin des Tuileries**, given their form during the Grand Siècle under Louis XIV, then head up to the elegant and opulent **Place Vendôme**, another of Louis XIV's creations.

Dinner: Dine in very Grand surroundings at **Le Grand Véfour**, within the grounds of the Palais Royal.

Evening: Take in a play by the **Comédie Française**, the heir to Molière's company, in the theatre of the Palais Royal.

Ten

Start: Métro St-Paul.

Breakfast: A late breakfast at **Le Loir dans la Théière**.

Morning: A wander around the **Marais**, with its numerous *hôtels particuliers* dating from the Grand Siècle, as well as the beautiful **Place des Vosges**, the former Place Royale.

Lunch: Splash out on a meal in the Place des Vosges at **L'Ambroisie**, grand cuisine in an elegant setting.

Afternoon: Cross the Seine to the **Hôtel des Invalides**, the Sun King's grandest Paris project, for an inside look at the military *gloire* that was so essential to the age.

Dinner: **Pierre à la Fontaine Gaillon**, in a *hôtel particulier*.

Evening: A ballet at the irrepressible **Opéra de Paris-Palais Garnier**; it's not Grand Siècle, but Louis would have loved it (*photo top*).

Food and Drinks

Sights and Activities

Nightlife

GRITTY CITY

Paris likes to see itself as the shop window of France, but behind the glamour and glitz and postcard views you can still find traces of the pre-sanitized capital, of old industries and dirty linen, that have managed to escape exile into the great grey *banlieux*, the suburbs that encompass the city. In some cases, Paris itself has made an attraction of things like sewers and skeletons that other cities keep in closets.

Eleven

Start: Métro Réaumur-Sébastopol.
Morning: A wander around the **Sentier**, Paris' Garment District, with visits to the **Passage Brady**, **Rue St-Denis**, the **Passage du Caire**, and the **Rue Montorgueil market**.
Lunch: Bustling **Tonneaux des Halles**, with its market atmosphere.
Afternoon: The **Catacombs** to look at the bones of Mirabeau, Rabelais and Madame de Pompadour, then walk over to see the relics of **Rue de la Gaîté**, and the church of

Notre-Dame de Travail – 'Our Lady of Work'.
Dinner: **Le Temps des Cerises** – don't confuse this workers' co-op with Les Temps in the Bastille.
Evening: Have a drink with the students and locals at **La Folie en Tête**.

Twelve

Start: Métro St-Denis-Basilique.
Morning: In working-class **St-Denis** visit the **abbey**, which was the first Gothic church, and royal tombs, smashed in the Revolution, then find out about the 1871 Comune in the **Musée de l'Art et de l'Histoire de la Ville de St-Denis**.
Lunch: **La Table Ronde**, serving hearty *choucroute*, *cassoulet* and the like.
Afternoon: Pick up a bargain, or maybe an antique, at **Les Puces de St-Ouen**, Paris' biggest and most famous flea market.
Dinner: **Chartier**, one of the last old-style *bouillons*.
Evening: Head up the road to **La Tartuffe**, with three one-man shows (nothing to do with Molière) a night.

Roots of the City

52 BC–AD 987: Early History

The natural crossroads of northern France, Paris has been occupied since the earliest times. The first inhabitants to leave their name were the Celtic Parisii, a fierce and warlike tribe who eventually settled down as boatmen on what is now the Île de la Cité, making a good living fishing and managing the river trade on the Seine.

Caesar, who came, saw and conquered in 52 BC, mentions the capital of the Parisii in his *Gallic Wars*, but most likely it was nothing more than a simple jumble of wattle-and-daub huts. The Romans made a proper town of it, called Lutetia, from a Celtic word that meant something like 'mudville'. Its modest forum, a low quadrangle containing a basilica and a temple, stood along Rue Soufflot, near the Panthéon.

After the barbarian invasions of the 5th century, Lutetia landed on its feet, becoming the capital of Clovis' new Frankish Kingdom c. AD 510. Under the rest of the Merovingian kings (named after Clovis' grandfather, the formidable chieftain Merovaeus) from 511 to 741, Paris kept its status; the Abbey of St-Denis was the dynasty's treasure house, and its place of burial. Their successors, the Carolingians, especially Charlemagne (768–814), preferred staying further east, and Paris became something of a backwater, ruled by a count.

The Vikings first raided Paris in 845; they came back again in force in 856 and 861. In 885 they found the city somewhat better defended, but rather than accept such an affront they put the town under siege. Count Eudes, depending entirely on the city's own resources, held them off – the first time anyone had ever managed to do so. Eudes' heirs, the counts of Paris (later dukes), would for the next century be the most powerful lords of France. One of them, Hugues Capet, finally became its king in 987; his house reigned uninterrupted for the next 805 years.

52 BC–AD 987

Abbey Basilica of St-Denis, for royal tombs from Clovis onwards, p.262
Crypte Archéologique du Parvis-Notre-Dame, for a Lutetian wall and other Roman traces, p.86
Musée de Cluny, for the remains of the Roman baths, p.218

987–1300: The Capital of the Middle Ages

'France', in the 10th century, was hardly even a geographical expression. Such a thing as the 'French nation' was not even dreamed of; over the centuries the kings created one, with Paris at its core. The monarchy brought Paris prestige and the trappings of power, but the real achievements were the city's own: trade and commerce that made it the metropolis of northern Europe, its university, the intellectual centre of Christendom, and its Gothic architecture, not to mention its schools of painting, sculpture and music that created much of the style of the Middle Ages.

Medieval Paris was divided into three parts: the Cité, home of the palace and cathedral; the university, on the Left Bank; and the busy, mercantile Right Bank. The Latin Quarter began its career in 1127, when nonconformist students expelled from the cathedral school of Notre-Dame settled in the relatively empty Left Bank. The teachings of Peter Abelard and his followers started an intellectual revolution, and the Left Bank filled up with eager scholars from all over Europe.

The Paris of the merchants got its start in the same manner as the old Parisii: shipping on the Seine. The old Company of Boatmen from Roman, or perhaps even pre-Roman, times had amazingly survived through so many centuries, and became the foundation of the city's economy and government. Its boats are the inspiration for the trim ship that sails today across Paris' coat of arms – although some say that the narrow-tipped island itself, the Île de la Cité, is the ship. By the mid-12th century trade had expanded so spectacularly that the new quarter was the most populous part of the city.

The first great royal benefactor of Paris was Louis VII (1137–80). Notre-Dame began to rise in his reign (1163), but the king's real contributions were of a more commercial nature, building the Place de Grève docks and a merchants' exchange near what is now Pont Neuf, and organizing the great fairs at St-Germain (Easter) and St-Lazare (All Souls').

Philippe-Auguste (1180–1223) decreed Paris' first street-paving programme, and built the first market buildings at Les Halles. He gave Paris a new wall, reflecting the considerable expansion of the city in the 12th century, and began the original, fortress-like Louvre to guard its western side. His reign, which saw a considerable tightening of royal control over all aspects of life in France, was naturally a great boon to Paris.

In the 13th century the momentum of growth continued. Paris' explosive economic expansion outstripped every other European city outside Italy. The city manufactured everything from luxury goods to armour, and it developed the first retail shops anywhere (interestingly, this trade began with books and art objects in the Latin Quarter). Organizing around itself the other cities and rich agricultural lands of the Île-de-France, Paris created a giant, integrated economic unit, and supplied the economic power for its kings to spread their rule across what is now France.

An advanced economy naturally brought with it some advanced problems. The hordes of provincial country folk pouring into Paris to find a better life made the city an overcrowded inferno. Public health and sanitation were in a wretched state. Beyond that, the exploited workers were organizing. Their proto-union, the *alliance*, was just taking shape when the felt-makers walked out for Paris' first strike in 1250. In 1270 everyone went out – perhaps the first general strike; they did it again in 1277.

By all accounts these struggles were never as bloody as they might have been, perhaps owing to the influence of St Louis (Louis IX,

> **987–1300**
> **The Latin Quarter**, for the most medieval corner of Paris, p.220
> **Notre-Dame and the Sainte-Chapelle**, the ultimate Gothic churches, pp.82 and 90
> **The remains of Philippe-Auguste's wall**, in the Marais, p.184

1226–70). This pious king, whose obsession with crusading greatly detracted from the good he could do his own kingdom, allowed Paris to set up its first free municipal government, under the direction of the guilds. And in the short time he did spend in Paris he made himself extremely popular, dispensing justice from under an oak in his palace garden on the island, or opening the palace and Sainte-Chapelle (his major architectural contribution) to the people for holidays and festivals.

1300–1450: A Century of Disasters

Paris began the terrible 14th century as by far the largest city in northern Europe, on a par with Venice and Milan; estimates of its population range from 80,000 to 200,000. It was a businessman's town, and its bourgeois élite had pretty much its own way – though labour troubles continued, with a strike in 1306 that turned into a full-scale rebellion. On the whole, business was bad. Things got worse with the onset of the Hundred Years' War, and the English invasion in 1338, followed by the Black Plague (1348), which hit overcrowded Paris especially hard, carrying off over a third of the population.

The Estates General, the assembly of the estates of France, looking across the channel to England, now began to demand a measure of real parliamentary control over royal policy and finances. Led by the Paris merchants' provost, Étienne Marcel, they refused any new taxes; Marcel seized control of the city and briefly held captive the dauphin (the future Charles V), while his father was captive in London, forcing him to sign a charter that would have set France

1450–1642: From Ruins to Renaissance

Recovery was a long, slow affair. The ethos of the medieval city was dead and cold, and not until the 17th century would a new Paris take form to replace it. It might never have recovered at all without government assistance. Kings issued decrees to repopulate the capital, offering cash grants at first, then offering freedom to killers and thieves if they would only consent to live there.

By the late 15th century, France was back on its feet and making trouble for its neighbours. Charles VIII (1483–98), Louis XII (1498–1515) and François I (1515–47) all spent most of their time fighting across the Alps. But instead of the French conquering Italy, the Renaissance Italians conquered France – with their art, music, poetry, clothes and cuisine. François and his son Henri II supported the showiest courts France had yet seen, in the royal palaces of the Marais and suburban digs such as Fontainebleau.

The momentum of the Renaissance was continued by Catherine de' Medici, who along with her entourage brought so much to France from her native Florence. A sucker for any occultist crank who came to court, she practised voodoo and black magic, and had a way with poisons; yet she often showed real skill in managing dangerous situations after the death of Henri II.

France's new plague was the Wars of Religion (1562–98), four decades of sporadic, nationwide civil war between Catholics and Protestants. Throughout the troubles, Paris stayed under the control of the Crown and the Catholics. In 1572 a truce was agreed, and many of the principal Protestant leaders

along the road to parliamentary monarchy. In July 1358, however, Marcel was killed in a riot; the exiled dauphin re-entered Paris in triumph and revoked the charter – the turning point in French history that wasn't meant to be.

As king, Charles V (1364–80) ruled with caution and skill, regaining lost lands and reviving the shattered nation. In Paris, he rebuilt the Louvre, gave the Right Bank a new wall (the route of today's Grands Boulevards) and moved his court to the Marais, making it the new fashionable quarter.

In the 1380s, under mad Charles VI, chroniclers noted a surreal atmosphere, like a permanent deranged carnival. The entire decade was a painful succession of popular revolts and riots. Paris and France unravelled completely in the 1390s, as the king's brothers fought continuous little wars, scheming to succeed Charles while the English ravaged the countryside. It got worse. From 1390 to 1420, Paris lived under an almost continual state of siege. Between the factions Paris changed hands seven times in that period, each change accompanied by new massacres and atrocities.

By 1420, when the English finally marched in, Paris' misery was complete. One third of the city's buildings were abandoned or completely wrecked, and possibly as many as three-quarters of its population had died or fled. Neither the well-meaning government of the Duke of Bedford, Paris' new English boss, nor the return of French rule (1436) brought improvement. Plagues returned four times between 1430 and 1450; wolves roamed outside the walls and occasionally crept inside by night to carry off a child.

returned to the capital. Here Queen Catherine, fearing a loss of influence, arranged the St Bartholomew's Day Massacre, which took care of the moderate leaders and some 10,000 followers, and guaranteed another 26 years of war. For most of this time Paris was dominated by the Dukes of Guise, ambitious ultra-Catholics who kept the wars going when nearly everyone else wanted them to stop. Henri de Bourbon, King of Navarre and rightful heir to France, who led the Protestant forces, besieged Paris and made it suffer before converting to Catholicism ('Paris is worth a Mass'); he ended the conflict with the 1598 Edict of Nantes, decreeing religious toleration. As Henri IV (1589–1610), he and his minister Sully did a lot for Paris, commencing an impressive building programme that included the Pont Neuf, Place Dauphine and Place des Vosges.

Henri ended his reign tragically, assassinated by a Catholic fanatic in Paris in 1610. His son, Louis XIII, took the throne at the age of 11. Louis' mother, fat and silly Marie de' Medici, controlled the government at first. In 1624 the weak-willed king was finally able to ease mum out of power, with the help of his immensely capable and devoted minister, Cardinal Richelieu, and so began the period that became known, rather misleadingly, as the Grand Siècle, which lasted until the end of the century. Both king and minister died in 1642, leaving France the strongest state in Europe.

1643–1715: An Unspeakable King

Louis XIV (1643–1715) became king at the age of five; the regent was his mother, Anne of Austria, and the minister was Richelieu's protégé, Cardinal Mazarin. Though corrupt to the core, Mazarin did well by France in extremely perilous times, beating back a Spanish invasion and surviving the civil wars of the Fronde (1648). 'Fronde' means a slingshot, a children's toy; this name, which the people of Paris conferred on the affair, captures perfectly its lack of seriousness. In succession, the anachronistic and useless Parlement de Paris, the greedy nobility and the long-oppressed bourgeoisie of Paris tried to take advantage of the child-king's weakness but, though briefly forced to flee Paris, Mazarin and the royal cause had prevailed by 1661.

Young Louis, enjoying total, personal power over France and the French when he reached his majority in 1659, chose as his chief minister Jean-Baptiste Colbert. A relentless overachiever, Colbert assumed total control of the national economy and tried to reform everything. None of the money Colbert made for Louis was able to rest in the king's pocket for long. As Louis grew older, his conceit and ambitions ballooned to incredible proportions, disturbing the peace of Europe with wars of aggression for almost 50 years.

Meanwhile, at home, Louis had put an end to the factionalism of the nobles once and for all. Following the example of Henri IV, he simply lavished money upon them, bribing them to spend all their time at court, where he could hold the chits for their gambling debts. Turning the entire ruling class into complaisant, mincing lapdogs at least ensured unity and civil peace. But surrounded by these noble sycophants – some 10,000 of them – Louis rapidly lost all touch with reality. Perhaps he never really believed himself to be the Sun incarnate, warming and illuminating this poor planet all by himself, but he did act the part, every hour of every day, and seemed to enjoy it. The bottom line for all this is simple: imagine the expenses of this court, and the insane new playpen that Louis built for them all at Versailles and then throw in the costs of the wars – France nearly went bust again.

By the end of Louis' long reign, misery was widespread and terrible famines gripped town and country alike. As if this wasn't enough, Louis also destroyed Henri IV's religious compromise. The Edict of Nantes was revoked in 1685, and torture and prison or exile became the lot of Protestants once more.

Louis' reign was rough on Paris, despite an ambitious building programme that included Place Vendôme and Place des Victoires, the Louvre colonnade, the Invalides and the Grands Boulevards. After the Fronde, the city lost its last vestiges of self-government, while Parisians were hard pressed by high taxes and bad policies. As for the poor, the wars of the Fronde had left Paris with some 40,000 unemployed and homeless. To Louis, this was a matter for the police. The luckier ones escaped to starve on their own; the unfortunates got dragooned into the new workhouses, such as the Salpêtrière, where they could starve while performing slave labour for Colbert's new industries.

1715–89: The Last of the Louies

Another century, another Louis. Louis XV, the Sun King's great-grandson, ascended the throne in 1715, at the age of five. This time the regent was the Duke of Orléans, who allowed Paris a refreshing interlude of decadence after the coma of the 'Great Reign'. When Louis XV began to reign in his own right, his people called him le bien-aimé, 'the well-beloved' Unfortunately, no. XV turned out to be a lethargic fool, who allowed France to be governed by flouncing favourites and court ladies, most notably the famous Madame de Pompadour (who gets a bad press, but was really the best of the lot).

France was stirring. This was the age of the salons and the philosophes : Voltaire, Diderot, Montesquieu and the rest, importing English political thought and common sense to the continent. The ills of France were discussed endlessly: the incredible privileges of the useless and all-devouring nobility and

Church; the economic oppression of every productive element of societ; and the total lack of justice, fairness and basic political rights. The solutions were obvious, but any hope of reform depended on the king, and he was not about to permit it. Louis really did say, 'Après moi, le déluge'. When the bien-aimé died in 1774, curses and rotten vegetables followed his coffin to St-Denis. Voltaire died four years later, regretting the coming Revolution he would not live to enjoy.

Under Louis XVI (1774–92) the last years of the ancien régime in Paris mixed progressive reforms with comical anachronisms. On the one hand, the removal of the stinking charnel house of the Innocents, and the decision eventually to demolish the Bastille (both in 1786); on the other, something foolish almost beyond belief, the wall of the Farmers-General (1784). The Farmers were tax farmers. The Île-de-France Farmers convinced the king to build an expensive new wall around Paris – not for defence, but so that they might better collect duties on goods entering the city. 'Le mur, en murant Paris, rend Paris murmurant', went a current joke. And it should be no surprise that this wall was one of the major causes of what came to pass in 1789.

1789–97: Paris' Own Revolution

Times were bad. By 1789, after a few disastrous harvests, the price of bread reached 4 sous a pound, while the average worker's daily wage was 16. The state's financial situation was desperate; Louis, having failed miserably on his own, made the fatal step of doing what every Frenchman demanded – he called the Estates General. They met at Versailles on 5 May 1789, for the first time since 1610. Accounts put off for 179 years were about to be settled.

The Third Estate, stymied in reform attempts by the noble and church delegates, swore the 'Tennis Court Oath' on 20 June, declaring themselves the National Assembly and promising not to break up until they gave France a constitution. On 12 July mobs sacked the customs barriers on the Farmers-General wall. Two days later, they went after the Bastille. Significantly, the Revolution that was gathering momentum was not really France's, but Paris'. After the capture of the Bastille, the Parisians formed a militia, commanded by Lafayette. Parisian radicals invented the tricolour, taking Paris' own red and blue, and adding the white of the royal flag. November brought the confiscation of the churches and monasteries, which had covered one-eighth of the area of Paris.

After the famous night of 4 August 1790, when the nobles and clergy in the Assembly renounced their privileges and feudal rights, the Assembly went to work remaking France. The Declaration of the Rights of Man was voted in, along with a liberal constitution. Louis and his family attempted to flee Paris in June 1791, and were kept from then on, almost as prisoners, in the Tuileries. Meanwhile, the émigrés, reactionary nobles who had fled France, were conspiring with foreign governments to overthrow the Revolution. The king was now obviously on their side. The summer of 1792 brought war with Austria and Prussia, and on 10 August the people of Paris stormed the Tuileries and imprisoned the royal family in the Temple.

Paris' government was now replaced by the radical Commune, and in September the new Convention Nationale declared France a republic. On 20 January 1793, the king was guillotined. The end of the House of Capet was as pathetic as could be imagined. Louis XVI, 'Citizen Capet', stood dumbfounded at the tribunal; noticing a plate of rolls on the judges' desk, he forgot all about having been king and could not concentrate on any of the questions put to him. Finally, in tears, he blurted out: 'Please, sir, might I have one of those rolls?' Just before his appointment with the National Razor he is reported to have put away sixteen pork chops.

In March, after military defeats, a dictatorial Committee of Public Safety was set up to manage the national defence (which it did brilliantly), along with a Revolutionary Tribunal to ferret out traitors. The stage was now set for a radical turn, and once more the Parisians were behind it. On 2 June the Commune, controlled by the radical Jacobins, seized the Convention and arrested the moderate faction, the Girondins.

In September the Terror began, egged on by the thoroughly insane, scrofulous Marat, a doctor-turned-journalist screaming for blood, and managed by the 'incorruptible' Robespierre, a provincial lawyer who was now virtual dictator of France. After Marat's assassination by sweet Charlotte Corday in July, the Terror really went to work; Robespierre sent to the guillotine moderate patriots such as Danton out of spite, and *ancien régime* celebrities such as Marie-Antoinette and 'Philippe-Égalité' (the Duke of Orléans who built the Palais Royal, and who had become a demagogic revolutionary) just for fun. After some 2,500 heads had rolled, not counting thousands more in the provinces, some courageous members of the Convention arrested Robespierre and his henchmen; the Terror ended with his execution on 27 July 1794.

The Convention's new constitution provided for government by a five-man executive, the Directoire. By 1797 the mood of the nation had changed considerably. Reaction was in the air, and a royalist party began to manoeuvre semi-openly. In Paris few cared for politics after such a glut of it; the working people who had supported the Commune were silent, battered by rampant inflation, and still without the right to vote. A powerful class of nouveaux riches had grown up, profiting from the wars. In such an atmosphere the divided and ineffective Directoire could command little authority or respect.

1797–1814: An Imperial Interlude

The victorious army had both authority and respect, and its most able general, Napoleon Bonaparte, had already saved the Republic from a royalist revolt in Paris in October 1795. Having beaten the English at Toulon, and conquered northern Italy from the Austrians in a campaign against overwhelming odds, he was the man of the hour. With his brother Jérôme as speaker of the national legislature, and his ally, the intriguer Siéyès, in control of the Directoire, the road was prepared for a coup that many clever politicians found desirable; like the German conservatives in 1933, they were sure they could 'handle' their man. On 9 November 1799, Napoleon bullied the legislature into leaving Paris for St-Cloud, where his troops were, the better to 'protect' its members. There he put an end to it, and to the freedom of France. Napoleon's control was solid enough for him to declare himself Emperor in 1804.

The precedents for turning France into a totalitarian, militaristic state were already in existence – thanks to Louis XIV and the tradition of tight, centralized control that had been in force ever since. As long as Napoleon was winning, and loot and art flowed into Paris, there was little need for a heavy hand. The real oppression came after 1810, when the economy was in disarray and the

cemeteries were starting to fill up. Eight new state prisons, meant for political dissenters, had just opened when the game was up in 1814. Napoleon had big plans for Paris; the Arc de Triomphe, the Madeleine and the colonnaded Rue de Rivoli survive to give a small taste of how Paris would have been rebuilt if the Emperor had had his way.

The last battle, excepting the comical post-script of the Hundred Days, was fought under the heights of Montmartre on 30 March 1814. The next day the Russian Tsar and the King of Prussia paraded down the Champs-Elysées, the first time foreign troops had occupied Paris since the Hundred Years' War. Paris was saved from a sacking by Tsar Alexander and the discipline of the Russian army; the Prussians, understandably, had wanted to have a little fun.

1814–70: Restoration, Rebellion, Reaction and Revolt

The Revolution had shaken France so thoroughly, and created so many opinions and so many grudges, that the rest of the century would be an impossible search for consensus and legitimacy; from 1790 to 1875, the Gallic banana republic/empire/monarchy lived through 13 regimes and 17 constitutions.

The king imposed by the allies was Louis XVI's old gouty brother, Louis XVIII (1814–24): 'partly an old woman, partly a capon, partly a son of France and partly a pedant'. France as a whole was content, and Louis had become mellow enough through long years of exile not to exact too much revenge, even permitting a charter (not quite a constitution) and a parliament. His successor was the third and youngest of the brothers, Charles X (1824–30). As Count of Artois he had been the head of the émigrés, and the most reactionary of the lot, the proverbial Bourbon who 'learned nothing and forgot nothing'. When he tried to gut the charter in July 1830, Paris revolted. A movement of journalists, secret political societies and Napoleonic

1814–70

Au Bon Marché, the world's first department store, p.213

Colonne de Juillet, commemorating the 1830 revolution in Place de la Bastille, p.186

Opéra de Paris-Palais Garnier, the supreme monument of the Second Empire, p.148

veterans seized the Hôtel de Ville, won over the troops, and tossed out the Bourbons once and for all.

The new king was Louis-Philippe of the Orléans branch of the family. Son of Philippe-Égalité, he had fought briefly in the Revolutionary army and later ended up teaching French in Boston. The 'bourgeois king', in his drab coat that became the prototype for the international businessman's uniform of today, entrusted government to Gradgrinds like the liberal Guizot, with his message to the poor: '*Enrichissez-vous!*' ('Get rich!'). The rich alone had the right to vote, while the workers were rewarded with laws more oppressive than anything the Bourbons ever dreamed of, such as the 1838 decree forbidding them even to discuss politics. Paris was packed with police spies to enforce it; anyone who didn't quite agree with the divine necessity of capitalist entrepreneurship got a one-way ticket to Devil's Island. After Guizot, the premier was Adolphe Thiers, a feisty bantam rooster from Marseille who became the model for Balzac's ambitious provincial, Rastignac. He completed the Arc de Triomphe, as a sop to Napoleonic loyalists, and effected some major improvements: mandating primary education and building France's first railways.

But after 18 years, with old Guizot back in power, no one but the industrialists could be found to support the increasingly corrupt and weak regime. A provocative Washington's Birthday dinner in Paris started the 'Revolution of Contempt' on 21 February 1848. The next day students and workers occupied the Place de la Concorde; Louis-Philippe soon abdicated, and the Second Republic was proclaimed. The winner of the first presidential elections turned out to be Napoleon's nephew Louis-Napoleon. Louis made a coup three years later and declared himself 'Emperor Napoleon III', sending some 26,000 political opponents off to the prison hulks in 1851 alone.

Under the influence of his wife, the fiery and reactionary Princess Eugénie, the new emperor, who had previously written a book called *The Extinction of Pauperism*, now found himself pampering a court of nouveaux riches, and presiding over a vulgar orgy of conspicuous consumption unmatched since Louis XIV's court at Versailles. The first 'fashion houses' attained prominence, and the first department stores were built (Au Bon Marché, 1852), feeding the idea of Paris as the 'city of luxury'. More than ever before, Paris had to be the showcase and symbol of an unloved regime, with the first of the great Expositions (1867), grandiose new monuments such as the Opéra, and the total replanning of the city by Napoleon III's prefect of the Seine, Baron Georges Haussmann.

Louis-Napoleon and Haussmann had ambitions for the city, and determined once and for all to make Paris safe for tyranny. The people of Paris had made three revolutions in 59 years, so the people of Paris had to be removed. They were – some 200,000 of them, evicted to form new and even more dire slums in Belleville, Ménilmontant and other eastern quarters. The 'other Paris' spent 90% of its wages on wretched housing and rotten food; those wages were falling far behind inflation, and child mortality was at an all-time high.

The Paris of privilege went over the top. Celebrity whores, the *grandes horizontales* such as Cora Pearl, went for as much as a million francs a night. The theatres and cafés had never been so brilliant (or at least so well dressed); the boulevards booming with shiny black carriages were the envy of the world. Culturally, the tyranny rewarded kitsch and held talent in suspicion. Poets such as Baudelaire and painters such as Courbet and Manet were constantly looking over their shoulders for the police.

1870–72: The Siege of Paris and the Commune

But by the end of Napoleon III's reign, the glitter was fading fast. The 1870 Franco-Prussian war was no contest. By 3 September, under woefully incompetent leadership, most of the surrounded army had surrendered, including the emperor himself. By 19 September the city was surrounded by Prussian troops.

But Paris did not care to fall. Under Louis-Philippe, Adolphe Thiers had begun a ring of fortresses around the city that made it almost impregnable to a 19th-century army. And the city of luxury was moving with skill and determination, raising a citizens' militia and converting city industries to make guns and ammunition. All France was galvanized when one of the new leaders, Léon Gambetta, escaped the city for Tours in a balloon, to organize the resistance and enrol new forces in the unoccupied zones. In Paris, people ate sawdust-laced loaves, and then the horses and the animals in the zoo, and finally tracked down even the cats and rats in the sewers. Balloons and microfilm-carrying carrier pigeons were the city's only contact with the outside world.

The Prussians defeated the new makeshift armies in the south, but Paris held; and so the city was incensed when a self-proclaimed government at Bordeaux – led by none other than old Adolphe Thiers – signed an armistice. Wilhelm II was proclaimed Kaiser of the new German Empire in Versailles' Hall of Mirrors, and his army was allowed a parade through the city it hadn't been able to capture. After the Germans left, women came out to scrub the streets where they had marched. Officials of the old regime, if recognized on the street, were liable to be strung up or bound and dumped in the Seine. The National Guard and the citizens met in a monster rally at the Place de la Bastille, some 300,000 strong, murmuring of 1792, 1830 and 1848. Paris was in a bad mood.

Thiers' government, now installed in Versailles, moved rapidly to disarm the city. When a detachment tried to confiscate the cannon on the heights of Montmartre, the National Guard resisted, killing two generals. Between 18 and 28 March 1871, the city's leaders declared the Paris Commune, a name that recalled the brave days of Étienne Marcel and the Revolution of 1789. The Commune wasn't really communist, as its opponents have always claimed; its biggest demand was for a free municipal government, and its reason for existing was to assuage the shame that Napoleon III and Thiers had brought on France, and to assure that no new clownish tyrant would arise to replace the old one.

However, the Commune was foolhardy, dilettantish and totally inept; with the sympathetic risings that were taking place all over France, particularly in Marseille, they might well have made a real revolution. Instead its leaders dithered, arguing endlessly and issuing manifestos while Thiers raised new troops. Versailles began bombarding the city in mid-April, causing tremendous damage in the *beaux quartiers* of the west.

Bloody Week, the taking of Paris, began on 21 May when an officer noticed that one of the main forts southwest of the city wasn't being defended. Troops poured into the city, meeting barricades at every important street corner. Resistance was effective in many areas, especially in Montmartre, defended courageously by a women's battalion under the poetess-revolutionary Louise Michel. Now the army that had been so badly embarrassed by the Germans began to take its revenge – against its own people. Versailles' policy was to shoot all prisoners and suspects, men, women and children alike. In response, the Communards began to shoot hostages, including the archbishop.

Paris was burning. Whether due to Versailles shells or Communard arsonists, hundreds of buildings went up in flames, including the Tuileries Palace and the Hôtel de Ville. The working class of Paris, knowing they could expect no quarter, set up the last desperate barricades around the Belleville *mairie*. On 27 May, the last 150 fighters to surrender were lined up against the wall of the Père-Lachaise cemetery and shot.

Some 20–25,000 Parisians were killed in the fighting, or massacred afterwards. Another 20,000 spent a year or more in prison hulks or camps in French Guiana. Entire quarters had been devastated; Thomas Cook was organizing special 'Ruins of Paris' tours. For over a year, little was done to rebuild – mostly due to the lack of tradesmen. In 1872 there was hardly a plumber or a roofer left in Paris, and the alleys of Belleville seemed populated solely by widows.

1872–1944: The Paris of the Third Republic

In the 1880s Paris was rebuilt – the regime that had destroyed it now naturally had to make its capital pretty again; Baron Haussmann's projects were completed just as he planned them. Republican prefects worked hard to bring Paris the benefits of modern technology; scores of new schools and hospitals were built, the Métro was begun, and Paris moved into the urban vanguard in everything from street lighting to garbage disposal.

The 1890s, the Belle Époque, was great fun, a continuous carnival for anyone in Paris with a few *sous* to get in. The entertainments included the first cinema, begun by the Lumière brothers in 1895 in a café on the Boulevard des Capucines, and the great Expositions Universelles. The Fair of 1889 gave Paris its definitive modern trademark, the Eiffel Tower.

During the First World War, Paris did more than simply keeping up the boys' morale. At the beginning, in the autumn of 1914, it looked as though the Germans might break through; the government had already decided to flee to Bordeaux when Joffre's troops saved Paris in the 'Miracle of the Marne' – made possible by the famous ride of the Paris taxis, carrying up to the front the reserves that turned the tide. Late in the war Paris came under the fire of the Zeppelins and the Big Bertha howitzer; these were ineffective, though they provided an unsettling look into the wars of the future.

The victorious French hosted the peace conference at Versailles, but Paris was looking poor and a little bedraggled. Its low rents and bonhomie in the 1920s made it the perfect setting for Americans fleeing from Prohibition, racial prejudice and conformity: Hemingway, Fitzgerald and Gertrude Stein shared an extremely lively decade with the modernist painters and the Surrealists, while Josephine Baker and jazz invaded the night clubs and Picasso painted stage backgrounds for Diaghilev's Ballets Russes. The Depression put a stop to such carrying on, and the Paris of the 1930s, marked by constant strikes, demonstrations and occasional street fights, simply wasn't much fun.

In May 1940, while the Nazi tanks were smashing through France's defences, a pathetic fatalism took hold of the city. The government quickly fled to Bordeaux, declaring Paris an open city; the Parisians were not startled to hear it, since half of them had already scrammed, blocking the roads and making any hope of a last defence even more unlikely. The Germans marched into town on 14 June.

Under the occupation, Parisians relearned to ride bikes and puzzled over ration cards, but on the whole daily life went on with eerie normality – the squalid death-in-life captured by the film *The Sorrow and the Pity*, the reality that French governments since the war have worked so hard to deny. Few occupied nations offered so many happy quislings. For every Parisian who worked in

The Vertigo of Modernism

It was as though in Paris Europeans saw a disease creeping into all their lives, and yet could not avert their gaze from the sick patient.

Richard Sennett, *The Fall of Public Man*

The disease was modernism, bringing with it the disorientation of rapid, unending change. Most of us late moderns have learned to cope with it after 150 years of being whirled about on its berserk merry-go-round. But consider the plight of those present at the creation – in Paris, the 'capital of the 19th century', where much of the new first appeared, and where the disruption and turmoil were the greatest.

The protagonists of modernism appeared in the 18th century: the (for lack of a better word) bourgeoisie, the people who were starting to enjoy riding their first carriage, who were importing new machines from England, studying science, reading and writing Paris' first newspapers. As someone wrote at the time: 'They knew they were different, but not exactly what they were.' They argued about politics in the Palais Royal gardens, and from there they surged out to storm the Bastille and change history for us all. Forty years later, under Louis-Philippe, the 'Bourgeois King', Paris belonged to them. Things were starting to pop. There were more Parisians than ever, traffic was booming, machines of all kinds appeared. Crowds formed to demonstrate, to buy gadgets from hucksters, to watch balloon ascents. The first railways were initiating Parisians into the allure of speed. By day Paris streets had become cramped pages of shop signs and advertising; by night gas lighting turned them into incredible fairy scenes.

With new dreams and new opportunities came new dangers. Mere things, for example, were starting to take on a life of their own. Shopkeepers such as Aristide Boucicaut, who founded the first department store in 1852, invented the tricks of modern merchandising to invest cheap, machine-made goods with an aura by associating them with aristocracy, youth, exotic desirability or 'good taste'. Overwhelmed, Parisians were the first to slide down the slippery road of defining themselves by what they possessed.

There were other dangers too. Mr Sennett's book, quoted above, notes how prior to the Revolution people's station in life could be guessed by their clothes – wives of artisans, for example, were forbidden to wear the same sort of frock as wives of craft masters. Now all that was gone, and in a city doubling in size every two decades, other people had become 'unknown quantities' – a mystery, perhaps a threat. Paris had become a city of strangers.

At the same time, Balzac and Flaubert were creating the modern novel. With their careful descriptive writing, they reinforced what people were learning in everyday life: that every item of dress, quirk of behaviour, or gesture might be a sign charged with hidden meaning. Not surprisingly, Parisians started to become self-conscious.

One result was that Paris, even more than London, invented the Victorian age. In the 1840s, city dress suddenly became more drab (and uglier) than ever before. Parisian men began to dress all alike: like undertakers, copying Louis-Philippe and his black suit. On the streets, in the theatre, they were learning to conduct themselves with a rigid,

---

the Resistance, another joined the fascist militias; police and bureaucracy assisted efficiently in deporting democrats and Jews to the death camps.

Liberation came two months after the Normandy invasions in 1944; Eisenhower's army graciously stepped aside to let the French under General Leclerc be the first to

enter Paris, on 24 August. The last week of the occupation had been dramatic enough. Resistance units came out of the sewers and catacombs to assume control of many Paris neighbourhoods, and policemen barricaded themselves inside the Préfecture on the Île de la Cité, bravely holding off German attacks for a week. Hitler, besides his other character

unflinching discipline. They were trying to hide themselves – from each other, and perhaps from Balzac. Women, reduced to chattels by the regressive Napoleonic code, suffered much worse: now came the time of deforming whalebone corsets, of female hysteria and constipation, of paranoia about virginity and purity. In 1857, Charles Worth opened the first fashion house and invented the fashion model; women learned to imitate mannequins, and to display themselves as commodities, just like the goods in Au Bon Marché.

On the stages of old Paris' theatre district, the 'Boulevard du Crime', melodrama was king, with displays of emotion and passion never before imagined; Frédérick Lemaître (the actor portrayed in *Les Enfants du Paradis*) was its greatest practitioner. In the whirl of the cities, an uncontrollable and quite nasty genie had slipped out of its bottle. Its name was personality, its currency, feelings. The repressed crowds were ready to worship anyone like Lemaître who was somehow free to express this powerful new force. For music, Parisians flocked to see dramatic showmen such as Liszt and Paganini. In politics, a poet-politician like Lamartine could briefly hold back the flood of the 1848 revolution by insulting and shaming the crowds, making them know that he 'felt' their pain, suffered more than they. But this new idea of political charisma would not be perfected until the next century – in Germany.

Other theorists, drawing on Paris' revolutionary heritage, invented the myth of 'the people', a collective sort of 'personality' that would also later be perfected elsewhere – in Russia. It did 19th-century Paris, and France, little good. The poet of the new era,

Baudelaire, talking about opinions and fashions, equated modernity with the ephemeral, but he could just as well have been talking about French politics. Throughout the century, rotten regimes rose and fell while the clocks in the railway stations ticked on.

More and more people were pouring into Paris all the time, cannon fodder for modernity's confusions: 25,000 slaughtered by their own army in 1871, a dozen times that from cholera, typhoid and other diseases of the slums. But more always came in to take their places, as Paris grew into a city of two million. Its soul and its symbol was in its streets, in the hurly-burly of all these people winning, failing or just getting by, birthing a new world as they struggled to come to grips with the incoherence around them. The street, their stage, spawned Balzac's *flâneur*, the passive, impotent observer of the crowd, the grandfather of the lost souls in Kafka and in Arthur Miller's *Death of a Salesman*.

But the street also created new life, new possibilities; among its masses were revolutionaries in politics, art and ideas. These Parisians began to express themselves in the Belle Époque of the 1890s, blowing off Victorian steam and creating modern art. This was the decade when glorious, disorderly creative urban life was at its height.

After the shock of the First World War, many began to have doubts about modernism and the unfathomable forces it unleashed. Anti-modernism turned modernism's tools on itself, and inevitably became concerned with social control: whether fascism or communism – or psychoanalysis, with its emphasis on 'adjusting' and conformity – or modern architecture.

flaws, turned out to be a very bad loser, ordering his military commander, General Dietrich von Choltitz, to blow Paris to smithereens. Fortunately for Paris, Von Choltitz was one of those few Germans who didn't just follow orders. He maintained a delicate balancing act for days, lying to Berlin and to the Gestapo spooks in Paris, while

secretly negotiating a surrender. After the war the city made Von Choltitz an honorary citizen. On 26 August came the military parades and De Gaulle's triumphal entry into the city. War correspondent Ernest Hemingway liberated the Ritz bar, while Parisians settled occupation scores: girls who had been too friendly with the

Germans got shaved heads and were paraded through the streets with swastikas gouged into their skins.

1944 Onwards: All Dressed Up and No Place to Go

The postwar era found Paris grumpy and out of sorts. Culturally, the city was dead indeed; art's avant-garde had moved to New York, while intellectual life revolved around the grim cult of the Stalinist-existentialist Sartre, capturing the spirit of the times as well as did the revolving-door governments of the Fourth Republic or the grey technocrats and nervous priggishness of the Fifth. Under De Gaulle, culture minister André Malraux tried to revive some civic spirit, illuminating monuments at night and forcing landlords to clean grimy building façades; at the same time government planners moved purposefully to get Paris ready for modern times – Les Halles was eliminated, as a vestige of the old and 'obsolete', while the towers of Maine-Montparnasse and La Défense, the new motorways such as the *périphérique* and endless miles of suburban tower blocks were built to proclaim their vision of the future.

Many Frenchmen, especially the leftists and old Resistance members, had hoped for a freer, more modern society in the postwar era. Instead – in politics and culture, in the factories and in the schools – they suffered under systems as regimented and undemocratic as ever. Following the 19th-century pattern, a long slow boil was followed by a sudden, unexpected eruption. It began, of course, in Paris, in May 1968, with the

students' occupation of the university; within a week the movement was nationwide. As many as nine million workers went out on strike. For one delirious month it seemed that France would really change; the government counterattacked skilfully, however, using its total control over television and radio to manipulate opinion, staging monster rallies of the silent majority in Paris, and finally winning a smashing victory in parliamentary elections in June.

De Gaulle himself would resign within a year, after losing an important referendum. A trend for greater democracy, openness and decentralization has been making slow headway in many facets of society ever since. The year 1977 brought a novelty: a measure of self-government for Paris, accorded by the State for the first time since the Middle Ages. The right-wing RPR (the old Gaullist party) rapidly assumed control not only of the office of Paris mayor, but initially of all 20 *mairies* in the city's *arrondissements*. Jacques Chirac, the first mayor, made the city his rock-solid power base in his quest for the presidency. Chirac's friends point out that he made Paris run like a Swiss watch: efficient services, cleanliness, comprehensive planning, and plenty of culture and amenities. His opponents note his close ties to building and real-estate interests, which devastated huge areas of the city under Chirac's rule.

Undoubtedly the most important phenomenon of the postwar years has been the near-total gentrification of Paris proper, and the consequent division between the rich, privileged centre and the gritty, neglected suburbs run by the Communists or Socialists. If Paris makes any contributions to culture in the coming decades, they may well come from the suburbs rather than the moribund centre; out in the terra incognita beyond the *périphérique* are the Nanterre branch of the University of Paris (Paris X), a stronghold of the 1968 revolt, some of France's most innovative theatre and dance groups, and a new subculture of *négritude* and French rap that is transforming popular music. Politically, the suburbs are stirring; a hopeless, futureless

No Dog Poo, Please, We're Parisians

In 1992, when Jacques Chirac was still mayor, a remarkable brochure appeared in every Parisian's mailbox. It was a full-colour comic book, printed at enormous expense by the City of Paris and devoted to the adventures of a dog named Archibald. We may assume Archibald to be of English extraction, not only from his name, but for his excruciating good manners and the fact that he wears a monocle. His purpose, which he accomplishes with aplomb, is to instruct less well-bred French dogs and thoughtless French humans on the importance of canine cleanliness. At the end of the story, Archibald puts to shame a dog named Rex, who only does it in the gutter when he feels like it. Then he helps his dog-sitter meet a nice girl with a poodle.

On the back of the brochure were the 'Ten Commandments of the Tidy Parisian Dog', as well as a helpful puppy chart to tell you how many *besoins liquides* and *besoins solides* your infant will be producing daily. For all dogs, the city recommended 'Always associate acts with words. Show him where to do it, while saying to him, "*Tes besoins!*" ' The city provided a number for its 'Hello Cleanliness' hotline, in case you had any further questions. Finally there was the Parisian Dog's Motto: 'Me, I do it where I'm told to do it.'

Who could fail to be impressed by the inexhaustible cleverness and resources of the Paris government? They were indeed getting serious about misplaced *besoins*. A trained Dog Poo Squad of a hundred undercover agents stalks the streets of Paris day and night. They travel in pairs, and when they spot an anti-social dog owner they move in, flashing their Propreté de Paris ID cards and serving malefactors with fines of €90 and up. The Propreté, funded with 20 per cent of the city's budget, doesn't fool around, as

---

atmosphere of unemployment, racism and marginalization is causing increasingly frequent disturbances.

The problems of the suburbs, though, are still of little interest to Paris and its eternal *classe politique*. Just before he died, François Mitterrand confessed that he had really been a man of the Right all along. His control of the Socialist Party provides a perfect example of how this small clique, made up of old schoolboys from the Grandes Écoles, has been able cynically to manipulate French public life with the all-important goal of keeping itself on top. Mitterrand's two terms as president (1981–95) were a high time for the *classe politique* and for Paris. Determined to leave his mark on the city, Mitterrand inaugurated his *grands projets* – the Louvre redevelopment, the Grand Arche at La Défense, a new Bibliothèque Nationale, Bercy, the Bastille Opéra, among others. Paris, and Mayor Chirac, had little say about them.

Apart from these, the Mitterrand era will probably be remembered best for corruption – political sleaze nearly on an Italian scale, though managed with more decorum. The

booty was shared by all parties and by the *classe politique*'s allies in business. France does have an increasingly independent judiciary, and a few courageous judges have been doing great work cleaning up the mess. Already scores of politicians and businessmen have received suspended sentences and fines; a few actually did time. The scandals are still coming out, notably in Paris. Here President Chirac himself, along with former prime minister Alain Juppé and former Paris mayor Jean Tiberi, were caught using city-owned housing and phantom jobs for their own benefit. So far the politically controlled state prosecutors have refused to issue indictments against such luminaries, but Paris showed its disgust in the municipal elections of 2001, voting in Bertrand Delanoë

1944 Onwards

La Défense, the grandest of the *grands projets*, p.258

Institut du Monde Arabe, for a glimpse of the future beyond the *grands projets*, p.238

Passerelle de Solférino, Paris' millennium bridge, p.56

even the casual visitor will notice. Their fluorescent green-clad legions can be seen scouring the streets at any hour. Besides washing out 1,650 miles of gutters daily, they have fleets of small green vans equipped with scrubbers, and even vacuum-equipped green motorcycles that weave in and out of pedestrian traffic on the pavements, frightening elderly ladies and children as they suck up offending gum wrappers and cigar butts.

Pampered Paris has money to burn for such whims – as well as for Grandes Arches, pyramids, art exhibitions of spray-can graffiti, gadgets built into the street that catch motorists who go through red lights, even a 100-page official colour monthly (called *Paris, le Journal*; strangely enough, most of the advertisers seem to be paving contractors). All this while strapped working-class suburbs lack money for basic services. But what's bothersome is not the obscene amounts France lavishes on its overindulged Babylon, but the way they spend it. The tidiness mania was just a minor manifestation of France's old evil genius – the urge to control everything, to rationalize, sanitize, homogenize, to stamp out all traces of diversity and spontaneity, and make the city an expanded version of some cadaverous bourgeois parlour in the 7e. The Bourbons gradually stifled Paris' medieval bonhomie, its street life and popular festivals; Napoleon III and Haussmann wiped out the old Ile de la Cité, and swept the poor out of Paris' centre. De Gaulle and Pompidou took care of the markets at Les Halles, and governments since have fostered the total gentrification of the entire city. Pity poor Jacques Chirac, an ambitious man – they left him nothing to do but mop up dog pies. Now that he's moved on to the Elysée Palace, the fever seems to have subsided; the green machines are less in evidence, and on some streets you'll have to watch your step once more.

– the first Socialist mayor ever, and the first openly gay politician to win a major office in France.

Despite being stabbed in the gut by a homophobic computer technician during a public party at city hall in 2002, Delanoë has been a very busy man. His new initiatives include political decentralization, giving more powers to the neighbourhood governments, the *arrondissements*, and a plan to even out the 'class segregation' of Parisian neighbourhoods by building or purchasing 64,000 flats in the west end, the Marais and the Left Bank for public housing.

Delanoë's top priority, though, is transport, and he isn't shy about taking radical steps to end what he calls the 'hegemony of the car'. Paris is building a new tram line around the city; it is taking huge amounts of tarmac away from cars and turning them into bus and bike lanes and pedestrian spaces.

The new mayor also wants Paris to have more fun. The party at which he survived the assassination attempt was part of the *Nuit Blanche* (sleepless night), an all-night festival around the city's major monuments that proved a great success.

An even greater success was *Paris-Plage* (*see* p.111), Delanoë's first big coup and a symbol of what he is trying to do for Paris, cleverly combining the festival spirit with the war on cars. In August 2002, the city temporarily shut down part of the riverside expressway that Georges Pompidou rammed through the city. Tons of sand were trucked in, and for the first time ever, Paris had itself a beach.

The motorists were apoplectic, but three million visitors with beach balls and umbrellas in the shadow of the Louvre found it delightful. Already, before Delanoë's election, visitors noticed that Parisians were gradually becoming a little less grumpy, a little more relaxed. As the city emerges, finally, from the grey postwar decades, the new mayor may have hit the public mood just right.

Art and Architecture

ART

The Middle Ages

The first Parisian artists were monks, the illuminators of medieval manuscripts. In the 13th century, when the new Gothic cathedrals created a demand for vast expanses of stained glass, artists adopted Byzantine-influenced pictures from the illuminators, although their styles gradually became freer and more natural (the best work is at Chartres, Sainte-Chapelle, Notre-Dame and St-Denis).

When the Capetian kings made Paris their capital, the artists in their courts held the same rank as servants, and they were expected to design buildings, pageants, tapestries, books, chairs, chess pieces and anything else the king might fancy (the Musée de Cluny is a treasure trove of such things). As the court expanded, royal artists began to specialize, while the king's favourite painter was elevated to the position of *premier peintre du roi*. This system remained intact until the Revolution.

By the 14th century, the university and court had sufficiently enhanced wealth and literacy in Paris for a new breed of artist, unattached to Church or nobleman, to live by selling painted books or accepting commissions. The same century saw Paris' first contact with 'International Gothic' painting, via the papal court at Avignon. The old Louvre was decorated with frescoes of flowery meadows and hunting scenes, while French sculptors, equally inspired by what they saw in Avignon, produced their delightful smiling, swivel-hipped figures of the Virgin, so popular that many were exported to Italy itself (examples can be seen in the Musée de Cluny).

In the lull in the Hundred Years' War before Agincourt, Flemish artists introduced their precise, detailed style. Their influence is shown in the few French paintings that have survived – among the best are the Louvre's *Portrait de Jean le Bon* and the *Parlement de Narbonne*. The most extravagant patron of the period was Charles VI's uncle, Jean Duc de Berry, who paid Flemish painters to produce the enchanting *Très Riches Heures du Duc de Berry* with its scenes of medieval Paris (now in Chantilly's Musée Condé).

The Renaissance and the School of Fontainebleau

A strong Flemish influence continued through the 15th century – in court painter Jean Fouquet (c. 1420–75, author of the Louvre's remarkable, melancholy *Portrait of Charles VII*, and the *Livre d'Heures d'Étienne Chevalier* at the Musée Condé), and in the so-called Maître de Moulins employed by the Bourbons (*Ste-Madeleine et une Donatrice* in the Louvre and *Charles II Bourbon* at the Musée Condé).

In 1497, Charles VIII's invasion of Italy brought back a number of paintings to Paris, beginning a taste for Italian art that became insatiable. His successor, François I, wanted not only the art, but the artists too: most notably Leonardo da Vinci (who is said to have died in the king's arms at Amboise in 1519) and, in 1528, Mannerist painters Rosso Fiorentino and Francesco Primaticcio and sculptor Benvenuto Cellini to decorate his new château at Fontainebleau. Although little survives of their original decorations, their stuccoes and the scheme of the painted panels remain to show the origins of the elegant long lines, clear colours and erotic tastes that figure in the 'School of Fontainebleau'.

In sculpture, the school's greatest master was Jean Goujon (1490–1561), whose Mannerist tendency was tempered by a study of the antique casts that adorned Fontainebleau's gardens (works in the Louvre, the Fountain of the Innocents and in the courtyard of the École des Beaux-Arts).

In painting, the earliest Fontainebleau style is epitomized in Jean Cousin the Elder's only known work and one of the first French nudes, *Eva Prima Pandora*, in the Louvre.

François I was also the first king to sit for many portraits, notably by the Flemish Humanist Jean Clouet (1486–1540); his son François Clouet (1510–72) performed the same role in the courts of Henri II and Charles IX (both in the Louvre).

The Age of Big Louies, or Art as Narcotic: The 17th Century

The massive rebuilding of Paris in the 17th century created a tremendous demand for art of all kinds. Henri IV had at least made it easy to find the talent by converting the Long Gallery of the Louvre into lodgings and studios for artists. Unfortunately, the taste of noble patrons demanded only works that were pleasing, decorative and pretentious, and few paintings done in Paris offer more than a slight, vacuous charm. The greatest French painters of the day, Claude Lorrain and Nicolas Poussin, fled Paris and spent most of their lives in Italy.

So Louis XIII was stuck with the insipid Simon Vouet (1590–1649) for his *premier peintre du roi*; his classical scenes in the Palais du Luxembourg hover dangerously near the chocolate box.

The greatest artist to work in Paris under Louis XIII was Rubens, in town to do the queen-sized scenes of Marie de' Medici's life (now in a special room in the Louvre). Some of his Flemish and Dutch assistants stayed behind; they influenced a notable set of non-court painters to tackle similar everyday subjects, especially the Le Nain brothers – Antoine, Louis and Mathieu. The best was Louis (1593–1648), whose *Repas de Paysans* in the Louvre attains a realistic nobility, void of the genre elements beloved by the Dutch. An even greater realistic artist was Georges de La Tour (1593–1652), whose solemn figures sculpted by darkness and candlelight are the most distinctive of the period.

Louis XIV's opinion of the Flemish and realist painters was well known: '*Enlevez-moi ces magots*' ('Get these apes away from me'). In 1648 the king founded the Académie Royale de Peinture et de Sculpture to supplant the Maîtrise, Paris' medieval painters' guild. The Académie lay dormant until 1661, when the indefatigable Colbert took over its direction. Colbert believed that art had but one purpose: to enhance the glory of his master, Louis XIV, and France. To make the propaganda credible, but also to contain the high cost of luxury imports and make France into an art exporter, Colbert demanded that the Académie dictate the highest standards to painters and sculptors, and to the weavers and furniture-makers at the newly established Gobelins. Astute flattery in the right places by Charles Lebrun (1619–90) earned him the position of the Académie's first director-dictator, and in 1675 he issued the magnificently flatulent *Tables de Préceptes*, the Académie's rules for art. Vast sums of money and Lebrun's bullying tactics produced an art organization unique in Europe. At the same time Colbert and Lebrun were snapping up paintings and sculptures for the royal collection. By 1709, 2,400 pictures were stashed in the Louvre, giving it a considerable head start in the art race (London's National Gallery had 38, when founded in 1834).

Under Louis, sculpture was largely a matter of public statues of the king to remind Parisians who was boss.

Lebrun, *premier peintre du roi*, spent his last 12 years directing the decoration of Versailles, painting the tedious Hall of Mirrors' ceiling celebrating the glory of Louis. Lebrun's archrival and successor as Académie director, Pierre Mignard (1612–95), was chiefly a portrait painter (see his Molière and Cardinal Mazarin in the Musée Condé). Other portraitists included Hyacinthe Rigaud (1659–1743), who painted the Louvre's *Louis XIV at the Age of 62* as a pompous old poof in a miniskirt and high heels; and Nicolas de Largillière (1656–1746), who had a lighter, more shimmering touch that fitted in nicely with the spirit of the next century.

The 18th Century: Rococo to Neoclassicism

Louis XIV's reign ended with a whimper of constipated religious art, and the echoes of Madame de Maintenon's footsteps in Versailles as she checked each Gobelins tapestry to make sure garments had been sewn over the nude figures. The old tyrant of tedium was still warm in the grave when Paris released all its pent-up frivolity in a wild orgy of indulgence and fun. The Regency launched the fashion for *rocaille*, or Louis XV rococo, with an abhorrence of straight lines and love of decorative foliage and shell shapes that soon spread across Europe. The first and finest painter to capture its whimsical spirit was Antoine Watteau (1684–1721). Watteau was the first independent artist working in Paris, patronized by the bourgeoisie and selling his work through dealers. When he was accepted into the Académie, it was as its first *peintre des fêtes galantes*, of courtship parties in the park; Watteau's world is exquisite but ephemeral and tinged with melancholy, as if aware that he and the society he painted were doomed. The Louvre has his masterpiece, *L'Embarquement pour l'Île de Cythère*.

Through engravings of his works, Watteau exerted a mighty influence on the French decorative arts of the 18th century, and he had a hundred imitators, most notably Nicolas Lancret (1690–1734) and Jean-Baptiste Pater (1696–1736), although their *fêtes galantes* often sink into mere genre scenes of pretty revellers. More solid bourgeoisie genre subjects typified the canvases of Jean-Baptiste Chardin (1699–1779), one of the most popular artists at the Académie's salons. Watteau also inspired *tableaux des modes*, engravings of people in fashionable costumes, and the *estampes galantes* that evolved into intriguing Norman Rockwellish records of everyday life in Paris. Louis-Léopold Boilly (1761–1845) was a master of the genre.

As Italian Baroque influences waned, the Académie reformulated its Rules for Great Art. History painting (which included mythological and allegorical scenes) was the only subject with prestige; the top painting prize, the *Prix de Rome*, was only given to the most convoluted historical tableaux, annually cooked up by Académie drudges. In 1734 the Académie decided to exhibit the works of its members in public salons and a new being, the art critic, was born to help people talk about what they saw. One of the first was Diderot, whose favourite painter was the deplorable Jean-Baptiste Greuze (1725–1805), but only because his paintings offered edifying moral tales.

Besides Chardin, one of the great stars of the first salons was Maurice-Quentin de La Tour (1704–88). He was the favourite of that great trendsetter of the day, Madame de Pompadour (see his portrait of her in the Louvre), who also favoured François Boucher (1703–70), a painter whose luscious nudes and light, mythological fancies were designed for rococo interiors and look like silly fluff on solemn museum walls. Jean-Honoré Fragonard (1732–1806) inherited his position as the chief decorative painter of the day, with an added touch of Watteau lyricism in his earliest works.

But rococo flew too much in the face of the basic Parisian taste for balance, classical harmony and right angles for it to endure for very long. Even as she patronized Boucher, La Pompadour's interest in the excavations at Pompeii pioneered the new, more classical style known as 'Louis XVI'. Painters of antique ruins, such as Hubert Robert (1733–1808), filled the new Louis XVI interiors; Jean-Antoine Houdon (1741–1828) supplied the cool, elegant statues. As for portraits, two of the leading artists were, for the first time, women: Elisabeth Vigée-Lebrun (1755–1842), Marie-Antoinette's favourite portraitist at Versailles (although her best work is *Madame Lebrun and Her Daughter* in the Louvre), and Madame Labille-Guyard (1749–1803), a friend of Robespierre, and a feminist who fought to abolish the

Académie's quota system for women and its ban against women teachers.

The Revolution and Napoleonic Art

The Revolution opened the salon to all, bringing in a flood of art – 3,000 paintings alone in 1795. The leading painter and art dictator of the Revolution, Jacques-Louis David (1748–1825), closed down the Académie's salon the next year and opened up a carbon copy called the Académie des Beaux-Arts. It held competitions for neoclassical patriotic pictures like his own, evocations of austere civic virtue, modelled on a ludicrous fantasy of ancient Rome. He led the government's nationalizing of art from royal palaces, churches and the châteaux of the émigrés. Another artist, Alexandre Lenoir, rescued sculpture from the *sans-culottes* (sometimes at the risk of his life) and during the Revolution opened the first public museum of French monuments.

In 1804, Napoleon made himself Emperor, mandating the new Empire style to decorate his residences while employing artists for political propaganda far more repugnant than even Louis XIV's. The best works are touched with the first whispers of Romanticism, as in the works of portrait painter Pierre-Paul Prud'hon (1758–1823) and sculptor François Rude (1784–1855) on the Arc de Triomphe. Napoleon found a willing toady in David (who had previously been Robespierre's), and gave him the task of recording the great moments of his career (*Le Sacre de Napoléon Ier* in the Louvre).

Besides imitating Louis XIV's use of art to sanctify tyranny, Napoleon shared his mania for the prestige of sheer accumulation. He booted the artists out of the Louvre and made it the Musée Napoléon, displaying loot from his conquests side by side with the national collection. But thanks to the little hoodlum, all the artists and art-lovers in Paris could freely go to study the Grand Masters – a crucial first step for the artistic revolutions that were to follow.

Early 19th Century: The Miasma of the Salons

The allies made the French return many of the paintings Napoleon had nicked, and the embarrassing blank walls became the venue of the new salon of the Académie des Beaux-Arts. Only David was absent, having gone into exile in Belgium on the fall of his master.

With David's departure, the chief artist remaining in Paris was his singularly irregular student, Jean-Auguste-Dominique Ingres (1780–1867). After tossing off a few high-kitsch Napoleonic propaganda pieces, Ingres went off to Italy, where he studied the Mannerists' distortion of the figure. His serpent-backed *La Grande Odalisque* (in the Louvre) was accused of being 'Gothic' (i.e. quirky and individual), but he had success with his historical troubadour paintings.

The Romantic movement finally reached Paris only after the prolonged neoclassical hangover of the Revolution and Napoleon. Romanticism soon manifested itself in painting; being encouraged to crank out 'Gothic' scenes made artists think about the old medieval spirit of freedom and individuality. Nor was it long before painters discovered that they, too, had plenty of lofty feelings to express, and they sought out subjects that they could respond to and paint emotively. The 1819 salon was shocked by its first Romantic painting, a barn-burner called *Le Radeau de la Méduse* (now in the Louvre) by Théodore Géricault (1791–1824).

In 1822, Eugène Delacroix (1798–1863), putative son of Talleyrand, made his salon debut and quickly became the leader of the Romantics. Like Géricault he painted topical subjects that moved him; his *Liberty Leading the People* (in the Louvre), the best-known image of the people of Paris at their barricades, was painted after the revolution of 1830. Considered an incitement to riot, it was hidden away until the Exposition of 1855, when its image of a bourgeois gent in a top hat next to a worker seemed safely impossible.

The Romantic emphasis on the emotions and individuality created the image of the artist as a bohemian, an eccentric outside respectable society. One group of painters – led by Théodore Rousseau (1812–67), and inspired by a desire to return to nature – went off to paint in Barbizon, a hamlet in the Forest of Fontainebleau. But the greatest landscape painter of the day was Camille Corot (1796–1875). Corot was the first painter inspired by photography (seen in his famous, fluffy, grey foliage); by mid-century, when the Académie and salon public had tacitly accepted the fact that the best an artist could do was mimic the camera, Corot was extremely popular, and artists were instructed to paint in his style, in various tones of grey.

'Paint what your eyes see' became the slogan of the realist painters who followed, although the first exponent, Gustave Courbet (1819–77), was even more Romantic and formal in vision than Corot. Courbet's declarations that his own judgement and appreciation of his art were all that mattered infuriated the salon and its public. He was persecuted as a 'dangerous socialist' and when his works were rejected at the Expositions of 1855 and 1867, Courbet set an example for future outsiders by putting on one-man shows at his own expense; after serving as chief art agitator in the Commune he died in poverty and exile. Two other distinctive artists working outside the pale were Honoré Daumier (1808–79), a painter of Goyaesque vision known only for his cartoons in his lifetime, who also died in poverty, and Charles Méryon (1828–64), Baudelaire's friend, whose dark watercolours and drawings of a haunted, sinister Paris, alive with spirits, gargoyles and swarms of black birds, are a world in themselves.

After 1852, Napoleon III became the new sugar daddy of the arts, and under his reign the salons reached new heights in titillating nudes (see the Musée d'Orsay's works by Bouguereau and Cabanel). After the Commune, the Third Republic took over the reins of patronage, leaving Paris a collection of enormous photograph-inspired historical scenes. The most distinctive painter to enjoy official favour was Pierre Puvis de Chavannes (1824–94), who looked back further than any, to quattrocento frescoes, adopting the forms and use of colour of the pre-Raphaelites (see the Hôtel de Ville, Panthéon and Sorbonne).

After Courbet, the salon next declared war on Edouard Manet (1832–83). When the salon jury of 1863 turned out so blatantly conservative that Napoleon III permitted a Salon des Refusés, Manet made Paris howl with outrage at the unclassical naked woman in his *Déjeuner sur l'herbe*; and his *Olympia* (1863) incited terrible derision. Although Manet concentrated on undogmatic everyday subjects such as horse races and café life, his vision was, like Corot's, inspired by photography; it was his bold new technique, his novel but masterful handling of paint, that offended the smoothies in the salon – and made him the idol of the Impressionists.

Impressionism and Beyond: Paris Gives Birth to Modern Art

In 1874, in the studio of the photographer Nadar on Boulevard des Capucines, the Société Anonyme des Artistes held their first exhibition – yet another protest against exclusion from the salon. What set it apart from other protest shows were the artists exhibiting: Degas, Renoir, Pissarro, Morisot, Sisley and Monet. Monet's painting of a sunrise entitled *Impression: Soleil levant* inspired a critic to call the whole group *Impressionnistes* – a name the painters adopted for their next seven exhibitions. They were not as interested in the realism of photography as in the science behind it, the discovery that colour completely owes its existence to light. The Impressionists have been aptly compared to a group of scientists in a laboratory; each followed his individual research and offered a colourful vision of the new, modern Paris of the boulevards, as well as old French favourites: landscapes and pretty women. Thanks to perceptive dealers such as Durand-Ruel, their works had achieved critical acceptance by the 1880s – although soreheads at the salon made sure that the state never spent any money on purchasing their works. Nearly all their paintings in the Musée d'Orsay are later gifts.

Impressionism became the benchmark that painters measured themselves against for the rest of the 19th century. Some of the most original artists committed the heresy of leaving Paris altogether: Gauguin, Emile Bernard and others moved to Pont-Aven and called their pictures 'Impressionist-Synthetist', and Cézanne went home to Provence to work on structure. Artists who remained, or who were drawn to Paris, included Georges Seurat (1859–91), the most scientific of the Postimpressionists, who invented Pointillism. In 1884 he took part in the founding of the Salon des Indépendants, open to all; those exhibiting included Henri de Toulouse-Lautrec (1864–1901), whose portraits of Montmartre and Paris' underworld have so powerfully affected the way the world looks at Paris, and Henri Rousseau (1844–1910), the first and greatest of naïve painters. At the same time, the expressive Romantic Auguste Rodin (1840–1917) was shaking sculpture awake from its stale neoclassical doldrums, causing furious controversies with his powerful, often radically distorted works – especially his Balzac on Boulevard Montparnasse.

In the 1890s, artists began to pour into the city, attracted by the *succès de scandales* of the Impressionists and Postimpressionists (and the commercial success some were beginning to enjoy). Dilettantes searched for ever more rare, exotic and exquisite stimulation – as in the works of Gustave Moreau (1826–98), who painted mythologies from his imagination, or Odilon Redon (1840–1916), who painted from his pre-Freudian dreams, and was much admired by Mallarmé and the Symbolists.

An unfortunate side effect of the 'decadents' is that their reputation tainted a genuine renaissance in European design, known in France as Art Nouveau. Best known for its long flowing lines, inspired by plants and the geometry of natural growth, Art Nouveau's complete devotion to craftsmanship put prices out of reach of the masses, and it never caught the popular fancy. The little success Art Nouveau had in Paris was mostly thanks to a German dealer in Oriental art named Siegfried Bing, who began to promote vases by Gallé, curvilinear furniture by Prouve, Vallin and Majorelle, and the virtuoso creations of Lalique, whose intricate, fairy-like jewellery, often in the form of dragonflies or beetles, delighted Sarah Bernhardt. La Bernhardt also loved to be depicted on the flattering Art Nouveau posters of Alphonse Mucha, a Czech illustrator living in Paris.

1900–40: Art Capital of the World

Among the poor bohemians living in Paris at the turn of the century were three painters inspired by the intense, pure colours of Van Gogh and the decorative Nabi group that grew up after Gauguin. Henri Matisse (1869–1954), André Derain (1880–1954) and Maurice de Vlaminck (1876–1958) first became known to the Paris public at an exhibition in 1905, when a critic labelled them Wild Beasts, or Fauves, for their uninhibited use of colour. Although Fauvism only lasted another three years, it was the first great avant-garde movement of the century.

The next movement followed quickly on its heels and lasted longer. In 1907, two hungry artists in Montmartre, admirers of the recently deceased Cézanne, Pablo Picasso (1881–1973) and Georges Braque (1882–1963), formulated Cubism, which liberated form in the same way that the Fauves liberated colour. Picasso and Braque aimed to depict the permanent structure of objects, and not the transitory appearance of the moment, by showing them from a number of angles at the same time. A second stage of Cubism, with stronger colours, greater sense of decoration, and the use of random elements such as newspaper clippings, was originated by Juan Gris (1887–1927) who, like Picasso and Braque, also designed stage sets and costumes for Diaghilev's Ballets Russes.

In 1910, Robert Delaunay (1885–1941) painted his vibrant Cubist paintings of the Eiffel Tower, and two years later went a step further from the austere Cubism of Picasso, Braque and Gris to a lyrical style of brightly coloured, nonrepresentational abstraction which the poet Apollinaire called Orphism. More new influences came from Eastern Europe: Constantin Brancusi (1876–1957; the Atelier Brancusi at Beaubourg); Ossip Zadkine (1890–1967); Marc Chagall (1887–1985), who, with his dreamy Russian-Jewish paintings, brought figurative painting into the avant-garde; and the Lithuanian Expressionist Chaim Soutine (1893–1943).

Meanwhile Parisian Marcel Duchamp (1887–1968) was causing the biggest outrage of all at the 1913 Armoury Show (New York's introduction to modern art) with his *Nude Descending a Staircase*. In 1915 he outraged the public even further with his 'ready-mades' – everyday items such as toilet seats displayed as art to challenge the typical attitudes towards taste. His anti-art ideas had followers on both sides of the Atlantic: Dada, founded in Zurich in 1916, arrived in Paris after the war with Picabia and Tristan Tzara. The Dadaists made it their business to shock and scandalize in the good old Paris tradition, with events such as The Vaseline Symphony. In a cross-cultural exchange, American Man Ray (1890–1976), inspired by Duchamp in New York, moved to Paris, where his 'Rayograms' (making photographs without a camera) endeared him to the Dadaists.

In 1924 a new manifesto announced that Dadaism was dead and a new movement with deeper aims, known as Surrealism, would take its place. As its theoretician, André Breton, explained it, Surrealism was 'to resolve the previously contradictory conditions of dream and reality into an absolute reality, a super-reality'. The police had to be called to stop the riots at the first Surrealist show in 1925: exhibitors included Man Ray, Picasso, the Catalan Joan Miró (1893–1983) and Max Ernst (1891–1976); in 1929 the group was joined by Salvador Dalí (1904–89) whose knack for self-publicity made him the most famous and controversial member of the group.

This was also the period when Maurice Utrillo (1883–1955) began to enjoy his first success for scenes of his native Montmartre, which he painted as therapy for a lifelong drink problem. He was encouraged by his mother, Suzanne Valadon (1867–1938), who began as a painter's model for Renoir and Degas, and later achieved her own vigorous personal vision in Fauve colours.

Postwar Paris

After the occupation, the Paris art scene reflected the grey, postwar malaise. Matisse had deserted Paris for Provence in the 1920s, and was followed by Picasso and Chagall (although the latter returned to paint the ceiling of the Opéra in 1964). In the 1940s the explosion of Abstract Expressionism in New York stripped Paris of its position in the avant-garde, leaving the galleries in St-Germain to display the weary imitative abstract *École de Paris*.

The most important noises of the time were made by the anti-artists, such as Jean Dubuffet (1901–85), who engaged in open warfare with France's culture czars; in his art he rejected professional technique in favour of spontaneity and authenticity, which he called *art brut* (raw art), inspired by his collection of the works of children, prisoners and the insane. In the early 1960s a playful group of artists known as the Nouveaux Réalistes emerged, inspired by the everyday items presented as art in the style of Duchamp's 'ready-mades' and by a disgust for contemporary culture: Niki de Saint-Phalle (b. 1930), Jean Tinguely (1925–92), Bulgarian-American Christo (b. 1935), César (1921–88), Ben, and Arman (b. 1928) gave Paris in the 1980s some of its most important (and amusing) monuments.

Finding Paris' Art

Boulevard Montparnasse, for Rodin's statue of Balzac, p.247

Espace Montmartre Salvador Dalí, for sculpture by the Surrealist, p.193

Hôtel de Ville, for the florid style of the Third Republic, p.165

Musée des Arts Décoratifs, to see medieval to 20th-century furnishings and decorative arts, including Art Nouveau, p.107

Musée de Cluny, one of the world's greatest collections of medieval art, p.218

Musée Condé, Chantilly, for the *Très Riches Heures du Duc de Berry* and an art collection ranging from Renaissance to neoclassical, p.293

Musée Delacroix, to see sketches, etchings and minor paintings by the artist, p.208

Musée Guimet, for art from India, China, Japan, Indochina, Indonesia and Central Asia, p.143

Musée Jacquemart-André, with works from the Italian Renaissance as well as French, Flemish and Dutch painting, p.117

Musée du Louvre, for a wide-ranging collection representing all periods from classical antiquity to the 19th century, including, of course, Leonardo da Vinci's *Mona Lisa*, p.98

Musée National d'Art Moderne, a superb collection of 20th-century art, p.163

Musée National des Monuments Français, for replicas of architecture and sculpture from the 9th to the 19th centuries, p.142

Musée Nissim de Camondo, for 18th-century furniture, tapestries, etc., p.118

Musée de l'Orangerie, for Monet's *Water Lilies* and more Impressionist works, along with some 20th-century painting (closed until 2004), p.112

Musée d'Orsay, for art from the transition to modernity, 1848–1910, and a particularly impressive collection of works by the Impressionists, p.122

Musée Picasso, with works by the long-time Paris resident in all his styles, p.179

Musée Rodin, for studies and works by France's greatest sculptor, displayed in his house and garden, p.129

Musée de la Sculpture en Plein Air, to see open-air sculpture by Brancusi, César and Zadkine, among others, p.239

Notre-Dame and Sainte-Chapelle, for the best of Gothic stained glass, pp.82 and 90

Opéra de Paris, for Chagall's paintings on the ceiling of the hall, p.148

Versailles, for the most lavish Grand Siècle furnishings and decoration, p.286

The current scene is best expressed in the thick, peeling layers of gallery posters on the walls of cafés and on billboards, each representing an exhibit with its own glittering vernissage, each discussed avidly for a moment before the next poster is pasted on top in an eternal search for the new.

ARCHITECTURE

Gothic: The Parisian Style

Nothing significant remains of Roman or Merovingian Paris, and little enough from the early Middle Ages. In the 12th century the city must have been packed with sumptuous churches and monasteries, though only a few works survive (St-Germain, apse of St-Martin-des-Champs).

Many minds and hands contributed to the technological revolution of Gothic architecture, but the worthy Abbot Suger of St-Denis gets the credit for actually erecting the first building (1130–44). Suger wrote that he wanted to 'make what is material immaterial', and Gothic builders pulled it off with an amazing array of new advances: the pointed arch, bearing more weight than the old round ones, flying buttresses to restrain the outward thrust of a wall, complex vaulting to roof over large areas, stained glass and rose windows to give the new churches an undreamed-of sense of openness and lightness. Gothic cathedrals were meant as a microcosm of creation, including a little of heaven and a little of earth. Their decoration, in sculpture and glass, has a place for everything, from mundane affairs like the zodiacal signs and the farmers' 'labours of the months' to the more profound mysteries of Scripture.

The first Gothic work in Paris proper was St-Pierre-de-Montmartre (1134); Notre-Dame was next, in 1163, and St-Julien on the Left Bank came three years later. Soon every town in the Île-de-France was building one, and the style spread outwards to all of Europe.

Sainte-Chapelle, begun by St Louis in 1245, is Gothic at the height of its power and sophistication: a tall chapel, its walls over two-thirds glass, one so bright and full of colours it seems less a mere building than a spiritual vision.

Little of medieval secular architecture survives: two beautiful, heavily restored mansions – the Hôtel de Cluny (1496) and the Hôtel de Sens (1475) – the Conciergerie and the 14th-century château at Vincennes.

The French Gothic tradition was continuing to evolve as late as the 17th century. In the 14th and 15th centuries it may be called Flamboyant Gothic, from the flame-like traceries in windows and sculptural decoration; St-Germain l'Auxerrois is a fine example. The last Gothic churches in Paris are really half-Gothic and half-Renaissance, built with no sense that these two styles might be incompatible; buildings such as St-Eustache (1530–1640) have a certain mongrel charm nonetheless.

A Renaissance Lost

With the Hundred Years' War came desolation and a national crisis of confidence; France wasn't quite in the mood for art in the quattrocento. The first truly Renaissance works in Paris were the Fontaine des Innocents and the Cour Carrée of the Louvre. An Italian would have said he was glad the French were finally catching on, but that the Louvre was a little over the top; Pierre Lescot's and Jean Goujon's ornate but harmonious Cour Carrée was nevertheless

ahead of its time, and must have been closely studied by Baroque Italians. French noblemen were starting to build new Renaissance hôtels particuliers in the fashionable Marais, such as the 1544 Hôtel Carnavalet, now Paris' city museum.

French Baroque and Academicism

Confidence most definitely returned with that excellent king, Henry IV. The Parisians bolted out of the gate in the 1610s with the first of the places royales (squares built as unified architectural ensembles, and usually dedicated to the ruling monarch): the Place des Vosges and the Place Dauphine. Claude Vellefaux, architect of the Place des Vosges, also built the 1607 Hôpital St-Louis in the same vein. Combining details from the Renaissance stylebooks with a French taste for brick, pitched roofs and gables, it could have been the birth of a lovely national style.

But France was still in a mood for imitation, and as before the new influences came from Italy. The Counter-Reformation Church was promoting a new wave of religious building; with St-Paul-St-Louis in the Marais (1627) began the fashion for tepid reworkings of Roman Baroque, and Italianate domes began springing up all over town (Val-de-Grâce, church of the Sorbonne). In secular buildings, imported Baroque translated into a more restrained, more French manner; its leading exponents were François Mansart (additions to the Hôtel Carnavalet) and Louis le Vau (Hôtel Lambert, much of Versailles and the Institut on the left bank of the Seine, 1661). Italian landscape gardening was adapted to French tastes by André Le Nôtre (gardens at the Tuileries, Vaux-le-Vicomte and Versailles).

Louis XIV and Colbert had long worked towards a total control of the arts, to ensure conformism and glorification of the regime. Like painting, architecture got its Académie in 1671. For the long-postponed completion of the Louvre, Louis and Colbert called upon the King of Baroque himself, Gianlorenzo Bernini, to design new monumental façades to surround the Cour Carrée. Bernini's foreign ideas and arrogance caused endless disputes; finally his plans were abandoned and the project was entrusted to Claude Perrault. The result was a classicist revelation, a remarkably original colonnade that has had a tremendous influence over everything built since in France. Another strikingly original work of the same period was Libéral Bruant's proto-rococo Hôtel des Invalides (1670).

Ten years later, however, Bruant's work suffered the intrusion of a huge church by Louis XIV's pet architect, Jules Hardouin-Mansart; the Dôme des Invalides is an aimless pile that the French to this day celebrate as one of the high points of their architectural achievement, perhaps because of its great size and gilded dome. Another sign of the academic rot setting in was the Observatory (1668), also by Perrault. Here, the architect insisted so strongly on following contrived rules of aesthetics that the result was almost unusable by the astronomers.

Elsewhere, the new academic servitors of the state produced pastiches of classical columns and pediments, combined with traditional French rooflines and fenestration, the most famous example of which is the king's stupendous garden-folly at Versailles. The greatest absurdities began to appear in the 18th century: the church of St-Sulpice (rebuilt 1719–40) and above all Jacques-Germain Soufflot's Panthéon (1755), also originally a church. One French critic has called this 'the first example of perfect architecture'. Yet it has no elements not borrowed from elsewhere, no coherence of the elements, not the faintest notion of proportion or symmetry. Soufflot, like Hardouin-Mansart, was a salon conversationalist, not an architect; his Panthéon can barely stand by itself, and is frequently closed to the public while engineers try to save it.

Neoclassicism

Ironically, both St-Sulpice and the Panthéon were harbingers of an 18th-century reaction against the tastefully vacuous work of the Sun King's reign. Still in the academic straitjacket, though influenced by the *philosophes* and, above all, Rousseau, architects attempted an even more direct copying of ancient Greek and Roman forms, and found it somehow liberating.

This trend produced a good deal of dross, and two remarkable successes. First, Jacques-Ange Gabriel's Place de la Concorde (1755–75), which marked a revolution in French planning – from a tightly-packed, introspective city to the expansive, horizontal and tree-lined Paris of today. Second was Claude-Nicolas Ledoux's 47 *barrières* for the new Farmers-General wall around the city (*see* p.32). All are simple as pie, playfully recombining classical domes, cylinders, colonnades and pediments in such a way that each was a little demonstration exercise in itself, and each referred to all of the others. Only four survive (Place de la Nation, Place de Stalingrad, Parc de Monceau, Place Denfert-Rochereau).

Neoclassicism, appropriate to an age that strove for virtue, continued through the Revolution (when little was built), through Napoleon and into the Restoration. Under Napoleon it reached its climax, with grandiose projects like the colonnaded Rue de Rivoli (1802), meant as a parade route for triumphal armies, the Bourse (A. T. Brongniart, 1808), the Madeleine (1806) and the Arc de Triomphe (1806).

A Revolution in Iron

The opening of the École Polytechnique in 1794 created a new sort of academicism, entirely separating the engineering side of architecture from the artistic. To be an architect, you had to attend the Beaux-Arts, the proud bastion of academicism. It was a fatal mistake. Paris, far ahead of any other European city, was on the verge of beginning a new architectural age, using durable, versatile iron and glass to make buildings fit for the Industrial Revolution and the new century dawning. As it is, Paris is full of brilliant works, daring and dazzling in the time when they were built, an achievement that everyone, with the exception of the Parisians themselves, appreciates and honours today.

Glass roofs were being put up over narrow shopping streets as early as 1776; the first proposal for a purpose-built, glass, light court came in 1780. Revolution and war interrupted progress, though iron bridges like the Pont des Arts (1803) and the Pont d'Austerlitz (1806) appeared, and the first of the *passages*, or arcades, were probably built in the 1790s. Economic recovery during the Bourbon Restoration brought a mania for arcade building; the 1820s saw beautifully appointed ones such as the Galeries Colbert-Vivienne and the Véro-Dodat. Precursors of the modern department store, the *passages* numbered some 130 in 1840; only a score of them remain today.

Other uses for iron and glass included churches, such as the graceful neo-Gothic Ste-Clotilde (1846), greenhouses (the Serre du Jardin des Plantes, 1830) and the railway stations, prime symbols of the Industrial Revolution that tried to marry the new technology to traditional French monumental architecture. The most surprising application – in libraries – was supplied by the visionary architect Henri Labrouste. His first experiment, the Bibliothèque Ste-Geneviève, was but an exercise for one of Paris' greatest masterpieces, the main reading room of the Bibliothèque Nationale.

Napoleon III and Haussmann: The Remaking of Paris

Few dictators anywhere have had such a will to build and transform, but then few dictators required people to address them as 'Emperor'. Louis-Napoleon knew nothing of this city, where he had never lived before

1848, but to aid him he found a brilliant and forceful native Parisian named Georges Haussmann, whom he made Prefect of the Seine *département*, the post that had almost total control over everything in Paris. Much of their work was badly needed: sewers, gas mains, water supplies, new schools and several of the city's parks. When they were done, Paris was as up-to-date as any city in the world.

Another aspect of their plans for Paris proved a little harder to swallow. To facilitate traffic, to enrich the unsavoury swarm of speculators that buzzed about the imperial throne, and to get the poor out of sight and out of mind, central Paris was nearly obliterated by a gargantuan programme of slum clearance and road building – Boulevards Sébastopol, St-Germain, Haussmann, St-Michel and Avenue de l'Opéra, among many others. No accommodation was made for the 200,000 or so displaced poor, and Haussmann showed absolutely no consideration for Paris' past; one of his most wanton crimes was the destruction of 80 per cent of the Île de la Cité, the city's ancient heart.

Architecturally, it was the heyday of the Beaux-Arts, with eclectic regime showpieces such as the completion of the Louvre and Charles Garnier's mammoth Opéra. But just as modern technology was enrolled to support Napoleon III's tyranny, it had to do the same for his art. Garnier, like Soufflot, was no architect, and he never could have made this marble pile stand by itself – iron girders hidden under the frippery do the job.

The Last Golden Age: 1870–1914

Recovery from the disasters of 1870–1 was slow, but by the 1880s the Third Republic was fostering inspired architecture once more. The 1889 Exposition was the apotheosis of iron, producing not only the Eiffel Tower but also the incredible Galerie des Machines (400m long), demolished in 1910. The tower is a magical apparition: a symbol for Paris, for its century, for all of modern industrial civilization – a building with no purpose, an ornament, yet one that delights everyone and makes intellectuals discuss and contemplate endlessly. By 1900, when Art Nouveau was beginning to flower, official architecture had lapsed back into eclecticism; a work such as the colonnaded, glass-roofed, lavishly decorated Grand Palais may seem to you magnificent or silly or both.

Sensuous, extravagant Art Nouveau seems a perfect match for the Paris of the Belle Époque, but in fact the style always met with a cool reception. Many restaurants and cafés (like Maxim's) to this day have conserved their Art Nouveau décors, but as for buildings there are only a few choice works by Hector Guimard. Greatly influenced by Gothic restorer Viollet-le-Duc and his rediscovery of organic forms in architecture, Guimard is famous for his métro entrances, most of which are now gone. He also did some singular apartment blocks in the 16e: the Castel Béranger and others on Rue La Fontaine, 142 Avenue de Versailles and 122 Avenue Mozart. His Left Bank counterpart, Jules Lavirotte, similarly adorned the 7e: Square Rapp and 29 Avenue Rapp.

Art Nouveau did have a big influence on another new feature of the Parisian scene – department stores. Since Au Bon Marché of 1852, these had been in the forefront of modernism, with huge light courts and grand staircases. At the turn of the last century they accepted Art Nouveau in a big way; you can see what has survived at the wonderful Samaritaine and the Galeries Lafayette. This era also produced some surprises only tangentially related to Art Nouveau, including two unique churches: St-Jean-de-Montmartre (1894), with lattice-work arches of reinforced concrete, and Notre-Dame-du-Travail in Montparnasse (1891), a workingmen's church with boldly exposed girders and rivets. Architects after 1900 put up some splashy buildings on Rue Réaumur, a busy street of the publishing and textile trades, that would look entirely at home in Chicago (especially the block at No.124, by Georges Chadanne, 1903).

The 20th Century: From Classicism to the *Grands Projets*

Instead of carrying bravely on with modernism, however, Parisian architecture inexplicably decayed into a heavy, tedious classicism – Louis XIV without the frills – as exemplified in the work of Auguste Perret (Théâtre des Champs-Elysées, 1911; Mobilier National at the Gobelins, 1931), and in the 1937 Exposition (Palais de Chaillot). After all the successes in the previous century, Paris had almost nothing to contribute to the 20th. Even examples of important non-Parisian architects are few and uninspiring: the UNESCO building (1958) behind the École Militaire, by Marcel Breuer, Pier Luigi Nervi and Bernard Zehrfuss; a pavilion at the Cité Universitaire by Lúcio Costa (1959). There is a clutch of buildings, mostly houses, by Le Corbusier, austere buildings with large window areas (Villas Roche-Jeanneret, Square du Docteur-Blanche; Salvation Army Hostel, Rue Cantagrel). Much more interesting than any of these are Le Corbusier's plans for Paris. So much did this man (and many of his contemporaries) hate the city, with its freedom and disorder, that he wanted to wipe it off the map. He submitted proposals for the never-built Voisin Project, in which much of the city centre was to be destroyed and replaced with tidy rows of tower blocks. Paris' elite saved the city for itself, but after the Second World War it imposed Le Corbusier's totalitarian vision on hundreds of thousands of Parisians, 'rehoused' in grim suburban concrete waste-lands. Occasionally this sort of thing has sneaked inside the Paris boundaries, as in the redevelopments at Belleville or the Front de la Seine.

Until 1968, architects were still being trained almost exclusively in the Beaux-Arts, guaranteeing a maximum of conformity and an allergy to creativity. This shows best in the huge office project of La Défense, begun in 1958, though most of the large buildings are

Finding Paris' Architecture

from the 1970s. Site planning has been notably unadventurous and unattractive, while the buildings themselves copy corporatist American firms such as Skidmore-Owings-Merrill. Paris suffered in many ways in the 1970s, from the destruction of Les Halles to the Right Bank expressway championed by President Pompidou. But the steadfastly modernist Pompidou also stood Paris on its ear with Richard Rogers' and Renzo Piano's Pompidou Centre, a controversial, high tech structure that has won fans even among traditionalists.

With the 1980s and President François Mitterrand, both Paris and its tutelary state were desperate to make up for so much lost time. Thus the Pharaonic era of the *grands projets*: the Grande Arche at La Défense, the Bastille Opéra, the Grand Louvre renovation that includes I. M. Pei's Pyramid, the Science Park at La Villette, the museum conversion of the Gare d'Orsay, all by foreign architects. Frenchmen were charged with designing the Ministère des Finances in Bercy and, biggest of all, the gruesome Bibliothèque Nationale. For a glimmer of optimism on the state of French architecture, the building that has won the widest acclaim in the last 20 years has been Jean Nouvel's marvellously elegant Institut du Monde Arabe (1987) on the Left Bank.

Perhaps fortunately, Paris hasn't the money for any more *grands projets*. Building continues on a more modest level, though. The ambitious new quarter at Bercy now includes Frank Gehry's long-delayed American Center, now redefined as a home for the Musée du Cinema. Another construction that has won public approval is the Passerelle de Solférino, a graceful pedestrian bridge linking the Quai des Tuileries with the Quai Anatole France.

Travel

GETTING THERE

By Air

Paris has two international airports, Roissy-Charles de Gaulle and Orly. Flights are plentiful; the question is finding one that meets your needs – whether it's flexible travel dates, cheap price or multi-stop itineraries. Prices vary wildly, depending on how far in advance you book and what kind of flight you are willing to settle for. But the offers are there. Travellers under 26 and students under 32 can pick up discounts through some of the specialist travel agencies.

From the UK and Ireland

It takes around 50mins to fly from London to Paris. Prices for a return flight vary from £30 on a low-cost airline to £300 for a high-season, full-fare ticket.

Scheduled Flights

Aer Lingus, **t** *(01) 886 8888*, **w** *www. aerlingus.com*. Flights from Dublin, Cork and Shannon to Charles de Gaulle.

Air France, **t** *0845 0845 111*, **w** *www. airfrance.co.uk*. Regular flights from London Heathrow, London Gatwick, London City, Birmingham, Bristol, Edinburgh, Glasgow, Aberdeen, Manchester, Newcastle and Southampton to Charles de Gaulle.

British Airways, **t** *08457 733 377*, **w** *www. britishairways.com*. Daily flights from London Gatwick or Heathrow to Charles de Gaulle. Also flies direct from Aberdeen, Belfast, Birmingham, Bristol, Cardiff, Edinburgh, Glasgow and Manchester.

British Midland, **t** *0870 6070 555*, **w** *www. flybmi.com*. From London Heathrow, Dublin, Belfast, Cardiff, Edinburgh, Glasgow, Leeds Bradford, Manchester, Teesside, Cork and East Midlands to Charles de Gaulle.

Flybe, **t** *08705 676 676*, **w** *www. flybe.com*. Flights from London Heathrow and City, Aberdeen, Bristol, Edinburgh, Manchester and Southampton to Charles de Gaulle and Orly.

Low-cost Carriers

The cheap no-frills carriers easyJet and Ryanair can sometimes get you to Paris from London for as little as £25 if you book well in advance. They often advertise special offers for even less, and you can book directly over the Internet. Prices go up the closer you get to your leaving date; fares booked at the last minute are sometimes not much cheaper than those of the major carriers. Tickets generally have conditions attached; often they are non-refundable and the date cannot be changed.

bmibaby, **t** *0870 264 2229*, **w** *www.bmi baby.com*. Flights from Cardiff and East Midlands to Charles de Gaulle.

Flights on the Internet

The best place to start looking for flights is the Web – just about everyone has a site where you can compare prices (see also the airlines listed in the main text), and booking online usually confers a 10–20% discount.

In the UK and Ireland

w *www.cheapflights.com*
w *www.flightcentre.co.uk*
w *www.lastminute.com*
w *www.skydeals.co.uk*
w *www.sky-tours.co.uk*
w *www.thomascook.co.uk*
w *www.trailfinder.com*
w *www.travelocity.com*
w *www.travelselect.com*

In the USA

w *www.air-fare.com*
w *www.airhitch.org*
w *www.expedia.com*
w *www.flights.com*
w *www.orbitz.com*
w *www.priceline.com*
w *www.travellersweb.ws*
w *www.travelocity.com*
w *www.smarterliving.com*

In Canada

w *www.flightcentre.ca*
w *www.lastminuteclub.com*
w *www.newfrontiers.com*

easyJet, *t 0870 6000 000*, *w www.easyjet. com*. Flights from Luton, Newcastle and Liverpool to Charles de Gaulle.

Ryanair, *t 08701 569 569*, *w www.ryanair. com*. Regular flights from Glasgow Prestwick, Dublin and Shannon to Paris Beauvais. Beauvais is 35 miles northwest of Paris; there is a bus link to Porte Maillot in central Paris.

Student and Youth Travel

CTS Travel, *t (020) 7290 0630*, *w www.cts travel.co.uk*.

Europe Student Travel, *t (020) 7727 7647*.

STA Travel, *t 08701 600599*, *w www.sta travel.co.uk*. Agents for STA Travel are based at many university campuses.

usit NOW, *Dublin t (01) 602 1600*, *w www. usitnow.ie*.

Packages

BA and Air France (*see* above) offer competitive packages with a selection of hotels.

From the USA and Canada

There are frequent flights to Paris on most of the major airlines. Direct flights can be expensive (going above US$1,000 in high season), but non-direct flights are much more competitive, especially with European carriers and if booked well in advance. During off-peak periods (the winter months and fall) you should be able to get a scheduled economy flight from New York to Paris from as little as $400–500.

It may work out cheaper to fly to London and then continue your journey to Paris from there, for example with a low-cost carrier.

Scheduled Flights

Air Canada, *t 888 247 2262*, *w www.air canada.ca*. Direct flights from Montreal and Toronto.

Air France, *USA t 800 237 2747, Canada t 800 667 2747*, *w www.airfrance.com*. Regular services from Altanta, Boston, Chicago, LA, Cincinnati, Houston, Miami, Montreal, New York (JFK and Newark), Philadelphia, San Francisco, Toronto and Washington.

American Airlines, *t 800 433 7300*, *w www. aa.com*. Flights from Boston, Chicago, Dallas, JFK and Miami.

> ### Airline Offices in Paris
> **Aer Lingus**: *t 01 55 38 38 55*
> **Air Canada**: *t 01 44 50 20 02*
> **Air France**: *t 08 36 68 10 48*
> **American**: *t 08 10 87 28 72*
> **British Airways**: *t 08 25 82 54 00*
> **Northwest Airlines**: *t 08 10 55 65 56*
> **United Airlines**: *t 08 01 62 62 62*

Continental, *USA t 800 231 0856, t 800 343 9195 (hearing impaired)*, *w www.continental. com*. Flights from Houston and Newark.

Delta, *t 800 241 4141, Canada t 800 221 1212*, *w www.delta.com*. Flights from New York JFK, Atlanta, Boston, Chicago, Cincinnati and Los Angeles International.

Northwest Airlines, *t 800 447 4747*, *w www. nwa.com*. Flights from Detroit.

Nouvelles Frontières, *5757 West Century Blvd, Suite 650, Los Angeles LA 90045, t 800 677 0720*, *w www.newfrontiers.com*. Discounted scheduled and charter flights from LA, New York and Oakland. They also offer packages.

United Airlines, *t 800 241 6522*, *w www. ual.com*. From Chicago, Los Angeles, Miami, New Orleans and Seattle.

Student and Youth Travel

CTS Travel, *t 877 287 6665*, *w www.cts travelusa.com*.

STA Travel, *t 1 800 781 4040*, *w www.sta travel.com*.

Travel Cuts, *t 1 866 246 9762*, *w www. travelcuts.com*.

By Train

Travelling by high-speed train is an attractive alternative to flying from the UK. **Eurostar** trains leave from London Waterloo and Ashford International in Kent, and there are direct services to Paris (Gare du Nord; 3hrs; from £70) and Disneyland Paris (3hrs; from £120; *see also* p.295). Fares are cheaper if booked at least seven days in advance (and get cheaper the further in advance you book) and if you include a Saturday night away. Check in 20mins before departure, or you will not be allowed on to the train.

Information and bookings:

Eurostar, *UK* **t** *0870 160 6600, USA* **t** *800 EUROSTAR*, **w** *www.eurostar.com*.

For details of other ways of getting to Paris by train, contact:

Rail Europe, *178 Piccadilly, London W1V 0BA,* **t** *08705 848 848,* **w** *www.raileurope.co.uk*.

Rail Europe, *226 Westchester Av, White Plains, NY 10064,* **t** *1 800 438 7245, Canada* **t** *1 800 361 72 45,* **w** *www.raileurope.com*.

SNCF, the French national rail company, runs an efficient network of trains within France. For information contact:

SNCF, **t** *08 36 35 35 35,* **w** *www.sncf.com*.

Disabled Travellers

Eurostar gives wheelchair passengers first-class travel for second-class fares.

The SNCF publishes a pamphlet, *Guide Pratique du Voyageur à Mobilité Réduite*, covering travel by train for the disabled (all high-speed TGVs are equipped) – contact Rail Europe (*see* above) for details.

By Car

Taking your car on a Eurotunnel train is the most convenient way of crossing the Channel between the UK and France. It takes only 35mins to get through the tunnel between Folkestone and Calais, and there are up to four departures an hour every day. Peak-time tickets for a car and passengers cost around £300 return in the low season, rising to £350 return in the high season. If you travel at night (10pm–6am), it is slightly cheaper. Special-offer day returns (look for them on the Web site) range from £15 to £50. Prices are per car less than 6.5m in length, plus the driver and all passengers.

Information and bookings:

Eurotunnel, **t** *08705 353 535,* **w** *www.euro tunnel.com*.

Driving in France

A car entering France must have its regis-tration and insurance papers. Drivers with a valid licence from an EU country, Canada, the USA or Australia don't need an international licence. If you're coming from the UK or Ireland, the dip of the headlights must be adjusted to the right. Carrying a warning triangle is mandatory; the triangle should be placed 50m (55 yards) behind the car if you have a breakdown. Seat belts are also mandatory; in addition, all cars in France are required to have rear seat belts, and these must be worn.

Drive on the right-hand side of the road. The speed limits are as follows: 130km/80mph on *autoroutes*; 110km/69mph on dual carriageways (divided highways); 90km/55mph on other roads; 50km/30mph in urban areas. Watch out for *priorité à droite*: the French rule of giving priority to the right at every intersection has largely disappeared, but there may still be intersections, usually in towns, where it applies. Petrol (*essence*) is relatively expensive in France (*see* p.66). Unleaded is called *sans plomb*; diesel is often called *gazole/gasoil*. If an attendant helps with oil, windscreen-cleaning or checking tyre pressure they will expect a tip. On *autoroutes* (motorways) tolls are quite high.

For information about driving in Paris, *see* 'Getting Around', p.66.

Disabled Travellers

The Channel Tunnel is a good way to travel by car since disabled passengers are allowed to stay in their vehicle.

Cars fitted to accommodate wheelchairs pay reduced tolls on *autoroutes*. An *auto-route* guide for disabled travellers (*Guide des Autoroutes à l'Usage des Personnes à Mobilité Réduite*) is available free from Ministère des Transports, Direction des Routes, Service du Contrôle des Autoroutes, La Défense, 92055 Cedex, Paris, **t** *01 40 81 21 22*.

By Sea

The most common route across the Channel to Paris is Dover–Calais. Dieppe and Le Havre, however, are actually closer to Paris, so it is best to ring round and check which service is offering the best deal at the time you want to travel (*see* contact details below). Fares vary according to season and demand. The most expensive booking period runs from the first week of July to mid-August; other pricey times include Easter and the school holidays. Book as far ahead as possible and keep your eyes peeled for special offers.

Information and bookings:

Hoverspeed Ferries, t *0870 240 8070,* **w** *www.hoverspeed.co.uk.* Seacats (catamarans) from Dover to Calais (35mins) and Newhaven to Dieppe (2hrs).

P&O Ferries, t *0870 600 0600,* **w** *www. posl.com.* Ferry and 'superferry' from Dover to Calais (45mins), Portsmouth to Le Havre and Portsmouth to Cherbourg.

P&O Portsmouth, t *0870 242 4999,* **w** *www. poportsmouth.com.* Day and night sailings from Portsmouth to Le Havre (5½hrs).

SeaFrance, t *08705 711 711,* **w** *www.seafrance. com.* Sailings from Dover to Calais (1½hrs).

Disabled Travellers

Most ferry companies offer special facilities if contacted beforehand.

By Coach

The cheapest way to get to Paris is by coach. The journey takes 8hrs. **Eurolines** has regular coach services from London to Paris, departing from Victoria Coach Station. If you book a week in advance, off-peak return tickets to Paris are as low as £33, peak-season (22 July–4 Sept) returns are from £39. There are discounts for anyone under 26, senior citizens and children under 12. In the summer, the coach can be the best bargain for anyone over 26; off-season you may be able to find an equivalently priced flight.

Information and bookings:

Eurolines, t *08705 143 219,* **w** *www.goby coach.com.*

SPECIALIST TOUR OPERATORS

The following list is a selection of independent companies offering city breaks to Paris, most catering to a special interest. A good place to look for further information and organizations is the Maison de France Web site at *www.franceguide.com* or the US Web site at *www.francetourism.com*, or a French government tourist office (*see* p.77). Other sources of information are The French Centre, 164–6 Westminster Bridge Rd, London SE1 7RW, **t** (020) 7960 2600, **e** info@ cei-frenchcenter.com, or the Cultural Services of the French Embassy, 23 Cromwell Rd, London SW7 2EL, **t** (020) 7838 2088/9, or at 972 Fifth Av, New York, NY 10021, **t** (212) 439 1400. Alternatively, check out the information at **w** *www.fr-holidaystore.co.uk.*

In France

Alliance Française, *101 Bd Raspail, 6e (S16),* **t** *01 42 84 90 00,* **e** *info@alliancefr.org,* **w** *www.alliancefr.org.* French classes at all levels (one month minimum).

Ecole Ritz Escoffier, *15 Place Vendôme, 75041 Paris Cedex (S9), **t** 01 43 16 30 50, **e** ecole@ ritzparis.com, **w** www.ritzparis.com.* Cookery courses at the Ritz.

Eurocentres Foundation, *13 Passage Dauphine (V13), 75006 Paris, **t** 01 40 46 72 00, **e** par-info@eurocentres.com, **w** www.euro centres.com; in the USA **t** (703) 684 1494, **e** alx-info@eurocentres.com; in the UK **t** (01273) 324 545, **e** bri-info@eurocentres.com.* Offers intensive general and business French courses in professionally equipped centres.

In the UK

Abercrombie & Kent, *Sloane Square House, Holbein Place, London SW1W 8NS, **t** 0845 0700 610, **f** 085 0700 608, **w** www.abercrom biekent.co.uk.* Quality city breaks, tailored to suit your interests.

BAC Sport, *BAC House, 112 Clerkenwell Rd, London EC1M 5TW, **t** (020) 7456 7100, **f** 020 7456 7110, **w** www.bacsport.co.uk, bacsport@ bac_london.com.* City breaks to coincide with sporting events.

British Museum Traveller, *46 Bloomsbury St, London WC1B 3QQ, **t** (020) 7456 7575,*

f (020) 7580 8677, *w www.britishmuseum
traveller.co.uk*. Art and architecture tours.

Cox and Kings, *4th Floor, Gordon House,
10 Greencoat Place, London SW1P 1PH,
t (020) 7873 5027*, *f (020) 7630 6038,
w www.coxandkings.co.uk*. Short breaks,
gourmet and escorted cultural tours.

Euro Academy, *77A George St, Croydon CR0
1LD, t (020) 8686 2363*, *f (020) 8681 8850,
w www.euroacademy.co.uk*. Art, cookery and
language courses.

Kirker Holidays, *3 New Concordia Wharf,
Mill St, London SE1 2BB, t (020) 7231 3333,
f (020) 7231 4771, w www.kirkerholidays.com,
e cities@kirkerholidays.com*. Tailor-made itineraries and packages.

Martin Randall Travel, *10 Barley Mow
Passage, Chiswick, London W4 4PH, t (020)
8742 3355, f (020) 8742 7766, w www.martin
randall.com, e info@martinrandall.com*.
Cultural tours of Paris with a lecturer
for company.

Page & Moy, *135–40 London Rd, Leicester
LE2 1EN, t 08700 106 212, f 08700 106 211,
w www.page-moy.com*. City breaks,
gastronomy and cultural tours.

Prospect Music and Art Tours, *36
Manchester St, London W1M 5PE, t (020) 7486
5705, f (020) 7486 5868, w www.prospect
tours.com*. Tours of the big museums.

Saga Holidays, *The Saga Building, Enbrook
Park, Folkestone CT20 3SE, t 0800 300 500,
f (01303) 771 010, w www.saga.co.uk*. Holidays
for the over-50s.

Shortbreaks Ltd UK, *t (020) 8402 0007,
f (020) 8402 1273, e info@short-breaks.com,
w www.short-breaks.com*. All-inclusive
Eurostar breaks.

Voyages Jules Verne, *21 Dorset Square,
London NW1 6QG, t (020) 7616 1000, f (020)
7723 8629, w www.vjv.co.uk*. Speciality tours,
including food and drink, art and history, and
single travellers.

Paule Caillat's Promenades Gourmandes,
*t (020) 7396 5550, w www.gourmetontour.
com*. Become Madame Caillat's apprentice
for a day: follow her around the market
then get hands-on and touch up your
culinary skills.

In Ireland

Abbey Travel, *44–5 Middle Abbey St,
Dublin 1, t (01) 804 7100, f (01) 873 3163,
w www.abbeytravel.ie, e information@
abbeytravel.ie*. City breaks.

Go Holidays, *28 North Great George's St,
Dublin 1, t (01) 874 4126, f (01) 872 7958,
w www.goholidays.ie*. City breaks.

In the USA

Abercrombie and Kent, *152 Kensington Rd,
Oak Brook, IL 60523, t 800 323 7308, w www.
abercrombiekent.com*. Quality city breaks.

Above and Beyond Tours, *230 North Via Las
Palmas, Palm Springs, CA 92262, t 800 397
2681, f 760 325 1702, e info@abovebeyond
tours.com, w www.abovebeyondtours.com*.
Gay city breaks.

Accent, *870 Market St, Suite 1026, San
Francisco, CA 94102, t 800 869 9291, t (415) 835
3744, f (415) 835 3749, e sfaccent@aol.com*.
Semester/year-long programmes at the
Sorbonne for all abilities.

EC Tours, *10153 1/2 Riverside, Toluca Lake,
CA 91602, t 800 388 0877, f 818 755 0999,
w www.ectours.com*. Tours and city packages.

Elderhostel, *75 Federal St, Boston, MA 02110,
t (617) 426 7788, f (617) 426 8351, w www.elder
hostel.org*. Courses in art, history and
gardens for older adults.

Jet Vacations, *880 Apollo St, Suite 243,
El Segundo, CA 90245, t 800 JET 0999,
f (310) 640 1700, w www.vacations.net*.
Independent travel packages and customized
group packages.

Kesher Tours, *347 Fifth Ave, Suite 706, New
York, NY 10016, t 800 847 0700, f (212) 481
4212, w www.keshertours.com*. Fully escorted
kosher tours, taking in London too.

Maupintour, *10650 W. Charleston Blvd.,
Summerlin, NV 89135, t 800 255 4266,
t (785) 331 1000, f (702) 260 3787, w www.
maupintour.com*. City breaks in Paris,
including at Christmas and New Year.

**National Registration Center for Study
Abroad**, *823 N. 2nd St, Milwaukee, WI 53203,
t (414) 278 0631, (414) 271 8884, w www.nrcsa.*

com. Language and culture courses at the Sorbonne and other centres.

Sportstours, *P.O. Box 457, New York, NY 10185 0457, t 800 879 8647, e info@sports tours.com, w www.sportstours.com.* Tours to the French Open tennis tournament in Paris.

ENTRY FORMALITIES

Passports and Visas

Holders of full, valid EU, USA, Canadian, Australian and New Zealand passports do not need a visa to enter France for stays of up to 90 days. If you intend to stay longer, the law says you need a *carte de séjour* (from your local *mairie*, or town hall), a requirement EU citizens can easily get around as passports are rarely stamped. Non-EU citizens had best apply for an extended visa before leaving home, a complicated procedure requiring proof of income, etc. You can't get a *carte de séjour* without the visa, and obtaining that is a trial run in the *ennuis* you'll undergo in applying for a *carte de séjour*. For further information contact your nearest French embassy/consulate (*see* p.72).

Customs

Duty-free allowances have been abolished for journeys within the European Union. For travellers coming from outside the EU, the duty-free limits are 1 litre of spirits or 2 litres of liquors (port, sherry or champagne), plus 2 litres of wine and 200 cigarettes.

Much larger quantities – up to 10 litres of spirits, 90 litres of wine, 110 litres of beer and 800 cigarettes – bought locally and provided you are travelling between EU countries, can be taken through customs if you can prove that they are for private consumption only. Shops at ports, airports and the Channel Tunnel continue to sell other products, such as perfume and cosmetics, at reduced prices. Non-EU citizens flying from an EU country to a non-EU country can still buy duty-free goods to take home.

ARRIVAL

Airports

There are two main airports in Paris: **Charles de Gaulle** (information **t** 01 48 62 22 80, **w** *www.paris-cdg.com*), 30km to the north of the city (also known as Roissy after the suburb in which it is located), and **Orly** (information **t** 01 49 75 52 52), 15km to the south.

Both airports are well equipped with tourist-information offices, car-hire firms, and places to eat and shop.

Getting to and from Paris Airports

By RER

Terminal 2 at **Charles de Gaulle** is on the RER B train line to central Paris (around 40mins to Gare du Nord; €7.50). Terminal 1 is linked to the RER B by airport bus only, so for travelling to or from this terminal a direct bus service from Paris is an option worth considering (*see* below).

Orly is linked every 4–8 minutes to RER B station Antony by an automatic train, Orlyval (€9 to Gare du Nord). All airport RER tickets allow you to transfer onto the métro to complete your journey.

By Bus

Both airports have good bus services (information **t** 01 41 56 89 00).

Charles de Gaulle: Air France buses run from both terminals to Porte Maillot and the Arc de Triomphe (€10), and to Gare de Lyon and Gare Montparnasse (€11.50). The slightly cheaper RATP (city) Roissybus goes to Rue Scribe, near the Opéra (€8). Allow an hour for the journey. Buses depart every 12–15mins from 5.45am to 11pm. There is also a night bus service via Gare du Nord and Châtelet.

Orly: Air France buses (€7.60) run from both terminals to Invalides and Gare Montparnasse; the RATP Orlybus (€5.50) goes to the RER station at Place Denfert-Rochereau. Buses depart every 15–20mins from 6am to 11pm; allow 45mins.

By Taxi

Airport taxis aren't the rip-off they are in some cities, but are only necessary if you have tons of baggage. It costs about €38 to central Paris from Charles de Gaulle, and €23 from Orly, depending on traffic.

GETTING AROUND

Maps

For detailed information, the *Michelin Paris-Plan 11* (2001) – the little blue book – is indispensable: brilliantly conceived, a cartographical work of art. For day trips into the outskirts of the city, Michelin's green *Environs de Paris 106* is the best.

Otherwise, most stationery stores sell the useful *Plan de Paris*, a little book that details every tiny street, métro station, and attraction you could ever hope to visit.

RATP

The Régie Autonome des Transports Parisiens is the authority that controls the buses and the métro. Their main office is at 54 Quai de la Rapée (métro Gare de Lyon; EE17). For recorded information call **t** 01 43 46 14 14. For a human being you have to pay €0.35 a minute; call **t** 08 92 68 7714. Lost property is on **t** 01 40 06 75 27.

The RATP Web site, with maps and information, is at **w** *www.ratp.fr*.

By Métro

The métro is a godsend to disorientated visitors; not only is it quick and convenient for travelling, but its stations serve as easy reference points for finding addresses. Contrasts with the London Underground are unavoidable. A ride in Paris costs less than half as much, and for that you get cleaner stations, faster service, fewer breakdowns, fewer fatalities, a staff a thousand times

Bus and Métro Tickets

It's not worth buying single tickets. Métro tickets are valid on buses and a *carnet* of 10 tickets can be bought at any métro station for €10, which works out as a 40% discount.

You can change métro lines as often as you want on the same journey for the same ticket, but the bus requires a new ticket with each bus you catch.

Passes

Compared to transport fares elsewhere, those in Paris will seem ridiculously cheap, but if you're going to spend a lot of time here, you can do even better. Most Parisians carry the basic pass, valid on buses, métro, RER and SNCF suburban trains. A weekly pass (*carte hebdomadaire*) is €13.75; a month (*carte orange*) is €46.05. These are good for two zones only; for more zones the fee is higher. Bring a passport photo when you buy and be sure to write the number of your carrying pouch on your ticket, otherwise you could end up with a fine. Note: these passes expire at the end of the week or month, so purchase them at the beginning of the period.

There is a special travel card, **Paris Visite**, starting at €18.25 for up to three days. This is a rotten deal, however, as you'll need to ride seven or eight times a day just to break even in comparison with a *carnet*, and none of the major attractions is included.

more helpful and courteous; most significantly, you get more air and space.

Trains run from 5.30am to 12.30am.

Which Line to Use

A minor complaint would be that the *direction* system is harder to read than the simple coloured maps in London, where each line has a name. To find the right train, it isn't simply a matter of looking for 'northbound' or 'eastbound'. You'll need to look at the map and remember the name of the **station at the end of the line**, in the direction you wish to travel. For example, if you wish to go north on Line 7 to Porte de la Villette, you're looking for a platform marked: 'Direction: La Courneuve–8 Mai 1945'.

The world's least offensive underground service is even struggling to achieve personality. Graphics and design have appeared in some stations to replace the ubiquitous white tiles from the 1930s, which leant a touch of clinical anaesthesia to the journey. Some métro stations have exhibits on art or the history of the locality: Louvre, Bastille (with part of the fortress' foundations built into the station), Hôtel-de-Ville, St-Denis-Basilique and St-Germain-des-Prés. Others have decorated platforms, such as the one at Cluny-La Sorbonne with mosaics on the ceiling or Varenne with replicas of Rodin's *Le Penseur* and Balzac sculptures. One of the best métro thrills is to take Line 6 from La Motte-Picquet past the Eiffel Tower to Trocadéro, one of its few sorties above ground and over the Seine within the city limits. Then there's the new automatic line, the Météor (Line 14), from Bibliothèque-F.-Mitterrand to the Gare St-Lazare, super efficient and hi-tech, but very noisy.

Always keep your ticket until the end, not only for spot checks, but because some of the bigger stations have automatic exit gates that gobble it up. In parts of some stations, like the phenomenally complex Châtelet-Les Halles with more than 2km of passages, there are two of these in a row. So you'll spend the rest of your life down there, unless you ask an employee for a get-out-of-the-métro-free card, a *contremarque*. They're used to it.

By Bus

Bus routes are more of a challenge than the dreary métro, but much more fun. There are simple rules for riding the buses: enter from the front of the bus and leave from the middle or the rear; press the *arrêt demandé* button just before your stop; you'll need to have your ticket stamped as you enter by the machine next to the driver (*oblitérer*).

Buses run very frequently 5.30am–8.30pm, with a reduced service 8.30pm–1.30am and on Sun. The **Noctambus**, Paris' night bus network, can be useful; there are 18 lines, many converging at Place du Châtelet from points around the edge of the city (map and information available from any métro station). Buses generally run once an hour, from 1.30 to 5.30am.

Route 29, through the Marais (from Gare St-Lazare to Gare de Lyon), features a modern version of the old Paris buses with open-back platforms.

L'Open Tour, a system of tourist buses with an open upper deck, follows a circular route of the principal sites with further loops out to Montmartre and to Bercy. Tickets cost €25.15 for two days; get on and off anywhere. **Balabus** (operated by RATP) runs from the Grande Arche along the river to the Gare de Lyon and back (from 1.30pm to 8pm Sun and holidays 15 April–15 Sept). Three bus tickets are required for the full one-way journey. **Montmartrobus**, another circular route, runs up, down and around Montmartre; get on or off anywhere. It takes one ticket per journey. Finally, you can ride the **Funiculaire de Montmartre** instead of climbing the steps of the Sacré-Cœur; one ticket each way.

BatObus, t 01 44 11 33 99, **w** *www.batobus. com*, is a river bus service operating up and down the Seine in the heart of Paris, with seven stops along the *quais* (March–Oct).

By RER

The Réseau Express Régional is Paris' suburban commuter train system, run jointly by the SNCF (Société Nationale des Chemins de Fer Français) and RATP, so it's separate, but part of the system, and you can use métro tickets on it within the Paris boundaries. It can come in handy for getting across town fast or for visiting places like the Musée d'Orsay and the Jardin du Luxembourg, where it has the closest station. From almost all the other stations, you can easily change onto the métro. The RER can also take you to Versailles, Disneyland and to the airports. Although some of the cars are marked for 1st class, the distinction has long been abolished. Trains run from 5.30am to 12.30am; for information call **t** 01 53 90 10 10.

By Taxi

There are 14,900 taxis in Paris. On the whole they are a pleasure to ride with honest drivers. They'll get you to the station on time if it kills you both – it's a matter of honour – while forcing you to defend your government's policies or telling you about their daughter's trip to Oklahoma City.

The Michelin *Paris-Plan* has all the city's taxi stands conveniently marked on the map with blue Ts. Radio taxis (*see* numbers below) can be especially helpful in rush hours, when cabs are hard to find. Fares are determined according to an arcane system, with three different base rates, corresponding to the three little fairy lights on top of the car, and those on the meter. The meter starts at around €2. Expect to pay about €10 for a journey within central Paris. Fares double after 7pm Mon–Sat and all day Sun. There are also extra charges for excess baggage, a pick-up from the station etc.

A taxi driver is required by law to: stop for you if the light on top is on (unless it's his last half-hour on duty); take you anywhere you want to go in Paris, or to Orly or Charles de Gaulle airports; follow whatever route you choose; accept all disabled passengers; and give you a receipt. He/she is not required to: take animals; take more than three people (an insurance regulation so don't waste your breath arguing); take an unreasonable amount of luggage; pick up passengers less than 50m from a taxi stand.

For a radio taxi, contact:

Alpha Taxi, t *01 45 85 85 85*
Taxis Bleus, t *01 49 36 10 10*
Taxi Étoile, t *01 45 01 85 24*
Taxi G7, t *01 47 39 47 39*

By Car

This is, of course, absurd. Parking is almost impossible in Paris, and battalions of the world's most elegant meter maids cheerfully await your every indiscretion. Paris tows away 1,200 cars a day. Towing is privatized and something of a racket – they don't have to wait for an officer to call them, they just take what they want along the clearways (*axes rouges*). You can usually avoid being towed by leaving a person in the car. If you catch them in the act, demand that they call a policeman (a legal nicety); they don't want to wait and lose business, so they'll probably just move on.

None of the smaller hotels and few even of the luxury variety have garages. Underground car parks are fairly common (shown on the Michelin map with a blue P). Rates are around €1.25–2.30 an hour, and €20 for 24 hours.

Paris traffic gets a bad press. Parisians are generally polite, tolerant even of indecision and the temporary blocking of narrow streets. When oncoming drivers blink their headlights at you, it means the *flics* (cops) are waiting just up the road with an anti-speeding camera: the commendable custom of a gracious and civilized nation. But on the abominable *périphérique*, look out for motorbikes streaking between the lanes.

Unlike New York, few motorists here will actually go out of their way to try to kill a pedestrian but, unlike London, pedestrian crossings in Paris mean next to nothing. The comparative accident statistics between France and Britain are, of course, indecisive and neither side wins. Compared with France there are twice the number of road accidents in Britain (which, given France's 60 million annual tourists makes the statistic even more significant). But the number of fatalities in France is twice that of Britain. Maybe most of the deaths are foreigners passing through.

The priority rules have changed in France in recent years. Priority is no longer automatically given to the right, although there may be some intersections where *priorité à droite* still applies. If so, they will be marked. Petrol (*essence*) at the time of writing is on average €1.10 a litre for *super* and €1 for unleaded (*sans plomb*), and never goes down following the world market, only up. For more information on driving in France, *see* p.60.

There are 24-hour petrol stations at:
118 Av des Champs-Elysées (L8)
6 Bd Raspail (S13)
152 Rue La Fayette (AA5)

Hiring a Car

This too has its drawbacks: high rental rates and the exorbitant cost of petrol. Unless sweetened in an airline or holiday package deal and booked from outside France, car hire is an expensive proposition (from €40 a day, including mileage for the smallest cars). Prices vary widely from firm to firm: beware the small print about service charges and taxes. The minimum age for hiring a car in France is around 21 to 25, and the maximum around 70.

Forget the big chains. Though convenient and dependable, they're always the most expensive by a long way and wouldn't survive without tax-deductible business trippers. Local firms that rent at reasonable rates include:

City Loc, *4 Av de la Porte-de-Villiers, 17e, t 01 40 68 96 96 (métro Porte de Champerret; off maps); and other branches.*

Rual, *78 Bd Soult, 12e, t 01 43 45 52 20 (métro Porte de Vincennes; off maps).*

SNAC, *118 Rue de la Croix-Nivert, 15e, t 01 48 56 11 11 (métro Félix-Faure; off maps).*

The international companies have offices at the airports:

Avis, *Charles de Gaulle, t 01 48 62 34 34; Orly, t 01 49 75 44 91.*

Europcar, *Charles de Gaulle, t 01 48 62 33 33.*

Handi Service, *t 06 86 18 19 43.*

Hertz, *Charles de Gaulle, t 08 25 88 97 55; Orly, t 08 25 88 92 65.*

LVEA, *t 06 86 18 19 43. For the disabled.*

By Bicycle

Fearless, experienced urban cyclists can hire bikes by the half-day, day or week. Contact:

La Maison du Vélo, *11 Rue Fénelon, 10e, t 01 42 81 24 72, f 01 40 16 98 49 (métro Gare du Nord; Y5–6).*

Paris à Velo C'est Sympa!, *37 Bd Bourdon, 4e, t 01 48 87 60 01 (métro Bastille; DD14).* Rentals and a variety of city bike tours.

Paris-Vélo, *4 Rue du Fer-à-Moulin, 5e, t 01 43 37 59 22, f 01 47 07 67 45 (métro Censier-Daubenton; AA19).* All-terrain bike rentals and city bike tours.

SNCF, *t 01 53 90 20 20.* Rents bicycles from some railway stations (e.g. Fontainebleau, Versailles, Rambouillet) between 16 May and 27 Sept.

New cycle lanes are being created on some of Paris' main boulevards and through the city centre under an initiative by Socialist mayor Bertrand Delanöe, but look out for delivery vans and scooters taking short-cuts. In summer 2001 an experiment closed the city's *quais* to all but bicycles and pedestrians. It remains to be seen whether this will be repeated every summer.

By Motorbike

To hire a bike try:

Free-Scoot, *144 Blvd Voltaire 11, t 01 44 93 04 03, w www.free-scoot.com (métro Voltaire).* Scooter rentals for around €25/day.

Motojet, *76 Rue des Tournelles, 4e, t 01 42 72 70 12, w www.motojet.com (métro Chemin-Vert; DD13).* The charge is €60 per hour.

Guided Tours

By Boat

The famous *bateaux-mouches* got their name (literally, fly boats), because the first ones were built in Lyon, on the Quai des Mouches. Dating back to the Universal Exposition of 1889, they have become victims of their own success, metamorphosing into floating *bateaux-lasagnas*, so wide that the arches of the Pont des Arts had to be rebuilt to let them through. The largest is equipped with a retracting wheelhouse to fit under the bridges.

It's a tourist experience, with the recorded narration droning on in all the popular languages; the embankments are so high you won't really see very much. But it can still be fun. Most charge around €8 for a 1hr tour, and most also offer more expensive lunch and dinner cruises.

Contact:

Bateaux-Mouches de Paris, *from Pont de l'Alma (north side),* *t 01 42 25 96 10 (métro Alma-Marceau; L10).* This has night tours in summer and a fancy dinner cruise for €77. Lunch available Sat (€46) and hols (€54).

Bateaux Parisiens, *from the Port de La Bourdonnais,* *t 01 44 11 33 44 (métro Bir-Hakeim or Iéna; J11–12).*

Canauxrama, *t 01 42 39 15 00,* *w www. canauxrama.com.* Reservation only for 3hr tours of the Canal-St-Martin (€12). Evening trips in summer.

Paris Canal, *t 01 42 40 96 97,* *w www.paris canal.com.* Goes from the Musée d'Orsay up the Canal St-Martin to La Villette, passing through old locks and under tunnels.

Vedettes de Paris, *from the Port de Suffren,* *t 01 47 05 71 29,* *w www.vedettesdeparis.com (métro Bir-Hakeim; I12–13).* Dinner cruises (€88.50). Book in advance.

Vedettes du Pont Neuf, *from Sq du Vert-Galant, on the Île de la Cité,* *t 01 53 00 98 98 (métro Pont-Neuf; V13).*

By Foot

The following companies run walking tours in English:

Association for the Safeguard of Historical Paris, *44–6 Rue François Miron,* *t 01 48 87 74 31 (métro St-Paul; AA13).* Historic neighbourhoods of Paris. Tours from €7.50

Paris Promenade, *t 06 78 93 23 21.* Themed tours from €20 (2½hrs).

Urban Walks and Introductions, *t 06 76 22 79 72.* Themed tours, including tours for children.

By Bicycle

See **Paris-Vélo** and **Paris à Velo C'est Sympa!,** above.

By Helicopter, Hot-Air Balloon and Limousine

You're not allowed to fly or float over the Eiffel Tower in a helicopter or balloon any more, but several companies offer trips on the outskirts, and you can still go into the centre in a limousine or rickshaw.

Aristo's Limousine, *12 Rue Martissot, 92110 Clichy,* *t 01 47 37 53 70,* *e aristos@ infonie.fr.* Sightseeing tours of Paris by luxury limousine.

France Montgolfières, *t 01 47 00 66 44,* *w www.franceballoons.com.* Tours around Paris by hot-air balloon.

Heli France, *from the heliport at Quai d'Issy,* *t 01 45 54 95 11,* *e helifrance@wanadoo.fr.* Helicopter trips for €122 per person.

Vélo-taxi, *76 Rue des Tournelles,* *t 01 42 72 70 12 (métro Chemin-Vert; DD13).* English- and French-language sightseeing tours in a rickshaw (€60 per hour for two people). They will pick you up.

Practical A–Z

Climate

In a little climatic anomaly, Paris and its suburbs get slightly more sun and less rain than almost anywhere in northern France; hence all the sidewalk cafés.

The worst months to visit are September and October. Although the weather and light are beautiful, the city is packed to the brim with visitors and trade fairs. Winter can be soggy, cold and grey, but the city's cultural life is in full swing, and there are fewer tourists. Paris in the spring can be meltingly romantic, warm and sunny or cool and drizzling, but also crowded with tourists and visiting school groups. Summer is usually a bit hot, but so many Parisians vacate in July and August the whole city slows down. Gourmets should note that most of Paris' chefs take their holidays in August.

Average daily temperatures in °C/°F

Jan	Mar	May	July	Sept	Nov
9 (48)	10 (50)	17 (62)	25 (77)	20 (69)	12 (54)

Crime and the Police

Nothing is likely to happen to you in Paris. For most Americans and British city-dwellers, in fact, coming here will be statistically less dangerous than staying at home. Streets are safe at night. There are a few good reasons for this: firstly, there is less widespread poverty and desperation here; secondly, the poor, and the criminals with them, are largely segregated out in the suburbs; thirdly, Paris is crawling with plain-clothes police, just as it was in the days of Louis XIV or Louis-Philippe: regular city cops, public transport cops, anti-dog-droppings cops, thirty-one flavours of cop in fact. But the ones to steer clear of are conspicuous enough: the boys in blue with big sticks and patches that say **CRS** (Compagnie Républicaine de Sécurité). Their presence means you have stumbled into an area where a major demonstration is taking place, or else a riot or revolution. Even the most peaceful demonstrations can be followed by gangs of *casseurs* (vandals), looking for an excuse to raise some hell.

Smile and follow the CRS's instructions, as they are uncouth and testy, and accountable to no one.

Besides the police, you will need to watch out for **pickpockets**, especially in the métro, in the flea markets (where everyone deals in cash), and wherever people are standing around to watch street performers (for instance, around Les Halles). Muggings are rare, but car thefts and thefts from cars (radios, etc.) are common.

Report **thefts** to the nearest police station; not a pleasant task, but the reward is the bit of paper you need for an insurance claim. If your passport is stolen, contact the police and your nearest consulate for emergency travel documents. By law, the police in France can stop anyone anywhere and demand ID; in practice, they only tend to do it to harass minorities, the homeless and scruffy, hippy types.

The **drug** situation is the same in France as anywhere in the West: soft and hard drugs are widely available, and the police only make an issue of victimless crime when it suits them (your being a foreigner may just rouse them to action). Smuggling any amount of marijuana into the country can mean a prison term, and there's not much your consulate can or will do about it.

Disabled Travellers

When it comes to providing access for all, France is not exactly in the vanguard of nations, but things are beginning to change. We have indicated in the listings where hotels have rooms especially designed for wheelchair access. There's one hotel with complete facilities for travellers with disabilities: the **Résidence Internationale de Paris**, 44 Rue Louis-Lumière, 75020, **t** 01 40 31 45 45, **e** *residence.inter@libertysurf.fr* (moderate). On the whole, **restaurants** do not have disabled toilets, and it is advisable to call ahead to ensure that you are seated at the most convenient table.

National **museums** offer disabled visitors free admission and usually have good wheelchair access. Newer buildings are inevitably better adapted for wheelchair users. In museum entries throughout this book, we use the term 'wheelchair access' for places that are most accessible to disabled travellers.

On **public transport**, only bus lines 88, 85 and 20, some of the RER stations and line 14 on the métro are accessible. The RATP and SNCF offer a *Compagnon de Voyage* service (**t** 01 45 83 67 77; €10/hr). Call at least 24 hours in advance. Taxis are required by law to accept all disabled travellers, whatever the circumstances, though only two taxis in Paris are equipped with wheelchair lifts (Mr Colas, **t** 06 07 49 58 92 and Mr Leconte, **t** 06 61 79 30 98). The Association Valentin Haüy (AVH), 5 Rue Duroc, 75007, **t** 01 44 49 27 27, publishes the *Guide du Métropolitain et du RER Intégral en Braille*, a Braille métro and RER map (€1.80). For information on facilities on transport to and from France, *see* individual sections in the 'Travel' chapter.

Detailed information is available by Minitel: 3614 HANDITEL (ask at your hotel or use the Minitel at any post office).

Organizations in France

Association des Paralysés de France, *17 Bd Auguste-Blanqui, 75013,* **t** *(01 40 78 69 00,* **f** *01 45 89 40 57,* **w** *www.apf.asso.fr.* A national organization with an office in each *département* providing in-depth local information; headquarters are in Paris.

Organizations in the UK

Access Travel, *6 The Hillock, Astley, Lancashire M29 7GW,* **t** *(01942) 888 844,* **f** *(01942) 891 811,* **e** *info@access-travel.co.uk,* **w** *www.access-travel.co.uk.* Travel agent for disabled people: special air fares, car hire etc.

Can Be Done, *11 Woodcock Hill, Harrow, Middlesex MA3 0XP,* **t** *(020) 8907 2400,* **f** *(020) 8909 1854,* **w** *www.canbedone.co.uk.* Tailored city breaks.

Holiday Care Service, *7th Floor, Sunley House, 4 Bedford Park, Croydon, Surrey CR0 2AP,* **t** *(0845) 124 9971,* **f** *(0845) 124 9972,* **e** *holiday.care@virgin.net,* **w** *www.holiday*

care.org.uk. Provides up-to-date information on travel, and can recommend suitable tour operators.

RADAR *(Royal Association for Disability and Rehabilitation), 12 City Forum, 250 City Rd, London EC1V 8AF,* **t** *(020) 7250 3222,* **f** *(020) 7250 0212, Minicom* **t** *(020) 7250 4119,* **w** *www.radar.org.uk.* Information and books on all aspects of travel, including specialist tour operators.

Organizations in the USA

Accessible Journeys, *35 West Sellers Av, Ridley Park, PA 19078,* **t** *800 846 4537,* **f** *(610) 521 6959,* **w** *www.disabilitytravel.com.* Group tours and independent travel tailored to your needs.

Mobility International USA, *PO Box 10767, Eugene, OR 97440, USA,* **t**/*TTY (541) 343 1284,* **f** *(541) 343 6812,* **e** *info@miusa.org,* **w** *www.miusa.org.* Information on international educational exchange programmes and volunteer service overseas for the disabled.

Rollaround Travel, *239 Commercial Street, Malden, MA 02148,* **t** *(781) 322 8197,* **f** *(781) 322 3031,* **w** *www.rollaround.org.* Specialist travel agency with contacts all over Europe.

SATH *(Society for Accessible Travel and Hospitality), 347 5th Av, Suite 610, New York, NY 10016,* **t** *(212) 447 7284,* **f** *(212) 725 8253,* **e** *sathtravel@aol.com,* **w** *www.sath.org.* Travel and access information.

Other Useful Contacts

Access Ability, **w** *www.access-ability.co.uk.* Information on travel agencies catering specifically to disabled people.

Access Tourism, **w** *www.accesstourism.com.* Pan-European Web site with information on hotels, guesthouses, travel agencies and specialist tour operators, etc.

Australian Council for Rehabilitation of the Disabled *(ACROD), PO Box 60, Curtin, ACT 2605, Australia,* **t**/*TTY (02) 6282 4333,* **w** *www.acrod.org.au.* Information and contact numbers for specialist travel agents.

Disabled Persons Assembly, *PO Box 27-524, Wellington 6035, New Zealand,* **t** *(04) 801*

9100, *e gen@dpa.org.nz,* **w** *www.dpa.org.nz.*
All-round source for travel information.

Emerging Horizons, *e horizons@emerging
horizons.com,* **w** *www.emerginghorizons.
com.* International on-line travel newsletter
for people with disabilities.

Electricity, Weights and Measures

Electricity

The voltage is 220V and plugs have small
round prongs; Brits will need only an adapter,
Americans a voltage converter for any radios
or appliances. The BHV department store at
52–64 Rue de Rivoli (métro Louvre; Z13) has a
good selection of such items.

Weights and Measures

France uses the metric system; below is a
conversion chart for quick reference.

1 centimetre = 0.394 inches
1 metre = 3.094 feet
1 kilometre = 0.621 miles
1 kilogramme = 2.2 pounds
1 litre = 0.264 gallons
1 inch = 2.54 centimetres
1 foot = 0.305 metres
1 mile = 1.6 kilometres
1 pound = 0.454 kilogrammes
1 ounce = 25 grammes
1 liquid pint = 0.473 litres
1 gallon = 3.785 litres

Embassies and Consulates

In Paris

Canada: *35 Av Montaigne,* **t** *01 44 43 29 00,*
w *www.amb-canada.fr (métro Franklin D.
Roosevelt; M9–10).*

Ireland: *12 Avenue Foch,* **t** *01 44 17 67 04
(métro Charles de Gaulle-Etoile; J7).*

UK: *36 Rue du Faubourg-St-Honoré,* **t** *01 44
51 31 00 (métro Madeleine; Q9).*

USA: *2 Rue St-Florentin,* **t** *01 43 12 22 22,*
w *www.amb-grandebretagne.fr (métro
Concorde; R10).*

Abroad

Canada: *42 Sussex Drive, Ottawa,
ON K1M 2C9,* **t** *(613) 789 1795,* **w** *www.amba
france-ca.org.*

Ireland: *36 Ailesbury Rd, Ballsbridge,
Dublin 4,* **t** *(01) 260 1666,* **w** *www.
ambafrance.ie.*

UK: *21 Cromwell Rd, London SW7 2EN,*
t *(020) 7073 1200,* **w** *www.ambafrance.
org.uk; 11 Randolph Crescent, Edinburgh EH3
7TT,* **t** *(131) 225 7954.*

USA: *4104 Reservoir Road NW, Washington
DC 20007,* **t** *(202) 944 6195,* **w** *www.info-
france-usa.org.*

Health, Emergencies and Insurance

Ambulance: *t 15*
Fire: *t 18*
Police: *t 17*

France has one of the best healthcare
systems in the world. Local hospitals are the
place to go in an **emergency** (*urgence*).

If it's not an emergency, the **pharmacies**
have addresses of local doctors, or you can
visit the clinic at a *centre hospitalier.*
Pharmacists are also trained to administer
first aid and dispense free advice for minor
problems. Pharmacies open on a rota basis;
the following pharmacies are open 24 hours:
Pharmacie Dhery, 84 Av des Champs-Elysées,
t 01 45 62 02 41 (métro George V; M8); and
Pharmacie Européenne, 6 Place de Clichy,
t 01 48 74 65 18 (métro Place de Clichy; S4).
Pharmacists that speak **English** and can help
match foreign prescriptions are: Pharmacie
Swann, 6 Rue de Castiglione, **t** 01 42 60 72 96
(métro Tuileries; S10); and British and
American Pharmacy, 1 Rue Auber, **t** 01 47 42 49
40 (métro Opéra; T8).

Condoms are available in pharmacies and
tobacconists and now in machines in many
métro stations.

There is a standard agreement for citizens
of EU countries, entitling you to a certain
amount of **free medical care** (75–80% of the
cost, reimbursed a week to 10 days later). Fill

out form E111, available from your local health authority (and from post offices in the UK). Non-EU travellers should check with their policies at home to see if they are covered in France, and judge whether it's advisable to take out additional insurance. However you're insured, you pay up front for everything, unless it's an emergency, when you will be billed later.

You should always make sure you have **travel insurance**, covering you for delays, lost baggage,theft, etc, and offering 100% medical refund and emergency repatriation if necessary. Ring around for the best deal. Be sure to save all doctors' receipts, pharmacy receipts and police documents (if you're reporting a theft).

Internet

Internet access is available at the following cybercafés:

Café Orbital, *13 Rue Médicis*, **t** *01 43 25 76 77*, **w** *www.orbital.fr* (*métro Luxembourg or Odéon; V16*). *Open Mon–Sat 10am–8pm, Sun 12–8pm*. Paris' first cybercafé has Macs and PCs to choose from. Food and drink available. 5 hours costs €30, but you can also pay per minute.

Cyberport Forum des Images, *Forum des Halles (Porte St-Eustache)*, **t** *01 44 76 63 44* (*métro Châtelet-Les Halles; X11*). *Open Tues–Sun 1pm–9pm, Thurs till later*. One of the nicest Internet cafés in Paris. First 30mins €5.50, subsequent 30min sessions €4.50. Free half-hour introduction to the Internet. Food and drink available.

easyInternetCafé, *31–7 Bd de Sébastopol*, **t** *01 40 41 09 10* (*métro Châtelet-Les Halles; Y12*). *Open daily 24hrs*. Parisian outpost of the popular British Internet café. Rates start at €3; the cheapest time is the evening.

Net@House, *48 rue Monge*, **t** *01 40 46 01 37* (*métro Place Monge*). *Open daily 9am–10pm*. New state-of-the-art café, with extremely cheap internet access, fax and international phone calls.

Le Web Bar Et L'Atelier, *32 Rue de Picardie*, **t** *01 42 72 66 55* (*métro Temple; CC10*). *Open*

Mon–Fri 8.30am–2am, Sat–Sun 10.30–2am. Cheap Internet access (€3 an hour) in one of the trendiest places in Paris; it's also a concert and exhibition venue.

Lost Property

The **Préfecture de Police**, 36 Rue des Morillons, 15e, **t** 01 55 76 20 20 (métro Convention; off maps), is the place to go for general lost property. It's open Mon, Wed and Fri 8.30–5, Tues and Thurs 8.30–8. Also report your loss at a local police station and keep a record for insurance purposes.

If you lose something on public transport, call **RAPT** on **t** 01 40 30 52 00. For credit-card hotlines, see 'Money', below.

Media

Newspapers: France has a long-established press scene and a wide variety of publications, though they never evolved into newspapers as known in the US or Britain. The best, and one of the youngest, is probably the mildly left-wing *Libération*, the first editor of which was Jean-Paul Sartre. *Le Figaro* is bulldog-rightist, very commercial, sometimes well written, sometimes repugnant. *Le Monde*, an ambitious journal founded just after the liberation of Paris, is certainly the most French and eloquent, which is not always the same as profound; real gems of erudition and wisdom appear in its pages, though finding them can require a lot of shovelling. *L'Humanité*, the Communist paper, used to be excellent, but has declined along with the party's fortunes. All the others are tabloid-quality. For politics, everyone reads the weekly *Le Canard Enchaîné*, with writing a little too colloquial and knowing for non-natives.

In English, the *International Herald Tribune*, which is published in Paris and good for superficial magazine-type articles about the city and French politics, is available everywhere; so are *USA Today* and the main British dailies. Also look for *Paris Free Voice*, a free community newspaper from the

American Church with reviews, cultural affairs and classifieds.

TV is similar to Britain, with competition between the heavier state-owned channels and the independents with lighter, international (read American) programming. News reporting is as bleak as elsewhere in the world, though special reports and documentaries can be exceptional. **TF1** is the popular leader among the independents with a strong interest in politics, but often sinks to lowest-common-denominator programming. **France 2**, state-owned and once the class act of French TV, is fumbling for a more plebian stance to justify its large subsidies (raised through an annual tax on TV sets). **France 3**, also state-owned, is the national voice for regional broadcasting and does come up with interesting shows or classic films. **Canal Plus**, a slick pay-TV station with links to Time-Warner, offers recent movies and porn together with a large selection of sports; also a chance for homesick anglophones to catch up the CBS nightly news at 7am (unscrambled). **La Cinquième** is another state station, devoted to educational programming during the day, but at 7pm it turns into **Arte**, an arty, highbrow German-French effort that produces something worth watching five nights out of seven. **M6** shows music videos mixed with business news and reruns of *The Avengers* (known in French as 'Bowler Hat and Leather Boots').

Radio airwaves are crowded, mostly with teenage ear candy, or rather, teenage ear *bonbons* since former President Mitterrand's government decreed that 40% of all music every station plays has to be French. Some exceptions: *Radio Libertaire* (89.4), anarchist-run, alternative news and music; *Beur FM* (106.7), North African; *Radio Latina* (99.0); *Radio Nova* (101.5), techno, acid jazz, and a range of unusual stuff; *Radio Classique* (101.1), classical; *FIP* (105.1), the ultimate in eclectic: opera back-to-back with Ella, followed by Lionel Ritchie, Chopin, and some little ditty from Iceland that you'll probably never hear again; and jazz only between 7.30 and 9pm.

And not to forget the state-run dinosaurs: *France Info* (105.5) gives 24-hour news; *France Musique* (91.7) mixes one-third classical and other music, and two-thirds commentary; *France Culture* (93.5) and *France Inter* (87.8) are also cultural, also mostly blah-blah-blah.

Money

On 1 January 1999 the **euro** became the official currency of France (and 10 other nations of the European Union) and franc notes and coins were no longer accepted after 17 February 2002. The euro is divided into 100 cents. Notes come in denominations of 5, 10, 20, 50, 100, 200 and 500 euros; coins come in denominations of 1, 2, 5, 10, 20 and 50 cents, and 1 and 2 euros. At the time of writing, the euro was worth UK£0.65, US$0.94 and C$1.47.

Traveller's cheques are the safest way of carrying money, but the wide acceptance of **credit and debit cards** and the presence of ATMs (*distributeurs de billets*), at banks and post offices, make using a card a convenient alternative. The types of card accepted are marked on each machine, and most give instructions in English. Check with your bank before you leave whether your debit/cash cards can be used in France. Credit-card companies charge a fee for cash advances, but rates are often better than those at banks. Visa is the most readily accepted of the international credit cards; American Express is often not accepted. Smaller hotels and restaurants may not accept cards at all. Some shops and supermarkets experience difficulties reading UK-style magnetic strips.

In the event of lost or stolen credit cards, call the following emergency numbers:

American Express: *t 01 47 77 72 00*
Barclaycard: *t (00 44) 1604 230 230 (UK)*
Diner's Club: *t 01 49 06 17 50*
Mastercard: *t 08 00 96 47 67*
Visa: *t 08 00 90 11 79*

Changing Money

Exchange rates vary, and nearly all banks take a commission of varying proportions.

Bureaux de change that do nothing but exchange money (and hotels and train stations) usually have the worst rates or take the heftiest commissions.

Opening Hours and Public Holidays

National Holidays

On French national holidays, banks, shops, businesses and some museums close; most restaurants stay open, as do tourist offices. The French have a healthy approach to holidays: if there is a holiday on a Tuesday or Thursday, they 'make a bridge' (*faire un pont*) to the weekend and make Monday or Friday a holiday too (this does not affect public services). *See* box for official public holidays.

Opening Hours

Banks: Banks are generally open 8.30am–12.30pm and 1.30–4pm; they close on Sunday, and most close either on Saturday or Monday as well.

Churches: Usually open all day, but some may only open for Mass. There are often admission fees for cloisters, crypts and special chapels.

Markets: Travelling food markets dwindle away at noon; most permanent street markets are open morning and afternoon Tuesday–Saturday and Sunday morning. Markets selling clothes, art, antiques, etc., are also open Sunday afternoon.

Museums: We've done our best to include opening hours in the text, but hours often

---

National Holidays

1 January New Year's Day
Easter Sunday March or April
Easter Monday March or April
1 May Fête du Travail (Labour Day)
8 May VE Day, Armistice 1945
Ascension Day usually end of May
Pentecost (Whitsun) and the following Monday, beginning of June
14 July Bastille Day
15 August Assumption of the Virgin Mary
1 November All Saints' Day
11 November Remembrance Day (First World War Armistice)
25 December Christmas Day

---

change with the seasons: longer summer hours usually begin in May or June and last to the end of September. Many museums (including the Louvre) are closed on Tuesday; a significant exception is the Musée d'Orsay, which is closed on Monday. National museums are free if you're under 18; otherwise admission charges range from €1.5–6 (often cheaper on Sundays).

Post offices: Generally open Mon–Fri 8am–7pm, and Saturdays 8am–noon. For two exceptions *see* 'Post Offices', below.

Shops: Normal opening hours in Paris are from 9 or 10am to 7 or 8pm, Tuesday to Saturday. Smaller boutiques may take 3 hours off for lunch (usually 1–4pm). Note that many shops in Paris close on Sundays and Mondays, with the exception of *boulangers*, grocers (some of which are always open Sunday morning and Mondays) and *supermarchés* (closed Sundays, open Mondays). Many small shops and restaurants still close for a holiday in August; this is gradually becoming less common, but it is a good idea to call ahead, just in case. We have tried to indicate places that close in the listings.

Photography

Developing photos in France is a little more expensive than in the UK or USA, as is the price of film.

Discount Tickets

The *Carte Musées et Monuments* (**w** *www. intermusees.com*) is available from tourist offices and participating museums (and some métro stations). As well as being a way to save money on museum admission, it also allows you to skip the queues. The card is valid for one day (€15), three days (€30) or five days (€45), and most of the major museums and monuments are included (among them the Arc de Triomphe, Musée du Louvre, Centre Georges Pompidou and Versailles).

Two chains that process photos overnight are Photo Station and FNAC Service. Both chains have branches throughout the city; central branches include:

FNAC Service, *19 Av de l'Opéra*, **t** *01 40 15 08 80 (U10); 84 Rue Mouffetard*, **t** *01 45 87 05 10 (Y18); 127 Rue de Sèvres*, **t** *01 43 06 33 23 (Q16)*.

Photo Station, *36 Av de l'Opéra*, **t** *01 43 12 32 79 (U9); 38 Rue de Rivoli*, **t** *01 48 87 21 29 (AA13); 24 Rue Soufflot*, **t** *01 40 46 02 55 (W16)*.

Post and Fax

Known as PTTs or Bureaux de Poste, post offices are easily discernible by their sign showing a blue bird on a yellow background. For general opening hours, *see* 'Opening Hours', above.

Two branches with longer hours are the main post office at 52 Rue du Louvre (métro Les Halles or Louvre-Rivoli; W10; *open 24 hours for all services*), and the branch at 71 Avenue des Champs-Elysées (métro George V; M8; *open Mon–Fri 8am–7.30pm, Sat 10am–7pm*). You can purchase stamps in tobacconists as well as post offices.

In Paris all **postcodes** begin with 75, the departmental number for Seine-et-Loire; 75001 means the 1er *arrondissement*, etc.

Most post offices have public **fax** (*télécopie*) machines and offer free use of the Minitel electronic directory.

Smoking

Tobacco and cigarettes are cheap in France and the French smoke a lot more than their British and American counterparts. Smoking is banned in public places (though this is often ignored), on public transport and in cinemas and theatres. Restaurants are required to have a no-smoking area, but this could well be a single table and near useless.

Students

The Latin Quarter is still the hub of the student community in Paris (although accommodation in the area is now mostly beyond any student's means), encompassing the second-hand bookshops and cheap eats around St-Michel and Paris' best-known college, the Sorbonne. The rest of the University of Paris is divided up and spread around the city.

Student **discounts** are available for most museums and often for cinemas, theatres, etc. You will need to show ID, such as an International Student Identity Card (ISIC; only valid in France if you are under 26).

The place to go for student **accommodation and information** is the Centre Régional des Oeuvres Universitaires et Scolaires (CROUS), 39 Av Georges-Bernanos, 5e, **t** 01 40 51 36 00 (RER Port-Royal; V18). It also supplies ISIC cards and student discounts for concerts, etc.

The largest place for student accommodation in Paris is Cité Universitaire, 19 Bd Jourdan, 14e, **t** 01 42 53 51 44 (RER Cité-Universitaire; off maps). Foreign students are also eligible to stay here. Prices depend on facilities. You'll need to apply in March or April for a place the following autumn.

Telephones

Nearly all public telephones have switched over from coins to *télécartes*, which you can purchase at any post office or newsstand for €6 for 50 units or €14.50 for 120 units. The French have eliminated area codes, giving everyone a 10-digit telephone number.

To make **international calls** from France, dial 00, wait for the change in the dial tone, then dial the country code, and then the local code (minus the 0 for UK numbers) and number. Country codes include: UK 44, US and Canada 1, Ireland 353, Australia 61 and New Zealand 64. Calls to the UK or USA cost around €1.10 for 7mins off peak (7pm–8am for the UK, 7pm–1pm for the USA). As everywhere, expect a big surcharge if you make any calls from your hotel room.

To call France from abroad, the international dialling code is **33**; then drop the first 'o' of the number.

The easiest way to **reverse charges** is to pay to phone the number and then give your number in France, which is always posted by public phones; alternatively, ring your national operator and tell them that you want to call reverse charges (for the UK dial 00 33 44; for the USA 00 33 11).

For national **directory enquiries**, call **t** 12; for international directory enquiries, call **t** 00 33 12 followed by the country code. Alternatively, try your luck and patience on the free, slow, inefficient Minitel electronic directory in every post office.

Time

Paris is 1 hour ahead of GMT, 6 hours ahead of US Eastern Standard Time, 9 ahead of Pacific Coast Time and 9 hours behind Sydney. Summer time (daylight-saving time) begins and ends on the same dates as in Britain (end of March and end of October). The question of summer time is under review in France, but in the meantime will continue unchanged.

Tipping

Almost all restaurants and cafés automatically add an extra 15% to the bill, and there's no need to leave any more unless you care to or in recognition of special service. The taxi driver will be happy with 10%, the cinema usher a few cents.

Toilets

That most fragrant and funky piece of Parisian street furniture, the sidewalk *pissoir* or *vespasienne*, has been replaced by the ugly beige spaceship toilets of the Decaux Company. They cost very little for 15 minutes of privacy, and are automatically sanitized after each user, although sometimes they're out of order or delinquents have made off with all the toilet paper.

Museums and most cafés have decent facilities; it's very unlikely you'll have to squat. However, you are more or less obliged to buy something or be sneaky. Train stations also make a small charge and fancier cafés with an attendant should be tipped.

If you're feeling nostalgic you can visit the last rusting *vespasiennes* in Paris in Boulevard Arago, in front of La Santé prison, in the 14e or near the Pont Mirabeau.

Tourist Offices

Abroad

Before you go, pick up more information from a French National Tourist Office:

Australia: *25 Bligh St, Level 22, NSW 2000 Sydney, t (02) 9231 5244, f (02) 9221 8682.*

Canada: *1981 Av McGill College, No.490, Montreal, PQ H3A 2W9, t (514) 876 9881, f (514) 845 4868, e mfrance@attcanada.net.*

Ireland: *10 Suffolk St, Dublin 1, t (01) 679 0813, e frenchtouristoffice@tinet.ie.*

UK: *178 Piccadilly, London W1V OAL, t 0906 824 4123 (calls charged at 60p/min), e info@mdlf.co.uk, w www.franceguide.com.*

USA: *444 Madison Av, New York, NY 10022, t (410) 286 8310, f (212) 838 7855, e info@ francetourism.com, w www.francetourism. com; 676 N. Michigan Av, Chicago, IL 60611, t (312) 751 7800, f (312) 337 63 39, e fgto@ mcs.net; 9454 Wiltshire Bd, Suite 715, Beverly Hills, CA 90212, t (310) 271 6665, f (310) 276 2835, e fgto@gte.net.*

In Paris

Tourist offices are called Syndicat d'Initiative or Office de Tourisme; they have bilingual staff who can help you find a hotel room, sell you a museum pass (*see* 'Opening Hours', p.75), fill you in on events, and tell you about places to see. Offices include:

Head Office: *127 Av des Champs-Elysées, t 08 92 68 31 12 (or for a recording in English of current events t 01 49 52 53 56), w www.paris-touristoffice.com (métro Charles de Gaulle-Etoile; K7–8). Open daily 9–8.*

Eiffel Tower: *Open May–Sept daily 11–6.40.*

Gare de Lyon: *Open Mon–Sat 8–8.*

Women Travellers

The French are certainly more chauvinist than the British or Americans, but that is not to say that women are any more in danger in

Paris than any other large city. Areas to beware of, particularly at night, are Les Halles and Rue St-Denis, around Pigalle and the Bois de Boulogne.

The Maison des Femmes, 163 Rue de Charenton, 12e, **t** 01 43 43 41 13 (métro Reuilly-Diderot; off maps), has a café and library and is a general meeting place and venue for exhibitions, classes, etc. for women. There's a **rape hotline** (toll free) on **t** 08 00 05 95 95.

Working and Long Stays

The first thing to know about trying to get settled in France is that the system is against you. If the sights, sounds, and eats are the reason you fall in love with the country, a trip to the *préfecture* may be the quickest way to cure yourself of any romantic notions. The laws change faster than you can imagine, so any attempt to sketch out possible options is nearly hopeless. Certain things remain constant, however: if you're not an EU national and you mean to stay longer than three months in Paris, the first thing is to make sure you get a residence visa (*visa de long séjour*) before you come to France, from the nearest French consulate in your country of residence. You can't get a visa once you're in France, and there's no way around it. Students or au pairs are eligible for a special visa but still need to get a residence permit once in France. For any visa, you'll need lots of papers and photos, including proof of financial support and insurance. Phone your consulate first to see what they require.

Once in France, EU national or not, the law says you have three months to get a **residence permit** (*carte de séjour*) from a Centre de Réception des Etrangers (or outside Paris, from the local *mairie*). You'll need one to work in France legally. Every office has its own interpretation of the requirements, but in addition to your visa you will need several photos, *timbres fiscaux* (government stamps, purchased at tobacconists), proof of means

(even EU nationals have to have a minimum sum in the bank), etc. They usually also require a medical examination. EU nationals have a legal right to work in France but do make sure it says so on the back of your *carte de séjour*. A *carte de séjour* with a work permit for non-EU citizens is nearly impossible to get unless you already have a job waiting in Paris (au pair jobs are the exception to this rule).

When it comes to looking for a job, teaching English (especially if you have a TEFL certificate), nanny/au pair work and working in bars are the standbys; language schools run ads for teachers in the *International Herald Tribune*, *FUSAC* (*France-USA Contacts*) and the *Paris Free Voice* (the last two magazines available free from stands near any Anglo-American restaurant or bookstore).

Avoid dealing with rental agents and their lofty fees (usually equal to a month's rent) if you possibly can. Of the newspapers, only *Le Figaro* has extensive rental listings, but there are several weeklies of classified ads (*J'Annonce* and *De Particulier à Particulier* are both available Thursdays for about €2–3 from news kiosks) where landlords and renters can cut out the middleman. The *Paris Free Voice* also has some listings, as does the *Herald Tribune* (luxury only) and *FUSAC*. Other possibilities are the bulletin boards at the American Church, 65 Quai d'Orsay, 7e (métro Invalides; N11) and the British Institute, 9–11 Rue de Constantine, 7e (métro Invalides; P12).

Landlords usually ask for two months' rent in advance, plus a security deposit. The minimum lease for a furnished flat is one year and three for unfurnished. Prices are by the square metre, which sounds more alarming than it usually is because most flats are definitely in the poky department. The beginning of September is a particularly bad time to look, as Paris is filled with students also looking.

The Islands

The Islands

Paris made its début on the Île de la Cité and, in their congenital chauvinism, the Parisians regard their river islet to this day not only as the centre of the city, but the centre of all France. Two of the most luminous Gothic churches ever built are reason alone for visiting, but there are other delights – shady squares and quays, panoramic bridges and the perfect symmetry of neighbouring Île St-Louis, an island-village of the *haute bourgeoisie*, concocted by 17th-century speculators and architecturally little changed since. Over the centuries, institutions of law and health have gobbled up the rest of insular Paris – the Conciergerie (the infamous 'antechamber of the guillotine'), the courts, the police and Paris' oldest hospital, the Hôtel-Dieu. But the sirens of their Black Marias and ambulances are whispers compared to the cacophony that used to rattle the Seine's bosom, when these were the most densely populated narrow lanes in Paris, and Parisians swarmed to hear the ballad singers on Pont Neuf or events like the *concert miaulique*, performed by 20 cats stuffed into a clavichord. On a Sunday morning you can hear a distant echo of the old din in Place Lépine's twittering bird market.

Highlights

Couples' City: The flower and bird market in Place Louis-Lépine, p.88

Parisian's City: A concert in the unforgettable setting of Sainte-Chapelle, p.90

Peace and Quiet: Watching the barges from the Square du Vert-Galant, p.92

Paris des Artistes: The brooding Baudelairian monsters on the roof of Notre-Dame, p.86

Grand Siècle Paris: An entire aristocratic neighbourhood, on Île St-Louis, p.93

Gritty City: The Conciergerie, the 'antechamber of the guillotine', p.89

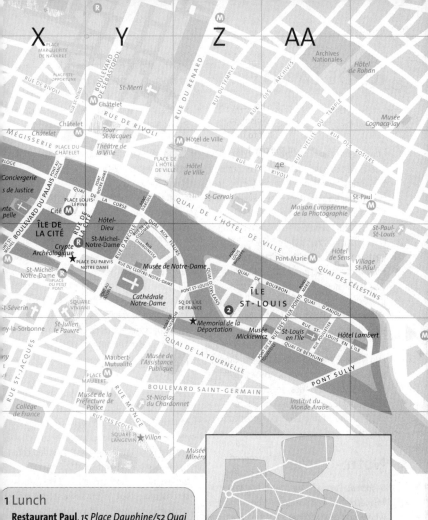

1 Lunch

Restaurant Paul, *15 Place Dauphine/52 Quai des Orfèvres*, **t** *01 43 54 21 48*; **métro** *Pont-Neuf*. **Open** *Tues–Sun 12–2.30 and 7–10.30.* **Moderate**. White damask tablecloths and red banquettes. A few tables outside overlooking the peaceful square.

2 Tea and Cakes

Le Flore en l'Ile, *42 Quai d'Orléans, Ile St-Louis*; **métro** *Pont-Marie*. **Open** *daily 8am–2am*. Great view over Notre-Dame, great tea, great Berthillon ice cream (straight and in exotic cocktails).

3 Drinks

Henri IV, *13 Place du Pont-Neuf*; **métro** *Pont-Neuf*. **Open** *Mon–Fri 12–10pm and Sat 12–4pm*. Long established and serving good snacks with a southwest flavour; Beaujolais and Loire wines.

ÎLE DE LA CITÉ

If the 19th-century revamping of the ancient Île de la Cité begun by Louis-Philippe and continued by Haussmann were 'progress' in any sense, then the Aztecs who queued up to have their hearts cut out by their priests were all the better for the operation. Extracting the dense medieval quarter from around Notre-Dame was especially cruel; 25,000 people who lived on a hundred colourful tiny streets were banished to the eastern slums, and although you can now see the cathedral from further away than ever, it will never look right without its proper setting and sits sad as a lone jewel in an empty box. Like the City of London and Wall Street, the area is dreary by day and deserted at night. Between the Conciergerie and Notre-Dame, just three huge buildings have replaced hundreds of houses, 16 churches, three priories, docks and warehouses, a prison, the Jewish ghetto, a hospital and a famous nest of prostitution called the Val d'Amour, the 'Valley of Love'.

Notre-Dame Y14

6 Place du Parvis-Notre-Dame, t 01 42 34 56 10; métro Cité, RER St-Michel-Notre-Dame; wheelchair access. Open daily 7.45–6.45, part or all of the cathedral will occasionally be closed for services; adm free; guided tours (about 1hr; free) in English Wed and Thurs at noon, in French Mon–Fri at noon, Sat and Sun at 2.30.

In the Middle Ages, the miracle plays and mystery plays put on by the confraternities were one of the major public entertainments. Often they were held in the **Place du Parvis-Notre-Dame**, where the magnificent porch of the cathedral could serve as 'Paradise', a word that over the centuries got mangled into *Parvis*. In those pre-Haussmann days, the Parvis was only a quarter the size it is now, and strollers down the web of lanes that once twisted here would marvel at the sudden sight of Notre-Dame looming up impressively before them.

Traced in the Parvis is the former route of Rue Neuve de Notre-Dame, laid out by Louis VII in the 12th century. When new, this was the widest street in Paris – all of 21ft across. To the right of the Parvis, a 19th-century, swashbuckling statue of **Charlemagne** occupies the site of the original Hôtel-Dieu.

History

This site has been holy ever since Paris was Lutetia, when a temple to Jupiter stood here (part of the altar, discovered in 1771, is in the Musée Cluny; *see pp.218–9*). In the 6th century, under Childebert, a small church was erected on what is now the Parvis, dedicated to the Virgin, St Étienne and St Germain. Sacked by the Normans in 857, it was quickly reconstructed but on the same scale, hardly large enough for the growing population of the Cité. A proper cathedral had to wait for Maurice de Sully, who became bishop of Paris in 1160; he raised the funds in spite of St Bernard, who preached jeremiads against such a worldly undertaking.

Cité and Citadel

The 3rd-century BC Parisii were always messing about in boats, and they naturally found a river island a convivial place to call home. The Romans had a soft spot for it as well, and although most of their Lutetia was on the Left Bank, the palace of the governors and central temple to Jupiter were here. When Clovis made Paris his capital, he moved into the Roman palace. In the 9th century, when the Normans began sailing up

river, the old palace was enlarged to make the Cité, Paris' citadel, where the whole population could take refuge. After Richard the Lionheart defeated Philippe-Auguste at Fréteval in 1194 and burned all his archives, kings always kept copies of documents in the Palais de Justice.

The kings remained in the palace until the 14th century, when Étienne Marcel's revolt suggested that living cheek by jowl with the Parisians was no longer safe.

Cities all over France were beginning great cathedrals. Notre-Dame came along on the crest of the wave; its architecture was destined to become the consummate work of the early Gothic. Because it was in Paris, the cosmopolitan centre of learning, Notre-Dame had a considerable importance in diffusing Gothic architecture throughout Europe; for over two centuries its construction site was a busy, permanent workshop, through which passed the continent's most skilled masons, sculptors, carpenters and glassmakers. Plans changed continually, as new ideas and new problems came up. The first masters, responsible for the basic design, are unknown. Later masters included Pierre de Montreuil, architect of the Sainte-Chapelle, who contributed most of the side chapels, the crossings and the Porte Rouge.

By 1302 the works were complete enough for Philippe le Bel to open France's first Estates General, or national parliament. Henry VI of England was crowned here in 1430; seven years later Charles VII was present at a solemn *Te Deum* to celebrate the retaking of Paris from the English. French coronations commonly took place at Rheims; the next one here would not come until 1804, the pompous apotheosis of Emperor Napoleon, brilliantly captured in the famous propaganda painting by David (*see* p.105).

During the Revolution, the Parisians first trashed Notre-Dame, wrecking most of its sculptures; then they decided to demolish it. A few subtle voices stood up for its 'cultural and historical value' and the cathedral was spared to become the 'Temple of Reason', where Reason's goddess, a former dancer, held forth. But while Notre-Dame could still be filled with crowds for political or religious pageantry, little upkeep had taken place for centuries. The building was literally falling to bits, its statuary eroding away, when Victor Hugo, with his novel *Notre-Dame de Paris*, contributed immeasurably to a revival of interest in the city's medieval roots. Serious restoration work began in the 1840s.

Eugène Viollet-le-Duc, a man who spent his life trying to redeem centuries of his country-men's ignorance and fecklessness, worked the better part of two decades on the site. His approach to restoration, especially to repairing the damage from the Revolution, was not scientifically perfect, but still far ahead of its time. Viollet-le-Duc's workshops produced original sculpture, attempting to capture the spirit of what had been destroyed or damaged instead of merely copying it. Since his time, Notre-Dame has continued to mark the important events in Paris' history, up to the celebrations of the Liberation on 26 August 1944, when a mysterious sniper took pot shots at De Gaulle.

The Façade

No one in the 18th century is ever recorded as having said a kind word about Notre-Dame, but the men of the Enlightenment could well have taken a lesson in form from the cathedral's powerful façade, a marvel of visual clarity and symmetry, as disciplined as a Napoleonic army and rather more graceful. To see this façade as it was intended, remember that, as with the temples of ancient Greece, originally all the statues and reliefs of a Gothic church were painted in bright colours. The statuary begins at the level of the rose window: Adam and Eve, on either side of the rose, and the Virgin Flanked by Angels. Below these, running the length of the façade, is a row of 28 Kings of Judah and Israel, the ancestors of Jesus. By the 18th century, popular belief held them to be kings of France, so all got their heads knocked off during the Revolution. A Catholic Royalist carefully buried them face down in a court-yard in Rue de la Chaussée-d'Antin, where they lay until their rediscovery in 1977 (they're now in the Musée de Cluny); the present kings are re-creations by Viollet-le-Duc.

Below the kings are the three portals, interspersed with four framed sculptural groups: St Stephen on the left; the Church and Synagogue on the two centre piers, representing the 'true and false revelations'; and on the right pier, St Denis.

The **left portal** is dedicated to the Virgin Mary, a lovely composition *c.* 1210. The tympanum is on three levels: the Coronation

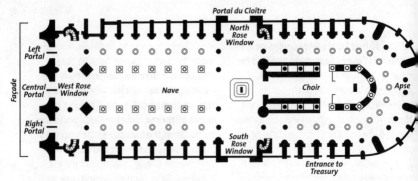

of the Virgin (on top), her Resurrection, and some of the kings and prophets who were her ancestors, with the Ark of the Covenant. Above are figures of angels, kings and prophets; below, the large statues of (unidentifiable) saints were replaced after designs by Viollet-le-Duc. Flanking the doors is a charming set of the zodiacal signs with the labours of the months corresponding to them. This is very common on medieval church doors, and one of the few secular subjects allowed in French Gothic works. In the Middle Ages, the New Year commonly began with the spring equinox; here that date is correctly marked by Pisces instead of Aries. Most other cathedrals (and all modern astrologers) have it wrong.

The **right portal**, dedicated to St Anne, is the earliest of the portals (mostly *c.* 1170); much of the sculpture may have come from an earlier church of Notre-Dame that stood where the apse of the cathedral is now. Why St Anne, the mother of Mary? Everything about the sculptural theme of Notre-Dame pertains to the Virgin, and the scenes here recount the earlier part of the story finished on the left portal. On the tympanum, scenes from the life of St Anne and Mary, below the Virgin in Majesty, are flanked by figures once (erroneously) believed to be King Louis VII and Bishop Sully, the cathedral's founders; below, you'll recognize the Annunciation, the Nativity and the Adoration of the Magi. On the trumeau (the pillar between the doors) is a strange sculpture (redone) of St Marcel trampling a dragon.

The **central portal** (finished *c.* 1220), featuring the Last Judgement, is the largest and most impressive of the three. Even

though everything else in the cathedral proclaims the glory of the Virgin, centre stage is nevertheless held by Christ, overseeing the distribution of saved and sinners. The surrounding angels bear symbols of the Passion, to remind us he saw some trouble too. From the bottom of the tympanum, the dead rise up and separate into upper and lower destinies. Note St Michael weighing souls, next to the Devil at the centre; this is an ancient motif that can be traced back through Venetian and Byzantine art to its roots in ancient Egypt. A statue of Christ occupies the trumeau. This, like the bottom levels of the tympanum, is a replacement since Soufflot (architect of the Panthéon) knocked out the original in 1771; he did it to make room for a processional cart to pass through. Viollet-le-Duc again designed the replacements. The saints that flank the door stand above small medallions picturing virtues and vices.

Such fine portals deserve **doors** to match. The hardware and hinges for those on the left and right, still in good nick today, were made by an ironsmith named Biscornet. They are quite artistically done, and a little mysterious; to this day no one has figured out how he forged them. Biscornet never let anyone watch while he worked, and a legend grew up that he sold his soul to the Devil for help with this important commission. Once installed, the doors refused to open until holy water was splashed on them; the mortified smith fled Paris and died soon after. Biscornet's central door, replaced long ago, witnessed the curious marriage of Henri IV and Marguerite de Valois in 1572; not yet in the good graces of the Church, Henri stood just outside the door, Marguerite just within.

The Interior

We can only guess what the interior furnishings looked like in the days before the Revolution. In the Middle Ages, when cathedrals were the great public living rooms of the cities and always open, there would have been no chairs, of course, just rushes strewn on the floor to soak up the mud from the hordes of people who passed through daily, gabbing, gambling, making business deals, eating lunch, waiting for the rain to stop or listening to the choir practice – Notre-Dame was the musical centre of medieval Europe, where much of the new polyphonic method was invented.

The decorations of the altar and chapels were more colourful and artistic than anything there now. Besides the gifts of kings and nobles, the city guilds competed ardently to embellish the cathedral for centuries. A late survivor of this tradition was the *may* of the goldsmiths, originally a live tree brought each year at May Day, later a tree of gold, and finally, up to 1709, a painting for one of the chapels. The guild went broke in that year, thanks to Louis XIV and his war taxes, but some of the *mays* can still be seen – there are two in the two chapels nearest the entrance in the right aisle.

Not all the décor was entirely religious. From an ancient custom, French generals victorious in battle were known as the *tapissiers* (drapers) *de Notre-Dame* for their habit of hanging captured flags and banners high in the nave. One of Notre-Dame's greatest marvels, a colossal Gothic statue of St Christopher, was removed by the clergy in 1785. It was considered good luck to see Christopher before a journey, so he was always made larger than life, but Notre-Dame's statue was exceptional – the congregation entered beneath his legs, heads brushing against his testicles for even more luck.

Today, we must be content with the architecture and the remnants of the stained glass, but it's more than enough. And it's big enough: 430ft long, with room for some 9,000 people, according to Viollet-le-Duc's calculations. The plan set the pattern for the other cathedrals of the Île-de-France: a wide nave with four side aisles, which curve and meet around the back of the altar. The side chapels were not original, but added in the 13th century to hold all the gifts pouring in from the confraternities and guilds. Today, sadly, there is not a single noteworthy painting or statue in any of them.

Most of the chapels were remodelled to suit the tastes of the 17th and 18th centuries, or wrecked in the Revolution. But this is nothing compared to the two incredible acts of vandalism committed in the age of the Big Louies. In the 18th century, nearly all of the stained glass was simply removed, to let in more light. And in 1708 the scoundrels began wrecking the high altar and choir. Louis XIII, slow in the sack and without an heir after 23 years of marriage, had vowed to dedicate all of France to the Virgin if she would do something about his problem. Louis should have wished for a watermelon, since the best Mary could come up with was the unspeakable Louis XIV. To thank the Virgin for being born, the Sun King ordered the florid, carved-wood choir stalls and a complete rebuilding of the choir, including a new altar, flanked by statues of His Majesty himself and his father. What could be more fitting for a Christian altar? It's interesting that no bishop since has had the nerve to remove them.

Thank God at least he spared the original **choir enclosure**, lined with a series of 23 beautiful reliefs of the life of Christ, done *c.* 1350 by Jean Ravy and his nephew Jean le Bouteiller; recently these have been repainted to approximate their original appearance. Another rare survivor stands at the entrance to the choir, a fine 14th-century **statue of Mary and child**.

We can be even more thankful they didn't take out the three great **rose windows**. The one in the west front, heavily restored by Viollet-le-Duc, expresses the message of this cathedral's art even better than the portals:

the Virgin sits in majesty at the centre, surrounded by the virtues and vices, the signs of the zodiac and the works of the months – all the things of this world. In the left transept rose (north), Mary is again at the centre, in the company of Old Testament prophets, judges and kings. In the right transept rose (south), a truly remarkable composition, she dominates the New Testament, amid the Apostles (in the square frames) and saints. As for the rest of the windows, much of the dull grey glass of the 18th century has been replaced, since 1965, by stained glass in abstract patterns. They were done with genuine medieval colours and techniques, but in a building where art is so meticulously organized, they still look a bit out of place. The fabulous organ (1867), back online after an 11-million franc restoration and computerization, thunders like no other instrument in France (there are concerts on Sunday afternoons).

The Treasury

*Entrance to the right of choir. **Open** Mon–Sat 9.30–6, Sun 2–6; **adm** €2.50.*

This has some excruciating 19th-century reliquaries and chalices, mostly donated by Napoleon III. Other exhibits include St Louis' linen tunic, cameos of all the popes up to Pius X, choir books and items related to the three archbishops assassinated by the Parisians. The Crown of Thorns and the other relics moved here from Sainte-Chapelle are displayed only during Lent and Holy Week.

The Towers

*t 01 44 32 16 72. **Open** Jan–Dec 10–5.30, April–Sept 9.30–7.30, July–Aug 9–7.30; **adm** €6.10, free on 1st Sun of the month.*

Charles Méryon was one of the great artists of the early 19th century, a visionary who laid bare the darker side of the Parisian psyche in scores of weird prints, showing the city's rooftops amid clouds of sinister black birds. One of his favourite subjects was the incomparable gallery of spooks (they are not gargoyles) that inhabit the upper regions of Notre-Dame. These are the work of Viollet-le-Duc, brilliant re-creations of the original monsters eroded to smooth lumps by centuries of wind. No one has ever come up with a satisfactory explanation for the hordes of fanciful beasts that inhabit medieval churches. They have no didactic religious meaning, and probably no esoteric meaning. They seem mere flights of fancy, though disconcerting ones. A Gothic cathedral is a microcosm of the Christian cosmos, and on its fringes lurk these wise, rather serene-looking creatures of the air: perhaps evil, perhaps only hinting of things undreamt of in the Christian philosophy.

To see these dark fancies at close quarters, you'll have to climb 238 steps. But it's worth it, not only for the monsters, but for a great Quasimodo's-eye view over the city. There are also the bells. In the south tower hangs a big-bellied one named the *Bourdon*, its 13,000 kilos packing a mighty F sharp heard only on holidays; in the north tower, the largest weighs over 2 tons, made from a melted-down Russian cannon captured at Sebastopol in the Crimean war. Its name is *Angélique-Françoise*, and it rings a C sharp. On the way up, there is a video presentation about the cathedral.

Crypte Archéologique du Parvis-Notre-Dame X14

*t 01 43 29 83 51. **Open** daily 10–6, closed some public hols; **adm** €3.30. Guided tour on some Saturdays.*

What was begun as an underground car park in 1965 had to become a museum when the excavations revealed the 3rd-century wall of Lutetia, traces of Roman and medieval houses, the Merovingian cathedral, 17th-century cellars and foundations of the Enfants Trouvés, or foundlings hospital of 1750, where unwanted children were left on a revolving tray. The archaeological work is faultless, and the foundations are labelled and explained with fastidious care, helping visitors to sort out easily this 3-D puzzle of stones covering over 1,500 years of history. But in truth there simply isn't much to see down here.

Musée de Notre-Dame Y14

10 Rue du Cloître-Notre-Dame, **t** *01 43 25 42 92.* **Open** *Wed, Sat and Sun 2.30–6;* **adm** *€2.50.*

This isn't a state museum, which explains its unusual opening hours. It is run by a society of friends of Notre-Dame, charming people who like to explain things to visitors and tell stories. The exhibits, mostly old prints, photos and plans, are fascinating, offering a wealth of detail on the history of the building and the quarter. There are drawings by Viollet-le-Duc, pictures of the old streets before Baron Haussmann demolished them, along with views of disappeared churches such as La Madeleine-en-la-Cité and St-Landry.

Almost directly across from the museum is Notre-Dame's northern portal (*c.* 1250), or the **Portail du Cloître**, since it once led to the cathedral cloister. Originally all of the island east of Rue d'Arcole was occupied by Notre-Dame's cloister, a veritable city within the city, enclosing 46 canons' houses, a round baptistry, a dozen small churches, as well as an episcopal school where Peter Abelard, St Dominic and St Bonaventure taught (now occupied by police garages).

The tympanum of the portal shows scenes from the childhood of Christ and illustrates the unusual legend of Deacon Théodore, who sold his soul to Old Nick but was saved by the grace of Mary; beneath, a figure of the Virgin is the only complete statue that survived the wrath of the Revolutionary mobs. Just to the left is another door, the Porte Rouge, from about the same date, with another Coronation of the Virgin on the tympanum, and various reliefs of the early 13th century to the left.

Around Notre-Dame

You can take a dip into what's left of the old Cité by wandering through the streets to the north of Notre-Dame, down **Rue Chanoinesse** (Y14), which has the last two canons' houses to escape demolition (Nos.22 and 24), and right into **Rue de la Colombe**

(Y14), where you can trace Lutetia's Gallo-Roman wall along the top of No.6, while the romantic little La Colombe restaurant conserves the doors and barrel vault of the Taverne Saint-Nicolas, founded in 1250.

Skirting the northern edge of the island is the **Quai aux Fleurs** (Y13–Z14), where No.9 sets the scene for a heart-rending tale, with a plaque and a pair of busts marking the site of the house of Canon Fulbert, the spiteful uncle of Héloïse (*see* 'Abelard and Héloïse' on the next page).

Square Jean-XXIII Y14

Until it was burned during the 'Three Glorious Days' of 1830, the archbishop's palace stood here, concealing much of the soaring apse of Notre-Dame. When Viollet-le-Duc built the archbishop a medievalish house south of the cathedral, the Square was left clear, except for a 19th-century fountain of the Virgin and a bust of the Venetian playwright Goldoni, who died in Paris in 1791.

But the apse steals the show; Notre-Dame is one of the few churches anywhere with a back end as beautiful as the front. The slender, delicate 312ft **spire** at the crossing, the highest part of the cathedral, can only be seen clearly from a distance. You'll never see the figures at its base, but one of them bears the features of Viollet-le-Duc, who rebuilt it. Even more astounding than this – as their proud architects no doubt meant them to be – are the **flying buttresses** that support the walls of the nave, 50ft arches of stone seemingly hanging in the air.

Mémorial des Martyrs de la Déportation Z15

Square de l'Île de France, **t** *01 46 33 87 56.* **Open** *daily 10–12 and 2–5, until 7 in summer.*

The Square de l'Île-de-France extends from the Quai de l'Archevêché to the very tip of the island, where vigilant mallards guard the stark Mémorial des Martyrs. Dedicated in 1962 by General de Gaulle, this is a solemn, moving memorial to the 200,000 French residents (i.e. Jews) sent by the Vichy government

Abelard and Héloïse

In 1118, in the golden age of troubadours, Héloïse was 18, and beautiful and intelligent enough to attract the attention of Notre-Dame's most brilliant scholar, Peter Abelard, then 38 years old, with such a reputation for continence and learning that when he approached Fulbert for lodgings, the old man quickly agreed, and asked in lieu of rent that the scholar tutor his bright young niece, 'authorizing me', wrote Abelard, 'to see her any hour of the day or night and punish her when necessary. I marvelled with what simplicity he confided a tender lamb to a hungry wolf...well, what need to say more: we were united first by the one roof above us, and then by our hearts.' Abelard was a talented harper, and soon his love songs to Héloïse were being sung all over Paris, beautiful songs 'that would have drawn the soul of any woman', as Héloïse herself described them.

The trouble began when Héloïse became pregnant; Abelard took her off to his sister's in Brittany, where she gave birth to a son, whom, trendy young couple that they were, they named Astrolabe. Abelard asked Héloïse to marry him, a proposal she strongly resisted, believing such a great philosopher should not tie himself down to one woman, and warning him that even marriage would not appease her uncle Fulbert's anger. But Abelard insisted, and a few months later, sure enough, the canon sent his heavies to 'punish me where I had most sinned' as Abelard admitted later. He took orders as a monk at St-Denis and Héloïse obeyed his command to become a nun, but was never reconciled to her vows and never stopped loving Abelard.

to the death camps. Each deportee is symbolized by a point; the prison-like interior of the monument, with its cold stone and iron bars, has inscriptions and a flame burns by the tomb of the Unknown Deportee.

But while the government can build memorials, it still cannot tell the truth about the willing complicity of thousands of French officials and police in the deportations. War criminals, such as those who led the Vel d'Hiv raid in 1942, in which 13,000 Parisian Jews were sent off to death, escaped prosecution for decades, protected by both right- and left-wing governments. If anything, this hypocritical memorial should be a reminder of how the French political class knows how to look after its own.

Until 1914, this site was occupied by the Morgue. Morgues are one of Paris' many gifts to the world, first set up in the 17th century. The word comes from *morguer*, 'to observe', for the whole point was to view (and identify) the corpses. By the 19th century it was one of Paris' biggest attractions: Charles Méryon and his friend Baudelaire haunted it, and Dickens confessed that whenever in Paris, 'I am dragged by an invisible force into the Morgue.'

Place Louis-Lépine X–Y13

Métro Cité, RER St-Michel-Notre-Dame. Flower market open Mon–Sat 8–7, bird market Sun 8–7.

In the middle of the island is Place Louis-Lépine, best known for its **Marché aux Fleurs** and **Marché aux Oiseaux**. Here, a daily flower market offers a haven of dewy green fragrances amid a desert of offices. The orchid stalls (in the first barn, off Rue de la Cité) are definitely worth a detour, or you can get a 10ft potted palm as a souvenir of Paris. On Sunday mornings a bird market takes over, a tradition dating back to the birds sold in the Middle Ages on the Pont au Change.

Overlooking the square is the **Préfecture de Police**, where a plaque tells how, just before the Liberation of Paris, the police barricaded themselves inside and held off a bloody German assault (with tanks) for a week.

Hôtel-Dieu X14–Y13

The massive bulk on the other side of the square, on Rue de la Cité, is the current incarnation of Paris' oldest hospital, the **Hôtel-Dieu**, founded in AD 660 by Bishop St Landry. Despite the very best of intentions, the

Hôtel-Dieu was for centuries a ripe subject for horror and black humour even beyond the borders of France. Patients could count on food and spiritual comfort, but until the 18th century, medical ignorance ensured that few who checked in ever checked out again. Financed by the revenue from hundreds of farms and houses in the Île-de-France, private donations and a tax on theatre tickets, the hospital could hold up to 4,000 patients. Up until the 17th century there were never more than eight doctors and often as few as two for the entire hospital. Although they developed a knack for setting fractures and removing gallstones, they had less luck with amputations (performed without anaesthetic, in sight of all the patients).

The beds were notorious for breeding disease and promiscuity, each designed for four to six people lying top to bottom. Such was the daily rush to clear out the beds for new arrivals that attendants sometimes dumped invalids who had merely fainted into the cemetery carts, and more than once the funerals were interrupted by indignant protests from the pile of corpses.

Today the Hôtel-Dieu is still a working hospital; and part of it is run as a hotel (see p.300).

Conciergerie W13–X14

1 Quai de l'Horloge, **t** *01 53 73 78 50;* ***métro*** *Cité,* **RER** *St-Michel-Notre-Dame.* **Open** *April–Sept daily 9–6, Oct–Mar daily 9–5, closed 1 Jan, 1 May, 1 and 11 Nov, 25 Dec;* ***adm*** *€6.10 (combined ticket with Sainte-Chapelle €9), Oct–May free on 1st Sun of the month; tours in English are listed at the entrance, guided tours in French at 11.15 and 3.*

To set the mood for a building known as the 'antechamber of the guillotine', the first of three round towers you pass along the quay is the Tour Bonbec (1250), or 'babbler', where prisoners were put to the question, their memories jogged by the rack, water torture (forced ingurgitation of hornfuls of water) or the boot (made of iron, in which pieces of wood were wedged). Justice could

be swift; a trap door under the prisoners' feet waited to pitch them into an *oubliette* lined with razor-sharp steel spikes; the Seine washed their mangled bodies away.

The Conciergerie wasn't always so grim. In its first, 4th-century incarnation it was the palace of Lutetia's Roman governors, a favourite retreat of Emperor Julian the Apostate. Clovis requisitioned the palace *c*. AD 500 and established the Frankish monarchy within its walls. In 987 Hugues Capet moved in, and it stayed in the family for the next 800 years. As the kings grew wealthy, their palace grew ever more splendid, so that by the time Richard the Lionheart came to call on Philippe-Auguste, it resembled a fairy-tale miniature in the Duc de Berry's *Très Riches Heures*.

In 1358, Étienne Marcel's partisans stormed the palace and assassinated the king's ministers as the Dauphin Charles V stood helplessly by. It was a lesson in the vulnerability of the royal person in Paris that subsequent kings forgot only at their peril; the immediate result was that Charles V ordered the construction of the less central and better fortified Louvre. Abandoned by the kings, the palace evolved into Paris' seat of justice and its prison. In 1914 the Conciergerie became a public monument.

As you enter the first room, the Gothic Salle des Gardes, note the first pillar to your left. The capital is carved with the lives of Héloïse and Abelard, culminating in the scene of Héloïse clutching like a giant lollipop the part of her lover they were both to miss sorely (see 'Abelard and Héloïse', above). Architecturally, the highlight of the Conciergerie is the adjacent guardroom, Philippe le Bel's Salle des Gens d'Armes (1314), one of the largest Gothic halls ever built (229 by 91ft). The spiral stair offered rapid access to the Throne Room above (now the Salle des Pas-Perdus); a passage under the stair leads to a kitchen (1350) built by Jean le Bon, with four fireplaces to placate the appetites of the royal household.

A grille separates the Salle des Gens d'Armes from a corridor called the Rue de Paris, named after 'Monsieur de Paris', a euphemism for the executioner during the Revolution. Here the poorest prisoners, unable to pay the price of the cell, slept on straw. A large percentage of the guillotine's more illustrious fodder passed through the dreary **Galerie des Prisonniers** just beyond: Marie-Antoinette (whose cell has been reconstructed), Danton, Desmoulins, Charlotte Corday and St-Just. All would have their collars torn and hair cut in Paris' grimmest Salle de la Toilette before boarding the tumbrils. Upstairs are other reconstructed cells, a room listing the 2,780 people condemned in Paris during the Revolution, the chapel where the unlucky Girondins feasted their last night on earth, and near the chapel a plaque marking the spot where Robespierre (whose favourite coat colour gave him the nickname of the 'seagreen incorruptible') spent his last hour in agony, with a jaw shattered from a failed suicide attempt, taunted by those who had feared him only the day before.

The corner of the Conciergerie next to the Pont au Change is closed by a square tower, the **Tour de l'Horloge** (X13). Built in 1371 by Charles V, it held Paris' first public clock; later centuries joked that it ran *'comme il lui plaît'*, and it ticks on to this day, though the innards have been replaced several times. The bridge was last rebuilt in 1639 and was originally lined with five-storey houses, headquarters for financial wheeler-dealers in the days before the Bourse.

Palais de Justice W13–X14

2 Bd du Palais, t 01 44 32 50 00; métro Cité, RER St-Michel. Open Mon–Fri 8.30–6.

The Palais de Justice itself is entered via the Cour du Mai; its façade conceals the Mercière, or gallery of shops, that once linked Sainte-Chapelle to the palace and provided rent money for the royal pocket. Although the name of the Cour du Mai recalls the May Day celebrations of Paris' lawyers, who in days of yore frisked merrily around a tree (a custom revived briefly with the Revolution's liberty trees), the courtyard is more sombrely

remembered as the Conciergerie's loading dock, where the gorged tumbrils rumbled away to the clicking knitting needles of a hundred Madame Defarges.

A grand stair from the Cour du Mai leads up into the hallowed **Salle des Pas-Perdus**, the 'cathedral of chicanery', according to Balzac, where the law was 'spiders' webs that let the big flies pass through while the little flies get stuck'. Originally the throne room of Philippe le Bel, it was rebuilt in 1871 and given its name, *pas-perdus* (mis-steps) as a constant warning that it takes but one false step here to ruin a career (there's another Salle des Pas-Perdus in the stock exchange). In the afternoon, you can study the stride of lawyers flapping by in their raven gowns, especially around the Première Chambre Civile. This was originally St Louis' bedroom, and then the seat of Paris' *Parlement*, and during the Revolution, Fouquier-Tinville's Tribunal that sentenced over 2,000 people to death in less than a year. The ornate ceiling was rebuilt in the style of Louis XII. To the right of its entrance, note the monument to the barrister Berryer in the company of a tortoise – a comment on the speed of justice.

Sainte-Chapelle X13

4 Bd du Palais, t 01 53 73 78 50; métro Cité, RER St-Michel. Open April–Sept daily 9.30–6.30, Oct–Mar daily 10–5, closed 1 Jan, 1 May, 1 and 11 Nov, 25 Dec; adm €6.10, combined ticket with Conciergerie €9, Oct–May free on 1st Sun of the month; tours in English are listed at the entrance.

'There's a sucker born every minute,' quoth the great circus entrepreneur Barnum, who in a former incarnation must have lived in the Holy Land, bamboozling French crusaders into spending their hard-plundered cash on old bits of wood and bones. If all the existing pieces of the True Cross were refitted together, the result would be the size of a California redwood. The Crown of Thorns (one of several) was sold, miraculously intact, to Baudouin, 'Emperor of Constantinople', who had to pawn it to the Venetians. In 1239

St Louis redeemed it for 135,000 *livres*, and there was still enough change left in his purse to pick up other holy real McCoys (now all in Notre-Dame), including the staff of Moses, several drops of the Virgin's milk, Judas' lantern, the sponge dipped in vinegar, and the front half of John the Baptist's head, which was found by the French in the abandoned palace of the Caesars when they sacked Constantinople in 1204. Considerably less was spent on the construction of the Sainte-Chapelle.

You might say he got his money's worth. The cliché in every art book is that Gothic buildings *aspire*, in grace, lightness and height. Sainte-Chapelle, the ultimate Gothic building, has *arrived*. Here, as at Notre-Dame, you will lose any notion you might have had about the Middle Ages being quaint and backward. Every inch declares a perfect mastery of mathematics and statics, materials and stresses. To put it briefly, the upper chapel is nearly 65ft high, and almost three-quarters of its wall area is glass. Unlike the case with most great cathedrals, here we know the architect's name: Pierre de Montreuil. Not only did he design Gothic's masterpiece, but he got it up in only 30 months and built it so well that not a single crack has appeared since the chapel was finished in 1248.

Sainte-Chapelle has an unusual plan, somewhat like a beaver lodge: the important part, the spectacular upper chapel, can only be entered from below, up a spiral stairway tucked in a corner of the lower chapel. As you go in, there's a clue as to why this double-deck arrangement was necessary – a flood marker from 1910 on one pillar shows how the Seine reached almost 6ft on this low-lying part of the island. Palace servants heard Mass in the lower chapel; the tombs belong to clerics of the 14th and 15th centuries, and the painted decoration is 19th century.

Emerging from the narrow stair into the upper chapel is a startling, unforgettable experience. The other cliché in the books is that Sainte-Chapelle is a 'jewel box' for Louis' treasured relics; this too is entirely apt, even

understated. Awash in colour and light from the tall windows, the chapel glitters like the cave of the Forty Thieves. The glass is the oldest in Paris (13th century), though much was restored a century ago according to the original designs. Of all the great French glass cycles, this one makes the most complete and concise 'picture Bible'. Almost all the major stories from both Testaments are represented. From the entrance:

First bay: left, Book of Genesis, including Adam and Eve and Noah's Ark; right, the Window of St-Louis, comparing his relic-collecting with St Helen's discovery of the True Cross.

Second bay: left, Exodus, the life of Moses; right, David and Solomon.

Third bay: left, Laws of Moses; right, Book of Esther.

Fourth bay: left, Books of Deuteronomy and Joshua, Israel's wanderings in the desert; right Books of Judith and Job (underneath is Louis' private oratory).

In the seven windows of the **apse**, from left to right: (**1**) Book of Judges, including the story of Samson; (**2**) Book of Isaiah and 'Tree of Jesse' (genealogy of Christ); (**3**) Life of the Virgin, the early life of Christ; (**4**) (central window) the Passion; (**5**) John the Baptist; (**6**) Book of Ezekiel; (**7**) Books of Jeremiah and Lamentations.

And opposite the apse, in the **rose window**, the Book of Revelations.

The atmosphere of the chapel is heightened by the lavish use of gold paint and the deep-blue ceiling painted with golden stars. This was part of the restoration, but in Louis' time it was probably much the same; this sort of heavenly decoration, fitting the Gothic sensibility so well, reached France in the 13th century, either from Italy or its original home, Byzantium.

Beneath the glass are 12 statues of the Apostles; many are reconstructions, but the originals are wonderfully expressive works. The crosses they bear are 'consecration crosses', recalling the custom by which a bishop, when consecrating a church, would mark crosses on 12 of the pillars, to symbolize

> ### The Patron Saint of Lawyers
>
> On 19 May, St Yves' day, a Mass is celebrated in Sainte-Chapelle for the souls of all the lawyers who have died during the year. St Yves, their patron, was a 14th-century ecclesiastical judge from Brittany who gave up his office to help the destitute. Despite his obvious piety, the legend goes that St Peter refused to let Yves past the Pearly Gates because he was a lawyer, so he sneaked in. Peter ordered him out. 'Only if a bailiff serves me an expulsion order signed by a judge,' countered Yves. Peter combed heaven, but, unable to find any members of the legal profession there, was forced to let Yves stay.

that the Apostles were the 'true pillars of the Church'. Above the statues are rare niello-work scenes of their martyrdoms.

The Western Tip of the Island

Pont Neuf W13–12
Métro *Pont-Neuf.*

By the late Middle Ages, the ancient umbilical bridges tying the mother island to the banks of the Seine had become eternally jammed with traffic, and on 31 May 1578 the cornerstone for a new bridge was laid by Henri III. It was completed in 1605 and, although often restored, retains its original form. Before the advent of public fountains, the Pont Neuf marked the downstream limit where the city's 20,000 water-carriers could legally draw water in the summer, but even then it was vile stuff.

Reliefs and grotesques decorate the Pont Neuf as seen from the river, portraying the pickpockets, charlatans and tooth extractors who used to harangue, amuse and prey on the passing crowds. For throughout the 17th century, the bridge was the place to see and be seen in Paris. When the police sought a suspect, they would post an agent on the bridge, and if after three days they failed to spot their man they assumed he wasn't in Paris. A big attraction was the singers of satirical and anti-government ditties (the Pont Neuf was the only place where they were tolerated). Strollers could hire parasols at either end of the bridge, a sybaritic touch that shocked foreign visitors.

The Pont Neuf had the first raised pavements in Paris, a much appreciated innovation in the mucky era when *décrotteurs* (shoe and stocking de-turders) did a brisk business. It was also the first bridge without houses or shops, and opened up a view down the length of the Seine that enchanted Parisians.

Square du Vert-Galant V–W13
Métro *Pont-Neuf.*

The Vert-Galant, or 'gay old spark', was a fond nickname for Henri IV, the most Parisian of kings and one whose incessant skirt-chasing endeared him to his subjects as much as his conversion to Catholicism. Little did the king suspect that his new Place Dauphine (*see* below) would be closed off on the Pont Neuf corner with his own memorial: a bronze equestrian statue by Giambologna, erected shortly after his assassination.

The original figure of Henri was only half as good as that of his horse. But artistic considerations never troubled the sleep of the mob of 1792, who smashed the horseman to bits. The next generation erected a new smiling Henri in 1818, made of bronze from the statue of Napoleon they had toppled off the Vendôme column. One foundry worker refused to see any humour in this recycling of idols and secretly deposited Napoleonic propaganda and a statuette of the little emperor in the belly of the horse.

The square marks the very prow of Île de la Cité, and the weeping willow at the tip, trailing into the river, is traditionally the first tree in Paris to burst into leaf. From here there are good views back to the Pont Neuf and its carvings, and ahead to the **Pont des Arts** (1803), one of the first, and most elegant, iron bridges built in France. You can embark on a tour of the Seine's other bridges on a *vedette du Pont Neuf*, moored at the north end of the square.

In the Middle Ages, the square was the tip of a muddy islet called Île aux Juifs, a favourite place for burning Jews and witches, and used on 12 March 1314 for the execution of Jacques de Molay, the Grand Master of the Templars. Before going up in smoke, De Molay cursed his accusers, Pope Clement V and Philippe le Bel, and predicted (accurately) they would follow him to the grave within a year.

Place Dauphine W13

Métro *Pont-Neuf or Cité.*

After the Templar barbecue, the Île aux Juifs was joined to Île de la Cité and made into a royal garden; in 1607, Henri IV allowed Achille de Harlay, president of the Paris *Parlement*, to convert it into a square named after the dauphin, the future Louis XIII, on condition that he make it a set architectural piece like Place des Vosges. The design, a triangle of identical houses of brick and stone with façades facing both the square and the river, has been sorely tried over the centuries: the east side was demolished in the 19th century to set off the pompous façade of the Palais de Justice, and only Nos.14 and 16 preserve something of their original appearance.

Now it is quiet, a leafy triangle in the cold stone officialdom that has usurped the Cité. It has always seduced lovers of Paris, although it took Surrealist André Breton to analyse the exact nature of Place Dauphine's charm: 'It is, without any doubt, the sex of Paris which is outlined in this shade.'

ÎLE ST-LOUIS

For 1,900 years, Île St-Louis was as neglected as the Cité was popular. Every now and then a medieval king would cross over to dub a knight or two (an old custom), but that was all. That this land, in the heart of one of Europe's most crowded cities, could have some practical value was only noticed in the wake of the Marais property boom. In 1614 bridge-builder and engineer Christophe Marie persuaded the king to let him bind the islets into one island, and tie it with bridges

to the Right and Left Banks. In exchange for the work, Marie and his speculator-associates Lugles Poulletier and François Le Regrattier were given several concessions, building and running a *jeu de paume*, a real-tennis court, and a *bateau-lavoir*, a wooden platform-boat floating beside the quay, where women paid a small fee to use the tubs for washing and rinsing and the roof for drying clothes (it remained a fixture of St-Louis' Quai de Bourbon until 1942). Most importantly, Marie and Co. could sell plots of the former cow pasture to developers. The simple grid of streets made subdivision easy, and aristocrats were more than welcome; their snob value increased land values and attracted the wealthiest members of the bourgeoisie – especially magistrates and financiers. The speculators, who didn't miss a trick, gave the quays a certain cachet by naming them after the royal houses of France. Its success was assured when the young, popular architect **Louis Le Vau** moved here in the late 1630s and became the chief speculator himself, designing and selling his elegant *hôtels particuliers*. In 1726 the island was given the name of its newly consecrated church.

Nearly all the houses on Île St-Louis went up between 1627 and 1667, bestowing on the island an architectural homogeneity rare in Paris. Although it charmed the Parisians of the Grand Siècle, it fell out of fashion in the 18th century, and in the 19th enjoyed a Romantic revival among bohemians such as Cézanne, Daumier, Gautier and Baudelaire, who were drawn by its poetic solitude. Since the last war property prices have rocketed to the stars. The fine *hôtels* have nearly all been restored or divided into flats; bijou restaurants sprout at every corner, and during Paris' big tourist invasions its famous village atmosphere decays into the gaudy air of an ice-cream-spattered 17th-century funfair.

Along the *Quais* Z–AA15

Although the inner streets and the island's dorsal Rue St-Louis-en-l'Île are too narrow for trees, the quays of Île St-Louis have some of the prettiest plane trees and poplars in Paris, casting dappled shadows across the façades of the *hôtels particuliers*. These were the first buildings to make river-views fashionable; one of the finest, complete with a shady garden, is enjoyed by the lucky residents of the **Maison du Centaure** at No.45 Quai de Bourbon, built by Le Vau's brother and named after its medallions showing Hercules fighting Nessus. Le Vau also designed the classy *hôtels particuliers* along the Quai de Béthune, originally called Quai des Balcons after the balconies that grace them.

Musée Mickiewicz Z–AA15

*6 Quai d'Orléans, t 01 55 42 83 83; **métro** Pont-Marie. **Closed** at time of writing; due to open some time in 2004, maybe later.*

This museums adds an exotic touch to Île St-Louis, with its 200,000-volume Polish Library of Paris founded in 1838. The first floor, devoted to Chopin, has original scores and the composer's death mask, while upstairs are ephemera on the life and times of poet and patriot Adam Mickiewicz (1798–1855), founder of Polish Romanticism.

Rue des Deux-Ponts AA15–14

Around the corner, the Rue des Deux-Ponts is a street widened in the early 20th century at the expense of all the houses on the odd-numbered side of the street. It ends at **Pont Marie**, named after the engineer who built it with his own money. Originally lined with houses, like most Paris bridges, it collapsed the day it opened in 1634, drowning 20 people. Since then it has continued to be one of Paris' more troublesome spans, and has often been rebuilt – since the 1790s, without the houses. Just to the left, the old cabaret **Le Franc Pinot**, with its decorative grille of grapes and vines, was until 1794 the home of the Renault family, whose daughter Cécile, inspired by Charlotte Corday, attempted to murder the tyrant Robespierre. She failed, and the whole family was sent to the guillotine.

Rue St-Louis-en-l'Île

This has always been the island's main commercial street, with enough little village shops to keep an islander from ever really having to cross over to the mainland. But there is one striking building as well, at No.51, the **Hôtel de Chenizot** (1730). A bearded faun's head and pot-bellied chimeras enliven its doorway, one of Paris' rare rococo works; countless others lost similar playful façades to the severe neoclassical fashion that came with the Revolution.

St-Louis-en-l'Île AA15

19 Rue St-Louis-en-l'Île, t 01 46 34 11 60. Open Tues–Sun 9–12 and 3–7.

The first, tiny chapel on the island, dedicated to the Virgin, was quickly deemed too dinky and common by the new islanders, and in 1664 Le Vau designed a new parish church, which remained unfinished until 1725. Although the big clock over the street is the only distinguishing feature of the boxy exterior, inside this is the perfect Baroque society church, a stone-and-gilt pastry for the spiritually untroubled.

Hôtel Lambert BB15

2 Rue St-Louis-en-l'Île.

Designed in 1641 by Le Vau for Jean-Baptiste Lambert, secretary to Louis XIII, this *hôtel particulier* was given lavish interiors painted by the top decorators of the day – Lebrun and Le Sueur; most of these decorations are still in place, minus a few squirrelled away in the Louvre. In 1831 it was saved from ruin by the exiled Polish leader, Prince Adam Czartoryski; it became the headquarters of the Polish government-in-exile, and a cultural rendezvous for émigrés such as Chopin, who taught piano to Polish princesses before running off to Majorca with George Sand. Today Hôtel Lambert belongs to the Rothschilds, and sometimes on weekdays they magnanimously leave the gate open so you can sneak a peek at the *cour d'honneur*.

The Grand Axe

The Grand Axe

There's little chance of getting lost along the Grand Axe – it's a perfectly straight line of about 8km (5 miles) and you can cover most of it on the bus. Frankly, its charms are few and – as a glance at the map will demonstrate – far between. But this is a part of Paris that every first-time visitor feels obliged to see. From the Louvre to La Défense, the monuments line up like pearls on a string: some natural, some cultured and some fake.

Paris' main drag recalls destiny and De Gaulle; its breadth and majesty still proclaim to the world that this is the place to be. It has been an irresistible magnet for parades ever since it was built: Napoleon's Grande Armée did it, and Bismarck made a Champs-Elysées promenade part of the armistice terms in 1870 – even though the Prussians couldn't capture Paris. And on both sides of the Atlantic, there are still plenty of stout fellows around who will never forget the day they did this walk in uniform, on 26 August 1944.

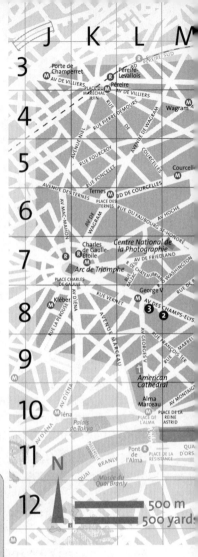

1 Lunch

Café Marly, *Louvre courtyard, facing the Pyramid;* **métro** *Palais Royal-Musée du Louvre.* **Open** *daily 8am–2am.* **Moderate**. New, beautifully designed chic hangout in the old ministries vacated for the Grand Louvre project. Especially pretty at night.

2 Tea and Cakes

Ladurée, *75 Av des Champs-Elysées;* **métro** *Franklin D. Roosevelt.* **Open** *daily 8am–midnight.* Exquisite and precious *salon de thé*, famous for its macaroons. Bring your laciest great-aunt along for tea.

3 Drinks

Le Fouquet's, *99 Av des Champs-Elysées;* **métro** *George-V.* **Open** *daily 8am–2am.* A Paris institution for the rich and famous.

Highlights

Couples' City: Stroll under the plane trees along the Champs-Elysées, p.113

Parisian's City: Lunch at the Louvre's trendy Café Marly, p.96

Peace and Quiet: Take refuge in the kings' parish church, St-Germain-l'Auxerrois, p.110

Paris des Artistes: The Louvre, one of their great meccas, p.100

Grand Siècle Paris: The Jardin des Tuileries, even in their stripped-down state, p.110

Gritty City: The traffic maelstrom in Place de la Concorde, p.112

MUSÉE DU LOUVRE U11–V12

*t 01 40 20 53 17, for information in English call t 01 40 20 51 51, w www.louvre.fr; **métro** Palais Royal-Musée du Louvre; wheelchairs available, plus plans indicating rooms with easy wheelchair access. **Open** Wed–Mon 9–6 (rooms start to close at 5.30), Mon and Wed eves until 9.30 (Wed eve everything is open; Mon eve Richelieu wing only; rooms start to close at 9.30), History of the Louvre rooms only open Mon (hours as above), museum closed some hols; **adm** €7.50, lower all day Sunday and after 3pm, free for under-18s and on 1st Sun of the month. Tickets can be bought in advance from branches of FNAC, Carrefour, Auchan and Virgin or at t 08 03 80 88 03 or t 08 03 34 63 46, or on the Web site. At weekends or on any day in summer, come early to avoid the long queues. Call the information number for details on which rooms are closed on any given day.*

The beginning of the Grand Axe, marked by a new glass Pyramid and the old Arc du Carrousel, is in the courtyard of the Palais du Louvre. This of course contains the delicious, often indigestible, 99-course feast that sooner or later all visitors to Paris must swallow. 'The Biggest Museum in the World' they call it, certain they have surpassed the Vatican, the Smithsonian, the British Museum and the other monsters. It isn't even as big as it used to be, for all post-1848 art has been moved to the Musée d'Orsay.

Risking total exhaustion, it can be done in a day if you concentrate on the highlights and do not follow your fancy too far. For a good look at everything, allow two full days, or a lifetime.

A Palace by the Seine

'Louvre' was the name of the area long before any palaces were dreamt of. The best guess anyone has to the origin of the name is 'leper colony', though historical evidence is lacking. The original castle was built some time after 1190 by Philippe-Auguste, perfecting his new city fortifications by protecting against attacks from up-river. Charles V rebuilt and extended it in the 1360s, after the revolt of Étienne Marcel taught him the value of having a well-fortified residence in turbulent Paris. During the worst of the Hundred Years' War, 1400–30, the kings abandoned the Louvre, spending their time in the Marais or among the châteaux of the Loire valley. The first to return was François I, in 1527; he demolished the old castle and began what is known today as the Vieux Louvre, the easternmost part of the complex, in 1546. François, a great patron of the arts, contributed more than anyone to building the Louvre's picture collection, the 'Cabinet du Roi'. Two works by his friend Leonardo da Vinci, the *Mona Lisa* and *Virgin of the Rocks*, originally hung in the royal bathroom.

After Henri II was accidentally killed in a tournament at his residence in the Marais (*see* p.183), his widow Catherine de' Medici decided to forsake east Paris; not caring for the half-completed Louvre, however, she commissioned Philibert de l'Orme, the greatest French Renaissance architect, to start yet another palace just to the west – the great Tuileries (1563). Catherine also began a long, stately gallery on the banks of the Seine, the present south wing of the Louvre, to connect the Tuileries with the Vieux Louvre. Unfortunately an old sorceress friend of Catherine's told her she would die in the Tuileries, and this most superstitious of all queens abandoned the works in 1572.

Henri IV, Louis XIII and Louis XIV all contributed in turn to the palace. Henri began the custom of housing artists in the Louvre, which continued until Napoleon booted the last of them out in 1806; among those who enjoyed room and board at state expense were Boucher, Fragonard and David. When Louis XIV abandoned the Louvre for Versailles in 1682, however, the palace fell on hard times. Louis rented out the rooms to just anyone, and the place was in such bad shape by the 1750s that there was talk of tearing it down.

The next royal resident, however unwilling, was Louis XVI, brought here by force from Versailles in October 1789 and installed in the Tuileries, where the National Assembly could keep a close eye on him. From here the royal family began its ill-fated flight to Varennes in June 1791. In June 1792 the Paris mob attacked the Tuileries and put a liberty cap on the frightened king's head, making him drink to the Revolution. Two months later, when it became clear that Louis was plotting with the émigrés to overthrow the Revolution, the mob came back in earnest, besieging and finally taking the Tuileries, massacring hundreds of the king's Swiss Guards after they surrendered.

Republican governments kept their offices in the Tuileries after 1795; they consolidated the art collections and made them into a public museum in 1793. Napoleon moved in in 1800, and started work on the northern wing. During the next 15 years, his men looted the captive nations of Europe for their finest paintings and statues, most of which ended up here. The picture of Napoleon as a sensitive art connoisseur is one of the sillier by-products of the Napoleonic myth. Like Hitler, he was a philistine, obsessed with art for the sake of status, and determined to make the Louvre – by then the 'Musée Napoléon' – the greatest, perhaps the only, museum in the world. In 1815 the allies made the French give most of the art back – though in a hundred towns in Italy and Spain, people remember stolen masterpieces that never found their way home.

The crowned heads of France chose to reside in the Tuileries from then on, though it brought them bad luck; out of five, only one (Louis XVIII) was allowed to finish his reign in peace. The last of them, Napoleon III, built more of the present Louvre than anyone else, including almost all the façades around the huge courtyards, the Cour Napoléon and Jardin du Carrousel. After his capture by the Prussians in the war of 1870, the people from the Paris provisional government inspected the Tuileries and were shocked to find the Emperor's pleasure-palace 'more like a brothel than a royal residence'. Public indignation over the exposés of life at the Tuileries contributed much to the onset of the Commune – and to the failure of monarchists to interest anyone in finding a new king after 1871. During the 'Bloody Week' of the repression of the Commune, the Tuileries was burned to the ground by a Communard officer; the rest of the Louvre nearly went with it.

It's been a quiet palace since. In 1981, his first year in office, President Mitterrand decided to shake it a up a bit with the *Projet du Grand Louvre*, a total refurbishing of the palace, museum and the adjacent Tuileries gardens. First the cars were chased out of the courtyards, which had become shabby parking lots. Then the Pyramid (*see* 'The Pyramid', overleaf) and the new museum lobby beneath it were begun. The entire north wing, which had housed the Ministry of Finance, was cleared to expand the museum space, and a giant underground car park and plush shopping mall was burrowed under the Jardin du Carrousel.

Arc du Carrousel

The burning of the Tuileries in 1871 made the Louvre's interior court a public affair – unfortunately, since it exposed to everyone's view one of the capital's greatest architectural embarrassments. Napoleon's architects, Beaux-Arts sycophants to a man, had been ordered to surpass the work of the Renaissance, and they replied with pastiche façades dripping with pointless statuary – all in cheap stone; the government is currently spending millions to clean and restore it.

There was a Place du Carrousel long before the Arc appeared. Before it became a merry-go-round, '*carrousel*' meant a knightly tournament, involving races, jousts and even singing. In the Place's centre, the Arc du Carrousel, like the other monument Napoleon built to himself, the Vendôme column, is a mere copy, in this case of the Arch of Septimus Severus in the Roman

The Pyramid

For a simple geometric bagatelle, architect I. M. Pei's 1988 entrance to the Louvre has certainly generated a lot of ink. *Le Figaro* called the controversy a revival of the 17th-century literary battle, the 'Quarrel of the Ancients and Moderns'. Another headline referring to President Mitterrand, Pei's sponsor, asked 'Who Does He Think He Is? Ramses II?' The structure is the crowning achievement or the ultimate atrocity from a decade of *grand projets* when Paris was transformed by metal and concrete. To some it was a cause célèbre of classical pure form, to others the Pyramid was a chilly, inhuman blast of rude geometry in the sacred precincts of art. Occultists, never lacking in Paris, are convinced that the Grand Axe pointing from here to La Défense can be followed in the opposite direction back to the Great Pyramid of Giza; they also claim it is a secret solar temple, noting (correctly) that the Pyramid is made of exactly 666 panes of glass, the sum of the numbers in the Sun's magic square.

The Pyramid and the Hall Napoléon beneath it are open until 9.45pm (except Tues), and that is the best time to come and see for yourself. Illuminated from inside, the structure is undeniably beautiful, inspiring almost. Behind the glass, the metal struts and cables make an intricate and delicate pattern, a marvel of intelligence and grace. An architecture that can be so provocative and so simple seems an advance of light years over the surrounding Second Empire buildings.

Much of the spilled ink deals with the eternal architectural conundrum of 'relating the building to the site' and Pei's solution was hardly one of respecting the surrounding buildings. The architect himself was silent about the theory behind his designs, but the most striking feature of his Pyramid is the contrast with the Louvre wings. Instead of the ponderous, pretentious Beaux-Arts, he has produced something light, almost immaterial. The most sophisticated technology available was employed (after four years of studies and calculations) to let the aluminium mullions be as thin as possible – the entire Pyramid weighs only 88.5 tonnes (90 tons).

It cost Mitterrand some 90 million francs, which works out at 1,100F (€167) a kilo – almost as much as a seafood platter from Fauchon. But compared with some of the other budget-busters among the *grands projets*, that was a pittance. A few minor problems have occurred since the opening: cleaning the glass, for one. When no machine could do the job, alpine guides were brought in; they devised a system of hooks and cables to support the intrepid window-washers.

Forum. The reliefs of Napoleon's army on its campaigns are done with remarkable verisimilitude, down to the buttons on the uniforms. On top, the Emperor placed the greatest prize of his career, the quadriga of four bronze horses he stole from St Mark's in Venice in 1805 (the Venetians nicked them from the Hippodrome in Constantinople in 1204; Constantine, who had placed them there, had stolen them from either Chios or Rome). In 1815 the allies made France give the famous ponies back. The current ones are copies; after 1815 an allegorical figure of the 'Restoration' was made for the chariot.

A sculptural ensemble in bronze in the **Jardin du Carrousel** appears to represent a crack ladies' rugby team at practice. In fact this is a collection of separate works by Aristide Maillol, a wonderful turn-of-the-last-century Catalan-French sculptor who started his career at the age of 40 and believed that any conceivable subject could be most effectively represented by female nudes of heroic proportions; the damsels represent 'the Night', 'Action in Chains' and 'Île-de-France', among others.

The Collections

Once through the door and down the long curving stairway, you are in the Hall Napoléon, where you can buy your ticket (*the correct change for the ticket machines will allow you to avoid the second queue*); there are also cafés and restaurants, an auditorium, a bookshop and space for exhibitions. From here you have a choice of three entrances into the labyrinth, up escalators marked **Denon**, **Sully** and **Richelieu**, the three sections into which the Louvre has been divided under the new organization scheme.

This scheme is somewhat irrational, not corresponding at all to the nature of the exhibits (Sully is the old Louvre, Denon the south wing, Richelieu the north wing, but that will do you little good when you're trying to find your way around inside). A free, colour-coded **orientation guide** is available at the front desk; as long as they keep it up to date, it will allow you to find the sections you're most interested in relatively easily.

If you take the Sully escalator, you can begin your visit with the History of the Louvre itself. From this exhibit, walk down to the crypt under the Cour Carrée to see the foundations of the wall and keep of Charles V's Louvre, unearthed in recent excavations and completely intact, as well as a detailed model of the castle.

Egyptian Art
Sully ground floor, Denon entresol (lower ground floor).

This may be the finest and most complete collection outside Egypt itself. Thanks to Napoleon, of course, the French got a head start. His 1798 expedition to the land of the pharaohs took along a fair-sized platoon of scientists and scholars interested in Egyptian antiquities. The army carted tons of art and mummies back to Paris, where Champollion, the director of the Louvre's new Egyptian department, deciphered the hieroglyphics.

A great granite **sphinx** from the 4th dynasty (*c.* 2500 BC) welcomes you in at the entrance (Sully). For most people, the greatest revelations here will be the earliest works. Under the first dynasties, in the third millennium BC, Egyptian artists were creating amazingly naturalistic painted statues, showing serene, likeable-looking folk like the *Majordomo Koki*,

Ambassador Kanefer and his wife Neferiret, and the Buddha-like *Seated Scribe*; see also the strange stele of the *Serpent King* from about 3000 BC, the very beginning of the Old Kingdom. Another very distinctive chapter in Egyptian art is the 'Amarna period', presided over by the original Sun King – Amenophis IV Akhenaton (1372–1354 BC), represented here by a striking statue. Pharaoh and prophet, Akhenaton moved the capital to his new city of Heliopolis, or Amarna, and created a short-lived religious revolution based on a transcendent sun god – as Freud wrote, the beginning of monotheism.

Sarcophagi there are in plenty, but keep an eye out for the surprises that make the subtle Egyptians come to life – like the dog with a bell around his neck, a sort of Alsatian, with a quizzical look. Or the pyramidal stone from the 30th dynasty with the 36 decan demons carved on it (three for each sign of the zodiac), representing an important theme in the later Egyptians' deep astrological mumbo-jumbo. Don't miss the **Mastaba of Akhetep**, a complete small funeral chapel (*c.* 2300 BC) from Saqqara. The interior walls are completely covered with a wealth of magnificently detailed reliefs: fish, birds, trees, oxen and donkeys, along with scenes of Akhetep's funeral feast and the preparing of his tomb.

The collection doesn't end with ancient Egypt, but carries on in Denon with exceptional exhibits of **Coptic Art** up to the Middle Ages. Building on a Greek-Hellenistic-Byzantine heritage, Egypt's Christians produced some remarkable work, especially in bronzes and embroidery; note the Roman-era sarcophagus of a girl, made of fabric strips woven in a wonderfully intricate pattern. There's an entire Coptic church here – the **Monastic Church of Baouit** (begun in the 6th century AD).

Middle Eastern Art
Richelieu and Sully ground floor.

Like the Egyptian collection, this is extremely rich and it goes on for ever. The various civilizations of **Mesopotamia** are well represented. As always, this necessarily means a preponderance of grim, arrogant works celebrating viciousness and raw power, and bragging about murders and conquests. It starts with what may be the oldest known historical monument, the Sumerian stele of the *Vultures*, with inscriptions from 2450 BC. Early Akkadian steles show kings trampling the bodies of their enemies.

You may have never heard of **Mani**, a great civilization centred on the Euphrates, now in Syria, that reached its height *c.* 1800 BC, but its people were some of the Middle East's most talented artists, represented here by statues and a rare surviving fresco. From Babylon, which destroyed Mani, there is a black monument carved with the **Code of Hammurabi**, the oldest known body of laws. For a fitting climax, there's the work of those sweethearts of antiquity, the Assyrians. A distinctly chilling touch permeates the weird, **winged bulls** of their palace façades, and especially the reliefs of those ever-victorious generals with those curly beards that must have taken their hairdressers hours to do.

Cultures on the fringe of the Fertile Crescent are also present, from Persia, Cyprus, Palestine and Syria. Finally, a room of **medieval Islamic** ceramics and metalwork (Richelieu *entresol*) includes the Font of St Louis, used to baptize future kings of France. Louis picked it up in Aleppo while crusading.

Classical Antiquity

Denon ground, Sully ground, lower ground and first floors.

Begin at the top of the 'Denon' escalator up from the Pyramid, with the *Atlantes* from the Theatre of Dionysos in Athens. Their presence in this conspicuous spot – four colossal, satyr-like creatures, each bemusedly contemplating his corkscrew-twisted John Thomas – proves that not only the Greeks but even the Louvre curators have a sense of humour.

From here follow stylized archaic **Greek works** such as the Egyptian-influenced *Lady of Auxerre* (late 7th century) and the headless *Hera of Samos* (really a *kore*, maiden). Some

exceptional works are displayed in the round hall; note the transitional-style, early 5th-century Pharsalian relief the French call the *Exaltation de la Fleur* (Robert Graves, who put the relief on the cover of his *Greek Myths*, thought it not a flower but the hallucinatory fly agaric mushroom, and that the ladies pictured were about to use it in a Dionysian ritual). Nearby are a number of fine reliefs from Olympia, including part of a series on the Labours of Herakles, and some from the Parthenon in Athens; these are a tease, with only a few beautiful fragments surviving.

Along with *Mona Lisa*, the reigning sex symbol of the Louvre has always been the *Vénus de Milo* (Sully) for whom neither date nor provenance is known, only that the villagers of Milos sold her to the French in 1820 to keep the Turks from getting her. Venus has led a charmed life; during the Commune she was hidden under a mountain of files in the Préfecture de Police, because officials were afraid that the Commune's art director, Gustave Courbet, meant to do her some harm (he was already partly responsible for blowing up the Place Vendôme column). During the *Semaine Sanglante* she survived a fire there only because a water pipe miraculously burst over her head.

Several large rooms are filled with **Roman-era copies** of Greek works – the main stock of any museum of antiquity. After these, continue by backtracking into Denon for **Etruscan art**. The talented Etruscans put on a good show: happy, sophisticated-looking folk like the smiling couple reclining on a 6th-century BC sarcophagus from Caere (modern Cerveteri) They liked to build in wood, with architectural decoration in painted terracotta, which accounts for many of the exhibits here, as in the exquisite scene of a religious procession, also from Caere.

The Etruscans' grim nemesis, **Rome**, comes next. Romans didn't show much interest in art until Augustus' time, and then their best work was in penetrating, naturalistic portrait busts: a good selection here includes Caligula, Nero, Hadrian, Marcus Aurelius, the Priestess Melitina and a cute little boy,

Caracalla. Note here a fine, classical relief of the preparation for a sacrifice, *c.* AD 150. The collections of carved sarcophagi and mosaics are superb. Much good mosaic work came from North Africa or around Antioch (the *Judgement of Paris*, and the spectacular Qabr Hiram mosaic from Lebanon, with intricate scenes of hunts and workers in the vineyard).

Some of the best antique works from all periods are assembled in the big **Cour du Sphinx**: the mosaic of the *Four Seasons* (another lovely work from Antioch), Hellenistic friezes of the *Battles of Greeks and Amazons* from Magnesia in Ionia, and a huge anthropomorphized *River Tiber* from the Isis temple in Rome. The section closes with a bang, in 5th–7th-century **early Christian art**, mostly from Syria. Suddenly the most artistically talented corner of the Western world is producing barbarically rough work with motifs of birds and snakes. Interesting reliefs show rare views of early churches (Syrian Greeks fleeing the Muslims probably contributed more than a bit to the beginnings of Romanesque); there is also *St Simeon Stylites*, the spookiest spiritual athlete of his day, squatting atop his pillar outside Antioch and preaching the word of the Lord.

But there's still more downstairs on the lower ground floor in Denon. On the stairs you'll pass the Hellenistic *Winged Victory of Samothrace* (2nd century BC), impressive for her dynamic sense of movement and skilfully carved flowing draperies – even if important bits are missing (a hand turned up in 1950; it's in a glass case to the right). There is a room of *objets d'art* from **Crete and Cycladic Greece**, and then a large but somewhat disappointing collection of **Greek vases**, including works from southern Italy and other parts of the classical Greek world, and finally ancient bronzes and jewellery.

Sculpture

Richelieu and Denon entresol (lower ground) and ground floors.

This means sculpture from the Middle Ages onwards. Since medieval times, the French have probably taken sculpture more seriously than other nations; they still do, and thus the work in Richelieu is predominantly French.

The **medieval section** is not one of the Louvre's richer collections, even though it was an age when French sculpture led Europe. When the Louvre became a museum, medieval art was still disparaged by most people, and work saved from all the demolished churches and cloisters is more likely to have ended up at the Musée de Cluny. Still, there are some good capitals and reliefs, including one capital of *Daniel in the Lions' Den* that shows how skilfully Parisians could sculpt in the 800s. There are excellent 12th-century statue columns of *Solomon and Sheba* from a church at Corbeil, and a lovely *jubé* (altar screen) from Bourges cathedral with scenes of the Passion. The imposing Gothic tombs include the *gisant* of Charles V and the uncanny **tomb of Philippe Pot** from the Abbey of Citeaux, a *gisant* held in the air by black-hooded monks (late 15th century).

The collection of **French Renaissance sculpture** is a must, not only for the quality of the work but also because there's hardly any of it in the rest of Paris. Sixteenth-century artists like Michel Colombe (*St George and the Dragon*) and Jean Goujon (mythological reliefs from the Fontaine des Innocents) recapture the brilliant, precise draughtsmanship of the Italian quattrocento, while giving it a flowing grace that is essentially French. Germain Pilon's creamy marble *Three Graces* (1560) was another work that helped determine the national aesthetic; it was made to hold the heart of Henri II.

After these triumphs French sculpture retained its high polish while growing more naturalistic. In the 17th century, like much of French culture, it renounced thought altogether; works in Richelieu's glass-roofed courtyards, such as Guillaume Costou's *Marly Horses* (c. 1740, the originals of the ones in the Place de la Concorde), are virtuoso productions as intellectually challenging as a chocolate éclair. In the same vein is the work of Provençal Pierre Puget (*Perseus and*

Andromeda) and Antoine Coysevox, a sculptor whose career consisted largely of flattering studies of Louis XIV. Empty mythological pastiches make up the bulk of French work through the 19th century, including the works of Napoleonic-era favourites Jean-Antoine Houdon and Antonio Canova. What some of the sculpture may lack in depth or interest, however, is more than compensated for by the sheer drama of the presentation. I. M. Pei and Peter Rice have designed a sculpture atrium of an unexpected openness and grace – as perfect a contrast with the palace's heavy stone archways as the sleek pyramid is to its ornate exterior.

Sculpture from other nations does have its place, notably from **Italy** (Denon), starting with a 13th-century wood polychrome *Deposition from Umbria*, and a *Virgin and Child* said to have once graced Dante's tomb in Ravenna. From the Renaissance, compare a group of other Madonnas from the quattrocento's greatest: Donatello, Luca della Robbia, Desiderio da Settignano, Jacopo della Quercia and Agostino di Duccio. On the ground floor look for Michelangelo's *Slaves*, sensuous, tormented, *non finito* figures 'in love with their own death' as Sir Kenneth Clark wrote, that were intended for the unfinished tomb of Pope Julius II in Rome.

French Painting
Chronologically arranged; Richelieu and Sully second floors.

The section begins with the earliest known French easel painting, a 1350 portrait of *King Jean le Bon*. Stricken by war and other troubles, the French missed out on the start of the Early Renaissance, but recovered *c.* 1450 with fine artists such as Jean Fouquet (*Portrait of Charles VII*) and Enguerrand Quarton (*Pietà d'Avignon*). The introduction of unfamiliar mythological subjects by the Fontainebleau painters, patronized by François I, brought a certain strangeness to French compositions, as in the lovely uncanny *Eva Prima Pandora* by Jean Cousin.

In the **17th-century rooms**, pearls are mixed with the dross – acres of tedious religious painting and Louis XIV fluff pieces like the giant battle scenes of Charles Lebrun, chief decorator of Versailles. But France at this time had a good many painters who rowed against the flow: Georges de La Tour, greatest of the French followers of Caravaggio, with startling contrasts of light and shadow (*St Joseph*, the *Adoration of the Shepherds*); and Louis le Nain (*Repas des Paysans*), who with his brothers Mathieu and Antoine was among the first to portray the everyday lives of simple folk. After these come two rooms of **landscapes**, including some by Lorrain and Poussin – the mysterious *Shepherds in Arcadia* that has caused no little comment in our time.

18th–19th-century French Painting
Richelieu and Sully second floor, Denon first floor.

Some of these are works of genius, among them Watteau's *Gilles*, the clown who now shares his secret sorrows amongst the merely amusing or downright awful – plenty of dogs, flabby mythological creatures and missal-picture madonnas. The exceptions are mostly portraits, bright-eyed Age of Enlightenment souls, like Jean-Baptiste Perronneau's *Madame de Sorquainville* or Nattier's *Portrait d'une jeune fille*. Chardin's *Boy with a Top* fairly casts a spell with its simplicity and quietude. In portraits after 1789 the bright eyes are gone and people tend to dress in black; mythological paintings have turned into cigar-box nudes (plenty of examples from David and Ingres). The section ends with delightful landscapes by Corot and the Barbizon school, forerunners of Impressionism.

The age of kitsch painting inaugurated by Napoleon bursts into full bloom downstairs in Denon. Not surprisingly, the Louvre has the best collection of its kind. Just as the Revolution had used classical motifs to equate an imagined Roman political virtue with the new age they wished to inaugurate, so Napoleon could use art to compare his own deeds with the great stories of antiquity. Mytho-kitsch (David's *Oath of the Horatii*) shades into military kitsch (David's *Leonidas at Thermopylae* or the many scenes of Napoleon's campaigns by Jean-Antoine Gros), and political kitsch (David again, with the *Sacre de Napoléon*, a colossal, Hollywood-pageant view of his self-coronation). And of course there is sex kitsch, where mushy proto-porn masquerades as art: here Picot's *Cupid and Psyche* is an early classic.

On the other hand, look at David's unfinished portrait of *Madame Récamier*, the famous Paris beauty, for a glimpse at everything that was best about the era, a breath of fresh air and simplicity, and a hint at the modern world that was dawning out of the wreck of Napoleon's Empire. Nearby are two other famous works: Delacroix's *Liberty Leading the People*, the Revolutionary icon painted for the revolt of 1830, where the bourgeoisie and workers fight side by side; and Géricault's dramatic *Radeau de la Méduse*, painted after a shipwreck that was very much in the news at the time.

While the Salle des États is closed for refurbishment (*see* below), this is also where you'll find Veronese's room-sized *Wedding at Cana* (a bit of Napoleonic plunder that never went back to Venice), which, besides Jesus and Mary, includes nearly all the political and artistic celebrities of the day: Emperor Charles V, François I and Suleiman the Magnificent sit at the table, while Titian, Tintoretto and other artists play in the band – Veronese himself is on viola.

Flemish, Dutch and German Painting
Richelieu second floor.

There are well over a thousand Flemish and Dutch paintings in the Louvre, thanks in large part to the acquisitiveness of Louis XIV and Louis XVI. Many of these are choice: fine 15th-century altarpieces by Van Eyck, Van der Weyden and Memling, Hieronymous Bosch's delightful *Ship of Fools*, an allegory of worldly folly (flying the Turkish flag), Joachim Patinir's gloomy *St Jerome in the Desert*, and some beautiful, meticulous works of Quentin Metsys (*The Moneylender and his Wife*). From the height of the Renaissance, from Duke Federico's Palace at Urbino, come 14 remarkable *Portraits of Philosophers*, a collaboration of Juste de Gand and the Spaniard Pedro Berruguete, a student of Michelangelo. There are two masterpieces of light and depth by Vermeer, the *Astronomer* and the *Lacemaker*, both from the 1660s and painted with the aid of a *camera obscura*. Also present are joyous scenes of peasant life by David Teniers, odd allegories from Jan Brueghel (*Air, or Optics, Earth, or the Terrestrial Paradise*; *Wind* and *Fire* are in Milan) and 15 Rembrandts (*Bathsheba* and a touching self-portrait in his old age).

Forget art for a minute. The real reason we've come to the Louvre is to see more than 1,000 square metres of unchained **Peter Paul Rubens**, recently installed up here. The edifying subject is the *Life of Marie de' Medici*. Besides Henry IV and her servants, Marie has cupids, sea-nymphs, angels, archangels, amoretti, spirits of the air, minor Olympian deities and satyrs to help her through the little crises of life. Rubensian buttocks fly every which way, in colours that Cecil B. de Mille would have died for. Among the best of the 21 queen-sized pictures are the *Presentation of the Portrait*, where Henri sees Marie's mug and says 'That's the girl for me!', and the *Apotheosis of Henri IV*, one of the most preposterous paintings ever attempted.

The Germans weigh in with a young Dürer self-portrait and Lucas Cranach's unsettling *Effects of Jealousy*, as well as Holbein's celebrated and moving *Portrait of Erasmus*. **English painting** isn't the Louvre's forte, but there are fine works by Reynolds and Gainsborough, an unfinished landscape by Turner and Henry Fuseli's outrageous sleep-walking *Lady Macbeth*.

Italian Painting: The Grande Galerie
Denon first floor.

For all the great works in the Grande Galerie, the star attraction is undeniably the room itself, running the length of the Louvre's south wing, flooded with light and full of pictures as far as the horizon. This is the room that gave the world its idea of what a picture gallery should look like. Somewhere in it you might chance upon Hubert Robert's 1796 scene of this very gallery, with quaintly attired folk strolling up and down or sketching, initiating themselves in the modern cult of Art. Clothes may change, but the democratic hordes that flood the place today seem little different.

Until recently, artists and periods were jumbled, much as they were when the Gallery first opened, but the new dispensation has given the floor to the Italians. At the far end is the oldest of these, what French critics, amazingly, still call 'primitives' – Italian art from the **late Middle Ages**: madonnas by Cimabue and Lorenzo Veneziano, Giotto's *St Francis Receiving the Stigmata*. **Early Renaissance** Florentines are here in force (a very representative work is Bernardo Daddi's *Annunciation*); the Sienese get a small glass case on the left (Sano di Pietro's *St Jerome Predella*, Sassetta's *Damnation of the Miser's Soul*), and north Italians one on the right (Pisanello's very stylized portrait of an Este princess).

One work familiar to many is the third (and least well preserved) part of the three-piece *Battle of San Romano* by Paolo Uccello, greatest and strangest of the Early Renaissance's slaves of perspective (the other two parts are in Florence's Uffizi and London's National Gallery). Further on come some fine late altarpieces by Botticelli (but he was never the same after he burned out and got religion), an eerie *Crucifixion* by Mantegna, and good works by Da Messina, Baldovinetti, Piero della Francesca (a portrait of Sigismondo Malatesta, Renaissance bad boy and builder of the famous 'Temple' in Rimini), Carpaccio and Perugino. Raphael's dreamlike *St Michael and the Dragon* and his portrait of the perfect Renaissance courtier, Baldassare Castiglione, are near the end, along with Leonardo da Vinci's haunting

Virgin of the Rocks and *Virgin and Child with St Anne*.

More Renaissance: The Salle des États
Denon first floor.

The rooms off the Grande Galerie have also been given over to Italian painting. The Salle des États is closed for refurbishment until the end of 2005, when it will be split in two to house Venetian Renaissance paintings (including the *Wedding at Cana*, see above) in one room and – in a room of her own – the **Mona Lisa** (currently on display at the other end of the Grande Galerie). *Mona Lisa* is the Louvre's undisputed superstar, 'the most famous artwork in the world', as a local guide trumpets her. She smiles from behind the glass (installed after she was slashed a few years back), as the tourists with their flash machines close in like paparazzi. Someone once claimed that the paintings in great museums tend to grow uglier over the centuries from 'too many ugly people looking at them'; *La Gioconda*, at worst, seems a little tired just now.

Late Italian and Spanish Painting
Denon first floor.

Continuing is a long stretch of **17th–18th-century Italian** art, the sort of paintings most prized by old French collectors (so naturally they often Frenchify their names: Zampieri or Domeniquin = Domenichino; Carrache = Annibale Carracci). There are some good works by Guido Reni and Caravaggio, but the Venetian Francesco Guardi's series of 12 works on *Venetian Festivals* (1763) steals the show, a sweet document of La Serenissima near the end of its career.

On the grand staircase (next to the *Winged Victory of Samothrace*) is one of the Louvre's treasures, a detached Botticelli fresco called *Venus and the Graces*: five perfect Botticelli maidens maintaining their poise and calm in the midst of the crowds. If this seems like a magic picture, perhaps it was intended as one. No one ever knows for certain what

Botticelli's pictures are about – the title given is an educated guess – but this one, like his famous works in Florence, is most likely a secret allegory, expressing some unrecoverable idea from the Neo-Platonic planetary mysticism current in the Florence of his day. We may expect that nothing in it is left to chance; the composition, proportions and colours would somehow mirror the symbolic concept behind the work.

The **Spanish painting** is neatly consolidated on the first floor in Denon. The collection is small but representative. From the 16th century, there is one El Greco *Crucifixion*; from the golden age of Spanish painting in the 17th century, at least one of each of the masters: Velázquez (*Infanta Margarita*), Ribera, and two Zurbaráns from the cycle of *St Bonaventure* – these were another unreturned Napoleonic theft, from Seville. Some of the several Murillos are stolen goods too; note the wonderful fantasy of the *Kitchen of the Angels*. There are several Goyas, the comically weird *Les Vielles* and the famous portrait of *La Marquesa de la Solana*, as Spanish as *churros* and chocolate.

Objets d'Art

Sully and Richlieu first floor.

This is a trip to Citizen Kane's Xanadu – except that instead of being a mere newspaper tycoon the mad collector had the resources of all the kings of France. The sumptuous clutter is stupefying: blinding jewels and heavy gold gimcracks, tapestries, delicate porcelain knick-knacks, watches, Renaissance bronzes, Merovingian treasure, chinoiserie, sardonyx vases... They've squirrelled away everything from George III's silverware to Marie-Antoinette's make-up case.

The greatest treasures are: Louis XIV's crown jewels (three cases full), Henri II's rock crystal chess set, Napoleon's crown and Josephine's earrings, the sword of the Grand Master of the Knights of Malta, Charles V's gold sceptre, Charlemagne's dagger, St Louis' ring, the jewellery of Arnegonde, wife of Clotaire I (*c.* 570), Louis XV's crown, and a

107.88 carat ruby in the shape of a dragon called *La Côte de Bretagne*.

While the Salle d'Apollon (Denon first floor) is closed for restoration (due to reopen sometime in 2004), they are on display with the rest of the collection on the first floor in Sully and Richelieu. Look also for the small bronze equestrian statue of Charlemagne, a rare and skilful work from the Dark Ages, and another relic from that time, the eagle of Abbot Suger, a porphyry vase enclosed in a golden eagle (*c.* 700) that once was the pride of the treasury of St-Denis, the richest in France. There is a small but rich collection of medieval and Byzantine reliquaries and trinkets, Renaissance bronzes from the master of the art, Andrea Riccio, and some beautiful majolicas from Moorish Spain and Renaissance Italy.

The Other Louvre Museums

If the cultural feast hasn't filled you up, the Louvre offers three further museums for dessert; these are entered from Rue de Rivoli.

Musée des Arts Décoratifs T–U11

107 Rue de Rivoli, t 01 44 55 57 50, w www. ucad.fr; métro Palais Royal-Musée du Louvre; wheelchair access. Open Tues–Fri 11–6, Sat and Sun 10–6; adm €5.40 (combined ticket with Musée des Arts de la Mode and Musée de la Publicité).

The biggest of the three, the Musée des Arts Décoratifs was founded in 1877, initiated by an organization now called the Union Centrale des Arts Décoratifs, dedicated to maintaining artistic standards in industrially made items. The museum's purpose was to show the public beautiful things so that people would be more demanding about what they bought for themselves. Until mid-2004 only the second floor is open due to renovation work.

Although it means confusing the chronology, the easiest way to visit is to take the lift to the **fourth floor** and work your way down. This floor offers a long expanse of

Louis XV and Louis XVI furnishings and trinkets: porcelain from Sèvres and other places in the Paris region, figurines, jewellery, snuffboxes with painted miniatures and an entire room of silverware. Madame de Pompadour's sauce dishes are on prominent display. In the opposite corridor are 19th-century decorative arts, beginning with the coldly elegant neoclassicism of the Empire style through to the Restoration, which was also partly a restoration of pre-1789 lightness and frivolity as well as the age when flowered wallpaper began to dominate the national consciousness. Eccentricity gathers momentum into the Second Empire, France's first great age of popular conspicuous consumption: enamelled plates with ferns, snakes and lizards for decoration; florid interiors, captured in paintings here, showing more gold, more colour, more exotica – more everything.

The excruciating **third floor** covers the age of Louis XIV, with the bastard Renaissance hand-me-downs that passed for design in the 'Grand Siècle'. It was a great age for faïence, however, mostly in provincial centres such as Moustiers, Marseille, Nevers and Strasbourg, all represented here. The opposite corridor covers France's timid flirtation with rococo, in the age of Louis XV.

On the **second floor** are works from the Middle Ages to the 16th century. Of course not much has survived of medieval decorative arts besides luxury goods like the lovely 15th-century Venetian ivories, or church paraphernalia and reliquaries. Much of the space is filled with paintings: a lot of Flemish works, and some good retables (a *Last Judgement* made in the 1420s for the Duke of Bedford, occupation governor of Paris). Among the most important furnishings, for those who could afford them, were tapestries, providing insulation and a lot of pretty greenery for houses with few windows; there's a good set here, with scenes from the all-time most popular medieval romance, the *Romance of the Rose*. Among the 15th–16th-century ceramics, the work from Italy and Moorish Andalucía stands out, as well as France's own enamelled work

from Limoges, with its distinctive dark, glistening colours.

Art Nouveau and the 20th century occupies the **ground floor**, by far the most popular part of the museum. The Art Nouveau hall is an attraction in itself: the glorious Salon de Bois saved from the 1900 Exposition (from a pavilion sponsored by the Union des Arts Décoratifs) and reconstructed here. It houses an exceptional collection of glasswork, showing the surprising breadth and imagination of the movement. The rooms that follow contain Art Nouveau furniture, including a bedroom suite by Hector Guimard; there is also a delightful exhibition of jewellery, from the 1900s through to Art Deco.

The collection goes right up to the present, though mostly concerned with those unexpected icons of modernity – chairs. From early experiments like Gerrit Rietvelt's 1934 do-it-yourself model and Marcel Breuer's famous 1932 design, the parade of chairs continues through the Scandinavians, to things you didn't know were art (the stackable plastic chair, a triumph of British design invented by Robin Day in 1963). American architect Frank Gehry contributes a practical cardboard rocker. And finally, an unforgettable parlour suite by Niki de Saint-Phalle.

Musée des Arts de la Mode T11

107 Rue de Rivoli, t 01 44 55 57 50, w www. ucad.fr; métro Palais Royal–Musée du Louvre. Open Tues–Fri 11–6, Sat and Sun 10–6; adm €5.40 (combined ticket with Musée des Arts Décoratifs and Musée de la Publicité).

France has a fashion industry managed by an enormously influential cabal of the top luxury-goods makers called the Comité Colbert. Governments have always supported the industry – since Colbert's time – but it was only during the rule of Socialist culture minister Jack Lang that the state's cultural machinery was enrolled in the effort. The Louvre is centre stage, with frequent fashion shows in the Cour Carrée, exhibitions of jewellery in the Musée des Arts Décoratifs, and above all this museum, opened in 1986 under the premise that women's clothing, if sufficiently expensive, is an art that enriches all our lives. The museum has a large permanent wardrobe of duds going back to the 16th century, as well as the collections of successful early 20th-century designers such as Poiret and Schiaparelli, though only a small part is on display, in changing temporary exhibitions.

Musée de la Publicité T11

107 Rue de Rivoli, t 01 44 55 57 50, w www. ucad.fr; métro Palais Royal-Musée du Louvre. Open Tues–Fri 11–6, Sat–Sun 10–6; adm €5.40 (combined ticket with Musée des Arts Décoratifs and Musée des Arts de la Mode).

The third part of the Union Centrale des Arts Décoratifs concentrates on the history of advertising, and in particular of the poster from the 18th century to today. Displays narrate the development of well-known brands such as Perrier and Benetton through their advertising campaigns, and show how the poster has become part of the make-up of the city. Famous poster artists – the best known of course being Toulouse-Lautrec – receive special treatment.

A Tour of the Exterior

The Louvre was 350 years in the building and is a veritable museum of French architecture. The best parts are the oldest. Start on the eastern end, on Rue de l'Amiral de Coligny. The majestic **colonnade** (begun 1668) marks the beginning of the French classical style. The key is in the decorative line, the graceful, precise line that you'll see in all the best work from the Renaissance up to the time of Napoleon, a line that redraws familiar classical motifs in such a way as to make them forever French.

The architect was Claude Perrault, brother of Charles, the writer of fairy tales. After the Bernini fiasco, in which the most fashionable architect of the age was called from Italy and failed three times to create a design that satisfied the king or Colbert, the job was entrusted to a committee that included Lebrun, Le Vau, Perrault and others; the plan

of Perrault, an amateur, won out, and no one ever regretted it. His ineffable colonnade has been slightly tampered with since; the relief on the pediment is from Napoleon's time, and the windows on the ground level replace Perrault's simple niches, perhaps intended for statues. The dry moat, part of the original design, was filled in the 18th century, a time when every sort of shack crowded around the walls of the half-abandoned Louvre. André Malraux, De Gaulle's culture minister, dug it up again for history's sake.

Walk under the central portal into the **Cour Carrée** (*usually open when there's not a fashion show inside; otherwise try the side portals facing the Seine or Rue de Rivoli*) and you will see a work as revolutionary in its time as the colonnade out front. The western side, the first to be completed, was a collaboration between architect Pierre Lescot and sculptor Jean Goujon (1546–70). Goujon's sculptural trim, anticipating the classical style, highlights a nervous, ultra-refined architectural composition well in tune with, and in some ways ahead of, the new Italian Mannerist architecture of the day. The architects of Louis XIV's time, who respected little of anything, at least respected this precocious work; Le Vau and Le Mercier completed the other three sides of the Cour Carrée in the 1640s to match it. Goujon's work can be seen framing the three round windows (west side): allegorical figures of 'abundance', 'war' and 'science'. On all four sides you can play the game of puzzling out the royal monograms built into the façades, from H, C and D on the original side for Henri II, Catherine de' Medici and Diane de Poitiers, the king's mistress; to LMT for Louis XIV and Marie-Thérèse.

The outer façades of the north wing, facing Rue de Rivoli, are contributions of Napoleon (right half, viewed from the street) and Napoleon III (left half); both lend much to the imperial dreariness of that street. As for the south wing, facing the Seine, the left half is the beginning of Catherine de' Medici's long extension; its completion (right half) was done under Henri IV.

The Napoleons, with their symmetrical brains, naturally had to make the Louvre symmetrical too; between them they more than doubled the size of the palace, expanding the south wing and building the northern one to mirror it, levelling an entire quarter in the process. Before the Communards burned down the Tuileries, which connected the two long wings, the Louvre must have been the only place in the world where a king could take a walk around the block without leaving his house – a walk of over a mile.

St-Germain-l'Auxerrois W12

2 Place du Louvre, t 01 42 60 13 96; métro Pont-Neuf or Louvre-Rivoli. Open daily 8–12.45 and 2.30–8; regular concerts.

Behind the Palais du Louvre, by the Pont Neuf, is the church of St Germain, a 5th-century bishop of Auxerre who died in Paris after distinguishing himself fighting heretics up in England. There has been a church in his honour on this site since Merovingian times, and today's version contains a bit of everything from the 12th century onwards; the oldest part is the Romanesque **bell tower**, visible from the rear of the church (next to the south transept). On 24 August 1572, the bells in this tower gave the signal for the St Bartholomew's Day Massacre; the Protestant leader, Admiral de Coligny, was staying on what is now Rue de Rivoli, where he was surprised and murdered.

From the 14th century on, whenever kings chose to live in the Louvre, St-Germain was the royal parish church. The rich decoration it received in this period largely succumbed to the pathetic taste of the 18th century; as at Notre-Dame, much good sculpture was destroyed, and even most of the stained glass was removed. Things got worse; the Revolution turned the church into a public granary, and it was only saved from demolition in the 1830s through the efforts of the writer Chateaubriand. Since the days when the scores of painters and sculptors working on the Louvre came here for Mass, St-Germain has been the artists' church in Paris.

St-Germain's best feature is a charming **porch**, built in the late 1430s. In the Middle Ages most of the churches in Paris were preceded by such works, but this one and the much less elaborate porch of the Sainte-Chapelle are the only ones that remain. Look closely to see the imaginative medieval bestiary discreetly included in the carved decoration: a monkey playing bagpipes, a hippo gobbling up a grimacing savage, cats chasing rats.

For all the troubles this church has suffered, a few noteworthy works of art remain inside. In the left aisle there is a remarkable Flemish altarpiece (*c.* 1530), Italian Renaissance tinged with the naïve in scenes of the Passion of Christ and the Life of the Virgin. In the right aisle, the Chapelle Paroissiale contains the original statue of the expressive, long-haired Ste-Marie-l'Egyptienne depicted on the porch (Marie, a 4th-century prostitute who became a holy hermit, was popular in France and often confused with Mary Magdalene). In the centre aisle, the royal family attended Mass in the 17th-century *banc d'œuvre*, designed by Charles Lebrun; further on, near the entrance to the enclosed choir, are 15th-century statues of St Germain and St Vincent. What is left of the original stained glass (16th century) survives in the transept windows on both sides.

Next to St-Germain, a complementary neo-Gothic façade was built in 1859 for the *mairie* of the *1er arrondissement*; its tower has a mechanical carillon that plays tunes by Rameau and other 18th-century composers (most Wednesdays at 1.30pm).

JARDIN DES TUILERIES R10–T11

Métro Tuileries or Concorde. Open summer 7am–9pm, winter 7am–8pm, open later for special events.

From the courtyard of the Louvre, the Grand Axe continues west up the Grande Allée of the Tuileries. In 1664, André Le Nôtre, gardener to Louis XIV, was given the task of redesigning these gardens; his elegantly classical reworking of the original plan (see 'From Tiles to Toilets'), which captured perfectly the mood of the Grand Siècle, made his reputation.

Although Le Nôtre's basic plan remains unchanged, there have been many minor alterations over the last two centuries. The biggest change, of course, was the disappearance of the Tuileries Palace, burned during the fighting in 1871. If you haven't been to Versailles (see pp.286–90), you may wonder what the fuss is about: without its original, meticulously kept flower beds and other decorations, Le Nôtre's design seems unexceptional. It still has plenty of statues; you'll see four by Rodin flanking the **Grande Allée** when you enter from Avenue du Général-Lemonnier. (There's also a gilded statue of Joan of Arc in Place des Pyramides, but don't walk out of your way to see it – it's a traditional meeting place for the far right.)

The centre of the park is shaded by avenues of chestnut trees, the *Quinconces des Marronniers*. Further up the Grande Allée, the **octagonal basin** is surrounded by statues that have survived from the Tuileries' days as a royal park: allegories of the seasons, French rivers and the Nile and the Tiber. Louis XIV's chief sculptural propagandist, Coysevox, sculpted Mercury and Fame on winged horses, the *Chevaux Ailés* (both copies) at the gates facing Place de la Concorde. Le Nôtre's plan included narrow raised **terraces** at the northern and southern ends, the Terrasse des Feuillants and the Terrasse du Bord de l'Eau; regrettably the latter has had its Seine-front view spoiled by Pompidou's Right Bank motorway, but both remain favourite tracks for Parisian joggers. At the Concorde end, the terraces expand into broader plateaus supporting buildings from the time of Napoleon III.

A recent scheme has seen the Quai des Tuileries and the quays to the east close down to traffic and receive 3,000 tons of sand to create **Paris-Plage**, a temporary beach which appears on the banks of the Seine in the months of July and August. Everything imaginable is set in place to give city-bound Parisiens a little beach holiday on their doorstep: palm trees, deckchairs, ice cream vendors and musical distractions abound.

From Tiles to Toilets

The first gardens on this site were built at the same time as the Tuileries palace, in the 1560s. It was Catherine de' Medici's idea, following the latest fashions in landscaping from Renaissance Italy; she purchased a large tract of land behind the palace, part of which had been a rubbish dump and part a tile works – hence the name *tuileries*. Her new pleasure park, designed by Philibert de l'Orme and others, was soon the wonder of Paris; symmetrical and neat, it became the model for Le Nôtre's work and all the classical French landscaping that followed. Contemporary accounts suggest it must have been much more beautiful, and more fun, than the present incarnation, with such features as a hedge maze, elaborate sundials and other astronomical devices, a 'grotto' lined with Sèvres porcelain and statuary, and a semicircle of trees planted to create an echo effect.

A story has it that during the time of Louis XIV, Charles Perrault, the controller-general of public works and author of the famous fairy tales (and brother of the Louvre's architect), convinced the king to open the park to the public. Louis, who never spent much time in Paris anyhow, was amenable, and the new Tuileries became Paris' most fashionable promenade.

It continued as such throughout the 18th century, featuring such novelties as Paris' first public toilets and first newspaper kiosk. The first gas airship took off from a spot near the octagonal pond in 1783, the same year as the Montgolfiers' pioneer hot-air balloon.

Musée de l'Orangerie R10

*Jardin des Tuileries, t 01 42 97 48 16. **Closed** for major renovations until early 2004.*

In the southwest corner of the park, the Orangerie has a permanent collection of paintings from the Impressionists to the 1930s, courtesy of Domenica Guillaume-Walter, who bequeathed the collections of her two husbands to the nation in 1977. Don't come here before you've seen the Musée d'Orsay and the Musée National d'Art Moderne in the Pompidou Centre. In the Orangerie, many of the big-name artists of the 20th century are represented, but the works are seldom among their best: dissolving landscapes of Chaim Soutine, Cézanne still lifes and portraits of his wife and son, rosy Renoir *fillettes* bathing or at the piano, Paris scenes by Utrillo, and a trio of Modigliani weird sisters.

Picasso contributes some formidable primeval women – the *Femmes à la fontaine* and the *Grande Baigneuse* (both 1921) – and from Matisse there's a series of *Odalisques*; these, and the several paintings by Derain, are later works, with little of the verve of the artists' Fauve days. For most people, the high point will probably be the luminous canvases by Monet, including one of the famous *Water Lilies*, and two wonderful pictures by the Douanier Rousseau, looking as out of place among the sophisticated moderns as his rustic subjects would among the Orangerie's visitors today: a nasty-looking *Little Girl with a Doll* (1907), and the pinched-faced provincial family on *Père Junier's Cart* (1910), a painting much beloved by the Surrealists.

Galerie National du Jeu de Paume R10

*1 Place de la Concorde, t 01 47 03 12 50; métro Concorde. **Open** Wed–Sun 12–7, Tues 12–9.30; **adm** €6 (can vary slightly according to the exhibition).*

This was built for real tennis, the crazy medieval game where the ball bounces off walls, roofs and turrets. It was all the rage in the 16th–18th centuries; under Henry IV there were even said to be 'more tennis players in Paris than drunkards in England'. After the game enjoyed a brief fad in the Second Empire, the building became the Impressionists' museum, but the collection has since been consolidated at the Musée d'Orsay and it now sits a bit forlorn, hosting contemporary art exhibitions.

PLACE DE LA CONCORDE Q9–R10

Métro Concorde.

Without the cars it would be a treat, the most spacious square and the finest architectural ensemble in Paris. The fourth in the series of Bourbon *places royales*, it was decreed by Louis XV just outside what was then Paris' western wall. An unusual location – but Louis owned most of the land around it, and no French king was ever averse to a bit of property speculation on his own behalf. Jacques-Ange Gabriel, a hitherto undistinguished architect (École Militaire, Petit Trianon), won the competition by coming up with something utterly, unaccountably brilliant and original. Breaking completely with the enclosed, aristocratic ethos of the other royal squares, Gabriel laid out an enormous rectangle, built up on one side only (the north), with the Seine facing opposite and the two ends entirely open, towards the parklands of the Tuileries and the Champs-Elysées. It was clear that Paris was growing rapidly, especially towards the west, and Gabriel intended his new square to be a colossal focal point for the city as a whole.

Later generations perfected (and frequently renamed, see 'Changing Places' opposite) the square. The **Pont de la Concorde** over the Seine opened in 1790; under Napoleon, the Madeleine (*see* pp.150–51) and Palais Bourbon (*see* p.129)

Changing Places

By 1836, what was originally Place Louis XV had changed its name six times, and seen more trouble than any square deserves. There was a bad omen in 1770, only six years after its inauguration, when a festival was being held to celebrate the marriage of the future Louis XVI with Marie-Antoinette; some fireworks misfired, and caused a panic in which over a hundred people were crushed to death. Twelve years later the name had been changed to Place de la Révolution, and Louis XV's statue, where the obelisk stands today, had already been melted down for munitions. That same spot now held a guillotine, the venue for all the most important executions under the Terror. Louis and Marie were the most famous victims, but neither the first nor the last – Danton, Desmoulins, Charlotte Corday and finally Robespierre himself held centre stage here while Madame Defarge knitted.

When the chopping stopped, the Convention chose the new name Concorde as a gesture of national reconciliation. The restored Bourbons would have none of that, but couldn't decide whether to give it its original name or call it after the martyred Louis XVI. In 1830 the revolutionaries proclaimed it Place de la Charte, after the charter they had obtained; only a few years later the authoritarian Louis-Philippe decided Concorde wasn't such a bad name after all.

were added to close the views on the Left Bank and complete the dazzling architectural ensemble. A new exclamation mark along the Grand Axe, the Egyptian obelisk (*see* below), appeared in 1836.

This is a square made for strollers and carriages. The fumes and menace of six lanes of traffic, zooming around the obelisk as fast as they can, has made its enjoyment nearly impossible – come at dawn on Sunday morning, or right after a rare big snowfall if you want some idea of the original effect. The centre island is an octagon, as Gabriel designed it, with allegorical statues of eight French cities at the corners (clockwise from the bridge: Bordeaux, Nantes, Brest, Rouen, Lille, Strasbourg, Lyon, and Marseille). Baron Haussmann's architect, Jacques Hittorff, added the ornate lampposts and two incredible bronze **fountains**, with rows of perplexed marine deities sitting on benches and cradling fishes, all looking as if they're waiting for the tram home from the market.

The **obelisk** comes from Luxor on the Nile, and dates from *c.* 1250 BC, the time of Ramses II. It was a gift from France's ally Muhammad Ali, semi-independent Ottoman viceroy of Egypt in the 1830s, and this spot was chosen for it because any political monument would have been a sure source of controversy in the future. Accepting an obelisk is one thing; floating the 221-tonne (225-ton) block to Paris and getting it upright again is a different matter. Look at the inscriptions on the base: scenes of the erection carved in intricate detail, with thanks in big gold letters to M. LEBAS, INGÉNIEUR, for managing the trick, 'to the applause of an immense crowd'. A battalion of artillerymen helped him raise it (you can see the machinery Lebas built for the job in the Marine Museum, p.142).

Gabriel's impressive pair of buildings on the north side of the *place* were meant as government offices. The one on the right, the **Hôtel de la Marine**, still is; it has housed the navy department since 1792. The one on the left saw the signing of the United States' first foreign alliance, the treaty of 1778 that brought diplomatic recognition and material aid to the new nation, and made all the difference in the War of Independence. Today it is the luxury Hôtel Crillon (*see* p.300). Across Rue Boissy-d'Anglas is the US Embassy complex, on the site of an 18th-century *hôtel* that formerly held the embassies of Russia and Turkey. Gabriel also laid out **Rue Royale** between his buildings, and planned for the future Madeleine to close its view. The architect built his own house at No.8; across the street, No.3 is the famous **Maxim's** (*see* p.317).

The Pleasantest Place in the World

In 1616 everything west of the Louvre was royal meadows and hunting preserves; in that year Marie de' Medici ordered the first improvement, a tree-lined drive along the Seine called the Cours la Reine (now part of the Right Bank motorway). In 1667, Louis XIV had Le Nôtre lay out a long straight promenade through the area, continuing the perspective of the Tuileries' Grande Allée. For almost two centuries, nothing more happened. Cows and sheep grazed the fields; gentlefolk took their Sunday drives, and a few bought land and built villas along the route. Their friends thought them eccentric, living so far from Paris. In 1709 the pleasure promenade took its present name, the 'Elysian Fields'.

British and Prussian troops camped here in 1814 after the defeat of Napoleon and cut down most of the trees. For the next few decades, the Champs-Elysées was a less aristocratic promenade; all Paris came on Sundays for a bit of fresh air. The upper part of the avenue, already partly built-up, saw a speculative boom in the reign of Napoleon III. The lower part, below the Rond-Point, was saved only because it served as a pleasure ground for all the late 19th-century exhibitions, a delightful bower of groves and avenues, elaborate flower beds, Chinese lanterns, brightly painted pavilions, ice cream and lemonade. There was a glassed-in Winter Garden, dancing and café-concerts under the trees, puppets and toy stalls for the children, buskers and jugglers, balloon ascents and Louis Daguerre's new-fangled photographic panoramas. The Champs-Elysées became Paris' greatest tourist attraction; all agreed that it was the pleasantest place in the world.

CHAMPS-ELYSÉES AND ARC DE TRIOMPHE

The Champs-Elysées

K7–Q10

The west edge of the Place de la Concorde is marked by a pair of winged horses, sculpted by Guillaume Coustou in the 1740s. Like their counterparts across the square, they came from Louis XIV's château at Marly, after it was destroyed in the Revolution. Today, they stand sentinel at the entrance to the second step in the creation of the Grand Axe: the **Champs-Elysées**. It isn't nearly the extravagant locale it was (*see* 'The Pleasantest Place in the World' above), but it's pleasing enough for a stroll.

The Grand Palais O9–10

3 Av du Général-Eisenhower, t 01 44 13 17 17; métro Champs Elysées-Clemenceau; wheelchair access. Open Thurs–Mon 1–8, Wed 1–10, mornings by appt, closed 25 Dec; Thurs–Mon last tickets 7.15, Wed last tickets 9.15; adm varies according to exhibition.

The Grand Palais, built for the 1900 Exhibition (*see* pp.140–41), is one of the biggest surprises in Paris, and beyond any doubt the capital's most neglected and unloved monument. The Grand Palais is closed for renovations until 2005, but its galleries are still open for art exhibitions. Peek through the glass doors into the grandest interior space in Paris, if not Europe: a single glass arcade 1,100ft long with a glass dome at the centre, flanked by tiers of balconies and a magnificent grand stair. Even now, standing forlorn and deserted, it astounds the eye. Its architects and the fair promoters built their folly in a pompous, eclectic style already obsolete, and adorned it with an allegorical jungle of florid sculpture and sententious figurines. The colossal horses and chariots at the corners represent 'Immortality Vanquishing Time' and 'Harmony Routing Discord'; sculptural reliefs bear titles like 'The Arts and Sciences Rendering Homage to the New Century'.

As much as the Eiffel Tower, the Grand Palais is a symbol of an age, of both France and Europe at the height of their power, empire and confidence. It reflects, more than any building except the lost Crystal Palace in London, the exuberance of an architecture that had just realized its technological capabilities. Now special world-touring art exhibitions are held in the northern end.

Palais de la Découverte O10

Av Franklin D. Roosevelt, t 01 56 43 20 21, w www.palais-decouverte.fr; métro Franklin D. Roosevelt or Champs Elysées-Clemenceau. Wheelchair access, except for mezzanines. Open Tues–Sat 9.30–6, Sun and some hols 10–7, closed 1 Jan, 1 May, 14 July, 15 Aug and 25 Dec; times for planetarium vary with the season; adm €5.60 (including planetarium €8.70). Some of the explanatory panels are in Braille.

The rear of the Grand Palais has been declared a palace in itself: the science museum or 'Palace of Discovery'. Before you go in, look at one of the glories of the Grand Palais' original decoration, a colourful frieze of Sèvres terracotta designed by Joseph Blanc. It represents *The Triumph of Art*, beginning in earliest times and passing through Greece, Rome, Charlemagne's empire, Renaissance Florence, Rome and Venice, and ultimately, of course, Paris.

Paris must be the only city in the world with three important science museums: the dusty Conservatoire (*see* pp.171–3), space-age La Villette (*see* pp.264–5) and this one, which opened in 1937 and still has a quaint flavour – particularly the astronomy section, reminiscent of old *Flash Gordon* serials on the planet Mongo.

You won't be bored, even if you can't read much French; there are lasers to play with, ant colonies, computers and white rats for whom you can design your own experiment. In the Eureka rooms there are hands-on games and tricks to learn about colours, optics and elementary physics. The scary stuff is kept at the back of the ground and mezzanine floors: generators that crank out over a million volts (but hardly any amperage; you can touch it, making your hair stand on end), and a nuclear exhibit where the kids can make various objects radioactive.

Place Clemenceau O–P9

Across the Champs-Elysées is **Place Clemenceau**, with a statue of '*Le Tigre*' in a billowing mac that makes him look more like a cod fisherman than French prime minister of the First World War. North of Clemenceau, the only buildings are a small pavilion renamed after Pierre Cardin and used for fashion exhibitions, and the circular **Théâtre de Marigny**. The iron fence across Avenue Gabriel marks the rear of the **Palais de l'Elysée** (*see* p.152).

The Petit Axe and Pont Alexandre III O11–9

One legacy of the 1900 Exposition was a new *petit axe*, opening a view from Place Clemenceau to the golden dome of the Invalides. The new boulevard, Av Tsar Alexandre III, was renamed **Av Winston-Churchill** after the Second World War in order to please the Brits and Stalin simultaneously.

For such a view, the Parisians borrowed a bridge from an opera: the **Pont Alexandre III**,

---

1900: The Coming Out of Modern Art

The Grand Palais building itself was an allegory: 'A Monument Consecrated by the Republic to the Glory of French Art'. In 1900, for a novelty, 22 Impressionist works – already a bit dated – were included in a separate room, something that would have been unthinkable in 1878 or 1889. When President Emile Loubet came to see the show, he thought he might take a look at the work of such notorious antisocial radicals as Pissarro, Renoir and Degas. A fashionable academician named Gérôme was showing him around; when they came to the Impressionists' room, Gérôme flung himself in front of the doorway, crying: 'Go no further, Monsieur le Président; here France is dishonoured!' It was but straw in the wind. The 1900 show in fact proved a turning point, where modern art made its first big breakthrough to a wider public.

(still) named after the Tsar at the height of Republican France's love affair with Imperialist Russia. The graceful 320ft steel arch is larded with sumptuous adornments that can be seen in all their glory since a complete renovation. The 50 million visitors who crossed in 1900 gaped at horseless buggies, X-rays, wireless telegraphs, Loie Fuller's Art Nouveau scarf dances, a film (synchronized to a phonograph) of Sarah Bernhardt playing Hamlet in the duel scene, and the prototype of Cinemascope (a balloon ascent on eight screens); they rode a mock Trans-Siberian railway, a Ferris wheel 330ft in diameter with 1,600 seats, and took the brand new métro to the Bois de Boulogne. An anarchist tried to spoil the show by throwing a bomb at the Shah of Persia, but he missed.

Petit Palais P10

Av Winston-Churchill, t 01 42 65 12 73; métro Champs Elysées-Clemenceau. Closed for renovation until winter of 2004/2005.

'Petit' is relative, for a building the size of the Opéra. It was designed for the Cult of Art at the 1900 Exhibition, holding a retrospective of 19th-century French works. The sculpture on the Petit Palais is just as flagrant as its grand brother, with the Four Seasons, the Seine and its Tributaries and, dominating the façade, the 'City of Paris Protecting the Arts'.

The present collection consists of plenty of 18th-century art and furniture (busts of Voltaire and Franklin by Houdon), a selection of medieval art and a smattering of works from the Renaissance, including Italian majolica and Venetian glass. The main attraction is still 19th-century French painting and sculpture, for which special exhibitions are usually mounted, including works from the Petit Palais' vast collection of prints and engravings.

Lower Champs-Elysées L8–Q10

After decades of decline, this area has undergone major renovation, including wider pedestrian pavements, a second row of *platanes* on each side, and new street furniture. Even the car dealers, hamburger stands, banks and obscure airline offices that took over in the 1970s have cleaned themselves up. Now the great avenue is always packed, and it's a considerably more lively and interesting place than it was 10 years ago. The north side is the more popular, attracting most of the sun and shops. Enjoy a *café crème*, sitting outside, while the world turns about you on its axe.

Arc de Triomphe J–K7

Place Charles-de-Gaulle, t 01 55 37 73 77, groups t 01 44 61 20 00; métro Charles de Gaulle-Étoile. Open April–Sept daily 9.30am–11pm, Oct–March daily 10am–10.30pm; open after the ceremonies on 8 May, 14 July and 11 Nov, closed 1 Jan, 1 May, 25 Dec; adm €7, free on 1st Sun of the month. Don't try crossing the frenetic Étoile; there's a pedestrian tunnel at the right-hand side of the Champs-Elysées.

This is *not* a tribute to Napoleon, although it certainly would have been had the Emperor been around to finish it. The arch commemorates the armies of the Revolution: the heroic, improvised citizen levy that not only protected their new freedoms against the *anciens régimes* of the rest of Europe, but actually liberated other peoples. It's a bit saddening that the French included Napoleon's brutal wars of conquest as a logical continuation of what was originally a fight for freedom.

In the 18th century, the Étoile was a rustic *rond-point* on the boundaries of the city; one of the *barrières* of the Farmers-General wall stood where the arch is today. Napoleon did have the idea for the arch, after his smashing victories of 1805–6; originally he wanted it in Place de la Bastille, but his sycophants convinced him that this prominent spot in the fashionable west end would be much more fitting. A life-size model was erected in 1810, to celebrate Napoleon's marriage to Marie-Louise of Austria.

Not surprisingly, work stopped cold in 1815. Eight years later, Louis XVIII had the really contemptible idea of finishing it as a monument to his own 'triumph' – sending an army to put down a democratic revolt in Spain. But by the reign of Louis-Philippe, the 'myth of Napoleon' had already begun its strange progress. Times were dull; Frenchmen had forgotten their two million countrymen Napoleon had sent to die for his glory, and the 18 years of tyranny and misery suffered by those left at home. The myth was helped along by the ex-Emperor's recently published memoirs, designed to whitewash his memory. A massive effort to complete the arch was mounted in 1832, and they had it finished four years later.

And four years after that, Napoleon's remains rolled under the arch, on a grey November day when the silence of the crowds was broken only by a few old veterans croaking 'Vive l'Empereur!' Napoleon III had Baron Haussmann make the Étoile into the showcase of Paris. Then, only five streets met at the circle; Haussmann added seven more (including Avenue Foch, originally named after Empress Eugénie and still the broadest street in Paris), and sent his architects to build a set of matching façades around the circle.

It isn't just the location and the historical connotations that make this such an important landmark. It's also a rather splendid arch, one of the finest examples of the dignified brand of classicism that came in with the Revolution and went out with Napoleon III. Much of the sculptural work is first-rate. Any Frenchman would recognize the group on the right side, facing the Champs-Elysées: the dramatic *Departure of the Volunteers in 1792*, also known as the *Marseillaise*. The sculptor, François Rude, has no other well-known works. Other scenes on the arch celebrate Napoleon's triumphs in battle.

Beneath the arch, an anonymous French soldier – killed in the First World War – is buried in the **Tomb of the Unknown Soldier**. An eternal flame commemorates those who died in both World Wars.

Inside is a small museum of the arch; from there you can climb up to the **roof** for a remarkable view of the Grand Axe and the pie-slice blocks around the Étoile (especially recommended after dark). Haussmann's new streets usually reserved the high-profile corner sites for the *hôtels particuliers* of the nouveaux riches (very new and very rich, mostly from property speculation). The Place de l'Étoile has a full circle of these wonders that mix Renaissance with Baroque and top it off with rococo.

Towards La Défense A3–K7

After the Arc, the Champs-Elysées becomes Avenue de la Grande Armée, and later Avenue Charles-de-Gaulle; there's nothing to see along either of these broad boulevards, but, if you dare, you can follow the Grand Axe to its logical conclusion, the spooky, high-tech corporate ghetto of **La Défense** (*see* pp.258–60).

NORTHEAST OF THE ÉTOILE

Centre National de la Photographie M7

Hôtel Salomon de Rothschild, 11 Rue Berryer, t 01 53 76 12 32, w www.cnp-photographie.com; métro Charles de Gaulle-Étoile. Open Wed–Sun 12–7 and Mon 12–9, closed 1 May and 25 Dec; adm €4.60, free Mon 7–9.

Temporary exhibitions are held in this beautiful old mansion, featuring cutting-edge photographers such as Sam Taylor-Wood. There is also support for young artists, who can exhibit in a new gallery, L'Atelier. The centre has a café overlooking the peaceful garden (access from the main building or from Rue Balzac).

Musée Jacquemart-André O7

158 Bd Haussmann, t 01 45 62 11 59, w www.musee-jacquemart-andre.com; métro St-Philippe-du-Roule. Open daily 10–6; adm €7.80 (inc. audioguide).

If one day you want to look at some beautiful pictures, but don't care to tackle the terrifying Louvre, there's probably no better choice than this museum, assembled by Edouard André and his wife Nélie Jacquemart at the turn of the century.

Nélie was a painter herself, and had a sharp eye. The works from the Italian Renaissance rival the Louvre's own collection, beginning with Paolo Uccello's dream-like *St George Slaying the Dragon* and Carpaccio's exquisite and fanciful *Embassy of the Amazon Queen*. Other greats represented include Mantegna, Pontormo, Cima da Conegliano, Alessandro Baldovinetti and Carlo Crivelli. And don't miss Tiepolo's fresco on the stairway, the *Reception of King Henri III in Venice*, commemorating one of the most spectacular parties of all time (1573).

French painters of the 17th and 18th centuries are also well represented, as are the Dutch artists; the collection includes two works by Rembrandt.

Musée Nissim de Camondo O5–6

63 Rue de Monceau; **t** *01 53 89 06 40,* **métro** *Monceau or Villiers.* **Open** *Wed–Sun, 10–5;* **adm** *€4.60.*

Nowhere more than here does one get the sense of French culture contemplating its navel. In a building modelled on the Petit Trianon are two floors full of 18th-century furniture, tapestries, ceramics, silverware, snuffboxes, soup tureens, candelabras, knick-knacks and geegaws.

Musée Cernuschi O5

7 Av Velasquez, **t** *01 45 63 50 75,* **métro** *St-Philippe-du-Roule or Monceau.* **Closed** *until mid-2005.*

A small and seldom-visited museum, bequeathed (along with the house) by another turn-of-the-century collector, this one is entirely devoted to Chinese art, from a serene 5th-century seated Buddha to a T'ang dynasty spittoon.

Parc de Monceau M5–O6

Bd de Courcelles, **t** *01 42 27 08 64,* **métro** *Monceau.* **Open** *summer 7am–10pm, rest of year 7am–8pm.*

As with the Palais Royal, Paris owes this rare oasis to Philippe d'Orléans (Philippe-Égalité), who had it landscaped in the 1770s and redone a decade later, shocking Parisians by hiring a Scotsman named Blakie to turn the grounds into the city's first large English garden.

Boulevard de Courcelles, the northern boundary of the park, follows the course of the Farmers-General wall (*see* p.32). One of Ledoux's less ambitious *barrières*, called the **Rotonde**, marks the park's main entrance.

Cathédrale Alexandre-Nevsky L6

12 Rue Daru, **t** *01 42 27 37 34;* **métro** *Courcelles.* **Open** *Tues, Fri and Sun 3–5.*

Just south of Boulevard de Courcelles, two blocks west of Parc de Monceau, Rue Daru has been the focus of Paris' Russian community for over a century. At its centre is the onion-domed cathedral, built in 1861. Nearby are the Russian library and a flurry of tea rooms and restaurants.

Musée d'Orsay
and the Invalides

05

Musée d'Orsay and the Invalides

Frankly, the Paris of quaint bistrots and narrow streets is rare in this chapter, mere refreshment stops on a death march of urban and national megalomania. Here at the self-designated centre of civilization, both the buildings and the spaces between them, baked through the centuries then iced and glazed by a succession of World Fairs, are on an heroic scale, a magnitude first set by the Sun King himself with the Invalides and Esplanade. This chapter covers not only the Invalides, but a slice of Art Nouveau, a whiff of Paris' sewers, and a topped-up grab-bag of museums, including the lovely Musée Rodin.

1 Lunch

L'Arpège, *84 Rue de Varenne*, **t** *01 47 05 09 06*; **métro** *Varenne*. **Open** *Mon–Fri 12.30–2.30 and 8–10.30*. ***Very Expensive***. Renowned chef Alain Passard devotes his menu almost exclusively to vegetarian dishes.

2 Tea and Cakes

Musée Rodin, *Hôtel Biron, 77 Rue de Varenne*; **métro** *Varenne*. **Open** *summer 9.30–6.30, winter 9.30–4.30*. There's no better place for a contemplative cup of tea on a lovely day than the café in the garden of the Musée Rodin.

3 Drinks

Le Sancerre, *22 Av Rapp*; **métro** *Ecole-Militaire*. **Open** *Mon–Fri 8am–10pm, Sat 3–10pm*. Red, white, rosé: pick your Sancerre and chow down at the oyster bar. Cosy, classy atmosphere with warmth.

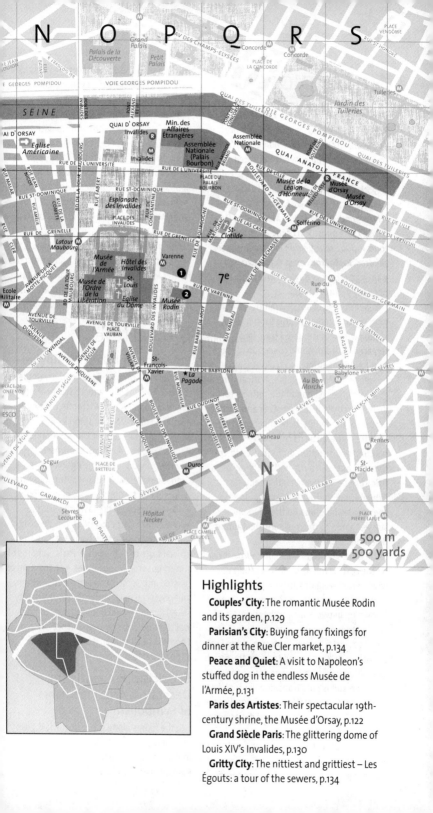

Highlights

Couples' City: The romantic Musée Rodin and its garden, p.129

Parisian's City: Buying fancy fixings for dinner at the Rue Cler market, p.134

Peace and Quiet: A visit to Napoleon's stuffed dog in the endless Musée de l'Armée, p.131

Paris des Artistes: Their spectacular 19th-century shrine, the Musée d'Orsay, p.122

Grand Siècle Paris: The glittering dome of Louis XIV's Invalides, p.130

Gritty City: The nittiest and grittiest – Les Égouts: a tour of the sewers, p.134

MUSÉE D'ORSAY S12

Quai Anatole-France, t 01 40 49 48 48,
w www.musee-orsay.fr; métro Solférino,
RER Musée d'Orsay; wheelchair access (wheel-
chairs and pushchairs available). Open
June–Sept Tues, Wed and Fri–Sun 9–6, Thurs
9–9.45; Oct–May Tues, Wed, Fri and Sat 10–6,
Thurs 10–9.45, Sun 9–6; last admission 5.15
(Thurs 9pm); closed 1 Jan, 1 May and 25 Dec;
adm €7, free on 1st Sun of the month; guided
tours include tours in sign language and for
children. Restaurant open 11.30–2.30 and
3.30–5.30 (Thurs 7–9.15); menu €14.50; café
open 10–5 (Thurs 10–9).

At peak times, count on waiting half-an-hour or so to get inside this former train station, where the engines have been replaced with a dynamo collection of the art that hauled painting and sculpture into the modern era. Moreover, it is specifically the art of Paris of the last half of the 19th century, when the city was both mother and battle-ground of modernity; here under one huge roof are gathered all its combative schools of painting and sculpture from 1848 to 1910, rounded out with a magnificent array of furniture, decorative arts, architectural exhibits and photography. You could easily spend a day here, and neither thirst nor starve, thanks to the museum's restaurant and rooftop café.

The Gare d'Orsay is itself a monument born on the cusp of the 19th century: a daring work of iron weighing more than the Eiffel Tower, with a nave taller than Notre-Dame, thrown up in two years for the 1900 World Fair to serve trains from the southwest. The architect, Victor Laloux, professor at the École des Beaux-Arts, was hired to make the façade a dignified foil for the Louvre across the river. The net result is pure Napoleon III rococola; unfortunately, the station's platforms were too short for modern trains, and it was abandoned in 1960.

Ten years later, the government decided to level it for a huge hotel. But the Parisians, after fatalistically letting Les Halles perish, would have none of it, and in 1973 Pompidou caved in and declared the station a historical monument. In 1977 a competition for converting the innards was won by the Italian Gae Aulenti, who came up with the idea of five levels of exhibition space set back along the sides, tucked full of little visual surprises, illuminated by as much natural light as possible. The undertaking foundered in financial and technical turmoil until 1981, when Mitterrand was elected and simply tripled its budget (he wasn't called Dieu for nothing). Inaugurated in December 1986, the Musée d'Orsay's core exhibits came from the former Jeu de Paume Museum and the 19th-century rooms of the Louvre. Plans are now afoot to rearrange the museum's layout.

Ground Level

Entrance and Nave: Sculpture

Sculptures command the entrance: Rude's piece of Romantic hyperbole, *Le Génie de la Patrie*, from the Arc de Triomphe, followed inside the main door by a Lion by Barye (d. 1875), animal sculptor extraordinaire, and Rude's *Napoleon Awaking to Immortality*, commissioned by the little egomaniac's Grenadiers. Below, the nave of the museum is dominated by the originals of large public works by Napoleon III's favourite sculptor, Jean-Baptiste Carpeaux (1827–75). Keeping them company is a selection revealing the official taste of mid-century Paris, a chorus of suffering, semi-erotic figures, either bound or twisted into some salon-approved position, and given classical names for respectability's sake. The Hollywood flabbergaster on the wall, *Les Romaines de la décadence* by Thomas Couture (Manet's teacher), won a top medal in the salon of 1849.

Classicism, Romanticism, Decorative Arts, Precursors of Symbolism

In the rooms along the wall, the last gasp of classicism is represented by some late Ingres (*La Source*, 1856), while its intense rival, Romanticism, checks in with Delacroix's *La*

Chasse au lion; note his inventive use of broken colour and 'drunken brush' strokes that presage the Impressionists. Beyond are gems from the Académie, including Cabanel's *La Naissance de Vénus*, a tasty tomato that tickled the salon of 1863. The next rooms (behind Couture's decadent Romans) offer **Decorative Arts from 1850 to 1880**: exquisitely crafted, pompous and over-wrought dust-magnets from Paris' World Fairs. The last set of rooms on the right is designated **Precursors of Symbolism**: the still, melancholy pastels of Puvis de Chavannes (*Le Pauvre Pêcheur*) and the Byzantine, mythological fantasies of Gustave Moreau (1826–98), who helped to invent one of the *fin de siècle*'s favourite motifs, the femme fatale (*Jason and Orphée*).

Salle de l'Opéra

At the far end of the ground floor is the Salle de l'Opéra, dedicated to Garnier's extraordinary folly, with Carpeaux's original *La Danse* from the façade. A model of the Opéra (from the 1900 World Fair) is cross-sectioned so you can see all the machinery behind the scenes. The room to the left bares the structure of the Gare d'Orsay as an intro-duction to the **Architecture of 1850–1900**; the several floors of a tower called the Pavillon Amont offer a compendium of Second Empire and Third Republic Paris façades and architecture from Viollet-le-Duc to Frank Lloyd Wright. Best of all is a massive 1855 *View of Paris* painted by Victor Navlet from a balloon floating over the Observatoire, when the outer Left Bank still had virginal meadows and farms, unstraddled by the Eiffel Tower.

Caricatures, Barbizon Landscapes, Courbet, Precursors of the Impressionists

Backtrack now towards the entrance and follow the rooms and galleries along the left side. The first room (closest to the entrance) contains what may come as a surprise: the works of the political satirist **Honoré Daumier** (1808–79), whose 36 terracotta caricatures of Louis-Philippe's political cronies, each representing a vice, prefigure *Spitting Image*. In painting he experimented with reducing detail to a minimum (*Crispin et Scapin*; also the mother and daughter of La Blanchisseuse). Following are several land-scapes from the **Barbizon School**, a movement inspired by photography and a longing to return to nature. Look for works by its theorist, Théodore Rousseau, and the lyrical, dissolving landscapes and figures (*La Dame en bleu*) from the last half of Corot's (1796–1875) career. A third member of the school, peasant-born Jean-François Millet (1814–75), worked making signs for taverns before he got a break at the age of 60. Here are his rainbow-lit *Printemps*, *L'Angélus*, and *Les Glaneuses*, which scandalized the 1857 salon for showing rural poverty and hard work instead of the frolicking shepherds preferred by the bourgeoisie.

The next room is dedicated to the greatest works of **Gustave Courbet** (1819–77), the formulator of realism and the first artist to completely buck the system. He horrified the salon in 1850 with his *L'Enterrement à Ornans*, a picture of an unsentimental, muddy country funeral in his home town. His huge *Atelier* (1855), an 'allegory of my last seven years as a painter', shows the artist in a motley crowd, including his naked muse, Realism, and his patrons and friends (among them Baudelaire, nose in a book). In 1869, Courbet went to the Mediterranean, and was mesmerized by the light (*Falaises d'Etretat après l'orage*), before his career was cut short by his political activities in the Commune.

The next rooms house a superb collection by artists generally lumped together as **precursors of the Impressionists**: for example, Eugène Boudin (1824–98), who in 1848 was the first to paint out of doors, so intent on capturing the atmosphere of his landscapes that he wrote in the margins of his paintings the date, the hour and direction of the wind (*La Plage de Trouville*, 1864). Others declared themselves followers of Delacroix, as seen in Fantin-Latour's *Hommage à Delacroix* (1864), a group portrait of the first rebels in the arts – including Whistler, Baudelaire again and **Manet** (1832–83). Manet was the direct, if reluctant, father of the Impressionists (*see* 'Blinded in the City of Light'), although he never showed his work at their exhibitions and never understood why the official salon and critics lashed out so violently against him. *Olympia* (1863), his most famous work here, made them spit venom when shown in the Salon des Refusés: not so much because of the nude (although Manet outraged many by giving her an erotic black cat instead of the usual dog, symbol of fidelity), but especially because Manet merely sketched in the bouquet of flowers – a photograph-inspired blur of movement that damned it in the eyes of his many critics.

Here too are Manet's *Le Fifre* (also refused by the salon), *Portrait of Zola* (painted in gratitude for the writer's support), *Clair de lune sur le Pont de Boulogne* and *Le Balcon* (one of the ladies is Berthe Morisot, Manet's sister-in-law). Adjacent rooms contain **Impressionist paintings before 1870**, when Monet, Renoir and Bazille (who died in the Franco-Prussian War) first took their easels out of doors: there's Bazille's sun-dappled *Réunion de famille* and a baker's dozen by Monet (1840–1926), filled with the freshness of new discoveries: *Coquelicots*, *La Pie*, *Pont de chemin de fer* and *Femmes au jardin*.

Next, tucked in a room of murky **realists**, are paintings by Monticelli, a native of Marseille who applied thick, unmixed paint with short feverish strokes and inspired Van Gogh's technique and his move to sunny Provence. The last room, **Orientalism**, displays sun-drenched canvases of exotic settings, a popular fad in the Second Empire, thanks to Delacroix's Algerian paintings.

Photography

The latest addition to the museum is devoted to antique photography, with a major focus on daguerreotypes. There are portraits from around 150 years ago, as well as some dream-like landscapes. Temporary exhibitions help fill out the gallery.

Upper Level: Impressionism and Postimpressionism

The reason for this unusual arrangement is the presence of overhead natural light, for light is the heart and soul of the treasures the museum has tucked under its roof: one of the world's most luminous collections of Impressionist paintings. Starring in the first room is Manet's *Déjeuner sur l'herbe* (1863), an updated version of Giorgione's *Concert champêtre* in the Louvre and the key inspiration for the Impressionists with its masterly, experimental handling of paint. Nearby is a portrait by an American friend of Manet, who in his delight for arty names called it *Arrangement in Grey and Black no. 1*, although everyone knows it as *Whistler's Mother*.

Impressionism 1870–80

Key works follow: Monet's *Régates à Argenteuil*, Pissarro's *Les Toits rouges*, and *L'Inondation à Port-Marly*, considered the masterpiece of Albert Sisley (1839–99), who was born in Paris of English parents and concentrated on the nuances of the changing colours and sensations of water, sky and mists. Of Paris, there's Monet's steam-filled *Gare Saint-Lazare* and his *Rue Montorgueil*, and by Renoir (1841–1919) an irresistible evocation of Paris' *bals-dansants*, the *Moulin de la Galette* (1876). This and *La Balançoire* nearby are not only masterful studies of light and shadow on the human figure, but an updating of the tradition of Watteau's *scènes galantes*. Renoir's *Chemin montant dans les hautes herbes* shows a charming if rarely used talent for landscape.

The next room contains paintings from the same decade by Manet, who after inspiring the Impressionists, was himself in turn inspired by their techniques in capturing outdoor light (*Sur la plage*), as well as depicting everyday Paris scenes (*La Serveuse de bocks*). His interests in turn influenced Berthe Morisot (1841–95), the *grande dame* of Impressionism, whose subjects from her life

Blinded in the City of Light

The blindness, or rather visual illiteracy, of the Paris public in response to Edouard Manet's *Déjeuner sur l'herbe* and *Olympia* led to national scandals in the 1860s that seem incredible today. One critic, Paul de Saint-Victor wrote: 'The crowd presses, as at the Morgue, before *Olympia*, reeking and horrible. Art descended so low doesn't even merit censure...Look, and pass on.' *Olympia*'s skin was 'dirty'; she was a 'female gorilla'. Manet was accused of purposely inflicting indecent pictures on a morally upright Paris as a ploy to gain notoriety. He was so universally despised that in 1866 Zola lost his job as art critic at *L'Evénement* for daring to prophesy that 'M. Manet's place is reserved in the Louvre...it is impossible – impossible, you hear – that one day M. Manet will not triumph and crush the timid mediocrities that surround him.'

Like many artists of the period, Manet was inspired by photography. 'If our works have a character that makes them seem like a protest,' Manet wrote in the 1863 catalogue for the Salon des Refusés, 'that is the result of sincerity, since the artist is only trying to render his impression.' Although the first to paint Impressionist scenes from everyday life, and to imitate the instantaneous effects of photography (as in his *Les Courses à Longchamp*), Manet cared little for subject matter and never injected any emotion into his work. He was what critics call a 'painter's painter', fascinated with the ineffable space between light and shadow.

Unlike many revolutionaries who followed, Manet never meant to provoke or challenge the Parisians. Son of a bourgeois family in Paris, he was born to please: a handsome charmer with a ready laugh, his studio was often crowded with society ladies. Manet longed to be accepted by the public, to win the Salon prize his followers disdained – but not at the price of compromising his art. After 1879, the year when his arch-enemy Albert Wolff, critic of *Le Figaro*, finally admitted in print that Manet had pointed the way to others, the artist responded by standing up with his arms extended like a signpost whenever he saw Wolff. In 1881 he finally won a second-class medal at the Salon, achieving his life's goal and paving the way for the public acceptance of the Impressionists, Manet's followers. Two years later he would be dead, at the height of his power; his last major painting, that uncanny scene of Paris nightlife called *Le Bar des Folies-Bergères* (now in London), was painted from a wheelchair.

Art critics have found in *Olympia* the first nude in 400 years (since Lucas Cranach's *Venus*) to portray a naked woman honestly, clean of the accumulated crust of the Academic conventions; after the initial shock, the painting opened the eyes of Paris to a new literacy in seeing. Some were better students than others. In 1890 the Louvre only accepted *Olympia* as a gift after lengthy negotiations, and only hung it in 1907, after Clemenceau intervened to make Zola's words come true.

and that of her friends form a woman's diary in paint (*Le Berceau*). The same room also contains works by **Degas**, whose unusual compositions were derived in part from the spontaneity of photography and Japanese prints; unlike the other Impressionists he never painted out of doors, but from memory (*A la Bourse, L'Absinthe, Les Repasseuses*). The ballet and race track became special interests of Degas after 1874, affording opportunities for unusual compositions and also for the study of movement. When his

failing eyesight precluded further painting, he modelled ballerinas in wax; a glass case holds the bronzes cast after his death.

Impressionism after 1880

Beyond are Impressionist works after 1880: **Monet** for his part continued to paint 'as the birds sing', ever surrendering himself to light and atmosphere, especially in his series that portray the same subject at different times of day: the museum has *Les Meules*, five of *Les Cathédrales de Rouen* and two versions of the water lilies (*Nymphéas*) painted at Giverny, where representation of form is so minimal as to verge on abstract constructions of pure colour. **Renoir** took a trip to Algeria (*Paysage algérien*, *Fête arabe à Alger*) and Italy, where he become disillusioned and convinced that the light touch he had cultivated (which was just becoming popular) was a cheat. After concentrating on line (*Danse à la ville*, *Danse à la campagne*) he developed his own pearly synthesis of line and colour, epitomized in *Les Grandes Baigneuses*, an extraordinary work from a man so paralysed by rheumatism he had his brushes strapped to his wrists.

The next room contains a large selection of Pissarro's landscapes, works by Morisot and the American Mary Cassatt (*Femme cousant*). The paintings collected by Van Gogh's art-loving friend Dr Gachet (Monet's *Chrysanthèmes* and Renoir's *Margot*) lead into a room of painting by **Van Gogh** (1853–90). Contact in Paris with the Impressionists (*La Guinguette*) lightened his palette before he journeyed to Arles and discovered colour as the only medium powerful enough to express his emotions: *L'Arlésienne*, *La Chambre de Van Gogh à Arles* and the merciless *Autoportrait*, painted during his first fit of madness in Arles. The most uncanny work of the collection, *L'Eglise d'Auvers-sur-Oise* (1890), is full of dark forebodings of his suicide; it was painted while Van Gogh was living with Dr Gachet.

Beyond are the works of the most pivotal figure in the museum, **Paul Cézanne** (1839–1906), who himself began with a heavy murky style (*Portrait d'Achille Empéraire*) before 1872, when he moved from his native Provence to the same Auvers-sur-Oise, where Dr Gachet was the first person to buy one of his pictures. Contact with Pissarro considerably lightened his colours: *La Maison du pendu*, which he showed in the first Impressionist exhibition in 1873, and *Une moderne Olympia*, inspired by Manet. The other Impressionists were not very impressed by him or vice versa, and after 1877 Cézanne spent most of his time in Aix,

becoming a legend towards the end of his life, the old grouch who thumbed his nose at Paris. Cézanne's goal was to give ephemeral Impressionism an intellectual, architectural underpinning of geometry, structure and composition, ever seeking new solutions for 'an art parallel to nature'; he was a superb colourist but never permitted himself any tricks or false bravura. The Musée d'Orsay has masterpieces of his three favourite subjects: a landscape (*L'Estaque*), figures (*Femme à la cafetière*, *Baigneurs* and *Les Joueurs de cartes*) and still lifes (*Pommes et Oranges* and *La Nature morte aux oignons*).

The next room is dimly lit to protect the subtle, refined colours of the **pastels by Degas**, whose experiments in the medium, especially his complex crosshatchings (*Danseuse au bouquet saluant sur la scène*), sparked a fresh interest in pastels in other artists, especially Toulouse-Lautrec.

Postimpressionism

The next rooms, devoted to the postimpressionists, offer another barrage of masterpieces, beginning with the last, great, unfinished painting by **Georges Seurat**, *Le Cirque*. The most scientific of painters, Seurat (1859–91) set out to rescue Impressionism from the charges of frivolity by developing his distinctive pointillist style, based on the colour theories of physicists Chevreal and N. O. Rood on the optic mixing of tones and the action of colour; when viewed from a distance, each dot of colour takes on the proper relationship with the dots around it, although remaining visible as an optic vibration. In *Le Cirque* Seurat was dealing with the problem of using linear rhythms to express movement and gaiety while preserving the serene, classical proportions of the Golden Section.

Pastels: Redon and Toulouse-Lautrec

Beyond, the **Salle Redon** is devoted to the works of the elusive Odilon Redon (1840–1916), master colourist and pre-Freudian painter of dreams, who belonged to no school but inspired the Symbolists, Surrealists and Metaphysical painters who followed (*Portrait de Gauguin*). There are several other rooms of pastels, culminating in the **Salle Toulouse-Lautrec**. Lautrec (1864–1901), a descendant of the counts of Toulouse, broke both legs as a child, which seriously impeded his growth. His physical afflictions may have contributed to his empathy in the penetrating portraits of 'occupationally distorted souls', especially of prostitutes, whom he drew while living amongst them. Lautrec strove to 'paint the truth, not the ideal' and he took the portrayals of the contemporary entertainment world by Degas to a unique level of individual portraiture, the most sincere of the Belle Époque (*La Goulue, Jane Avril Dansant, La Clownesse Cha-U-Kao*).

Galerie Bellechasse: Rousseau, Gauguin

The long Galerie Bellechasse kicks off with another unique painter, Henri Rousseau (1844–1910), known as 'Le Douanier' from his job in a customs bureau. Rousseau generally is classed as a naïf, which distracts from his intuitive mastery of the same architectural problems that Seurat wearied himself into an early grave trying to solve (*La Guerre* and the magical *La Charmeuse de serpents*). Next come the painters of **Pont-Aven**, a fishing village in Brittany where Gauguin (1848–1903) first fled in his search for a simpler life. Younger painters followed, especially Émile Bernard (1868–1941), who with Gauguin formulated **Synthetism** (although the egocentric Gauguin never acknowledged Bernard's work). Another reaction against the 'mindlessness' of Impressionism, Synthetism was based on the subordination of objects in a picture to one overall rhythm, 'synthesizing' them to bring out the meaning the whole evoked in the artist. Admirers of primitive art for its power and simplicity, the Synthetists similarly ignored perspective to simplify forms into large, expressive, coloured patterns with dark outlines, a style sometimes called cloisonnism for its resemblance to medieval cloisonné enamels: note

Gauguin's *Les Lavandières à Pont-Aven* and *Les Meules jaunes*, painted after his 1888 period with Van Gogh in Arles. Hanging nearby are works by other Pont-Aven painters, Sérusier and Émile Bernard (his masterpiece, the haunting *Madeleine au Bois d'Amour*, modelled on his sister).

After cold, wet Brittany comes the sensuous tropical breeze of Gauguin's lush paintings from the South Seas, where he escaped 'diseased' civilization to rejeuvenate art by becoming 'one with nature': *Femmes de Tahiti, Le Repas, Cheval blanc, Et l'or de leur corps*. There are examples of his sculptures, *Oviri* and the carved lintel from his door in the Marquesas Islands, where he died in 1903, ill, broke, depressed, at odds with the colonial authorities whom he accused of exploiting the natives. Gauguin's work, fanatical attitude and long slow suicide have had a powerful influence on subsequent artists, both as a guide and a warning.

The Nabis and Fauvism

Following are the works of another school that developed out of Pont-Aven, the **Nabis** (Hebrew for 'prophet'), born in 1889 when Gauguin showed Sérusier how to paint a forest scene on a wooden cigar-box lid (*Le Talisman*). Sérusier (1864–1927) took it back to his young comrades of the progressive Académie Jullien, who decided that they, too, would rejeuvenate art. In 1890 their precocious spokesman, Maurice Denis (1870–1943), wrote the essential dictum of all modern art: '...a painting, before being a warhorse, a naked woman, some anecdote or whatnot, is essentially a flat surface covered with colours arranged in a certain order' (see his *Taches de soleil sur la terrasse* and *Les Muses*). Edouard Vuillard (1868–1940) was the decorative Nabi of intimate bourgeois interiors and gardens, perhaps because he lived with his mother until well into his 50s (*Au Lit*); Bonnard (1867–1947) was the most inspired by Japanese prints (*Les Femmes au jardin, Le Peignoir*); Félix Vallotton (1865–1925) painted the most innovative compositions (*Le Ballon*); and Aristide Maillol (1861–1944) was a Nabi who went on to sculpt monumental women (*La Femme à l'ombrelle*). The logical conclusion of Maurice Denis' dictum was **Fauvism**, represented by André Derain's *Le Pont de Charing Cross* (1902) in the Kaganovitch collection in the last room on this floor (along with more by Van Gogh and Gauguin); the Pompidou Centre's Musée d'Art Moderne chronologically continues from here.

Middle Level

After all these Upper Level fireworks, the Middle Level starts out by showing you the art that people actually bought at the time, whose creators lived like princes: after Toulouse-Lautrec, Bouguereau's *Birth of Venus* in the gaudy old hotel ballroom seems little more than a hussy painted for bar-room winks. Then come six rooms from the official **salons from 1870–1914**, huge trumpeting white elephants – pseudo-prehistoric subjects such as Cormon's *Le Fils de Caïn*, or patriotic pieces (the plaster *Le Forgeron* by Dalou, cast in bronze for the monument honouring the Republic in Place de la Nation), or picturesque everyday life (*The Docks of Cardiff* by Lionel Waldem), or violence from battle of the Commune (André Devanbez's *La Charge*). One room has a marble bust of Sarah Bernhardt and works by the Divine Sarah herself.

Beyond is a hotchpotch selection of artists classed as **Symbolists**: *The Wheel of Fortune* by Burne-Jones, who made the Pre-Raphaelites popular in France, *Summer Night* by Winslow Homer, the famous *Portrait of Proust* by Jacques-Emile Blanches, *Le Rêve* by Puvis de Chavannes, *Nuit d'été* by Munch and the extraordinary, pastel-coloured *École de Platon* by Jean Delville, where naked youths with Gibson-girl hairdos languidly listen to philosophy under the wisteria.

Along the museum's central nave is a second terrace of sculpture: Frémiet's model of St Michael and the dragon for Mont St-Michel; and *L'Age mûr* and other works by Camille Claudel (1864–1943), Rodin's ill-starred student, model and mistress. There are original plasters by Rodin (1840–1917) of

his works in the Musée Rodin and in Meudon: *Ugolin*, *Balzac*, *La Muse* (from the monument to Whistler) and *La Porte de l'Enfer*.

Off the terrace, a series of rooms is devoted to the extraordinary renewal of fine workmanship and design known as **Art Nouveau**: dragonfly jewellery by Lalique, furniture by Guimard (*Banquette avec vitrine*), a desk by Henry Van de Velde, glass by Tiffany (his *Au nouveau cirque*, after a drawing by Lautrec) and Émile Gallé (*Plat d'ornement*). Don't miss Robert Carabin's *Library*, with its Symbolist allegories on the Triumph of l'Esprit over Ignorance. Near Rodin's sculpture, the **Tour Guimard** displays furniture designed by architects: beautiful chairs by Guimard, Gaudí, Bugatti, Mackintosh and Frank Lloyd Wright; others are in three small rooms along the south (Rue de Lille) galleries. The sculptures on the terrace here are by Rodin's contemporaries (Bartholomé and Bourdelle) and his successors, Maillol (*Méditerranée*) and Joseph Bernard.

The last set of rooms along this terrace is devoted to **Paintings after 1900**, and the careers of artists who began as Nabis: more interiors by Vuillard, who worked with egg tempera for its fresh fresco colours (*Coolus*, and the large *Bibliothèque*); Maurice Denis, who remained closest to the original ideals (*Jeu de volant*) and Bonnard (*En barque*).

Musée de la Légion d'Honneur R11–12

*2 Rue de la Légion-d'Honneur; **métro** Solférino, **RER** Musée d'Orsay. **Closed for renovations until sometime in 2005.***

The **Hôtel Salm** (1783) is French neoclassicism at its most graceful, small in scale, with a miniature triumphal arch and Ionic colonnade around its forecourt. This is a replica (the original was burned in the Commune); there's another copy in San Francisco. The museum, however, is a reminder that one of the first tasks of any French regime was to create a system of Brownie points; the Revolution no sooner abolished the monarchy's orders of merit than it created a

'Victor of the Bastille' pin for those who participated in the riot. Then in 1802 Napoleon created the far grander Legion of Honour. His councillors protested: weren't medals 'the baubles of monarchy'? *'Eh bien,'* replied the little cynic, 'it is with baubles that men are led.' Besides medals, the museum contains other Napoleana.

THE INVALIDES

Assemblée Nationale P–Q11

33 Quai d'Orsay, t 01 40 63 60 00, w www.assemblee-nationale.fr; métro Invalides or Assemblée-Nationale, RER Invalides. Open for guided tours (in French; around 1hr) on Sat at 10, 2 and 3 (admission to sessions by prior application only); adm free.

The Assemblée seats its 577 members in the Palais Bourbon on the Quai d'Orsay (although when the French refer to the 'Quai d'Orsay', they mean the Ministry of Foreign Affairs next door). The palace-building Bourbon this time was the daughter of Louis XIV and Mme de Montespan, who completed it in 1728. Louis XV purchased it in order to change its façade to harmonize with his Place de la Concorde, a plan that had to wait until 1807, when Napoleon required a matching temple bookend for his Madeleine. In 1827 it became the seat of the French parliament. Inside, the best bits are concentrated in the library, its domes and pendentives decorated with Delacroix's grand murals on the History of Civilization (1838–45), its shelves lined with the records of Joan of Arc's trial, Rousseau's manuscripts, and more. But don't count on seeing it during the tour.

Basilique Ste-Clotilde Q12

12 Rue de Martignac, t 01 44 18 62 60; métro Solférino, Varenne or Invalides. Open Mon–Fri 9–7 and 2.30–5.30, Mass daily at 12.15; closed hols (if not religious).

Confronting the Defence Ministry across Square Rousseau, Ste-Clotilde is a perfect 13th-century Gothic church – designed in 1840 by F. C. Grau. Its innovative use of iron upset conservatives, and construction was delayed until after Grau's death in 1853. There's a surplus of academic painting to see but nothing else, although fans of *Tropic of Cancer* may find a visit irresistible after Henry Miller's description of his first and last Catholic Mass, when he and a friend wandered into Ste-Clotilde at dawn after a night's revels: 'A weird, unearthly noise assailed my ears...No music except this undefinable dirge manufactured in the subcellar – like a million heads of cauliflower wailing in the dark...That this sort of thing existed I knew, but then one also knows that there are slaughterhouses and morgues and dissecting rooms.'

Musée Rodin P13

Hôtel Biron, 77 Rue de Varenne, t 01 44 18 61 10, w www.musee-rodin.fr; métro Varenne. Open April–Sept Tues–Sun 9.30–5.45, garden until 6.45, last admission 5.15; Oct–Mar Tues–Sun 9.30–4.45, garden until 5, last admission 4.15; adm €5, garden only €1.

The Hôtel Biron (1731) was built after a plan by Jacques-Ange Gabriel for Peyrenc de Moras, who made a fortune by getting out of John Law's 'Mississippi Bubble' scheme before it popped. It is one of the most charming and best-preserved mansions in Paris from the period (several rooms have their original woodwork), fitted with distinguished façades overlooking both the front courtyard and back gardens. When Auguste Rodin moved here in 1908, he was 68; his reputation as France's greatest sculptor was in the bag, and it was agreed that he would leave the state his works after he died (in 1917, 10 days after marrying his mistress of over 50 years).

Rodin was the last of the great Romantics. He sculpted the literary subjects of the day, but with a personal vision, intensity and integrity that liberated sculpture from its stagnant rut as mere portraiture, public decoration or patriotic propaganda. He studied Michelangelo in Italy and came back to cause his first sensation in 1876 with *The Age of Bronze* (*L'Age d'airain*, Room 3), so realistic that he was accused of casting a live man in bronze. In 1880, Rodin was commissioned to make a bronze door for a museum of decorative arts, resulting in the *Gates of Hell* (in the garden). Although never completed, the Gates fired the sculptor's creative imagination, and many of the 200 figures he planned for their decoration became sculptures in themselves. Studies are scattered throughout the museum: the *Three Shadows*, Paolo Malatesta and Francesca da Rimini in *The Kiss* (Room 4) and *The Thinker* (outside), in a pose reminiscent of the Lost Soul in Michelangelo's *Last Judgement*. The famous *La Main de Dieu* (1898) in Room 4 inaugurated Rodin's departure from academic tradition in a composition purely from his imagination.

Room 6 is dedicated to sculptor Camille Claudel, sister of poet Paul and Rodin's model for his *La France* and *L'Aurore*; here too are examples of her work before she went mad, a portrait of Rodin and her masterful *L'Age mûr*. Room 8 has portraits of society ladies Mrs Potter Palmer, Lady Sackville-West and the poignant *Mother and her Dying Daughter*, the faces and hands almost engulfed, overwhelmed by the raw marble, an emotional device Rodin often employed, inspired by Michelangelo's *nonfiniti* in the Louvre.

Upstairs, studies and models trace the evolution of Rodin's two great public monuments, *Balzac* and *The Burghers of Calais*. Here, too, are paintings that Rodin owned and left to the state, notably Van Gogh's *Les Moissonneurs* and *Père Tanguy* (a portrait of the kind-hearted colour dealer), and Monet's *Paysage de Belle-Isle*.

Outside, amid the roses of the **Cour d'Honneur** are Rodin's *Thinker* and other masterpieces. The delightful **garden** is filled with studies for the Burghers, and a serene duck pond contains the most harrowing sculpture of all, *Ugolino and his Sons*.

As you leave, note the plaque by the gate commemorating poet Rainer Maria Rilke, who was Rodin's secretary from 1908 to 1911.

Hôtel des Invalides O–P13

t 01 44 42 37 72, *w www.invalides.org*; *métro Latour-Maubourg, Varenne or Invalides, RER Invalides.*

Esplanade des Invalides O13–11

The dome of the Invalides glows like a second sun over its Esplanade, stretching 550 yards down to the Seine. This vast expanse was laid out in 1720 and recently spruced up, but it is still too formal and crisscrossed by traffic to be very inviting.

This was the Plain of Grenelles in 1670, when Louis XIV's under-minister of war, Louvois, persuaded his warmongering king to provide a hospital for old soldiers (most of whom lived in disgraceful penury), which could incidentally double as a monument to the military glory and triumphs of Louis himself. The latter consideration called for nothing less than the grandest Paris project of the Sun King's reign, financed by taxing monasteries and markets, and docking the miserable pay of active soldiers. The competition for the design was won by Libéral Bruant: a rhythmic 650ft façade with pavilions at either end, a crown of dormer windows shaped like armoured torsos and a central doorway in a magnificent built-in arch rising to the roof. This frames an equestrian relief of Louis XIV, flanked by Justice and Prudence, two virtues hoodwinked to bear the tyrant company. These are copies; the originals by Coustou were smashed in the Revolution, which began here the morning of 14 July 1789, when the mob clambered over the now-dry moats and broke into the subterranean armouries, pillaging 28,000 rifles to capture the Bastille.

Cour d'Honneur O13

Hôtel des Invalides. **Open** summer daily 10–6, winter daily 10–5.

Even if you don't visit the Invalides museums, do step under the arch into

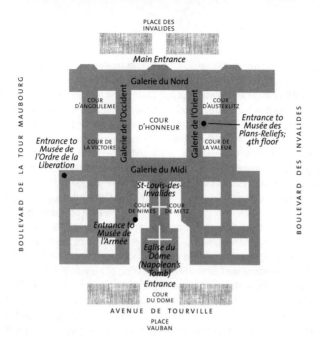

Bruant's majestic cobblestoned courtyard, the Cour d'Honneur. Bristling with cannons, its double-decker arcades were inspired by the cloister of El Escorial in Spain, although Bruant's corners project inwards and his arcades playfully resemble rows of windows. More sculpted trophies adorn the round dormer windows; the fifth on the left, along the central arcade, is encircled by wolf paws as if it were the eye of a wolf (*le loup voit*), a mason's pun on Louvois' name.

St-Louis-des-Invalides O13

Hôtel des Invalides, **t** *01 44 42 37 65; wheelchair access.* **Open** *summer daily 9.30–5.30, winter daily 9.30–4.30; adm on same ticket as Musée de l'Armée.*

The façade of this church closes the south end of the Cour d'Honneur, guarded by a statue of Napoleon, 'the little Corporal', in his old grey coat and hat. This held pride of place on the Vendôme column from 1833 until 1863, when Napoleon III replaced it with a silly statue of his uncle modelling the latest in togas.

The Invalides has Siamese-twin churches, head-to-head, originally sharing the same altar and chancel: St-Louis for the old soldiers and staff, and the Eglise-du-Dôme (*see* pp.132–3) for royals. St-Louis was designed by Bruant but built by his rival, Jules Hardouin-Mansart when Louvois fired Bruant.

A few dozen flags, including swastikas, hang like forgotten laundry above the gallery; during the Revolution, St-Louis was converted into a 'Temple of Mars' and the captured enemy banners that had hung for centuries in Notre-Dame's nave were moved here, but briefly; in 1814, when the allies entered Paris, the governor of the Invalides threw 1,417 of them into a bonfire.

As you leave the church, the arcade to your left enshrines one of the 700 Paris taxicabs requisitioned during the night of 6 September 1914 to transport 7,000 soldiers 35km to the front and save Paris at the Battle of the Marne.

Musée de l'Armée O–P13

Hôtel des Invalides, **t** *01 44 42 37 72, infos-ma@invalides.org.* **Open** *April–Sept daily 10–5.45, Oct–Mar daily 10–4.45, closed 1 Jan, 1 May, 1 Nov and 25 Dec;* **adm** *€5.70; tickets, sold under the right arcade, are valid for two consecutive days and include entry to the other museums below. Wheelchair access.*

Bête comme la paix ('as stupid as peace') is an old Parisian expression, one that seems to sum up the spirit of this unmatched horde of military paraphernalia. The sections in the east arcade cover the 17th to 19th centuries, the period of France's obsession with *gloire*. On the ground floor huge wall paintings of Louis XIV's Flanders campaign of 1672 decorate the veterans' refectory, now hung with French battle banners and Ingres' portrait of *Napoleon I on the Imperial Throne*, while a second gallery holds a remarkable collection of silly cavalry uniforms and not so silly rifles.

The first floor displays 100,000 more uniforms in at least as many rooms. A large section is devoted to Napoleon, with his coat and hat, his stuffed dog and white horse, paintings of his retreat from Moscow and *Napoleon at Fontainebleau*, the Emperor like a little boy slouching in his chair with a sulky look on his face as he abdicates for the first time; further on are locks of his hair, his death mask and a reconstruction of the room where he died on St Helena.

Napoleon's military genius was intuitive and, unlike the strategies of subsequent French generals, completely void of dogma. His only theory was to rally his *grognards*, or 'grumblers', to strike unexpectedly and deliver a decisive blow in one big battle, a tactic that perfectly fitted the French tradition of personal, gallant bravery and (often futile) gestures. In the displays on the second floor, you begin to note how after Napoleon French military tacticians were always one battle behind – as De Gaulle warned in the 1930s, while the French were building their Maginot line. The most interesting exhibits relate to the siege of Paris and the Commune – ration tickets and petrified bread made from sawdust (*brioche dynatique, 300g par jour*), photographs of the barricades and balloons, machine guns (Paris' secret weapon of 1870, but not used until it was too late), and a rare survival of a *Panorama* (a 360° painting that spectators would view from the middle to relive an event, in this case the 1870 Battle of Rezonville).

The exhibits continue across the courtyard, in the ground-floor refectory of the west arcade, where murals of Louis XIV's Dutch campaigns of 1672–8 look down on ancient Greek, Merovingian, medieval and Renaissance weapons and armour. Adjacent galleries hold swashbuckling Turkish, Chinese and Japanese weapons. On the first-floor landing, a case of Gulf War exhibits is already in place, while the first floor is jammed with material relating to the First World War – paintings, models of a trench and the battlefield at Verdun, and one of Krupp's three Big Berthas.

The new General de Gaulle wing, which starts on the third floor, is devoted to the Second World War, the Free French and *la France combattante*. Events are displayed chronologically over three floors, describing the effect of the war on France from 1940 until the Liberation in 1945. The efforts of De Gaulle and the Resistance are highlighted, and the events are brought to life through every conceivable media: maps, photos, objects, uniforms, guns, recordings, and black and white footage. The recordings are all in French, but most of the accompanying panels are translated into English.

Musée des Plans-Reliefs O–P13

*Hôtel des Invalides, **t** 01 45 51 95 05. **Open** summer daily 10–5.45; winter daily 10–4.45; closed 1 Jan, 1 May, 1 Nov and 25 Dec; **adm** on same ticket as Musée de l'Armée (see above).*

The museum is housed on the top floor, under the massive joists of the roof of the Invalides. Louis XIV began to collect these huge scale relief models of France's fortified cities and towns on Louvois' advice in 1686. Some of these fill entire rooms; until 1927 they were considered a military secret.

Église-du-Dôme O13–14

*Hôtel des Invalides, **t** 01 44 42 37 72. **Open** April–June daily 10–6, July–Sept daily 10–7, rest of the year daily 10–5, closed first Monday of every month and 1 Jan, 1 May, 17 June, 1 Nov and 25 Dec; **adm** on same ticket as Musée de l'Armée (see above).*

Designed by Hardouin-Mansart and completed in 1706, the pointy dome is so impressive that the church was named after it, and as a prominent feature of the Paris skyline it was regilded with 27½lbs of gold for the Revolution's bicentennial in 1989. What most books on the Invalides omit is how closely the architect copied the dome of Ste-Anne-la-Royale, a Paris church begun in 1662 by Guarino Guarini, the master Baroque architect from Turin, but demolished in 1823.

Beneath his dome, Hardouin-Mansart designed a Greek cross plan, with radiating circular chapels, while the altar is under a copy of St Peter's baldachin. Though unusual, the interior leaves so cold an impression that in 1800 Napoleon made it a military pantheon, when he installed the remains of Louis XIV's Marshal Turenne (whom he admired for his strategy of surprise attacks).

The greatest main-chancer in history, responsible on his own estimate for the deaths of 1,700,000 Frenchmen, Napoleon died on 21 May 1821, vomiting from stomach ulcers (caused either by the poisonous 'Paris green' in the plaster of his room, or by the fact that his French chef on St Helena retired, abandoning him to English cuisine). His request, inscribed over the bronze doors to the crypt – 'I wish to be buried on the banks of the Seine, in the midst of the people of France, whom I have loved so dearly' – was imprudently granted by Louis-Philippe in 1840 as a bid to gain popularity (although all it gained was unfavourable comparisons between the heady days of the Grande Armée and his own stolid bourgeois regime). Napoleon's body was fetched from St Helena by a committee headed by Louis-Philippe's son; before loading the coffin aboard ship the committee took a peek inside and were amazed to see old Boney 'perfectly intact', his toenails sticking through his boots. The official record omits the fact that someone lopped off the imperial organ and pickled it – a shrivelled, inch-long curiosity that occasionally appears in London auctions. Still, the aura of Napoleon was so uncanny that once the authorities had him back in Paris, they packaged him up in six coffins of mahogany, tin and lead, all fitted like Chinese boxes within an enormous 43ft by 21ft porphyry sarcophagus the colour of dried blood. The design of the tomb in the circular crypt is by Louis Visconti – by far the most restrained proposal submitted in the tomb competition.

Napoleon's last resting place exacerbates the ambiguity of his memory; 12 winged statues of Napoleonic Victories guard his tomb, while the passage around the crypt displays a series of bas-reliefs of the dead man apotheosized as Caesar or Jupiter bragging of his accomplishments (the quotes are taken from his self-serving *Las Cases* memoirs written on St Helena). Politically, the French are grateful that Bonaparte's hatred of liberalism, contempt for democracy and obsession with patriotism and *la gloire* have survived only in France's far right wing. As a myth, however, he has a frightening resilience.

Three other Bonapartes are buried here: Napoleon II, King of Rome (in the crypt); Napoleon's big brother Joseph (1768–1844), the unhappy King of Naples and later of Spain; and Napoleon's youngest and favourite brother Jérôme (1784–1860), who became the King of Westphalia, where he was popularly known as the 'Merry Monarch'. In the far right-hand chapel, Marshal Foch (1851–1929), hero of the final battles of 1918 and commander of the British and French forces at the end, has an impressive monument supported by eight soldiers.

The park in front of the church is the one place where you might meet some of the 70 current long-term patients (compared to the 6,000 accommodated when the Invalides opened in 1674). And there's yet another museum to the west, facing Boulevard de La-Tour-Maubourg: the **Musée de l'Ordre de la Libération** (*open April–Sept daily 10–6, Oct–Mar 10–5; adm free*), with items relating to the Ordre de la Libération, created by De Gaulle in 1940 to reward all who joined him.

La Pagode P15

57 bis Rue de Babylone, t 01 45 55 48 48; métro St-François-Xavier.

One of the last vestiges of the craze that swept Paris after 1868, when Japan opened its ports to the West and exported the prints that fascinated Van Gogh, Degas and nearly every other artist working in Paris, this pagoda was built in 1896 as a *petite folie* by Mme Boucicaut, wife of the owner of Au Bon Marché (*see* pp.213–4). Her receptions were so much in vogue that people would rent the balconies of adjacent flats to watch them through binoculars.

Transformed into a cinema in 1931, La Pagode was where Cocteau premiered *Le Testament d'Orphée* in 1959. The exterior was extensively restored in the late 1990s.

QUARTIER GROS CAILLOU

Edible and Architectural Confections L–N11–13

If you're not in a hurry, explore the 'goose foot' of streets between the Esplanade des Invalides and the Champ de Mars known as the Quartier Gros Caillou. Unlike the Faubourg St-Germain, east of the Invalides, this didn't become a residential area until the mid-19th century; it has trees, shops and a large dollop of street life.

Rue Cler, closed to traffic, is the centre of one of Paris' most exclusive food markets. At the end closest to the river, it meets Gros Caillou's other main shopping street, **Rue St-Dominique**; at No.64 the Boulangerie Excelsior has kept its 1900 Art Nouveau décor by Benoist and a ceramic floral ceiling. To the west at No.110 is another ornate bakery (1896), this time in the Louis XV style.

Further along is the charming neoclassical **Fontaine de Mars** (1806), showing the Greek health goddess Hygeia in the form of a circus snake woman caring for Mars, an allusion to a military hospital that once stood here.

In nearby **Rue Sédillot** you can see the exuberant **Liceo Italiano** with its circular door (No.12), one of three buildings in the neighbourhood by **Jules Lavirotte** (1864–1928), Paris' craziest Art Nouveau architect.

An even more marvellous Lavirotte confection is to be found on **Avenue Rapp** at No.29: this 1903 apartment house visually ambushes the unwary passer-by with its luxuriant, fluid stone, ceramics and extraordinary detail, especially the nymph and dead poodle and the lizard-shaped door handle.

To recover from the shock, try the old fashioned delights to be found at No.27, the **Chocolatier Puyricard**, before continuing south to **Square Rapp**, with more examples of Nouveau/Deco architecture and a latticework trompe l'œil wall. Here Lavirotte shows himself to be a slightly indigestible precursor of Dr Seuss, his building sporting the quirkiest, crookedest tower in Paris, his asymmetrical balconies stretching over rows of children's faces all holding their breath.

Les Égouts L11

*Entrance on the corner of the Quai d'Orsay and Place de la Résistance, opposite 93 Quai d'Orsay, **t** 01 53 68 27 82; **métro** Alma-Marceau, **RER** Pont de l'Alma. **Open** May–Oct Sat–Wed 11–5, Nov–April Sat–Wed 11–4, closed 2 weeks in Jan; **adm** €3.80.*

Although Baron Haussmann is best known for Paris' boulevards, he was personally more interested in its sewers, which he entrusted to an engineer named Belgrande: Paris, Haussmann realized, would never be a modern city as long as its inhabitants risked being washed away on rainy days. Victor Hugo, in his long digression on Paris' intestines in *Les Misérables*, gave these drains a peculiar romance to match their aroma, and ever since the World Fair of 1867 visitors have descended to the sewers (1,274 miles of them), originally to be pulled along in little torchlit wagons. These were replaced by boats, which since 1972 have been replaced by a silly film, a museum and a stroll along a smelly sewer.

It's reassuring to learn that this humid underworld has its own street signs corresponding to the ones above, in case you ever fall down one of the 26,000 manholes.

Eiffel Tower and Trocadéro

1 Lunch

Jules Verne, *Eiffel Tower (private lift to the 2nd platform)*, **t** *01 45 55 61 44; be sure to reserve and insist on a window seat; **métro** Bir-Hakeim. **Open** daily 12–2.30 and 7.15–9.30. **Very Expensive**. Haute cuisine as highly rated as its position, 400ft above Paris; succulent poulet de Bresse* with mushrooms, and much more.

2 Tea and Cakes

Maison du Japon, *101 bis Quai Branly*, **t** *01 44 37 95 95*, **w** *www.mcjp.asso.fr*; *RER Champs de Mars-Tour Eiffel.* **Open** Tues–Sat 12–7pm. Salon de thé on 1st floor, with traditional tea-making ceremony every Wed.

3 Drinks

Le Totem, *Palais de Chaillot (Musée de l'Homme), 17 Place du Trocadéro;* ***métro*** *Trocadéro.* **Open** daily 12pm–2am: lunch 12–2.30, salon de thé 2.30–7.30, dinner 7.30–midnight, bar midnight–2am. A popular and trendy bar and restaurant, Le Totem has a terrace with an amazing view of the Eiffel Tower.

Eiffel Tower and Trocadéro

Paris' most famous landmark reminds you of the good Paris of light and magic, the city that could first imagine, and then weave, iron in the air – as opposed to the Paris of rigid state control and power, of the Louvre and the Invalides, squatting upriver waiting to pounce and squash. The Eiffel Tower could only dance.

This chapter contains other relics of this effervescent, popular Paris, scattered around what were the busiest of the World Fair grounds. To recapture some of the old thrills, when cosmopolitan fairgoers swarmed to and fro over the Seine, come for the Bastille Day fireworks, which erupt behind the Eiffel Tower.

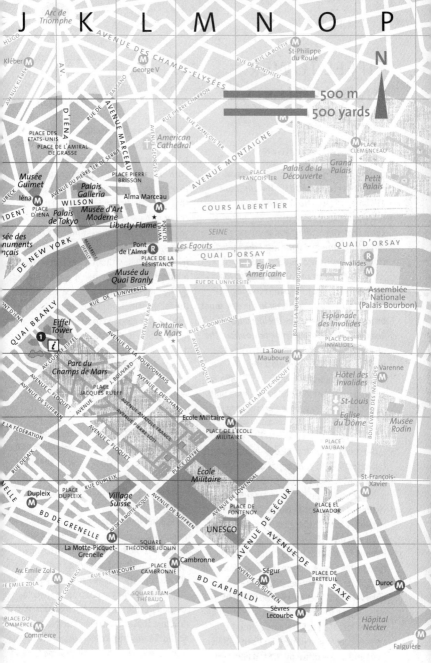

Highlights

Couples' City: Romantic dining on top of Paris, at the Jules Verne, p.136

Parisian's City: Rollerblading around the Jardins du Trocadéro, p.141

Peace and Quiet: The serene Japanese garden of the Musée Guimet, p.143

Paris des Artistes: The Eiffel Tower, one of their favourite subjects, p.138

Grand Siècle Paris: An overview of its architecture, in the Musée National des Monuments Français, p.142

Gritty City: Nautical grit in the Musée de la Marine, p.142

EIFFEL TOWER AND AROUND

Eiffel Tower (Tour Eiffel) J13–K12

*Champ de Mars, **t** 01 44 11 23 23, **w** www. eiffel-tower.com; **métro** Bir-Hakeim, Ecole-Militaire or Trocadéro, **RER** Champ-de-Mars; wheelchair access via North Pillar entrance. **Open** Sept–May daily 9.30am–11pm, June–Aug 9am–midnight, last adm 1hr before closing, stairs close at 6.30pm; **adm** to 1st platform €3.70, to 2nd platform €7, to top platform €10.20 (by lift), stairs to 2nd platform €3.30. If you arrive later in the day, count on a good hour's wait for the lift to the 1st, 2nd and 3rd platforms. Think twice about the ascent if it's hazy. You even have to pay to walk up as far as the 2nd platform.*

The incomparable souvenir of the 1889 Fair, 300m (1,000ft) of graceful iron filigree built to celebrate the Revolution's centenary and the resurrection of France after her defeat by Prussia in 1870, Eiffel's tower has been derided as 'a suppository', 'a giraffe' and 'a criminal, sinister pencil-sharpener' (*see* 'The Offensive Erection'); it has also been the scene of 370 suicides and one birth (in a lift). Belly-up between its four spidery paws, its 9,700 tons may look menacing, but they sit with extraordinary lightness on the soft Parisian clay, exerting as much pressure as that of a man sitting in a chair (4kg per sq cm, or 57lb per sq in). It was erected in two years, for less than the estimated 8 million francs, welded together with 2,500,000 rivets and built without a single fatal work accident. Until 1930, when it was surpassed by the Chrysler Building in New York, it was the tallest structure in the world.

The tower reverted to the state in 1909, and was about to be destroyed when at last it found a practical use, as a meteorological station and wireless antenna. As the latter it played an important role in the First World War, especially after the Germans' code was broken in 1915; a series of mysterious

The Offensive Erection

The competition for the design of a 1,000ft tower resulted in 700 proposals, including a giant lighthouse, a sprinkler to cool Paris off in August and a guillotine in memory of victims of the Terror. In the end a 'functionless' entry from the workshop of Gustave Eiffel was given the nod. Eiffel was already famous for his bold bridges and viaducts; in 1886 he had designed the structural frame of the Statue of Liberty, defying all the naysayers who said her arm would surely blow off. In return for building his '300-metre flagpole' as he called it, Eiffel was granted a 20-year concession (it paid for itself within a year) and a cosy office by the top platform that you can peek into through the window.

In its day, such engineering daredevilry bent quite a few Parisians out of shape. Residents around the Champ de Mars feared it would fall on their heads. The artistic élite, led by Charles Gounod, Charles Garnier and Alexandre Dumas, signed a vitriolic petition against the profanation and dishonour of the capital; Guy de Maupassant left Paris for good so as never to look upon its 'metallic carcass' again, insulted in his soul that the best his generation could produce resembled 'a factory chimney'.

The Eiffel Tower has proved a litmus test of modernity. Georges Seurat painted it soon after it was built, anarchists tried to blow it up, Hitler saw it and sniffed 'Is that all?' In a city as self-conscious as Paris, it has been the subject of volumes of poetry and speculation; Roland Barthes was fascinated by it as a structure that was nothing but metaphor, a symbol 'in the grand itineraries of dream' of nothing and everything at the same time, of communication, science, the 19th century, a rocket, a phallus, a lightning conductor, an insect. In 1924, René Clair may have had the last word in his film *Paris qui dort*, in which an evil spell puts the whole world to sleep – except for a handful of people visiting the top of the Eiffel Tower.

messages about a certain 'H 21' led to the arrest and execution of Mata Hari, who only a few years back had performed her pseudo-Javanese dances in the first platform's restaurant. For the 1925 Exposition des Arts Décoratifs, André Citroën paid to make the Eiffel Tower the world's largest advertising sign. In 2003 20,000 lamps were installed in the structure, allowing the tower to sparkle and shimmer until around midnight each evening.

Originally the tower was painted several tints, lightening to yellow-gold at the top, so its appearance dissolved and changed according to the time of day and weather; now every five or six years, forty painters cover it with 7,700lbs of a sombre maroon colour called *ferrubrou*. On a very clear day, about an hour before sunset, the view from the top (899ft) extends 50 miles into the environs of Paris.

Over six million people a year visit the Eiffel Tower, but apparently that's not enough, nor are there enough places for them to spend money: there are plans to dig a hole at its feet and fill it with restaurants, a museum, a car park and shops.

Champ de Mars J13–M14

Gabriel converted this space, originally market gardens, into a parade ground for the cadets of the École Militaire (*see* below). In 1780 it was opened to the public, providing space for essential Parisian activities such as balloon ascents and horse racing. On the first anniversary of Bastille Day in 1790, the Festival of Federation was held here, featuring Talleyrand and 300 priests chanting Mass while Lafayette and Louis XVI led the crowd in oaths of allegiance to France and its constitution. Four years later Robespierre staged his massive Festival of the Supreme Being to inaugurate the new state cult. In 1889 much of the Champ de Mars went under the roof of the extraordinary Galerie des Machines, the horizontal counterpart to the Eiffel Tower, a pavilion in iron measuring 1,390ft by 380ft. This marvel

was demolished in 1910, an act Walter Benjamin labelled 'artistic sadism'.

Mur pour la Paix

Currently located on the Champ de Mars at the foot of the Eiffel Tower, the Mur pour la Paix was inspired by the Wailing Wall in Jerusalem. Designed by Clara Halter and erected in 2000, it is made of metal and glass and engraved with the word 'peace' in 32 languages. Visitors are encouraged to post their own messages of peace in the slots made for that purpose. Eventually the wall will be moved to a permanent location in front of Paris' UNESCO building (*see* below). Messages can also be sent and read on the Web site, **w** *www.murpourlapaix.com*.

École Militaire M14–N15

Although the feckless Louis XV took no interest whatsoever in founding a royal military academy, the real king of France, Mme de Pompadour, approved the idea in 1751. It was Beaumarchais who suggested raising funds by taxing playing cards, and the plans for the school were confided to Jacques-Ange Gabriel, who created one of the most palatial barracks of all time. The Place de Fontenoy façade, with its colonnaded wings, pediment, four massive Corinthian columns and steep roof fits squarely into the tradition begun by Perrault's Louvre, while the more austere north façade (originally the back) has the great view down the formal gardens of the Champ de Mars to the Eiffel Tower.

The École Militaire's star pupil was the Corsican lying in the porphyry box in the Invalides, who left in 1780 as an 18-year-old artillery lieutenant.

UNESCO M15–N16

*7 Place de Fontenoy, **t** 01 45 68 10 60 (information in English), **w** www.unesco.org; **métro** Ségur or Cambronne; wheelchair access. **Open** Mon–Fri 9.30–12.30 and 2.30–5, closed hols and during conferences; **adm** free.*

Designed in 1958 by the Italian Nervi, Frenchman Zehrfuss and American Breuer,

The Compulsive Exhibitionist

As cities go, Paris has long been the champion show-off. From the Middle Ages to the Revolution, it drew crowds from all over Europe to its trade fairs, especially the annual luxury fair put on by the abbots of St-Germain. The first modern public exhibition was organized by the Directory in 1798. But when Britain astounded the world with its dazzling display of industrial prowess in the Crystal Palace in the Great Exhibition of 1851, an upstaged France had to respond.

Set in the muddy old parade field, the Champs de Mars between the Champs-Elysées and the École Militaire, the 1855 Exhibition turned out a poor imitation of the London show, a pastiche of ugly Second Empire glass and iron pavilions. Undismayed, the Parisians tried again in 1867 with an Exposition Universelle. Again, consumer goods were the Exhibition's *raison d'être*: there was everything from Sèvres porcelain to locomotives. Adolphe Sax had a stand to promote his new saxophone, and the star of the Prussian exhibit was the advanced Krupp cannon, which Bismarck would soon be using on Paris itself. Fifteen million visitors came to try out the first *bateaux-mouches* and make balloon ascents with the photographer Nadar. Prostitutes and cabarets featuring the latest Second Empire dance, *le chahut* or cancan, did a roaring trade. When critics complained that the Exposition showed Paris as the capital of orgies rather than a competitor in industry, the Comte de Fleury shrugged: 'In any case, we had a devilish good time'.

Paris then decided to make fairs a habit, hosting one every 11 years or so. The next show, in 1878, was even bigger and better, the first modern, truly international Exposition – even Japan and China put up small pavilions. The telephone and phonograph were crowd favourites, along with the Statue of Liberty's head (the only part Bartholdi had finished) and, most amazing of all, a machine that manufactured ice. With a main pavilion on the Champ de Mars almost a half-mile long, the French government had spared no expense; after the traumas of 1870–71, it was imperative to show the world that France was back on its feet.

Progress was the religion of the 19th century, and the World Fairs were its holy shrines. They were the ultimate spectacle, combining technology, nationalistic pageantry, art and music, fantasy architecture, fashion and exoticism, business and

---

the headquarters of the squabbling UN cultural agency is in the shape of a big Y perched on stilts. Usually no one cares if you want to poke around in the lobbies to see the works by Picasso, Arp, Le Corbusier and Giacometti among others. At the east end there's a quiet Japanese garden by Noguchi; at the west, along Avenue de Suffren, there's a curious trapezoidal Assembly Hall, pleated like a concrete accordion, as well as a clanking mobile by Alexander Calder, a monumental *Figure en repos* by Henry Moore and two walls by Miró.

Village Suisse K15–L14

78 Av de Suffren/54 Av de La Motte-Picquet; métro La Motte-Picquet-Grenelle. Open Thurs–Mon 10.30–7.

To the north of UNESCO, up Avenue de Suffren, the Village Suisse was a favourite kitsch attraction in the 1900 Exhibition. Now enlarged, it holds a large collection of antiques dealers.

Musée du Quai Branly K12–L11

15 Rue Jean-Baptiste Berlier, t 01 56 61 70 00, w www.quaibranly.fr. RER Place de l'Alma.

This museum, due to open in 2006 on a site overlooking the Seine near the Eiffel Tower, has raised great expectations. The architect is Jean Nouvel, whose other Parisian projects include the Fondation Cartier and the Institut du Monde Arabe. The museum will be built on stilts, with colourful protrusions bulging out from its flanks and a

pleasure. The Expositions offered a glimpse of a richer, faster future, full of colour and light and delightful mechanical toys. The one in 1889 was bigger still, drawing 32 million visitors. Queen Victoria boycotted this one, as did many other monarchs – it commemorated the centenary of the Revolution. Later, they regretted missing it. The star was the Eiffel Tower, and to match the Tower, engineers drilled a thousand-foot well into the Trocadéro gardens; visitors went down in elevators to the mysterious quarries and tunnels of underground Paris.

The city's decision to hold a fair in 1900 was announced only two years later, in the hopes of undermining any attempts by hated Berlin to try to upstage Paris with its own fair. The 1900 version was the height of the phenomenon – no Fair before or since made so much money. Over the main gate, a voluptuous naked statue of the Fairy Electricity welcomed everyone in to a wonderland of technology: some of the first commercially available cars, a huge wall of constantly changing coloured electric lights, a 330ft version of that recent American invention, the Ferris wheel. The Tsar sent Eskimos and Cossacks; the English sent the Prince of Wales.

Paris missed its date with 1911, but the 1925 Exposition des Arts Décoratifs proved a fitting showcase for the creative Paris of the 1920s – and gave the world the term 'Art Deco'. In 1931 the government sponsored a lavish Exposition Coloniale, a celebration of imperialism in the Bois de Vincennes, which included a replica of the Angkor Wat temple in Cambodia.

Parisian Exhibitionism went out with a whimper in 1937, a half-hearted affair doomed by the malaise of the times and infighting between the Popular Front government and its rightist enemies. But crowds came to see television, Picasso's *Guernica*, Georges Simenon in a glass cage cranking out an Inspector Maigret detective novel in a week, and the Pavilion of Asbestos, the Wonder Mineral, where visitors were invited to immerse themselves in a roomful of the stuff.

The myth of Progress, and the Parisian urge to show off, would never be the same. Paris hasn't tried one since, and the other postwar Expositions around the world have all been notably lacking in inspiration – where Paris a century ago created the Eiffel Tower for a centrepiece, in 1992 Seville could offer only a big orange.

---

restaurant at the top. The gardens are to be designed by Gilles Clement, who co-designed the Parc André Citroën.

The new museum will tackle the art and civilizations of Africa, Asia, Oceania and the Americas, with collections being redistributed from the Musée de l'Homme (*see* p.142) and the Musée des Arts d'Afrique et d'Océanie (*see* p.268).

TROCADÉRO AND MUSEUMS ALONG THE NORTH BANK

The main feature of the Place du Trocadéro is the superb view from the courtyard of the Palais de Chaillot across the river and to the south. Note the alignment: from Foch's nose (the Field Marshal was supremo of the Allied forces in 1918; his statue is in the centre of the Place), exactly between the ears of his horse, geometrically up the cracks in the middle of the courtyard, through the centre of the fountains below, unerringly down the middle of Pont d'Iéna, precisely between the legs of the Eiffel Tower, lined up with the centre of the little lake in the very mid-point of the Champ de Mars, between the ears of another horse, this one carrying Joffre (French commander in 1914 and victor of the Marne), and finally up to the pinnacle of the flag pole on top of the roof of the École Militaire.

By standing on the lower level of the upper terrace of the courtyard, you can manoeuvre the Tour Montparnasse in behind the left legs of the Tour Eiffel and make that black monstrosity disappear from view completely.

The name Trocadéro is derived from the name of a fort near Cádiz captured by the French in 1823, part of a campaign that helped to restore a diehard reactionary government in recently democratic Spain. The gardens stretching down to the Seine were laid out for the 1878 fair and restored in 1937; today they are home to a 1900s carrousel and the fattest, most complacent colony of stray cats in all Paris.

Palais de Chaillot H12–I11

*17 Place du Trocadéro; **métro** Trocadéro.*

The palace is one of the legacies of the very last World Fairs, the 1937 Paris Exposition Universelle (*see* 'The Compulsive Exhibitionist' on the previous page). The giant sententious epigrams in gold letters wrapped around the building were composed by Paul Valéry, and defy any meaningful translation. Today, the Palais de Chaillot provides a home for four museums, along with a theatre.

Musée National des Monuments Français I11

*In the east wing, **t** 01 44 05 39 10.*

Viollet-le-Duc had the idea of creating a central collection of exact, lifesize copies of France's finest architectural features, sculptures and mural paintings from the early Romanesque period to the 19th century. The result was first exhibited at the 1889 World Fair; over the years the collection has grown to 2,000 replicas, all arranged to help you study the evolution of French art and architecture.

The redevelopment taking place at the time of writing will expand the collection into the whole wing; the Musée du Cinéma, which has been closed since a fire in 1997, will reopen in the Rue de Bercy (*see* p.270) in late 2004.

Musée de l'Homme H–I11

*In the west wing, **t** 01 44 05 72 72. **Open** Wed–Mon 9.45–5.15, closed hols; **adm** €3.*

This once excellent anthropology museum, which opened the year after the 1937 World Fair, offers lots of dusty display cases and long explanations in French of things you never dreamed existed. Due to vast reorganisation of Paris's museums, much of the ehnology collection (the most interesting in the museum) is collecting dust in some warehouse en route to the Musée du Quai Branly (*see* p.140). The prehistoric and human biology sections are still open, while the temporary exhibitions can be fun. There's also a good restaurant too, Le Totem (*see* p.136).

Musée de la Marine H12–I11

*In the west wing, **t** 01 53 65 69 53, **w** www.musee-marine.fr. **Open** Wed–Mon 10–5.50, closed 1 Jan, 1 May and 25 Dec; **adm** €7; guided tours for children and deaf/blind visitors on reservation. Wheelchair access.*

Haughty Brits may turn a blind eye, like Nelson, but France has its own proud tradition on the sea, and you'll get an extra helping of it here. As you might expect, gloriously detailed model ships make up the bulk of the exhibits: Cousteau's *Calypso*, the carrier *Clemenceau*, pride of the modern French fleet, a room-sized 120-gun, *L'Océan*, from Napoleon's time, and on and on. Historical reconstructions enable you to see how an ancient Roman galley or a Renaissance galleass looked and worked. There are carved wooden figureheads, entire ships, such as Napoleon's gilded state barge of 1810, Joseph Vernet's 18th-century series of paintings on the ports of France, and another series Louis XVIII had commissioned on the naval battles of the War of American Independence. Don't miss the collection of navigational instruments, and numerous compasses, all pointing in different directions.

A restoration programme is currently under way, to be completed in 2005; the museum will remain open throughout.

Cinémathèque I11

7 Av Albert-de-Mun; t 01 56 26 01 01 for recorded programme (in French), or consult Pariscope.

A cinema showing vintage films which will move to Bercy (*see* p.269) along with the Musée du Cinéma.

Théâtre National de Chaillot I11

1 Place du Trocadéro, t 01 53 65 30 00, w www.theatre-chaillot.fr.

The legendary actor and director Jean Vilar, who ran this famous subsidized theatre (formerly known as Théâtre National Populaire, or TNP) in the 1950s, opened it to new audiences by providing cheap tickets and subscriptions. Today it has one large auditorium and two studio-style venues, where the classics and new plays are performed by stars of the stage and screen. There's a restaurant, and often pre-show music in the foyer.

Musée National des Arts Asiatiques-Guimet (Musée Guimet) J10

19 Av d'Iéna, t 01 56 52 53 00, w www.museeguimet.fr; métro Iéna; wheelchair access. Open Wed–Mon 10–6, Sun 10–4, last tickets 5.30; adm €5.50, free on 1st Sun of the month, free audioguide. Restaurant t 01 56 52 54 18, lunch menus €14 and €17.

Founded in 1879 by an industrialist from Lyon, Émile Guimet, this is one of the world's richest collections of art from India, China, Japan, Indochina, Indonesia and Central Asia. The collection of Khmer art from the 8th century to the mid-12th (the period of Angkor Wat and meditative smiles) is the best outside Cambodia. There are magnificent bronzes and shadow puppets from Java, paintings from Nepal and Tibet, Chinese ivories from as far back as the 17th century BC and a superb collection of lacquerware. Masterpieces from India include the torso of the *King Serpent of Mathoura* (2nd century AD) and a *Cosmic Dance of Shiva*.

The fascinating Salle Hackin proves ancient commercial and artistic links between East and West in Hellenistic times, producing some charming, sensual works – *Préparatifs du grand départ*. On the second floor of the museum are works from Japan (a 17th-century screen showing the arrival of the Portuguese) and a 3rd-century Korean crown. The first, second and third floors house a collection of Chinese ceramics, paintings, calligraphy and decorative arts from Ancient China up to the Qinq dynasty.

The **Panthéon** next door (*same ticket and hours as the museum*) holds Guimet's unique collection of Buddhas and figures of the Six Hierarchies from Japan and China, dating back to the 6th century. Afterwards, you can put your feet up in the peaceful Japanese garden in the back.

Musée de la Mode et du Costume Palais Galliera K10

10 Av Pierre 1er de Serbie, t 01 56 52 86 00; métro Iéna or Alma-Marceau. Open for exhibitions only Tues–Sun 10–6; adm €7.

The pseudo-Italian Renaissance Palais Galliera (1894) was built to house the 17th-century Italian art that the Duchess of Galliera meant to donate to Paris, until she changed her mind and gave it to Genoa instead. Paris did get the palace, however. Today, it's the snooty municipal museum of fashion, alternating a permanent collection with exhibitions. Because of space and the fragility of its 16,000-piece collection, the museum devotes itself to two exhibitions a year, by designer, period or theme.

Palais de Tokyo K10–11

11 Av du Président-Wilson, t 01 53 67 40 00, w www.palaisdetokyo; métro Iéna or Alma-Marceau. For opening hours, see individual museums.

Like the Palais de Chaillot, this is a relic of the 1937 Fair; the similarities don't end there: it too houses museums.

Musée d'Art Moderne de la Ville de Paris K10–11

*In the east wing. **Open** Tues–Sun 10–5.45 for the permanent collection, Tues–Fri 10–6 and Sat–Sun 10–7 for temporary exhibitions; **adm** €4.50, free adm to permanent collection Sun 10–1, extra charge for temporary exhibitions. Wheelchair access on ground floor only.*

There's a small permanent collection of works from Matisse onwards, as well as changing exhibitions, usually on contemporary artists. The café has an outside terrace with a view of the Eiffel Tower.

Site de Création Contemporaine K10–11

*In the west wing, entrance at 2 Rue de la Manutention, **t** 01 47 23 54 01, **w** www.palais detokyo.com. **Open** Tues–Sun 12–12; **adm** €6, free 1st Sun of month.*

This new exhibition space for contemporary art opened in the Palais de Tokyo in 2002. It features a changing programme of temporary exhibitions covering art, video, music, fashion, etc. by French and international artists. It also serves as a lively forum for discussion and innovation, and hosts lectures, concerts and fashion shows. Due to lack of funds, the building has been only partly restored; cement stairs lie naked, surfaces are bare and cracked, and entrances appear to have been punched through the walls by giant demolition balls. A shop, restaurant and bar encourage visitors to linger well into the night.

Place de l'Alma L10

***Métro** Alma-Marceau.*

To the east of the Palais de Tokyo, Avenue du Président-Wilson extends to Place de l'Alma, by the bridge of the same name. It was underneath this square that Diana Princess of Wales was killed in 1997. A previously ignored monument, a reproduction of the flame from the Statue of Liberty standing over the site, has become a memorial for spontaneous public sentiment.

The bridge is the launch point for one of the main *bateau-mouche* companies offering boat rides along the Seine (*see* pp.67–8).

Opéra and
Palais Royal

1 Lunch

Les Noces de Jeannette, *14 Rue Favart,*
t 01 42 96 36 89; métro Richelieu-Drouot.
Open *daily 12–1.30 (last orders) and 7–9
(last orders).* **Moderate.** A re-minimalized
classic with some wonderful dishes.

2 Tea and Cakes

A Priori Thé, *36 Galerie Vivienne; métro
Bourse.* **Open** *Mon–Fri 9–6, Sat 12–6.30, Sun
12.30–6.30.* English tea and cheesecake under
the glass-roofed *passage*.

3 Drinks

Harry's Bar, *5 Rue Daunou; métro Opéra.*
Open *daily 10.30am–4am.* Since 1911 the
most famous American bar in Paris.

Opéra and
Palais Royal

The area around the Opéra was to the Paris
of the early 19th century what the Champs-
Elysées would be later in the century: the
city's showcase and playground of the élite.
It's still the home of all luxury, the main
source of what the French call *articles de
Paris*; here you'll find the gilded fashion
houses and the jewellers whose names are
known around the galaxy and beyond.

Its proximity to the Louvre meant that
this corner of town attracted monumental
projects from three of France's most
unpleasant despots: Louis XIV's Place
Vendôme, Napoleon's self-memorial that
became the Madeleine, and Little Napoleon's
incomparable Opéra. These men, and the
style of the buildings they left behind, set
the tone for the area, which is a little stuffy,
a little faded, more than a little over the top
and eternally, unashamedly Parisian. It's a
must if you're looking forward to window-
shopping at places such as Pierre Cardin.

It offers a contrast to Palais Royal and the
area to the north of it, the most unabashedly
retro quarter of Paris. Dusty, dignified, quiet
and very obsolete in a number of unimpor-
tant ways, it hasn't really been popular with

Parisians or tourists or anybody else since
the 1830s. But exploring this area and its
cluster of *passages* (*see* the walk on
pp.276–9) may turn up some of Paris' most
unexpected delights: it's all about old books,
pretty things and good architecture; in other
words, the elements of civilization.

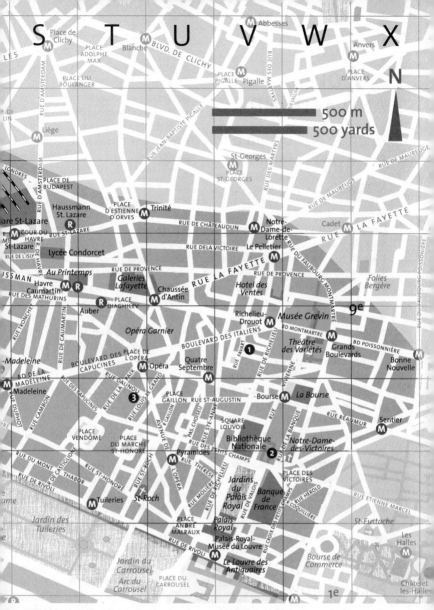

Highlights

Couples' City: Shopping for delicacies in Place de la Madeleine, p.151

Parisian's City: Dress up to the nines and prowl the Faubourg St-Honoré, p.151

Peace and Quiet: The reading room in the Bibliothèque Nationale and the Cabinet des Médailles, p.156

Paris des Artistes: Inside the Opéra, where Degas and Chagall painted, p.149

Grand Siècle Paris: Hardouin-Mansart's elegant Place Vendôme, p.152

Gritty City: No grit, but plenty of dust in the Musée Grevin, p.150

THE OPÉRA AND AROUND

Avenue de l'Opéra and Place de l'Opéra T8–U10

Métro *Opéra.*

The **Avenue de l'Opéra**, sloping up from the Louvre, was cut by Baron Haussmann in the 1860s to give the Opéra a proper setting; originally it was called Avenue Napoléon. There are no trees, thanks to Charles Garnier, who insisted they would spoil the view of his masterpiece, but its drabness has not prevented it from becoming one of the major tourist strips of Paris, with travel shops predominating. Then there's Harry's New York Bar, just around the corner on Rue Daunou, which never lets anyone forget it is the 'birthplace of the Bloody Mary' or that Hemingway frequently got stewed here; the grandpa of all the world's 'Harry's Bars' has been here since 1911.

The Japanese have moved in on the east side in a big way, especially Rue Ste-Anne, which is lined with oriental restaurants, shops and private clubs.

Place de l'Opéra was one of the status addresses of late 19th-century Paris; it was also the site of the original Grand Hôtel, opened for the World Fair of 1867.

Opéra de Paris-Palais Garnier T8

Place de l'Opéra, t 01 40 01 22 63, w www.opera-de-paris.fr; métro Opéra, RER Auber. Open (museum) daily 10–5, last admission 4.30, restricted access when matinées or special events are held, closed hols; adm €6; tours in English Saturday at 12.30 (get there at 12.15), 90mins, €10. Tickets for shows t 08 36 69 78 68 or from box office Mon–Sat 11–6.30 and 45mins before performance.

The supreme monument of the Second Empire was conceived in 1858, after Napoleon III was leaving a slightly more intimate theatre and one of the rabble got close enough to try to assassinate him. A competition was organized for a new Opéra, and the plan chosen was the largest, submitted by a fashionable young architect named Charles Garnier. After winning the competition, Garnier still had to convince a sceptical Napoleon and Eugénie. Asked what style his work was supposed to be, the architect replied: 'It is no style. Not Greek or Roman; it is the style of Napoleon III.' That won the Emperor over immediately (and he reportedly added: 'Don't worry about my wife; she doesn't understand anything').

It took 14 years to build, partly because of the massive foundations that were necessary – the first excavations revealed a subterranean lake on the site. Also, work was interrupted by the Prussian siege and the Commune. After the unfinished building was taken by the Versailles troops, some dozens of Communards were massacred among the foundations and covered up; bodies are still occasionally found during repair work.

Finally opened in 1875, three years after Napoleon's death, the biggest and most sumptuous theatre in the world soon passed into legend, much of it due to Gaston Leroux's novel *Le Fantôme de l'Opéra*, about a mad engineer named Erik who worked on the foundations and sneaked off to build himself an underground palace on the lake. There were controversies, such as the one over Carpeaux's flagrant statuary outside. The artist's rivals pretended to be shocked (naked women, in Paris!) and threw bottles of ink at them. Anarchists plotted to blow the place up, and everyone whispered about the famous Opéra masked balls ('great festivals of pederasty', one writer called them). In 1896 one of the giant chandeliers fell on the audience during the climax of Faust; miraculously only one woman was killed, and the morning headlines screamed '200,000 Kilos on the Head of a Concierge!'

Envied and copied throughout the world, this building contributed much to the transformation of opera into the grand spectacle and social ritual it became in the Belle Époque, that world of top hats and lorgnettes designed for Groucho to tease Margaret Dumont, and for Harpo to drop sandbags on pompous oily tenors. It may have seemed that way to François Mitterrand, when in the 1980s he decided on the overtly political gesture of sentencing opera to the proletarian Bastille. Today the behemoth sits a bit forlorn, home only to its dance company, controversially run until a few years ago by the late Rudolf Nureyev. Major foreign ballets also call here, and occasionally there's even an opera.

Circumnavigating its vast bulk is an experience. Asked how one should consider his building, Garnier recommended 'silent awe'. Its very size prevents us from noticing its height – 224ft to the silly golden Apollo on top of the dome, enough height for a 17-storey building. On the western side, notice the double ramp for carriages up to the Imperial Box, meant to protect Napoleon III from those pesky assassins. Of the exterior embellishments, only Jean-Baptiste Carpeaux's allegory *La Danse* stands out, the second group from the right on the lower level of the façade. This is a copy (by Jean-Paul Belmondo's dad, like many others in Paris); the original, still with traces of ink on it, can be seen in the Musée d'Orsay.

The Interior

The inside is just as impressive, awash with gold leaf, frescoes, mosaics and scores of different varieties of precious stone, from Swedish marble to Algerian onyx. Amazingly, the 'world's biggest theatre' seats only some 2,100 people; the rest of the space is given over to grand lobbies and marble staircases dripping with more mythological statuary, along with the rooms of the French national dance academy (where Degas painted many of his pretty ballerinas). The highlight of the tour may be the hall itself, with its ceiling (1964) painted by Marc Chagall; the nine scenes, lovely if perhaps incongruous in this setting, are inspired by some of the artist's favourite operas and ballets.

The **Musée de l'Opéra** is in the Imperial Pavilion; it has a collection of memorabilia and art, including a portrait of Wagner by Renoir.

The Grands Boulevards R9–W8

To the east and west of Place de l'Opéra stretch the Grands Boulevards: **de la Madeleine**, **des Capucines**, **des Italiens** and **Montmartre**, part of Haussman's great chain of thoroughfares extending east to Place de la République. A century ago these were the brightest promenades of Paris, home of all the famous cafés and restaurants. Today the glamour is gone but the streets are crowded just the same; they're a good place to take in a movie – and have been since the world's first public film show was put on by the Lumière brothers at No.14 Boulevard des Capucines, on 28 December 1895. (Of the 22 punters who attended, only five thought that moving pictures had any future; one of the five was to become the first great French director, Georges Méliès).

Boulevard Haussmann, to the north of the Opéra, is one of Paris' liveliest shopping districts, where the managers still send hucksters out on to the street to demonstrate vegetable choppers and dab cologne on the ladies. Down the street to the west you will see **Au Printemps**, a grand old department store (1889–1911); the lovely cupolas, a Paris landmark, are all that remain of a once-spectacular building now thoroughly homogenized (take the escalator to the rooftop café for a fine view).

But directly in front of you is **Galeries Lafayette** (1900), which has been more fortunate. Have a look inside for the wonderful glass dome and Art Nouveau details. Once there was a spectacular grand staircase from the same era. According to the girls in the perfume department, the management ripped it out almost overnight when they heard the city was considering a preservation law that would force them to keep it.

Musée Grévin W8

*10 Bd Montmartre, t 01 47 70 85 05, w www.
musee-grevin.com; métro Grands Boulevards;
wheelchair access. Open Mon–Fri 10–5.30,
Sat–Sun 10–6, last admission 6; adm €15.*

The Musée Grévin now contains more than 300 wax figures. New additions to the roll of honour include the French actor Jean Reno (*Subway*, *Le Grand Bleu*, *Léon*), Victor Hugo and Esmeralda, and British faces such as Sean Connery and Naomi Campbell.

The Grévin occupies an old theatre lobby, and the delicious 19th-century brass-and-upholstery setting quite upstages the wax dummies, which aren't that lifelike anyhow.

Maybe the admission is so high because in the past they have had problems protecting the exhibits. Excited Frenchmen are constantly molesting dummies of politicians, voodoo worshippers stick pins in pop singers, and a few years back the Basque ETA admitted knocking off King Juan Carlos' head in a daring daylight *attentat*. The most recent outrage came when celebrity chef Paul Bocuse went missing. Either he took a walk, or he's holding the dishcloths in a rival's kitchen.

Towards Gare St-Lazare R6–S7

Northwest of the Opéra, Rue du Havre leads up to Gare St-Lazare, passing the **Lycée Condorcet** (1783), one of the purest and finest works of *ancien régime* neoclassicism. The architect, Alexandre-Théodore Brongniart, went on to design the Bourse 25 years later. Like Perrault's Louvre façade, this is one of the key works in defining the French manner: classical forms reinterpreted in original arrangements, austerity lightened by a small dose of sculptural ornament, and an emphasis on cornices and rooflines. It may seem hard to believe, but this elegant building was originally a Capuchin monastery. It became an élite *lycée* under Napoleon in 1804; alumni include Proust and Verlaine.

The **Gare St-Lazare** (1889) itself is a good example of 19th-century cultural schizophrenia: all efficiency, iron and glass inside with a 17th-century-style façade pasted on to make it respectable. Don't miss Arman's witty sculpture in front of the station, a column of old suitcases bronzed and welded together, called *Consigné à Vie*.

LA MADELEINE AND FAUBOURG ST-HONORÉ

La Madeleine R8

*Place de la Madeleine, t 01 44 51 69 00;
métro Madeleine. Open Mon–Sat 8.30–7,
Sun 7.30–7, hols 9–7, closed some hols and
some Suns 1.30–3.30. For information on
concerts call the number above, or see
l'Officiel or Pariscope.*

The façades of Rue Royale, leading up to La Madeleine, formed part of architect Gabriel's overall scheme for the north side of what was then Place Louis XV – now Place de la Concorde (*see* pp.112–3). To close the street vista, he provided for a building at the end of the street, which eventually became **La Madeleine**.

Construction was begun in 1764, but this church was fated to see many changes before its completion. The death of the architect in 1777 occasioned a complete rethink; the new man opted for a neoclassical Greek cross plan, imitating Soufflot's Panthéon (*see* pp.228–9). It was only a quarter finished by 1792, when the revolutionary government pondered over a new use for the project – perhaps the seat of the National Assembly, the Banque de France or the National Library. But Napoleon knew what was best – a Temple of Glory, dedicated to himself and his Grand Army.

The previous plans were scrapped, the foundations razed, and in 1806 architect Barthélemy Vignon came up with an imitation Greek temple. Napoleonic effi-ciency got the colonnades up in nine years, but once more, political change intervened; after 1815 the restored Bourbons decided to make it a church after all. The exterior was kept as Vignon planned it, not a proper Greek temple, more the Romantic souvenir of one. The arrangement of the columns, about which the ancients were very particular, follows no conventional pattern; but it's a fine building just the same. The reliefs on the pediments and the Corinthian capitals are carved with a grace and precision that the French had been working towards for two centuries.

After the chilly perfection of the Madeleine's exterior, the inside comes as a surprise: windowless and overdecorated, creamy and gloomy, more like a late Baroque Italian church – or ballroom. The rustic cane chairs contrast with the gilded Corinthian columns and walls covered with a dozen varieties of expensive marble, in imitation of the Pantheon in Rome. The combined efforts of its 19th-century artists will never convince you that this building, the scene of Paris' high-society marriages and funerals, could possibly have anything whatsoever to do with the Christian religion. The crowning touch, near the entrance, is an intrusive glass booth with a sign reading 'Priest on Duty' in five languages. There he sits, at a desk with a telephone, reading the newspaper.

Place de la Madeleine R9–S8

Métro *Madeleine.*

The square surrounding the church is one of Paris' gourmet paradises, with famous restaurants such as Lucas Carton and many of the city's finest food shops, all on the north side: small places specializing in caviar (No.17) or truffles (No.19), the Confiserie Tanrade, Hédiard and the incredible Magasins Fauchon, with just about anything you could imagine. The window displays here are entirely over the top – delicacies that go for over €150 a kilo, and all-too-beautiful

plates in gelatine that have the appearance of embalmed food. The place also has a small but cheerful **flower market** (*open Mon–Sat 8–7*), the poshest public toilets in Paris (well worth a visit) and the *kiosque-théâtre*, where you can get cheap tickets for most of the plays in town.

Chapelle Expiatoire R7

29 Rue Pasquier, Square Louis XVI, t 01 44 32 18 00; métro St-Augustin. Open Thurs–Sat 1–5, closed hols; adm €2.50.

During the Restoration, Louis XVIII had this dolorous **chapel**, north of the Madeleine, built to the memory of his brother, Louis XVI. Previously, the site had been the cemetery of the Madeleine, where the royal family and some 3,000 other victims of the Terror had been buried in unmarked graves. Most are still somewhere under the grass, including Charlotte Corday and Philippe-Égalité, to whom there are small memorials, as well as Danton, Hébert, the Desmoulins and Madame du Barry. The royal family was exhumed and rested for a short time in the chapel before being removed to St-Denis. If it really was them, that is. They were sure about Marie-Antoinette (they recognized her knickers) but the body they claimed as Louis XVI was just a guess; many believed it was really a vile toady of Robespierre's named Henriot, one of the men most responsible for Louis' execution.

Rue du Faubourg-St-Honoré and Rue St-Honoré K6–X12

Rue du Faubourg-St-Honoré, running west off Rue Royale just south of the Madeleine, is another big-name, window-shopping street. On the other side, Rue St-Honoré continues east as far as the Palais Royal. This street hasn't always been so posh: in the 1790s, it was the radical hotspot of Paris: on the corner of Rue du Marché-St-Honoré stood the convent that became the chief nest of radical revolutionary intriguers – the Jacobin Club.

As well as shops, the Faubourg-St-Honoré is thick with *les flics*, charged with protecting the British Embassy at No.39 (built for Napoleon's tart of a sister, Pauline Borghese), as well as the Americans and the Japanese, not to mention the President of France, who resides under the hundred chandeliers of the **Palais de l'Elysée** (1718). Napoleon signed his abdication here in 1815, and Napoleon III lived here from his election in 1849 until he decided to make himself Emperor two years later. The *hôtel* has been the official residence of the head of state since 1873.

Place Vendôme S–T9

Métro Madeleine or Opéra.

The second of Louis XIV's 'royal squares', after Place des Victoires (*see* p.156), was laid out in 1699 by the same architect, Jules Hardouin-Mansart. The king's sycophants were at first divided between calling it 'Place Louis le Grand' or 'Place des Conquêtes', but posterity settled the issue by giving it the familiar name of a *hôtel* that had previously occupied the site, that of the Duc de Vendôme (one of Henri IV's bastards). The most satisfactory of all 17th-century French attempts at urban design, the square seems the utter antithesis of a building like the Opéra – though both were built to impress. Here, however, Hardouin-Mansart does it with absolute decorum. Situated midway between the Madeleine and the Opéra, only two streets lead into the square, which was conceived as a sort of enclosed urban parlour for the nobility. Balls were sometimes held in it, but cafés or anything else that would encourage street life or spontaneity were forbidden.

Originally, the square was to house embassies and academies, but the final plan proposed the present octagon of eight mansions, with uniform façades, and an equestrian statue of – guess who – in the centre. From the start, the buildings were occupied by the wealthiest bankers; later residents included John Law and Chopin (who died at No.12). Today the square still has a not-too-discreet aroma of money about it, home as it is to the Ritz Hotel, Cartier, Van Cleef & Arpels and a fleet of other carriage-trade jewellers who never put prices in the window displays. Shed a tear at No.12 when you pass by, not only for Chopin but for the 200-year-old jewellery house of Chaumet. In a wonderful moral tale of the 1980s this family firm went spectacularly bust, partly from the Chaumet brothers' 18th-century approach to book-keeping, but mostly from extending credit to a clientele of jet-set deadbeats that included Arab princesses and third-world dictators. The brothers, pious Catholics both, trusted until the last minute, then tried some charmingly inept financial prestidigitation to cover up the losses. When the end came, they assumed personal responsibility and went off to the calaboose in majestic silence. A New York conglomerate owns the place now.

Leading north from the square is **Rue de la Paix**, which has been a swank shopping street ever since it was laid out in 1806. The first of the great couturiers, Englishman Charles Worth, opened his house at No.7 in 1858, just in time for the conspicuous consumption orgy of the Second Empire. Fashion houses have favoured this area ever since.

In the centre of the square, where Louis' statue presided before the revolutionaries melted it down to make cannons, is the **Vendôme Column**. Nothing could more eloquently capture the philistine emptiness of the first Napoleon's reign than this rather elegant bronze abomination. The Louis XIV statue here had been dressed as a Roman emperor, but Napoleon's men came up with something even better, a precise copy of Trajan's Column in Rome. Napoleon himself can be seen in several places on the spiralling reliefs, beating everyone's armies, dedicating bridges and bestowing on grateful conquered helots the benefits of French civilization and the metric system. Throughout the 19th century, the statue of the Emperor

Artistic Licence

The entire Vendôme column is actually a copy of a copy, thanks to the Communards of 1871, and in particular Gustave Courbet. As artistic director of the Commune, the painter led the campaign to destroy this symbol of blind militarism – he also complained that it 'offended him aesthetically'. The demolition was made into a public festival, on 16 May, and the crowds and soldiers fought over the bronze scraps for souvenirs. A year later, as one of the final ironies of the Communal comedy, a republican government ordered it rebuilt and made an example of Courbet by sentencing him to prison for six months and billing him 250,000 francs for the reconstruction; the painter chose exile in Switzerland.

at the top was a weather-clock marking changes in French politics. The original, with Napoleon in a toga like Louis, was replaced during the restoration with a Bourbon lily. Louis-Philippe put up a new Napoleon in a more modest military uniform; you can see it today in the Invalides. Napoleon III put his uncle back in Roman gear; a copy of that is what you see today (see 'Artistic Licence').

St-Roch T10

24 Rue St-Roch, t 01 42 44 13 28; métro Pyramides or Tuileries. Open for tours Mon–Fri 1–5; for info about concerts t 01 42 44 13 26.

There were outbreaks of plague in France as late as the 17th century; to be on the safe side, Parisians finally decided to build a church to St Roch, the medieval plague saint from Montpellier. Louis XIV helped lay the cornerstone in 1653, but with increasing financial problems work on this low-priority project ground to a halt. Finished in the 18th century, thanks to funds from a lottery and a big gift from banker John Law (see p.171), St-Roch became one of the society churches of Paris. Famous folk buried here include Diderot, Le Nôtre and Corneille.

The church had the misfortune to be in the way of the final act of the French Revolution. On the 13th of Vendémiaire, l'An 6 (5 October 1795), the Royalists of Paris rose in revolt against the new constitution of the Directory. A column of rebels was marching down Rue St-Honoré on its way to the Tuileries, when it was intercepted by a loyal force commanded by General Napoleon Bonaparte. Napoleon, who always believed in massed artillery, had had the presence of mind to bring some along. Firing point-blank into the rebels, he won the day and made a name for himself in Paris (he had already negotiated his price for saving the Republic – the command of the Army of Italy that was to be his stepping-stone to power). The results of his work on that day can still be read, just barely, in St-Roch's pockmarked façade (which is currently undergoing extensive restoration).

Inside, it's just another overblown and insincere church of the Age of the Louies. Like the goods in the designer shops that infest the quarter, the church displays its 'SR' monogram everywhere, as if it were a trademark. The best part is the frothy Lady Chapel behind the altar, a large circular work with a pleasing unity of equally dubious 18th-century painting, sculpture and glass. On the right, note the tomb of Admiral de Grasse, who helped make American independence possible by trapping the British at Yorktown.

PALAIS ROYAL AND AROUND

Palais Royal U11–V10

Métro Palais Royal-Musée du Louvre.

Originally it was the Palais du Cardinal. Richelieu built it for himself, beginning in 1629; perhaps he was fed up with being kept awake at night by duellists under his window in Place des Vosges (see pp.183–4). Naturally he willed it to the king, whose money he was playing with, long before his death in 1642. Anne of Austria and four-year-old Louis XIV moved in soon after, but left for the more defensible Louvre when the uprising of the Fronde got hot. Louis' childhood memory of the danger to his life made him hate the place, and he gave it to his brother Philippe, Duke of Orléans (usually known simply as 'Monsieur'); the palace stayed in his family until the Revolution.

Much rebuilt since Richelieu's time, the Palais Royal currently houses the Conseil d'État, which advises on proposed laws and serves as an appeal court for administrative decisions.

Théâtre-Français U11

The theatre was attached to the Palais Royal complex in 1786 and ever since it has been home to the **Comédie-Française**, the company founded by Louis XIV out of Molière's old troupe. Louis' motives were predictably dishonourable; the king was much less interested in supporting the theatre than having it under his thumb. All French rulers until the 1970s upheld the tradition, keeping the Comédie not merely state-funded but state-controlled.

In the lobby, Houdon's famous statue of Voltaire is displayed along with the chair on which Molière died – after collapsing on stage, ironically playing the lead in his *Le Malade Imaginaire* in the Palais Royal's original theatre.

Cour d'Honneur U1–V12

Passing under the arch between the theatre and the palace you enter the Cour d'Honneur. In 1986 a sculptor named Daniel Buren was permitted to transform this space into an abstract ensemble of grey, striped columns, making it look somewhat like a factory roof. Considerable controversy has been aroused by these concrete stumps and the equally incongruous big steel balls on the court's two fountains. The state realized its folly and tried to stop the Frankenstein they had commissioned – but too late. Buren was nobody's fool, and his lawyers got the courts to affirm 'the artist's right to finish his work'. No one has a good word for it, but there are no plans for its removal. To the right is the last remaining bit of Richelieu's

original palace, decorated with prows of ships, reminding us that the cardinal was, among other things, Minister of the Navy.

Jardin du Palais Royal V10

Open April and May 7am–10.15pm, June–Aug 7am–11pm, Sept 7am–9.30pm, Oct–Mar 7.30am–8.30pm; no dogs.

The gardens lie just beyond the Cour d'Honneur. The last descendant of 'Monsieur', who was also Duke of Orléans, the notorious 'Philippe-Égalité' of Revolutionary fame (*see* p.33), had in 1781 hit on the idea of cutting down his enormous debts by selling off part of the gardens for building lots. His architects chopped the greenery down by a third, and enclosed it with an arcaded quadrangle of terraced houses, à la Place des Vosges. The new development was an immediate success, if not entirely as respectable as its predecessor in the Marais. Under the arcades, several cafés soon opened (Caribbean rum, a novelty in Paris, was the trendy poison); gambling houses and bordellos thrived. The latter were quite refined establishments, fronting as hat shops or even furniture shops; one madam printed brochures showing the latest styles in beds, along with the 'rental prices' for each. Napoleon, arriving in Paris in 1787, got his first tumble here, like many lads from the provinces. The police couldn't do a thing about it. They could not, in fact, even enter the Palais grounds without the duke's permission – such were the privileges of princely families before 1789.

Ironically enough, this privilege helped make the Palais Royal gardens, and the cafés in its arcades, one of the birthplaces of the Revolution. Like the Tuileries, it was one of the bastions of the *nouvellistes*, or newsmongers. But in the Tuileries, as every Parisian knew, one talked about fashions and court gossip. You came here, among the 'unorganized and invisible empire' of free thought, the only opposition possible under *ancien régime* despotism, if you wanted to argue politics. Typically, the attack on the Bastille was spontaneously conceived here, when Camille Desmoulins jumped onto a café table and started talking, on the morning of 14 July. (And four years later, minus a day, Charlotte Corday stopped here to purchase a knife at No.177 on her way to see Marat.)

Under Napoleon, and for a long time after him, the Palais gardens continued to be Paris' public forum for vices, if no longer for political ideas. In 1814, under the occupation, the allied commanders (all except for the priggish Duke of Wellington) actually took up lodgings here. Parisians claim the amount fleeced from them at gambling was greater than the entire amount of war reparations levied against France; Prussian Field Marshal von Blücher, the real victor of Waterloo, lost a million francs in one night at the bezique table. Fashion and vice both moved to the Grands Boulevards after 1838, when Louis-Philippe closed the gambling houses; ironically enough, as Orléans heir, he owned the place. Later, because the Dukes of Orléans were pretenders to his throne, Napoleon III confiscated both the gardens and the palace, which had to be partially rebuilt after the Communards torched it in 1871.

Ever since, the garden has kept well out of the mainstream of popularity. The arcades that were once packed day and night now hold only a few quietly fascinating shops selling antiques, military models or recycled designer clothing from the 1950s. There is a rotating sculpture exhibition and a few restaurants, including the celebrated Grand Véfour at No.79, around since 1784 and still appointed with most of its original décor and furnishings.

The gardens themselves are well clipped and neat, a peaceful retreat. Hang around long enough and you may see a dignified, well-dressed gentleman with the white clown face of a Pierrot and pockets full of birdseed, who comes nearly every day. In an instant, the numerous sparrows of the gardens line up on a fence before him to do their tricks. With the panache and flourish of an orchestra conductor, he makes them sit on his fingers or spring in the air after the seed. Every few minutes, he will pull out a notebook and jot something down. 'There are a few of them I still do not know yet,' he explains.

Rue de Rivoli R10–BB13

The long, busy street of imposing buildings whose arcades are copied throughout the world runs south of the Palais Royal in a straight arrow from Place de la Concorde to the Marais. The part to the west was begun by Napoleon, who conceived it as a personal monument, a 'triumphal way' for military parades, to be bordered by arcades – the forerunner of the Grand Axe up the Champs-Elysées before the completion of the Arc de Triomphe. The east end of Rue de Rivoli, from the Hôtel de Ville and into the Marais, was only completed after 1848.

The only French branch of the stationer W. H. Smith, at the Concorde end (see p.360), is a good place to buy English books. A few doors down is the famous Salon de Thé Angelina, which is still known for serving the best hot chocolate in Paris.

The *Passages*

Paris' 19th-century glass-roofed arcades (also known as *galeries*), once the height of fashion, had fallen into disuse by the start of the 20th century, but in the 1970s several were restored and revived and now make charming places for a stroll. We suggest a route for a walk through the *passages* on pp.276–9.

Some of the most interesting *passages* are in the area north of the Palais Royal. Just south of the Banque de France is the *passage* where our walk starts, **Galerie Véro-Dodat** (V11–12), one of the oldest and prettiest. To the east of the Bibliothèque National is the **Galerie Vivienne** (V10–9), the smartest arcade, with a marble floor, an elegant café and expensive shops (Jean-Paul Gaultier has an outlet here).

Finally, up near the Grands Boulevards is the **Passage de Panoramas** (W8), actually a series of arcades which were among the first to be built.

Banque de France V9–W10

*39 Rue Croix des Petits Champs; **métro** Palais Royal-Musée du Louvre. Not accessible to tourists.*

In this huge monolithic building the national cent-pinchers work amidst gilt-edged 18th-century splendour; the blank façade, added after 1870, hides a palace that was built by François Mansart for La Vrillière, Louis XIII's secretary of state.

Place des Victoires W10

Métro *Bourse.*

The second of Paris''royal'squares (after Place des Vosges, although this one was a private development, not a royal command) was laid out by Hardouin-Mansart in 1685 to accommodate an equestrian statue of Louis XIV, commemorating his series of lesser victories against the Dutch and the annexation of the Franche-Comté. Like its predecessor, the piazza was planned as an intimate, enclosed public space. Hardouin-Mansart designed both the square and the uniform circle of buildings around it with no little skill; the proportions were related to each other and to provide the best sight lines for the bronze centrepiece (melted down in the Revolution; the present statue dates from 1822).

Over the last century, the Parisians have done their best to spoil the effect. Façades were altered, and in 1883 Rue Étienne-Marcel was cut through the Place, entirely wrecking its dignified and enclosed atmosphere. By the 1950s it had reached a nadir of tackiness, jammed with zipper wholesalers, news offices and advertising signs.

Lately there has been a clean-up; the place now attracts very expensive high-fashion shops – the sort that paint the mannequins silver or black – and has definitely found its way back.

Notre-Dame-des-Victoires W9

*Rue Notre-Dame, **t** 01 42 60 90 47; **métro** Bourse. **Open** daily 7.30–7.30.*

Begun in 1629 for the monastery of the Petits-Pères (now demolished), several well-known architects (Libéral Bruant among them) got their oar in on this church before the last roof tile was laid in 1740, resulting in a blasé work with the air of a mortuary chapel. The thousands of *ex-voto* plaques add to the effect – this active church is the destination for a pilgrimage to the Virgin Mary (but this may be ending; the shop across the street that sold the plaques has been replaced by a British clothes designer). Somehow, somewhere there might be a reader impassioned enough about 18th-century religious painting to appreciate Carle van Loo's seven scenes of the *Life of St Augustine* in the choir. The French think very highly of them.

Bibliothèque Nationale V9–10

*58 Rue de Richelieu (enter from Rue de Richelieu or Rue Vivienne), **t** 01 47 03 81 26, **w** www.bnf.fr; **métro** Bourse. **Open** Mon–Sat 9–6, closed hols. **Salle Labrouste** open Mon–Sat 10–7; adm free; guided tour 1st Tues of the month at 2.30 (€7; 90mins) – turn up or call **t** 01 47 03 86 87. **Cabinet des Médailles et Antiques**, **t** 01 47 03 81 10; open Mon–Sat 1–5, Sun 12–6; adm free. Temporary exhibitions are shown in Galeries Mazarine and Mansart.*

With some 13 million books, not to mention 15 million prints and photographs, and a few million miscellaneous manuscripts, pamphlets, maps and sound recordings, plus 24 shelf-miles of periodicals, the Bibliothèque Nationale claims to be the largest library in the world (in eight different buildings) and is the library of record for everything published in France. This original building is now called Richelieu to distinguish it from Tolbiac, the unofficial name for the huge new high-rise library complex in the 13e (*see* p.270).

The first inventory of a royal library comes from the 1370s; in those troubled times, the king only had a choice of some 900 books to toddle off to bed with. But they did let them pile up over the years. A decree of 1537 inaugurated the *dépôt légal*, the requirement that anyone publishing a book must send a copy to the king – they were less concerned with building the library than with making sure they had a look at anything that might be seditious. Louis XIV's minister, Colbert, put the library on a sound footing when he consolidated all the king's holdings in two adjacent *hôtels particuliers* he owned on Rue Vivienne. Now, after various additions and remodellings, the library occupies the entire block.

You can't use either of the facilities without a reader's card, but by all means do have a look inside at the old building. Through a big glass door, you can see one of the architectural masterpieces of Paris, the main **reading room**, the Salle Labrouste. Henri Labrouste had already pioneered the use of iron for a library hall at Ste-Geneviève; here, in 1863, he took the structural freedom that iron afforded to make an incredible flight of fancy. A few spindly columns with gilded capitals support the entire hall; nine intersecting domes soar high over the readers' heads, each with a glass oculus at its centre. This is architecture a century ahead of its time. Blending strangely well with the anachronistic décor – blue-green landscape murals, gilt trim and endless shelves of dusty leather-bound books – the total effect is unforgettable.

The **Cabinet des Médailles et Antiques**, occupying its own wing of the Bibliothèque complex, is an amazing little museum that not one visitor to Paris in a thousand has heard of, let alone seen. The collection, really the treasure-trove of the kings of France, goes back at least to Philippe-Auguste in the 12th century. Nationalized during the Revolution and combined with the confiscated church treasures of St-Denis and the Sainte-Chapelle, it contains the 1st-century AD *Camée de Sainte-Chapelle*, the biggest cameo ever made, showing Emperor Tiberius and Germanicus his son, and the Treasure of Berthouville, an impressive hoard of Gallo-Roman jewellery, to compare with Greek, Roman and Etruscan jewellery. Just as surprising are the Oriental items in the next room: a rock crystal cup *c.* AD 700 decorated with scenes of the legendary King Khusrau, and the exquisite Moorish sword of Boabdil, the last King of Granada.

There's more that glitters, including the splendidly barbaric Treasure of Childeric, with state-of-the-art Merovingian goldsmiths' work from the 5th century, as well as King Dagobert's throne. Coins, medals and commemorative medallions follow, in which the show is stolen by a fine collection from the Italian Renaissance, by the undisputed, all-time greatest master in this medium, Pisanello.

Now that all the books have been moved to Tolbiac, Richelieu has permanent exhibitions featuring manuscripts, maps and plans, music, seals and photographs, as well as the collection of medals and coins described above, which is being expanded. A National Institute for the History of Art is being formed, which will be located in the Salle Labrouste.

Behind the Bibliothèque, the Square Louvois is a little park with a pretty fountain (1844) allegorizing the 'Four Rivers of France': the Seine, Loire, Garonne and Saône; the last is an unusual choice, replacing the usual Rhône.

Palais de la Bourse W9

4 Place de la Bourse, t 01 49 27 55 55, w www.bourse-de-paris.fr; métro Bourse. Open to visitors by appt only; adm €8.50; tours last 90mins.

This pile of pretension was slain by the humble silicon chip in 1999, when traders' yells and finger signs were replaced with screens and buttons. No one seems to know what will become of the place (the security guard at the gate thinks it would make an original night club); at the moment it houses nothing more than a museum. After John Law (*see* p.171), modern capitalism had a bad name in France, and open stock trading was not organized until the opportunist free-for-all of Napoleon's time.

The Bourse (1808) is the masterpiece of neoclassicist Alexandre-Théodore Brongniart. The finely sculpted Corinthian colonnade, similar to that of the Madeleine (*see* pp.150–51), defines the structure; the building was carefully extended with two short, identical wings in 1907 to give it its cruciform shape. Also like the Madeleine, it gives a good idea of how Napoleon would have transformed Paris, had he won.

Bric-a-brac markets are held on the last Friday of each month in the square in front.

Beaubourg
and Les Halles

08

1 Lunch

Tonneaux des Halles, *28 Rue Montorgueil*, *t 01 42 33 36 19; métro Étienne-Marcel. Open Mon–Sat 8am–midnight, lunch 12–3, dinner 7.30–12.* **Moderate**. You'd think that the market porters were still around and about to crowd in through the door. The genuine article, friendly, chaotic and excellent.

2 Tea and Cakes

Au Père Tranquille, *16 Rue Pierre Lescot*, *t 01 45 08 00 34; métro Les Halles. Open daily 9am–midnight.* A large café opposite the Forum des Halles, with seats outside and a range of snacks and cakes.

3 Drinks

Le Sous Bock, *49 Rue St-Honoré, t 01 40 26 46 61; métro Châtelet. Open Mon–Sat 11am–5am.* Complicated cocktails and the best imported beers; snacks of mussels and *frites*; 45 varieties of whisky and 400 beers.

Beaubourg and Les Halles

This is the site of the old Paris of merchants and markets, the only area on the Right Bank without either a royal palace or a royal square; its history is entirely lacking in powdered noblemen, subtle philosophers, *grandes dames* of the salon, soldiers or clerics. It was – at least until lately – the Paris of the Parisians, the place where you would go to buy your turnips, pick up a strumpet or start a revolution. The streets are medieval, and their names betray the gritty workaday spirit of the place: Street of the Knifesmiths, of the Goldsmiths, Goose Street.

Only 40 years ago, there were indeed knifesmiths, goldsmiths and geese, and these streets were crowded with handcarts and barrels night and day. No part of Paris has seen greater changes in those 40 years, and those changes are certainly not for the better. The megaprojects of the Fifth Republic – the Forum/Les Halles shopping mall and the Beaubourg/Pompidou Centre –

squat amidst the scant remnants of medieval conviviality like conquerors from space. Once the Halles was a vast colourful wholesale distribution market for all Paris and surrounded by slums. The porters' guild, *Les Forts des Halles*, ruled the streets, shouldering real sides of beef through narrow alleys and eating three-course dinners for breakfast to give them strength. Today the opportunity created by the relocation of Les Halles, the redevelopment of the slum Ilot I and the expenditure of billions of francs by the most mercilessly efficient city government in the world looks to have been all completely wasted. The failure of this process is worth a visit just to see for yourself what the experts are capable of. The Forum is a subterranean labyrinthine 'new town' of failing shops, the park is as full of life as a cinder cemetery and the streets are bleak un-spaces of plannerized compromise dominated by skateboarders and fast food outlets. Yet compared to the City of London, Paris' old business centre got off lightly; old streets and buildings remain intact, where the human scale makes for good ambling.

Highlights

Couples' City: Views of Paris from La Samaritaine's rooftop café, pp. 166 and 324.

Parisian's City: Go to a show, at the Châtelet or Théâtre de la Ville, p.166

Peace and Quiet: The holy halls of ingenuity in the Conservatoire des Arts et Métiers, p.171

Paris des Artistes: The superlative collection in Beaubourg's Musée National d'Art Moderne, p.163

Grand Siècle Paris: The triumphal arches of Louis XIV, Porte St-Martin and Porte St-Denis, p.173

Gritty City: The working end of Paris – Rue St-Denis and the Rue Réaumur garment district, p.173

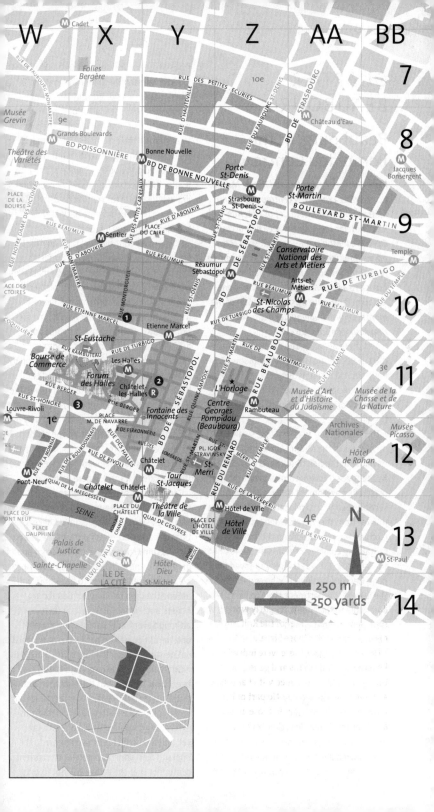

QUARTIER BEAUBOURG

Beaubourg, or the Pompidou Centre Z12–11

Place Georges-Pompidou and Rue St-Martin,
t 01 44 78 12 33, w www.centrepompidou.fr;
métro Rambuteau, Châtelet or Hôtel-de-Ville,
RER Châtelet-Les Halles; wheelchair access.
Open Wed–Mon 11am–10pm, closed 1 May;
adm exhibitions €4.50–7.50 (includes adm to
museum); day pass €10; for guided visits call
t 01 44 78 46 25. Museum open 11am–9pm,
last adm 8pm; adm €5.50, free 1st Sun of the
month; English audioguides extra. Atelier
Brancusi open Sat–Sun 1–7.

And there it stands, the Centre National
d'Art et de Culture Georges Pompidou. Most
Parisians call it simply 'Beaubourg'. The big
tilted open space in front is the Place
Georges-Pompidou, known to one and all as
the 'Plateau de Beaubourg'.

The 'Beau Bourg' was a village, swallowed
up by Paris in the Middle Ages, that has lent
its name to the neighbourhood ever since.
By the 1920s it had become a grey, unloved
place; the government cleared a large
section, meaning to relocate the flower
market from the overcrowded Halles.
Nothing happened, leaving the void as a
tantalizing challenge to Paris planners until
the late 1960s. It was the grey, unloved president, Georges Pompidou, who came up with
the idea of a 'department store for culture'
accessible to the widest possible public, a
development that was to rival the Sacré-
Cœur and the Eiffel Tower in its indifference
to Parisian architectural traditions.

The design finally chosen was the most
radical of all those submitted. The architects,
Richard Rogers and Renzo Piano, turned
traditional ideas of building upside down –
or rather, inside out. To allow larger, more
open spaces on the inside, and to expose
frankly what a modern structure really is,
they came up with a big rectangle of girders,
from which the insides are hung, a kind of
invertebrate architecture, with an insect's
shell instead of a skeleton. Much more
provocative was the idea of putting the technological guts of the building on the outside
– celebrating the essentials instead of hiding
them, and painting them in bright colours
keyed to help the observer understand how
it all works: electrics in yellow, air condition-
ing in blue, white for ventilation ducts, etc.
These are best seen on the back of the
building, along Rue Beaubourg.

It was more controversial than anything
since the Eiffel Tower. Critics grumbled about
connections with the Martian war machines
from *War of the Worlds*, and complained
about the lack of respect for the 'historic
architecture' of the quarter (you'll have
noticed by now that Beaubourg has hardly
any). After the centre opened in 1977,
Parisians and tourists voiced their opinion by
making it overnight the most visited sight in
the city, surpassing even the Eiffel Tower. The
'Plateau' in front, redesigned by Piano into an
austere, sloping rectangle decorated only by
surreal ventilation shafts from the car park
below, became an instant happening that
even Georges Pompidou might have enjoyed
(from a safe distance), where Paris' old
coterie of repulsive oral tricksters – sword-
swallowers, cigarette-munchers and
bicycle-eaters – performed amid buskers,
tramps, backpackers and portrait sketchers.

As its shiny surfaces have weathered and
grown dull, the ballyhoo has died down a
bit, and the centre seems to fit right in
among the drab buildings of Beaubourg.
Rogers' and Piano's hi-tech architecture,
although eventually accepted by the city
and the critics, has become a postmodernist
cul-de-sac with few followers. The crowds
now are not quite so large, and there have
been complaints about the management
of the centre and the lack of imagination in
its exhibits. But Beaubourg is still far from
exhausting its potential. No one can say
yet that the architecture won't go into the
books as a brilliant precursor of the current
century, or that the centre will not find its

role as a cultural clearing-house for some future Renaissance.

Musée National d'Art Moderne

The major permanent feature of the centre is this superlative, millennium-edition collection of 20th-century art (excellent audioguide available), presented over two floors of open white space punctuated at every turn with plate-glass windows which alternate stunning views over Paris with flat, still lakes of water setting off stone and iron sculptures.

The **top floor**, Art 1905–60, takes up where the Musée d'Orsay leaves off: at the turning point of modernity, when the Fauves (Derain, Vlaminck, Matisse, Marquet) liberated colour from its age-old function of representing nature. Van Gogh had blazed a trail by using colour to express emotions. The Fauves went a step beyond, applying colour and line on a two-dimensional surface as an intellectual expression, the way a poet uses words on a piece of paper (see the work of Matisse, the most lyrical and profound of the Fauves, especially his *Bocal de poissons rouges* (1914) and *Nu sur fond ornemental*).

Fauvism flickered out after only four years, but set off an immense burst of creative energy. Picasso formulated the creed of modern art when he wrote: 'I don't work after nature, but before nature – and with her.' New developments happened at a dizzying pace. 'We were like alpinists, all linked to one another,' said Braque, and one of the first examples of this linkage is his own *Viaduc à L'Estaque* (1908), hanging in the room of Fauves but painted in homage to Cézanne. As Van Gogh was a prophet for the Fauves, Cézanne's experiments in rendering volume with nuances of colour inspired Cubism. The Cubist works of Picasso, Braque, Juan Gris and Duchamp analyse form by depicting it simultaneously from a hundred points of view on a flat surface; note, too, Léger's *La Noce*, a rare Cubist work depicting movement instead of a still life. A prism of aftershocks fills the next rooms, especially the first abstract works, born of Wassily

Kandinsky's imaginative Expressionism and the geometric fundamentals of Mondrian and his De Stijl followers.

There are important works from most of the big-name artists who continued modernism's sometimes amusing and delightful, sometimes distressing and painful inquiry into art, expression and its meaning: stylized figurative painters Chagall, Soutine and Rouault; the Dadaists Picabia and Man Ray; the Surrealists Dalí (his funny *Six Images of Lenin on a Piano*), Magritte, Tanguy, Masson and Ernst; Jean Dubuffet, who in 1948 founded the Compagnie de l'Art Brut to sell the work of mental patients and questioned the very meaning of culture (he came out against it). Don't miss the recently acquired *Mur d'André Breton*, the great surrealist's collection of Asian and South American masks and bric-a-brac, as well as presents from friends and a stuffed dog.

At every point the display and organization of the museum's works explores the cross-pollination between pure and applied art, combining a Mondrian canvas of flat squares and defined boundaries with sculptures composed of squares and flat planes, alongside 1920s architectural models by Paul Nelson and Le Corbusier, where the same principles have been used to transform the spaces we live in. Further on are more naturalistic paintings such as Bonnard's *L'Atelier au mimosa*, whose vibrating colours are only barely contained by the vertical and diagonal lines of the window-frames and balustrade, and works by Fernand Léger, whose chunky human forms mark a return to figure painting but stylized into ovals and squares edged in thick black lines.

The effect of war and the collapse of political idealism is painfully explored, and from the 1950s onwards you can see the rapid hurtling towards the modern art of today, with monochrome canvases of pure texture, white on rippling white by Piero Manzoni, or Yves Klein's wall-sized rectangle of deep blue to drown in.

The audioguide is especially helpful on the **lower floor**, Post 1960, where the familiar images of Pop Art and new realism, and displays of space-age plastic furniture give way to the explorations of artists' cautionary responses to new technology in the 1960s: Robert Rauschenberg's *Oracle* and Sigmar Polke's *Pasadena*, questioning the truth of the sudden flood of media images, information and advertising pouring over an unprepared public. The art on this floor is participatory, kinetic, interactive – Yaacov Agam's *L'Antichambre à l'Elysée* and Dorothea Tanning's textured *La Chambre 202, Hôtel du Pavot* shift their colours with each changing viewpoint – and there are installations such as Joseph Beuys' 1985 *Plight*, two rooms of rolled felt enclosing a silenced and sick piano, that embrace a particularly modern and self-absorbed kind of uncertainty.

Also on this floor are a Graphic Art Gallery and a New Media Centre. On other floors you'll find a public **reading library** (the BPI) and musical research institute (IRCAM), a gift shop with goods inspired by the modern art collection, a bookshop, a café, a swanky new restaurant (Chez Georges; *see* p.322), halls for temporary exhibitions, two cinemas, two concert spaces, and, outside on the Plateau, the **Atelier Brancusi**, a reconstruction of the Paris studio where the Romanian sculptor lived from 1925 to 1957.

Place Igor Stravinsky Y–Z12

Built at the same time as the Centre Pompidou behind it, this broad sheet of water serves as a play pool for a collection of monsters created by that delightful sculptress from Mars, Niki de Saint-Phalle. Her colourful gadgets are each dedicated to one of Stravinsky's works (it isn't always easy to guess which); at any moment, they are likely to start spinning around and spraying you with water. The black metal mobiles between them are the work of Jean Tinguely.

St-Merri Y12

76 Rue de la Verrerie, t 01 42 71 93 93; métro Hotel-de-Ville. Open daily 3–7, closed Aug; free

concerts Sat 9pm and Sun 4pm; guided tour one Sun a month, call ahead to check times.

Saint Merri, or Medericus, was an abbot of Autun buried here in the early 8th century. A chapel was built over his relics, on a site then on the outskirts of the city; in the Middle Ages, with all the bankers and cloth merchants in this area, it became one of the richest parish churches of Paris. The present building was begun *c.* 1500, in a late Flamboyant Gothic style, and not completed until 1612. The last part to be finished was the bell tower, which contains a 14th-century bell called the Merri, the oldest in the city. Only a century and a half later, Paris found St-Merri impossibly old-fashioned; Michelangelo Slodtz was commissioned to prettify the interior, with the help of his brothers. (Don't laugh; Slodtz, who spent 20 years in Rome and whose work can be seen in St Peter's, was actually one of the more accomplished sculptors of his time.)

During the Revolution, St-Merri served the nation as a saltpetre factory. The mobs did a fairly thorough job of trashing its façade, so what you see on it today are largely replacements from the 1840s, including the statues of saints and the little winged, supposedly hermaphroditic demon that leers over the main portal. Inside, the Slodtz brothers didn't do too much mischief; their major contribution is the neoclassical remodelling of the choir and altar; several of their carved saints can be seen around the church. From the original church, there remain some 16th-century stained glass (along both sides of the nave), and a majestic organ ensemble carved in wood by Germain Pilon in the 1640s.

Quartier de l'Horloge Z11

Métro Rambuteau.

Just north of the Plateau Beaubourg in Rue Rambuteau, Zadkine's statue of Prometheus stealing the fire points the way into this often-maligned project of the 1970s – but look again, at one of the modest but meaningful successes of Paris' redevelopment. Intimate, protected from cars and built on a

human scale, the design avoids brash architectural pretensions in favour of a
comfortable community for people to live
and work in. Halfway down Rue Brantôme is
the project's centrepiece, **Le Défenseur du
Temps**. This golden mechanical clock, the
work of Jacques Monestier (1979), portrays a
curious fancy, the 'defender of time' battling
with his sword each hour against a monster
of the earth (a dragon), of the air (an eagle)
or of the sea (a crab). At noon, 6pm and 10pm
he must take on all three.

HÔTEL DE VILLE
AND CHÂTELET

Place de l'Hôtel-
de-Ville Y–Z13

Medieval Paris never gave too much
thought to urban amenities. If any Right
Bank burgher wanted to stretch his legs,
about the only place to do it was this square,
the only large open space in the city. Back
then it was called Place de Grève ('of the
strand'). Laid out as a merchants' yard in 1141,
the square quickly evolved as Paris' business
centre and key to the growth of the Right
Bank. It never was the most tranquil place for
the burghers to promenade; its expanse
would have been swarming with a cosmopolitan crowd of merchants and boatmen,
along with their stacks of bundles and
barrels – salt fish from the North Sea for
Friday, wines from the Champagne (but no
sparkling champagne yet, not for another
400 years), iron nails and tools from
Germany, novelties and luxuries from
Byzantium via Venice (many of these bound
for England).

But there was room enough in the Place
de Grève for all sorts of other activities.
Executions were commonly held there, it
being the only space large enough to accommodate the crowds. From medieval times, on
any weekday men looking for work would
mill about in one corner, and prospective

employers knew they could find help there.
To 'do the Grève' became a synonym for
being out of work. Gradually, *grève* came to
mean a strike, and a new word was thus
added to the French language. As *grèves* had
become a frequent threat to the established
order by the 19th century, the name was
changed to the innocuous 'Town Hall Square'
when Haussmann redesigned it.

Hôtel de Ville Z13

Place de l'Hotel-de-Ville, **t** *01 42 76 54 04,*
w *www.paris-france.org;* **métro** *Hotel-de-
Ville; wheelchair access. Visits by appt only.*

As local government developed out of the
ancient establishment of the boatmen's
guild, it was only natural that the first organization of the Commune, or city government,
should have its headquarters here. A
medieval landmark facing the square was
the small **Maison des Piliers**, the 'columned
house', fronted by a portico built in an
attempt to re-create the architectural
grandeur of Roman times. Étienne Marcel
commandeered it for his new city *commune*
in the 1350s, and a Hôtel de Ville in one form
or another has been on the site ever since. It
has witnessed many events in the city's
history: here Louis XVI was forced to accept a
tricolour cockade from the mob in 1789; here
Robespierre was arrested, five years later,
ending the Reign of Terror. Crowds besieged
the building in 1830 and again in 1848, when
they were cowed by the insults of the poet
Lamartine. Behind, on Rue de Lobau,
Napoleon constructed an army barracks still
in use today. A tunnel underneath Rue de
Lobau permits soldiers to occupy the Hôtel
de Ville in minutes – as they've had to do on
at least a dozen occasions since 1800.

The current incarnation isn't as old as it
looks. After the Prussian victories of 1870, the
Hôtel de Ville was seized by the provisional
government and fortified. Its fall to the mob
on 18 March 1871 marked the beginning of
the Paris Commune; throughout the fighting
it was the nerve centre of the Communards,
and was burned to the ground in the last

days. The new building, begun in 1874, generally follows the design of its predecessor, covered with over a hundred statues of famous Frenchmen and lit with 142 Baccarat crystal chandeliers. Inside there are big, colourful paintings in almost every room, all in the most florid late 19th-century manner.

Châtelet X13–Y12

The Quai de Gesvres, enjoying fine views over the Seine and the Île de la Cité, opens into Place du Châtelet, adorned with a memorial column to Napoleonic glories. The square is named after a little medieval castle, demolished under Napoleon, that once guarded the approaches to the Pont au Change.

Two Theatres

Nowadays two theatres define the Place du Châtelet. On the east side is the **Théâtre de la Ville** (*see* p.355), the Paris municipal theatre, offering a highly varied, reasonably priced repertoire of dance, theatre and music.

On the west side is the **Théâtre du Châtelet** (*see* p.350), a typically lavish work of the Second Empire. This used to be called the Sarah Bernhardt. The great actress was flush enough in 1899 to buy it and name it after herself, and she spent the rest of her career here, bumping about histrionically on her wooden leg in ripe productions like *La Dame aux Camélias*.

Tour St-Jacques Y12

*Place de la Tour St-Jacques; **métro** Châtelet. Closed to visitors.*

The butchers of medieval Paris always had one of the wealthiest and most powerful of the city guilds. This was their quarter, where names like Slaughter Street and Skinners' Street were changed to something less piquant in the prissy Victorian Paris of the Second Empire. St-Jacques-de-la-Boucherie was the butchers' church, one of the grandest in Paris and a famous meeting place for French pilgrims on their way to Santiago de Compostela. That did not stop the Revolutionary government from levelling

it in 1797 and renting out the land to a manufacturer of cheap clothes. Only the 170ft tower survives (1523) in its small green square, one of the last and most glorious works of Flamboyant Gothic in the city. The platform at the top is eccentric enough, graced with a huge statue of St James as well as a bull, a lion and an eagle (symbols of the Evangelists, with James doing service as the man, the fourth symbol). The windy tower has been the city's meteorological station since 1891; at its base is an equally eccentric statue of Pascal, with a broken nose and a big thermometer, reminding us that the great mathematician and Christian mystic, author of the *Pensées*, also did some pioneering scientific work on the weather in the 1640s.

Around the Pont Neuf

Quai de la Mégisserie W12–X13

Here, near the Pont Neuf is one of the strongholds of the *bouquinistes* with their old books and postcards, while on the street itself are still a few traders in the quay's traditional specialities: seeds, bulbs and birds. The **Pont Neuf** itself, together with the twin façades of the Place Dauphine (*see* p.93), makes an exceptionally graceful cityscape.

La Samaritaine W12

*Rue de la Monnaie/Rue de Rivoli, t 01 40 41 20 20; **métro** Pont-Neuf. **Open** Mon–Sat 9.30–7, Thurs until 10.*

One of the greatest Art Nouveau events of Paris is not a palace or a public building but a department store. The name comes from a statue atop the old pumping station, built on the Pont Neuf under Henri III and long a city landmark. Ernest Cognacq started his business nearby in 1869, about the same time as Boucicaut's Au Bon Marché (*see* pp.213–4), but he was not able to build his great palace of consumption until 14 years after his Left Bank competitor. Architect Frantz Jourdain designed the building in 1900, with a façade that is a remarkable marriage of graceful technology and sheer whimsy. The exposed ironwork, painted with colourful floral motifs, was a revolutionary feature; it both defines the structure brilliantly and permits huge areas of glass, including at the street level Paris' first big shop windows. In spite of the present management's attempts to make the Samaritaine look like every other department store in the world, the most important features of the original interior survive: a flowing grand staircase under a glass skylight and more Art Nouveau fantasy decoration: peacocks and passion flowers are the predominant theme.

The main part of the building, facing the Seine, was unfortunately altered in 1927. Three years later, the still-growing business built an addition across the street in a sadly subdued brand of Art Deco; there's a restaurant under the roof and a rooftop café with stunning views across Paris (*see* p.324).

LES HALLES

Incredibly, the lanes around slanting Rue des Halles are part of the old medieval street plan of Paris that has been least changed, although what was once the liveliest part of the city has been turned into a thoroughfare of high-speed traffic darting in and out of tunnels, of run-down shops and imitation 'non-stop' pubs, of graffiti and tacky tourism. In other words, you are now approaching a triumph of modern city planning (*see* 'Les Halles: Past, Present, Future', overleaf).

Forum des Halles X–Y11

Métro Les Halles, RER Châtelet-Les Halles.
The escalators on all sides will lead you down into the belly of the beast, the underground of the Forum des Halles. The pigeons are already making themselves at home here, swooping over your head down the escalator shafts and gleaning the concourses for crumbs of pizza and *croque-monsieur*. It isn't likely the planners considered them, though they did go to great lengths to make this something more than just another shopping mall. Besides the ice cream and chain

stores, there is plenty of modern art (note the big mural along Rue des Piliers, a strange panorama of human progress from the Stone Age up to Louis Armstrong, appropriately falling to bits), as well as questionable cultural amenities like the 'Pavillon des Arts' and the 'Maison de la Poésie'; you can shoot a game of inscrutable French billiards (no pockets) or watch the young at the indoor swimming pool next to a tropical garden where orchids and a banana tree grow behind a glass wall. At the **Vidéothèque de Paris** (*see* p.355) you can while away an afternoon watching old French television shows, movies or newsreels; there are booths for individual viewing and also an auditorium with continuous showings, usually of films about Paris.

At its eastern end, the Forum rises up above ground into a row of pavilions, sheathed in glass and shaped like girolle mushrooms.

Jardin des Halles W–X11

About three-quarters of the new Forum is underground, and most of the old marketplace is now the uninviting Jardin des Halles. Habitués come with a bottle of beer and sit quietly with looks of dismal resignation on their faces – the buskers, the crowds and anything that's alive shun it like the plague and stick to the old streets to the east. Current Mayor Delanoë has plans to revamp the gardens.

The circular **Bourse du Commerce** (the Merchants' Exchange, 1889) closes the western end of the park. In medieval times an important palace, the Hôtel de Nesle, stood on the site; later there was a convent and then the exquisite Hôtel de la Reine built by Philibert Delorme for Catherine de' Medici. The next occupant was an extension of the Halles, the Halle aux Blés, from which the current building takes its circular shape.

One curious fragment of Catherine's palace remains: the tall column called the **Colonne de Médicis**, now standing at the southeastern corner of the building on Rue de Viarmes. Inside, a spiral staircase leads to a platform where Catherine and her

Les Halles: Past, Present, Future

The great market, the 'Belly of Paris' as Emile Zola called it, was an 800-year-old institution before it was sacrificed in 1969 on the altars of private greed, bureaucratic incompetence and political compromise. Les Halles began in the reign of Louis VI, a simple open place in Les Champeaux ('little fields') on the edge of the Right Bank. About 1183, Philippe-Auguste laid out a proper market, roughly on the site of today's Forum, with central buildings for clothes, furs and luxury goods, a vast open space around it for food and a surrounding wall – for the king to collect his taxes as the farmers and merchants brought in their goods.

The people of the market, organized in their various corporations, soon began to feel themselves representative of Paris as a whole, and they often played a hand in political affairs. It became the custom for the ladies to call on the king with a basket of lilies of the valley every first of May, on which occasions they might politely mention some popular grievance that they felt had not come to the royal attention. This custom is maintained today with the Fête des Fleurs on the same date, when lilies of the valley are for sale on every street corner of the city.

The Halles was a world in itself, engulfing all the streets around the market proper. Each was dedicated to a particular trade. Some of these are remembered in the names, encompassing every possible business from Rue de la Ferronnerie ('of the smiths') to Rue aux Ours (originally not 'bears' but *oies*, 'geese') Rue des Lombards

was home to the Italian moneychangers and bankers, like Lombard Street in London, and the seamier side of the market area is frankly remembered in Rue de la Grande Truanderie and Rue de la Petite Truanderie – dedicated respectively, it seems, to felonies and misdemeanours.

Napoleon reacted just as you'd expect he would. After a brief tour in 1810, he said, 'I don't like this mess...there is no discipline here. This market isn't worthy of the capital of an empire.' His architects made the first plans for a covered market, but it was not until the reign of Napoleon III that anything was done. Architect Victor Baltard designed the famous, graceful green pavilions in 1851, which became the model for new markets all over Europe. Other iron pavilions continued to be built here until 1936, by which time the complex covered some 9 acres.

This Halles was in its way as much fun as its medieval predecessor. It lived by night, when the loads of meat and produce came rolling in from across France. Bars and bistrots thrived on its fringes; they stayed up all night too, giving the poets and prostitutes and insomniacs a place to refresh themselves while they relaxed in the company of the market people.

Although there had been talk of closing Les Halles since the 1920s, a serious effort had to wait for De Gaulle's new regime in the late 1950s. The general's favourite technocrats groaned about the market's 'inefficiency', and especially about the way it tied up traffic on surrounding streets. The hidden agenda behind their gripes was an infernal marriage

astrologers (including, briefly, Nostradamus) would contemplate the destinies of the dynasty and of France.

St-Eustache X11

Place du Jour, **t** *01 42 36 31 05;* **métro** *Les Halles,* **RER** *Châtelet-Les Halles.* **Open** *daily 9–7.30, organ recitals Sun pm.*

One small redeeming feature of the Halles project was that it opened up the view of the

the market's own parish church, St-Eustache, behind Henri de Miller's huge stone egghead, listening to the secret currents in Paris' bowels.

The entrance is on Place du Jour. The façade, a pathetic neoclassical pudding, was added in the 1750s to 'improve' one of Paris' last and significant Gothic buildings. The other three sides remain unmolested, revealing an exotic late bloom of medieval architecture, Flamboyant Gothic in design

of two forces. First, suiting the mood of the times and the inclination of the politicians, was the desire to sanitize and homogenize. Convivial and informal as they are, markets make such types nervous; not only do they seem disorderly, as they did to Napoleon, but they make it harder to collect taxes (the new market at Rungis has lots of computers, and records are kept of everything). Second, a perverse conspiracy grew up between the government, developers and property interests. Here was an opportunity – the only one possible – to redevelop a vast space in the very heart of Paris, replacing small businesses with large ones and promising fat profits for anyone who got in early.

Although the vast majority of Parisians were shocked by the proposed scheme of tall buildings, high densities and a 'world trade centre', little organized opposition appeared until it was too late. The conservationists were not aroused, as the district had no fine *hôtels particuliers* to save like the Marais. Even the leftists were confused, as a further aspect of the grand scheme was to demolish the infamous Ilot I, designated the worst slum in Paris as far back as 1908.

When opposition did start to form, and the initial plan came back before the city council for reconsideration, the events of 1968 overtook the entire process. Three years later the digging began for *le grand trou*, the biggest urban hole in the world and by 1977 the last of Baltard's pavilions had disappeared – the same year that London closed down Covent Garden (one of the structures was reconstructed at Nogent-sur-Marne, *see* p.269).

Confusion reigned while the hole deepened. Finally, inevitably, the bureaucrats decided what the area really needed – a shopping mall. The Forum des Halles opened in 1979.

And what was the result of the efforts of these planning geniuses? The boom in property values and development that was supposed to accompany the Halles' demise never happened. The Trou has been compromised by a blighted neighbourhood of soulless architecture surrounding a heartless bunker of blank windows and piped music. The market people work in supposedly efficient new metal sheds out in the suburbs – though a third of the merchants, the smaller ones of course, were driven out of business by the transition. Every restauranteur who remembers the old days will tell you that the food isn't nearly as good or as fresh as it used to be, though it is definitely more expensive. The displacement created a new class of middlemen whose job is to get the food into Paris; they take their cut, and their vehicles help create new traffic jams on the roads leading into the city.

Probably no greater crime has been committed against a modern city in the name of progress. The joke is that it was unnecessary. If Les Halles had been left alone, it would naturally have declined a bit by now; modern chain supermarkets take care of themselves and have little need for old-style wholesale markets. A smaller Halles would have been much less offensive to the motorists; it would still be there to give Paris a heart, purchasers a choice, and night owls a place to wander.

---

although a bit Baroque in spirit; note how the typical pointed arch over the windows has turned into a heart shape. Once there was a glorious spire over the crossing, like that of Notre-Dame. The French took it down in the 19th century because it was in the way of some telegraph wires.

The original St-Eustache, like the market, began in the time of Philippe-Auguste. Jean Alais, a rich burgher who was also chief of the mystery players, had loaned money to

the king and gained a tax concession in the fish market in return. He grew so wealthy from it, and felt so guilty collecting all the dosh without work, that he decided to finance a chapel for the Halles. St-Eustache, begun in 1532, soon became one of the most important churches in the city, second only to Notre-Dame. Richelieu, Molière and Madame de Pompadour were baptized here, and Louis XIV had his first communion. Among the notables buried inside was

Colbert, whose tomb can be seen in one of the ambulatory chapels.

The **interior** shows the plan typical of great Parisian churches since Notre-Dame: five aisles, leading into ambulatories around the broad apse, and with a transept built into, rather than projecting from, the church. The forest of pillars and pointed arches is grand and impressive – though it's a little disconcerting to see Corinthian columns in a supposedly Gothic building. The art inside, meticulously detailed on the displays posted at the entrance, is disappointing: a slim collection of second-rate works, mostly by Italian painters, half-hidden among the gloomy furnishings and clutter. St-Eustache offers its parishioners one novel service: in the right aisle you'll see a small wooden box marked 'Messages for Souls in Purgatory'.

Whatever you do, do not miss the forlorn **chapel** in the left aisle, near the entrance, entirely filled with Raymond Mason's 1969 work, *The Departure of the Fruits and Vegetables from the Heart of Paris*, a funny, very moving diorama of solemn, dignified market people, carrying their leeks and tomatoes and turnips in a sort of funeral procession, away from the Baltard pavilions and into suburban exile.

A homogenized shadow of this old conviviality still exists in the **Rue Montorgueil market** (*open daily except Monday*), beginning near St-Eustache's apse.

Square des Innocents X12

***Métro** Les Halles, **RER** Châtelet-Les Halles.*

The crowds of young people, who have made this square their main city-centre rendezvous, can be seen literally dancing on the graves of their ancestors: there has been a cemetery on this spot from Merovingian times (*see* 'A Grave Stench').

Philippe-Auguste built a wall around the Innocents, but by no means was it cut off from the life of the city. Even fashionable Parisians liked to make their evening promenades here. Prostitutes frequented it at night, along with lovers making their

A Grave Stench

The atmosphere of the old Halles was perhaps chiefly characterized by its singular aroma. For until 1786, the entire neighbourhood was perfumed by a ripe stink of decaying corpses from the Halles' neighbour, the Cimetière des Innocents.

In the Middle Ages it acquired its name from the adjacent church. Renowned for its soil, reputed to 'rot out a body in nine days', it became by the 1100s the main depot for the carcasses of Parisian paupers and other folk who had made no prior arrangements. The methods were refreshingly simple. Bodies were dumped into huge trenches; when they filled up, earth was piled on top and a new trench begun. When the corpses had entirely decomposed, they would be dug up and carted out of town – if the beggars from the nearby Cour des Miracles (*see* p.174) didn't steal them first; apparently after a few weeks in the ground the bones burned rather well and were used as firewood.

The Innocents' function, and its social scene, changed little from medieval times to the reign of Louis XVI. The decision to get rid of it was only made when the corpses, and their attendant hordes of crazed, flesh-eating rats, started pushing through the walls of the neighbours' cellars. In 1786 the cemetery was demolished, the bodies were moved off to the catacombs (*see* pp.249–50) – though there must still be lots of forgotten ones lurking under here – and the cleared site was converted into a market, and later into the present square.

midnight trysts among the heaps of corpses. During the day it was the home of the public scribes, gents with little tables who would crank out anything from a petition to the king to a billet-doux for the illiterate. The embellishment of the cemetery was entirely appropriate. A marble statue of a skeleton held pride of place in the centre of the courtyard, and in the early 15th century the Duc de Berry had his painters do the outside walls with a *danse macabre* of grinning skeletons carrying off the Pope, the King, the Knight, and everyone down to the Workman and the Child.

Nowadays, the centre of the square is marked by the **Fontaine des Innocents**, which previously stood outside the cemetery. The only surviving Renaissance fountain in Paris (1549), this is the work of Pierre Lescot, though the lovely decorative reliefs are from the hand of Jean Goujon – mostly copies; the originals were hustled off to the Louvre.

To the south of the square is a collection of streets dotted with bistrots, street characters and some rather pathetic sex shops. Among them, narrow **Rue Quincampoix** (Y12–11) is worth exploring if you have the time, with a number of pretty iron balconies and carved portals on the old *hôtels*. It had an interesting mix of tenants in the old days – whores and bankers; at what is now No.54 stood the headquarters of the most infamous banker of all, John Law (*see* 'John Law').

RÉAUMUR, ST-DENIS AND THE SENTIER DISTRICT

Conservatoire des Arts et Métiers Z9–AA10

60 Rue Réaumur, t 01 53 01 82 20, t 01 53 01 82 00 (recorded info), w www.cnam.fr/museum; métro Arts-et-Métiers or Réaumur-Sébastopol. Open Tues–Sun 10–6, Thurs 10–9.30, closed hols; adm €5.50.

Along with St-Germain on the Left Bank, St-Martin-des-Champs was one of medieval Paris' two great monasteries. Today no more rural than London's St Martin-in-the-Fields, it was well outside town in Merovingian times, when an oratory is recorded here, dedicated to France's original patron saint; according to legend, Martin cured a leper on this site. The first monastery was destroyed by the Normans in the 1060s and rebuilt

John Law

John Law was a man ahead of his time. Failing to interest Britain or any other state in his advanced ideas about credit and stock schemes, he brought them to nearly-bankrupt France in 1716 and soon gained the favour of the Regent. His first venture was the Mississippi Company, a state-backed monopoly of trade and development in the Louisiana Territory. Two years later, his success allowed him to combine the company with what was meant to be the first proper national bank, which could drive the economy by holding state funds and making loans off them.

In his own life, Law had learned how rolling over paper could make real wealth, and he sincerely believed it could work for everyone. It was an instant success. Law had invented speculation, or rather speculation had invented itself. Shares in the company seemed a magic passage to instant wealth, and Law helped the boom along by ingenious advertising methods, such as parading gilded Indians through the streets and publishing prints showing mountains of solid silver in Louisiana. Even Paris' poor scraped together their *sous* to buy in. Rue Quincampoix turned into a rowdy outdoor stock market where everyone jostled for paper bargains and bid up the prices.

Law was on top of the world. By 1720 over a million Frenchmen had a piece of the company, which had grown into a system controlling France's tax system and financing its national debt. It was no swindle. Law was utterly honest, and invested his own fortune in the company. Consequently, when the inevitable bust came in the autumn of 1720, he was completely ruined. Left alone, he might well have been able to save his system and learn from the experience, but by October 1720 his enemies had him banished from France. Law ended up in Venice, making a miserable living at cards, while in Paris the wealthiest aristocrats, many of whom had been burned, carved up the company and divided its assets among themselves. The small fry didn't get back a penny.

almost immediately, growing over the next century into a walled complex that ruled over scores of other monasteries. St-Martin owned much of the Right Bank, and had the right of administering justice in 'fifty streets' of the city.

Consequently, the monks ran a rather large prison. The kings had taken this over by 1718, when John Law (see above) had a bright idea to make use of the inmates: he talked the authorities into marrying 190 of them to 190 jailed prostitutes, and shipped them over the ocean to populate just-founded New Orleans. During the Revolution, the monastery served as an arms factory until the Conservatoire, a scientific laboratory and technical school, was established in 1798. Some important work was done here. The first balloon ascent for scientific purposes left from the courtyard in August 1804; the researchers went up to 13,000ft and learned, among other useful things, that it was damned chilly up there.

In 1802, Jacques Vaucanson, a maker of machines and automata, contributed his own collection to start the Musée des Techniques, the world's original museum of technology. In the years since it has grown into an enormous, odd and dusty hoard of gadgets and models, scientific break-throughs and techno-dinosaurs, with more junk than any junkyard and more mad-scientist gear than the Universal Studios properties department.

Before going in, have a look at the monastery from the outside. The church, visible from Rue Réaumur, is (again, along with St-Germain) one of the only two impor-tant Romanesque works left in Paris. The façade and nave are rebuildings, but the truncated bell tower and the lovely choir and apse, with its radiating chapels, survive from the 1130s. The narrow arches and intricate floral capitals show a Byzantine influence; the rows of tiny human and monster heads under the cornice are essentially French (and traceable back to the ancient Gauls, who liked to decorate their sanctuaries with the real heads of their enemies).

The main buildings, facing Rue St-Martin, were rebuilt from 1712 in a surprisingly graceful style; more like a Marais *hôtel* than a monastery. The entrance to the museum is in the main courtyard, guarded by statues of French inventors Nicolas Leblanc (who thought up a method for extracting sea salt) and Denis Papin (who made a sort of steam engine a century before Watt). The museum was reopened in 2000 after a complete reno-vation, and the visit now starts on the second floor, leading you through a procession of galleries dedicated to scientific instruments, construction, communication and energy. Highlights include the first calculating machine, designed by Blaise Pascal, and a magnificent collection of 18th-century clocks.

For readers of Umberto Eco's *Foucault's Pendulum*, the main highlight of the museum will be the interior of St-Martin's church, now stuffed full of cars, aircraft engines, pumps and some heavy bits that defy all identification, incongruously sprawling under the medieval vaulting. One of Stephenson's early locomotives is here, along with the very first automobile, Joseph Cugnot's 1771 steam-powered *fardier*. Designed to pull cannons, the thing never did work right. Amadée Bollée's 1873 *L'Obéissante* was one of the first steam coaches; it ran from Paris to Le Mans at 12mph, and looks almost comfortable.

The mystic **pendulum** (1855) has been restored to its former place in the choir. Léon Foucault, who also first measured the speed of light, thought up this toy, which proves the rotation of the earth by tracing a daily circle in its oscillations (the earth turns underneath it). The original experiment, conducted in 1851 under the dome of the Panthéon, had a swing wide enough to keep it going a full day. This one doesn't, but there's nothing magic about it; timed elec-tronic magnets, hidden in the base, keep the pendulum moving. Of course nobody in 1851 doubted that the earth rotated, but this bagatelle did find some scientific importance: as a precursor of relativity, when it led later scientists such as Mach to reconsider Newton's false idea of a possible 'absolute motion'. Eco fans might be disappointed; not only are the church and its exhibits far less weird and sinister than he portrayed them, but the pendulum itself is a small, trifling thing, its wire too thin to hang a literary editor.

St-Nicolas-des-Champs Z10

252 bis Rue St-Martin, t 01 42 72 92 54; métro Arts-et-Métiers or Réaumur-Sébastopol. Open Mon–Fri 9.30–1.15 and 3–7.15, Sat 10.30–1 and 3.30–7.30, Sun 9.45–12.30 and 4.30–6.30.

Facing the Conservatoire across Rue Réaumur is the church of St-Nicolas-des-Champs. In the 12th century, the monastery of St-Martin had become such a large and wealthy concern that it could build this substantial church just for its servants. The present building was begun in the 15th century, a fine Flamboyant work with a bit of playful asymmetry on the window over the main portal. The 16th-century south portal is just as good, carved with nervous, wiry Renaissance grotesques after a design by Philibert Delorme. Don't expect anything particularly edifying inside; much of the interior, and all the stained glass, succumbed to the tastemakers of the 18th century. Now St-Nicolas is a simple parish church, its busiest altar the one to St Rita, patroness of unappreciated housewives, where there are always a few candles burning.

The Triumphal Arches of Louis XIV Z8–AA9

When the course of the Grands Boulevards (*see* p.149) was still Paris' city wall, the two grandest and most important of the gates stood here, at Rues St-Denis and St-Martin; both were castles in themselves, crowned with sculpted turrets and pinnacles. Something had to replace those venerable landmarks, and what better than another tribute to the glories of His Solar Majesty.

Both these precursors of the Arc de Triomphe and the Grande Arche celebrate military victories in Holland and along the Rhine. The **Porte St-Martin**, built in 1674, is unusually austere, more like an 18th-century neo-classical work than something from the Grand Siècle. The **Porte St-Denis** (1672), two streets west, is much more in keeping with the spirit of the age, a veritable cascade of flowery sculptural allegories and trophies.

Rue St-Denis X12–Z9

You might find a stroll through this breezy, sleazy paragon of urban depravity a breath of fresh air in such an otherwise tidy town.

In upper **Rue St-Denis**, police and prostitutes have reached a civilized truce. They manage it in a way only the French could, without any of the Puritan stupidity and violence of American cities, or the capitalist sex-kitsch of Hamburg or Amsterdam. The ladies (a selection of the very ugliest from three or four continents) stand in doorways, dressed for the role but conservative about the make-up; they chat in a matter-of-fact way while waiting for clients, like suburban matrons gossiping over the back fence. They share St-Denis with Turkish restaurants and lingerie shops with names like the 'Mae West' and the 'Flying Skirt'. Somehow it all seems so wholesome and normal; if you're looking for exoticism, romance, danger or anything besides a pleasant and polite business transaction, this may not be the right city. Watch the ladies who are not prostitutes: they will stand in a doorway, to check the weather or wait for a friend, without feeling self-conscious in the least.

North of the Grands Boulevards, the street becomes **Rue du Faubourg-St-Denis**; there are still plenty of whores, amidst a raucous bazaar of gentlemen with earrings, doner kebabs, unintelligible languages, fluorescent orange pastries, large menacing dogs, half-plucked chickens, and a lingering scent of cumin.

The centre of the action is the incredible **Passage Brady**, running two blocks from

St-Denis to St-Martin. This is the unofficial capital of the Indian and Pakistani communities in Paris. The arcade, one of Paris' oldest, was the headquarters of the avant-garde Nabi painters of the 1890s; they fuelled up and issued their manifestos from a long-gone bar. Today, the Brady boasts a Muslim barber, Bengali fast food and shops selling linoleum, blue polyester lingerie and giant aluminium pots. Lakes appear on the pavement whenever it rains.

The Sentier District X9–Y10

This is no picturesque backwater, but the quarter of Paris that perhaps works hardest for its living. The Sentier stitches together France's clothes, everything from the heights of designer glitz to T-shirts with 'Naf Naf' printed on them. Anyone from New York will recognize the place immediately – it's a Parisian double of the Garment District: huge shops that sell nothing but buttons or silk ribbons, frantic lunch counters brimming with weird, coded conversation, overdressed, languid shopgirls, slow, serene Hasidim, and young men in sweatshirts bowling you over with their speeding trolleys along Rue d'Aboukir. The exotic names of the Sentier – Aboukir, Alexandrie and Caire – stem from enthusiasm over Napoleon's victories in Egypt. Today, the **Passage du Caire**, two streets north of Réaumur off Rue St-Denis, is a dingy but respectable showcase for the Sentier's manufactures (it's also the oldest surviving *passage*, opened in 1799). Until 1667, though, this was the most notorious quarter of all Paris, the ghetto of thieves and beggars, called the **Cour des Miracles**.

The Sentier has a remarkable main street, **Rue Réaumur**. For two decades after 1897, when it was cut through the old neighbourhood, Réaumur bade fair to become the commercial centre of Paris. Publishing and fashion businesses rushed to buy in, while developers threw up ostentatious, ultra-modern buildings of iron and glass to accommodate them. The boom was cut off

The Cour des Miracles

An old aristocratic property like the Palais Royal, where the police could not go, the Cour des Miracles in the 17th century became the centre of Paris' huge population of predatory beggars. The 'miracles' occurred every evening when the scoundrels came home – the blind regained their sight, the lame were healed, and crutches and wooden legs were packed away for the night. When not begging, the Cour's inhabitants cleaned the pockets of Paris' crowds. La Reynie, Louis XIV's famous police chief, finally got the royal authority to clear out the Cour in 1667, and he managed it with panache. One night his men surrounded the area and announced that the last nine men leaving it would be hanged. The Cour was empty in ten minutes.

by the First World War, and Réaumur never achieved its early promise. Small-time fashion houses rent most of the space now, where many of Paris' 75,000 seamstresses stitch away.

Rue Réaumur makes a fascinating architectural museum of early 20th-century passions and folly; many of the buildings won the city's annual *concours* ('competition') for new façades, and on almost all of them the architects have proudly signed their names. Beginning at Boulevard de Sébastopol, there's the florid and silly **Rotonde Félix Potin** (1910), former headquarters of the now defunct grocery chain. No.100, on the north side of the street, looks like a department store but really was the home of the newspapers *L'Intransigeant* and *Paris-Soir* (1924). No.116 won the *concours* in 1897, as did its neighbour, No.118; this 1900 work of Guiral de Montarnal is a seminal piece of Parisian Art Nouveau, with a front all curves and nearly all glass. Georges Chedanne's No.124 is stunning and uncompromisingly modern, boldly showing off its girders and rivets in a way that the Parisians of 1903 must have found profoundly shocking. Finally, another work of De Montarnal is at No.130 (1898), with a well-preserved original lobby and grand stair.

Marais and Bastille

1 Lunch

Jo Goldenberg, *7 Rue des Rosiers; métro St-Paul*. **Open** *daily 9am–1am*. **Moderate**. The Marais branch of Paris' most famous delicatessen. You'll think you're in New York.

2 Tea and Cakes

Le Loir dans la Théière, *3 Rue des Rosiers; métro St-Paul*. **Open** *Mon–Fri 11–7, Sat and Sun 10–7*. Tranquil and popular tea room/restaurant in the Marais; intellectual atmosphere.

3 Drinks

Les Vins des Pyrénées, *25 Rue Beautreillis (south of Rue St-Antoine); métro Bastille or St-Paul*. **Open** *daily 12–2.30 and 8–11.30*. One of the last non-trendy wine bars *à l'ancienne*.

Marais and Bastille

One of the less frantic corners of old Paris, the Marais is the aristocratic quarter *par excellence*. Charles V enclosed this area of reclaimed marshland within his new wall in the 1370s, and set the tone by moving in himself. Nobles and important clerics followed and built imposing *hôtels particuliers*. What really made the Marais' fortune was Henri IV's construction of the Place des Vosges in 1605. For the rest of the century, even after Louis XIV moved the big show out of Paris to the Palace of Versailles, the Marais was the place to be. By the time of Louis XVI, although by then the area had clearly lost out in popularity to the Faubourg St-Germain, and whatever lingering spark of glamour there might have been was extinguished by the Revolution, when most of the great mansions were divided up.

Being out of fashion for two centuries did the place no harm, and recently the most ambitious restoration effort in Paris has spruced the quarter up, ready for your inspection. The main attractions here are the grand *hôtels particuliers* of the 16th–18th centuries and the museums they contain: on Paris, Picasso, locks and keys, hunting and

fishing, historical documents, Victor Hugo, Paris again, and so on. In the area that has perhaps changed the least over the last 300 years, take time to look for details, like the 17th-century street signs carved into many old buildings or the subtle sculptural decoration on scores of old *hôtels particuliers*.

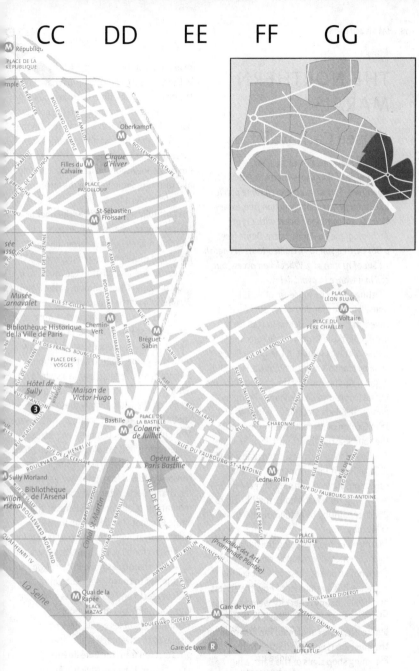

| CC | DD | EE | FF | GG |

Highlights

Couples' City: The serene Place des Vosges, one of Paris' most lovable squares, p.183

Parisian's City: The Musée Carnavalet, packed full of curiosities on the city, p.178

Peace and Quiet: A stroll along the unusual Promenade Plantée, p.188

Paris des Artistes: The Musée Picasso, with works by the long-time Paris resident, p.179

Grand Siècle Paris: The entire Marais and its elegant *hôtels particuliers*, pp.178–85

Gritty City: France's biggest collection of locks, in the Musée de la Serrurerie, p.179

THE NORTHERN MARAIS

Musée Carnavalet BB13

23 Rue de Sévigné, t 01 44 59 58 58,
w www.paris.fr/musees; métro St-Paul.
Open Tues–Sun 10–5.40, closed some public
hols; adm permanent collection free, exhibi-
tions €5.50, combined ticket with Crypte
Archéologique du Parvis-Notre-Dame (see
p.86) €5, free Sun 10–1. Guided tours in English
1st Sat of month at 3. Wheelchair access, but
call in advance to avoid delay.

Fittingly, the city museum of Paris is
housed in the grandest of all the *hôtels parti-*
culiers in the Marais. Begun in 1548 for a
president of the *Parlement de Paris*, the Hôtel
Carnavalet was rebuilt in the Grand Siècle
style by François Mansart in 1660. From the
original survive most of the ground floor and
loggia (court off Rue des Francs-Bourgeois),
and some reliefs around the windows by
Jean Goujon or his followers, representing
the Four Seasons (court off Rue de Sévigné).
The City of Paris purchased the mansion in
1866 to turn it into a museum, and the
collections have grown steadily ever since –
everything from Napoleon's toothbrush to a
Boucher painting of 'Mademoiselle
O'Murphy's foot'.

Carnavalet, besides being the name of a
former owner, also means a carnival mask;
you'll notice one of these carved over the
entrance. It is a reminder of how the streets
of old Paris, or any other city, were an empire
of symbols and pictorial allusions in the days
before everyone could read. The first room of
the museum is entirely devoted to the
charming **shop signs** of this Paris: a big
Persian king carved in wood for a dealer in
cashmere, St Anthony and his pig for a
butcher, an inn at the sign of the Three Rats.

The rooms that follow, devoted to ancient
and medieval Paris, are rather scanty, but
there are plans and models of ancient Lutetia
and Merovingian Paris, and a fascinating,
mad model of Paris in 1527, made by a monk
in the early 20th century. It must have been
the passion of a lifetime: every last building
is present, made of paper, with the details
painstakingly drawn in and painted. On the
first floor, the 17th and 18th centuries are
more than well represented, with the
emphasis, inevitably, on interior decorating
and furniture. From here there's an abrupt
jump to modern times, with such exhibits as
the faithfully reproduced **bedchamber of
Marcel Proust**, where he would accept his
morning madeleine (always on the same
plate) and muse on fate and memory.

If you're nodding off after too much bourgeois plushness, the **ballroom of the Hôtel
Wendel** will startle you to your senses. This
hotel, formerly on Avenue de New-York, gave
Catalan artist José-María Sert carte blanche
in 1924 to create a venue that would draw
the avant-garde. Done in subdued monochrome paint over gold leaf, in a style faintly
reminiscent of Tintoretto's chiaroscuros, the
scenes on the walls portray the Queen of
Sheba leaving to meet Solomon, with dwarfs,
Mongols, ostriches, tumblers, elephants,
potted palms and astrologers in attendance,
all ephemeral in their flowing draperies and
conspiring towards an informed parody of
the Grand Siècle. After that comes an earlier
monument of abstruse modernism, the
entire **Fouquet jewellery shop** from Rue
Royale, *c.* 1901. Alphonse Mucha, famous for
his posters for bicycles, cigarette papers and
Sarah Bernhardt, designed this Art Nouveau
monument to conspicuous consumption,
with peacocks and stained glass, wood carvings, fountains and mosaic floors.

Fouquet's baubles would have been
displayed to advantage in the next tableau, a
private room from the **Café de Paris** (formerly
41 Avenue de l'Opéra), showing Art Nouveau
at its sweetest and most unaffected.

The next section is devoted to **paintings**.
Those of Jean Béraud (1849–1936) stand
out, faithful recordings of Parisian life of
photographic quality.

From here, you'll digress in time to the
Revolution. This section begins starkly, with

naive allegorical paintings by a contemporary named Dubois. The first, from 1791, celebrates Louis XIV, the 'father of a free people'; another is a mystic work from the same year, declaring the 'hope of a golden age'. Dubois also paints the taking of the Bastille, with greater realism. Keys to the Bastille are on display – opposite a glass case with young Louis XVII's toys.

The revolution of 1830 is well documented, with paintings of the fights around the Louvre and Porte St-Denis, and a loony diorama of Louis-Philippe addressing a crowd at the Hôtel de Ville. The paintings go on and on – in 19th-century Paris there were so many events and so many painters to chronicle them. For the events of 1870, the best artists are the duo of Didier and Guiaud, with a heroic scene of Gambetta's *Balloon Escape from Paris* (almost life size), and fascinating views of bread queues and enlargements of the messages brought in by pigeons. Other artefacts fill out the atmosphere of Paris under siege, including ration cards, carrier-pigeon feathers and a careful portrait of a rat that went to make some Parisian's dinner.

The Carnavalet's back garden gives onto Square Georges-Cain, where you can contemplate the house François Mansart designed for himself in 1666 (No.5). In 1903 it became the 'Temple of Humanity' for the positivist religion founded by the followers of Auguste Comte, and the front was altered to match the sect's original temple in Rio de Janeiro. Facing the square is the late 15th-century Hôtel de Marle, now the Swedish Cultural Centre; and on its right, the Hôtel de Chatillon, with an ivy-covered courtyard.

Hôtel de Lamoignon BB13

24 Rue Pavée, t 01 44 59 29 40; e bibhup@free. fr; métro St-Paul. Open Mon–Sat 9.30–6, closed public hols and 1–15 Aug. Bring ID and photo.

Opposite the Musée Carnavalet, this *hôtel* was begun in 1580 for Diane de France, an illegitimate daughter of Henri II (notice the allusions to the mythological huntress Diana in the decorative reliefs). Everything is original except for the main portal closing the courtyard, added in 1718. It now houses the **Historical Library** of the City of Paris.

Musée Cognacq-Jay BB12

Hôtel Donon, 8 Rue Elzévir, t 01 40 27 07 21; métro St-Paul. Open Tues–Sun 10–5.40, last adm 4.30, closed hols; adm free. Wheelchair access, but call in advance.

It's somewhat ironic that Ernest Cognacq, the thoroughly modern department store magnate who founded the Samaritaine department store (*see* pp.166–7), should have devoted his free time to accumulating bric-a-brac from that quaintest of centuries, the 18th. The collection of ladies' cosmetic boxes will leave you speechless. They keep company with ornate furniture and a good collection of paintings by Chardin, Boucher, Rembrandt, Tiepolo, Guardi and Canaletto, among others.

Musée de la Serrurerie (Musée Bricard) BB12

1 Rue de la Perle, t 01 42 77 79 62; métro St-Paul or Chemin-Vert. Open Mon–Fri 8.30–12.30 and 1.40–5.30, closed hols; adm €5.

Louis XVI, who enjoyed his hobby of locksmithing much more than any affairs of state, would have loved this place. The museum is housed in the 1685 Hôtel Libéral-Bruant, built by the architect of the Invalides for himself. The Bricard company, which makes (can you guess?) locks, has assembled a small collection of door and window hardware from Roman times to the present. Highlights include some fancy Renaissance door-knockers from Venice and a reproduction of an old Parisian locksmith's shop.

Musée Picasso BB12

Hôtel Salé, 5 Rue de Thorigny, t 01 42 71 25 21; métro St-Sébastien-Froissart or St-Paul. Open April–Sept Wed–Mon 9.30–6, Oct–March Wed–Mon 9.30–5.30, closed 25 Dec and 1 Jan; adm €5.50, Sun €4.

The 'Salted Palace' (1656), restored in the 1980s, takes its name from its original occupant, Jean Bouiller, a collector of the hated *gabelle* (salt tax) for Louis XIV. And modern France's taxmen have supplied the collections inside – Picasso's heirs donated most of the works here to the state in the 1970s in lieu of inheritance taxes. Few really famous pictures are here, but representational works can be seen from all Picasso's diverse styles: a 'blue-period' *Self-portrait* of 1901 through the Cubist *Man with a Guitar* (1912) and beyond. Works from the early 1920s, such as the *Pan's Flute*, show a classicizing tendency, while those from the later 1920s and 30s are the most abstract of all. This is Picasso at the top of his art, exquisite draughtsmanship and the most skilful use of colour, especially in the series of *corridas* and *minotauromachies*, employing mythological elements later seen in *Guernica*.

One room of the museum contains paintings from Picasso's personal collection, including works by Corot, Matisse and Cézanne. There is also a covered sculpture garden of the master's works from many periods, and an audiovisual room with slide shows and films.

Hôtel de Rohan BB12

Corner of Rue des Quatre-Fils and Rue Vieille-du-Temple, t 01 40 27 60 96; métro Rambuteau. Open for special exhibitions only.

This is one of the last and most ambitious of all the Marais mansions. The Rohan family, magnificent chisellers even by the standards of 18th-century French nobility, made their living off the Church. Four family members in succession were cardinals and bishops of Strasbourg – although they preferred to stay here in Paris, living off the income from Strasbourg and scores of other absentee clerical holdings around France. One of the last Cardinals de Rohan got caught up in the 1785 'Affair of the Diamond Necklace' with Marie-Antoinette and Cagliostro. The first of them, Armand de Rohan-Soubise, had this *hôtel particulier* built in 1705.

In the courtyard, over the door to the Rohans' stables, is a masterpiece of rococo sculpture, Robert le Lorrain's theatrical *Horses of Apollo* (entrance at 87 Rue Vieille-du-Temple; once inside go through the arch to the right). These high-relief beasts, ready to spring right off the calm sandstone wall of the court, make an unforgettable contrast with the restrained, neoclassical architecture of the palace.

The Hôtel de Rohan is part of the National Archives (*see* below), but during special exhibitions it is open to the public. The interior is one of the best preserved in Paris, and it's worth keeping an eye out for an occasion to gain an insight into the world of the Rohans, in such decadent-but-cute fantasies as Boucher's *Chinese Suite* or the grinning monkeys of the *Cabinet des Singes*.

Archives Nationales AA12

60 Rue des Francs-Bourgeois, t 01 40 27 60 96; métro Rambuteau. Museum open Wed–Mon 10–12 and 2–5.30, Sat and Sun 2–5, closed hols; adm €3.

Where Rue des Francs-Bourgeois meets Rue des Archives stands the huge neoclassical bulk of the Archives Nationales. The oldest part is a turreted gateway built in the 1370s, while the grand horseshoe-shaped courtyard facing the Rue des Francs-Bourgeois belongs to the main part of the Archives, the **Hôtel de Soubise**. Seized during the Revolution, it has held the National Archives since 1808. The part you can visit, the **Musée de l'Histoire de France**, isn't for everyone, but with a little knowledge of French and an interest in history, this collection of documents can be utterly fascinating. Each is accompanied by a concise commentary and a copy of the text in modern French (Latin in Merovingian cursive can be a bit of a strain).

The earliest document is about (naturally) real estate, a decree of Dagobert I, *c.* 630, written on papyrus. The heavy seals of the Merovingian and Carolingian kings add the proper feudal touch, along with the weird pictographs that Charlemagne and others used for a signature. The first document in French, fittingly, is a tax schedule for merchandise from 1223 – the ancestor of VAT. There's a letter from Joan of Arc to the people of Rheims, encouraging them to resist the English, and the first copy of the Declaration of the Rights of Man (1790). But the best thing in the museum is a painting on the far wall: a gigantic, hysterically funny 16th-century allegory of the *Ship of Faith*, piloted by the Jesuits (from whom it was seized in the 1760s, when they were expelled from France), and rowed by priests and nuns, smiling beatifically down at the drowning sinners who missed the boat.

South of the museum, down Rue des Archives, is the 15th-century **Maison de Jacques Cœur** (No.40), discovered under a coat of stucco in a 1971 restoration. Cœur, a merchant of Bourges, was a fascinating man ahead of his time, a proto-capitalist, who got a little too big for the king's liking. Falsely accused of poisoning the royal favourite, Agnès Sorel, Cœur escaped prison and ended up in Rhodes, fighting the Turks.

Further down at No.22 is the **Temple des Billettes**, an 18th-century monastic church now belonging to the Lutherans, with the only Gothic cloister left in Paris.

Musée de la Chasse et de la Nature AA11

60 Rue des Archives, t 01 53 01 92 40; métro Rambuteau. Open Tues–Sun 11–6, closed hols; adm €4.70.

François Mansart designed the Hôtel de Guénégaud around 1650, which you can visit because the passion and money of a big-game hunter named Sommer have turned it into a museum. Along with Sommer's trophies there are antique weapons, elephant tusks and a surprising collection of art – hunting and wildlife scenes from Rembrandt to Monet.

North to République

In any medieval view, you'll notice what seem to be baby walled cities just outside the walls of Paris. This isn't the medieval imagination at work; they really existed. Two of the largest were on what is now the northern fringes of the Marais, up Rue des Archives or Rue du Temple towards Place de la République: the Abbey of St-Martin-des-Champs (*see* p.171) and, in particular, the 'Quarter of the Templars' (*see* 'The Knights Templars'). The centre of the site is now occupied by the **Carreau du Temple** (BB10), a small park built by Haussmann with an iron bandstand. To the east of the square across Boulevard du Temple is the **Cirque d'Hiver** (*see* p.372), probably the most famous circus venue in the world. Originally this delightful round building was the Cirque Napoléon. Hittorff, Napoleon III's favourite architect,

The Knights Templars

The Knights Templars, an order of the noble élite founded in 1119 to protect pilgrims and defend the newly conquered Holy Land, attracted so much talent, land and money that it soon found it was a European power in its own right. Vows and piety went by the board; learning to move money around Europe and the Middle East to finance their activities, the Templars stumbled on the idea and methods of banking. By the 12th century they kept the royal treasury, and pretty much managed the economy of the nation. They owned most of the Marais; about the turn of the century they began building their extramural complex, partly for greater security, and partly to make even more money by sheltering merchants and artisans shut out by the monopolistic guilds of Paris.

Some estimates put the population of the Templars' new city as high as 4,000. After the lightning seizure of the order and its property by Philippe le Bel in 1307, their enclave (given to the Knights of Malta) gradually dwindled as it was swallowed up by the expanding city. Confiscated by the Commune of Paris, it became the prison of Louis XVI and Marie-Antoinette. Napoleon had it demolished in 1808 to keep Bourbon loyalists from turning it into a shrine. Today not a single stone of the Temple remains.

designed it in 1852, when the golden age of the circus was just beginning. Part of Fellini's *The Clowns* was filmed here.

Place de la République BB9–CC10

Métro *République.*

It isn't pretty, but this is understandable, for the square was less an urban ornament than a military installation, a key strongpoint in the never-ending job of defending Paris from the Parisians.

République took its present form under Napoleon III; the big barracks he built along its northern face are still occupied. The boulevards that radiate in all directions gave the troops easy access to all points in radical, working-class east Paris. To expand the square to its present dimensions, Baron Haussmann demolished the greater part of the Boulevard du Temple, the legendary theatre district that Parisians of the 19th century knew as the 'Boulevard du Crime' from the cops-and-robbers melodramas the public loved. Among the theatres knocked down was the Funambules, home of the great actor Frédérick Lemaître. All this will be familiar to anyone who has seen Marcel Carné's *Les Enfants du Paradis* (1943). In the memorable opening scene of the film the whole boulevard is displayed, with its teeming crowds, its jugglers and mountebanks. It was all reconstructed, the most expensive film set ever made in France, in a studio in Nice – and in the middle of the German Occupation.

THE JEWISH QUARTER

Rue des Rosiers (AA12–BB13) has been the centre of a small Jewish community since the 18th century; a wave of immigration from Eastern Europe in the 1880s and 90s made it what it is today – one of the liveliest, most picturesque little streets in Paris. Recently, a number of Sephardic Jews from North Africa have moved in, adding to a scene that

includes bearded Hasidim, old-fashioned *casher* (kosher) grocery shops, snack stands and famous delicatessen restaurants such as Jo Goldenberg (*see* p.176). There are also fine pâtisseries (especially at No.29) with Eastern European treats such as poppy-seed rolls, and kosher pizza by the slice at No.11.

The synagogue at 10 Rue Pavée is designed with a stunning curvilinear façade by Hector Guimard.

Musée d'Art et d'Histoire du Judaïsme AA11

*71 Rue du Temple, t 01 53 01 86 60; **métro** Rambuteau or Hôtel-de-Ville; wheelchair access. **Open** Mon–Fri 11–6, Sun 10–6, closed some Jewish hols; **adm** €6.10. For children's activities call t 01 53 01 86 62.*

Housed in the Hôtel St-Aignan, a beautifully restored 17th-century Marais mansion, the museum's permanent collection explains the central tenets of Judaism – the festivals and rites of passage – and emphasizes the importance of the written word. Each section is illustrated with a wealth of paintings, religious objects and ornaments, including exquisite examples of illuminated *ketoubbah* (marriage contracts), and a 19th-century wooden *succah* (tabernacle) decorated with a naïf fresco of Jerusalem. Scroll ornaments from around the world illustrate Judaism's diversity: Italian Renaissance examples feature mythological figures, Polish ones have biblical symbolism and North African ones reflect Moorish designs.

The fate of the Jews who lived in this *hôtel* before the Second World War is recalled by an installation by the artist Christian Boltanski, *Les Habitants de l'Hôtel de St-Aignan en 1939*, which features posters roughly stuck on the wall of an internal courtyard. Each poster states the name, place of origin and occupation of the residents in 1939. Some also include the date of their deportation from Paris. In many cases this is the final piece of information known about them. The museum also arranges a changing programme of temporary exhibitions.

PLACE DES VOSGES AND RUE ST-ANTOINE

Place des Vosges CC13

Métro *Bastille or St-Paul.*

This lays claim to being Paris' first proper square, and possibly the first in northern Europe; London's first attempt, Inigo Jones' original Covent Garden, appeared in 1630. The inspiration seems to have come from Catherine de' Medici, who cleared the site when her husband, Henri II, met an untimely death in a palace that stood here (*see* 'Just a Joust'). The idea was probably a memory of the fashionable, arcaded Piazza SS. Annunziata back home in Florence. In 1605, Henri IV finally began the building of what would be known as the 'Place Royale', a centrepiece that the sprawling Marais badly needed. Its architects are unknown; though the square is Italian in concept, the adaptation became something a 17th-century Frenchman could love – hierarchical, elegant and rigorously symmetrical.

In a way this square is the predecessor of Versailles. Behind the uniform façades were 36 palaces; the only buildings that stood out were the pavilions of the king and queen, at the north and south entrances – a public place in an aristocratic setting, mirroring in its design the subjection of the nobility to the king. The Place Royale was Henri's pet project, and he visited the works most days.

It was not completed, however, until after his assassination, in 1612. The opening ceremonies ironically included another joust, a perfect prelude for the scenes witnessed in the Place's first decades. Besides stately promenading, the nobles of the age were fondest of duels. Despite Richelieu's attempts to outlaw them (he once lived on

Just a Joust

The Place des Vosges' association with royalty began long before the square ever appeared. The Hôtel des Tournelles, a turreted mansion built here in the 1330s, had belonged to a chancellor of France, a bishop of Paris and a pair of dukes before Charles VI purchased it in 1407. Later kings occasionally used it for councils and state ceremonies. One such event was the going-away party for Henri II's daughter Catherine de France, who was off to marry Philip II of Spain. The celebrations included an old-fashioned joust, in which the king participated (in the grim and reactionary 16th century, nobles revived this archaic custom). Wearing the colours of his celebrated mistress, Diane de Poitiers, the unfortunate Henri took a shot right through the visor from Montgomery, the captain of his Scots Guard. He died ten days later and his widow, Catherine de' Medici, commanded that the cursed palace be demolished.

the square, at No.21) the reign of Louis XIII was the golden age of the sport. Rapier in one hand, torch in the other, the hotbloods put on regular midnight shows for the neighbours who might still be awake. What put an end to the custom was not Richelieu's police but the decision of the property owners in 1685 to enclose the square's centre with a fence and make it a garden – this time imitating the new fashion from London.

During the Revolution, when all the names of *ancien régime* streets were changed, the Place Royale must have been one of the last; the revolutionaries could find nothing better to call it than the awkward Place de l'Indivisibilité. Napoleon handled it even worse, giving it its present moniker, Place des Vosges, in honour of the first *département* to pay its share of the new war taxes.

Today the square is one of the loveliest surprises sheltered by the Marais, a favourite with tourists, Parisians, groups of schoolchildren and everyone else. It's utterly pleasant under the clipped linden trees, and the statue of Louis XIII (an 1825 replacement for the original melted down in the

Revolution) looks fondly foolish with his pencil moustache and Roman toga. The architecture, totally French and refreshingly free of any Renaissance imitation, invites contemplation. If you do so, you'll notice a lot of the 'brick' is painted plaster; even aristocrats can cut corners.

Maison de Victor Hugo CC13–14

6 Place des Vosges, t 01 42 72 10 16; wheelchair access. **Open** *Tues–Sun 10–5.40, closed hols;* **adm** *free.*

The master (*see* pp.251–2) lived here between 1832 and 1848, and the place has been turned into a somewhat lugubrious shrine. Of interest, besides Hugo's charming mock-Chinese dining room, are original illustrations from his books and a good number of Hugo's own peculiar drawings.

Rue St-Antoine BB13–DD14

Lively Rue St-Antoine is the main artery of the Marais, following the course of a Roman road. In the Middle Ages it was the city's widest street because it was used for so many popular festivals and processions.

Hôtel de Sully CC14

62 Rue St-Antoine, t 01 44 61 20 00; métro St-Paul. **Open** *Tues–Sun 10–6.30, closed hols;* **adm** *to exhibitions €4.*

A contemporary of the Place des Vosges, this offers an extensive bookshop and rotating photography exhibitions. These are organized by the Patrimoine Photographique, which is in charge of the national photographic collection, a record in photos and documents of the 20th century.

QUARTIER ST-PAUL

St-Paul-St-Louis BB13–14

99 Rue St-Antoine, t 01 42 72 30 32; métro St-Paul. **Open** *Mon–Wed and Fri 8–8, Thursday 8–10.30, Sun 9–8. Mass at 9am and 7pm.*

In the late 16th century, there developed in Italy the architectural fashion that art historians used to call the 'Jesuit Style'. Combining the confident classicism of the decaying Renaissance with a sweeping bravura to be perfected in the dawning Baroque, this architecture was a key part of the Jesuits' plan to forge a swank, modern image for the Counter-Reformation Church. It took some 70 years for the style to find its way to Paris; the construction of St-Louis began in 1627, and Cardinal Richelieu himself celebrated the first Mass in 1641. From its opening, this church was the showcase of the new Catholicism in Paris: its gloomy façade hiding the most sumptuous interior, the Jesuits' best orators delivering vague but sonorous sermons, music supplied by Lully and Charpentier (both organists here), and all the lights of society present in the congregation.

From their base here, the intelligent, determined Jesuits quickly became a power in France, the confessors of kings and educators of the élite (Voltaire, for one). Thoroughly trashed in 1792, the church lost almost all of its treasures – even the statues on the façade are later additions – and it became a 'temple' in the Revolution's cockamamie 'cult of Reason'. There's little to detain you inside. The design follows that of the Gesù in Rome closely, including the discreet dome: one of Paris' first, inspiring the Italianate domes of the Invalides and others. The sculptural decoration around the dome and crossing by Martellange, the church's original architect, is fine, intricate work and very Grand Siècle. There is a statue of the Virgin sculpted by Germain Pilon (1586) in the chapel to the left of the choir, where the hearts of Louis XIII and XIV were kept (until they were ground up for paint: *see* 'Val-de-Grâce', p.250).

Around St-Paul-St-Louis

Just south of the church down Passage St-Paul is Rue Charlemagne and the **Village St-Paul** (BB14; *open Thurs–Mon 11–7*), a modern housing development that includes small courtyards filled with antique shops and art dealers. A little further south is the

Right Bank's only remaining stretch of the 12th-century **wall of Philippe-Auguste**.

Musée de la Curiosité et de la Magie BB14

11 Rue St-Paul, t 01 42 72 13 26; métro St-Paul. Open Wed, Sat and Sun 2–7; adm €7.

A museum of magic, with historical items related to magic, games and demonstrations of conjuring tricks (*see* p.372).

Hôtel de Sens AA14

1 Rue du Figuier, t 01 42 78 14 60; métro Pont-Marie or St-Paul. Open library Tues–Fri 1.30–8.30, Sat 10–8.30, closed 1–15 July; exhibitions Tues–Sat 1.30–8; adm varies according to the exhibition (around €3).

Strangely enough, Paris did not become an archepiscopal see until 1623; for over a thousand years, its bishops were subject to the archbishops of the little town of Sens. In the Middle Ages these influential clerics spent most of their time in the capital. One of them, *c.* 1475, built this medieval confection overlooking the Seine (today the river is two streets away). Another rented it to Henri IV; he used it to park the amazing Queen Margot (Marguerite de Valois) whose scandalous behaviour was becoming an embarrassment at court.

For three centuries, the archbishops rented out the old palace to increasingly less elegant tenants; by 1916, when purchased by the city, it was half in ruins and being used as a laundry. Now almost completely reconstructed, it is one of the loveliest buildings in Paris, an impertinently asymmetrical fantasy of gables, turrets and pinnacles. The palace is now Bibliothèque Forney, a remarkable institution dedicated to the old crafts and industries of France.

Maison Européenne de la Photographie BB13

5–7 Rue de Fourcy, t 01 44 78 75 00, w www.mep-fr.org; métro St-Paul and Pont-Marie; wheelchair accessible (wheelchairs available).

Open Wed–Sun 11–8, closed hols; adm €5, free Wed 5–8. Café open Wed–Sun 11–7.30.

North of the palace, Rue de Fourcy (with a rare 18th-century cobblers' shop sign) joins **Rue François-Miron**, a venerable street of character that began as a Roman road. On the corner is this centre for contemporary photographic art, offering exhibitions, a library and various activities.

St-Gervais-St-Protais Z13

Place St-Gervais, t 01 48 87 32 02; métro Pont-Marie or Hôtel-de-Ville. Open daily 6am–9pm, Thurs open all night.

The blank façade of this church may not seem impressive nowadays, but it is a minor landmark of an architectural revolution, one of the first in Paris to attempt a classically inspired style instead of the good old tradition of French Gothic. Louis XIII laid the first stone for the façade in 1616. The rest of the building, begun in 1494, is the latest incarnation of a church that has been on this site since the 6th century. In March 1918, when the Germans were trying a last-ditch effort to terrorize France out of the war, a shell from Big Bertha came through the roof and killed over a hundred people.

There isn't much inside: some good stained glass in the Lady Chapel behind the altar, heavily restored in the 19th century, and Paris' oldest organ (1601), where eight members of the Couperin family, including the famous composer, held the post of organist until 1856.

AROUND BASTILLE

Place de la Bastille DD14

Métro Bastille.

Every gate in the walls of Paris had some sort of castle to defend it. This *bastille* (the Porte St-Antoine) lay on the main road to the east, and was situated very close to the royal residences of St-Pol or the Tournelles; consequently it was the best defended of all.

Begun in 1370, the Bastille's original purpose was keeping the English out. It was a proper castle, a tall, grim rectangle with eight round towers and very few windows; its outworks covered an area as big as the square today. But well built as it was, militarily the Bastille never had any luck; seven times it was besieged during rebellions or civil wars, and six times it was quickly taken.

Under the English occupation, the Bastille garrison was commanded by Sir John Fastolf, sometimes claimed as a model for Shakespeare's Falstaff (but Fastolf, a tough and capable commander over many campaigns in France, gets a bit role himself in the first part of *Henry IV*). It was Richelieu who determined the Bastille's role as a prison, and it soon became the most important calaboose in the realm, hosting the Man in the Iron Mask and later Voltaire, who made two visits, one for over a year. More than anywhere else, it was a place where delicate cases could be held at the king's pleasure, under the notorious *lettres de cachet* – letters bearing the king's seal ordering imprisonment or exile without due process. Accommodation in the Bastille was not all that awful, at least for the wealthy, who might bring in their servants, and could afford the choicer dishes on the governor's bill of fare. Privileges – walking along the ramparts, using the library, being able to order dinner from outside – were at the discretion of the Lieutenant of Police, an arbitrary regime but not always unkind.

There's nothing to see of the famous fortress today, of course (*see* 'The Storming of the Bastille') – unless you arrive on the no.5 métro, coming from the Gare d'Austerlitz, where some of the foundations survive around the platform. The square has been redesigned, with the outline of the fortress set into the pavement (see the outline of a tower curving across the street a few yards down Rue St-Antoine).

This is the only square in town created not by kings or planners but by the people of Paris. Since they cleared the space back in 1789, the Place has been the symbolic centre of leftist politics, the setting for monster celebrations like the one that followed Mitterrand's election in 1981. The *motards* (bikers) of Paris also make a traditional but non-political contribution to the square, holding their beery bike-ins on Friday nights.

Colonne de Juillet DD14

At 153ft, the Colonne de Juillet is the centrepiece of the Place de la Bastille, commemorating the Revolution of 1830. Napoleon had planned to decorate the spot with a gigantic elephant, surmounted by a tower (along with golden bees, elephants with towers or obelisks were one of Napoleon's personal symbols, representing little more than the Emperor's whimsy and possibly inspired by the emblem of Catania, Sicily, or a Bernini sculpture in Piazza Minerva, Rome). The 50ft bronze mammoth was actually built, its trunk designed to spout water into a fountain. Napoleon took a great interest in the work, but after his defeat in 1815 the beast sat in its workshop (where the Bastille Opéra is now) for 31 years until the government sold it for scrap.

The 'July column', restored for the bicentennial of the Revolution, was erected over the unfortunate elephant's pedestal in honour of those who died in the 1830 revolt. Ironically, it became a shrine to the overthrow of the regime that built it; in 1848 a new crop of revolutionaries burned Louis-Philippe's throne next to the column. On top is a figure of the 'Genius of Liberty'.

Opéra de la Bastille DD14

120 Rue de Lyon, t 01 40 01 17 89, advance bookings t 0836 69 78 68, w www.opera-de-paris.fr; métro Bastille; wheelchair accessible. For excellent guided tours (in French only) call t 01 40 01 19 70 for times and buy a ticket from the office; disabled visitors t 01 40 01 18 50, children t 01 40 01 22 46. Tickets €10–109 (opera) and €7–67 (ballet).

As part of Mitterrand's notions of 'bringing culture to the people', he conjured up the startling façade of the Opéra de la Bastille.

The Storming of the Bastille

By the 1780s there were very few prisoners still kept under *lettres de cachet*, which were abolished in 1784. The government had already appropriated the funds to demolish the Bastille when the Revolution struck.

Two weeks before Bastille Day, one of the last few prisoners got himself into trouble, shouting out of his window through a sort of bullhorn made from a drainpipe that he and the rest of the inmates were about to be massacred, pleading for the people to come and save him. This was, of all people, the Marquis de Sade, inside since 1784 for his usual offences against public propriety and servant girls. The governor shipped him to the madhouse at Charenton on 4 July 1789.

On the 11th, the king dismissed his minister Necker, and the people of Paris, losing all hope of reform, began to arm themselves. On the morning of the 14th, after a rousing speech by Camille Desmoulins in the Palais Royal (*see* pp.154–5), some 600 people, including women and children, advanced across Paris to the grim fortress that had become a symbol of royal despotism. They battled all afternoon against a small garrison of Swiss Guards and retired veterans until, at about 5pm, the arrival of a detachment of revolutionary militia decided the issue. The gates were forced, the governor and many of the defenders massacred, and the last seven inmates of the Bastille were acclaimed as heroes: the prisoners comprised four swindlers who were about to be transferred to another prison, an English idiot named Whyte, a gentleman whose family had petitioned the king to lock him up for incest and one genuine political prisoner, who had been in the Bastille for some obscure conspiracy since 1759 and didn't want to leave.

The demolition commenced the following day. Although started by popular enthusiasm, a clever rascal named Palloy quickly took charge of the work, intending to make a profit from the Bastille in any way possible. Besides organizing patriotic dance parties on the site, 'Citizen Palloy' sold off the stones to build the Pont de la Concorde, and to repave the Pont Neuf and a few score Paris streets. His greatest coup was having stones carved into models of the fortress, and sending off one each to the 83 *départements* into which France had just been divided – accompanied by his salesmen, peddling smaller souvenirs to all and sundry.

There used to be a small railway station here, the Gare de la Bastille. The buildings included a métro pavilion that was one of the finest works of Hector Guimard. The government planners typically levelled it without a second thought when they began clearing the site for the Opéra in 1985.

Uruguayan-Canadian architect Carlos Ott was chosen personally by President Mitterrand in 1983 as the winner of the worldwide design competition, out of 787 entries. Ott probably wishes that he had never even heard of Paris. The architectural criticism has been harsh; Ott was up against popular ideas about what an opera house should look like, reaching back to Charles Garnier, who wrote the book on the subject with the old Paris Opéra.

On the inside, Ott did everything you could ask of an architect; the sight lines and acoustics are excellent, if less intimate than the old – this is a stage meant for spectacle rather than the singer-to-audience and heart-to-heart communication of classic Italian (or French) opera.

It is on the outside that the problems start, and not just with 50lb fascia tiles falling on passers-by from the façade. The heroics of 'everyman architecture' have produced a squared and geometrical look reminiscent of a French school notebook, recalling a stifling *dictée*, the more-than-perfect tense and all the other manifestations of anal retentiveness in French culture. The bile-tinted hue of the exterior glass was intended to reflect the weathered copper of the Colonne de Juillet. But that connection is simply non-existent in the streaked, pigeon-daubed glass of the real thing. And the absence of traditional Parisian monumentality in the design, intended to make opera appear *d'accès facile*, resulted in little more than a homogenized exercise in polite modernism.

Finally the official *raison d'être* of the opera house – to bring culture to the people of the city's east end – has been quietly abandoned. In 1992, Pavarotti singing *Un Ballo in Maschera* was beamed out into the square on wide screens for the common man. Since then, all pretence at anything but highbrow at high prices has been quietly forgotten. The real purpose of the building will be harder to forget: a three-billion-franc monument to Tonton himself, and a vast opportunity for Tonton's cronies to soak up some public money. 'Let them bawl,' Mitterrand cried during one of the many storms of criticism during his reign, 'History will judge!'

Arsenal CC15

1 Rue de Sully, off Bd Henri-IV, **t** *01 53 01 25 25,* **w** *www.bnf.fr;* **métro** *Sully-Morland.* **Open** *Mon–Fri 10–6, Sat 10–5;* **adm** *free.*

In 1512 the state commandeered the old Celestine monastery here for the manufacture of munitions. After an explosion in 1563 took part of the neighbourhood with it, the arsenal moved across the Seine to La Salpêtrière, leaving only the name behind. Since 1797 the buildings have housed part of the Bibliothèque Nationale, including many of the libraries confiscated from nobles and monasteries during the Revolution, and some lavish 18th-century apartments.

Pavillon de l'Arsenal BB15

21 Bd Morland, off Bd Henri-IV, **t** *01 42 76 33 97.* **Open** *Tues–Sat 10.30–6.30, Sun 11–7.*

Since 1988 this has been a special exhibition dedicated to Paris, its history and the planning for its future. The exhibits, beginning with a 540-sq-ft model of the entire city that lights up to point out sites and stages in its development, are as high-tech as the *grands projets* themselves; the whole thing is relentlessly educational, and does a good job of presenting the planners' doubtful case.

Faubourg St-Antoine EE14–GG16

Métro *Ledru-Rollin or Gare de Lyon.*

From Place de la Bastille, the new Opéra seems to hide the entire quarter; walk about behind it, and you'll find one of the most attractive of the city's old working men's areas, which in recent years has undergone a speedy gentrification. The main street, Rue du Faubourg-St-Antoine, has long been famous for its furniture-makers; the few that survive make 18th-century imitations.

The old Faubourg still survives around the touristy, bar-lined Rue de Lappe, the trendy Rue de Charonne, and the Place d'Aligre, which hosts a market, the Marché d'Aligre (*every morning until 12.30*). It got its start centuries ago, when a good-hearted abbot of St-Antoine, who owned the land, allowed traders to sell clothes to the area's poor, providing they kept the prices very low.

Promenade Plantée EE15–GG17

Métro *Bastille or Gare de Lyon.*

A short walk from Place de la Bastille down Rue de Lyon takes you to Avenue Daumesnil and one of Paris' latest not-so-grand projects. The old railway viaduct high above the avenue has been converted into a charming garden walk, which will eventually lead all the way from Bastille to the Bois de Vincennes. As you follow the long-gone tracks, the garden narrows and cuts between apartment blocks, affording views into the second-floor windows of houses that used to rattle to the passing of trains.

Below the Promenade, along the length of Avenue Daumesnil, the railway arches now house ateliers of high-class specialized craft, in what is known as the **Viaduc des Arts**: furniture, glass, art paper, aromatherapy oils, wood, lampshades, and restaurants modishly make the most of their reclaimed setting.

Montmartre and the North

Montmartre and the North

From the Eiffel Tower or the top of the Pompidou Centre, Montmartre resembles an Italian hill town from Mars, gleaming white under the beehive domes of the palace of Emperor Ming the Merciless. A closer inspection reveals honky-tonk tourist Paris at its ripest, churning euros from the fantasy-nostalgia mill for the good old days of Toulouse-Lautrec, cancan girls, Renoir and Picasso. On the other hand, the Butte has some of Paris' last secret alleys and picturesque streets, just as pretty as they were when Utrillo painted them. Down at the bottom near Boulevard Barbès is a completely different world: the Goutte d'Or quarter, grotty, cosmopolitan and alive, home to many immigrants and Paris' cheapest shops; it's an agreeably urbane and funky place, but one where you may not feel comfortable at night.

1 Lunch

Chez Ginette, *101 Rue Caulaincourt*, **t** *01 46 06 01 49*; **métro** *Lamarck-Caulaincourt*. **Open** *Mon–Sat 8am–2am*. **Moderate**. Very reasonable, with plenty of fun.

2 Tea and Cakes

L'Été en Pente Douce, *23 Rue Muller*; **métro** *Château-Rouge*. **Open** *daily 12–12*. Ideal location for tea and pâtisserie on a lovely terrace with a view, east of Sacré-Cœur (but not worth staying for the full meal).

3 Drinks

Le Relais de la Butte, *12 Rue Ravignan*; **métro** *Abbesses*. **Open** *daily 12–11pm*. Old-fashioned, friendly and plant-filled wine bar with plenty of wines by the glass.

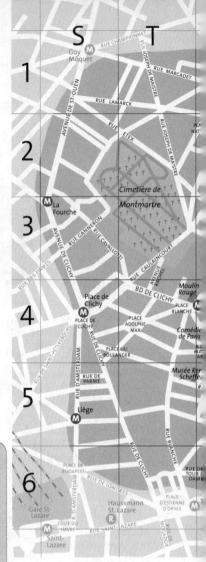

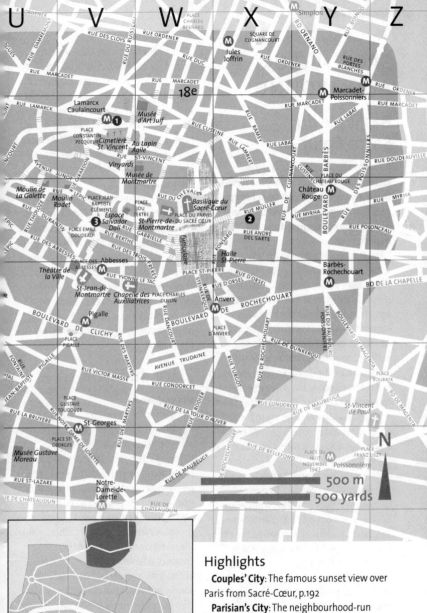

Highlights

Couples' City: The famous sunset view over Paris from Sacré-Cœur, p.192

Parisian's City: The neighbourhood-run Musée de Montmartre, p.197

Peace and Quiet: The atmospheric Cimetière de Montmartre, p.196

Paris des Artistes: Wander around their old haunts – *see* Trailing the Artists, p.194

Grand Siècle Paris: Come up here to escape its weight; Montmartre was outside the walls

Gritty City: Buy a whole new wardrobe at Tati for next to nothing, p.200

SACRÉ-CŒUR AND AROUND

Basilique du Sacré-Cœur W3

*Parvis du Sacré-Cœur, t 01 53 41 89 00; métro Abbesses or Anvers (take the funicular to the steps of Sacré-Cœur). **Open** basilica daily 6.45am–11pm, dome and crypt daily 9–6.30; **adm** basilica free, dome and crypt €5.*

The story goes that between 1673 and 1689 Jesus Christ appeared to a nun from the Royal Abbey of Montmartre, demanding a church to the glory of his Divine Heart 'to serve France and repair the bitterness and outrages that have wasted her'. The project was put to every regime that followed, but nothing happened until the rise of the Commune and the fall of Rome (Napoleon III had been protecting the pope from the Italians, who captured Rome in 1870). These events brought a new urgency to the task. An influential band of fervent Catholics made 'a national vow' to build Sacré-Cœur to 'expiate the sins' of France.

Many Parisians regard the resulting puffed-up excrescence of Romano-Byzantine lard looming over their city with some embarrassment, and not only for its architecture. The national vow was imposed on the city by a vote in the National Assembly in 1873, despite opposition by radicals and many Montmartrois, who claimed it would ruin the character of the Butte (it has, drawing 6 million visitors a year).

In the design competition the most pompous entry, by Paul Abadie, was chosen. It drove Adolphe Willette (the designer of the Moulin-Rouge) crazy: 'It isn't possible that God, if he exists, would consent to live there,' he declared. On the day the first bit, the crypt chapel, opened, he ran in and shouted: '*Vive le diable!*' To thank him, the Montmartrois gave his name to a square at the foot of Sacré-Cœur's stairs.

Every hour around the clock since 1885, even in 1944 as bombs shattered the windows, there has been someone on duty praying for the sins of the Commune. After visiting Sacré-Cœur, however, you may think that the Communards' real sin was losing Paris, allowing the city to be devastated and some 20,000 Parisians slaughtered at the hands of the self-righteous regime that built this basilica.

For a descent into the abyss, visit the clammy **crypt**, with its neglected chapels, broken chairs, dingy cases of relics salvaged from the Royal Abbey of Montmartre, overgrown statues of praying cardinals, and a slide show on the building of Sacré-Cœur. The view from the **dome** isn't that much more spectacular than the view from the *parvis* below, but you can look vertiginously down into the awful interior of the basilica.

Place du Tertre W3

Métro Abbesses.

This was once the main square of Montmartre village, but it's hard to imagine a more blatant parody of the Butte's hallowed artistic traditions. Unless you come bright and early, you can scarcely see this pretty square for the easels of 200 artists (the law permits two per square metre) waiting to immortalize you. A plaque at No.6, the restaurant Chez la Mère Catherine, marks the invention of the word *bistrot*: the Cossacks, who formed part of the Allied army of occupation in 1814 but were forbidden alcohol by their captains, would demand their drinks on the sly and 'quickly, quickly' ('*bistro, bistro*', in Russian). The current owner led the successful fight against the deforestation of Place du Tertre proposed by the city, which regards old trees as a menace to society.

Place du Calvaire, just off Place du Tertre, must be the dinkiest square in Paris; it affords one of the most tremendous views over the capital, and is the best possible viewpoint for the Bastille Day fireworks.

St-Pierre-de-Montmartre W3

2 Rue du Mont-Cenis, t 01 46 06 57 63; métro Abbesses. Open daily 8–7.30. Also hosts concerts – see l'Officiel or Pariscope.

At the east end of Place du Tertre, the Butte's oldest church is disguised with a 19th-century façade. St-Pierre is the last relic of the Royal Abbey of Montmartre (*see* 'The Butte Sacrée' overleaf), which disappeared in the Revolution when the elderly, blind and deaf Mother Superior was condemned to death by Fouquier-Tinville for 'blindly and deafly plotting against the Revolution'.

The church was consecrated in 1147 by Pope Eugenius III. The tunnels and quarries underneath have so undermined the foundations that the columns of the nave bend inwards like a German Expressionist film set. Otherwise there is little to see – two 7th-century Merovingian columns near the entrance, 1950s stained glass resembling African textiles and the ghostly tombstone of foundress Adélaïde of Savoy (d. 1134), wife of Louis VI the Fat, who spent her last years at the abbey.

Just north of St-Pierre-de-Montmartre, in **Rue du Chevalier-de-la-Barre**, stood temples to Mercury and Mars, though the last traces of them vanished in the 19th century (*see* 'The Spirit of Mars').

Espace Montmartre Salvador Dalí V3

11 Rue Poulbot, t 01 42 64 40 10, w www. dali-espacemontmartre.com; métro Abbesses. Open Sept–June daily 10–6, July and Aug daily 10–9; adm €7.

This permanent collection of Dalí's sculptures and book illustrations is displayed in a dark, dramatic setting with choreographed spotlights and a soundtrack of the artist's voice. The souvenir shop sells reproductions.

Halle St-Pierre X3–4

2 Rue Ronsard, t 01 42 58 72 89, w www.halle saintpierre.org; métro Anvers. Open daily 10–6, closed August; adm €6. Salon de thé

The Spirit of Mars

The violent spirit of the war god has dominated this area, which may explain why this street bears no trace of Mars' temple today. Under Henry IV, however, enough remained intact for the king to use it as a platform to bombard Paris.

The street is named after the 18-year-old Chevalier de la Barre, who failed to raise his hat before a religious procession in Amiens. His sentence, confirmed by the Paris *Parlement*, was to have his hand cut off and his tongue torn out, followed by decapitation. This did not happen during the Counter-Reformation witch hunt but in 1766, in the middle of the Enlightenment (Voltaire's blistering pen made it a *cause célèbre*), which shows how *ancien* the *ancien régime* could be 33 years before the Revolution.

open daily 10–6. Children's activities Wed, Sat and Sun 3–4pm (plus Mon–Fri during school hols), €6; marionette shows Wed, Sat and Sun, and school hols, €3.

Originally built by a student of Baltard in 1868, the old glass-and-iron market of St-Pierre has been converted to hold two museums: the **Musée d'Art Naïf Max Fourny**, with some 500 works by naïf painters from around the world, and a children's **Musée en Herbe**, with changing exhibits.

MONTMARTRE'S WESTERN SLOPES

Place des Abbesses V4

Métro Abbesses.

The pretty square's pride and joy is its **métro entrance**, one of Guimard's originals and the only one (along with Porte-Dauphine) with its glass roof intact.

The outlandish church decorated with turquoise mosaics is another of Paris' architectural milestones, the neo-Gothic **St-Jean-de-Montmartre**, the first important building in reinforced concrete (the bricks are

The Butte Sacrée

The Romans called this 423ft 'mountain' Mons Mercurii, after its hilltop shrine to the god of commerce, but he lost his billing in the 9th century when the abbot of St-Denis renamed it the Hill of Martyrs – Montmartre, the Butte Sacrée. Foremost among the martyrs was Paris' patron, Denis, although he didn't care for the place; after the Romans gave him the chop in the 3rd century, he picked up his head and walked to the northern suburbs (see p.262).

In 1133, Louis the Fat and Adélaïde of Savoy founded the Royal Abbey of Montmartre on the site of the first Merovingian church to St Denis, leaving the rest of Montmartre a modest hamlet amid vineyards, windmills and gypsum quarries (hence the renowned plaster of Paris). Only Henri IV briefly interrupted its tranquillity in 1589, when he lugged his cannons up the Butte to besiege Paris.

Montmartre became a *commune* (pop. 638) during the Revolution and was renamed Mont Marat. Napoleon wanted to build a temple of peace on the Butte, but the Allied occupation (1814–17) after the final defeat at Waterloo precluded such hypocrisy. The population of the hill soared as workers took refuge from Baron Haussmann's demolitions, but Paris came after them and gobbled up Montmartre itself in 1860.

In February 1871, after the fall of Paris, members of the National Guard made off with 170 cannons that were meant to be surrendered to the Prussians; the money for the cannons had been raised by public subscription, so the Guardsmen reasoned

---

sham), built between 1894 and 1904 by Anatole de Baudot, a pupil of Viollet-le-Duc; step inside to see Baudot's innovative play of interlaced arches.

Chapelle des Auxiliatrices V–W4

11 Rue Yvonne-Le-Tac, **t** *01 42 64 59 29 or* **t** *01 42 23 48 94; métro Abbesses.* **Open** *daily 3–6.*

Although Roman Prefect Sisinius Fescennius ordered Paris' first bishop, Denis, to be executed on the summit of the Mons Mercurii, the executioner was far too lazy to walk all the way up, and Denis was separated from his head here. Although Denis post humously walked off in search of holier ground, the Christians of Montmartre thought the plot sufficiently sanctified and had themselves buried in what became known as the Martyrium. Thomas à Becket visited the shrine during his exile from England, and Jeanne d'Arc made a pilgrimage, starting a trend that lasted until the Revolution. On 15 August 1534, the former Basque soldier and Paris University student Ignatius of Loyola led his fellow Basque St Francis Xavier and five other companions to the Martyrium to recite the initial vows that led to the founding of the Jesuits.

This present chapel was erected in 1887; it has a 7th-century altar and a 13th-century bas-relief of Denis' martyrdom.

Trailing the Artists U4–V2

Leafy, lovely asymmetrical **Place Émile Goudeau**, with its Wallace fountain, steps and benches, is the antithesis of the classic Paris square down on the 'plain' below; note the curious perspective down Rue Berthe which, like many other streets up here, seems to lead to the end of the world. This square, most famously, was the site of the **Bateau Lavoir** (No.13), a leaky, creaking wooden warehouse that Max Jacob named after its resemblance to the floating laundry concessions on the Seine. Among the 'passengers' who rented studio space here were Braque, Gris, Van Dongen, Apollinaire and Picasso. Life was spartan; in winter the tea in the communal pot froze every night and had to be reheated for breakfast, but inspiration was far from lacking. In 1907 Picasso painted his *Demoiselles d'Avignon*, the girls with multiple profiles (not from Avignon, but some prostitutes he knew in Barcelona) and invented Cubism.

they were rightfully theirs and dragged them to the summit of the Butte. On 8 March, before dawn, the regular Army was sent up to seize the guns, but forgot the horses to pull them, causing a fatal delay; by morning schoolteacher Louise Michel, the 'Red Virgin', had sounded the alarm, bringing out a sea of angry, tense and neurotic Guards and civilians. They captured two generals, Thomas and Lecomte, and summarily executed them. Montmartre's 29-year-old mayor, none other than Georges Clemenceau, arrived after the fact, crying '*Pas de sang, mes amis!*' and burst into tears when he saw that he was too late. Meanwhile Thiers and the national government fled to Versailles and Paris' revolutionary leaders, caught by surprise, scrambled to improvise the ill-fated Commune.

The first artists, poets and composers had already moved into Montmartre in the mid-19th century with the workers, drawn by cheap rents and the quality of its air and light. The police knew the village rather as the resort of *apaches*, gangs of Parisian toughs distinguished by their wide berets and corduroy trousers; when Eric Satie began his career playing piano in a Montmartre cabaret, he came to work armed with a hammer. After the First World War the bohemians moved off to the lower rents of Montparnasse, leaving their reputation to the sideshow artists who obligingly provide the tourist busloads something to spend their money on. Off the main stampedes, however, exists a Montmartre that evokes better than any other quarter what Parisian streets looked like before the Second Empire.

One critic of the Bateau Lavoir artists was Montmartre prankster Roland Dorgelès, who thought to fool their spokesman, Apollinaire, by tying a paintbrush to the tail of an ass and calling the result *Et le soleil se coucha sur l'Adriatique*, by a certain Boronali. It was a great success at the Salon des Indépendants, sold for 400F and fooled all the snobs – except Apollinaire. The rest of Montmartre laughed itself silly. In 1970, just as the Bateau Lavoir was to be converted into a museum, it burned down and has been replaced by 25 more comfortable if less picturesque studios; there's a small display on its predecessor in the window.

Among the wooden houses reminiscent of the Bateau Lavoir is **No.5 Rue d'Orchampt**, Paris' first prefab house, brought here from the 1889 World Fair. A big plaque at whimsical No.11 marks the last residence of the 1970s pop singer Dalida, who since her death has become something of a cult figure among the romantic middle classes, and now has her own *place* complete with statue on the other side of the hill. Rue d'Orchampt leads you on to winding **Rue Lepic** and the last two of Montmartre's 30 windmills, **Moulin du Radet** (now an Italian restaurant) and to the left, the **Moulin de la Galette**, built

in 1640 and converted in the early 19th century into a popular *guinguette*, painted by Renoir (*The Ball at the Moulin de la Galette*, 1876, in the Musée d'Orsay).

Rue Tholozé, running south from here off Rue Lepic, is home to the Right Bank's first art cinema, named Studio 28 after the year it was founded. Even it had its rough moments: when Buñuel and Dalí's *L'Age d'Or* was premiered in 1930, Catholic conservatives ripped the screen to shreds.

A stairway passage from Rue Lepic climbs up to **Avenue Junot**, the 'Champs-Elysées of Montmartre', laid out in 1910 in a former wasteland. Now it's a rare street of peaceful Art Deco houses with gardens (Anouk Aimée lives here). No.13 is decorated with mosaics designed by Francisque Poulbot (d. 1946), the artist otherwise guilty of those cloying postcards of Montmartre urchins; at No.15 is the **house of Tristan Tzara** (1926) designed by Viennese architect Adolf Loos.

Tzara read the first Dadaist (anti-war, anti-sense, anti-everything) manifesto in a Zurich café on 8 February 1917, with Hans Arp sitting in with a *brioche* hanging from his nose. After the war, Tzara joined Picabia in bringing Dada to Paris, causing riots with his 'poetry readings' chosen at random from the newspaper or telephone directory, and announcing 'Cubism is a cathedral of *merde* (shit)'. For his own pad, however, Tzara wasn't having any nuttiness; the austere functionalist Loos was himself the author of a manifesto, *Ornament and Crime*.

Have a look at peaceful cul-de-sac Villa Léandre (at No.25), one of the most desirable addresses in Paris, then continue up Avenue Junot and turn right up Rue Simon-Dereure, which narrows into the romantic, ivy-covered Allée des Brouillards (up the stairs). To the right is the entrance to the little **Square Suzanne-Buisson**, where children play and old men toss their *boules* under the strange watchful gaze of a statue of St Denis, head in hands (he stopped at a fountain here to wash the blood off).

Rue Cortot cuts through to Rue du Mont-Cenis, passing the water tower that pokes its way into all the views of Sacré-Cœur. Cobblestoned **Rue St-Rustique**, the oldest street in Montmartre, ducks west off here. At the end of the lane is the **Place Jean-Baptiste-Clément**, named after the composer of the song *Le Temps des Cerises* (hence the cherry tree in the square), the cherries symbolizing the Red Flag of the Commune and the hope that it would one day fly again (the other smash hit born of the Commune was the *Internationale*, with words by a worker named Pottier).

Cimetière de Montmartre S2–U3

20 Av Rachel, t 01 53 42 36 30, métro Place de Clichy. Open summer Mon–Fri 8–6, Sat 8.30–6, Sun 9–6; winter closes 30mins earlier.

Despite the viaduct overhead, this is one of Paris' most romantic graveyards, a favourite last pasture for composers, painters, actors and writers.

There's Berlioz, one of Montmartre's first arty residents, and further up Avenue Berlioz the great German poet Heinrich Heine (who spent long agonizing years dying in Paris, threatening to report God to the Humane Society), film director François Truffaut,

painter Fragonard, poet and critic Théophile Gautier, Alexandre Dumas Jr., Edgar Degas (De Gas on the family tomb), Foucault of pendulum fame (*see* p.172), Offenbach (in the northwest corner), Nijinsky, the Goncourt brothers, Stendhal (whose potty epitaph reads: 'To live, to love, to be a Milanese'), Frédérick Lemaître (the great actor portrayed in *Les Enfants du Paradis*), the celebrated beauty Juliette Récamier, who is said to have died a virgin, and, back near the entrance and exit, the beautiful courtesan Alphonsine Plessis (1824–47), the model for Marguerite Gautier, *La Dame aux Camélias*, who really did die of consumption in the arms of Alexandre Dumas Jr., who made her the literary saint of unrequited love.

NORTHERN MONTMARTRE: ALONG RUE DES SAULES

The Vineyard V2

Rue des Saules; métro Lamarck-Caulaincourt. Not open to the public.

Montmartre's **Vineyard** was planted by the Montmartrois in 1886 in memory of the vines that once covered the Butte. If nothing else, the harvest is an excuse for a colourful neighbourhood wine crush. This results in some 400 bottles of weedy gamay called Clos de Montmartre, the perfect accompaniment, perhaps, for a roast Paris pigeon fed on cigarette butts; it is sold to raise money for the Butte's old folks.

Au Lapin Agile V2

22 Rue des Saules, t 01 46 06 85 87; métro Lamarck-Caulaincourt. Open Tues–Sun 9pm–2am; adm €24 (see p.353).

This, the oldest surviving nightspot in Montmartre, opened in 1860 as the Cabaret des Assassins, but in 1880 a painter named

Gil painted the sign of a nimble rabbit avoiding the pot, a play on his name: the *lapin à Gil* or the *lapin agile*. In the early days, when it was a favourite of Verlaine, Renoir and Clemenceau, customers would set the table themselves and join in singsongs, originating an informal style the French call *à la bonne franquette*. In 1903, Aristide Bruant (*see* p.198) purchased the place to save it from demolition, and thanks to the good humour of his friend Frédé it enjoyed a second period of success. Poor artists could pay for their meals with paintings – as Picasso did with one of his *Harlequins*, now worth millions.

Cimetière St-Vincent V2

*Off Rue St-Vincent, entrance is a sharp right turn on Rue Lucien-Gaulard; **métro** Lamarck-Caulaincourt. **Open** for group visits with a guide; reserve in advance, **t** 01 46 06 29 78.*

Buried here are Swiss composer Arthur Honegger, film actor Harry Baur (d. 1943, after being tortured by the Gestapo), proto-Impressionist Boudin, Belle Époque poster artist Jules Chéret, and Maurice Utrillo (1883–1955), son of artist Suzanne Valadon, who taught him to paint as therapy for adolescent alcoholism. The feeling of solitude in his haunting, empty street scenes of Montmartre (he often painted the **Maison Rose**, on the corner of Rue des Saules) was no accident. Utrillo, like Sartre, thought hell was other people; he reacted so violently whenever a woman appeared in the street (he was prone to exposing himself and shouting: 'This is what I paint with!') that he was only allowed out with a chaperone.

Note the tomb of a couple named Platon and Papoue Argyriades, which resembles a little house; it has a curtained window with a painting of Platon and Papoue looking out. After all the grieving angels and other pomp it is sweetness itself, reminiscent of the pagan tombs, the 'little sitting rooms of the soul', under St Peter's in Rome. The artist Théophile Steinlen (1859–1923), famous for his cats and satirical cartoons of Paris, was originally buried here, but now you'll find him under the statue of an embracing couple in nearby Place Constantin-Pecqueur.

Musée de Montmartre W2

*12 Rue Cortot, **t** 01 46 06 61 11; **métro** Lamarck-Caulaincourt. **Open** Tues–Sun 10–12.30 and 1.30–6, closed 1 Jan, 1 May and 25 Dec; **adm** €4.50.*

Although this may look to be a contrived attraction, it is in fact a genuine neighbourhood museum, set up in the oldest house on the Butte and run by the people of Montmartre. Behind a pretty courtyard full of fuchsias, so healthy they are turning into trees, you'll see prints, pictures and souvenirs that tell the real Montmartre story: the old gypsum quarries that made most of the hill unbuildable until the 19th century, pictures of soldiers chasing revolutionaries through the quarries in 1848 and the old Montmartre skyline of windmills. There are plenty of old photos and maps of the area, some of Toulouse-Lautrec's posters and even the original sign from the Lapin Agile. One little exhibit is absolutely chilling – an overview of a 1933 city plan to partially level the hill, eradicate all of old Montmartre and create a new gridiron street plan for the developers.

PIGALLE

When it's not called Pigalle, the area south of Montmartre is grandly known as Nouvelle Athènes, presumably after its neoclassical architecture, mostly neo-boring and filled with insurance companies. The most attractive parts are **Rue de la Tour-des-Dames** east of Ste-Trinité church (T6) and the **Square d'Orléans** (entrance 80 Rue Taitbout, U6), where George Sand and Chopin lived opposite one another.

On the whole, however, the area around **Place Pigalle** (V4) owes its renown less to the Romantic than to the Erotic. Jean-Baptiste

Sleazy Serge

He was probably le Petit Prince...and became, in face of the tragic reality of life, a touching Quasimodo.

Brigitte Bardot

Even the most flighty American tourist in Paris on 2 March 1991 sensed something was amiss. Glum looks and solemn murmurs filled the cafés; tearful crowds and journalists milled in Rue Verneuil. And then the tourist understood. Paris was mourning one of its own: alackaday, Serge Gainsbourg had kicked the bucket – the ice bucket, in his case. Then perhaps the tourist looked blank, and the Parisians attempted to jog the old memory bank.

Who could forget Serge's cheesy hit songs and films – Bardot in hot pants straddling a bike in *Harley-Davidson*? Or *Bonnie and Clyde* with BB as Bonnie and sulky Serge as Clyde? Or with Jane Birkin in the 1968 heavy-breather with the ding-a-ling melody,

Je t'aime...moi non plus? Or perhaps *Lemon Incest*, the video filmed with Serge lying (albeit clothed) in bed with his pubescent daughter Charlotte?

Like the cigarettes and booze that stole Serge from his adoring public, French pop music should have a health-warning label. But Serge's success, confirmed by the recent issuing of a commemorative CD library of every note he ever croaked, wasn't altogether the result of his songs, or his loopy Franglais lyrics (although once on television he simply belched and farted along to the music) but rather his role as king of insults, the great provocateur, the obscene drunk, the old rogue who burnt a 500F note on television ('not many of you can afford to do this,' he commented with a twinkle). His best mate Jane Birkin helped him create his scruffy image: ill-shaven, dishevelled hair, cigarette dangling, rumpled scout shirt and jeans. Serge had ears you could hang pianos

---

Pigalle was a neoclassical sculptor, and he would be pained if he knew his name conjured up live sex shows instead of his graceful *Mercury Tying his Sandal* in the Louvre. But times are hard in the highly taxed and thoroughly regulated porno industry in Paris, and the selection of seedy sex shops does not compare with New York or even London, confirming the area's transition toward a larger and wider retail sector.

The first taverns and *guinguettes* appeared here in the 18th century, just beyond the Farmers-General wall where booze was cheaper. The **Café de la Nouvelle Athènes**, once at 9 Place Pigalle, was a favourite of Manet and the Impressionists, who had a permanently reserved table. East of the square stood two famous nightspots: the 1807 *guinguette* **Elysée Montmartre** (72 Boulevard de Rochechouart, crowned by a pretty if crumbling bas-relief) and the much later **Le Chat Noir** (No.84) founded in 1881, featuring arty, satirical songs in Parisian slang, accompanied by shadow puppets. It owed part of its tremendous success to the fringe literary clubs that camped out here –

the *Hydropathes*, the *Hirsutes* and the 'Epileptic Pickled Herrings'. The *chansonnier* Aristide Bruant (1833–1925) got his start here, always dressed in the same red shirt, black scarf and wide black hat that Toulouse-Lautrec made famous. Bruant later took over the premises and opened his own club, **Le Mirliton**, which drew the slumming *bourgeoisie* who in their thousands paid to be insulted and provoked (*see* 'Sleazy Serge').

Moulin Rouge T–U4

82 Bd de Clichy, t 01 53 09 82 82; métro Blanche. Open for dinner at 7pm, 1st show daily 9pm, adm €92; 2nd show Sat and Sun only 11pm, adm €82.

Place Blanche, west of Place Pigalle, is embellished with the red wooden sails of a Paris landmark as familiar as the Eiffel Tower: the Moulin Rouge.

It was founded by an ex-butcher named Zidler, who was the first to understand the immense business potential in Paris' congenital vulgarity. Zidler's inspiration was the Elysée Montmartre (*see* above) where people

from, but vacant singers and starlets found him an irresistible Svengali.

In Paris, the best poets and writers have often been bad boys, from François Villon, a murderer and thief who barely escaped the scaffold, to Rabelais, who spent his life dodging a Sorbonne-sponsored auto-da-fé for heresy. Medieval Paris had a grand old tradition of chanson drinking clubs with names like The Society of Peeing Cats or The Liberated Squirrels, each wittier than the next and liable to be closed down for cutting too close to the quick. For Serge's direct role model, however, we have to race ahead a few centuries to Aristide Bruant, the *chansonnier* of Montmartre's cabarets in the late 1880s and 90s. Bruant was a shrewd businessman: he had a trademark stage costume, and made a fortune from insulting the Parisians, who came from all over town to be bullied and lambasted as mugs, pigs, camels and worse. For all that, Bruant was a real poet; he

updated Villon's slangy ballads to create a new genre of French song, a kind of sung poetry performed, according to one critic, with 'the most cutting voice, the most metallic voice I have ever heard; a voice of rioting and the barricades...an arrogant and brutal voice which penetrated your soul like the stab of a switchblade into a straw man'. Bruant's songs also opened the eyes of the bourgeois to the homeless and jobless, the prostitutes, pimps and *apaches* and toughs who end up at the guillotine, and Paris' 'little people'.

Bruant had many followers: Yvette Guilbert, Edith Piaf, Jacques Prévert, Georges Brassens, Juliette Gréco – and even Serge in his way, without poetry or sincerity, but a lot of flab, cynicism and shock for the sake of shock. For the time being, Paris can't provide much better. A deeply conformist culture needs its Quasimodos and court jesters and, as sleazy as Serge was, Paris misses him.

came to dance the *chahut* ('noise, mayhem, high spirits'), as well as its more difficult offspring, a Second Empire quadrille called the *cancan*, performed by women only – thumping and sweating, the most extrovert and erotic dance of the day, with its frilly-knicker-revealing high kicks, cartwheels, *grands écarts* (splits), *port d'armes* (holding a foot as high as possible over one's head), and saucy displays of one's bottom, all to the lilting tunes of Offenbach's popular operetta.

The cancan became orgasmic when danced by the Elysée's La Goulue, who started life as a laundress, and whose name 'the glutton' came from her greedily sucking up the dregs of every pleasure. Her partners included the gaunt, rubbery Valentin-le-Désossé ('the boneless one'), by day a mild-mannered wine merchant, at night a dancing fool, and a dignified girl known as 'Grille-d'Égout' ('sewer grating') because of the spaces between her teeth. All were immortalized by Toulouse-Lautrec, that insatiable moth who haunted Montmartre's cabarets with his sketchbook.

Zidler bought an old dance hall, and left its decoration to a painter, Adolphe Willette,

who stuck a mock windmill on the façade and purchased a plaster elephant with a tiny stage in its gut from the 1889 World Fair, just the thing for hoochie-coochie dancers. From the day it opened on 6 October 1889, the Moulin Rouge was a roaring success: not only did Zidler lure away La Goulue, Valentin-le-Désossé and Grille-d'Égout from the Elysée, but his PR techniques made it respectable for *tout Paris* to attend the show. Perhaps Zidler's greatest theatrical coup was in 1892, when he starred Joseph Pujol of Marseille, 'Le Pétomane', who played all the popular songs of the day with his specially gifted aspirating anus; the king of the Belgians made a special trip to Paris just to hear him. Other regulars of the Moulin Rouge were the *chanteuse* Yvette Guilbert of the long black gloves, the Edith Piaf of her day, and Jane Avril, or Jane la Folle, who came to dance for her own pleasure with a sinuous rapture that personified decadence to the connoisseurs. In 1894, Zidler left the Moulin Rouge, and if it didn't decline, it lost its innovative spark (and Jane Avril) to its competitors. Still going over a hundred years later, however, the Moulin

Rouge has lurched into the new millennium with stars the calibre of Janet Jackson and Vegas kitsch extravaganzas. It still manages to pull the crowds in (and there are still plenty of bare breasts).

Further west on Boulevard de Clichy, the poet **Jacques Prévert** lived and died in the alley of Cité Véron; across the boulevard, note the little **chapel of Ste-Rita**, the patroness of unhappy women and the special church of Pigalle's prostitutes.

ROCHECHOUART AND THE GOUTTE D'OR W4–Z2

Métro Barbès-Rochechouart.

The east end of the 18e is the lively capital of North African and Middle Eastern Paris; during the day, it's a veritable souk full of bargains that draws shoppers from all over Paris. In 1991, when the National Front's high poll ratings made racism fashionable, Mayor Jacques Chirac embarrassed nearly everybody when he walked down the area's main Boulevard Barbès proclaiming that real French people didn't like the smell of foreigners' cooking and complaining about 'polygamists who bring over three or four wives and a dozen kids to live off the state'. In reality this aspect of Paris is here to stay, especially under a Socialist administration that wants as many _sans papiers_ as possible made legal because they all vote left. And this neighbourhood meets a strong need; Rue Livingstone and environs offer the cheapest textiles in France, attracting a cosmopolitan crowd of women who offer a display as colourful as the fabrics.

The souk's main thoroughfare is manic **Boulevard de Rochechouart**, where the pink-plaid plastic bags sprouting from every hand all hail from the massive kinetic vortex of Tati (4 Boulevard de Rochechouart, and at the corner of Rue d'Orsel and Rue de Steinkerque). Although other outlets have opened across the city, this is still _the_ place to come for an exciting scrum around the bins of clothes priced next to nothing.

Adjacent Boulevard Barbès is the border of the **Goutte d'Or**. The name 'golden drop' comes from a white wine produced here in the misty past, but it is a name that has evoked a certain piquancy ever since Zola made it the street where the courtesan _femme fatale_ of his _Nana_ grew up in poverty. Now immigrants from some three dozen different countries live together. Pavement stands spilling into the sidewalks offer kebabs and spicy snacks, and North African music sends its fatalistic laments from the cafés.

St-Germain

St-Germain

France is one country where brainy philosophers get respect, and St-Germain was their citadel; in the postwar decades there were enough eggheads here to make omelettes, sizzling and puffing away with the latest fashionable philosophy. Since the 1960s it has cooled considerably, and in the inevitable urban cycles the haunts of the avant-garde have now been gentrified; one writer recently compared it to Monaco. But despite the absurd rents and surplus posers, St-Germain's essential conviviality remains intact. In spite of the invasion of designer shops, its narrow streets, scarcely violated by the planners, its cafés and bookshops, and the Luxembourg gardens cluttered with chairs all invite you to gas the day away in the spirit of those first eggheads, Voltaire and Diderot, if not Camus, Sartre, Simone de Beauvoir, Foucault and the more recent *germanopratine* sages – yes, this quarter even has its own adjective.

1 Lunch

Le Petit Vatel, *5 Rue Lobineau, t 01 43 54 28 49; métro Mabillon. Open Mon–Sat 12–3 and 7–10.30; closed hols and part of Aug. No smoking.* **Cheap**. When they say *petit* they mean minuscule but good *grand-mère* style meat and vegetable dishes at a good price.

2 Tea and Cakes

Café Procope, *13 Rue de l'Ancienne-Comédie, t 01 40 46 79 00, métro Odéon. Open daily 11.30am–1am.* Paris' oldest café, restored for the Revolution's bicentennial; also has lunch menus.

3 Drinks

Bar du Marché, *75 Rue de Seine; métro Mabillon. Open daily 7.30am–2am.* In the thick of the action, a trendy bar where your drinks money will go a little further. Glamorous crowd packed into narrow rows of tables.

Highlights

Couples' City: Dinner in a private alcove at Lapérouse, p.331

Parisian's City: Play a pick-up chess game in the Jardin du Luxembourg, p.211

Peace and Quiet: The serene Musée Delacroix and the painter's bit of garden, p.208

Paris des Artistes: St-Germain's once cutting-edge galleries and its hallowed cafés, p.205

Grand Siècle Paris: The Académie and library in the Institut de France, p.204

Gritty City: The lancet used on the Sun King's fistula in the Musée de l'Histoire de Médecine, p.210

ALONG THE RIVER

Palais de l'Institut de France V13

*23 Quai de Conti, t 01 44 41 44 41, w www.
bibliotheque-mazarine.fr; métro Pont-Neuf or
Odéon. Open for guided tours Sat, Sun and
hols 3pm; adm free. Bibliothèque Mazarine
open Mon–Fri 10–6, closed 1–15 Aug; bring ID
and two passport photos; 48hr pass free.*

Long ago this was the site of the baleful
Tour de Nesle that marked the west end of
Philippe-Auguste's 1188 wall around Paris.
It was later used as the retreat of the widow
of Philippe V, Jeanne de Bourgogne (d. 1329)
who, when tired of her lovers, stuffed
them into sacks and chucked them out of
the window.

On his deathbed France's ace grafter,
Cardinal Mazarin, willed 2 million *livres* to
construct the Collège des Quatre Nations to
educate 60 students from Alsace, Artois,
Piedmont and Roussillon, the four provinces
incorporated into France during his regime.
To honour his wishes Louis XIV plumped for a
new quay in 1662, toppled the infamous Tour
de Nesle and commissioned Le Vau to design
the college. As a nod towards Mazarin's
Roman origins, Le Vau gave the college a
strong Italian flavour, complete with a
bundle of *fasces* over the door and an oval
dome à la Bernini, which along with its
curved wings forms a handsome Baroque set
piece complementing the Cour Carrée of the
Louvre across the Pont des Arts.

In 1805 Napoleon made the college the
seat of the Institut de France, a body created
in 1795 to unite the Académies of Sciences,
Inscriptions et Belles Lettres and, the grand-
daddy of them all, the Académie Française. If
you're game for the dull, pedantic tour the
highlight is **Mazarin's tomb** by Hardouin-
Mansart, a masterpiece of 17th-century
French sculpture.

Otherwise, pop in to see the **Bibliothèque
Mazarine**, which in 1643 (in another location)
was Paris' first public library. It has since been

The Académie Française

The Académie Française was born in 1635,
when the preciosity of salon hostesses (one
lady would greet guests with: 'Do satisfy the
desire that this chair has to embrace you')
drove a handful of literary men to meet
informally on their own. Richelieu got wind
of their meetings and, ever suspicious,
offered them his 'protection', which they
could hardly refuse. It solved the eternal
problem of what to do with potentially dis-
affected intellectuals: recruit them into an
académie to serve the state. This they do by
'defending' the French language, especially
from the hundred-headed Hydra, Franglais.
Every Thursday afternoon they meet to
compile their official dictionary; they're
closing in on the second half of the alphabet.

Although everyone knows that the writers
not admitted into its ranks (Diderot, Flaubert,
Balzac, Proust, Camus, etc.) make a far more
distinguished list, membership of the
Académie is still a plum to campaign for. In
1980 novelist Marguerite Yourcenar broke
the sex barrier to become the first
'*Immortelle*'. Now there are three.

restored to its original ochre and green
appearance. Travellers used to visit to
ogle the statue of skinny old Voltaire in
the nude, but the Academicians have since
tucked him away somewhere for their
own delectation.

École des Beaux-Arts U13

*14 Rue Bonaparte, t 01 47 03 50 00,
w www.ensba.fr; métro St-Germain-des-Prés.
Courtyards open daily 8–8, otherwise adm
only during exhibitions; guided tours of
building available, call for information.*

Temporary exhibitions are held in the
oldest buildings on this site, Queen
Marguerite de Valois' Chapelle des Louanges
and a chapel (with elegant doors by Goujon)
built for an Augustine monastery after
Marguerite's death. These were built in 1606
and 1619 respectively. The Chapelle des
Louanges boasts Paris' first dome.

During the Revolution, the painter Alexandre Lenoir hijacked the monastery as a depot for 'worthy' religious art (especially the kings' tombs from St-Denis) that he salvaged from the sledge-hammers of the *sans-culottes*. From 1795 to 1814, Lenoir put his collections on display as a museum of French monuments, where the hitherto despised Romanesque and Gothic art – displayed in a shadowy, mysterious, 'medieval' atmosphere – made a great impression on visitors and nurtured a Romantic revival of the Middle Ages. In 1816 the convent became the School of Fine Arts. The main courtyard contains a collage of architectural fragments, most notably the central façade of Henri II's Château d'Anet (1548), with another fine door by Goujon. Other bits were wrecked in May 1968 by art students, an insolence the authorities continue to punish by banning the annual Beaux-Arts ball.

Rue des Beaux-Arts U13

This is one of the main axes of the slowly churning St-Germain art world. The original galleries opened in the 1920s, when they shocked the public by being the first to show modern and abstract works. It's hard to be shocked any more, although you may fall into a trance as you stroll past the rows of big picture windows, inadvertently juxtaposing works of rare enchantment with brain-dead dog meat. Among the galleries here you'll find Di Meo and Patrice Trigano, both specializing in the abstract *École de Paris*, and Claude Bernard, who shows figurative works by Hockney, Bacon, Botero and others.

In 1900, Oscar Wilde, aged 46 but broken by his prison term, came to die 'beyond his means' in the former Hôtel d'Alsace (No.13). At least he kept his good taste to the very end. 'Either this wallpaper goes, or I do,' he grumbled, and died. Anyone who has spent much time in older French hotels knows just how he felt. In the 1840s the poet Gérard de Nerval lived at No.5, in the company of a pet lobster that he took for walks with a blue ribbon around its neck.

Hôtel des Monnaies V13

11 Quai de Conti, **t** *01 40 46 55 35,* **w** *www. monnaiedeparis.fr;* **métro** *Pont-Neuf or Odéon.* **Open** *Tues–Fri 11–5.30, Sat and Sun 12–5.30;* **adm** *€8; tours of the medal workshops Tues and Fri at 2.15, but go early to get a place;* **adm** *€3.*

Jean-Denis Antoine, charged by Louis XV to design the Mint, bucked every lingering rococo urge of the day in favour of clean lines and minimal decoration. The interior offers decidedly more: a fine double-curving stair by the main entrance, handsome courtyards (one with a marker indicating the Paris meridian), and the **Musée de la Monnaie** – not dusty cases of coins and medals, but a vivid, historical display that makes money indecently engrossing.

Although a new mint has been built near Bordeaux, until recently the Hôtel des Monnaies produced all the francs in France; it still produces commemorative medals, a Renaissance art inspired by ancient Roman coins. No one familiar with the taste of Napoleon III will be surprised to see his new railways commemorated with medals of naked ladies stroking big locomotives; more recent medals are on sale in the shop.

Along the *Quais* V13–W14

East along the river stretches Paris' oldest quay, the Quai des Grands-Augustins (1179). The 'big' Augustines who used to live in a convent here would have been shocked to know that their old wine shop at No.51 would in the 1860s become the restaurant **Lapérouse** (*see* p.331). Those watery pictures of game and oysters enclose a sumptuous interior that was famous not for its food but for upper-crust hanky-panky: the intimate alcoves on the first floor were booked by lawyers and politicians, who, according to a convenient French law, could not be arrested for adultery in what was technically a public place. The cooking has since improved, but the waiters still knock before entering your little bower of bliss.

The stately *hôtel particulier* at No.7 Rue des Grands-Augustins was from 1936 to 1955 Picasso's last and most luxurious address in Paris, as well as the setting for Balzac's *The Unknown Masterpiece*. Picasso painted a masterpiece here that is hardly unknown – *Guernica* – and remained here throughout the Occupation, far too monumental for even the Nazis to harass, as much as Hitler despised his politics and art.

The frenetic **Rue Dauphine**, laid out in 1607 as the southern extension to Pont Neuf, was so fashionable that it was chosen for France's first street lamps in 1763, which shone so brilliantly that Paris earned the name 'City of Light'. The *hôtel particulier* at No.31 has beautiful 18th-century ironwork, while next door at No.33 was **Le Tabou**, the most renowned of the postwar existentialist jazz cellars, where Juliette Gréco and Boris Vian sang to slouching young Parisiennes in black turtlenecks, black nails and black lipstick.

PLACE ST-GERMAIN-DES-PRÉS

Philosophers' Haunts U14

Place St-Germain-des-Prés, at the crossroads of Rue Bonaparte (the only street in Paris named after Napoleon) and Boulevard St-Germain, which Baron Haussmann slashed through the heart of the Left Bank in 1880, has four *germanopratine* institutions.

Whether the first, **Les Deux Magots** café (*see* p.334), is indeed '*le rendez-vous de l'élite intellectuelle*', as claimed by its own menu, or the 'Two Maggots' of American teenagers, it does offer grandstand views of St-Germain. Inside, the two statues of Chinese mandarins, or *magots*, date from the shop's original vocation: selling silks. The name was retained when it became a café in 1875; Mallarmé, Verlaine and Rimbaud gave it its literary seal of approval in the 1880s, and the

café has distributed its own literary prize since 1933. A few doors down, its rival **Le Flore** (*see* p.334) opened in 1890. It too attracted a brainy clientele; Picasso and Apollinaire would edit art magazines in the back, Sartre and Camus were regulars, only to stalwartly ignore each other's presence.

On the south side of the boulevard, **Le Drugstore**, a groovy hangout in the 1960s, has made way for Emporio Armani, although its neighbour, **Brasserie Lipp**, still packs Paris' *Who's Who* in with a *choucroute* unchanged since 1920.

Église St-Germain-des-Prés U14

3 Place St-Germain-des-Prés, t 01 43 25 41 71; métro St-Germain-des-Prés. Open daily 8–7.

Outside this church, one of the most venerable in Paris, sits a statue of Diderot, quill in hand, who seems to be studying it for an article in his *Encylopédie*.

Perhaps it would read like this: when Childebert I, son of Clovis, returned from the siege of Saragossa in 543, his booty included a piece of the True Cross and the tunic of St Vincent. Germanus, bishop of Paris, convinced Childebert that he should found an abbey to house the relics, and the king endowed it with land stretching from the Petit Pont to the suburb of Meudon. When Germanus himself was canonized, the church changed its name to St-Germain – 'St-Germain the Golden', people called it, for all its shimmering treasures and mosaics. It was one of the most important Benedictine monasteries in France, and until Dagobert (d. 639) it was the burial place of the Merovingian kings. After the Norman pillage of 866, a new St-Germain was rebuilt and protected by high walls and turrets. Of this early Romanesque church, little has survived: capitals (now mostly in the Musée de Cluny) and the base of the massive tower on the west front. The nave, choir, east and west towers were rebuilt in 1193. Architect Peter de Montreuil added a Lady Chapel, as beautiful as his Sainte-Chapelle.

The Intellectual Life

If urbanity is St-Germain's middle name, it owes much to its parent, the Benedictine abbey of St-Germain-des-Prés. Like the Temple and the Latin Quarter, it was a walled fiefdom for hundreds of years, a law unto itself but ruled by abbots with a certain cosmopolitan flair (one was a retired king of Poland). The scholarly monks, specialists in ancient manuscripts, set the intellectual tone of the quarter; art, food and fashion from the rest of Europe and the East were introduced into Paris through the abbey's month-long fair. Theatres prospered; the first coffee houses opened here; and actors, Protestants, foreign artists and workers outside the pale of Paris' monopolistic guilds could live in independent St-Germain, so that by 1697 the population included 16,000 foreigners, far more than in any other quarter of Paris. Ideas circulated more freely as well; if Rousseau and Voltaire got short shrift at the Sorbonne, they were published and discussed in St-Germain. Local cafés later became hotbeds of Revolutionary activity.

The two wives of Henri IV, Marguerite de Valois and Marie de' Medici, started the fashion for building *hôtels particuliers* and palaces in St-Germain and its more illustrious Faubourg. Aristocratic presence helped to preserve the area from 19th-century modernizers, and even from the worst of the Occupation. In its cafés (the coffee was ersatz, but the stove fires were irresistible) Paris' intellectuals kept the spark alive in a circle around Jean-Paul Sartre and Simone de Beauvoir, the notebook-scribbling high priest and priestess of St-Germain. After the war the spark spread into smoky jazz cellars, private clubs and galleries spilling over with abstract works of the *École de Paris*. Everyone was tremendously cool, which meant being tremendously bored; jaded youth stewed in existential *ennui*, divesting its unwanted consciousness on pinball machines, Le Drugstore and the latest Godard film.

Today, jaded youth can hardly afford a coffee in Boulevard St-Germain, and switched-on couples go deep into debt to buy a former maid's room tucked under the steep slope of a mansard roof. The contemporary Parisian art world has flown over the river to the Marais, Beaubourg and Bastille quarters, while the arteries of St-Germain's galleries harden around well-established artists and plain old antiques.

It became the custom for the king to appoint abbots, or for the abbots to become kings: the grandfather and father of Hugues Capet were abbots, as was Hugues himself before becoming king in 987. Royal patronage enabled St-Germain to do as it pleased, and in 1530 its scholars were the first to translate the Bible into French, in face of violent opposition from the Sorbonne and *Parlement*.

In 1789 St-Germain's precious tombs and reliquaries were destroyed, the famous library confiscated (to become the core of the Bibliothèque Nationale), while the church was converted into a saltpetre factory. The damage had only just begun: in 1840 Victor Hugo led a campaign for St-Germain's restoration, and for the next 20 years much of what the Revolutionaries missed fell victim to the hacks hired to save it.

To create Rue de l'Abbaye, the beautiful Lady Chapel, cloister and refectory were sacrificed. Fragments of it, with the chapter house (against the wall) and refectory (ruined window), can be seen on the corner of Place St-Germain-des-Prés and Rue de l'Abbaye in Square Laurent-Prache. Here, too, is a bronze *Head of a Woman* by Picasso (1959), a memorial to his friend, poet Guillaume Apollinaire, who died in 1918.

The restorers were just warming up. Next two of the church's three towers were truncated, fine details were bashed or replaced by cheap copies, and the walls botched by Ingres' pupil Hippolyte Flandrin (1854–63) – murals so excruciating that a score of petitions have been circulated to have them painted over.

The front porch of St-Germain had already undergone an act of vandalism, in the 17th century, and only a damaged carved lintel survives from the original entrance. Squint past Flandrin's colours to appreciate the proportions of the church – the choir, with its mix of ogival and rounded arches and five radiating chapels is an especially lovely example of the transition from Romanesque to Gothic. The marble shafts in the short columns above the arcade are from the 6th century, the only Merovingian work *in situ* in Paris.

The second chapel in the choir contains the remaining bits of **René Descartes** (1596–1650), who died in Stockholm, his frail health a victim to Queen Christina's insistence on having her philosophy lesson at 5am, even in the middle of a Swedish winter. When Descartes' writings began to attract attention, France demanded his body, but his skull is in the Musée de l'Homme. In the north transept lies John Casimir (d. 1672), king of Poland, who preferred to spend his last years as abbot of St-Germain.

At 5 Rue de l'Abbaye stands the **Palais Abbatial**, one of the few Renaissance buildings to survive the storms of Paris. It was built in 1586 by the Cardinal-Abbot Charles of Bourbon, who in 1589 let himself be proclaimed King Charles X by the Catholic League in place of the rightful heir, his nephew Henri IV. When Henri captured Paris, he bagged his presumptuous uncle as well, who died a year later of chagrin. The courtyard of the abbot's palace is now the dainty **Place Furstemberg**, with its paulownia trees, a serendipitous gem of urban design.

Musée Delacroix U14

*6 Rue de Furstemberg, **t** 01 44 41 86 50, **w** www.rmn.fr; **métro** St-Germain-des-Prés. **Open** Wed–Mon 9.30–5, last **adm** 4.30; **adm** €4, free on 1st Sun of the month.*

This was the last home of Eugène Delacroix, who moved here in 1857 to be close to St-Sulpice. Sketches, etchings and a dozen minor paintings hang in his lodgings and atelier, and there's a quiet garden that suited the old bachelor to a T. For despite the romantic, exotic pre-Impressionistic fervour of his paintings, Delacroix liked his peace and quiet. Soon after painting his most famous work, *Liberty Leading the People*, he wrote to his mistress: 'Those people (the republicans) nauseate me. I wish I were an Austrian.'

Square F. Desruelles and Rue Mabillon U14

St-Germain's flying buttresses (among the first in France) form a handsome backdrop to Square F. Desruelles, on Boulevard St-Germain.

The now-dingy glazed portico on the wall was made for the Sèvres factory pavilion in the 1900 Exposition. Two hundred years ago this was the abbey's **cemetery**, near the abbey prison; in September 1792 a mob of thugs, fresh from hacking up 116 Carmelites in Rue Vaugirard, took over the prison and held mock trials before butchering 318 more monks in their own graveyard.

Running south of the square is **Rue Mabillon**, once the centre of the famous fair of St-Germain (*see below*), the main source of funding for the abbey.

The St-Germain Fair

From 1482 until the Revolution this was the biggest fair in Paris, beginning on 3 February and lasting until Palm Sunday. It sold everything except weapons or books: fabrics the first week, crockery and porcelain the second, and luxuries the third (dressing gowns from Marseille, Siamese bonnets, Milan cheeses, gold necklaces, cement to fill smallpox scars). The third week drew the greatest crowds – commoners during the day, and the gentry, including the king himself, at night, when the fair was illuminated like fairyland. The distractions were nonstop: acrobats, operas, comedies, fortune-tellers, games of chance and cabarets offering the finest wines. The Marché de St-Germain in Rue Mabillon was built over the main fair pavilion, while the buildings on the left mark the ground level in the fair's heyday.

EAST ALONG BD ST-GERMAIN

Rue de l'Ancienne-Comédie and Around

The Old Comédie Française V14

*14 Rue de l'Ancienne-Comédie; **métro** Odéon.*

The building where the old theatre company trod the boards is distinguished by a figure of Minerva by Le Hongre, reclining lazily across its façade.

In 1680, the better to control the content of Paris' theatres, Louis XIV ordered Molière's old troupe to merge with a company at the Hôtel de Bourgogne to form the Comédie Française (to distinguish it from Comédie Italienne). The combined company moved to a *jeu de paume* (an enclosure for real tennis) here and converted it into the first Italian-style hemicycle theatre in France, with seating for 1,500 arranged in three tiers. The Comédie lost its lease in 1770 and moved to the Odéon (*see* below).

Opposite is Paris' oldest coffee house, **Café Procope** (*see* p 334), which relocated here from Rue de Tournon to be near the theatre. Coffee came to France by way of Turkey and was first sold by street vendors at the St-Germain fair. In spite of warnings that it caused impotence, the new beverage swept Paris by storm. Armenians opened the first cafés, but it was an enterprising Sicilian nobleman turned waiter named Procopio dei Coltelli who in 1686 hit on the right formula, serving coffee, chocolate, alcohol and food, while encouraging customers to smoke and gamble. It was so successful that France's greatest historian, Jules Michelet, wrote that coffee led indirectly to the Revolution because it made people talk more than ever.

Rue de l'Ancienne-Comédie ends at the Carrefour de Buci, the most fashionable crossroads of the Left Bank in the 18th century, and **Rue de Buci**, today host to the city's most fashionable market (particularly at weekends).

Cour du Commerce-St-André V14

To the east, off Rue St-André-des-Arts, is the cobblestoned Cour du Commerce-St-André, opened in 1776. This is Paris' oldest *passage*, built before new iron and glass engineering techniques were to make them the marvel of the Right Bank (*see* pp.276–9).

Midway along it, to your left, extend three minute courtyards known collectively as the **Cour de Rohan**. In the first courtyard, the gentle Dr Joseph-Ignace Guillotin and a carpenter named Schmidt used sheep to test their decapitation machine, a design improvement on the 15th-century *mannaja* used in Italy, Provence and Edinburgh. Guillotin claimed that the victim felt only a cool 'puff of air on the neck', but to the end of his life (he died peacefully, in bed) protested against the use of his name for the device.

There's a pretty Renaissance house covered with vines in the second courtyard, part of the *hôtel* of Diane de Poitiers; the iron tripod in the corner was a once-common urban sight, a *pas de mule* (horse mount).

Around Carrefour de l'Odéon

Place Henri-Mondor V14

Métro Odéon.

Before Haussmann got his mitts on it, this was the site of Danton's house, where Robespierre's toadies arrested 'the tribune of the people' in April 1794. 'I would rather be guillotined than a guillotiner,' Danton declared. 'Besides, my life is not worth the trouble, and I am sick of the world.' When Danton and his neighbour, Camille Desmoulins, went to the scaffold on the same day, the Revolution lost its last advocates of humanity and moderation and Paris sank into the Terror.

Danton is remembered by an unflatteringly corpulent statue, but one that helpfully points motorists the way down one-way Boulevard St-Germain.

Maison Auguste Comte V15

10 Rue Monsieur-le-Prince, on the second floor, t 01 43 26 08 56; métro Odéon. Open Tues 2–5, or by appointment; adm free.

This is the capital's murkiest museum, maintained as a shrine to the 'Father of Sociology'. Born in 1798, Comte was an apostate disciple of social reformer Saint-Simon before he cooked up his six-volume *Cours de Philosophie Positive* (1830–41), based on the loopy theory that everything could be known through pure science – taking mathematics as the base of knowledge, wisdom rose in a strict hierarchy through physics, chemistry and biology to reach the ultimate science: sociology. This pyramid of wisdom gained a sentimental side in 1844, when Comte met his ideal woman, Clotilde de Vaux. She died two years later, and Comte devoted the rest of his life to her cult, which he called the 'Religion of Humanity', a mix of science, social improvement and mumbo-jumbo that found most of its converts in Brazil.

Musée de l'Histoire de la Médecine V14–W15

12 Rue de l'École de Médecine, in the Université René Descartes, t 01 40 46 16 93; métro Odéon. Open Mon–Wed, Fri and Sat 2–5.30, closed hols; adm €3.50. Guided tour on Tues at 2.30; adm €8.

The Faculté de Médecine, a fine-proportioned neoclassical number built in 1776, makes the most of its available space with an upper floor that runs over the traditional screening wall. Within (ask or you'll never find it) is the museum. In 1992, on the night it reopened after major restoration, a fire brought down the roof. Fortunately its prizes survived, and amid paintings of medicine's early movements and lots of damsels in medical distress, there's the very first stethoscope (invented by Laënnec in 1817, just in time to hear the dying heartbeats of Madame de Staël); a 3,000-piece wooden skeleton commissioned by Napoleon; a 17th-century Japanese mannequin showing acupuncture points; and the lancet used on Louis XIV's anal fistula in 1687, an operation of momentous import to posterity because it was the first time a surgeon performed the actual cutting instead of talking a barber through it. There was one casualty. In beating out the time of a Te Deum celebrating the king's recovery, the composer Lully struck himself in the foot with his cane and died of the infected wound.

Université Paris VI V–W15

Opposite the museum, you can go into the courtyard of the Université Paris VI (*schooldays only 10–6*). Originally this was Paris' most important Franciscan convent, known as the Cordeliers after the ropes the friars wore instead of belts. The Franciscans were chucked out in the Revolution, and within their walls Danton founded his club, a rival to Robespierre's hard-hearted Jacobins on the Right Bank. The convent was demolished in the 19th century for the medical school, but in the courtyard, the Flamboyant Gothic refectory and dormitory (1370) stand apart from the bustle, a sweet forget-me-not from the past.

JARDIN DU LUXEM-BOURG, ODÉON AND ST-SULPICE

Palais du Luxembourg and Petit Luxembourg U15–V16

15 Rue de Vaugirard (the longest street in Paris); t 01 42 34 20 00; métro Odéon, RER Luxembourg. Closed to the public. Musée du Luxembourg: 19 Rue de Vaugirard, t 01 42 34 25 95. Open Tues–Thurs 10–7, Sat–Sun 10–9, Mon and Fri 10–10.30; adm €9.

'Twas a dark and stormy night when the newly widowed Marie de' Medici, Regent of France, ordered her coachman to drive her to the Bastille, where she brazenly pinched all the money her husband, Henri IV, had set aside in case of war. Marie used it to buy land south of Rue de Vaugirard to be near her favourite Italian intriguers: Concini (whom she made a *maréchal* of France) and his wife, Leonora Galigaï. And in 1612, on the death of the Duke of Luxembourg, Marie added his *hôtel particulier* (now the **Petit Luxembourg**) to her estate. But the regent's ambitions were hardly *petite*; in fact, she dreamed of a replica of her girlhood home, Florence's vast Pitti Palace.

Architect Salomon de Brosse managed to dissuade her in favour of a more traditional French mansion, but decorated it with Florentine touches, such as the rusticated bands of stone that give it a corrugated look, and its 'ringed' Tuscan columns. Marie's enjoyment, however, was cut short when she was exiled to Cologne, where she spent her last 10 years after conspiring against Cardinal Richelieu. Since 1958 the palace has been the seat of the French **Senate**, but terrorist bombings in 1995 made it touchy about visitors.

Facing the Senate, under the portico at 17 bis Rue de Vaugirard, the wall is marked with a **metre**, a rare survivor of the Revolution's campaign to familiarize the population with its newfangled measure.

At the west end of the big palace, the delightful Petit Luxembourg was Paris' first public art gallery, and still offers temporary exhibitions in its **Musée du Luxembourg**.

Jardin du Luxembourg T17–V15

Bd St-Michel, t 01 42 34 20 00; RER Luxembourg. Open April–Oct daily 7.30am–9.30pm, Nov–Mar daily 8.15–5. Théâtre de Marionnettes, t 01 43 26 46 47. Open Wed at 4, Sat and Sun at 11 and 4; adm free.

In the time of Julian the Apostate, this was a military encampment called Lucotitius (hence the gardens' old nickname 'Luco'). Now a very welcome Left Bank oasis, the Jardin du Luxembourg remembers its

foundress with the long pool of the **Fontaine de Médicis**, located near the gate, just east of the big palace. Dating from 1624, it's one of the most romantic rendezvous in Paris, dappled by the shade of plane trees and adorned with 19th-century statues of the lovers Acis and Galatea about to be ambushed by the jealous cyclops Polyphemus. They are only the first of a cast of marble men and women big enough for a Cecil B. de Mille costumier. The godawful Marie de' Medici herself figures among the Great Women of France posing around the central basin; in the trees towards Rue Guynemer, there's a midget *Statue of Liberty* by Bertholdi, who modelled her on his mom and gradually made her bigger (as on the Île des Cygnes) and bigger (as in New York).

Metal chairs are scattered under the trees, although the scarce lawns are out of bounds, unless you're in the company of a toddler. The kids have all the fun – on an opulent carrousel designed by Charles Garnier, riding pony carts and mini-cars, sailing boats in the Grand Bassin, or watching Guignol in the **Théâtre de Marionnettes**.

Théâtre de l'Odéon V15

1 Place Paul-Claudel, t 01 44 41 36 36; métro Odéon, RER Luxembourg. Open for performances only.

Built by Louis XV in 1782, the neoclassical Théâtre de l'Odéon (full name Odéon-Théâtre de l'Europe) was the first public theatre in Paris designed exclusively for drama. Its austere Doric façade is attractively set in the semicircular Place de l'Odéon, while porticoes on either flank integrate the building into the square itself. The design was a hit; after fires in 1807 and 1818, the theatre was faithfully reconstructed as it was.

For decades, however, the Odéon was a commercial flop. During the Revolution its troupe split, the pro-Republican actors going off to the Comédie Française and the Royalists sticking it out here until they were carted off to the slammer. In the next century the theatre had a few successes

(Bizet's *L'Arlésienne*, in 1872), but it only became popular after the Second World War when Jean-Louis Barrault and Madeleine Renaud quickened its pulse with contemporary drama. In May 1968, Barrault and Renaud even took their enthusiasm to the streets, distributing Roman helmets from the wardrobe to protect student skulls from billy clubs. They were immediately sacked.

Rue de Tournon V14–15

Métro Mabillon.

You could fill a wax museum with the luminaries who once graced Rue de Tournon, a street of distinguished 18th-century *hôtels particuliers* and bookshops. Many are remembered with plaques: Balzac, Musset and André Gide (at various times) lived at No.2; the American Revolutionary admiral John Paul Jones died at No.19, after serving in the navy of Catherine the Great; Casanova lived at No.27; the Concini conspirators, and later Louis XIII (during the crisis over Cardinal Richelieu), lived at No.10, the Hôtel des Ambassadeurs. At No.6, the **Institut Français d'Architecture** (*t 01 46 33 90 36; open Tues–Sun 12.30–7; adm free*) offers imaginative exhibits and displays on architectural projects going up around the world, while at No.8 lived the very first of St-Germain's 'amazons', **Théroigne de Méricourt** (*see* 'The Amazon of St-Germain').

St-Sulpice U15

Place St-Sulpice, t 01 46 33 21 78; métro St-Sulpice. Open daily 7.45am–7.30pm.

The centrepiece of Place St-Sulpice, the **Fontaine des Quatre Evêques** (1844), is punningly known as the Fontaine des Quatre Points Cardinaux – each bishop faces a cardinal point, but none were ever (*point*) made cardinals. Behind rises **St-Sulpice**, a church with the charm of a train station.

In the 12th century the abbots of St-Germain founded a church to St Sulpicius (a 6th-century archbishop of Bourges) for the peasants of their domain, who were

The Amazon of St-Germain

Few women had better Revolutionary credentials than Théroigne de Méricourt: she was awarded a sabre of honour for her role in the taking of the Bastille, and in October 1790, painted red, dressed in feathers and armed with the aforementioned sabre, pistols and smelling salts (against the stench of the unwashed Parisian mob), she led the march of women and children on Versailles, where she boldly gave Marie-Antoinette a piece of her mind. Later, she would lead a column of women on the assault of the Tuileries (20 June 1791).

Théroigne de Méricourt's boudoir in this *hôtel particulier* was as famous for its decorations – prints of the executions, weapons and copies of the Declaration of the Rights of Man – as for its visitors: Danton, Camille Desmoulins and the 'Archangel' Saint-Just. On Revolutionary playing cards her likeness replaced the queen of spades. Her flamboyant speech and dress (she wore nothing but tricolour costumes and facepaint) and countless lovers infuriated Robespierre's prudish Madame Lafarges, who ambushed, stripped and whipped her one day as she went to the Assemblée Nationale. This display of fury from a fellow woman deranged her, and she ended up running about naked on all fours, howling in the madhouse at the Salpêtrière.

not allowed in the snooty monastic church. St-Sulpice's present incarnation dates from 1646, but by the time the builders reached the façade in 1732, the original Baroque plan seemed old-fashioned, resulting in a competition, won by an even more antique design by a Florentine named Servandoni. Other architects stripped Servandoni's plans down to a double-decker Doric and Ionic loggia bookended by factory-chimney bell towers, never crowned with the soaring pinnacles Servandoni intended.

Inside the grey, cavernous nave, railway clocks tick down the minutes to the next TGV to heaven. The organ is one of the most seriously overwrought in Paris; the holy water stoups are two enormous clam shells, gifts from Venice to François I. In such a setting, the lush, romantic murals by Delacroix in the first chapel on the right literally radiate warmth: *Jacob Wrestling with the Angel* and *Heliodorus in the Temple* (1858–61). The last chapel before the right transept contains the Hallowe'en tomb of Curé Languet de Gergy (1750) by Michelangelo Slodtz. The copper strip across the transept traces the Paris meridian, and if you come at the winter solstice you'll see a sunray strike the centre of the obelisk.

THE FAUBOURG ST-GERMAIN

The western reaches of Boulevard Saint-Germain form a genuine border, between regular old St-Germain of the 6e *arrondissement* and its blue-blooded Faubourg of the 7e. High heels crack like rifles in hushed streets hemmed in by aristocratic mansions where, by communal consent, nothing ever happens. Bigwigs began migrating here in the 17th and 18th centuries from the Marais, often by way of Versailles, where they had been bored to tears. The descendants of those lucky enough to keep their heads still live in the same apartments, although ministries, institutes and embassies now occupy the grandest *hôtels particuliers*. Others around Rue des Saints-Pères have become antique shops; the street hosts an antiquarians' fair in May.

The Faubourg isn't the most inviting place for tramping about unless you mean to do some serious window shopping, but there are a few sights to be seen as you go.

Rue du Dragon T14

Métro *St-Germain-des-Prés or St-Sulpice.*

Paintings were a popular buy at the St-Germain fair (*see* p.208), especially those by the colony of foreign (often Protestant) artists who did not belong to the official artists' guild, the Maîtrise. Many of these 'pirates' had their ateliers in **Rue du Dragon** (most notably No.37). To transport their works to the fair they had to cross 200 feet of land belonging to the city of Paris – where guild members lay in ambush to seize and destroy their 'illegal' paintings. The artists retorted by hiding their canvases in loaves of bread, up ladies' skirts, and outrunning guildsmen in the middle of the night.

At the end of Rue du Dragon is the **Carrefour de la Croix Rouge**. In the 16th century a ruined temple of Isis still survived, attracting a few infidels on the sly until priests exorcized the bogeys with a giant crucifix painted red. Paganism has made a comeback, however, in the saucy *Centaur* – Paris' homage to Picasso – contrived of metal bits and bobs by César in 1985. The tail resembles the contents of a gardener's shed, and it comes equipped, unlike classical centaurs, with male pokers at the front and back.

Square Boucicaut and Au Bon Marché R–S15

Métro *Sèvres-Babylone.*

Presiding over Square Boucicaut is a white marshmallow statue of the plump and caring Madame Boucicaut as an allegory of charity. Her husband Aristide was the founder of **Au Bon Marché**, the world's first department store, just across Rue Velpeau. Au Bon Marché caused a revolution in retailing and consumer attitudes when it opened its doors in 1852. Boucicaut's innovations were in essence three: prices fixed and clearly marked on each item (compared to the old bazaar-like haggling); low price mark-ups to encourage volume sales (thanks to the new Industrial Age glut of machine-made goods); and the concept of browsing through *entrée libre* – free entrance to anyone, whether or not they wanted to buy (previously, merely to enter a shop implied a purchase). But what made the department store a success from the start (turnover rose from 450,000 francs in 1852 to 7 million francs in 1863) was a phenomenon Marx called 'commodity fetishism': Boucicaut's ingenious displays, juxtaposing the most incongruous items in exotic settings, gave consumer goods a magical mystique and a status far removed from their use. Objects became desirable in themselves, so instead of saving money in department stores, people spent more.

To accommodate the masses of entranced shoppers, Louis-Charles Boileu and Eiffel designed a new Au Bon Marché in 1878. Based on the iron and glass *passages* of the Right Bank (*see* pp.276–9), the store features a central glass-roofed well, surrounded by hanging iron galleries. The basic structure survives behind a 1920 façade, minus the grand staircase that was once its glory.

On the other side of Rue du Bac a second Au Bon Marché building (1900) offers an array of gastronomic fetishism.

Along Rue du Bac R15–T12

Between the buildings of the Bon Marché stretches Rue du Bac (named not after the dreaded exam to get into university, but the old ferry over the Seine).

Chapelle de la Médaille Miraculeuse R15

140 Rue du Bac, t 01 49 54 78 88; métro Sèvres-Babylone. Open Wed–Mon 7.45–1 and 2.30–7, Tues 7.45–7.

You'll notice most of the traffic pulls up in front of No.140; what from a distance appears to be a common Parisian garage entrance is in fact the bizarre Chapelle de la Médaille Miraculeuse, where in 1830 the Virgin made the first of a string of appearances in France. She asked a young Fille de Charité named Catherine Labouré to mint a holy medal with her image on it, promising that 'all who wear it around their necks will

receive great rewards'. Since then, 500 million have been sold. The nuns will sell you one if you like.

Musée Maillol/Fondation Dina Vierny R14

59 Rue de Grenelle, t 01 42 22 59 58, w www. museemaillol.com; métro Sèvres-Babylone or Rue du Bac. Open Wed–Mon 11–6, closed hols; adm €7.

Located on one of the most important streets of the 7e, the Musée Maillol is dedicated to the Catalan sculptor who believed any aspect of creation could be represented by an heroic female nude. In the 1730s, the merchants' provost Etienne Turgot thought to supply the area (next to the museum) with much-needed water and panache by commissioning the fine theatrical rococo **Fontaine des Quatre Saisons** (1739) from the sculptor Bouchardon. The allegory represents the city of Paris, enthroned between the Seine and the Marne, while bas-reliefs of the four seasons pose on the wings.

At No.51, **Barthélemy** provides the presidential table with the best-ripened cheeses in Paris.

Northwest towards the River

Maybe it's the ghosts of Proust and Edith Wharton, the lack of trees, the heavy blank faces that its *hôtels particuliers* turn to the streets, but there's something Florentine and mysterious about this part of the *quartier*. It was the first purely residential area in Paris, and shops or cafés remain scarce. The increasing police presence hints that you are nearing the **Hôtel Matignon** (in Rue de Varenne; métro Rue du Bac; Q14), the second most expensive hotel in Paris and the official residence of the prime minister.

The Latin Quarter

1 Lunch

Le Balzar, *49 Rue des Écoles*, **t** *01 43 54 13 67*;
métro Maubert-Mutualité. **Open** *daily
8–12pm*. **Expensive**. The classic brasserie (bar-
restaurant) of the quarter, with old-
fashioned leather seats and lots of mirrors,
packed with academics at lunch time.

2 Tea and Cakes

La Fourmi Ailée, *8 Rue du Fouarre*; *métro
St-Michel or Maubert-Mutualité*. **Open** *daily
12–12*. A cosy atmosphere in a former glassworks, fire in the fireplace, good salads,
scones and excellent desserts.

3 Drinks

Le Piano Vache, *8 Rue Laplace*;
métro Maubert-Mutualité. **Open** *daily
12pm–2am*. Relaxed, noisy and fun student
bar, offering killer cocktails.

The Latin Quarter

The Latin Quarter is one of Paris' great
clichés, where Abelard taught, Villon fought,
Erasmus thought and Mimi coughed. Its
name was bestowed by a student named
Rabelais, for Latin (with an excruciating
nasal twang) was the only language
permitted in the university precincts, spoken
by the blackhearted judges of the Sorbonne
down to their sooty kitchen scullions, until
Napoleon said *non*. Napoleon's 19th-century
successors tended to regard the Latin
Quarter itself as an anachronism, and
rubbed most of its medieval abbeys, colleges
and slums off the map. The quarter's main
street, Boulevard St-Michel ('Boul' Mich'),
was laid out in 1859, but its original paving is
anchored under thick asphalt, having proven
too convenient for slinging at the police in
May 68. Since then, most of the students
have been dispersed throughout Paris and
its suburbs.

But once you too have dispersed any lingering romantic or operatic notions that the
Latin Quarter evokes, it can be good fun,

especially at night, when it becomes the
headquarters for an informal United
Nations of goodwill.

There's plenty to see during the day
as well: Gothic churches, the Panthéon,
two generally ignored museums (of the
police and public assistance) full of Paris
trivia, and – best of all – the Musée de
Cluny, with its sensational collection of
medieval art.

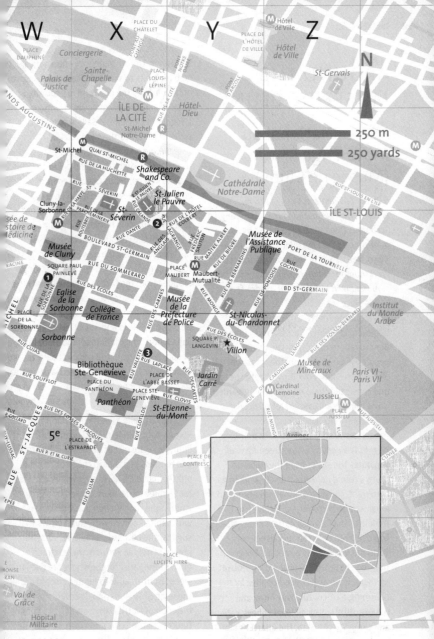

Highlights

Couples' City: The exquisite medieval charms in the Musée de Cluny, p.218

Parisian's City: Light a candle at the shrine of the city's patron saint in St-Étienne-du-Mont, p.227

Peace and Quiet: The hallowed halls of the Panthéon, p.228

Paris des Artistes: Seek out works by Pierre Puvis de Chavannes, favoured painter of the Third Republic, pp.225 and 229

Grand Siècle Paris: The Chapelle de Ste-Ursule-de-la-Sorbonne, the first Baroque church in Paris, p.225

Gritty City: Crime and punishment, Paris style, in the Musée de la Préfecture de Police, p.222

AROUND THE MUSÉE DE CLUNY

Musée National du Moyen Age (Musée de Cluny) W15

*6 Place Paul Painlevé, **t** 01 53 73 78 16, **w** www.musee-moyenage.fr; **métro** Cluny-La Sorbonne. **Open** Wed–Mon 9.15–5.45 (last adm 5.15), closed 1 Jan, 1 May, 25 Dec; **adm** €5.50, free 1st Sun of the month. Summer workshops for children. Medieval concerts in summer on Fri 12.30 and Sat 4; adm €5.50.*

This place is old. The baths, or Thermes de Cluny (dating from c. 215), overlooking Boulevard St-Germain, are the most impressive Roman relic in Paris. They survived because people lived in them until the 1330s, when the Benedictine abbey of Cluny bought the land and converted them into a hanging garden.

The abbey's adjacent *hôtel particulier* is one of only two Gothic/early Renaissance residences to survive in Paris. As in many later *hôtels particuliers*, a screening wall separates the street from the Hôtel de Cluny's *cour d'honneur*, a lovely work in its own right. The warm cinnamon walls peak in a balustrade and openwork gables; in the middle of the façade a narrow hexagonal tower, carved with the cockleshells of Santiago, encloses a spiral stair. The colonnade on the left probably held the house kitchens, while water was supplied by the charming 15th-century well head.

A beautiful Gothic porch leads into one of the world's greatest collections of medieval art. It began in 1832, when Alexandre du Sommerard rented the first floor of the Hôtel de Cluny to hold his private museum of medieval art. Although Du Sommerard was considered a junk-collecting oddball at first, interest in his museum leapt as the writings of Ruskin and Hugo brought the Middle Ages back into fashion. In 1844 the state purchased the collection, baths and *hôtel* for

a museum. Unfortunately for you, there are no boring bits to skip, but a continuous trove of the rare and the beautiful in exquisite detail to linger over for hours.

Highlights include: in **Salle II**, a delightful series of six tapestries called *La Vie seigneuriale* on the good life 500 years ago, contemporary with the Hôtel de Cluny itself; in **Salle III**, a gorgeous English leopard embroidery believed to have been the saddlecloth of Edward III; in **Salle V**, 15th-century alabasters from Nottingham.

Salle VIII, the Roman section of the museum, contains the newest exhibit: 21 sad, solemn, erosion-scarred heads of the Kings of Judea from the façade of Notre-Dame (*see* p.83). In **Salle IX** are lively, ornate 11th- and 12th-century Romanesque capitals from St-Germain-des-Prés and Ste-Geneviève, and in **Salle X** don't miss four magnificent statues of apostles made in the 1240s for Sainte-Chapelle, or the narwhal's tusk that was once thought to belong to a unicorn.

The *Thermes*

Lofty, vast **Salle XII** is the *frigidarium* of the Roman baths. Wide-arched openings admit light; there are niches in the walls for statues and remains of drains in the floor. It is the only Roman bath in France to have kept its roof – three barrel vaults linked by a groin vault in the centre, ending at the corners with capitals carved with ships' prows that suggest the baths were built by or for the powerful *nautae Parisiaci*, the boatmen's guild of the Parisii. In the centre are five large blocks from an altar to Jupiter, erected during the reign of Tiberius and discovered under the choir of Notre-Dame: among the Roman figures are the Celtic gods Tavros Trigarnus (the bull with three cranes perched on his back), Cernunnos (the god sprouting antlers), and more reliefs of the *nautae Parisiaci*. There's also a 4th-century statue of Julian the Apostate, who, before becoming emperor, would have bathed here.

The Lady and the Unicorn

Upstairs, **Salle XIII** is a rotunda containing Cluny's greatest treasure: the six Aubusson tapestries of *La Dame à la Licorne*, dating from the late 15th century. Woven for Le Viste, a Lyonese noble family (whose arms are incorporated into each scene), the tapestries were only rediscovered in the 19th century, rolled up and mouldering away in an obscure château in the middle of France. The lady, unicorn and lion appear in each scene, on a blue foreground and red background called *millefleurs*, strewn with a thousand flowers, birds and animals, evoking the early Renaissance's delight in nature. The first scenes appear to be allegories of the five senses, but the meaning of the sixth, where the legend on the tent reads *A mon seul désir* and the lady is either taking or returning a necklace from or to a coffer, will always remain a charming mystery.

Salle XIV, a long gallery of retables, painting and sculpture, contains two master-pieces: the *Pietà de Tarascon* (1450s), influenced by Italian and Flemish artists who painted in the papal entourage of Avignon, and a moving figure of *Marie Madeleine*, sculpted in Brussels *c.* 1500. Cast a glance at **Salle XV**'s curious lead tokens dredged up from the bottom of the Seine, some impressed with the symbols of Paris' guilds, others with religious themes, perhaps fallen off the hats and staves of passing pilgrims. All that glitters really is gold in **Salle XVI**: barbarically splendid 7th-century Visigothic crowns; a rare golden rose, of the type distributed by medieval popes to their friends and allies; reliquaries (including a 15th-century container for Jesus' umbilical cord); 4th-century lion heads in rock crystal, and exquisite works in gold and enamel. In **Salle XVIII**, where you can leaf through a 15th-century Book of Hours, the walls are hung with the first of 23 tapestries on the *Life of St Stephen* (1490) from the cathedral of Auxerre. The chapel (**Salle XX**) is a flam-boyant gem, its rib vaulting supported by a central palm-tree pillar, while a little spiral stair descends from the ornate doorway in the corner. **Salle XXI** features a late 15th-century tapestry series on the Life of the Virgin from the cathedral of Bayeux, while

Salle XXIII contains ivories (diptychs, chess pieces, etc.) from the 4th–12th centuries.

Place Paul-Painlevé W–X15

Outside the museum, this little square is an important one for students: it sports a **statue of Montaigne**, a 1988 copy of the original, that nearly had its feet completely rubbed off by exam-takers hoping for good luck. The square also contains a monument to the painter Puvis de Chavannes, and a statue of Romulus and Remus. In the centre, flowers and grasses have been left to grow wild.

BOULEVARD ST-GERMAIN TO THE RIVER

St-Séverin X14–15

1 Rue des Prêtres-St-Séverin, t 01 42 34 93 50; métro St-Michel, RER St-Michel-Notre-Dame. Open daily 11–8; for details of concerts call ahead or look in l'Officiel or Pariscope.

St-Séverin, one of the oldest churches in Paris, greets you with a row of sinister, serpentine gargoyles jutting 3ft out over Rue St-Séverin, threatening to puke rain-water on your head.

Séverin was a 6th-century hermit whose most notable feat was talking Clovis' grandson Cleodald into taking religious orders; Cleodald took them so seriously that he was canonized as St Cloud. The original Merovingian church here was rebuilt in 1031, though its Romanesque replacement took the next 450 years to complete and gradually evolved into Flamboyant Gothic. Still, it failed to suit the fickle taste of Louis XIV's cousin, the ornery Grande Mademoiselle, who no sooner joined the parish than she paid Lebrun to redecorate the interior. Lebrun's mischief can never be completely undone – columns remain ridiculously fluted; pointed arches were rounded off.

The carved 13th-century **portal** in Rue des Prêtres-St-Séverin was brought over from St-Pierre-aux-Bœufs, a church on the Île de la Cité demolished in 1837. It has a fine rose window, but is obscured inside by the rococo organ (1745), an otherwise fine instrument whose ivories Saint-Saëns and Fauré would come to tickle on Sunday afternoons. Lacking space to expand lengthwise, the 14th- and 15th-century builders of St-Séverin added a whole extra set of aisles and chapels, creating a rare visual breadth that culminates in St-Séverin's most remarkable feature: a palm-ribbed double ambulatory that seems to unwind organically from the twisted spirals of the centre column. Even the smeared, dirty watercolour stained glass added in 1966 can't spoil the effect. Other details are concentrated in the first three bays of the nave, the only part of the church to survive a 15th-century fire: exquisite Flamboyant tracery in the vaults and the Romanesque capitals, and 15th- and 16th-century stained glass in the clerestory.

St-Séverin's peaceful **garden**, enclosed by arcades, is actually the last charnel house in Paris. When the graveyard became too crowded, bones were dug up and embedded in the arches, half of which still stand.

Around St-Séverin X14–15

Outside the church in **Rue St-Séverin**, you will see a two-bit cabaret at No.12: it was over this that the Abbé Prévost d'Exiles wrote *Manon Lescaut*, the only one of his hundred-plus novels remembered today.

On the other side of the church is **Rue de la Parcheminerie**, named after parchment makers, who manufactured Paris' first 'paper' from degreased lambskins; a complete folio would require a whole flock of sheep. Along with the illuminators the parchment makers moved here from the Petit Pont in the 1200s to be nearer the university. It was the beginning of the Left Bank's leading role in French publishing, a status confirmed in 1666 when Colbert corralled all of Paris' printers into the Latin Quarter to keep a close eye on them.

Medieval Trails and Tales between Boulevard St-Germain and the River

This is one of the rare corners of Paris to preserve the pre-Haussmann higgledy-piggledy of a Charles Méryon drawing.

Around Rue de la Huchette X14
Métro St-Michel, RER St-Michel-Notre-Dame.

The 13th-century 'street of the little trough' is a suitable name for a vocation the lane holds to this very day, except that the fat *rôtisseurs* ('meat roasters') described in awe by so many medieval visitors have been replaced by smaller greasy spoons serving kebabs. On weekend evenings the aroma draws half of the students in the world. If Rue de la Huchette seems a squeeze, take a look down **Rue du Chat-qui-Pêche** (named after an old inn sign of a fishing cat). At 6ft it's the narrowest street in Paris, and the last really medieval one, giving an idea of what Haussmann demolished.

The jazz cellar of the **Caveau de la Huchette** at 5 Rue de la Huchette is even more retro than its music; some historians believe it was a secret Templar meeting place linked to the Petit Châtelet dungeons. No.10 was a hotel in 1795, where a certain Brigadier-General Bonaparte lived while he schemed his way to the top. The little **Théâtre de la Huchette** at No.23 produces Paris' equivalent of London's eternal *Mousetrap*: Ionesco's *La Cantatrice chauve* and *La Leçon* premièred here in 1957 and are still going strong.

Boulevard St-Michel V18–X14
Métro St-Michel, RER St-Michel-Notre-Dame.

The street peters out in **Place St-Michel**, a traffic vortex laid out under Napoleon III and decorated with a striking fountain by Davioud of St Michel slaying the Dragon. It marks the beginning of the Latin Quarter's busy thoroughfare **Boulevard St-Michel**, or simply Boul' Mich, laid out in 1859, its paving stones now covered by a coat of asphalt.

Rue St-Jacques U21–X15

Lutetia's main street was named **Rue St-Jacques** after the thousands of cockle-shelled pilgrims who walked along it to Santiago de Compostela. It was linked to the Île de la Cité by Paris' first bridge, built in the time of Julius Caesar at the narrowest point of the Seine; the **Petit Pont** (1853) spans the same stretch today.

Square René-Viviani X15–Y14
Métro Maubert-Mutualité.

This spot of green by the Seine replaced a fetid sick ward attached in 1602 to the Hôtel-Dieu on the Île de la Cité. To link the two, the hospital built the **Pont au Double**, named after the double toll it charged – one to get on and another to get off (today's Pont au Double is a modern reincarnation). Until 1835 the bridge was lined with sickrooms, and the hospital-bridge-annexe formed a fascinating U-shaped ensemble that positively reeked. Square Viviani's Gothic odds and ends, melted by wind and rain, were found near Notre-Dame; the tree on concrete crutches is the oldest in Paris. It's a false acacia, called a *robinier*, after Robin the botanist who planted it in 1602.

St-Julien-le-Pauvre X14–15
1 Rue St-Julien-le-Pauvre, t 01 43 29 09 09; **métro** *St-Michel,* **RER** *St-Michel-Notre-Dame.* **Open** *daily 9.30–6.30; sung Mass Sun 11am.*

Dating back to 587, the diminutive transitional Gothic church St-Julien is a last token of a score of chapels founded at the same time as Notre-Dame. It provided hospitality for pilgrims to Santiago de Compostela, and enlarged in 1208, it became the university's assembly hall, an association that went sour when a student riot in 1524 left the church half-ruined. All members of the university were henceforth banned, and migrated up the hill to St-Étienne-du-Mont (*see* p.227), while poor St-Julien was practically abandoned. In 1651 it was on the verge of collapse when the roof was lowered and the nave lopped off (the ruins on the left show the original size) and it was made the chapel of

the Hôtel Dieu. The fine Gothic vaulting in the right aisle is original, and although the arches in the chancel (1180) are pointed, the builders went back to the Romanesque for the arcade in the nave. Two Romanesque capitals survive in the chancel, one portraying not angels but harpies from Greek mythology. Perhaps they have felt more at home since 1889, when St-Julien was given to the Greek Catholic rite.

Rue Galande X14–15
Métro Maubert-Mutualité.

Rue Galande, just south of St-Julien-le-Pauvre, was once the start of the bustling Roman road to Lyon. These days the action happens on weekends at the Studio Galande, local perpetuator of *The Rocky Horror Picture Show*. Over its door is a somewhat incongruous 14th-century bas-relief depicting a scene from the legend of St Julian the Hospitaller, who came home one day to find a couple in his bed. Thinking his wife had a lover, he slew the pair, only to learn they were his own parents. In despair he and his wife sailed up the Seine and founded a hostel to serve the poor. One day a leper asked Julian and his wife to ferry him across the river, and revealed himself to be the forgiving Christ. Other houses on Rue Galande are medieval, but have been much restored. No.65 has a rare gable roof, while the Auberge des Deux Signes (No.46) contains Gothic fragments from St Julian's chapel of St-Blaise and, appropriately, the monks' old refectory.

At its eastern end, Rue Galande meets **Rue du Fouarre**, a mere stump of a street that in the 12th century was the very embryo of the university; it's named after the straw bales (*fouarre* in Old French) that served as benches for the first students. Tradition has it that Dante attended classes here in 1304.

Shakespeare & Co. X14
Métro Maubert-Mutualité.

Rue de la Bûcherie, running parallel to the river one street back from the Quai de Montebello, shelters what must be the most famous English-language second-hand bookshop on the continent, **Shakespeare & Co.** (*open daily 12–12*). This is the namesake of Sylvia Beach's bookshop that stood in Rue de l'Odéon between the wars. Beach's kindness and free lending library made her a den mother for many expat writers, but none owed her as much as James Joyce. After the *Ulysses* obscenity trial in 1921 precluded the publication of the book in Britain or the USA, Beach volunteered to publish it herself. Joyce returned the favour by handing back galley proofs with 10,000 smudgy corrections.

George Whitman, great-grandson of Walt Whitman, has continued the old tradition, sometimes providing temporary employment or a few days' shelter to impoverished writers.

Rue de l'Hôtel Colbert and the School of Medicine X15–Y14
Métro *Maubert-Mutualité.*

The circular structure on the corner of Rue de l'Hôtel-Colbert housed Paris' first **School of Medicine**. The buildings date from 1472, except for the triple-tiered, circular **amphitheatre** inaugurated in 1745. In between those two dates were long years when only a handful of students gathered to discuss questions that still seem pertinent today: does debauchery make men bald? Can a woman turn herself into a man? Dissections, banned by the Church, could only take place in the winter, when the weather preserved the corpses swiped from the church yard of St-Séverin.

Much of what we know about stolen bodies in Paris has come down in the writings of Restif de la Bretonne (1734–1806), literary police informer, self-proclaimed *espion de vice* and pervert, who lived at No.16 (replaced by a 19th-century building). Restif's masterpiece, a series of fragmented sketches called *Les Nuits de Paris* (1789), has inspired urban writers from Baudelaire to Henry Miller. But paper could hardly contain all of Restif's thoughts, and he took to carving notes in Latin on the bridges to Île St-Louis. Passers-by could follow his separation from his wife (*Abiit hodie monstrum*: 'the monster

left today'), his liaison with Sara Devée in 1776 (*Data tota – felix*: 'she gave herself completely – happy'), and even his meals (*Coena ad belved*: 'had supper on the boulevard'). Although he died in poverty amid well-founded suspicions of incest with his daughters, a cortège of 2,000 admirers, from whores to duchesses, buried him in style.

Place Maubert Y15
Métro *Maubert-Mutualité.*

Place Maubert is the Platea Mauberti of 1202 and medieval centre of the Latin Quarter. The word Maubert is said to be an elision of Maître Albertus – the philosopher Albertus Magnus, who gave alfresco lectures on dialectic in this square. Albertus had as his assistant a magic, know-it-all brass head until one of his students, Thomas Aquinas, smashed it to smithereens, beginning the sorrowful tale of Place Maubert's 700 year decline. Lectures gave way to low taverns, while grim Sorbonne theologians made it a barbecue pit for the three H's: humanists, heretics and Huguenots, staging so many autos-da-fé that Place Maubert was for centuries a pilgrimage site for Protestants. The most famous victim was Étienne Dolet, who published unauthorized, unexpurgated versions of *Gargantua* and *Pantagruel*. These days a civilized street market takes place on Tuesdays, Thursdays and Saturdays, amid the Vietnamese and Thai grocers.

Musée de la Prefecture de Police Y15

1 bis Rue des Carmes, **t** *01 44 41 52 50;* **métro** *Maubert-Mutualité.* **Open** *Mon–Fri 9–5, Sat 10–5, last adm 4.30, closed hols;* **adm** *free.*

The Parisians, for all their fine manners, can be a rascally herd of cusses. The Fronde uprising in Louis XIV's minority revealed how many weapons were loose in the streets; although only gentlemen and soldiers on active duty were allowed to carry swords, in practice the whole city was armed to the teeth. People were openly robbed, even on the Pont Neuf, and no one disagreed when the satirist Boileau wrote in 1660: 'The darkest forest is a safe haven after Paris.'

Louis XIV reacted to this crime wave by founding the ancestor of the modern Paris police in 1667. His lieutenant was the tough but fair-minded Nicolas-Gabriel de La Reynie, (*see* 'Mean Streets of the Grand Siècle'). La Reynie and his successors, with their teams of sergeants and informers, not only policed but governed Paris, taking responsibility for the city's security, equipment and modernization, and also its morals, religious affairs and public health. Louis himself didn't give a fig for Paris, but he would summon La Reynie to Versailles to hear the latest gossip of dukes caught singing rude ditties or pissing out of windows, which always made him chuckle before he sent notes threatening them with the Bastille.

This museum, on the second floor of the modern police station, has a fascinating collection of archive material: from Louis' *lettres de cachet* to the criminal report on Verlaine and Rimbaud; there are police uniforms, a guillotine blade, a model of Fieschi's assassination machine (which failed to blow up Louis-Philippe), anarchist bombs, documents on the ex-convict Vidocq (who, like Ahmed the Moth in *The Arabian Nights*, was appointed chief over a unit of reformed crooks in the 1830s), and Grandville's hilarious engraving of conspiring umbrellas called the *Cauchemar du Préfet de Police*. The biggest exhibit covers *anthropométrie* – the method invented by commissioner Alphonse Bertillon to identify crooks by photographing and measuring their noses, ears and eyes. In 1903 Bertillon obtained the first conviction in Europe using fingerprints as evidence, a mere 1,400 years after the Chinese.

Musée de l'Assistance Publique Y–Z15

47 Quai de la Tournelle, t 01 40 27 50 05; métro Maubert-Mutualité. Open Tues–Sun 10–6, closed hols; adm €4.

The museum is a handsome 17th-century *hôtel*, originally occupied by Madame de Miramion and her Filles de Ste-Geneviève,

Mean Streets of the Grand Siècle

One disadvantage of Louis XIV's policy of grinding the poor was that it made thieves not only more numerous but also more rapacious. In Paris, muggers were not satisfied with your purse; they'd have your shoes and clothes too, along with your underwear if you were wearing any. Nicolas de la Reynie, the king's capable chief of police, had 800 boys on the street, looking dapper in their blue uniforms with silver stars. But they couldn't be everywhere in an unlit city of half a million, full of dark cul-de-sacs.

And if the crooks didn't get you, you were at least sure to step in something, or have something splash on your head; sanitary conditions had not improved an iota since the Middle Ages, and if anything they had worsened. La Palatine, writing in the 1660s, records the smell of rotting meat and fish in every street, and 'crowds of people pissing everywhere'. The king's household set the example; it was noted that underneath every balcony of the Louvre was a steaming heap of *ordures et immondices*. All this was La Reynie's business – everything was his business. This unsung hero from Limoges, who took the job in 1667, was a sympathetic fellow who often managed to protect poor Parisians from the whims of the king, and who probably did more for Paris than anyone in its long history. Besides initiating the first street lighting (at least when there was no moon, a penny-pinching custom that lasted until the 19th century), he forced landlords to build latrines, widened streets, forbade the carrying of swords and canes, paved the quays of the Seine, required shop-owners to sweep the streets in front of their doors, and closed down the *asiles*, noble properties that were off-limits to the police and had become the haunts of robbers and predatory beggars, such as the famous 'Cour de Miracles' (*see* p.174).

who comforted the ill. Although most cities would prefer that visitors judge them by their public monuments, Paris' hospitals have gamely created this museum to chronicle the city's treatment of the down-and-out.

Their fate has varied with society's attitudes, from the medieval view that poverty was a Christ-like virtue to be graced by works of charity, to the ungenerous 16th-century position (familiar today) that the poor are a menace to society. In 1656, in the wake of the Fronde uprisings, Cardinal Mazarin and Louis XIV solved the poverty 'problem' by creating the infamous Hôpital Général. The scheme kicked off with a Grand Renfermement, in which archers at the crossroads of Paris rounded up 40,000 misfits – the blind, paupers, madmen, orphans, prostitutes, alchemists, homosexuals, idlers, unemployed soldiers, heretics, blasphemers, witches and thieves – and forcibly confined them in workhouses. Naturally it was 'for their own good'. Grimmest of all was the fate of abandoned infants. In 1638 a priest named Vincent de Paul discovered that foundlings were being sold off for a few coins to beggars, who broke their arms and legs to excite the pity of passers-by. Appalled, Vincent founded a foundling hospital by Notre-Dame, although this was quickly overwhelmed as poverty increased: the 438 foundlings dropped off in 1660 rose to 7,676 in 1772, or roughly 21 abandoned children a day. Five whose fate is unknown were fathered by J.-J. Rousseau, who forced his mistress to abandon them.

The Church's opposition to dissection and to doctors attending births limited medical progress until the end of the 18th century. In 1776 the Hôpital Necker became Paris' first institution founded exclusively for treating the ill. By the early 19th century nearly all the hospitals had followed suit, releasing the prostitutes and poor to fend for themselves.

The museum contains a wide assortment of memorabilia: early medical instruments, pharmaceutical jars, bead bracelets that parents left with foundlings as identification, in case they ever had the means to retrieve the child, and works of art from the hospitals, from the richly illuminated *Livre de Vie Active* (1482) by Jean Henry, Proviseur of the Hôtel-Dieu, to a stupefying *Louis XIV Admired by the Universe*, which used to hang in the Salpêtrière (*see* p.240).

Outside on the *quai*, there's a delicious prospect of Notre-Dame pinioned by its flying buttresses.

THE LEARNED QUARTER

These few blocks are the ancient confines of Paris University, an institution founded in spirit by Peter Abelard, one of the greatest thinkers of the Middle Ages (*see* 'The University of Paris'). Old and new university buildings are scattered about the quarter; others have spread west to St-Germain and southeast into Mouffetard (*see* p.237).

The Sorbonne W16–X15

47 Rue des Ecoles, t 01 40 46 22 11; métro Cluny-La Sorbonne or Maubert-Mutualité. Group visits by appointment – call ahead; flat rate of €46 per group (max 30). Or take a peek at the Cour d'Honneur via 17 Rue de la Sorbonne.

Paris' first college, supplying room and board to poor students, was founded in 1180 by a Londoner named Josse, and among the scores that followed was this one, founded in 1257 by Robert de Sorbon, chaplain to St Louis. It differed from its predecessors by offering teaching in the 'sacred studies', and eventually it evolved as the headquarters of Paris' dread Faculty of Scholastic Theology.

In the 1630s the college was rebuilt on an ambitious scale by its titular chancellor, Cardinal Richelieu, but even that was judged too small and replaced in the 19th century by the current ponderous buildings. These have been reduced from their once glorious status as the seat of the university to merely housing Paris branches III and IV.

The University of Paris

In 1099, Peter Abelard left his native Brittany to attend the school of Notre-Dame. The 20-year-old Abelard chose Paris just to hear one man: the celebrated Guillaume de Champeaux, Notre-Dame's master of dialectic – the art of reasoning through debate. Dialectic was the hottest subject of the day, and it didn't take the gifted Abelard long to talk the pants off Champeaux and formulate his own doctrine, called 'conceptualism'. Conceptualism holds that abstract ideas, or universals, exist only as mental concepts and have no objective existence. Abelard's lectures were famous for their brilliance, and soon students from all over Europe flocked to Paris to hear them.

In 1118, when his affair with Héloïse ended with the unkindest cut of all (see 'Abelard and Héloïse', p.88), Abelard retired to the monastery of St-Denis. Yet his disciples continued to pour into Paris, 3,000 of them, clamouring for his return until the bishop of Notre-Dame booted them out. They took refuge on the Left Bank's Montagne de Ste-Geneviève and by popular demand Abelard joined them, lecturing in the vineyards, daring to subject sacred Church dogma to the rigours of dialectic and principles of logic based on Aristotle, whose books had just recently resurfaced from the Dark Ages. This was too much for St Bernard of Clairvaux, who manoeuvred to have the teachings of Abelard condemned as heresy at the 1140 Council of Sens. Abelard appealed to the pope and in 1142, en route to Rome to defend himself in person, he died.

But the cat was out of the bag. In Paris the high standards of enquiry and scholarship set by Abelard made the Left Bank a 'paradise of pleasure' for intellectuals and students from across Europe. Private citizens and religious orders built college-hostels to house the scholars. In 1180, Philippe-Auguste enclosed the whole area, walls that until the 18th century defined the University Quarter.

The heady freedom of thought that made Paris University great in the 13th century drew the leading thinkers of the day: Albertus Magnus from Germany, Thomas Aquinas from Naples and Roger Bacon from England. In 1255 it took the revolutionary step of making all the known works of Aristotle mandatory in its syllabus. 'France is the oven where the intellectual bread of humanity is baked,' marvelled a visiting papal legate. High spirits came in the yeast, and boys will be boys. Scholars interpreted the privileges granted by the king and the pope as a licence to rob, murder and rape. In 1223 a town-and-gown battle ended with 320 dead scholars pitched into the Seine. Subsequent high jinks were more subdued, although during the Renaissance theology students had to be chastised for attending church in drag, wolfing down roast chicken during Communion, satirizing the Mass responses and playing dice in the chapels.

Chapelle de Ste-Ursule-de-la-Sorbonne W15–16

Entrance from the Cour d'Honneur at 17 Rue de la Sorbonne, t 01 40 46 22 11. **Open** *rarely for temporary exhibitions; also part of tour (see above).*

This domed chapel (1630) is all that survives of the Sorbonne from Richelieu's day. Modelled after the Gesù church in Rome, it was the first in Paris in the new 'Jesuit' or Baroque style. The interior decoration was destroyed when the *sans-culottes* converted it into a 'Temple of Reason', except for paintings in the spandrels by Philippe de Champaigne and the white marble **tomb of Richelieu** (Lebrun, 1693). The latter only escaped by the hair of the Cardinal's chinny-chin-chin, when monument-monger Alexandre Lenoir (see p.205) threw himself between the revolutionary smashers and the tomb, only to receive a bayonet in the leg for his trouble.

If you come between lectures (or can manage to sit through one – they're free), take a look in the **Grand Amphithéâtre** to see the celebrated fresco in lollipop colours of *Le bois sacré* by Puvis de Chavannes.

Sadly, 'the intellectual bread of humanity' had already begun to grow mould by the late 1200s. Aristotelian logic coagulated into the blind scholastic formulae mocked by Villon and Rabelais, a stilted conformism that drove serious scholars to Oxford, Cambridge, Padua and Cologne. When Philippe le Bel convinced the theological judges at the Sorbonne that they should condemn the Knights Templars in 1312, he cursed the university with a political role that compromises its independence to this day. The Hundred Years' War came close to compromising its very existence. The university supported the English and Burgundian claims, and at the trial of Joan of Arc the Sorbonne supplied the prosecutor who sent the Maid to the stake.

In 1470 three Germans were invited to the Sorbonne to start the first printing press in France, beginning a renaissance of intellectual life on the Left Bank. Unfortunately by then the Sorbonne was too reactionary to satisfy the new thirst for knowledge and in 1530 an alternative, the humanist Collège de France, was founded to teach Greek, Hebrew and forbidden classical authors. During the Counter-Reformation things got worse: after giving its approval to the St Bartholomew's Day massacre, the Sorbonne concentrated not on printing books but on burning them. Richelieu, appointed chancellor in 1622, tried to revive the Sorbonne's flagging status with an extensive rebuilding of the college. Nothing he could do, however, halted the

Latin Quarter's decline into a volatile slum. The Revolution had no qualms about closing the whole university down as the rubber stamp of King and Church, and deconsecrated its beautiful Gothic abbeys, churches and colleges. Left empty, they fell prey to speculators in the 19th century.

Napoleon resuscitated the university, but there was no going back to the old ways – if the Sorbonne was political, so were the post-Revolutionary students, who played important roles in the upheavals of the 19th century, who battled the Nazis in Place St-Michel, protested against the war in Algeria and in May 1968 shocked the government by rising up against the mandarin structure and archaic teaching methods of the university itself. The nervous government overreacted and sent police into the university's sacred precincts, provoking demonstrations in the streets and further repressions, until in true Parisian tradition up went the barricades on 10 May. What had begun as a protest against the state of the university had spread to a rebellion against the boredom and apathy of the De Gaulle era, with a succinct motto: 'It is forbidden to forbid.' The result: one student killed, hundreds wounded and arrested, and a debate over university reforms that continues to this day. But the government has accomplished its agenda: the rebellious Sorbonne has been blasted into a centreless prism of 13 blandly numbered campuses scattered throughout Paris.

Collège de France X15–16

11 Place Marcelin-Berthelot, t 01 44 27 12 11; métro Maubert-Mutualité. Not open for visits.

As the Sorbonne became mired in reactionary scholasticism and arguments over angels dancing on the head of a pin, humanists led by Guillaume Budé petitioned François I for an alternative, a 'republic of scholars' where they could study Hebrew and 'pagan' Greek and Latin texts banned at the Sorbonne. In 1530 the king complied, and to this day the Collège de France maintains its scholastic independence, although the State

provides all its funds. The older buildings around the courtyard date from 1778, decorated with statues of its famous scholars – Champollion, who cracked Egyptian hieroglyphs with the Rosetta stone (by Bartholdi, 1875), Budé, the historian Michelet, and the physiologist Claude Bernard (d. 1878), a pioneer in research on diabetes and the pancreas gland. Paul Valéry, Roland Barthes and Michel Foucault gave lectures here. Altogether, the intellectual bread served up here has proved no more nutritious than the Sorbonne's: despite its prestigious status, this college was the source of much of the cynical, pointless psychobabble that infects universities today, especially in America.

Along Rue des Écoles W15–Z12

Further east along Rue des Ecoles is the former **École Polytechnique**, founded by the Convention in 1794 and one of France's most élite Grandes Écoles. One of its alumni, Valéry Giscard d'Estaing, was President of France in 1977 when it was decentralized to the suburbs, leaving this building to be taken over by the Ministry of Research and Technology. It overlooks Square Paul-Langevin, occupied by a **statue of François Villon** (1431–63), the virile if rather sooty archangel of the Latin Quarter – student, murderer, thief and the greatest lyrical poet of his day (*see* 'François Villon').

MONTAGNE STE-GENEVIÈVE

Rue Clovis (X–Y16) is the summit of the Gallo-Roman Mont Lutèce, known since the Middle Ages as Montagne Ste-Geneviève after the city's patron saint (*see* 'The Patron Saint of Paris', overleaf).

When Clovis converted to Christianity ('Oh, if only my Franks had been there!' he sighed, when first learning about the Crucifixion), he built on Montagne Ste-Geneviève a basilica dedicated to SS Peter and Paul. In 512 he was buried there, next to his wife Clotilde and Geneviève. Such a cult grew around the miracle-working **tomb of Geneviève** that the church was expanded and renamed after the thwarter of Attila; an abbey was erected and the Montagne covered with vineyards, providing an open-air classroom for the rebellious Peter Abelard (*see* 'The University of Paris', pp.225–6).

So many students moved into the quarter that a new chapel, St-Étienne, was built next to Ste-Geneviève to accommodate them. In 1802 old Ste-Geneviève was demolished to

---

François Villon

Although a master of the highly structured verse forms bequeathed by the troubadours, Villon wrote with a remarkable directness on subjects from his own wayward life, using an idiomatic language rich in Parisian slang. He excelled in complicated, 13-line, double-rhyme stanzas called *rondeaux*, the form of his exquisite *Ballade des Dames du Temps Jadis* with its bittersweet refrain *'Mais où sont les neiges d'antan?'* ('Where are the snows of yesteryear?'). He composed his last known masterpiece, the poignant *Ballade des Pendus*, while sitting on death row in Paris in 1462. Villon's sentence was lightened to exile from the capital for 10 years, whereupon he vanished from history.

---

make way for Rue Clovis, leaving only its tall Romanesque tower, the **Tour Clovis**, a captive within the walls of the élite Lycée Henri IV (23 Rue Clovis).

At **No.3 Rue Clovis**, you can see a stretch of the wall Philippe-Auguste built around the Latin Quarter, minus its crenellations.

St-Étienne-du-Mont X–Y16

Place Ste-Geneviève, t 01 43 54 11 79; métro Cardinal-Lemoine. Open Mon 12–7.30, Tues–Fri 7.45–7.30, Sat 7.45–12 and 2.30–7.45, Sun 8.45–12.30 and 2.30–7.45, closed hols.

Charming, asymmetrical St-Étienne was begun in 1492, to squeeze in the great press of students. Accounts of the university's four annual processions from St-Étienne to St-Denis claim that the rectors in front would enter St-Denis *before* the last students had left St-Étienne, a feat that would require at least 30,000 students, teachers and support staff.

Charles VII's invasion of Italy in 1494 gave the French their first toe-dip in the Renaissance. They made St-Étienne their sampler; although it had been begun in Flamboyant Gothic in the choir, they made the façade their own, stacking up three different pediments like building blocks. Inside, the Renaissance nave is closed off by a

The Patron Saint of Paris

In 451, fresh from pillaging and deflowering 11,000 virgins in Cologne, Attila and the Huns marched towards Lutèce looking for more fun. The Roman citizens fled in terror, but the Parisii stuck around when Geneviève, a holy virgin living on this hill, assured them that God would spare the city. And indeed, at the last minute, the Huns veered off and sacked Orléans instead – precisely where Paris' Romans had fled. Scoffers have long claimed that Geneviève's intervention was less decisive than Attila's discovery that Paris was no place to look for virgins.

very fetching arched *jubé*, or rood screen – the only one surviving in Paris – flanked by two openwork spiral stairs, galleries and balustrades, Gothic in structure but entirely coated in Corinthian frosting. A few other details survived the Revolution, when St-Étienne became the 'Temple of Filial Piety': the great organ of 1630, a carved pulpit of 1650 with a baldachin, and Renaissance stained-glass windows.

In the ambulatory are the graves and epitaphs of one of France's greatest thinkers, Blaise Pascal (d. 1662), and one of her greatest playwrights, Racine (d. 1699), both of whom lived among the fleshpots and died pious and austere Jansenists. Just beyond them, surrounded by *ex-voto* plaques and paintings, is the **Chapel of Ste-Geneviève**, still one of the busiest pilgrimage sites in Paris. Whenever the city needed some really big juju, especially against inclement weather or invasions, her reliquary, so big that it required 10 men just to lift it, would go on procession through the city, joined by a host of other saintly relics before ending up at Notre-Dame. Although Geneviève rarely let Paris down, in 1793 anti-clerical revolutionaries melted down her reliquary, burned her bones and tossed the ashes into the Seine.

A replacement reliquary holds a stone from her original sarcophagus, but Geneviève has shown that she can still occasionally hold the Huns at bay: as one *ex-voto* reads, a

three-day prayer vigil here in September 1914 preceded the Battle of the Marne.

Before leaving, take a look at the deep-coloured, 17th-century enamelled glass windows in the **Galerie des Charniers**, all that remains of the old charnel-house cloister where the bodies of Mirabeau and Marat lay after their ejection from the Panthéon (Mirabeau's remains are now in the catacombs, while Marat's were lost after he was tossed into a gutter). The iconography of the windows contrasts Old and New Testament scenes.

THE PANTHÉON AND AROUND

The Panthéon x16

*Place du Panthéon, t 01 44 32 18 00;
métro Cardinal-Lemoine, RER Luxembourg.
Open April–Sept daily 10–6.30, Oct–Mar
10–6.15, last adm 45mins before closing;
adm €7, free 1st Sun of the month Oct–Mar.*

After a close call with the grim reaper in 1744, Louis XV vowed to construct a new basilica to hold the relics of Paris' patroness. Unfortunately the Crown was flat broke, and only after 10 years of lotteries did construction begin, in 1755. It had just been completed in 1790 when the Revolution kicked off its muddled history by co-opting it as a Panthéon to honour its Great Men.

The trials and tribulations of this 'dunce cap on a hill' really began when Louis XV commissioned Jacques-Germain Soufflot (otherwise best known for demolishing Notre-Dame's magnificent central portal) as architect. Soufflot's stated aim, that he would synthesize the perfect harmonies of the Greek temple and the central basilica with the audacity of the Gothic cathedral, hint at mental delusion on a grand scale – 367ft by 274ft to be precise. Some French critics trumpet the result as 'the first example of perfect architecture', when in fact the Panthéon is a textbook case of how not to build, an impoverished bastard of design that has always had difficulties fulfilling even the most basic tenet of architecture: standing up. In 1985, when stones came plummeting from the vaults, it had to be closed. After lengthy repairs, most of the building is open again for visits.

The project was ridden with difficulties from the start. Although the building was supported by flying buttresses hidden in the walls and iron staples secreted in the masonry, Soufflot made the interior columns too slender to support the structure and, in his neoclassical daydreams, forgot he was in cold, humid Paris instead of dry, sunny Athens: the roof terraces and vast unprotected stone surfaces let the rain sink in and rust the aforementioned iron staples, rot the murals, and warp and bend the windows out of shape. Cracks developed in the walls even before the building was finished, and Soufflot, as stressed out as his structure, died of anxiety in 1780. The dome, copied from London's St Paul's, was meant to have been supported by columns, but subsidence was so great that Soufflot's successor, Rondelet, had to opt for 10,000 tons of solid walls and pilasters. And like St Paul's, it's a trick – there are actually three domes fitted like Chinese boxes one inside the other – so that from the inside the dome would seem to float over the planned baldachin that would have sheltered Geneviève's relics. It never did, but in 1851 the dome came in handy when Foucault hung his pendulum from the top to prove the rotation of the earth.

To be fair, had the whole worked out according to Soufflot's plans, the interior would have been filled with a refined play of light and shadow. The sun was to have filtered between the columns, pouring not only through the openings in the dome but also through 42 enormous windows that were walled up by the Assembly in 1791 when the church was converted into the 'Temple of Glory and Immortality'. Even this didn't start on the right foot: two of the first pantheonized corpses, those of Mirabeau and Marat, were given the bum's rush as

soon as politics changed. Napoleon reconverted the Panthéon to a church, and the remains of two other inmates, Rousseau and Voltaire (who disdained each other in life), were shunted off into an unmarked closet. Louis-Philippe thought the church was better as a Panthéon, and had David d'Angers replace the temple pediment (this was in 1837; it was the fourth pediment in 50 years) with a frieze of Liberty handing palms to La Patrie, who doles them out to France's civilian and military heroes, beginning with Napoleon. His presence perhaps ensured the frieze's survival in 1851, when monks persuaded Napoleon III to reconvert the building to a church. In 1871 the cross was turned into a pole for the red flag when the Panthéon became the Left-Bank headquarters of the Commune. It went back to a church again until 1885, when Victor Hugo died (see pp.251–2). Hugo was so inflated that no ordinary tomb would hold him, and his funeral inaugurated the building's current status as the Panthéon of France's Great Men. The best thing inside is Puvis de Chavannes' mural on the Life of Sainte Geneviève, in the right aisle.

The **crypt**, intended for the monks of Ste-Geneviève, is certainly grand and gloomy enough for Great Men – Voltaire, Rousseau and Soufflot himself in the first section; then Hugo and Zola, Louis Braille, Jean Jaurès, Resistance leader Jean Moulin, Jean Monnet (a founder of the EU), René Cassin (author of the UN Declaration of Human Rights), 40 dignitaries from the First Empire, Gambetta (although only his heart is here), and André Malraux, pantheonized in 1996. And in 1997, the second woman entered the hallowed halls: both Marie and Pierre Curie were reburied here to great acclaim.

Place du Panthéon X16

Soufflot is also responsible for the cold stone field called the **Place du Panthéon**, and designed its twin curved buildings, now the Faculté de Droit and the *mairie* of the 5e *arrondissement*.

Hôtel des Haricots (Mean Beans)

In the Middle Ages, the site of the Bibliothèque Ste-Geneviève was occupied by the Collège de Montaigu, 'the cleft between the buttocks of Mother Theology', an institution notorious for its harshness, beatings and forcing scholars to recite long verses in Latin while kneeling in salt. Beds were too much of a luxury here: students slept on the stone floor with swarms of bugs and they ate beans so often that the school's other nickname was the 'Hôtel des Haricots'.

Not surprisingly, Montaigu's alumni turned out to be either proto-fascists or proto-hippies: they included Calvin and Ignatius de Loyola (both admired it) and Rabelais and Erasmus (both wanted to burn it down).

On the north side, the building covered with the names of writers is the **Bibliothèque Ste-Geneviève** (*10 Place du Panthéon,* **t** *01 44 41 97 97; reading room can be visited by appointment; call at least 24 hours ahead; adm free*), containing the only monastic library to survive the Revolution. Built on the site between 1843 and 1850 by Henri Labrouste, it may seem a mild-mannered neo-Renaissance building from the street, but it hides a magnificent reading room, crowned by a twin-naved, barrel-vaulted iron roof. It was the first time that iron was used in 'serious' architecture, and its success encouraged Labrouste to create the incredible reading room at the Bibliothèque Nationale (*see* pp.156–7).

The first centre of Paris was just a block up: the corner of Rue St-Jacques and Rue Cujas, laid out by the Roman surveyors as the *cardo* and *decumanus* of Lutetia.

Jardin des Plantes

Jardin des Plantes

This area, east of the medieval walls that cradled the Latin Quarter for most of its history, offers an unusual cocktail of sights and smells that hardly seems to belong to the same city as the Eiffel Tower and Champs-Elysées – gossipy village streets, a tropical garden, a Maghrebi mosque and old geezers playing *boules* in a Roman arena.

Rue Mouffetard market really comes into its own at weekends, but closes down on Mondays.

1 Lunch

Le Buisson Ardent, *25 Rue Jussieu*, **t** *01 43 54 93 02*; *métro Jussieu*. **Open** *Mon–Fri 12–2 and 7.30–11, closed Aug*. **Moderate**. Much recommended French classic with quality *à l'ancienne*. Try *confit de canard*, *pommes à l'ail* or *riz de veau à la crème*. Lunch menu €15, full evening menu €28.

2 Tea and Cakes

Café of the Grande Mosquée, *39 Rue Geoffroy-St-Hilaire*; *métro Place Monge*. **Open** *daily 9am–11.30pm*. A delightful café where you can sip mint tea in a garden patio built in the style of the Alhambra.

3 Drinks

Cave la Bourgogne, *144 Rue Mouffetard*; *métro Place Monge*. **Open** *Tues–Sun 7am–2am*. Good wine and everything else to drink, plus excellent sandwiches.

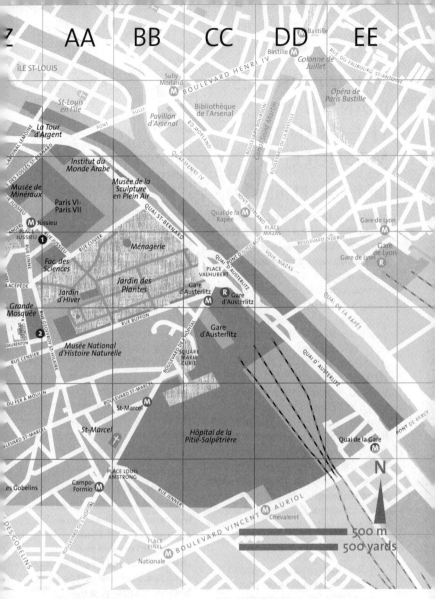

Z AA BB CC DD EE

Highlights

Couples' City: Visit the Institut du Monde Arabe, with its magical windows, p.238

Parisian's City: Bar-hopping along Rue Mouffetard on a Saturday night, p.237

Peace and Quiet: The gardens and greenhouse of the Jardin des Plantes, p.234

Paris des Artistes: The riverside Musée de la Sculpture en Plein Air, p.239

Grand Siècle Paris: Louis XIV's workhouse, now the distinguished Salpêtrière, p.240

Gritty City: Paris' worst building – the asbestos-ridden Université de Paris VI and VII, p.238

THE JARDIN DES PLANTES AND THE GRANDE MOSQUÉE

Jardin des Plantes Z17–CC19

57 Rue Cuvier, t 01 40 79 30 00, w www.mnhn. fr; métro Jussieu or Gare d'Austerlitz, RER Gare d'Austerlitz. Open summer daily 7.30am–8pm, winter daily 7.30am–5.30pm; adm free. Café open daily 10–5.

In 1626 doctors Jean Hérouard and Guy de La Brosse convinced their best-known patient, Louis XIII, to establish a botanical garden of medicinal plants in the capital, similar to the one his father Henri IV founded at the university of Montpellier in 1593. Some of France's most famous botanists – the three Jussieu brothers, Daubenton and especially the Comte de Buffon (1707–88), the great 18th-century curator – travelled around the world to collect 2,500 species of medicinal plants and exotic trees. In 1793 the Convention created the School and Museum of Natural History, and galleries and research laboratories went up along the flanks of the gardens. In one pavilion along Rue Cuvier radioactivity was discovered in 1896 by Henri Becquerel, who shared the Nobel Prize with the Curies.

The Rue Cuvier entrance into the park is marked by the **Fontaine Cuvier**, honouring Georges Cuvier, father of comparative anatomy. Although it quaintly depicts Mother Nature musing among her lieutenants – a lion, a contortionist crocodile, a walrus, an eagle and a veritable seafood platter – there is something disconcerting about it, a lost 19th-century pedantic but slightly contemptuous attitude towards nature that also haunts the unloved buildings in the Jardin des Plantes.

The most endearing feature of the garden is a 17th-century dump that Buffon converted into a labyrinth (up on the little hill just to the right), topped by a small bronze temple with a sundial called the **Gloriette de Buffon** (1786). Near the maze towers a **cedar of Lebanon**, a seedling from Kew Gardens brought to Paris in 1734 by Bernard de Jussieu. And south of the Grand Amphitheatre (really a small neoclassical building near the entrance), look for one of the oddest trees, the ironbark from Iran.

Jardin d'Hiver (Serres Tropicale et Mexicaine) AA17

57 Rue Cuvier. Open Wed–Mon 1–5, April–Sept open until 8 at weekends, closed 1 May; adm €2.50.

Just south of the Grand Amphitheatre, a tropical forest is sheltered in one of the world's first iron and glass pavilions (1830, by Rohault de Fleury). The contents seem to have been lifted directly from the works of the Douanier Rousseau (*see* p.127), complete with mini-waterfall, stream and turtles; a second hothouse at the back bristles with cacti. In front of the pavilions, a fence encloses the 2,600 labelled plants of the **Botanical School gardens** (*open 8–11 and 1.30–5, closed Sat, Sun and hols; adm free*).

Muséum National d'Histoire Naturelle AA18

36 Rue Geoffroy-St-Hilaire, t 01 40 79 54 18, w www.mnhn.fr; métro Jussieu or Gare d'Austerlitz, RER Gare d'Austerlitz; wheelchair access. Open Wed–Mon 10–6, Thurs 10–10, closed 1 May; adm €6 (€8.50 including exhibitions). Signed visits and visits for the blind available, t 01 40 79 54 18.

At the far west end of the formal parterres looms the impressive Zoology Building, now the centre of the Jardin des Plantes' recently expanded and modernized ensemble of museums. After being closed for 30 years, the former zoology section is back with a vengeance as the **Grande Galerie de l'Evolution** – with every sort of interactive exhibit and audio-visual trick in the book, all on the theme of evolution and the diversity of life (pull-out English translations are slotted in the benches). The environmental message is relentless in exhibits from the dodo to modern man. The old stuffed critters are still present too, including hundreds of butterflies and a blue whale.

The long building beyond it houses the **Galerie de Minéralogie et de Géologie** (*open April–Oct Wed–Fri and Mon 10–5, Sat and Sun 10–6, Nov–Mar Wed–Mon 10–5, closed 1 May; adm €5*), displaying giant crystals from Brazil that imprison rainbows in hundreds of kilos of quartz, as well as meteorites and the museum's treasure – two rooms of precious gems on their own and in schmaltzy *objets d'art* that belonged to Louis XIV. A cross-section of a 2,000-year-old sequoia on the porch was donated to the soldiery of France by the same of California, although it was barely a twinkle in Ma Nature's eye compared to the other tree displayed here – a petrified stump from the marshes that covered the Paris basin 33,000,000 years ago.

Galerie de Paléontologie BB–CC17

*2 Rue Buffon; **métro** and **RER** Gare d'Austerlitz. **Open** April–Oct Wed–Fri and Mon 10–5, Sat and Sun 10–6; Nov–Mar Wed–Mon 10–5, closed 1 May; **adm** €5.*

The last and most surreal of the Jardin des Plantes' museums is in a massive brick building overlooking the Gare d'Austerlitz. The bas-reliefs of bugs, scorpions and violent battles (man v. bear, man v. crocs) that decorate the exterior reach a climax just inside the door, with a huge statue of an orang-utan strangling a man. The displays, with their little Latin tags, haven't been touched for decades – skeletons of mammoths, mammals and giant birds, burdened with names like Mégaptère Boops, march in frozen ranks down the centre of the galleries, along wth a rhinoceros that once belonged to Louis XV. Along the walls, glass cases contain a nightmarish collection of disembodied, greyish organs in bottles – a tiger's liver; a giraffe's uterus; camel, rhino and elephant willies; a two-headed baby named Marie et Christine; and a plaster model of ostrich guts. The first floor has the dinosaur bones, the second floor breathtakingly

boring exhibits on the palaeontology of the Île-de-France.

In front, by the Place Valhubert gate, is a **statue of Lamarck** (1744–1829), the great biologist whose theory of evolution held that what we do and learn in our lifetime can be passed on to our offspring, an idea mocked by biologists for over a century, but one that seems ever more topical in the light of the nurture/nature debate.

Ménagerie BB17

*3 Quai St-Bernard/57 Rue Cuvier, **t** 01 40 79 37 94; **métro** and **RER** Gare d'Austerlitz. **Open** April–Sept Mon–Sat 9–6, Sun 9–6.30, Oct–Mar daily 9–5, closed hols; **adm** €6. **Microzoo** open daily 10–12 and 2–5.30 (children must be over 11). **Restaurant and café**.*

Opposite the formal parterres of the Jardin des Plantes, and east beyond the rose gardens, Allée de Jussieu leads to the Ménagerie. In 1793 the Commune ordered all the wild beasts in circuses and travelling zoos to be sent to the Jardin des Plantes to form a public menagerie. The tattered horde was richly augmented two years later during the Flanders campaign, which bagged the entire zoo of the Stadtholder of Holland. Some animals became celebrities – the giraffe given by the Pasha of Egypt to Charles X in 1829 was the first ever seen in France, and set a veritable giraffe fashion mania. There was Jacqueline the chimp, who wore gloves and slept in a bed with sheets with her pet dog and cat; and then there was a homicidal brown bear, who permanently k.o.'d an Englishman on a bender who had only wanted to box, and later devoured one of Napoleon's impoverished veterans, who had jumped into his pit believing that the gold-coloured button the bear played with was a *louis d'or*. The Parisians named the bear Martin after the soldier, and to this day all bears in the Ménagerie are named Martin.

Humanity had its revenge during the siege of Paris in 1870, when the zoo appeared on the famous Christmas menu at Voisin's: stuffed head of ass (the hors d'oeuvre), *consommé d'éléphant*, roast *camel à l'anglaise*, *civet de kangourou*, bear ribs sauce *poivrade*, leg of wolf *sauce chevreuil*, roast cat with a side dish of rats, *terrine d'antilope aux truffes*, all washed down with a Mouton-Rothschild 1846 (wine was one item the Parisians never had to ration out during the siege). Nowadays larger zoo creatures are kept at Vincennes (*see* p.268), while the Ménagerie has smaller animals, to be viewed up close: reptiles, birds of prey, fetus-like albino axolotls, insects, deer, monkeys, big cats and a pair of Martins. The **Microzoo** looks at micro-organisms.

Grande Mosquée de Paris Z–AA18

*Rue Georges-Desplas, **t** 01 45 35 97 33 for prayer times, **t** 01 43 31 38 30 for all other info (in French and English), **e** recteur@mosquee-de-paris.com; **métro** Place Monge. **Open** for visits Sat–Thurs 9–12 and 2–6, closed Muslim hols; **adm** €3. Tour in French on request. **Hammam** open to men Tues 2–9pm and Sun 10am–9pm, to women Mon, Wed, Thurs and Sat 10am–9pm, Fri 2–9pm; **adm** €15, scrub €10, massage €10–30, combined packages available (some include meal); no children under 12. **Restaurant** open daily 12–3 and 7.30–10.30, **café** open daily 9am–11.30pm. **Shop** open daily 11am–7pm.*

Opposite the Jardin des Plantes, across Rue Geoffroy-St-Hilaire, yet another world awaits within this exotic white and green Maghrebi mosque, built between 1922 and 1926 in remembrance of the Muslim dead in the First World War and as a symbol of Franco-Moroccan friendship. It is nominally the central mosque for France's four million-plus faithful. A series of interior courtyards gives on to the sumptuous prayer room, where the domes were decorated by rival teams of Moroccan artisans competing in geometric ingenuity. The muezzin has not chanted the call to prayer from the minaret for years, in a move to mollify non-Muslim neighbours. During Ramadan the mosque is well attended and a fair of religious items is held in the main courtyard, but at other times the place is almost deserted. Politics is the reason: since its founding, the mosque has been under the control of the Algerian government, now, ironically, a secular state at war with the Islamic Salvation Front, which makes for conflicting loyalties among the French Muslim community.

Behind the mosque, at Nos.39 and 41 Rue Geoffroy-St-Hilaire, there's a Turkish bath (hammam), a quiet café serving mint tea and oriental pastries, a couscous restaurant and an arts and crafts shop.

MOUFFETARD AND AROUND

Place de la Contrescarpe Y17

Picturesque and piquant, the square at the northern end of Rue Mouffetard dates only from 1852, when the 14th-century Porte Bourdelle was demolished. For the next hundred years Paris' tramps flocked here, and now, even though most of the houses have been fixed up, it still has a bohemian atmosphere, especially at weekends. Rabelais, Ronsard, Du Bellay and the other Renaissance poets of the Pléiade would come to make merry at the Cabaret de la Pomme de Pin, at the corner of Rue Blainville (plaque at No.1).

Just off the Contrescarpe, at 50 Rue Descartes, another plaque shows the original appearance of Porte Bourdelle with its drawbridge; further along, there's another Hemingway-was-here plaque, and one at No.39 (now a restaurant) commemorating Paul Verlaine, who died in 1896 in a squalid hotel. In his last years, after his fiery affair with Rimbaud ended in pistol shots and a prison term, the poet had become Paris' most famous antihero, a wasted, pathetic figure, haunting Left Bank cafés to extinguish his brain cells in absinthe, often in the company of his 'secretary', a drink-cadging charlatan named Bibi-la-Purée.

Leading off Place de la Contrescarpe is **Rue Rollin**, a treeless street of blonde stone houses more Mediterranean than Parisian. A plaque at No.14 marks Descartes' address in Paris. A good Catholic, he nevertheless preferred the Protestant Netherlands, and sniffed that while in France 'what most disgusted me was that no one seemed to want to know anything about me except what I looked like, so I began to believe that they wanted me in France the way they might want an elephant or a panther, because it is rare, and not because it is useful'.

Rue Mouffetard Y17–19

This lively, narrow street is named after the *mofette* (stench) that rose from the tanners and dyers along the Bièvre, a once bucolic tributary of the Seine that rolled through woodlands and meadows. Over the centuries it became an open sewer and had to be covered over.

Rue Mouffetard itself is one of the most ancient streets in Paris, following the path of the Roman road to Lyon. Ever since then it has been lined with inns and taverns for the wayfarer; while strolling down the 'Mouff' and poking in its capillary lanes and court-yards you can pick out a number of old signs, such as the carved oak at No.69 for the Vieux Chêne, which began as a Revolutionary club.

Rue du Pot-de-Fer owes its name to the **Fontaine du Pot-de-Fer**, one of 14 fountains donated by Marie de' Medici when she reno-vated a Roman aqueduct to feed the fountains in the Jardin du Luxembourg. In 1928, 25-year-old George Orwell moved into a seedy hotel at 6 Rue du Pot-de-Fer to live off his meagre savings while he learned the craft of writing; when he was robbed, he was reduced to washing dishes in a hotel in the Rue de Rivoli – the source for his first published book *Down and Out in Paris and London*.

Further south, beyond Rue de l'Epée-de-Bois begins Rue Mouffetard's **market**, where shops spill out to join pavement stalls, cascading with fruit and vegetables, cheeses, seafood, pâtés, sausages, bread and more, with an occasional exotic touch such as the African market in Rue de l'Arbalète.

St-Médard Y18–19

141 Rue Mouffetard, t 01 44 08 87 00; métro Censier-Daubenton. Open Tues–Sun all day (closed for lunch 12–2.30), Mon only for 7pm Mass.

At the bottom of the street, St-Médard occupies the site of an old village church founded in the 9th century where the road crossed the Bièvre. It was rebuilt from the 15th century onwards, and is a pleasant if unremarkable building with a few windows from the 1620s. But in the 18th century its cemetery (now replaced by a garden) was the scene of a peculiar hullabaloo (*see* 'St-Médard', overleaf).

RUE MONGE NORTH TO THE SEINE

Arènes de Lutèce Z17

Rue Monge, t 01 45 35 02 56; métro Jussieu or Place Monge. Open summer daily 9am–9.30pm, winter daily 8–5.30.

'Passer-by, dream before the oldest monu-ment in Paris,' reads the plaque of 1951, commemorating the city's second millen-nium. 'May the city of Paris also be the city of the future and of your hopes.'

The slight remains of Lutetia's Roman amphitheatre (now a garden, football pitch and *boules* court) date from the 2nd century. Originally it could seat 10,000: half the entire population of Lutetia. A unique feature was the stage at the east end, adaptable for glad-iator fights or less brutal theatrics. The amphitheatre was too convenient a quarry to survive the Dark Ages, when its stone went into fortifying the Île de la Cité. What remained was forgotten until rediscovered in 1869, restored in 1917 and, incredibly, almost demolished in 1980 for a housing project.

St-Médard

François Pâris, son of a city councillor, had renounced a prosperous legal career and a rich inheritance to help the needy of Faubourg St-Marcel (*see* below) in the most direct fashion possible, even learning to knit so he could make them socks. Too humble to aspire to the priesthood, he served merely as a deacon at St-Médard, and when he died in 1727 at the age of 37, he was buried here. The good deacon's mourners were many; his simple goodness greatly appealed to those austere fundamentalists, the Jansenists, who regarded him as a saint at a time when they were being persecuted by the Jesuits. At his graveside a few teenage girls became so emotional that they were seized with convulsions. The fits were contagious: within two years the *convulsionnaires* numbered over 800 young women, jumping and spinning in the cemetery, barking like dogs or mewing like cats, eating soil from the deacon's grave and drawing huge numbers of curious onlookers. Miracle cures and prophecies followed in quick succession. In 1731, St-Médard's pious carnival took an ugly turn, as the *convulsionnaires* began to whip and beat themselves in a frenzy of volup-tuous pain. The most extreme asked to have their hands and feet nailed to planks. In January 1732, Louis XV ordered the cemetery closed, and on the gate posted the notice:

De par le roi, défense à Dieu
De faire miracle en ce lieu.

Not only was God forbidden to perform any more miracles, but the *convulsionnaires* were faced with imprisonment and went underground, where they convulsed until 1761 – the same year that the Jesuits were expelled from France.

In the quiet gardens that encompass the arena, don't miss the knotty beech, the crookedest tree in Paris.

Paris VI and VII Z16–AA17

Rue des Boulangers, behind the Arènes, is a remarkable village street of 17th- and 18th-century houses and tiny gardens. It curves down gently to **Place Jussieu**, where abruptly the scene changes. The looming sinister steel, glass and concrete vortex is **Paris VI and VII**, the university's science faculty and a text-book case of the failure of architectural modernism.

Originally this was the site of the famous abbey of St-Victor, founded in 1108 when Guillaume de Champeaux, master of dialec-tics at the École de Notre-Dame, retreated here with his disciples after being upstaged by his pupil, Peter Abelard. Made a royal abbey in 1113, St-Victor was destroyed in the Revolution, replaced by a *halle des vins* that was in turn swept away in the 1960s for this malignant fairy-ring of bleak, wind-whipped towers on stilts. The project was scarcely complete when students scaled the glacial cliffs of its entrance to cover the finishings with Maoist slogans. Rather than paint over them, the authorities connected the letters to form evil alien messages, which blend in perfectly with the massive, harrowing tile-mural of a primal scream. The ordinary *frissons* offered by the fight-to-the-death decorations of the Galerie de Paléontologie (*see* p.235) seem naïve before this relic of the know-it-all world of science nerds. The joke's on them; the entire complex is laced with asbestos, and it's too dangerous to gut it and renovate, or even to knock it down and try again.

Appropriately enough, the only thing to see is a small **Musée des Minéraux** in Tower 25 (*34 Rue Jussieu,* **t** *01 44 27 52 88; open Wed–Mon 1–6, closed hols; adm €4.50*) and its rare specimens of lapis lazuli, malachites, quartz and uranium. You may find yourself uncon-sciously looking for anti-radiation iodine tablets in the university vending machines.

Institut du Monde Arabe AA15–16

1 Rue des Fossés-St-Bernard, **t** *01 40 51 38 38,* **w** *www.imarabe.org;* **métro** *Jussieu or Cardinal-Lemoine; wheelchair access.*

Open *museum and exhibitions Tues–Sun 10–6; **adm** €4; library Tues–Sat 1–8.*

Completed in 1987, this coolly elegant riverside structure is nearly everyone's favourite contemporary building in Paris. The competition for the Institut's design was won in 1981 by Jean Nouvel (a Frenchman, for once), who came up with a pair of long, thin buildings, one gracefully curved to follow the line of the quay. Their walls are covered with window panels inspired by ancient Islamic geometric patterns, but equipped with photo-electric cells that activate their dilation or contraction according to the amount of sunlight – with a gentle hi-tech whoosh that takes you by surprise the first time you experience it.

The Institut is financed by the French government and 22 Arab countries, with the goal of introducing Islamic civilization to the public and facilitating cultural exchanges. Besides an extensive library (on the third floor, around a great spiral ramp) there are rotating exhibitions, a shop of books and crafts, and recordings and films to see in the *Espace Son et Image*. The **museum**, spread out on several floors, displays examples of the art and exquisite craftsmanship of the Arab world, beginning with pre-Islamic times (2nd- and 3rd-century stone and alabaster carvings from Yemen, Hellenistic art from north Arabia and funeral busts from Palmyra) and continuing to ceramics, tiles, textiles, brass, carpets and astrolabes from the Middle Ages to our day, accompanied by explanatory mini-videos, some in English.

Skirting the Seine Z15–CC17

Opposite the Institut du Monde Arabe is the **Musée de la Sculpture en Plein Air**, set up in 1980 and modelled after one in Tokyo. As you walk the length of Quai St-Bernard, you'll see all the usual river activities, along with sculptures by the likes of Brancusi, César and Zadkine.

The **Pont de la Tournelle** (1656, enlarged in 1851) is named after a pair of medieval towers (*tourelles*) that stood on either bank,

---

La Tour d'Argent

In the earliest days the *patron* of the Tour d'Argent would get up at the crack of dawn to shoot the day's menu in the marshlands of what is now Île St-Louis. Henri III knighted him for his heron pie, and according to tradition the king learned how to use a fork here (although it was more likely that Henri, who had spent an extraordinary week being entertained in Venice, where forks were commonplace, introduced the utensil to the Parisians). The pressed duck remains the stuff of legend, and France's gourmet bibles continue to lavish stars on this grand old (and furiously expensive) restaurant (*see* p.334), with the longest gastronomic tradition of any in the capital of cuisine.

---

linked by a chain ready to barricade the river at a moment's notice. The tower on the Left Bank was converted in 1582 to an inn known as **La Tour d'Argent** (*see* above). Although the original tower was demolished in the Revolution, a new Tour d'Argent was resurrected on the same site. Clients of the restaurant can visit a little museum, with famous menus, autographs, china and the 'table of three emperors', set as it was in June 1867 for the future Kaiser Wilhelm I, Bismarck, Tsar Alexander II and the future Tsar Alexander III, who were all in town for the Exhibition.

FAUBOURG ST-MARCEL

Faubourg St-Marcel, the southeastern corner of the 5e on the way to the 13e, was a working-class village annexed to Paris in 1702. 'There's more money in one house in Faubourg Saint-Honoré than in all of Faubourg St-Marcel,' Sébastien Mercier wrote in his *Tableaux de Paris*. 'Here, far from the traffic in the centre, hide ruined men, misanthropes, alchemists, maniacs, narrow-minded rentiers, and a few studious sages, who truly seek solitude.' Needless to say, these are no longer allowed to exist, at least not so close to the centre of Paris.

The sleepy streets around here scarcely remember when this was Paris' boisterous, odoriferous and cacophonous horse, pig and dog market; the only memories of this are a few old signs. In the old days, the corner of Rue Buffon reverberated with the croaks from the weekly *marché aux crapauds*, or toad market. The buyers? British, and later French, gardeners plagued by slugs and other pests, and young ladies who would have soothsayers read their fortunes in the toads' entrails.

The church of **St-Marcel** (Coptic Christian, with well-attended charismatic services on Sundays), just south of St-Marcel métro station in Boulevard de l'Hôpital (AA–BB19), was unfortunately replaced in 1966, in the middle an architectural dark age.

Hôpital de la Salpêtrière BB19–DD20

One of Paris' largest hospitals, this is a relic from an earlier dark age of public morality. Enter through the main gate off Boulevard de l'Hôpital and past the square named after **Marie Curie** (b. Poland, 1867–1934). In 1911 she became the first woman to win the Nobel Prize (for research into radioactivity and atomic chemistry) and then the first person to win twice, before she died from an overdose of radiation.

Originally the arsenal of Louis XIII, the Salpêtrière (the saltpetre works) was converted by Louis XIV in 1654 into a prison-workhouse for orphans and the poor under the auspices of the Hôpital Général. Locking

up *les misérables* proved to be so effective that the Salpêtrière was expanded to take in female criminals, prostitutes, repudiated wives and the insane. By the number of 'patients' it was the world's largest hospital at the time of the Revolution, although it had only begun to care properly for its inmates when an infirmary was installed in 1783.

After the Revolution abolished the work-houses, the 'Pavilion of the Mad' remained at the Salpêtrière, and evolved into a leading centre of research into mental illnesses and diseases of the nerves. At first conditions were appalling. Patients were chained or left naked in filthy rooms. If it was a slow day at the Morgue (*see* p.88), visitors could come and stare for a few *sous*. Conditions began to improve in the 1790s when Dr Pinel (whose statue is to the left of the entrance in Square Marie-Curie) took the radical step of unchaining his patients from the wall. In the 1880s a young neurologist named Sigmund Freud worked for six months here as an intern; his observations of the then current use of hypnotism to treat hysterics contributed to his theory of the unconscious.

The Salpêtrière's central building, by Libéral Bruant (1677), has the same austere grandeur as the architect's Invalides, crowned this time by an octagonal dome with a lantern. The remarkable geometric church it protects, **St-Louis-de-la-Salpêtrière**, has radiating from its high altar four large naves divided by chapels, in order to isolate the patients by their degree of physical or social contagious-ness. The interior is strikingly plain and unadorned, somehow having been over-looked in the 19th-century urge to gussy up churches with bad art.

Montparnasse

1 Lunch

L'Amuse Bouche, *186 Rue du Château,* *t 01 43 35 31 61;* **métro** *Mouton-Duvernet.* **Open** *Tues–Sat 12–2 and 7.30–10.15.* **Moderate.** A tiny place run by the former chef of Jacques Cagna, serving food to warm the cockles of your heart.

2 Tea and Cakes

Calabrese Glacier, *15 Rue d'Odessa;* **métro** *Montparnasse-Bienvenüe.* **Open** *daily 10am–midnight.* The Leonardo da Vinci of ice-cream inventions, home of the famous vanilla and cinnamon *soupe anglaise*.

3 Drinks

Le Rallye Peret, *6 Rue Daguerre;* **métro** *Denfert-Rochereau.* **Open** *Tues–Sat till 8pm, closed Aug.* Owned by the same family for over 80 years, with the biggest variety of bottles to choose from on the Left Bank.

Montparnasse

'Ne va jamais à Montparnasse!' was the note André Breton posted to himself over his desk in Montmartre, not wanting to join the post-First World War art exodus from the Butte Sacrée to this pagan Left Bank usurper. Nearly everyone else went, and Montparnasse, with its cheap rents, became the vortex of the avant-garde and its -isms in the 1920s.

There was scarcely anything picturesque or beautiful about Montparnasse then, and there's certainly nothing now; Parisians lovingly call it an 'exquisite cadaver'. But Montparnasse and the hinterland of the 14e still boasts a high density of art studios; advertising and cinema people flock to its cafés and trendy restaurants and during the weekend evenings it's jam-packed.

For the daytime stroller there are things to see as well: straight and unconventional architecture, statues and fountains, billions of dead Parisians in the Cimetière du Montparnasse and Catacombs, the ateliers of the sculptors Bourdelle and Zadkine, and a post-office museum.

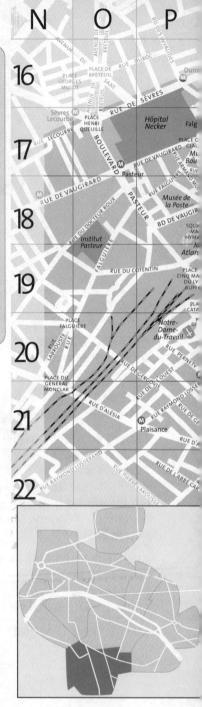

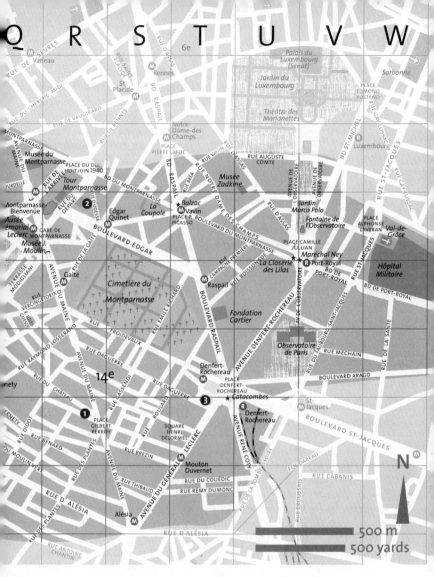

Highlights

Couples' City: An evening in the Lost Generation cafés along Boulevard de Montparnasse, p.246

Parisian's City: Goldoni and Pirandello in French at the Comédie Italienne, p.246

Peace and Quiet: The shady groves of the Cimetière du Montparnasse, p.250

Paris des Artistes: Bourdelle and Zadkine's studios, with collections of their works, pp.245 and 248

Grand Siècle Paris: Louis XIV's stately, if astronomically useless, Observatoire, p.248

Gritty City: Into the bowels of Paris, on a guided tour of the catacombs, p.249

AROUND TOUR MONTPARNASSE

Paris' Mount Parnassus began its career as a weedy heap of tailings from the many Roman quarries in the area, a mound where students came to frolic with bottles of wine and buxom muses – hence its tongue-in-cheek name taken from the holy mountain of Apollo, the god of art and poetry. In the Middle Ages, Montparnasse ground the flour for Left Bank baguettes; in 1780 there were still 18 working windmills. The first houses date from the 17th century, when Louis XIV built the Observatoire to create an *axe*, or prospect, with the Palais de Luxembourg, and laid out the Grand Cours du Midi (now Boulevard du Montparnasse). Land was still cheap enough in the early 19th century for Montparnasse to experience a first flush of fashion with its dance halls, *guingettes* and cabarets. After the construction of the Gare Montparnasse (the terminus from Brittany), a piquant workers' quarter grew up south of the Boulevard du Montparnasse; even today the area boasts a strong Breton flavour.

In the 1870s, Verlaine, Anatole France and Sully-Prudhomme called themselves 'The Parnassians', giving Montparnasse its first genuine link to the arts. Other Parnassians arrived in the early 20th century: Modigliani and Apollinaire in the lead, fleeing rising prices in Montmartre. Art connoisseurs Gertrude and Leo Stein moved in just behind them; Lenin, Trotsky and so many other revolutionaries lived here that the Tsarist police had a special Montparnasse unit.

After the First World War, these pioneer Monparnos were followed by artistic and literary pilgrims and refugees from all over the world. Others, the Hemingways, Fitzgeralds and so on, came as refugees from Prohibition. Made instantly rich thanks to the exchange rate, the Americans helped to create the frenzy of *les années folles*, as the French call the 1920s, partying the night away in Montparnasse's cafés. As Sinclair Lewis described the Café Dôme: 'It is the perfectly standardized place to which standardized rebels flee from the crushing standardization of America.'

After the Second World War, the scene changed again; the culture vultures retreated to St-Germain and the north side of Boulevard du Montparnasse, while the neighbourhood where Americans drank themselves silly was singled out for the city's first experiment in American-style property development, in a toadstool project called **Maine-Montparnasse**. Planned back in 1934 but begun only in 1961, this incorporated Paris' first skyscraper, a new railway station to replace the old Gare Montparnasse, a shopping mall and a concrete wasteland of urban anomie. This and similar displacements since 1975 have resulted in the 14e losing a fifth of its population, nearly all of them workers forced out into the *banlieue*.

Tour Montparnasse R17–18

Place Raoul Dautry, entrance in Rue de l'Arrivée, **t** *01 45 38 52 56,* **w** *www.tourmont parnasse56.com;* **métro** *Montparnasse-Bienvenüe. Viewing platforms* **open** *summer daily 9.30am–11.30pm, winter daily 9.30am–11pm, last ascent 30min before closing;* **adm** *€7 (56th floor), €8 (59th floor).*

The Montparnasse station is named after Fugence Bienvenüe, the engineer who designed the first métro line in 1896. Until London's Canary Wharf, the tower above was the tallest in Europe at 656ft, sticking up like a sore tombstone, way out of proportion to the rest of the Paris skyline. The closed-in 56th floor offers not only views but a bar, Ciel de Paris ('the highest in Paris!') and a film of aerial views over the city; the 59th floor is an open terrace. On a clear day you can see for 25 miles, with the added plus of *not* seeing the Tour Montparnasse. The ungainly, submerged shopping mall in front overlooks Place du 18 Juin 1940, the date of De Gaulle's famous BBC speech encouraging the French to fight on.

Mémorial du Maréchal Leclerc de Hauteclocque et de la Libération de Paris, et Musée Jean Moulin Q18–19

23 Allée de la Deuxième D.B., t 01 40 64 39 44; métro Montparnasse-Bienvenüe; wheelchair access. Open Tues–Sun 10–5.40; adm €4, free Sun 10–1.

This museum overlooking the Jardin Atlantique, a rather bleak garden above the station, offers exhibits and audio-visuals on the wartime career of the general and the great Resistance leader, located here because the surrender in 1945 was signed in the old Gare Montparnasse.

The station had already entered Parisian mythology in 1898, when the brakes of a train speeding at 37 miles an hour failed just as it approached the station. The guard applied the Westinghouse brake and saved the passengers, but the engine went hurtling through the glass wall and came to a halt halfway across the square, crashing into a kiosk where it killed an old woman. A post-card showing the accident was so popular it had to be reprinted seven times.

Musée Bourdelle Q17

18 Rue Antoine-Bourdelle, t 01 49 54 73 73; métro Montparnasse-Bienvenüe. Open Tues–Sun 10–6, last adm 5.45, closed hols; adm free.

Antoine Bourdelle (1861–1929) was a student of Rodin, whose maxim was *L'art fait ressortir les grandes lignes de la nature.* Even more prolific than Rodin, he left some 900 statues and studies in this curious red-brick building.

Bourdelle's great obsession was Beethoven, whom he carved 62 times, using his death mask as a model; here too are bas-reliefs from the Théâtre des Champs-Elysées (1912) inspired by Isadora Duncan, and the violent *Héraklès Archer* (1909). Even if you don't want

to go in, look at the courtyard: a monumental petrified garden party gate-crashed by the Trojan horse.

Musée du Montparnasse Q17

21 Av du Maine, t 01 42 22 91 96, e musee dumontparnasse@wanadoo.fr; métro Montparnasse-Bienvenüe or Falguière. Open Tues–Sun 12.30–6.30; adm €4.

Exhibitions featuring Montparnasse artists, from Picasso and Modigliani to those living in the neighbourhood today.

Musée de la Poste P18

34 Bd de Vaugirard, t 01 42 79 23 45; métro Montparnasse-Bienvenüe. Open Mon–Sat 10–6, closed hols; adm €4.50.

Just behind the Gare de Montparnasse, this cream-coloured building wrapped in concrete prisms has five floors covering postal history, from ancient letters on clay tablets to the modern PTT. There's a complete collection of French stamps (note the lovely, meticulous engravings on issues up to the 1960s), as well as memorabilia from the siege of 1870.

PLAISANCE

This old working-class quarter to the south of the Montparnasse complex got its name from its many pleasant *guinguettes* in the 18th century. Though increasingly threatened by high rents, and by office blocks sprouting like toadstools all around the Tour Montparnasse, it still lives up to its name – one of the few places anywhere in Paris with a genuine neighbourhood feel to it.

The older, chummier parts of Plaisance are to the south, around **Rue Pernety** and **Rue Raymond-Losserand** (P20–Q21). To the north, on the other side of Avenue du Maine, lies another street that helped to give Montparnasse its reputation in the old days: **Rue de la Gaîté** (R19–18). This will be a sad trek for anyone who remembers the Montparnasse of even 20 years ago, especially since its last great music hall, Bobino, was converted into a disco. Like its counterparts in Montmartre, this old 'street of gaiety' grew up outside the Farmers-General tax wall, where the tax on drink was cheaper. One old-timer, the **Théâtre de la Gaîté-Montparnasse** at No.6, still has its stucco masks; at No.17 the **Comédie Italienne** (*see* p.356) still performs Goldoni and *commedia dell'arte*, just as in the days of Watteau. There's no plaque for the street's most famous resident, Trotsky, amidst the dilapidated sleazola and capitalist sex shops.

Place de Catalogne Q19

Métro Gaîté.

Designed by the neo-neo-neoclassical Catalan architect Ricardo Bofill, this monumental colonnaded and pedimented amphitheatre (1974) may look like a Stalinist project of the 1950s, but it has the advantage over the other bunker buildings in the area in that it replaces old working-class housing with affordable flats (425 subsidized units out of 574). It's a sorry sign of our times that Place de Catalogne doesn't even pretend to be a place where residents can meet and linger; traffic spins around a centre entirely hogged up by a pretentious fountain called *The Crucible of Time*, where water (sometimes) flows up and spills over the tilted disc, made of 500,000 blocks of Breton granite.

The pedestrian zones and lawns are to the south: **Place de l'Amphithéâtre** and, through a giant arch, grassy **Place de Séoul**, surrounded by angular reflective glass and closed off by two lonely Doric columns the size of sequoias.

Notre-Dame-du-Travail P20

59 Rue Vercingétorix, t 01 44 10 72 92; métro Pernety or Gaîté. Open Tues–Sat 10–12 and 2–6, Mon 2–6 and Sun 10–12.

Plaisance has a remarkable parish church: a monument to its *abbé* Soulange-Bodin

(1861–1925), who spent his career founding mutual-aid societies, food cooperatives and working men's clubs. His idea for 'Our Lady of Work' was to make a 'universal sanctuary' for workers, and as the funds for its building were raised by popular subscription, it was built as economically as possible. The result is Paris' most striking and honest ironwork church, designed by Jules Astruc (1899–1901); his delicate use of girders in the nave and chapels has had few imitators. The frescoes in the apse show the patron saints of the trades dressed in workers' smocks of the time.

ALONG BOULEVARD DU MONTPARNASSE
Famous Cafés S17–U18

Métro Montparnasse-Bienvenüe or Vavin.

Boulevard du Montparnasse has been devoted to pleasure ever since it was the knoll where medieval students sang and danced. Before the First World War, **La Rotonde** (at No.102, now prettified beyond recognition) was a favourite of Picasso, Apollinaire, Trotsky and Lenin. Trotsky often gave fiery speeches, while Lenin bided his time playing chess or enjoying the charms of his favourite prostitute, who after his rise to power complained to anyone who would listen that the cheapskate still owed her money. **Le Sélect** (No.99) has kept its original décor intact; it was famous for its fights in the 1920s, and is still the noisiest of the four. **Le Dôme**, with an interior designed by Slavik, is the quietest and most touristy. **La Coupole**, a few doors down, is still one of the trendiest spots to be seen in in Paris; recently restored as much as possible to its original 1920s appearance, its 24 pillars are decorated with paintings by Othon Friesz and 30 other artists.

Near here, at 26 Rue Vavin, don't miss the bizarre 'Bathroom Building' covered with blue and white tiles and built in 1912 by Henri

Sauvage, who wanted to create inexpensive, 'hygienic' housing for the poor.

Rodin's Balzac T18

Métro *Vavin.*

Where Boulevard Montparnasse crosses Boulevard Raspail, Rodin's statue of Balzac lords it over the parked motorcycles. No work by Rodin, and few other statues, stirred up such a bitter row (*see* 'The Scandal of Balzac').

La Closerie des Lilas U18

Further east, where Boulevard du Montparnasse crosses Avenue de l'Observatoire, the famous *guinguette* **La Closerie des Lilas** opened its doors in 1847, in an immense grove of lilacs. Baudelaire, Verlaine and Mallarmé were regulars of this first version; after the First World War it was reborn here as a bar and restaurant, a favourite rendezvous of the Surrealists, who on occasion swung from the chandeliers. A plaque in the bar marks the spot where Hemingway stood (a victim of haemorrhoids) while writing *The Sun also Rises*.

Fontaine de l'Observatoire V18

RER *Port-Royal.*

In 998, when Hugues Capet's son Robert the so-called Pious was excommunicated, he built himself a pleasure palace called Château de Vauvert which stood just north of the Boulevard Montparnasse and Avenue de l'Observatoire intersection. As it fell into ruin, devils were said to have moved in – rumours encouraged by the cutthroats and robbers who made it their lair to such effect that even today the French say '*aller au diable Vauvert*'. In 1259, St Louis gave Vauvert to the Carthusians, who cleared away the devils, put in exotic pear orchards (now in the Luxembourg gardens) and dug quarries. The latter were converted to wine cellars so vast that one poor fellow out for a secret tipple lost his way in the subterranean labyrinths,

The Scandal of Balzac

When a monument for Balzac's centenary was commissioned in 1891 by the Society of Men of Letters, Zola (the then president) swung the choice of sculptor to Rodin, in the face of die-hard reactionaries, who hated the fact that the Minister of Fine Arts had declared the experimental, avant-garde Rodin France's greatest living sculptor.

Artistically, Rodin's greatest problem was reconciling Balzac's magnificent, leonine head with a short, pudgy body, deformed by decades bent over a writing desk. A preliminary nude Balzac (now in the Musée Rodin) was quickly rejected, and after years of delay due to the sculptor's ill health, a plaster of the statue was finally revealed to a thunderstruck public in the salon of 1898: Rodin had rendered the novelist not as a man but as something more elemental, a rugged monolith surging from the earth crowned by a tragic, dramatic head, a wonderfully imaginative if unconventional evocation of mind over matter. The reaction was violent: the Men of Letters refused the statue and although Rodin's supporters raised funds to have Balzac cast and put up in public, Rodin refused to be drawn into the battle. He paid back his advance with interest, and took the statue out to his country house, while a banal substitute was put up in Rue Balzac in the 8e. In 1939, 22 years after Rodin's death, he was finally vindicated by the placing of his great *Balzac* here.

only to be found 15 years later in skeletal form. After the Revolution, the Carthusians were cleared away to perfect the perspective from the Palais de Luxembourg to the Observatoire. This is the perfect setting for the **Fontaine de l'Observatoire** (Observatory Fountain, 1875), where sassy tortoises spit in the eyes of rearing horses with seal tails. On top, four naked girls carved by Carpeaux have sent old Atlas out to pasture, by supporting the world as easily as a beach ball. Near here, Rue Michelet is guarded by the fantastical Assyrian-Egyptian brick **Institut d'Art et d'Archéologie**.

Gertrude Stein

The area north of the Musée Zadkine nurtured American writers from Pound to Hemingway, all dreading or hoping for an invitation from Gertrude Stein, the 'Mother Goose of Montparnasse', who in 1903 moved into 27 Rue de Fleurus, to the north off Rue d'Assas. With her brother Leo, Gertrude Stein was among the first to understand and support new artists and the -isms that crowded the early 20th century – neo-Impressionism, Fauvism, Futurism and especially Cubism (she drew the line at Dadaism and Surrealism, apparently because it infringed on her own turf). Stein gave the Lost Generation its name; her *Autobiography of Alice B. Toklas* is among the classic documentaries of Paris in the 1920s. One of the greatest nonsense writers of all time, she had no doubt of her genius. 'Joyce is a third-rate Irish politician. The greatest living writer of the age is Gertrude Stein.'

Musée Zadkine U17–18

*100 bis Rue d'Assas; t 01 43 26 91 90; **métro** Vavin. **Open** Tues–Sun 10–5.40, closed hols; **adm** €3.30, free Sun.*

Here you can visit the delightful garden and sculptor's studio of the Ukrainian Ossip Zadkine, who purchased this charming house in 1928. 'Come see my folly d'Assas,' he once invited a friend, 'and you will understand how the life of a man can be changed because of a dovecote, because of a tree.' Among the works displayed here is a model of his masterpiece, *The Destroyed City* (1947), in Rotterdam.

AROUND THE OBSERVATORY

L'Observatoire U19–V20

*61 Av de l'Observatoire, t 01 40 51 22 21, w www.obspm.fr; **métro** Denfert-Rochereau. **Open** by appt only: write 2 months ahead to* join the guided tours usually held on the first Sat of each month at 2.30; **adm** €4.50.

As Sun King, Louis XIV was a natural patron of astronomers, and he commissioned Louvre architect Claude Perrault to build them an observatory. The result, a parcel of perfect symmetry, was begun on the day of the summer solstice in 1667, each corner orientated to a cardinal point, its centre pierced by the Paris meridian (2°20'17" east), a longitude that rivalled Greenwich as the base measure of the entire world until 1884, when Greenwich was universally adopted – except in France and Ireland, which held out until 1911.

Despite all this, when the observatory was half-completed, the Academy of Science's director, Giandomenico Cassini, complained to Louis that the building would be useless for observations unless Perrault redesigned the top floor. Perrault and the king categorically refused. The debate grew sharp, and Cassini, realizing that they were more interested in the observatory's appearance than its function, began like a good Italian to argue and gesticulate at the Sun King, who slowly eclipsed at such disrespect. Colbert saved Cassini from the Bastille by whispering to Louis: 'Sire, this babbler doesn't know what he's saying.' There was no saving the Observatory, however, which was completed to Perrault's plans (the white, ball-shaped dome is from a later date), and Cassini was forced to erect his tubeless, cranelike 150ft long 'air telescope' on its lawn, where he was the first to see four of Saturn's moons. But the greatest contribution of Louis XIV's scientists was their measurements: the calculation of the earth's circumference, confirming the ancient Greek estimate; the distance between the earth and the sun – 20 times greater than what Ptolemy had believed (very gratifying to a Sun King, who wanted to be as far above humanity as possible); and the speed of light, which the Greeks had never thought of measuring.

The academy's zest for measurements continued during the Revolution. To replace a thousand higgledy-piggledy medieval

The Discoverer of Neptune

The statue gracing the front of the Observatoire is of Urbain-Jean Leverrier (1811–77), one of its greatest astronomer-measurers. Studying the hitherto mysterious perturbations in Uranus' orbit, Leverrier calculated the existence of another planet, its orbit, mass and distance from the earth, and in 1846 wrote to a colleague in Berlin, suggesting that if he pointed his telescope in a certain direction on a certain day, he would see a new planet. Leverrier was perfectly right. He modestly declined giving his name to what we know as Neptune, and when offered the chance in Paris to view his discovery through a telescope himself, refused. He had known in his mind that the planet was there; he needed no proof.

measures used under the *ancien régime*, the academicians invented the metric system in 1791, as logical as pie; its metre was calculated as one ten-millionth of a quarter of the distance from the North Pole to the Equator. The Observatoire continues to measure away: under the monumental stair, a path leads 92 ft down to a subterranean quarry where the temperature never varies, the perfect atmosphere for the Coordinated Universal Clock that keeps France's official time, calculated to a millionth of a second.

In front of the Observatoire is a statue of Urbain-Jean Leverrier (*see* 'The Discoverer of Neptune').

Place Denfert-Rochereau T20–U21

Métro *Denfert-Rochereau.*

Around the back of the Observatoire is Place Denfert-Rochereau, once known as the Tombe d'Issoire, after a giant Saracen who came to destroy Paris in the time of Charlemagne but was cut down and buried on the spot. Now it is one of the Left Bank's busiest traffic fandangos, guarded by the sphinx-like *Lion de Belfort*, a beast designed by Bartholdi to commemorate Colonel Rochereau's defence of Belfort in 1870, the sole 'victory' the French salvaged from the Prussian fiasco. Despite grabbing Alsace and Lorraine in the peace treaty, Bismarck let France keep Belfort in exchange for the humiliation of Paris: a Prussian triumphal march down the Champs-Elysées.

The two pavilions with carved friezes survive from the Barrière d'Enfer, or 'tollgate of hell', in the Farmers-General wall. An apt name, as one of the pavilions (No.1) serves as the entrance to the Catacombs.

The Catacombs W20–21

1 Place Denfert-Rochereau, t 01 43 22 47 63. **Open** *Tues 11–4, Wed–Sun 9–4, closed hols;* **adm** *€5. Take a torch.*

Down the 90 steps of a spiral stair wait pictures of the old gypsum quarries that make Paris a gruyère cheese under all her fine frippery. Next it's a tramp through damp and dreary tunnels to a toytown Fort of Port Mahon (Menorca), hollowed out of the wall by a bored caretaker once imprisoned there. Then there's a vicious blue puddle called the *source de Léthé*, inhabited by little pale-eyed creatures who dine on bone moss. Then the doorway inscribed: 'Halt! This is the empire of the dead.' But of course you don't halt at all, for beyond is the main attraction: the last earthly remains of Mirabeau, Rabelais, Madame de Pompadour and five to six million other Parisians removed here, beginning in 1786, from the putrid, overflowing cemetery of the Innocents (*see* p.170) and every other churchyard in Paris. Tibias are stacked as neatly as the tinned goods in a supermarket. Skulls, with a nice patina of age, are arranged decoratively in cross or heart shapes.

The ossuary was dubbed the '*catacombes*' in Paris' eternal effort to ape Rome, and, like the morgue (*see* p.88), it soon became a tourist attraction. The acoustics are so remarkable that in 1897 a midnight concert took place featuring the Danse Macabre; heavy-metal attempts to follow suit have been quashed by the authorities. During the war, the Nazis never suspected that the catacombs were the headquarters of

Resistance hero Colonel Rol-Tanguy. Pinching souvenirs must be common, for bags are thoroughly checked at the gate.

Fondation Cartier pour l'Art Contemporain T19

261 Bd Raspail, t 01 42 18 56 72,
w www.fondation.cartier.fr; métro Raspail.
Open Tues–Sun 12–8pm; adm €5.

The Fondation Cartier hosts international contemporary art exhibitions in a spectacular building by Jean Nouvel, who also designed the Institut du Monde Arabe (*see* pp.238–9).

Abbaye Royale du Val-de-Grâce W18–X19

1 Place Alphonse-Laveran, off Rue St-Jacques,
t 01 40 51 51 94; RER Port-Royal. Open Tues and
Wed 12–6, Sat and Sun 1.30–5; adm €4.50.
Gregorian chant Sun 11am.

Before the Revolution, vast areas of Paris were covered by wealthy monastic complexes; Val-de-Grâce is the only one to survive intact. Anne of Austria, wife of Louis XIII, installed the first Benedictine nuns here in 1621 and built for herself a small pavilion – complete with a false floor – directly over the gypsum quarries, where she kept a nest of Spanish spies to abet her plots against Richelieu. The cardinal got wind of what was going on in 1637 and abruptly banned further religious retreats by the queen. Miffed, Anne vowed to build a magnificent church in exchange for a little Louis, and proved that God was on her side by giving birth after 23 childless years. François Mansart drew the plans, and a seven-year-old Louis XIV laid the foundation stone in 1645. Progress was slow, because of difficulties shoring up the gypsum galleries; Anne impatiently fired Mansart and hired Lemercier to complete the task. The gypsum galleries came in handy later when Anne had a point of access drilled from her quarters, 'the hole in the service of Madame the Queen', a wondrous innovation in the days when French kings received

visitors while unburdening themselves on a *chaise percée*.

The church itself is cold potatoes, but then few French architects ever got a handle on Baroque. Val-de-Grâce's plan is a copycat of Palladio's Redentore in Venice; over the altar rises a quasi-clone of Bernini's baldachin in St Peter's; in the lofty dome (also modelled on St Peter's) Pierre Mignard's fresco, the *Gloire des Bienheureux*, has a cast as big as an old Broadway musical and figures three times life-size, all pap: just like St Peter's. In a niche under the chapel to the left, the embalmed hearts of queens and kings were buried in canopic lead cases until the Revolution, when Val-de-Grâce became the military hospital it is today. The lead cases were melted down into bullets destined for other royal tickers, while their contents were auctioned off to a pair of painters, St-Martin and Martin Droling, who ground up the hearts to make a much sought-after brownish glaze for oil paintings.

A door from the St-Louis chapel leads out to the cloister and gardens, where you can take a look at Anne of Austria's pretty pavilion, supported in part by rusticated columns, and the monumental façade of the old convent with its mansard roof. In the west wing a little **Musée des Armées du Service de Santé** has items on the history of military medicine. A new hospital stands at the end of the gardens, where French researchers are developing methods to zap brain tumours with lasers and 3-D cameras.

CIMETIÈRE DU MONTPARNASSE R18–T20

3 Bd Edgar Quinet, t 01 44 10 86 50;
métro Edgar Quinet or Raspail, RER Port-
Royal. Open mid-Mar–Oct Mon–Fri 8–6,
Sat 8.30–6, Sun 9–6; Nov–mid-Mar Mon–Fri
8–5.30, Sat 8.30–5.30, Sun 9–5.30; adm free.

The third-largest cemetery in Paris, Montparnasse saw its prestige grow along

Baudelaire and Hugo, Progress and Spleen

One can simultaneously possess a special genius and be a fool. Victor Hugo proves that to us well – the Ocean itself is tired of him.

Baudelaire

The Chinese curse 'May you live in interesting times' fell upon Paris' two great poets of the 19th century, Victor Hugo (1802–85) and Charles Baudelaire (1821–67). It was also the only thing the two had in common. Hugo consumed life whole: the noble and the grotesque, injustice and poverty, politics and religion, until he himself swelled up bigger than life. Where ennui, inertia and ill health (and a trial for offending the public morality) oppressed Baudelaire, Hugo possessed the literary and sexual energy of a volcano. No poet since has enjoyed such popular idolatry, and it's a sobering lesson for anyone disgusted with today's crass commercialism to learn that in the 19th century you could buy Hugo ink or 'Soap of the Muses' with Hugo's picture, or a gas lamp in the form of Hugo's head with the inscription: 'He beams his rays through all of nature and becomes a sun for the human race.'

Certainly as the man who saw Notre-Dame as a giant 'H' – a projection of his own name – he was the perfect poet laureate for a city whose deadly sin is vanity. After all, Hugo's Paris novels were powerful enough to influence real life: *Notre-Dame de Paris* (1831) led

directly to the restoration of the collapsing cathedral, while *Les Misérables* (1862) inspired many readers to fight for social justice in the ill-fated Commune (Hugo, rather than join them, slunk off to Belgium).

The poet–city relationship was symbiotic. Paris could always count on Hugo to trumpet *le mot juste* for each occasion, from the city's first Exposition in 1855 ('Progress is the Footstep of God!') to the introduction for an 1867 guidebook to Paris ('A coach passes flying a flag; it comes from Paris. The flag is no longer a flag, it is a flame, and the whole trail of human gunpower catches fire behind it'). During the Prussian siege, Hugo tried to shame Bismarck for his impudence in trying to capture the French capital: 'It is in Paris that the beating of Europe's heart is felt. Paris is the city of cities. Paris is the city of men. There has been an Athens, there has been a Rome, and there is a Paris...' When André Gide was asked to name France's greatest poet, he made his famous reply: 'Victor Hugo – alas!' Gide acknowledged Hugo as the supremely gifted craftsman, an incomparable virtuoso, but one whose unfailing lack of vision responded to the momentous changes of the 19th century by smothering them in words.

Like Hugo, Baudelaire wrote best when he wrote about Paris, but it might as well have been a city from another planet, the ever-tantalizing, ever-changing urban hell of the 19th century. Baudelaire was the first to

---

with fashion as the quarter's habitués decided to spend eternity on the Left Bank, enjoying a view of the Tour Montparnasse rising behind the tombs.

Even if cemeteries give you the heebie-jeebies, walk briefly down Rue Émile-Richard (the only municipal street in Paris with no living residents) and take the first path to the left to see the lighthearted Tomb of the Famille Charles Pigeon. M. Pigeon invented the non-exploding gas lamp, and is depicted here in the matrimonial bed next to his sleeping wife, reading by the light of his miraculous invention. Other famous folk

buried east of Rue Émile-Richard include André Citroën, Bartholdi (sculptor of the Statue of Liberty), César Franck, Guy de Maupassant and Alfred Dreyfus.

In the new, larger section to the west, there's a cenotaph to **Baudelaire**, with a bust of the poet overlooking a cocooned body near the corner of Rue Émile-Richard and Avenue Transversale (he is actually buried on the far side of the cemetery, under the name of Aupick, his mother's second husband; *see* 'Baudelaire and Hugo, Progress and Spleen'). Here too lie Sartre, Simone de Beauvoir, Brancusi, Rude, Houdon, Bourdelle,

understand the collapse of the age-old relationships between the individual and society (*see* 'The Vertigo of Modernism', pp.38–9); his *Tableaux Parisiens* in *Les Fleurs du Mal* and the prose poems in *Paris Spleen* have lost none of their evocative, disturbing power.

Baudelaire stands in an urban literary tradition that began with François Villon, Montesquieu and Diderot. It was updated during the Revolution by Louis-Sébastien Mercier, who wandered the streets of Paris by day, gathering material (*Tableau de Paris* and *Nouveau Paris*), and Restif de la Bretonne, who took the night shift (*Les Nuits de Paris*), two innovative figures who have never really had their due even in France. Both wrote their sharp, detailed observations in sets of fragmentary sketches, a new form for a new age.

As 19th-century Paris convulsed from one upheaval to the next, the search for meaning from the streets was continued by the elusive Gérard de Nerval; his *Les Nuits d'Octobre* was inspired by Restif, but Nerval enriched what he saw with images from the dream world, forays into the subconsciousness that presage the Surrealists' exploration of Paris' mysteries: Louis Aragon's masterpiece, *Le Paysan de Paris* (1926), André Breton's *Nadja* (1928), or Philippe Soupault's *Les Dernières Nuits de Paris* (1928), with its evocative epigram: 'To choose is to grow old.' And closer to our own time are Henry Miller's Paris books, and the Italian Giovanni Macchia's *Les Ruines de Paris* (1988), evoking the perpetual destruction, the slow, sweet apocalypse of this Sodom and Gomorrah on the Seine.

But it was Baudelaire the opium smoker, the *flâneur* outside the pale, a man clawed apart by the paradoxes within himself, who 'saw the elephant', as opium addicts say when the drug wears off and leaves a vision of naked reality. What makes Baudelaire compelling reading today is that his 'elephant' is still with us. While Hugo gushed over progress with a capital P, Baudelaire pondered in the very same year, 1855, 'whether [humanity's] indefinite progress might not be its most cruel and ingenious torture; whether...shut up in the fiery circle of divine logic, it would not be like the scorpion that stings itself with its own tail – progress, that eternal desideratum that is its own eternal despair!'

But poets, unlike progress, come to an end. When Hugo, 'the sun for the human race', had his supernova, he was given the biggest funeral in Paris' history. Black crêpe was hung over the Arc de Triomphe; two million people filed past his coffin; and the church of Sainte-Geneviève was converted once and for all into the Panthéon to become his last resting place. Baudelaire, in contrast, doesn't even get his own name over his modest grave in Montparnasse cemetery: you have to look under 'Aupick', the name of the stepfather he hated.

Saint-Saëns, Serge Gainsbourg (*see* pp.198–9), Jean Seberg, Soutine, Zadkine, and Vichy premier and German collaborator Pierre Laval, who committed suicide by swallowing arsenic the night before his execution was due, but was strapped to a chair and shot anyhow.

In the southwest corner of the cemetery stands the truncated 15th-century tower of Montparnasse's last windmill, which once stood in a farm where the young Voltaire was wont to roam. Just north of the windmill, in Allée des Sergents-de-la-Rochelle, take a look at the bittersweet statue exiled from the Luxembourg Gardens for offending public morality, called **La Séparation d'un Couple**, the woman sending a last kiss to her lover from beyond the grave.

Outside the Centre

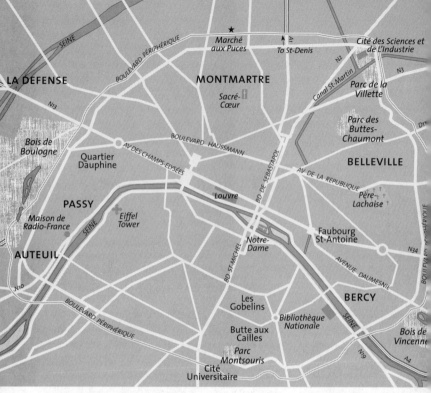

These are mostly what planners poetically call 'urban grey areas', where not even Haussmann's boulevards can dispel the prevailing anomie. It is *cinéma vérité* country, and if you spend enough time here you'll begin to understand the nihilism that pervades the life of Parisian intellectuals and informed the *Nouvelle-Vague* films of the 1960s. But you should have seen it back in the old days. Perhaps the reason why Parisians are traditionally so introspective is that, before the railways, any trip outside the holy city meant traversing a desert of refuse heaps and open graves, haunted by vicious robbers and hungry vermin.

The one landmark on the northern side was the Gibbet of Monfaucon, a scaffolding of 5ft-thick tree trunks, built in 1233 near what is now the St-Louis hospital. The kings or the city provosts could hang 60 men at a time on it when necessary. It was dismantled in 1790 as a humanitarian measure; the French had invented a much kinder way to do the job: the guillotine.

Now you're in the mood, let's begin on the Seine, at the west end of the Right Bank, and continue around Paris more or less clockwise, ending in the westernmost *arrondissement* of the Left Bank.

16e: PASSY AND AUTEUIL

The 16e gets a bad press, especially from Parisians: monied and neat, a *quartier* out of touch with the real life of the rest of Paris. The residents of 16e are presumed to be DCBG (*bon chic, bon genre* – 'good taste, good types'), obsessed with their magazine lives, with appearances and networks. Yet it also has some of the most elegant streetscapes in Paris, the best examples of a planned city based on a unified classical architecture. Avenue Foch in the spring is magnificent, and both Avenue Victor-Hugo and Avenue Kléber are masterpieces of concept and execution. The area is essentially residential and very comfortable too, but there are some worthwhile visits for the tourist: a few museums, most of them minor, and most of the life's work of Art Nouveau master Hector Guimard.

The terrain of the 16e used to be the farm-land of two villages: **Auteuil**, to the south, and **Passy**, the centre of which still bears traces of its village origins around Place de Passy and Rue de l'Annonciation.

Passy and its Museums

Musée Marmottan C12

2 Rue Louis-Boilly, at the edge of Jardin du Ranelagh, **t** *01 44 96 50 33,* **w** *www. marmottan.com;* **métro** *La Muette.* **Open** *Tues–Sun 10–5.30, closed 1 May and 25 Dec;* **adm** *€6.50. Ask about guided tours for children.*

Here you will find some of Monet's best works, collected by the the Marmottan family along with medieval miniatures, tapestries and Napoleonic art and furniture. The Monet works are the highlight, however: some of the *Nymphéas* (Water Lilies), a view of the Pont de l'Europe behind Gare St-Lazare, one of the *Cathédrales de Rouen* and a view of the British Houses of Parliament.

Musée du Vin H12–13

Rue des Eaux, 5 Sq Charles-Dickens, **t** *01 45 25 63 26,* **w** *www.museeduvinparis.com;* **métro** *Passy.* **Open** *Tues–Sun 10–6, closed 25 Dec– 1 Jan;* **adm** *€6.50.* **Restaurant** *open for lunch.*

This has didactic exhibits and wax dummies set in old quarries that were converted into wine cellars by monks in the 15th century. Ticket price includes a *dégusta-tion* at the end.

Maison de Balzac G13

47 Rue Raynouard, **t** *01 55 74 41 80;* **métro** *Passy or La Muette.* **Open** *Tues–Sun 10–6, last adm 5.30, closed hols;* **adm** *free (€3.30 for temporary exhibitions).*

The great novelist had a dozen Paris addresses in his lifetime, but he spent seven years here, working like a slave to pay off his creditors. **Rue Berton**, behind the house, is one of the few streets unchanged from the times when Passy was a rustic village.

Maison de Radio-France F14

116 Av du Président-Kennedy, **t** *01 56 40 15 16 for details of concerts,* **t** *01 56 40 21 80 to book a tour;* **métro** *Ranelagh.* **Open** *for tours only, daily at 3pm (in English; minimum 2 people); no need to book;* **adm** *€4.*

Every Parisian knows the 16e's most imposing landmark, a round aluminium-and-glass complex prominently positioned on the banks of the Seine. Begun in 1953, it is the perfect symbol of postwar Paris: a weird, inhuman tribute to unchained technology, housing a weary, state-controlled media bureaucracy. Some of its own employees call the place 'Alphaville' after the spooky 1960s science-fiction film by Godard. The architect, Henry Bernard, had been a winner of the academics' Holy Grail, the *Prix de Rome*.

The **Musée de Radio-France** has exhibits on the beginnings of French TV, going back to the first broadcast in 1931 (America didn't manage one until 1939). Before privatization, this building was also the home of ORTF, the television monopoly that acted as a shame-less propaganda organ for the government in the De Gaulle years.

From here, you can see the Seine divided by the thin **Île des Cygnes**, which according to legend is made of the bones of horses, and once was a favoured spot for duels. The familiar lady at the southwestern end is Paris' largest model of the *Statue of Liberty*, a gift in 1885 from the American colony of Paris.

Auteuil, Architecture and Art Nouveau B18–E14

Métro Jasmin or Michel Ange-Auteuil.

Running south beyond the Maison de Radio-France is **Rue La-Fontaine**, a poor area that in the 1880s was not even paved. Little did it know it was destined to become the showcase of France's greatest Art Nouveau architect. The first building, at No.14, is Guimard's most famous work, the **Castel Béranger** (1894), built as a simple middle-income apartment block of the 1890s; the

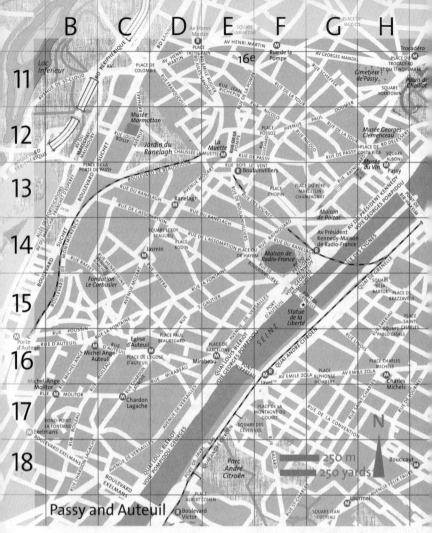

details, including the wrought-iron decorative work and the doors and windows, are wonderful, and as these are private apartments, they are all you'll get to see.

Further along the street are more fine Guimards: at Nos.17 (the **Bar Guimard**), 19, 21 and 60, as well as around the corner on **Rue François-Millet** at No.11.

No.65 Rue La Fontaine, the Studio Building, is by the interesting, early 20th-century architect Henri Sauvage of Bathroom Building fame (see p.246).

There's more Guimard in the surrounding streets: further south at No.34 **Rue Boileau**, and on **Avenue Mozart**, at No.120 (his own house, built in 1909) and No.122. For Guimard's later works, already

experimenting with Art Deco, seek out No.10 **Rue Jasmin**, and No.18 **Rue Henri-Heine** (1922), where the architect lived before moving to New York in 1938.

For a building that at least equals the Castel Béranger, walk a few blocks south to the extraordinary block of flats at 142 **Avenue de Versailles**; don't miss the stairway.

A few streets away, you can familiarize yourself with the next generation of architects (see below).

Fondation Le Corbusier C14

*8–10 Square du Docteur Blanche, **t** 01 42 88 41 53; **métro** Jasmin. **Open** Tues–Fri 10–12.30 and 1.30–6 (Fri until 5 only), Mon 1.30–6, closed hols, Aug and 24 Dec–2 Jan; **adm** €2.40.*

The Fondation manages the Villa Jeannevet (which houses the library) and the Villa La Roche, a Cubist building in white concrete, steel and glass, built in 1923. There are exhibitions about Le Corbusier and his contemporaries in this, his best Parisian work.

Jardin des Serres d'Auteuil Off maps

3 Av de la Porte d'Auteuil (off map), t 01 40 71 74 00; métro Porte d'Auteuil. Open summer daily 10–6, winter daily 10–5; adm €0.70. Occasional tours in French and English.

These are the greenhouses where plants and flowers are grown especially for Paris' green spaces. Seasonal displays can be spectacular. The **Jardin des Poètes** next door is a less formal garden dedicated to famous French poets. Rodin's statue of Victor Hugo is the garden's centrepiece.

Jardins Albert Kahn Off maps

14 Rue du Port, Boulogne, t 01 46 04 52 80; métro Boulogne-Pont de St-Cloud. Open May–Sept Tues–Sun 11–7, Oct–April Tues–Sun 11–6; adm €3.50. Café.

A beautiful water garden influenced in particular by gardens in Japan and England, and worth visiting year round. The museum shows temporary exhibitions from the collection of banker Albert Kahn, reflecting life at the beginning of the 20th century.

BOIS DE BOULOGNE Off maps

Métro Les Sablons (north, on Av Charles de Gaulle), Porte Maillot (northeast, on Av de la Grande Armée), Porte Dauphine (northeast, on Av Foch), or Porte d'Auteuil (southeast, on Av de la Porte d'Auteuil); RER Av Foch (north-east on Av Foch) or Av H. Martin (east on Av Henri Martin); bus nos.43 (to Neuilly), 73 (Porte Maillot), 63 (Porte de la Muette), 32 (Porte d'Auteuil) or 52 (Porte d'Auteuil).

After the Eiffel Tower, the Bois de Boulogne was, not so long ago, the most-visited place in Paris: 'the world capital of prostitution' no less, where every day over a million francs changed hands. Now all the access roads are blocked off at night, but driving through it in the evening can still be an eye-opener: scantily clad ladies ply their trade along the roads.

It was a venerable tradition. François I built the Château de Boulogne here, where he installed his mistress, La Ferronnière, about whom it is said that he died of loving her too fervently. Other kings installed their own loves: Diane de Poitiers and Gabrielle d'Estrées both lived here. Even after the Revolution, when the château was razed, the park kept its reputation for love. In the 17th century its bowers were full of impetuous couples; as one Parisian wrote at the time: 'There are two types of public gardens in Paris. In the first, one goes to see and be seen, and in the second, one goes not to see nor be seen by anyone.'

The Bois owes its current appearance to Napoleon III, who spent his early years in London and gave the Bois to the city as its own Hyde Park, crisscrossed by roads, riding and walking paths. The most scenic spots include the **Lac Inférieur** (*RER Av Henri-Martin or métro Ranelagh*), with its islets and emperor's kiosk; the **Shakespeare garden**, by the open-air theatre in the Pré Catelan; the **Grande Cascade**, an artificial Swiss Alps waterfall, just east of Longchamp; and for garden and rose lovers, the sumptuous **Parc de Bagatelle** (*15mins walk from métro Pont de Neuilly or take bus no.244 from métro Porte Maillot or RER Rueil-Malmaison; open spring and summer daily 9am–8pm, autumn daily 9–6, winter daily 9–4; adm €3*). The best (and cheapest) way to enjoy lunch in the Bois is to take a picnic, although the park does have restaurants and cafés (*see p.338*).

Jardin d'Acclimatation Off maps

In the north of the park, near the Porte des Sablons, t 01 40 67 90 82, w www.jardin dacclimatation.fr; métro Les Sablons; Le Petit Train links it with Port Maillot Wed, Sat and

*Sun (daily school hols) 11–6, every 15 mins, free. **Open** July and Aug daily 10–7, rest of the year daily 10–6; special activities at weekends and during school holidays; **adm** €2.50.*

This has nearly every possible activity for kids: camel and canal-boat rides, a small zoo, playgrounds, a doll's house with antique toys, a *guignol* (puppet show), children's theatre, bumper cars, crafts and games.

Musée National des Arts et Traditions Off maps

*6 Av du Mahatma-Gandhi, **t** 01 44 17 60 00; **métro** Les Sablons. **Open** Wed–Mon 9.30–5.15; **adm** €4, free on 1st Sun of the month.*

Near the Jardin d'Acclimatation, this museum is a good bet for older kids (and especially for adults). The functionalist building (1969) houses beautiful displays of pre-industrial art and cultural artefacts from France's provinces, arranged according to the dictum of Claude Lévi-Strauss: 'All human civilization, no matter how humble, presents two major aspects: on one hand, it is in the universe, on the other, it is a universe itself.'

Quartier Dauphine

At the east end of the Bois de Boulogne is the Quartier Dauphine, where the Porte Dauphine métro is the most beautiful of the original Art Nouveau stations built by Guimard. The district also has three small museums that may pique your curiosity.

Musée d'Ennery and Musée Arménien Off maps

*59 Av Foch; **metro** Porte Dauphine. Both closed at the time of writing; call Musée Guimet, **t** 01 56 52 53 00, for info.*

Houses Far Eastern art, puppets, masks and especially netsukes (fantastically carved Japanese buttons).

Musée de la Contrefaçon Off maps

*16 Rue de la Faisanderie, **t** 01 56 26 14 00; **métro** Porte Dauphine. **Open** Tues–Sun 2–5.30, closed hols and weekends in Aug; **adm** €0.50.*

Run by Paris' Manufacturers' Union, this museum displays the very thing it hates most: counterfeits. Cartier watches, rum labels, Lacoste shirts; some are pretty good and some ludicrous, but as long as the name is spelled differently (Channel No. 5, Contreau Triple-Sec) they're legal.

Avenue Victor-Hugo and Musée Dapper I8–J7

*Museum: 35 bis Rue Paul-Valéry, **t** 01 45 00 01 50; **métro** Victor-Hugo. **Open** during exhibitions Wed–Sun 11–7; **adm** €5, free on last Wed of the month.*

Walk up the Avenue to **No.50** for the 1902 masterpiece of Art Nouveau architect Charles Plumet (1861–1928), more popular than Guimard for his references to French classical styles. At the end of its courtyard is the entrance to the **Musée Dapper**, which puts on first-rate exhibitions of pre-colonial African art. Nearby, in Place Victor-Hugo, you can see a good Tintoretto (*Adoration of the Shepherds*) in the church **St-Honoré-d'Eylau**.

LA DÉFENSE Off maps

***Métro** Grande-Arche-de-La-Défense, **RER** La Défense.*

Fifty years ago this end of the Grand Axe was a dismal suburban industrial area, its only feature a *rond-point*, laid out by Madame de Pompadour's brother back in 1765 when the area was still a noble park and hunting preserve. (The idea of *rond-points* started with such parks; a hunter could stand in the middle and see deer crossing the paths in any direction.) After the siege of 1870, a statue commemorating the defence of Paris was set up here: 'La Défense' gradually gave its name to the whole area. In 1955 the national government (not the Ville de Paris) decided to make a modern, American-style business district out of the vacant land as part of the drive to make France a great economic power and Paris an influential world business centre. A state development corporation called EPAD was set up to do the job.

As the biggest construction project in France since the Maginot Line started digging, they weren't fooling three years later. The site was expanded to three square miles and over 25,000 people had to be relocated, together with some 700 factories and businesses. By 1960, glass towers were sprouting like toadstools, a surreal scene for older Parisians. French film directors were not slow to seize on La Défense's cinematic potential. Jacques Tati's poor bewildered Monsieur Hulot was baffled by glass doors and accosted by Germans demonstrating appliances in the sweet 1960s film *Playtime*. In *The Little Theatre of Jean Renoir*, one of that director's last films, there is a vignette of a modern woman who falls hopelessly in love with her electric floor polisher; the tidy corporate people of La Défense provide a Greek chorus, singing her tragic fate as they march up and down the métro entrances.

With bad times in the 1970s, building slowed and EPAD almost went bust; Prime Minister Raymond Barre intervened in 1978 with another infusion of money. The government induced 14 of the top 20 French corporations to move in, with a little bribery and a good deal of discreet arm-twisting, and La Défense really took off. Today, about 150,000 people work here ('two-thirds of them executives or managerial class', EPAD's literature brags), and there are also 55,000 residents.

In the pharaonic atmosphere of the Mitterrand decade, EPAD went entirely out of control, planning a series of monster buildings during the boom years before 1990; of these only the Grande Arche ever saw the light of day. More office towers have appeared recently, notably PB6, a stylish glass curve designed by Peï and partners, originators of the Pyramid at the other end of the Grand Axe. It's an improvement on the earlier architecture, the corporate-American buildings of the 1960s and 70s that exploited the austerity of the International Style to mask a total lack of inspiration and skill. Later works, like the huge Elf Tower, tended to be lukewarm rehashes of reflecting-glass postmodernism from across the Atlantic. The worst atrocities include the grim Japan Tower on the western fringes, and especially the **Quartier du Parc**, La Défense's main residential area. You can catch a glimpse of this from the Grande Arche (to the south), a nest of amoeba-shaped towers with round windows, painted in camouflage patterns of brown, white and blue.

Much like the Pompidou Centre, La Défense exposes for all to see the best and the worst of French ideas about planning and architecture. On the good side is the audacity and can-do spirit of the enterprise. It got built, it worked, and if the public expenditure was large, it wasn't all wasted or gobbled up in corruption (until Mitterrand, anyhow). The extension of the Grand Axe was a brilliant *tour de force* of cultural continuity, connecting the Paris of the centuries to the Paris of the future. And the segregation of modern business in a new quarter undoubtedly saved central Paris from some horrors of speculative building. On the other hand, basic planning and design are primitive. Cars and people may be laudably kept separate, but the formless labyrinth of pedestrian spaces is chilly and anomic, inevitably lined with blank walls; almost everything is inside or underground – you'll notice people scurrying nervously between the buildings like bugs, afraid of getting squashed.

Climb the stairs from the bus stop, and find your way through the maze to the **Parvis**, also called the Podium or the Dalle, the long pedestrian mall aligned with the Grand Axe. Wander at your leisure among these sorry monoliths, dubbed with corporate acronyms such as GAN, COFACE, PFA CNIT and SCREG, interspersed with a wealth of abstract sculptures and mosaics. At the eastern end, with a broad view over Paris, is the **Takis Fountain**, illuminated in the evenings with coloured lights. In the centre, near the Agam Fountain, is the original sculpture of the 1870 'Défense'. At the western end stands one of the project's first buildings, a huge American-style shopping mall called **Les Quatre Temps**; outside it the 50ft red '*stabile*' was the last work of Alexander Calder. The colourful giants scattered about this part of the Parvis are from works by Joan Miró.

The Grande Arche

Parvis de la Défense, **t** *01 49 07 27 57,* **w** *www. grandearche.com.* **Open** *summer daily 10–8, winter daily 10–7;* **adm** *€7.50.* **Restaurant** *on 35th floor,* **t** *01 49 07 27 32; open daily for lunch, in summer also Sat for dinner.*

Since its opening in 1989, François Mitterrand's personal monument has been the undisputed star of the show. The first two proposals for filling this space were backed by Presidents Pompidou and Giscard d'Estaing – Giscard threw out Pompidou's, and Mitterrand cancelled Giscard's, both for 'reasons of economy'. But money proved to be no object when Mitterrand started to take a personal interest in it. Here was a chance to plant a monument on the most conspicuous spot available in Paris, and the president wasn't about to leave this plum to his successor. One big problem was finding a purpose for whatever would eventually be built; the original proposal was for an 'International Communications Centre', but no one could explain just what this might comprise. Another plan was to make it the seat of the 'Foundation for the Rights of Man'. No such foundation existed, unfortunately – but now that they've got a building, one has been created.

By 1983 the government stopped worrying about such trivial matters and decided to build. A competition was proclaimed; the winner, selected by Mitterrand himself, was an obscure architect named Otto von Spreckelsen, whose previous projects numbered only a few churches in his native Denmark. In the late 1980s work went on at a furious pace, in an attempt to get the monster ready for the Revolutionary Bicentennial; on one memorable day the girders went up for eight entire storeys. The Arche opened in grand style on 14 July 1989,

with the president hosting a meeting of the (then) G-7 heads of state at the top. Filling it up still proved a problem. The government was able to sell most of the space at bargain-basement prices, but interestingly enough the deal included having them rent half of it back; the left side of the Arche now houses the entire Ministry of Transport and Public Works.

Criticism of the Arche has come from all angles. David Gentleman called it a 'television with a blank screen'. Architects have also noted that about half the space inside is wasted, unusable for offices. Right-wing papers decry the 'democratic Caesarism' of Mitterrand's plans, and above all the mismanagement that resulted in a 1.3 billion franc project ending up running over budget by more than 100 per cent; luxuries such as 350 sq ft of Carrara marble don't come cheap.

Some facts and figures would be appropriate: the Arche's official name, which never caught on, is the *Arche de la Fraternité*; it weighs some 300,000 tons, and its publicists never fail to remind us that Notre-Dame, or the broad Champs-Elysées could fit easily through the hole in the middle (we think both are untrue, but no two sets of published dimensions for the thing are the same; intentional obfuscation is suspected). You'll notice it isn't exactly aligned to the Grand Axe; subsurface conditions made this impossible, but Von Spreckelsen managed to tilt it at an angle of 6°33', exactly the same as the deviation of the Louvre courtyard. There are other subtleties for archaeologists to puzzle over in some distant future age: the Arc du Carrousel measures 25m (82ft), the Arc de Triomphe 50m (164ft), and Von Spreckelsen continued the ratio, making his exactly 100m (328ft), though this statistic too may not be accurate; nobody knows.

Visiting it is surreal; speakers hidden in the trees regale you with Serge Gainsbourg tunes as you make your way to the top for the panoramic view of the city. You can either climb or take a ride through the air in the lift, which runs up a glass tube through the hole.

Musée de l'Automobile

1 Place du Dôme, Colline de La Défense,
t *01 46 92 45 50;* **métro** *Grande-Arche-de-La-Défense; wheelchair access.* **Open** *daily 12–7, Sat until 9pm.*

A historic collection of cars, mostly French, and auto memorabilia.

MARCHÉ AUX PUCES DE ST-OUEN Off maps

Métro *Porte de Clignancourt (not métro Porte de St-Ouen); walk down Av de la Porte de Clignancourt and under the Périphérique motorway.* **Open** *Sat, Sun and Mon 7am–6pm.*

We include **Les Puces** here, instead of in the shopping section of this book, because while you may not have room in your grip for a Louis Quinze chair, a visit can still be one of the most entertaining things to do in Paris. Paris has in fact three permanent flea markets, but the biggest and most famous is just outside the city at St-Ouen. The other two are the trendy **Puces de Vanves** (*métro Porte de Vanves; open Sat and Sun*) and the shabbier **Puces de Montreuil** (*métro Porte de Montreuil; open Sat, Sun and Mon*).

All around Paris, the cleared space outside Adolphe Thiers' city wall of 1841 became the Zone, a weird desolation inhabited by the most unfortunate of Paris' poor. Many of them went into the junk and old-clothes trades, and by the 1880s it became a custom to visit the Zone to buy such things. Around 1920, when the walls were demolished, the dealers coalesced into regular markets, just in time to be discovered by André Breton, looking for bizarre and incongruous items of refuse with which to haunt the dreams of respectable folk.

Les Puces (literally, 'the fleas') has been upscaling ever since. Today it harbours every sort of flea, from posh antiques merchants to desperate rag-pickers. Had it been a few hundred yards south, in Paris proper, it would have been gentrified or destroyed by the government long ago. As it is, in the tatty suburb of St-Ouen, it has troubles enough, between an unsympathetic Communist government and the Paris developers who have bought up some of the buildings.

Les Puces starts south of the Périphérique with a vast expanse of cheap clothes stands, typical of those you'll see in any French market. Beyond the motorway, if you continue straight down Avenue Michelet you'll find the entrance to the first and perhaps poshest of the covered markets, the **Marché Biron**: lots of fancy gilt atrocities from the Second Empire, and choice Art Nouveau and Deco pieces. There's less ambitious stuff in the back alley: a good shop for posters and reproductions at No.140, beautiful nautical and scientific instruments at Nos.173 and 181. Beyond the Biron on Avenue Michelet is the domain of the leather stands, along with stands that sell hardware and ten-a-penny nails.

The far end of the Biron opens onto **Rue des Rosiers**, the main drag of Les Puces, where the entrances to most of the other covered markets are. There are more antiques in the **Marché Dauphine**, a modern metal barn with palm trees and a fountain in the centre, and a delightful mural of market life at the entrance. The **Marché Paul-Bert**, currently fashionable, was begun in 1945, its spaces reserved for dealers who had their businesses confiscated during the German Occupation. The **Marché Serpette** is newer, with mostly 20th-century serious antiques and kitsch items, while the **Marché Vernaison** is the biggest and the most like London's Camden Lock; the trendiest and most popular of all is the **Marché Malik**, with clothes and bric-a-brac from the 1960s and Americana.

For an ambience no place in France can match, visit the Funky Broadway of the Puces, **Rue Jean-Henri-Fabre**, parallel to the Périphérique. Everyone has music playing, with Peruvian pipe bands and Barry White as favourites. The metal buildings and concrete pylons are decorated with posters for Kurdish

Communist groups and the latest offerings of the local cinema, films such as the *Two Twat Tango*. The pavements are lined with stands selling old postcards, Rastafarian paraphernalia, wigs and books (lots of used Tintins with crayon marks); behind are sheds where you can buy ladders by the dozen or bulk lots of toilet paper. Between the stands, three-card monte (*bonneteau* in Parisian slang) artists prey on chumps. Saddest are the areas at the end under the overpasses of the Périphérique. Buyers and sellers alike are dressed in grey; goods displayed on cloths include tampons, dead televisions and grimy rubber ducks.

ST-DENIS AND THE ORIGINAL GOTHIC CHURCH Off maps

Métro St-Denis-Université. The métro is the only way to get to this close-in northern suburb; it's the last stop on the no.13 line (direction St-Denis-Université).

Climbing out of the métro stop – especially on market days – it will seem as if you have been magically transported to a lively village. Paris is a world away, and you are surrounded by crowds of Frenchmen doing what Frenchmen were born to do: haggle good-naturedly over oysters, geese and asparagus.

St-Denis, with its great abbey that was the necropolis of the kings of France, is today one of the classic *banlieues défavorisées*. Communist-run, gritty and poor, it saw its transformation from rural idyll to industrial inferno in the 19th century, when some 60 factories making everything from cars to pianos moved in. Today the old village is only the centre of a suburban agglomeration of over 100,000 people. It's well run, and still has a noticeable sense of civic pride, as you'll learn talking with the folks at the local **tourist office** (*1 Rue de la République, t 01 55 870 870*), across the street from the abbey. One of these charming ladies is probably

responsible for St-Denis' new slogan: 'The city of dead kings and a living people'.

The Abbey Basilica

1 Rue de la Légion d'Honneur, t 01 48 09 83 54; métro Basilique de St-Denis, RER St-Denis. Open April–Sept Mon–Sat 10–6.30, Sun 12–6.30; Oct–Mar Mon–Sat 10–5.15, Sun 12–5.15; adm €6.10; guided tours 11.15 and 3.

St Denis, who shambled up here, head tucked under his arm from Montmartre (*see* p.194) to begin his career as patron of France, is a truly shadowy character. Like so many other French saints, such as St Pol (Apollo) or St Saturnin (Saturn), he may be a half-conscious fabrication, papering over survivals of paganism that early missionaries had assimilated into the new faith. And what would be more natural than retaining Denis (Dionysus) as guardian deity of the wine-quaffing Gauls?

In any case, this has been the site of a cemetery from Roman times, and an abbey from perhaps the 5th century, favoured by Dagobert and other Merovingian kings, who began the tradition of making it the site for royal burials. St-Denis' present glory is entirely due to its rebuilding under the remarkable Abbot Suger (1081–1151). Diplomat, counsellor to Louis VI and Louis VII, and ruler of France while the latter was away on the Crusades, Suger also found time, according to his own accounts, to invent Gothic architecture single-handedly. Perhaps his architects had something to do with it too, but the good abbot, constantly cajoling and suggesting over the sculptor's shoulder and even helping hoist the stones, must get a fair share of the credit; his ideas may well have been decisive in the use of Gothic pointed-arch vaulting and rose windows.

To promote his beloved abbey, Suger wrote influential works on history and government, practically creating by himself the mythology of the sacred kings of France, while empha-sizing the importance of the abbey and the role of St-Denis as protector of all the kings since Clovis. After his death, St-Denis seems to have become a regular forgery factory, as monks cranked out false chronicles, charters and bequests dating from as early as Charlemagne's time to prove certain rights of the abbey and its royal patrons. Wealth, influence and royal cadavers accumulated over the centuries, and not surprisingly St-Denis and its 'frightful reminders of our former tyrants' became one of the chief targets of the revolutionaries of 1793. Twelve hundred years' worth of anointed bones were tossed into a pit; the revolutionaries trashed the tombs and carted off France's richest church treasure (much of which finally found its way to the Cabinet des Médailles in the Bibliothèque Nationale; see pp.156–7). Under the restoration, Louis XVIII started fixing the place up, and Viollet-le-Duc came to finish the job in 1859.

The basilica's **façade** is one of the triumphs of Suger and his architects, a marvel of clarity and order that pointed the way to all the Gothic cathedrals that followed; the sculptural trim on the upper levels and the three carved portals became a Gothic commonplace (thanks to the revolutionaries almost all the reliefs and statues are copies). **Inside**, notice that the nave and transepts are in a different style, a confident mature Gothic; they weren't completed until the mid-13th century under the masterful eye of Pierre de Montreuil. The unassuming choir is the real Gothic revolution, with its ribbed vaulting. The lovely rose window, with seasons and signs of the zodiac, is one of the few remaining bits of medieval glass, as are the Tree of Jesse and Life of the Virgin in the apse behind the main altar.

From the right aisle, you begin the tour of the **royal tombs**. These too have been heavily restored after the desecrations of 1793 and few are of interest, even though they go as far back as Dagobert, who died in 639 (for all the early kings, gisants – horizontal effigies atop the sarcophagi – were remade during the Middle Ages). Some that stand out: near the entrance to the tombs, François I, praying with his wife Claude de France, on an elaborate Renaissance tomb, designed by Philibert

de l'Orme; beyond these, Charles V, with his faithful Constable of France Bertrand du Guesclin, who helped keep the English out in the Hundred Years' War; on the left side of the choir, Louis XII and Anne de Bretagne, another Renaissance spectacular, largely the work of Germain Pilon. In the right ambulatory hangs the *oriflamme*, the flame-covered battle standard of the French kings, a 15th-century copy of the medieval original, lost in the Hundred Years' War.

Musée de l'Art et de l'Histoire de la Ville de St-Denis

*22 bis Rue Gabriel-Péri, t 01 42 43 05 10. **Open** Wed–Fri and Mon 10–5.30, Sat–Sun 2–6.30, open until 8 on Thurs, closed hols; **adm** €4.*

St-Denis has a delightful museum, housed in an old Carmelite convent. From nun memorabilia and an exhibit on medieval daily life, the scene changes to modern industrial St-Denis: paintings by local artists of the canals and gas works, old shop fronts and the *roulottes* (caravans) many workers lived in. The biggest exhibit is devoted to the 1871 Commune: a floor of paintings, posters, cartoons and newspapers relate the story more thoroughly than you'll ever see it in Paris.

IN AND AROUND PARC DE LA VILLETTE Off maps

30 Av Corentin-Cariou, t 01 40 03 75 75, w www.la-villette.com; métro Porte de la Villette, Porte de Pantin or Corentin-Cariou. For a different way to start a day's excursion, take a boat up Canal St-Martin to La Villette (see p.68).

From 1867 on, this corner of northeastern Paris was the city's stockyards, a vast complex of market halls, slaughterhouses and marshalling yards, a place where tired Parisian males would go to get a hot glass of bull's blood to pep them up (or, like Marcel Proust, they'd go just to ogle the butcher boys). In the 1960s the government began a new complex – a juicy political pork-barrel scandal, built when old-fashioned stockyards were disappearing thanks to refrigerated transport. The huge building – the biggest slaughterhouse in the world – stood abandoned until Giscard d'Estaing picked it up for one of his *grands projets* in 1974.

All around Science City stretches the Parc de la Villette, the 'Park of the 21st Century', designed by American Bernard Tschumi. The grass has taken hold, and the little trees are growing gamely, but the place still has something of a stockyard's air to it. The **Canal de l'Ourcq** runs right through the middle, and scattered around are a dozen bright red follies. These interesting constructions, each a variation on a single hi-tech architectural theme inspired by Le Corbusier, house various activities: video and plastic arts workshops for kids (*come Sat or Sun at 2.30*), an **information centre**, a café, and a chain hamburger stand. One is the entrance to the **Argonaute**, a 1957 submarine open for your exploration (*open Tues–Sun 10–6.30; adm included in adm to Cité des Sciences, or €4 on its own*). Also for the children, there are three delightfully innovative **playgrounds**, the Jardin des Vents for toddlers, the Jardin des Voltiges and the Jardin du Dragon.

The park is full of surprises; there's a witty Claes Oldenburg 'monumental sculpture', the **Buried Bicycle**, a **Garden of Mirrors**, a **Bamboo Garden** with a strange sort of stone cylinder in the middle 'for meditation' and **Le Cinaxe**, a vibrating film theatre set on hydraulic jacks that simulates space flight.

Cité des Sciences et de l'Industrie

t 01 40 05 80 00, **w** www.cite-sciences.fr; wheelchair access. **Open** Tues–Sat 10–6, Sun 10–7; **adm** €7.50 (includes Explora, Cinéma

Louis-Lumière); Planétarium **adm** *€2.50, Argonaute* **adm** *€3; joint tickets with other attractions also available.*

The metamorphosis of the slaughterhouse into a rectangle of glass and exposed girders reminiscent of the Pompidou Centre has led Mitterrand's critics to have their fun with this project too. As a science museum, it duplicates the fine **Palais de la Découverte** (*see* p.115), off the Champs-Elysées, only it's a little flashier and more up to date.

A little flashier? It has its own internal television station, its staff of smartly costumed *animateurs* speaking 15 different languages, its computerized magneto-sensitized tickets, its 'infra-red headphones', giving a running commentary of what you're seeing, and its lasers, buzzing gimcracks and whirling gizmos. Bring the children to help you get through alive.

The main part is called **Explora**, comprising three floors of hyperactive exhibits, video shows and gadgets, including some 60,000 video screens.

Level 1

Space, with a model of the *Ariane* rocket with a simulated space voyage; a working model of the new French bathyscape, the *Nautilus*; ecological exhibits where you can manipulate the environment and foul it up all by yourself; a hi-tech greenhouse; a pseudo-nuclear reactor; experiments with sound, sight and photography you can do: the most fun part of the museum.

Level 2

Here you are constantly pestered by talking robots. There are some captivating astronomical exhibits; a biology section where you can test your own body; a transportation section that includes a simulated ride on the Airbus 310. There are **Planétarium** shows (with English translations) and **3-D films** in the Louis Lumière cinema.

Ground Floor

This is home to the **Cité des Enfants** (*t* 09 82 69 70 72 to reserve; activities (1½hrs) Tues, Thurs and Fri at 9.45, 11.30, 1.30, 3.30; Wed, Sat and Sun at 10.30, 12.30, 2.30, 4.30; adm €5;

children must be accompanied by an adult), a brilliant place for children to experiment with plants, animals and computers, with expert attendants to help. There are two sections: one for ages 3–5, one for 5–12. **Techno Cité** (*open only during the school year on Wed and Sat*) is designed for children from age 11 up.

Géode

24 Av Corentin-Carion, **t** *01 40 05 79 99,* **w** *www.lageode.fr; book in advance or try to get a ticket as soon as you arrive at the park;* **adm** *€8.75.*

The giant steel marble sitting in a pond next to the Cité is the **Géode**, housing yet another theatre: a 180°, 4,000 sq-ft screen showing overwhelming 70mm science films.

Cité de la Musique

221 Av Jean-Jaurès, **t** *01 44 84 44 84;* **métro** *Porte de Pantin; wheelchair access.* **Open** *Tues–Sat 12–6, Sun 10–6;* **adm** *€6.10.*

Across the Canal de l'Ourcq from the Cité and the Géode, the southern half of the park is occupied by the two new white asymmetrical buildings of the Music City, designed by French architect Christian de Portzamparc: concert halls (one with hyper-acoustics designed by Pierre Boulez), the **Conservatoire** of dance and music, and a **Musée de la Musique** with 4,500 instruments, including Stradivarius and Guarnieri violins, and Beethoven's clavichord, all cosily gathered together in one place.

The **Zénith** concert hall is a popular rock and schlock venue. In a rare fit of softheartedness, the government passed up a chance to demolish another fine old building. Instead they turned the market house of the old stockyards, the **Grande Halle**, into a place for jazz concerts (Salle Boris-Vian). The magnificent 780ft glass and iron hall, built in 1867 by Jules de Merindol, is perhaps the least known of 19th-century Paris' architectural wonders. It's a no-nonsense, utilitarian building, yet one

inspired by the Crystal Palace and at the ends strangely reminiscent of Pisa cathedral.

Rotonde de la Villette

From the Parc, the **Bassin de la Villette** stretches southwest towards Place Stalingrad, connecting the Canal de l'Ourcq and the Canal St-Martin. This wide spot in the canal system was intended as a place of recreation when it was built under Napoleon, the 'Champs-Elysées of the East'; it isn't much to look at now.

At the Stalingrad end stands the largest of Claude-Nicolas Ledoux's surviving *barrières* from the Farmers-General wall. The sandstone **Rotonde** (1784) looks too grand to have been a customs house; it has been beautifully restored, but the city hasn't found a better use for it yet than to house a library.

Canal St-Martin

Once home to Paris' less than affluent, the long banks of the old canal between Rue du Faubourg-du-Temple and Rue Louis-Blanc (*métro République or Goncourt or Louis Blanc*) are fast coming to life as hip Paris' new zone. The **Quai de Valmy** and **Quai de Jemmapes** are being developed into modern apartment blocks, clearly competing for the oddest balcony prize; fathers and sons on in-line skates race between the raised gardens, and fishermen dangle their feet along the cobbled banks beneath the green iron bridges. At 95 Quai de Valmy, the pink, green and yellow façades of the assorted Antoine et Lili shops and wholefood café make a colourful splash between the green trees. At 102 Quai de Jemmapes is the site of the **Hôtel du Nord**, made famous by Marcel Carné's 1938 film with Arletty and Louis Jouvet; it now serves traditional French cuisine in a setting full of *atmosphère*. 167 Quai de Valmy hops after 10pm to the strains of live jazz.

Despite its ambitions it's not quite Amsterdam, and there are still long stretches of building sites in between the clusters of trendy bars, but it's a relaxing place for a summer evening stroll.

BELLEVILLE AND PARC DES BUTTES-CHAUMONT

Belleville Off maps

Once upon a time this was a pretty village where people went to get away from Paris. Belleville in particular was one of the major pleasure grounds of the city in the 18th and early 19th centuries, its main street, Rue de Belleville (then Rue de Paris!), lined with cabarets and *guinguettes*, unpretentious café-gardens for dancing; half of Paris would come up on any warm Sunday afternoon.

In the 1850s Belleville started to fill up with working people as Paris expanded outwards. Haussmann annexed the district in 1860, and used it as a sort of overflow tank for the tens of thousands his new projects were dispossessing. Seemingly overnight, the area changed from a garden suburb to the worst slum Paris had ever seen: little water, no sanitation and no building controls. The *guinguettes* became dangerous dives, ruled by young thugs who had read Wild West stories and called themselves *apaches*. Belleville became the heart and soul of the Paris Commune, and the Communards' last stands were around the *mairie* and Père-Lachaise cemetery.

The 20th century brought waves of immigration. Not so long ago a rather charming quarter of old houses and neighbourhood character, Belleville has now been swamped by vast tracts of redevelopment hideous even by Parisian standards.

Parc des Buttes-Chaumont Off maps

Rue Manin (main entrance on Place Armand Carrel), **t** *01 53 35 89 35;* **métro** *Buttes-*

Chaumont or Botzaris. **Open** *May–Sept daily 6.45am–11pm, Oct–April daily 6.45am–9pm.*

Belleville still has Paris' loveliest park, another Haussmann creation. A rocky haunt of outlaws in the Middle Ages, well known to François Villon (*see* p.227), the park was begun in 1867. In an age when the 'picturesque' was fully in vogue, the natural charms of the Buttes weren't quite good enough. Haussmann's designers brought in thousands of tons of rock and created the artificial cliffs that are its fame today. The centrepiece is a familiar landmark, a steep island in a lake, crowned by a small classical **temple**, modelled after the Temple of the Sibyl in Tivoli. The climb rewards you with a seldom-seen view over Montmartre and the northern parts of Paris; before the Eiffel Tower was built this was the favourite spot for suicides.

Musée Edith Piaf

5 Rue Crespin du Gast, **t** *01 43 55 52 72;* **métro** *Ménilmontant.* **Open** *Mon–Wed 1–6, Thurs 10–12, visits by appt only, closed Sept;* **adm** *donation.*

Edith Piaf (*see* opposite) was literally born on the streets below the Parc des Buttes-Chaumont, under a streetlamp, shielded behind the cloak of a kindly gendarme (there's a plaque at 72 Rue de Belleville).

In 1967 her fan club, Les Amis d'Edith Piaf, set up a museum full of Piaf memorabilia in a friend's flat in Ménilmontant.

CIMETIÈRE DU PÈRE-LACHAISE

Two main entrances: Porte Principale on Bd Ménilmontant and Porte Gambetta on Rue des Rondeaux; three smaller entrances: Porte des Amandiers on Bd Ménilmontant, Porte de la Réunion on Rue de la Réunion and Porte de la Rue du Repos on Rue du Repos; **t** *01 55 25 82 10;* **métro** *Père-Lachaise, Philippe-Auguste, Gambetta or Alexandre-Dumas.* **Open**

Edith Piaf

Daughter of an itinerant singer and an Italian acrobat, Piaf and her half-sister were raised in a provincial whorehouse before taking to the streets of Belleville to sing for their supper. Edith's voice soon attracted attention, and her career as Paris' most beloved singer and songwriter was launched. She eventually bought a *grand hôtel particulier* at Boulogne, but used her ornate marble bathtub with gold taps for her goldfish; she went through life with dirty feet.

16 Mar–5 Nov Mon–Fri 8–6, Sat 8.30–6, Sun and hols 9–6; 6 Nov–15 Mar Mon–Fri 8–5.30, Sat 8.30–5.30, Sun 9–5.30; adm free.

Père Lachaise had the best job in France. As Louis XIV's confessor, he held the keys to heaven for a king who was both superstitious and rotten to the core. It isn't surprising that Lachaise got lots of presents, which he converted to real estate here in what would later be the centre of the 20e. In 1804, under Napoleon's orders, Prefect of Paris Nicholas Frochot bought the land for cemetery space, something Paris was in dire need of at the time. Frochot was a clever fellow; it's said he thoroughly fleeced the baron who owned the land, then later sold him back a plot at a ridiculously high price. To popularize the new development, the prefect invited in a couple of celebrity corpses: Molière's and La Fontaine's. They didn't mind a bit.

The 'most famous cemetery in the world', and the largest in Paris, Père-Lachaise has always been a favourite place for a stroll; Balzac said he liked to come here to 'cheer himself up'. Thinking you might like to do the same, we've made it into a walk (*see* pp.279–81).

Leaving the cemetery through the main gate and turning right onto Boulevard de Ménilmontant, you'll be heading towards one of the city's newest hot neighbourhoods. Its centre is Avenue Oberkampf, where, having been priced out of the Marais, Bastille and the entire Left Bank, the young, hungry and outrageous have set up shop. Amid some of the city's blocky 1960s and 70s architecture and quaint houses from a bygone era, a multicultural mix of artists, models, and other creative types have given birth to a variety of boutiques, cafés, and music clubs that stretch toward Belleville and the Canal St-Martin, adding new flavour to these old *quartiers populaires*.

BOIS DE VINCENNES

Métro Porte Dorée for the zoo; métro Château de Vincennes, RER Vincennes for the castle. Open daily dawn to dusk.

This is another good place for a picnic. Like the Bois de Boulogne, its matching bookend at the other end of Paris, Vincennes owes its existence to the French kings' love of hunting. They set it aside for that purpose in the 1100s, and Philippe-Auguste even built a wall around it to keep out poachers. In the 14th century the Valois kings built its castle: a real fortified castle, not just a château, for this was the time of the Hundred Years' War. As long as the nearby Marais was fashionable, so was Vincennes, but when Louis XIV left Paris for Versailles, the neglected hunting ground was turned into a public park. During the Revolution most of it became a space for military training grounds and artillery practice, and it had to be almost completely reforested in the 1860s.

Aquarium Tropical de la Porte Dorée

239 Av Daumesnil, t 01 44 74 84 80; métro Porte Dorée. Open Wed–Mon 10–5.30; adm €4.

In 1931, Paris felt compelled to put on another World Fair, the first in six long years. This one was a little different: the Exposition Coloniale was a government effort put on to show the French how wonderful it was to be imperialists, and how much money they were earning by it. The White Man's Burden was a commonplace in France up to the

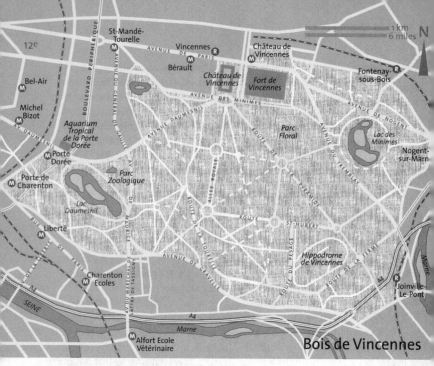

1960s, not surprising in a country that has always felt it had a *mission civilisatrice*, even vis-à-vis its immediate neighbours.

The fair, the first not to be held around the Champs-Elysées, took place in the Bois de Vincennes and surrounding areas; the star attraction was a life-size lath-and-plaster replica of the central temple of Cambodia's Angkor Wat. The one permanent building was the 'Museum of the Colonies' which became after the war the 'Museum of Overseas France'. Though necessity meant the name changed again, the museum lasted until 2003: not just a relic of a silly pretension, but one of the best collections of African and Pacific Islands art anywhere in Europe. However, the museum's entire collection is being moved to the Musée du Quai Branly (*see* p.140), along with collections from the Musée de l'Homme (*see* p.142).

The excellent tropical aquarium in the basement is still open to the public. The 300 species on display are often spectacular, though the yellowing, dog-eared signs leave you wondering what you are looking at. There are coral reefs, nautiloids, a crocodile pit, electric eels and lots of unusual species such as longfish and gobies, which can breathe air and are thought to be the ancestors of amphibians.

Zoo

53 Av de St-Maurice, **t** *01 44 75 20 10,* **w** *www.mnhn.fr;* **métro** *Porte Dorée.* **Open** *summer daily 9–6, winter 9–5.30, last adm 30mins before closing;* **adm** *€6.* **Restaurant**.

Besides the open spaces of the Bois de Vincennes, the main attraction is the Zoo, one of the largest in Europe. It offers giant pandas and a 67m (220ft) artificial mountain (which has started to collapse). Adjacent is one of the prettier parts of the park, the Lac Daumesnil with its islands, one blessed with a fake romantic ruin like the one in Buttes-Chaumont.

Parc Floral

Entrances: Esplanade du Château or Route de la Pyramide, **t** *01 55 94 20 20,* **w** *www.parc floraldeparis.com;* **métro** *Château de Vincennes.* **Open** *April–Sept daily 9.30–8, Mar and Oct daily 9.30–6, Nov–Feb daily 9.30–5;* **adm** *€3 (summer), €1.50 (winter).*

South of the Fort de Vincennes are these flower gardens, with water lilies, orchids and dahlias. It's a good place to bring the kids at weekends, with rides, special entertainments and places to eat.

Château de Vincennes

Av de Paris, Vincennes, t 01 48 08 31 20; métro Château de Vincennes (northern edge of park). **Open** *summer daily 10–12 and 1–6, winter daily 10–12 and 1.15–5; short guided tours (45mins) and long guided tours (1 hour 15mins) five times daily;* **adm** *€6.10*

The finest example of medieval secular architecture in Paris, this 'Versailles of the Middle Ages' shows what the French could build, even in the sorrows of the 14th century. Begun under Philippe IV in 1337, it was completed in 1380 in the same half-fortress, half-residence style of the old royal palace on the Île de la Cité: a walled enclosure with a keep built into the walls, and inside, state buildings and a Sainte-Chapelle (currently under restoration), just like the one on the island.

Under Cardinal Mazarin the complex was modernized, just in time for Louis XIV to go off to Versailles and forget about it. Louis was always short of prison cells (no other king in French history locked up so many political prisoners) and Vincennes made a convenient calaboose; in the 18th century Mirabeau spent three years here on a *lettre de cachet*.

Napoleon, another ruler who liked to keep his cells full, made it a prison again while rebuilding the fortifications just in case. Unwittingly, he provided Vincennes with a chance for a short but brilliant military career; it was the only bit of Paris that never surrendered in the Napoleonic Wars. The hero of the story is General Daumesnil, who had lost his leg fighting the Austrians and was given the easy job of commandant here. When the Allies took Paris in 1814, peg-legged Daumesnil refused to submit; he sent them a message: 'The Austrians got my leg at Wagram; tell them to give it back or else come in and get the other one.' Daumesnil stood fast until the Hundred Days, but after

Waterloo he was besieged again. And he held out again, until he could surrender Vincennes to a Frenchman, King Louis XVIII. During the First World War the trenches around the castle were used for shooting spies; Mata Hari was one of them.

The highlight of the tour, the 14th-century *donjon*, or keep, is unfortunately closed for several years for restoration work. Strong and taciturn outside, it hides a beautiful residence within, containing stained glass and excellent sculptural work. In the bedroom on the second floor England's King Henry V died in 1422; they parboiled him in the kitchen to keep him nice for the trip home to London.

Nogent-sur-Marne

RER Nogent-sur-Marne; the Pavilion is just left past the Syndicat d'Initiative (Tourist Office), in Av Victor-Hugo.

On the back fringes of the Bois de Vincennes, you can seek out the last magnificent glass-and-iron Baltard Pavilion from Les Halles, reconstructed as a kind of mini-convention centre.

12e: BERCY FF19–II21

Métro Bercy.

South of the Gare de Lyon, along the Seine, the old village of Bercy used to make its living by unloading all the wine and grain that came down the river. Today it is the biggest redevelopment area in Paris. The *grands projets* already completed include the monolithic, grey bunker of the Ministère des Finances (1989) stretching away from the Seine as if it were a continuation of the adjacent Pont de Bercy.

The area's most obvious landmark is the **Palais Omnisports de Paris-Bercy** (*8 Bd de Bercy, t 01 40 02 60 60, w www.popb.fr; métro Bercy; tickets also available from FNAC and Virgin*), a major venue for concerts and sporting events, including the Paris Tennis Open.

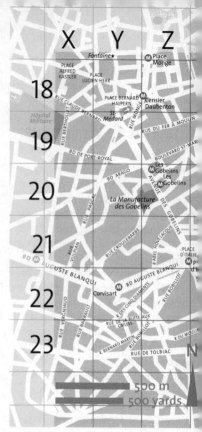

The latest *grand projet* is 51 Rue de Bercy, Frank Gehry's American Centre, which is being transformed into a space devoted to cinema and is due to open in late 2004 on the edge of the Parc de Bercy (*w www.51ruedebercy. com; métro Bercy or Cour St-Emilion*). The Musée du Cinéma will be reopened here (having closed due to a fire in the Palais de Chaillot in 1997), alongside a film archive and cinema screens.

The **Parc de Bercy** is a delightful green space with ponds, vines and a kitchen garden, plus masses of flowers growing wild. In 2004, Bercy will be linked to the TGB (*see below*) by a footbridge. Bercy Village has been created from the old wine warehouses and you can now have a drink or a bite to eat (from Tex-Mex to sushi), or browse in lifestyle boutiques. On the Parc's riverside terrace are the massive whimsical bronze sculptures of Algerian artist Rachid Khimoun, entitled 'Les Enfants du Paris'. Close inspection reveals that they are constructed from the imprints of drains and sewer covers from around the world.

13ᵉ: LES GOBELINS AND AROUND

Bibliothèque Nationale EE20–GG21

11 Quai François-Mauriac, t 01 53 79 59 59, t 01 53 79 49 49 for tours, w www.bnf.fr; métro Bibliothèque François-Mitterand or Quai de la Gare. Open Tues–Sat 10–8, Sun 12–7, closed hols; adm one-day pass €3, exhibitions €5.50; 90min tours by appointment from 2pm; library open to all over 16 years.

Traditionally one of the poorest *arrondissements* in Paris, the 13ᵉ emerged even worse from the planning yoyos of the 1950s and 60s. It's a desolate place, characterized mainly by wall after wall of soulless blocks of flats stretching south to the Périphérique with not a blade of green between.

In this most woebegone corner of Paris, Tonton Mitterrand planted his definitive *grand projet*, the Bibliothèque François Mitterrand, forming part of the Bibliothèque Nationale and known informally as the Tolbiac Site, or the TGB – Très Grande Bibliothèque. In 1989 a hitherto unknown Frenchman, Dominique Perrault, won the design competition with an ultra-Modernist nightmare of four 280ft towers, surrounding sunken gardens and reading rooms. Construction was under way before anyone started listening to the librarians' complaints that glass-walled skyscrapers provide the worst possible conditions for keeping old books. The TGB came out so breathtakingly ugly and dysfunctional that no one wanted to move in, but there was nothing to be done about it.

Butte aux Cailles Y22–Z23

***Métro** Corvisart and walk south.*

'Quails' Hill' was the landing point of history's first manned balloon flight, and an old quarter that had the gumption to unite

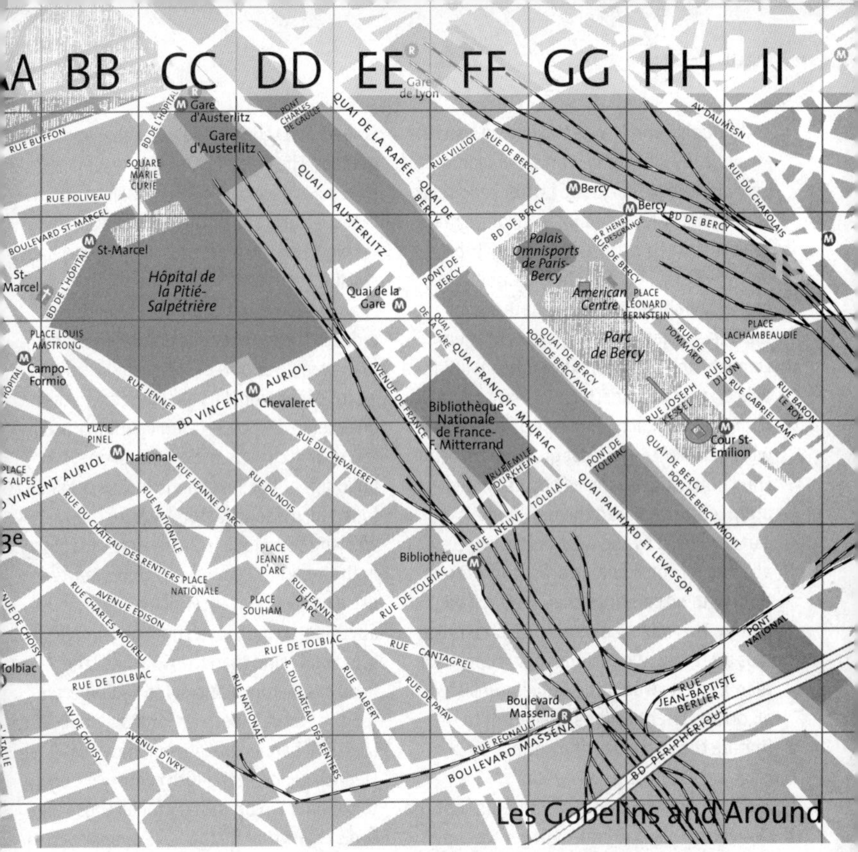

Les Gobelins and Around

Map labels (grid A–II):

Gare d'Austerlitz · Gare d'Austerlitz · Gare de Lyon · Bercy · Bercy · Av DAUMESN · RUE BUFFON · RUE POLIVEAU · SQUARE MARIE CURIE · BD DE L'HOPITAL · RUE DE BERCY · RUE VILLIOT · RUE DE BERCY · BD DE BERCY · RUE OU CHAROLAIS · BOULEVARD ST-MARCEL · St-Marcel · St-Marcel · QUAI D'AUSTERLITZ · QUAI DE LA RAPÉE · QUAI DE BERCY · R HENRI DESMARRIE · BD DE BERCY · RUE DU CHAROLAIS · Hôpital de la Pitié-Salpêtrière · St-Marcel · BD DE L'HOPITAL · Palais Omnisports de Paris-Bercy · PLACE LOUIS ARMSTRONG · PONT DE BERCY · American Centre · PLACE LÉONARD BERNSTEIN · PLACE LACHAMBEAUDIE · Campo-Formio · RUE JENNER · BD VINCENT AURIOL · Chevaleret · Quai de la Gare · QUAI DE LA GARE QUAI FRANÇOIS MAURIAC · Parc de Bercy · QUAI DE BERCY · POST DE BERCY AVAL · RUE JOSEPH KESSEL · RUE DE DIJON · RUE GABRIEL LAMÉ · RUE BARON LE ROY · Cour St-Émilion · PLACE PINEL · Nationale · PLACE S VINCENT AURIOL · RUE DU CHEVALERET · Bibliothèque Nationale de France-F. Mitterrand · RUE DUNKERQUE · PONT DE TOLBIAC · QUAI DE BERCY · PORTE DE BERCY AMONT · QUAI PANHARD ET LEVASSOR · PLACE JEANNE D'ARC · PLACE NATIONALE · RUE DU CHÂTEAU DES RENTIERS · RUE NATIONALE · RUE JEANNE D'ARC · RUE DUNOIS · RUE NSUVE TOLBIAC · Bibliothèque · PONT NATIONAL · 3e · Tolbiac · RUE CHARLES MOUREU · RUE DE TOLBIAC · PLACE SOUHAM · RUE DE TOLBIAC · RUE CANTAGREL · RUE ALBERT · RUE DE PATAY · Boulevard Massena · RUE JEAN-BAPTISTE BERLIER · RUE DE CROISY · AVENUE EDISON · AV DE CHOISY · AVENUE D'IVRY · RUE NATIONALE · RUE DU CHÂTEAU DES RENTIERS · RUE REGNAULT · BOULEVARD MASSENA · BD PÉRIPHÉRIQUE · RUE D'ITALIE

against the cement mixers. This is one of the few neighbourhoods in Paris with a strong sense of community, as well as several good restaurants and bars.

Chinatown BB23–DD24

Métro *Porte d'Ivry.*

Paris' Chinatown, the southeastern corner of the 13e roughly south of Rue de Tolbiac and east of Avenue de Choisy, encompasses a dozen nationalities, many of whom came to France as refugees from Cambodia, Vietnam and Laos.

La Manufacture des Gobelins Y–Z20

42 Av des Gobelins, t 01 44 08 52 00; **métro** *Les Gobelins.* **Open** *only for short guided tours in French, Tues–Thurs at 2 and 2.45 (arrive 15mins ahead), closed hols;* **adm** *€8.*

Up until the 19th century, the little river Bièvre still flowed openly through here, its banks lined by tanners and dyers. The most famous of the latter was a family named Gobelin, who owed their great fame and fortune to the discovery of a prized scarlet dye. Ironically, the Gobelins have gone down in history for tapestries, an art they themselves never touched.

In 1520, with all the pretensions of the nouveaux riches, the Gobelins built themselves a castle (follow the dusty courtyard of workshops back to No.4 bis Rue Gustave-Geffroy). This strange, grey-towered relic was called the Château de Reine Blanche after a 14th-century castle located here, built for either Blanche de Provence or Blanche de Bourgogne, wife of Charles IV.

Since 1940 the three state weaving factories – the Gobelins, the Beauvais and the Savonnerie – have been consolidated here at the old Gobelins site, producing as they have for the past 300 years all the tapestries, rugs and furniture covers required by the French state.

Although Henri IV was the first to have the idea of a royal tapestry works, the plan was only put into action in 1663, after Fouquet's extraordinary fête at Vaux-le-Vicomte made Louis XIV green with envy (*see* 'Day Trips', pp.296–8). Colbert bought the Gobelins' property, built factories and housing for 250 tapestry-makers (three-quarters of them Flemish) and put them under the insufferable Charles Lebrun. The goal was to furnish the royal residences and especially Versailles with items of the highest quality – made in France. Artistic squabbles began immediately. Lebrun replaced the traditional cartoons used by the weavers (which allowed for considerable artistic interpretation) with oil paintings they were to copy strictly. This mixing of media became ridiculous after 1748, when under new supervisor Jean-Baptiste Oudry the Gobelins insisted on 36,000 different colours, the better to imitate the subtleties of paintings by Mignard, Watteau and Poussin.

After the Revolution, governments kept the Gobelins around to crank out servile copies of paintings that flattered their egos. Only when half of the factory was burned down during the Commune in 1871 did the authorities consider renewing the true, decorative art of weaving. After the Second World War all 18th-century models were dropped for good (except when replacing or repairing worn-out items in the Elysée palace, for instance) and now all three factories rely on designs by 20th-century artists, such as Dufy, Chagall and Picasso. With very few exceptions their works are still for the state, which stores them in the adjacent Mobilier National and distributes them to offices and ministries as it sees fit. A weaver can spend seven years on a large project and never discover its eventual destination. Prices are just as secret, although it is estimated that the few private commissions that are permitted average €12,160 per square metre.

The Gobelins remains a village enclave remote from Paris and the 20th century. It has pretty cobbled courtyards with statues of Colbert and Lebrun, its own chapel and shady gardens. The serene 17th-century workers' housing is decorated with medallions on the tapestry craft, and of the hundred Gobelins weavers (mostly women since the war) half still live there. Neither has the technology changed, although chromatic science has reduced the number of colours to a more manageable 14,000 or so. The tall vertical looms of the Gobelins are identical to the ones set up by Colbert. Similar looms, used for making carpets, are over in the newer buildings of the Savonnerie (it was originally founded in a soap factory), where the weaving technique is the reverse of tapestry. In the adjacent Beauvais section, weavers use a horizontal warp which must, if anything, be more of a strain on the eyes, spine and mind than the Gobelins'. The Beauvais factory was created by Colbert in 1664 to weave tapestries for individuals after Louis XIV banned private purchases of Flemish goods. In the 19th century it began to specialize in upholstery for all those big Louis chairs that fill the halls of upper-crust French officialdom, although now, as at the Gobelins, most work is based on cartoons by contemporary artists.

The tour leaves you next to the vast Mobilier National, built in the 1920s over the Gobelins' orchards (free fruit used to be one of the tapestry-workers' perks) and where all the state tapestries and furnishings are stored.

PARC MONTSOURIS AND THE CITÉ UNIVERSITAIRE Off maps

Parc Montsouris

***Métro** and **RER** Cité-Universitaire.*

'Mount Mouse', with its lawns, old-fashioned merry-go-round and exotic trees, is the second-largest park in Paris *intra muros*, after Buttes-Chaumont. The highest point of the park is occupied by the Bardo, an impressive replica of the palace of the beys of Tunis built for the World Fair of 1867; it now serves as a Tunisian cultural centre.

The Pavillon Montsouris (see p.340) is one of the nicest places to eat in Paris.

Cité Internationale Universitaire de Paris

Main entrance 1–6 Bd Jourdan, t 01 44 16 64 00; métro Cité-Universitaire. Swiss pavilion open daily 10–12 and 2–5.

The Cité was originally founded in the 1920s, in the spirit of the Latin Quarter's medieval colleges, to offer students decent accommodation.

The campus, stretching south of Parc Montsouris, was a vast expanse of land set aside for various nations to build pavilions for their Parisian scholars. The 35 pavilions offer a curious architectural sampler: note the geometrical Dutch Pavilion (1928) by Dudok; the Swiss Pavilion (1932) by Le Corbusier, one of his first buildings set up on *pilotis*, or stilts; and next door, the rougher-edged Brazilian Pavilion (1959), Le Corbusier's last Paris work, designed with Lúcio Costa.

Maison-Musée Lénine

4 Rue Marie-Rose (between Rue du Père-Corentin and Rue Sarrette), t 01 43 21 89 04; métro Alésia. Open by appt; adm free.

Lenin spent his last four years in Paris in this house, now a little museum where you can see items relating to his stay, including his dishes and chess set (donated by Gorbachev in 1986).

15e: SOUTHWEST PARIS

The 15e is the largest and most populous *arrondissement* in Paris with some 200,000 souls, but it has nothing very compelling to show for it, unless you count the thrills on the waterslides at the huge sport complex, **Aquaboulevard** (see 'Sports and Green Spaces', p.369).

La Ruche Off maps

Passage de Dantzig; métro Porte de Versailles.

'The Hive' was Paris' first *cité* for artists and its most singular historical monument. Designed by Eiffel as the wine pavilion for the 1900 World Fair, the Ruche was scheduled for demolition in 1902 when a mediocre academic sculptor, Alfred Boucher, purchased it and several other cheap pavilions and relocated them to this site, then within ear-shot of the slaughterhouse. In all, *père* Boucher created 140 studios and flats (the 24 in the Ruche itself were triangular wedges so narrow they were nicknamed coffins), which he leased to his 'bees' – impoverished painters and sculptors – at a nominal or uncollected rent. Many of the first residents, Brancusi, Soutine, Chagall, Zadkine, were *émigrés* from Eastern Europe.

During the First World War, the Ruche was requisitioned to house refugees (Chagall returned to find all his paintings gone, except for a handful used to roof the concierge's rabbit hutch). To this day, some 80 'bees' still buzz in the hive.

Institut Pasteur and Musée Pasteur N19–O18

25 Rue du Dr-Roux, t 01 45 68 82 83; métro Pasteur. Open Mon–Fri 2–5.30, last adm 5, closed Aug and hols; adm €3.

Founded by Louis Pasteur in 1888, the prestigious Institut today continues his research into vaccinations; in recent years it made the news in the controversy over who discovered the AIDS virus first.

A tour of the museum takes in Pasteur's apartment, drawings and portraits as well as items relating to his career and to the Institut. After Pasteur's death the government wanted to stick him in the Panthéon, but his family preferred him to lie where he had worked, in the crypt.

Book-browsing and Parc Georges-Brassens Off maps

Métro Porte de Versailles or Convention. Book market open Sat and Sun 8am–7pm.

At weekends, Rue Brancion is the site of an excellent second-hand **book market**. This skirts **Parc Georges-Brassens** (1985), named after the singer-songwriter who spent his last years nearby, in Rue Santos-Dumont. It replaced the old Vaugirard abattoir – hence the two bronze bulls at the entrance by Rue des Morillons.

Rue du Commerce J17–K16

Métro Av Emile-Zola or Commerce.

This charming, if slightly dilapidated, street was the main artery of the old village of Grenelle, annexed to Paris in 1860. As you stroll down it, note No.78, one of the oldest butchers in Paris; a bit further south, at No.24 Place Etienne-Pernet, stands an enchanting Art Nouveau building full of vegetative flourishes. From here, walk down Avenue Félix-Faure to see other pretty buildings: No.13 with a ceramic frieze, No.31 with sculptures, and best of all No.40, with a sculpture representing La Fontaine's fable of the crow and the fox.

To the north of Rue Commerce, **Boulevard de Grenelle** is the great divider between the chic (rubbing shoulders with the aristo 7e) and the unchic (i.e. Rue du Commerce). At the top, near the Eiffel Tower, is one of the saddest sights in Paris: the **Place des Martyrs Juifs du Vélodrome d'Hiver** (I13–14), where in July 1942 the Paris police rounded up 13,152 Parisian Jews for Auschwitz. Only a handful survived.

Walks

16

THE ART OF SHOPPING: A WALK THROUGH THE *PASSAGES*

This is a perfect walk for a rainy day, since most of it will find you in the shelter of the *passages*. The precursors of the modern department store, the first of these arcades appeared in Paris in 1776. To begin with, they were merely narrow shopping streets, covered up by landowners trying to boost trade by giving shoppers a place to get their feet out of the urban muck. About 1780 someone came up with the idea of covering them with glass – the beginning of the iron-and-glass revolution in architecture, the first step towards the Crystal Palace and the Louvre Pyramid. Fashionable, purpose-built *passages* became the craze in the 1820s. Paris once had 200 of them, and the idea spread to cities around the world.

Now well out of the mainstream of commerce, their charm is perfected. In any city where there are arcades, it's the same; they attract old-book dealers, stamp and coin shops, men who carve pipes by hand, doll hospitals and specialists in music boxes: all the fond foolishness that an angel of cities would find worthy of her protection. If you need a birthday present for any of your favourite crazy people, look no further.

The start of the walk, fairly in the shadow of the Louvre, is on a little back street, Rue Jean-Jacques Rousseau, where a graceful arch welcomes you into the **Galerie Véro-Dodat**. Built in 1826, the Galerie is one of the

oldest and prettiest of Paris' *passages*; it initially wowed the Paris crowds with its mahogany, marble and bronze decoration, as well as its use of a new technological marvel: gas lighting. Véro and Dodat were two butchers who made it big; riding the crest of the new fad for arcades, they went out of their way to impress. Today, the ornate columns and *putti* (cherubs) still glisten, though it could all use a coat or two of varnish. There are some interesting shops both new and old, a smattering of galleries and one of Paris' eternal wonders: **Robert Capia**'s curiosity shop at No.26. Paris' leading antique-doll expert, Capia likes everything else that is old and unusual; the stuff in the windows is fascinating, and inside it's jammed up to the ceilings.

From either end of the arcade, head back towards the Louvre and turn right onto Rue St-Honoré. Since this walk is all about shopping, you might as well have a look inside the enormous **Louvre des Antiquaires** on your left. Don't expect any of the charm of the arcade shops or the flea markets out in the suburbs. Built into a converted department store, this is literally an enormous shopping mall for antiques, packed with sumptuous shops and tiny booths. If you're ready for a coffee by now, you could stop off at Café Marly, the Louvre's chic new café.

Going back to Rue St-Honoré, you'll be facing the twin hulks of the Comédie-Française and the Palais Royal. Pass under the arch between them to enter the **Jardin du Palais Royal**. A cousin to the *passages*, this was the place to be in the 1780s, when the enclosed garden was surrounded by shops and cafés. A few quaint old shops still survive, selling antiques and lead soldiers.

Leaving through the opposite end of the garden, a right on Rue des Petits-Champs will take you to the entrances of the **Galerie Colbert** and **Galerie Vivienne**. This elegant pair of glass-roofed arcades was built in the 1820s, and along with the Véro-Dodat they are the most luxurious survivors of the genre in Paris. Light and airy, with neoclassical reliefs and mosaic floors, these arcades

Start: Métro Louvre-Rivoli.
Finish: Rue Richer.
Walking time: An hour and a half, though you might see enough in the shop windows to keep you half a day.
Lunch and drinks stops: Café Marly, *see* p.318; Le Grand Colbert, *see* p.322; A Priori Thé, *see* p.323; L'Arbre à Cannelle, *see* p.323.

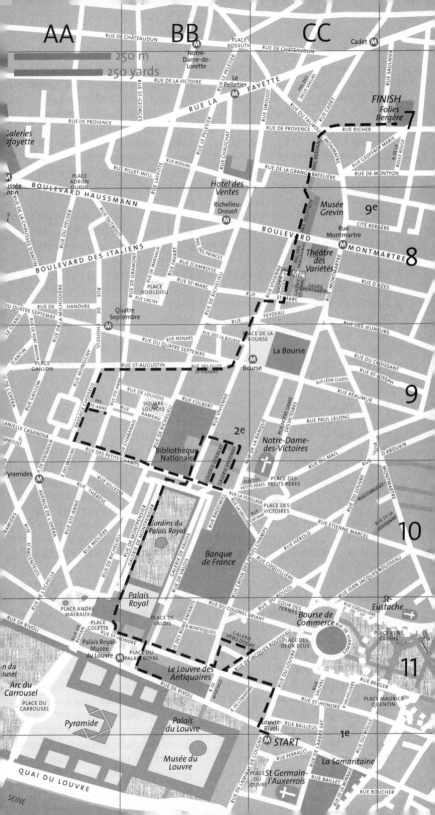

provide a dreamy setting for their little shops and cafés. Both arcades have been well restored, though sadly the Colbert has had most of the life squeezed out of it by the Bibliothèque Nationale, which has taken over most of the space for its bookshop and a deathly art gallery; they'll soon be sharing it with the Institut National de l'Histoire de l'Art. The Colbert does have the fancier restaurant of the two, though, **Le Grand Colbert**, where you can indulge in lunch in opulent surroundings. If your budget doesn't stretch that far, there's a simpler lunch menu at **A Priori Thé**, in Galerie Vivienne.

To see the next of the *passages* will require circumnavigating the vast bulk of the old Bibliothèque National. This block contains the original buildings of France's national library, first established under Louis XIV. From the end of the arcade facing the library turn left, then right at the corner, onto Rue des Petits-Champs. Three streets down, the entrance of the lively **Passage Choiseul** and **Passage Ste-Anne** will be on your right. These passages come alive at lunch time, with local workers popping in for cheap lunches in the sandwich bars, or to browse in the well-stocked art shop and ubiquitous second-hand book dealers.

The opposite end of Passage Choiseul leaves you in Rue St-Augustin. Turn right, follow this street to the end and turn left onto Rue Vivienne, passing the front of the old Paris Bourse, forlorn after technology made it redundant in 1999. Two streets further, a right on Rue St-Marc will take you to the biggest nest of *passages* in Paris, collectively known to Parisians as the **Passage des Panoramas**. Robert Fulton, the American pioneer of submarines and steamboats, also invented the popular entertainment called the 'panorama', in 1796. This was a huge circular painting, illuminated from behind and plotted in exact perspective to give spectators inside the circle the impression of being in the middle of a scene from ancient history, or a famous battle. Though such static spectacles were only to be a passing fashion, big theatres were built for them in

major cities, including the one here (demolished long ago), built in conjunction with one of the first of Paris' arcades (1800).

Five distinct arcades intersect here (Galeries Feydeau, St-Marc, des Variétés, Montmartre and the long Passage des Panoramas), to make a little self-contained city of a hundred shops. Mostly they're utilitarian establishments, with a few stamp and coin shops, printers and even a Turkish bath. Have a look in the windows of **Graveur Stern**, a print shop in business here since 1840, which loves to put its best work, along with some curiosities, on display. **L'Arbre à Cannelle** is a cosy *salon de thé* here.

Follow the Passage des Panoramas to its end, and you'll be on the Grands Boulevards – Boulevard Montmartre, to be specific, the centre of Parisian high life in the 19th century. The **Théâtre des Variétés**, a few doors to the right on the boulevard, has changed little since it was built in 1807. In its 1860s heyday this was a famous venue, one where Offenbach put on such famous operettas as *La Belle Hélène*, *Les Variétés* and *La Périchole*.

Right across the street from the Passage des Panoramas, however, you can continue the arcade trail through the **Passage Jouffroy**. If you still haven't come to love the peculiar little world of the *passages*, this one might do the trick. A pretty play of dappled shadows lights up the faded grandeur of this busy 1846 arcade, which boasts its own hotel, and a wax museum, the **Musée Grévin**, which seems perfectly at home in this rare setting. The arcade shops offer antique toys, oriental rugs, Cinédoc, a great shop for cinema books, posters and memorabilia, and an outlandish selection of antique walking sticks and canes at **Segas**, No.36, under the moose antlers.

Passage Jouffroy continues directly across Rue de la Grange Batelière as the **Passage Verdeau**. Ten years ago this was the shabby end of the *passage* trail, lined with empty shop fronts and Chinese self-service places. Recently restored, it now houses mostly old book and print shops. It's a popular lunchtime hangout for the people at the

Hôtel des Ventes Richelieu-Drouot, just around the corner on Rue Drouot (*t 01 48 00 20 20; open Mon–Sat 11–6*). Paris' version of Sotheby's or Christie's, Drouot was established in 1851.

The end of the Passage Verdeau leaves you in Rue Richer, not far from the old **Folies-Bergère** at No.39. Today, it's a poor shadow of its former erotic glory; all that remains is the Art Deco relief of a nude on the façade. This is where the walk ends; from here you can head back down for more mainstream shopping on the Grands Boulevards.

A TOUR OF PÈRE-LACHAISE

Ever since the prefect Nicholas Frochot (*see* p.267) relocated the ashes of Molière, La Fontaine, Héloïse and Abelard here in the early 19th century, the cemetery named after Louis XIV's confessor has been a favourite place for an afternoon stroll, far from the hurly-burly of the city. Over the years it has expanded from its original 42 acres to 108, making it by far the largest cemetery in Paris, where over 600,000 await the trump of Judgement Day.

In design, Père-Lachaise is a cross between the traditional, urban sort of French cemetery, with ponderous family mausolea in straight rows, and the modern, suburban-style model. Brongniart, the architect of the Bourse, laid it out like an English garden; its romantic curving lanes and greenery influenced later cemetery designers, even in Britain. Lastly, Père-Lachaise is an outdoor museum of 19th-century French sculpture: David d'Angers, François Rude, Charles Garnier and Hector Guimard have all left works along these leafy alleys.

Free maps are available at the main and métro Père-Lachaise entrances, or are on sale in the flower shops. Once you've entered, there are few signs to help you find the tombs you're looking for, except rock poet Jim Morrison's; his fans have thoughtfully

decorated everybody else's monuments with directions in felt pen.

The main entrance, at Boulevard de Ménilmontant and Rue de la Roquette, leads into the original part of Père-Lachaise. Right near the front, in section 4, you'll find the graves of **Colette [1]**, **Rossini [2]** and the poet **Alfred de Musset [3]**, although the ashes of the latter were sent back to Italy. Opposite Colette, a right down Avenue du Puits will take you to section 7 and the tombs of Père-Lachaise's senior residents, **Héloïse and Abelard [4]** (*see* p.88 for their story). Legend says that when the sepulchre was opened to put in the body of Héloïse, Abelard held out his arms to receive her. In the 17th century prudish abbesses would pry their remains apart and put them in separate tombs, and romantic abbesses would reunite them. In 1792 they were moved and placed in a double coffin, with a lead barrier between them 'for decency's sake'.

For **Jim Morrison [5]** (d. 1971), follow the crowds to section 6. The cops keep a constant eye on the place, and once-common sights, such as wild-looking Germans cooking sausages on a camp stove, or naked trippers sprawled over other graves and chanting in tongues, are no longer common. Devotees today leave flowers, smokes and playing cards (face cards only), incense and small toys. There is no proof, incidentally, that Morrison is actually buried here; many people claim he isn't even dead.

From Morrison, backtrack up across Avenue Casimir-Perier to section 11 for **Chopin [6]**, who died in Paris in 1849 and is commemorated with a statue of Erato, the muse of music. For true romantics, white roses are the token of remembrance (*available at the eastern entrance*). This a favourite section for musicians, with the tombs of **Cherubini [7]**

> **Start**: Métro Philippe Auguste.
> **Finish**: Métro Alexandre-Dumas.
> **Walking time**: About two hours.
> **Lunch and drinks stops**: Bring your own provisions; otherwise, there are a couple of options nearby (*see* p.338).

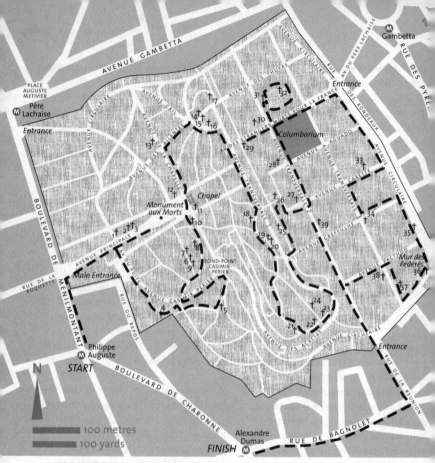

and **Bellini [8]** (who was reburied in Italy) and jazz pianist **Michel Petrucciani [9]**.

Adjacent section 12 has the painter Géricault **[10]** (with a relief of his *Le Radeau de la Méduse* in the Louvre) and the monumental tomb of **Adolphe Thiers [11]**. Responsible for the massacres of the Commune, he felt no irony in choosing to be buried near the spot where the last of the shootings took place, but Parisians don't forget; the tomb has been desecrated regularly since 1877.

Across from Thiers is the cemetery **chapel**. In the sections to the north of it you can seek out the painter **David [12]** (section 56); **Bizet [13]**, along Avenue de la Chapelle (section 68); **Balzac [14]**, marked by a bust by David d'Angers (turn up Avenue des Ailantes to section 48); poet **Gérard de Nerval [15]** (section 49), and **Delacroix [16]** (section 49). Near the latter's lava sarcophagus is a 52ft

phallic something, the strangest tomb in the whole cemetery. It immortalizes one **Félix de Beaujour [17]**, a judge during the Revolution, and from the decoration it is impossible to tell if Félix was the high priest of a shadowy cult or if he simply wanted a tomb in the style archaeologists of the time thought was 'ancient Etruscan'.

From here head south down Avenue Transversale 1 to the oldest and loveliest part of Père-Lachaise, with florid statuary and dead politicians centred around the Rond-Point Casimir-Perier. This section holds **Corot [18]** (section 24), **La Fontaine [19]** (section 25) and **Molière [20]**. Whether the bones here are really Molière's is a matter of debate; when he died suddenly in 1673, it took some special pleading from the king himself to have such a creature as an actor buried in Christian ground. The Church, however, insisted on only two priests and no mourners at the grave site, and from the beginning rumours flew that France's greatest dramatist had been secretly dumped in a ditch with the unbaptized.

A clique of Napoleon's marshals rests quietly in adjacent sections 28, 29 and 39: **Ney [21]**, **Masséna [22]**, **Murat [23]** and **Cambacérès [24]**. Avenue Transversale 1 (with Félix's monument closing the view at the northern end) neatly bisects the cemetery, and on the other side of it, back towards the centre, lies British Admiral **Sidney Smith [25]**, who helped beat the French in the Napoleonic Wars and always loved Paris.

Just beyond Smith, you can visit actress **Sarah Bernhardt [26]**, **Auguste Blanqui [27]**, a leader of the 1848 revolt and the Commune, and **Simone Signoret and Yves Montand [28]** (section 44). Northwest of the divine Sarah is a small tomb that draws as many worshippers as Morrison's: that of **Allan Kardec [29]**. Kardec, born Léon Rivail in 1804, was one of the fathers of 19th-century spiritualism. His followers are still numerous enough, in Paris, to keep up a near-permanent vigil around the flower-bedecked shrine. Don't fool with these people; they will come after you if you hang around too long, or if you try to photograph the tomb. But take time to read the incredible notice posted behind Kardec by the City of Paris, a calm and reasoned philosophical tract warning against the folly of adoring the remains of a mortal being.

Nearby are **Apollinaire [30]** (section 86) and **Proust [31]** (section 85), along with an unpleasant outsider, **General Rafael Trujillo [32]**, dictator of the Dominican Republic until 1961 and one of the champion nasties of that nasty century.

The large structure in section 87 is the **Columbarium**, in which are kept the ashes of Surrealist painter **Max Ernst**, diva **Maria Callas** (although her ashes were later exhumed and scattered over the Aegean), violinist **Stéphane Grappelli** and **Isadora Duncan**, the American dancer who wowed Paris and died so tragically.

Avenue des Étrangers Morts pour la France leads alongside the Columbarium, straight to the eastern gate of the cemetery. Turn right before the exit, and you'll come to section 89 and one of the grandest tombs of all, Sir Jacob Epstein's tribute to **Oscar Wilde [33]**. As everyone knows, Oscar is here due to certain character flaws in the people and institutions of his native land. Epstein's memorial, a sort of looming Egyptian Art Deco deity, ensured that Wilde would find no peace even in the afterlife. The statue's prominent winkie became the talk of Paris. First a fig leaf was put on it, and then in 1922 an unidentified Englishwoman who apparently knew the deceased batted it off, fig leaf and all; the busted member was last seen serving as a paperweight on the cemetery keeper's desk.

Press on to the far southeastern corner of the cemetery; in section 94, the fellow with the dynamo in his lap is **Théophile Gramme [34]**, a Belgian who invented the thing in 1869. Near the wall in 94 are **Gertrude Stein and Alice B. Toklas [35]**

In the far corner is section 97; this was the last bit of free Paris in 1871, where the Versailles troops lined up the last 150 Communards against the wall (the **Mur des Fédérés**). The wall is a place of pilgrimage for French leftists, many of whom are buried nearby, including 1950s Communist chief **Maurice Thorez [36]**, and there are memorials to the Parisians deported to the Nazi camps during the Occupation. But the most famous resident of 97 is no doubt **Edith Piaf [37]** (*see* p.267). Just up from her, in section 96, is **Modigliani [38]**. For one last political martyr, there's **Victor Noir [39]**, in section 92. Noir was a brave journalist who criticized Napoleon III; a cousin of the Emperor shot him in cold blood in 1870, and got off in a fixed trial, causing big demonstrations. His bronze *gisant*, paid for by national subscription, shows him exactly as he was when he died, with an apparent state of excitation that Parisian girls used to come and rub for good luck.

From here head back down to the exit at Rue de la Réunion, from where it's a short walk to Alexandre-Dumas métro.

MONTMARTRE BY NIGHT

When night falls, half of Paris heads for the hills, or rather the hill, the Butte Montmartre. This is nothing new. Montmartre has been a night-time rendezvous since the 18th century, not so much for its picturesque qualities – although old descriptions of the village, with its garden plots, vineyards, fountains and creaking windmills, make it sound like something out of an operetta – but because it was outside the tax farmers' wall and drink was cheap. Rents remained low, too, after Haussmann's boulevard-building revolution; and side by side with villagers going about their business a bohemian colony grew up that led a nocturnal life all its own. Small flats for illicit trysts of all descriptions were easy to find. By the 1880s, Montmartre was already the city's lesbian district, where it was common to see women dressed as men dancing with other women in bars.

Montmartre in its heyday was never as carefree as the studenty Latin Quarter; old accounts claim it literally reeked of absinthe – cheap wine fortified with wormwood. For the poorer habitués, the charm of the deadly tipple came from the hours one could spend in a café, nursing a single glass while obliterating unwanted consciousness. Billions of brain cells were prematurely wiped out before absinthe was made illegal in 1915.

The Impressionists, wanting to capture fleeting moments, loved Montmartre, and Cubism was born here too, with Picasso's *Demoiselles d'Avignon* in 1908 (detractors at the time suggested that absinthe had something to do with it). By the 1920s, soaring rents drove the artists and writers out of Montmartre. One who stayed was André Breton, who posted a note to himself

> **Start**: Métro Lamarck-Caulaincourt.
> **Finish**: Place de Clichy.
> **Walking time**: About two hours, plus stops.

'Ne va jamais à Montparnasse!' and then invented Surrealism.

These days Montmartre may have about as much of an edge as a butter knife, but it still has a nightlife of its own high above the rest of Paris. This is partly nostalgic, here in the 'world capital of nostalgia', and partly due to the old neighbourhood's intrinsic charm, which takes on a certain magic when the sun goes down. Expect plenty of company from all over the world – one thing Montmartre still is is lively, although most of the noise is made by tourists.

Climb the steps behind the métro to reach Rue Calaincourt. On your left is **Chez Ginette** [1], 101 Rue Caulaincourt (*see* p.330), where you can have an old-fashioned Montmartre night out, with a singsong around the piano. Another traditional favourite, **Bar Au Rêve [2]** (*see* p.331), is down at No. 89, and won't break the bank. A left after Chez Ginette will take you up to Rue des Saules; turn right up more steps to **Au Lapin Agile [3]**, 22 Rue des Saules (*see* p.353), an old cottage converted in 1860 into one of the most celebrated cabarets in Paris; Utrillo painted it endlessly. Inside, the low ceiling, smoke, dimmed lights and works of art and artlessness paid by poor artists in lieu of their tabs, remain the same, while every evening *animateurs* gamely attempt to recapture the atmosphere , trying to get befuddled Japanese tourists to join in the songs.

The historic importance of drink to Montmartre is recalled up the other side of Rue St-Vincent at the oldest **vineyard** in the city limits, planted in 1886 by the Montmartrois who still remembered the good old days when their *Butte Sacrée* supplied Paris with plonk.

Just after the vineyard, turn right down Rue de l'Abreuvoir, an old Montmartre street made more evocative by the discreet street lighting. Have a look down the romantic Allée des Brouillards (the 'Lane of Fogs') then head left up Rue Girardon to Rue Norvins and charming **Rue St-Rustique**, the oldest street in Montmartre; it was here that Van Gogh painted one of his best-known

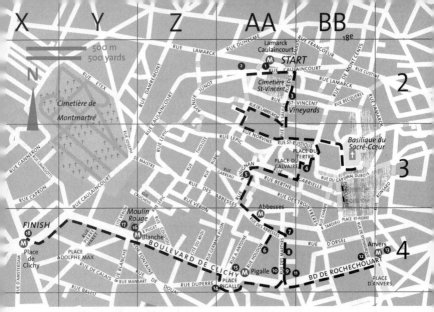

Paris paintings, *La Guinguette* (in the Musée
d'Orsay) at A la Bonne Franquette.

Follow Rue du Chevalier around to the
Basilique du Sacré-Cœur, by day 'a heavy,
somnolent whiteness, like the belly of a
faded woman', as Henry Miller put it, by night
illuminated to resemble an iridescent palace
for a pooh-Bah from another galaxy. From
the *parvis* in front of Sacré-Cœur the City of
Lights twinkles magically at your feet, while
the Eiffel Tower lights up like a giant sparkler
on the hour.

Backtrack around Rue du Chevalier to **Place
du Tertre**, packed with tourists and artists
drawing their portraits and caricatures. **La
Cremaillére [4]**, on the square (*see* p.330), is a
gaily touristy place serving decent food on a
terrace; you may even be serenaded by an
enthusiastic accordionist for the True Paris
Experience. For the spectacular view minus
the tunes, stroll over to tiny adjacent **Place
du Calvaire**.

Stepped Rue du Calvaire leads down to Rue
Gabrielle; turn right and follow Rue Ravignan
around to Place Émile Goudeau, stopping off
for a glass of wine at **Le Relais de La Butte [5]**,
12 Rue Ravignan (*see* p.343), overlooking the
Butte. Place Émile Goudeau is the most
romantic of Montmartre's squares, with its
trees, old houses and Wallace fountain
spilling down the steps, a corner of dream
Paris waiting for Gene Kelly and Leslie Caron

to whirl through in dream Paris Technicolor. If
you had come this way just over a hundred
years ago, however, you would probably have
wondered at the racket coming out of the
Bateau Lavoir, which stood at No.13. In 1908,
while still living here in picturesque misery
and just finishing the aforementioned
Demoiselles d'Avignon, Picasso held his
famous banquet in honour of the then 60-
year-old Henri (Le Douanier) Rousseau (*see*
p.127), hanging the Bateau Lavoir with flags
and Venetian lamps. Yet what was meant to
be a sincere celebration of a great painter
(something that only Picasso and a select
few realized at the time) was misinterpreted
as a cruel joke at an old man's expense.

From the square take Rue Ravignan, turn
left onto Rue des Abbesses, then second right
onto Rue Houdon, where you can pop in at
Chez Cerisette [6], on the left side of the
road, for a glass of wine or a bite to eat.

Head back up Rue Houdon, turn right again
onto Rue des Abbesses then left onto Rue des
Martyrs, address of several popular night
spots: **Chez Claude et Claudine [7]** at No. 94
(*see* p.330), which stays open late at night,
ladling out bowls of onion soup (among
other tasty dishes); **Michou [8]**, at No. 80
(*see* p.353), offering a popular drag show and
satires of French celebrities; and **La Fourmi
[9]**, nearby at No.74 (*see* p.345), which is
always packed with a bohemian crowd. Then

just down at No.75, one of the city's best world music clubs, **Divan du Monde [10]** (*see* p.352), sashays most nights to South American sounds.

Below, Rue des Martyrs runs into the neon-bright boulevards where the legend of 'Gay Paree' was born in the Naughty Nineties, sparkling like champagne, frivolous and kicking higher than anyone had ever kicked before, exposing erotic inches of bare flesh under the petticoats. Although part of old Montmartre, today this area is better known as **Pigalle**, Paris' red-light district. In the 1930s, a young Edith Piaf sang in the streets while picking out potential rich women for the pimp she loved, who would then move in to seduce, then rob them in the alleys. The city's literature contains a thousand similar stories; now local businesses take pride in the fact that Pigalle at night is the safest place in Paris.

If upper Montmartre is forever linked in nostalgia's eye to Renoir's lighthearted *Moulin de la Galette*, these nether regions are tinted by Manet's absinthe drinkers and Toulouse-Lautrec's unblinkered depiction of the Parisian demi-monde: its prostitutes, singers and dancers. Even after Pigalle became respectable for the bourgeoisie to visit with the Paris Exposition of 1889, tales of quiet desperation surfaced with regularity, tangible on winter days, when the trees are bare and a greyness seizes it by the throat. This is the world of manic gaiety and tragedy fictionalized by Zola's *Nana* and Dumas' *La Dame aux Camélias*; the beautiful real-life model for the latter, Alphonsine Plessis, died aged 23 and lies buried in the Cimetière du Montmartre (*see* p.196), just behind the bright lights of Boulevard de Clichy.

At night, however, you just may pick up the lingering perfume of Gay Paree. If you turn left at the bottom of Rue des Martyrs onto

Boulevard de Rochechouart, the first old Montmartre institution you come to, the old vaudeville theatre **La Cigale[11]**, at No.120 (*see* p.351), has morphed into a rock concert venue. At No.72, the **Elysée Montmartre [12]** (*see* p.347) was the first cabaret on Montmartre's boulevards, founded over two centuries ago during the reign of Napoleon III. The cancan got its start here, and although the idea and its stars were lured away to the Moulin Rouge, the Elysée is a survivor, and in its current incarnation is one of the best places in Paris to dance to alternative or world music. At No.62, the **Canotier du Pied de la Butte [13]** (*see* p.353) is a long-time favourite of the French, who come to join in the singsongs until dawn.

From here backtrack along the boulevard to the square that gave its name to the quarter, Place Pigalle. You may want to earmark the **Folie's Pigalle [14]**, 11 Place Pigalle (*see* p.352), for later reference; here no one bats an eye if you turn up for a drink at 7am, just as the rest of Paris is waking up to go to work. The **Chao Ba Café [15]**, overlooking the square (*see* p.345), is a trendy nightspot with comfortable bamboo chairs, cocktails and Indo-Chinese food.

Follow Boulevard de Clichy to Place Blanche, the epicentre of Montmartre by night. Here the **Moulin Rouge [16]**, 82 Boulevard de Clichy (*see* p.198), from the same vintage as the Eiffel Tower, still spins its famous sails, its legend renewed yet again by the recent film. If watching the cancanning Dorris girls over a bottle of champagne is too much of a historical burp, you can strut your own stuff on the three storeys of dance floors at **La Locomotive [17]** nearby (*see* p.348). Finish up in Place Clichy, where there's the 1930s style **Charlot Roi des Coquillages [18]** (*see* p.329), with oysters and other shellfish, open nightly until 1am.

Day Trips

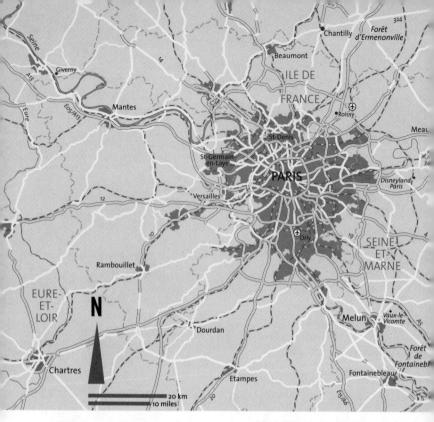

VERSAILLES

t 01 30 83 77 77, *w* www.chateauversailles.com; no pushchairs allowed in château. **Open** May–Sept Tues–Sun 9–6.30, Oct–April Tues–Sun 9–5.30, closed hols; **adm** €7.50, reduced adm after 3.30pm, free 1st Sun of the month Oct–Mar (Grands Appartements and Galerie des Glaces only; very busy); gardens free summer 7–dusk, winter 8–dusk. No credit cards. Buy in advance to avoid queues. Entrance A: Grands Appartements/Galerie des Graces/Appurtement de la Reine. Entrance C: tour with an audioguide (€4 extra). Entrance D: guided tours in English (€4 extra for 1hr tour, €6 extra for 90min tour) covering different parts of the château. Guided tour of gardens €3; horse-drawn carriage rides around park from €7.

'Don't copy my liking for war or my taste in building.'

Louis XIV, on his deathbed, to Louis XV

Versailles' name comes from the clods that the farmer turns over with his plough, referring to the clearing made for a royal hunting lodge. And so Versailles remained until the young Louis XIV attended the fatal bash at Fouquet's Vaux-le-Vicomte (*see* pp.296–7), which turned him sour with envy. He would have something perhaps not better but certainly bigger, and hired all the geniuses Fouquet had patronized to create for himself one of the world's masterpieces of megalomania: 123 acres of rooms. They are strikingly void of art; the enormous façade of the château is as monotonous as it is tasteful, so as not to upstage the principal inhabitant. The object is not to think of the building, but of Louis, and with that thought be awed. It is the shibboleth of France, the albatross around her neck.

Versailles contributed greatly to the bankruptcy of France: Louis, used to overawing his subjects, began to hallucinate that he could bully nature as well. He ordered his engineers to divert the Loire itself to feed his fountains, and when faced with the impossible, settled on bringing the waters of the Eure through pestilent marshes to Versailles by way of the aqueduct of Maintenon, a 10-year project that cost nine million *livres* and the lives of hundreds of workmen before it was abandoned. Too much sacrifice and money has been concentrated here for the French to shake the albatross loose; they are part of it.

If there's no art in Versailles, there is certainly an extraordinary amount of skilful craftsmanship. Besides its main purpose as a stage for Louis (Versailles and its gardens were open to anyone who was decently dressed and promised not to beg in the halls; anyone could watch the king attend Mass or dine), the palace served as a giant public showroom for French products, especially from the new luxury industries cranked up by Colbert. As such it was a spectacular success, contributing greatly to the spread of French tastes and fashions throughout Europe. Today, Versailles' curators haunt the auction houses of the world, looking to replace as much of the original decoration as

Getting There

By Train

Trains from Gare Montparnasse and Gare St-Lazare go to Versailles-Rive Droite, from where it's a 15min walk. The RER C goes to Versailles-Rive Gauche, which is 700m from the château. Make sure you take the train showing the correct destination (the code on the front of the train will begin with the letter V). The journey takes about 45mins from the centre of Paris.

By Bus

Bus no.171 from Paris Pont de Sèvres (end of métro line 9) stops at Versailles Place d'Armes. The journey takes about 30mins.

By Car

Versailles is 20km west of Paris towards Rouen, accessible from the D10 or A13 (take the Versailles-Château exit). The journey should take about 30mins, and there is parking (for a fee) in the Place d'Armes in front of the château.

Tourist Information

2 bis Av de Paris, **t** 01 39 24 88 88, **f** 01 39 24 88 89, **e** *tourisme@ot_versailles.fr*. There's also an information desk at each entrance.

Special Events

Musical Fountains

Open April–mid-Oct; *adm* €6. Throughout the summer the musical fountains in the gardens are switched on. All of them still use their original plumbing.

Grandes Fêtes de Nuit

Held on four Saturdays between 3 July and 18 Sept; to book tickets through FNAC or Spectacles Châteaux, call **t** *08 92 70 18 92 or* **t** *01 30 83 78 96.* An annual extravaganza featuring fireworks, illuminated fountains and a 'historical fresco'.

Eating Out

Café in Cour de la Chapelle, *Château de Versailles,* **t** 01 39 50 58 62. **Open** *daily 9.30–6.30.* Sandwiches, pastries, coffees, etc. to eat in or take away.

La Flotille, *Parc du Château, near Grand Canal,* **t** 01 39 51 41 58. **Open** *daily 12–2 and 6.30–12.* Some tables outside. Classic French cuisine – *sole meunière,* etc. A la carte €30.

Place d'Armes is convenient but overcrowded. Try the following instead:

Brasserie du Théâtre, *15 Rue des Réservoirs,* **t** 01 39 50 03 21. Classic brasserie dishes like duck *confit* or *escargots.* A la carte €30 plus.

La Brasserie du Musée, *2–4 Place Gambetta,* **t** 01 39 50 18 08. **Open** *Tues–Sun 10–5. Salon de thé* near the château. Menu €16, à la carte €17; offers take-away too.

Le Terminus de Mille, *4 Place Lyautey,* **t** 01 39 51 10 65. Brasserie five minutes from the château, with a terrace. The €10 menu make it a cheap and popular choice.

Rue Satory and Place du Marché are a little further from the château, but more peaceful.

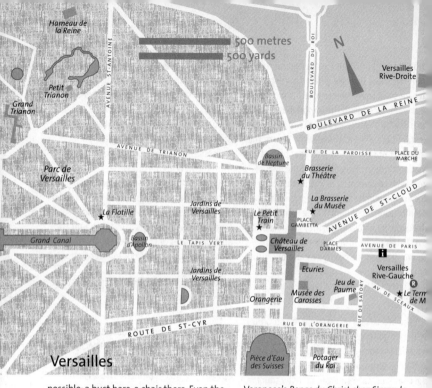

Versailles

possible: a bust here, a chair there. Even the gardens have been replanted with Baroque bowers, as they appeared in the time of Louis XIV. One thing the restorers don't care to recreate is the palace plumbing. A mere three toilets catered for the estimated 20,000 residents, servants and daily visitors.

After Louis XVI and Marie-Antoinette were evicted by the Paris mob on 6 October 1789, Versailles was left empty, and there was talk of razing it when Louis-Philippe decided to restore it as a museum.

Grands Appartements

These are the public rooms traditionally open to all in Louis XIV's day, though when it's crowded, you may feel as squeezed as toothpaste in a tube. There's the elliptical, two-storey Chapelle Royale, the architectural highlight of Versailles; a historical gallery of rooms lined with portraits of royal relatives and views of Versailles; the Grands Appartements, a series of tiresome gilded drawing rooms, each dedicated to a Roman deity. The Salon d'Hercule is designed around the one good painting in the palace,

Veronese's *Repas du Christ chez Simon le Pharisien*; the Salon de Diane has a gutsy bust of Louis by Bernini.

Beyond are the Salle de Guerre and Salle de Paix, linked by the famous 241ft **Hall of Mirrors**. This is still crowned with Lebrun's paintings of the first 17 years of Louis XIV's reign, but lacks the original solid-silver furniture, which Louis had to melt down to pay his war debts. The famous 17 mirrors with 578 panes are post-1975 copies, put in place after a disgruntled Breton blew up the originals; facing the windows, they reflect the sunlight into the gardens, a fantastical conceit intended to remind visitors that the Sun himself dwelt within. He would have become decidedly overcast had he known that on 18 January 1871 another empire – and one that had just completely humiliated France – would create its first *kaiser* here. On 28 June 1919 the Allies, with a fine sense of irony, ended the horrific Act Two of the conflict, by staging the signing of the peace treaty in the same spot.

Beyond the Salle de Paix are the formal apartments of the queen. The rooms required a colossal reconstruction to achieve their current appearance; shreds of fabric were found and rewoven in the original designs, and Savonnerie carpets copied from old designs. The Chambre de la Reine was used for the public birthing of Enfants de France. In the Antechamber, note the portrait of *Marie-Antoinette and Her Children* by Madame Vigée-Lebrun. The Salle du Sacre was created by Louis-Philippe to receive a copy of David's painting of Napoleon's coronation in the Louvre; David actually preferred the copy to his original.

At the far end of the north wing is the Opéra Royal (visitable on the guided tour only), a gem designed by Gabriel for Louis XV in 1768, which is all wood, painted as marble, but designed 'to resonate like a violin'.

Gardens

Then there are the gardens, last replanted by Napoleon III, with their 13 miles of box hedges to clip, and the 1,100 potted palms and oranges of the Orangerie, all planted around the 'limitless perspective' from the terrace fading into the blue horizon of the Grand Canal. Not by accident, the sun sets straight into it on St Louis' day, 25 August, in a perfect alignment with the Hall of Mirrors. On either side, Le Nôtre's original garden design – more theatrical and full of surprises than any of his other creations – is slowly being restored. Meanwhile, hundreds of trees have been sacrificed in the name of new vistas of the château, inspired by Louis XIV's guidebook to the gardens, the *Manière de Montrer les Jardins de Versailles*. In it he devised a one-way route for his visitors, for even at their best Le Nôtre's gardens are essentially two-dimensional, and best appreciated when seen from just the right angle.

Louis kept a flotilla of gondolas on his Grand Canal, to take his courtiers for rides; today the gondoliers of Venice come to visit every September for the Fêtes Vénitiennes. The rest of the year you can hire a boat to paddle about in, a bike to cycle through the gardens, or even catch a little zoo train.

Restoration work began in 2003 on 25 sites around the castle and gardens; sections of the king's apartments will be restored, as will the derelict Orangerie.

Grand Trianon and Petit Trianon

Open *April–Oct daily 12–6.30, Nov–Mar daily 12–5.30; adm €5. Le Petit Train does round trips from the Parterre Nord to the Trianons; fare €5.*

Far more interesting than the main palace, the Grand Trianon is an elegant, airy Italianate palace of pink marble and porphyry with two wings linked by a peristyle. It was designed by the staff of Hardouin-Mansart in 1687 for Louis XIV ('I built Versailles for the court, Marly for my friends, and Trianon for myself,' he said). After his divorce, Napoleon brought his new Empress Marie-Louise here, who did it up attractively in the Empire style.

The gardens in this area were laid out by Louis XV's architect, Jacques-Ange Gabriel, who also built the rococo Pavillon du Jardin des Français and the refined Petit Trianon nearby, intended for Louis XV's meetings with Madame de Pompadour. Louis XVI gave the Petit Trianon to Marie-Antoinette, who spent much of her time here. On a torpid afternoon around 5pm on 10 August 1901, two Englishwomen, Miss Moberly and Miss Jourdain, were wandering through the wood near here when they went into an uncanny time warp: through the trees they saw a woman in white, dressed in the 18th-century fashion, a man running urgently, a gardener and ladies playing a 'Chinese ring' game. Feeling increasingly uneasy, the two women withdrew; when no one could explain what they had seen, they researched the site, and came to the conclusion that the woman in white was none other than Marie-Antoinette and the man running was a messenger warning her that the Parisians were marching on Versailles; the Chinese ring game, long forgotten, was rediscovered by archaeologists, who confirmed other details as well. The story draws a crowd of wannabe time travellers to the same spot every 10 August. Beyond the Petit Trianon is the Hameau de la Reine, the delightful operetta farmhouse built for Marie-Antoinette, where she could play shepherdess.

Petites Ecuries

Fifty metres from the entrance of the palace on Av Rockefeller, t 01 39 02 07 14. Open Tues–Fri 9–1, Sat–Sun 11–2; adm €7. Musical performances Sat and Sun 2.15–3; adm €15.

A new incentive, under the direction of the famous horse-trainer Bartabas, has brought the horses back to Versailles. The royal stables are now open to the public, and every morning you can witness the training of the equerries and their horses inside the prestigious main arena. For the ultimate horsey show, take in the musical performance, every weekend. This features the equerries' carousel plus an equestrian improvisation.

Musée des Carosses

Right next door to the Grande Écurie, t 01 30 83 77 88. Open March–April, Sat–Sun 2–5.30; May–Sept, Sat–Sun 2–6.30; adm €1.90

This small museum presents a collection of both noble and royal coaches used for baptisms, weddings, coronations, funerals and the like. Among these fairytale carriages are the royal sleighs, which were used along the frozen Grand Canal in the wintertime.

Le Potager du Roi and Salle du Jeu de Paume

Garden: entrance at 6 Rue Hardy, on the left side of Place des Armes, t 01 39 24 62 62, f 01 39 24 62 01. Open April–Oct daily 10–6; adm Mon–Fri €4.50, Sat and Sun €6.50. Guided tours Sat and Sun every hour 10.30–4.30; book ahead by phone. Jeu de Paume: 1 Rue du Jeu-de-Paume, t 01 30 83 77 88. Open May–Sept Sat–Sun 2–5; adm free.

Nothing escaped Louis XIV's attention: even his carrots and cabbages were planted in geometric rigidity in his immaculate vegetable garden, the Potager du Roi, arranged to please all five senses. The adjacent Parc Balbi, a romantic park planted by the Comte de Provence (future Louis XVIII) fo his mistress, is no longer open to the public.

As an antidote to Versailles, visit the little Museum of the Revolution in nearby **Salle du Jeu de Paume**, where the Third Estate made its famous Tennis Court Oath on 20 June 1789 to promise France a constitution.

CHARTRES

A world away from Versailles in spirit, Chartres lies at the edge of the Beauce, a flat, pleasant country that has always supplied the capital with much of its grain. But the famous photo view of France's greatest cathedral, with its Gothic towers rising over the horizon from a field of wheat, is becoming harder to find these days as the growing town spreads out over the surrounding countryside.

The Romans found this part of Gaul inhabited by a tribe called the Carnutes, after whom Chartres is named. The village, built around a sacred well, was an important religious site from the earliest times. As such it was a key target for the Christians. They may have taken it over as early as the 4th century, substituting the worship of the Virgin Mary for that of the ancient mother goddess, who ruled over wells and underground springs. A primeval wooden statue of the goddess, recycled as Mary, was worshipped here as late as 1793. The first Christian basilica was built in the 4th century and rebuilt several times.

Chartres Cathedral

Chartres, t 02 37 21 59 08. Open May–Oct 8–8, Jan–April and Nov–Dec 8–7.15; adm free. Mass on Mon, Wed, Thurs and Sat 11.45am and 6pm; Tues and Fri 9am, 11.45am and 6pm; Sun 9.15am (Gregorian Mass), 11am and 6pm. Guided tours in English May–Oct Mon–Sat 12 and 2.45; meet at entrance to gift shop.

Getting There

By Train

There are regular departures from Gare Montparnasse. The journey takes around 1hr.

By Car

Chartres is southwest of Paris. Either take the A6 *autoroute* from the Porte d'Orléans towards Bordeaux-Nantes, followed by the A10 and A11 towards Nantes; or take the RN10 from the Porte de St-Cloud towards Rambouillet. The journey takes about 1¼hrs.

Tourist Information

Place de la Cathédrale, **t** 02 37 18 26 26.

Eating Out

Brûlerie les Rois Mages, *6 Rue des Changes*, **t** *02 37 36 30 52*. **Open** *Tues–Sun 9.15–12.15 and 2–7.15, Mon 2–7.15*. *Salon de thé* near the cathedral.

Brasserie Bruneau, *4 Rue du Maréchal-de-Lattre-de-Tassigny*, **t** *02 37 21 80 99*. **Open** *Mon–Fri lunch and dinner, Sat dinner*. **Inexpensive**. Traditional brasserie near the town hall.

Le Buisson Ardent, *10 Rue au Lait*, **t** *02 37 34 04 66*. **Open** *Thurs–Sat and Mon–Tues 12–2 and 7.30–9.30, Sun 12–2*. **Inexpensive**. Popular and easy-going restaurant overlooking the cathedral.

Au P'tit Morard, *25 Rue de la Porte-Morard*, **t** *02 37 34 15 89*. **Open** *Thurs–Sat all day; Mon, Tues and Sun for breakfast and lunch, closed 2 weeks Feb and 3 weeks Aug*. **Inexpensive**. A restaurant in the lower part of town with a terrace. Book.

Don't wonder that such a small town should have managed such an impressive cathedral. Medieval Chartres, about the same size as the present version, was relatively much more important; in the 11th century its cathedral school was an internationally known centre of learning, a rival to Paris itself. The current building took form after a fire in 1194 destroyed a brand-new cathedral. Rebuilding commenced immediately and contributed much to the legend of pious community participation in cathedral building. Everyone pitched in with labour or funds to complete the inspired new design for the 'Palace of the Virgin' – even Kings Philippe-Auguste and Richard the Lionheart, who were then fighting over the area. By 1260 the building was nearly complete; the rapidity of the work allowed Chartres to have a stylistic unity seen in few other medieval cathedrals. Its construction also shows many advances in the new Gothic architecture, such as the carving of thick pillars into apparent bundles of slender columns, to accentuate the verticality and lightness of the building.

Chartres also perfects the concepts of roof vaulting and the flying buttress, allowing it to be the widest of all Gothic cathedrals, while letting in more light with big windows in the clerestory and especially in the magnificent apse, which is nearly all glass.

In the words of Émile Mâle: 'Chartres is medieval thought in visible form.' More than 10,000 figures in stone or glass complete the encyclopedia in stone, which would take a thorough knowledge of Scripture and medieval philosophy and a lifetime's work to decipher properly.

The **west porch** survived the 1194 fire, and is the oldest part of the cathedral. Besides the exquisite statues of saints that flank the doors, note on the left door the zodiac signs and works of the months, one of the loveliest of the Gothic 'stone calendars'. While the tympanum of the central portal is dedicated to Christ (in an almond-shaped mandorla, surrounded by the symbols of the Evangelists), those on the sides belong to Mary: an *Annunciation* (left) and *Assumption* (right). The façade's south tower is original; the northern one was struck by lightning and rebuilt in the Flamboyant style in the 14th century.

The **south porch** honours the saints: the martyrs (right door), Apostles (central door) and confessors (left door), surmounted by nine choirs of angels: seraphim, cherubim, thrones, dominations and all the rest. The

north porch, less extravagant, includes a tympanum of the *Adoration of the Magi*.

Inside, your attention will be caught between the brilliance of the architecture and the finest **stained-glass windows** ever: 173 of them, mostly originals. In Chartres it was the custom for the city guilds to supply these; look at the bottoms of the windows along the nave, and in many you will see scenes of the contributing guild's members at work: goldsmiths, bakers, weavers, tavern-keepers, blacksmiths, moneychangers, furriers and many others. Especially good are the windows in the apse, picturing the life of Christ (a *Tree of Jesse*, etc.), and the great rose windows, especially the *Rose de France* in the north transept, celebrating the Virgin. The rose in the south transept represents Christ in Glory, as in the Book of Revelation.

On the floor of the nave, the famous labyrinth (sometimes covered by chairs) is now almost unique in France; many other Gothic cathedrals had similar ones, but most were destroyed in the 18th century. A large exhibition erected off the nave attempts to explain the Christian meaning of the maze, but it's an utter fabrication; there simply isn't one. The symbolism of labyrinths since the remotest times has always had something to do with the passage of the soul and with astronomy; here it may also reflect the patterns of a dance, a survival of pre-Christian times. Originally, there was a bronze relief of Theseus and the Minotaur at the centre of this one. Below, in the crypt, the ancient sacred wells still survive.

Just behind the cathedral, to the left, the **Musée des Beaux-Arts** (*29 Cloître Notre-Dame*, **t** *02 37 36 41 39. Open summer Wed–Sat 10–12 and 2–6, Sun 2–6; winter Wed–Sat 10–12 and 2–5, Sun 2–5; adm €1.50*) has a fine collection of tapestries and Renaissance paintings.

GIVERNY: MAISON DE MONET

Fondation Claude Monet: *Rue Claude Monet,* **t** *02 32 51 28 21,* **w** *www.fondation-monet. com.* **Open** *April–Oct Tues–Sun and Mon hols 10–6; adm €5.50.* **Musée d'Art Américain**: *99 Rue Claude-Monet,* **t** *02 32 51 94 65,* **w** *www. maag.org.* **Open** *March–Oct/Nov Tues–Sun 10–6, closed last 2 weeks in August; adm €5.50. Pleasant café-terrace.*

The Impressionists' Impressionist Claude Monet moved out to this charming house in 1883 and stayed here until he died in 1926, immersed in his Japanese prints and the gorgeous chromatic gardens and water lily ponds he designed, each section arranged to bloom in a predominant colour. A subterranean passage links the ponds and gardens, separated in Monet's day only by a seldom-used railway line. The huge studio he

Getting There

By Train

The nearest train station to Giverny is 6km away in Vernon (35min from Gare St-Lazare; take trains for Rouen). From Vernon there are bus and taxi connections to Giverny, as well as bikes for hire.

By Car

Take the A13 west of Paris towards Rouen via Vernon. The journey takes about 1½ hrs.

Eating Out

Ancien Hôtel Baudy, *81 Rue Claude Monet*, **t** *02 32 21 10 03.* **Open** *April–Oct Tues–Sat* 9am–9pm and Sun lunch. A bistrot with a menu for €18.50.

Restaurant Les Nymphéas, *Rue Claude Monet*, **t** *02 32 21 20 31.* **Open** *April–Oct Tues–Sun and Mon hols 9–8.* **Moderate.** Snacks, salads and ice creams.

Charcuterie Michel Vauvelle, *60 Rue Claude Monet*, **t** *02 32 51 28 29.* **Open** *Tues–Sun 8am–7pm (Nov–Mar closed 1–3).* Good for picking up a picnic or a sandwich to take away.

La Terrasse, *87 Rue Claude Monet*, **t** *02 32 51 36 09.* **Open** *April–Oct Tues–Sun and hol Mons 10–7.* Inexpensive *salon de thé* and shop with regional specialities.

designed for his water lily canvases is now a boutique. May, June and July, the best months to visit, are simply drunk with colour.

To see what Monet's American colleagues were up to, visit Giverny's Musée d'Art Américain, up the road.

ST-GERMAIN-EN-LAYE

Château de St-Germain-en-Laye and Musée des Antiquités Nationales

Place du Château, **t** *01 39 10 13 00; wheelchair access.* **Open** *Wed–Mon 9–5.15;* **adm** *€4.*

Getting There

By Train

RER A to the end of the line: St-Germain-en-Laye (about 20mins from the Étoile).

By Bus

Bus no.258 goes between La Défense and St-Germain, but the RER is the most sensible way to get there.

By Car

Take Avenue de la Grande Armée from the Étoile towards La Défense and follow signs to St-Germain. The journey takes about 30mins.

Tourist Information

38 Rue au Pain, **t** 01 34 51 05 12, **w** www.ville-st-germain-en-laye.fr.

Eating Out

La Feuillantine, *10 Rue des Louviers,* **t** *01 34 51 04 24.* **Open** *daily 12–2 and 7.30–10.* **Expensive.** Cosy and busy restaurant serving good-value reliable fare. Booking advisable.

La Petite Province, *16 Rue du Vieil Abreuvoir,* **t** 01 39 73 88 88. **Open** *Tues–Sat 12.30–9.30.* Wine bar also serving food (€30).

Tarte Julie, *3 Rue du Vieil Abreuvoir,* **t** 01 39 73 95 11. **Open** *Tues–Sun 11.30–6.30,* **closed** *Sun in July and Aug. Salon de thé.*

West of La Défense, the old town of St-Germain-en-Laye grew up around a priory founded by Robert the Pious in 1050. The priory became a château, lavishly rebuilt in brick by François I, and it saw the dawn of the Sun King, who spent most of his first 40 pre-Versailles years here and hired Le Nôtre to lay out the long **gardens**. There are regular tours of the château. The excellent museum has an archaeological collection ranging from Lower Palaeolithic to Merovingian France.

Musée Départemental Maurice Denis-Le Prieuré

2 bis Rue Maurice Denis, **t** *01 39.73 77 87.* **Open** *Tues–Fri 10–5.30; Sat, Sun and hols 10–6.30;* **adm** *€3.80; guided tour Sun 3.30 (€1.50 extra).*

The Marquise de Montespan's old digs houses richly coloured Symbolist and Nabis paintings by Denis, Bonnard, Vuillard and Co.

CHANTILLY

Beyond suburbia lie the former domains of the Montmorencys, a pretty piece of real estate picked up by these wealthy counts through marriage. The family château in Chantilly is now a museum.

Château et Musée Condé

t *03 44 62 62 62.* **Open** *Mar–Oct Wed–Mon (Aug daily) 10–6, Nov–Feb 10.30–12.45 and 2–5;* **adm** *€6.50.* **Park** *open March–Oct daily 10–7, Nov–Feb daily 10.30–5;* **adm** *€2.50.*

Chantilly, birthplace of whipped cream, has long been rich and coveted. It began as an island in a bog topped with a Roman fort, which in feudal times the Montmorencys made into a castle with a moat. This was rebuilt in the Renaissance by a boy named Anne, the Grand Connétable Anne de Montmorency, who had 29 other estates to live in while work progressed.

Getting There

By Train

Chantilly is on the line to Compiègne or Creil (30mins). RER D also goes to Chantilly. The Château is 2km from the station.

To get to Ermenonville, take RER B3 to Charles-de-Gaulle I and then the bus.

By Car

Take the A1 *autoroute* north of Paris. The journey should take about 45mins.

Tourist Information

60 Av du Maréchal Joffre, **t** 03 44 67 37 37, **w** *www.ville-chantilly.fr*.

Eating Out

Capitainerie du Château, *Château de Chantilly*, **t** 03 44 57 15 89. **Open** Wed–Mon lunch only. **Moderate**. Convenient self-service restaurant for a snack or a full meal.

Restaurant Le Goutillon, *61 Rue du Connétable, Chantilly*, **t** 03 44 58 01 00. **Open** daily 12–3 and 6–12. **Moderate**. Friendly restaurant with stone walls and wooden beams. Snails a speciality.

Musée Vivant du Cheval Restaurant. **Open** Wed–Mon 12–4. **Inexpensive**. Good for lunch and snacks.

Anne's granddaughter Charlotte caught the roving eye of Henri IV, who thought the best way to have his evil way with her would be to marry her off to a complaisant husband, Henri de Bourbon-Condé; the plan backfired when the groom refused to recognize the king's *droit de seigneur*, and the old skirt-chaser showed his displeasure by exiling the young couple. They were able to return to Chantilly in 1643, after the king's death, and left the estate to their son, the Grand Condé, who brought the château its greatest fame, commissioning gardens and fountains from Le Nôtre.

The grandson of the Grand Condé, who knew he would be reincarnated as a horse, built for his future self the Grandes Écuries, one of the most palatial stables in the world. These have endured as the Musée Vivant du Cheval (before the château, near the edge of Chantilly's prestigious racecourse; *see* below), while the Renaissance château was destroyed in the Revolution, rebuilt and destroyed again in 1848. What you see today is the fifth in the same spot, overlooking the former bog – now a mirror of waters.

Inside the château, the art collection of the **Musée Condé** is one of the best in France outside the Louvre: a fine if somewhat dottily hung selection from the Italian Renaissance, with works by Annibale Carracci, Palma Vecchio, Raphael, Andrea del Sarto, Filippino Lippi, Mazzolino, a sad sweet *Virgin* by Perugino, a very linear *Autumn* by Botticelli, a

surreal Sassetta and from oddball Piero di Cosimo the *Portrait of Simonetta Vespucci*, wearing a viper around her neck. There are exceptional French works: by François Clouet Watteau, Poussin, and Jean Fouquet's *Livre d'Heures d'Étienne Chevalier* (1460); beautiful monochrome windows in the Galerie de Psyché on the Legend of the Golden Ass, made by a follower of Raphael for Anne de Montmorency; Ingres' *Antioche et Stratonice*, a famous piece of neoclassical kitsch; and portraits: of the 'Big Bastard of Bourgogne' (Flemish, 15th century), of Talleyrand (who does look like a 'living corpse', as one Englishman described him), of Molière about to cock a brow and laugh (by Pierre Mignard) of Louis XIV daintily lifting his fleur-de-lys skirts (by Hyacinthe Rigaud), of Bonaparte, First Consul (by Gérard), the only picture covered with glass, as if the administrators expected someone to spit on it, and a *Déjeuner de Jambon*, by Watteau's follower Lancret, a typical scene of gluttony, enjoyed by French nobles as much as the petite bourgeoisie of the Dutch genre painters. The jewel of the collection, the **Très Riches Heures du Duc de Berry**, that unparalleled masterpiece of early 15th-century illuminator's art, is hidden in the library, where you have to go with a guide, and even then all you are permitted to see are well-made facsimiles.

So much for great art; but it's the horse palace built by Condé's grandson that gets most of the visitors these days (*see* below).

Musée Vivant du Cheval

Château stables, **t** *03 44 57 40 40.* **Open** *Wed–Mon 10.30–6.30; three dressage demonstrations daily, call for times;* **adm** *€8.*

There are 30 beautifully groomed horses of nearly every conceivable breed, some 31 rooms of horsey artefacts and toys, audio-visuals and models of everything Old Paint or Black Beauty is useful for, except those Parisian horseburgers.

Forêt d'Ermenonville

Mer de Sable: **t** *03 44 54 00 96.* **Open** *summer only daily 10.30–6.30, weekends until 7;* **adm** *€15.50, child €13.50.*

Chantilly has the most beautiful forest in the Île-de-France, dividing it from the A1. This is where Rousseau spent his last months, as a guest of the Marquis de Girardin, and where he died and was buried before being Pantheonized. If you have a car and children, consider the forest's 50-acre Mer de Sable on the N330: a sea of sand dunes left over from the Tertiary Age, fitted out with all the usual kids' activities, including rides, a train, shows, and camel excursions.

DISNEYLAND

Disneyland Paris is in Marne-la-Vallée, about 20 miles east of Paris. Booking from UK **t** *0870 606 6800; booking from USA* **t** *33 1 60 30 60 81; booking from France* **t** *01 60 30 60 53 (lines open daily);* **w** *www.disneylandparis.com; wheelchair access,* **t** *01 60 30 10 20 for visitors with special needs.* **Open** *July–Aug 9am–11pm, rest of the year 9am–8pm;* **adm** *adult passport high season: 1 day €39, 3 days €107; it's usually worth booking a package and staying on site for the full experience and better value for money. Tickets are available at the*

Getting There

By Train

From April–Sept **Eurostar** (**t** 08705 186 186; **w** *www.eurostar.com*) runs a daily service from London Waterloo/Ashford International to Disneyland Paris which takes just 3hrs (2hrs from Ashford). If booked in advance it can cost as little as £100 return. For package trips on Eurostar call **t** 0870 167 67 67. At other times it is best to change at Lille for a TGV, which will take you direct to the park.

From Paris, RER A goes direct to the park (direction Marne-la-Vallée-Chessy). From central Paris (e.g. Etoile, Auber or Châtelet) it takes about 40mins. Remember to buy a ticket before you travel as the usual métro tickets are not valid.

By Bus

There are transfers direct from Orly and Roissy airports which run every 45mins: Roissy Mon–Thurs and Sat 8.30am–7.45pm, Fri and Sun 8.30am–9.30pm; Orly daily 8.30am–7.30pm, Fri also at 8.30pm, 9.15pm and 9.45pm. The journey time from either airport is about 45mins. The shuttle stops at all the hotels in the park and near the main entrance. Adults €14 one way. Tickets can be bought on board the shuttle, at Aéroport de Paris desks in the terminal buildings or at your travel agents before you travel.

By Car

Take the A4 motorway east toward Metz-Nancy. Follow signs for Marne-la-Vallée until junction 14.

Tourist Information

City Hall, on the left-hand side of the entrance to Main Street, USA, is the park's central information point. There is also a seasonal information point at the far end of Main Street, USA, in Central Plaza. If you still have any unanswered questions or concerns head for the guest-relations window situated to the right-hand side of the main entrance as you approach the theme park, under the railway arch.

Eating Out

Disneyland has a wide range of restaurants, cafés and snack bars catering for all tastes and appetites.

entrance to the park, but it might be more efficient to buy them in advance, from: any Disney Store in the UK; the Disney Store on the Champs-Elysées in Paris; Virgin Megastore on the Champs-Elysées in Paris; Thomas Cook Bureaux de Change at the UK Eurotunnel Passenger Terminal, and Dover and Portsmouth ferry terminals; on board P&O Stena Line Ferries between Dover and Calais; or tourist offices at Orly and Roissy airports and on the Champs-Elysées in Paris. You can also order a brochure from the telephone numbers given above. Age/height restrictions apply to some rides.

Back in the 1930s, Walt Disney put out a cartoon version of Pinocchio, in which at one point the naughty puppet and other truants end up in an amusement park for bad boys, where they have so much mindless fun they turn into donkeys, and are then captured and sold by the evil owners. The idea must have put a seed in old Walt's brain; the results may now be seen in California, Florida, Tokyo and, since 1992, in the far suburbs of Paris.

'A cultural Chernobyl at the heart of Europe' snarled theatre director Ariane Mnouchkine although, as the French themselves have pointed out, culture in Europe must be pretty thin gruel if it can be threatened by a cartoon mouse. The French government helped bring the fox into the chicken coop – an RER line and TGV line linked up to Marseille, Lyon, Lille, Charles de Gaulle airport and eventually London, and land made available on very favourable terms. Although the first three years were characterized by a brutal baptism in red ink and farcical Franco-American misunderstandings, Disneyland Paris appears to have settled down under French management; the new regime has none of the brash, hip-shooting swagger of the first, American-run years, and no one frets any more about cultural pollution leaking out of Marne-la-Vallée.

The park is a fifth the size of the city of Paris – 1,943 hectares (4,800 acres), protected from the outside world by 30ft sloped dikes. Six large theme hotels are run with that guaranteed 'Have a nice day' friendliness and chocolates-on-the-pillow approach. Besides the rides, the corporate-processed fun includes infinite 'shopping opportunities', special shows, food (American, Mexican, Italian and other European), discothèques and weird American nightlife at the Festival Disney complex. There's also the new Walt Disney Studios, a working cartoon and television studio.

If you go in summer, bring a good book: Tinkerbell herself must have designed the enchanted queue routes for the rides that curl in and out, up and down, all the better to keep you believing you're almost there when there's still half the population of Europe waiting in front of you.

VAUX-LE-VICOMTE AND FONTAINEBLEAU

If you're considering hiring a car for a day trip, make it this one: that way you can combine both châteaux and the sights around the forest of Fontainebleau.

Vaux-le-Vicomte

*t 01 64 14 41 90, w www.vaux-le-vicomte.com. **Open** March–Nov daily 10–6; at other times by appointment, call t 01 64 14 41 90. Fountains: 2nd and last Sat of month 3–6; romantic candlelight tours: May–Oct Sat (and Fri in July–Aug) 8pm–midnight; audioguides available in English; **adm** €12, candlelight tours €15.*

Vaux was the prototype for Versailles but is much prettier: designed by Louis Le Vau and decorated by Charles Lebrun, it is set in the original *jardin à la française* by André Le Nôtre, who had a scale vast enough to play with vanishing points and perspectives to his heart's content. The whole shebang was paid for and masterminded by Nicolas Fouquet, Louis XIV's minister of finances, who adopted

Getting There

By Train

Trains from Gare de Lyon go to Melun (61km); from there take a taxi or shuttle bus 6km to the Château de Vaux-le-Vicomte.

The train to Melun continues to Fontainebleau, 65km from Paris. Get off at Fontainbleau-Avon, then take bus A or B from the station to the centre.

By Bus

City Rama runs tours from Paris on Mon, Thurs and Sat at 1.45. Visits last 5 hours, including a visit to the château. Tours in English are available; call **t** 01 44 55 61 00 for information.

By Car

Fontainebleau is southwest of Paris. Take the A6 or follow signs to Fontainebleau. The journey takes about 1hr.

Tourist Information

4 Rue Royale, Fontainebleau, **t** 01 60 74 99 99, **f** 01 60 74 80 22. Sells detailed maps and hires out bikes, so you can explore the ancient forest paths.

Eating Out

Ty Koz, 18 Rue de la Cloche, Fontainebleau, **t** 01 64 22 00 55. **Open daily 12–11pm (may close some afternooons)**. A crêperie where à la carte costs around €12.

L'Espérance, 117 Rue Grande, Fontainebleau, **t** 01 64 22 23 86; wheelchair accessible. **Open Mon–Sat 7am–1am. Closed 2 weeks in Aug. Inexpensive**. Brasserie with terrace.

Le Caveau des Ducs, 24 Rue de Ferrare, Fontainebleau, **t** 01 64 22 05 05; wheelchair accessible. **Open daily 12–2 and 6–10. Moderate**. Classic French food, including seafood, with a view of the château and terrace.

Hercules as his patron, just as Louis fancied himself as Apollo.

Even if Fouquet aped a decorative mythology on the level of Disney's *Fantasia*, the concept of Vaux was undeniably Herculean. Not only did Fouquet unite the greatest talents of his time (Madame de Sévigné and La Fontaine were among his other 'discoveries'), but he created this country palace and gardens in only five years, employing 20,000 masons, decorators and gardeners, all with one aim in mind: to form a suitable stage for a grand fête to impress one single person, the king, on 17 August 1661. It was, by all accounts, the most splendid party in the history of France. The choicest dishes were prepared on gold and silver plates by Vatel, the famous *maître d'hôtel*; the great Lully composed music for the occasion, the *comédie-ballet* was by Fouquet's friend Molière, 1,200 jets of water danced from the fountains, elephants decked in jewels lingered among the orange trees, while Italian fireworks wizards astounded all with their artistry. The 23-year-old Louis was certainly impressed; and so miffed that he refused to sleep in the *chambre du roi* built just for him.

Vaux was used as lavish proof of Fouquet's graft and cited in his embezzlement trial three years later, but it wasn't the expense that got Louis' goat that famous night; after all, limitless graft by treasurers was built into the still-feudal system, and Cardinal Mazarin had filched much more. What niggled Apollo was that Hercules, a mere mortal, had upstaged him not only in extravagance but as an arbiter of taste (Vaux suggests that style Louis XIV should really be called style Fouquet). And like Apollo, who was often cruel, Louis punished Fouquet's hubris, personally intervening in his trial to insist on a sentence of solitary confinement for life. The king confiscated all Fouquet's property. Then he confiscated Fouquet's ideas to create Versailles, hiring Le Vau, Lebrun and Le Nôtre to repeat their work at Vaux, but on an appalling scale; Fouquet's tapestry weavers and furniture makers were employed to form the nucleus of the Gobelins factories (*see* pp.271–2); Louis hired Fouquet's firework makers to illuminate his own fêtes; he even carted off Fouquet's 1,200 orange trees for his Orangerie at Versailles.

In the 19th century, Le Nôtre's gardens, with their clipped hedges, statues and elaborate waterworks, were restored. Period furnishings and tapestries from the Gobelins and Savonnerie complement the surviving decorations, which include Lebrun's portraits of Fouquet in the Salon d'Hercule and his poignantly unfinished ceiling in the **Grand Salon**. Another salon honours La Fontaine, who wrote *L'Elégie aux Nymphes de Vaux* for his fallen patron, a touching tribute from one of the Classical Age's sweetest characters, if the most absent-minded. (Once he walked past his own son, and asked, with a puzzled air: 'Haven't I seen that young man somewhere before?') Vaux's stables contain the **Musée des Équipages**, full of beautiful antique carriages. Lastly, look for the carved squirrels, Fouquet's family symbol (because they hoard all their goodies).

Fontainebleau

Château de Fontainebleau

*t 01 60 71 50 70. **Open** June–Sept Wed–Mon 9.30–6, Oct–May Wed–Mon 9.30–5; closed 1 Jan, 1 May, 25 Dec; **adm** €5.50. Petits Appartements and museum tours by appt only, t 01 60 71 50 60; **adm** €3. **Park** open summer daily 9–7, winter daily 9–5.*

At weekends half of Paris seems to be here; the forest, with its wonderful variety of flora – including 2,700 species of mushrooms and fungi – oak and pine woods, rocky escarpments and dramatic gorges, is the wildest place near the metropolis. It was always exceptionally rich in game and by 1150 had already been set aside as the royal hunting reserve of Louis the Fat. The medieval kings managed with a fortified castle/hunting lodge, but then along came François I, who chose Fontainebleau to be his artistic showcase. Down went most of the old castle and up went an elegant château, fit to be decorated by the artists the king had imported from Italy, especially the great Rosso Fiorentino, a student of Michelangelo, but a man so badly shaken by the brutal sacking of Rome in 1527 that he was half-mad and ended up committing suicide. Rosso and his fellow Mannerist Primaticcio (Primatice, in

French) had a decisive influence on the French artists of the first École de Fontainebleau (led by Jean Goujon, Jean Cousin and Antoine Caron), whose hallmarks were an extreme refinement and eroticism. Work on the château continued under Henri II and the exquisite architect Philibert de l'Orme. Henri IV added two courts decorated by Flemish artists, who influenced a second, if less original, École de Fontainebleau. Every subsequent ruler to Napoleon added to the place; the Revolution destroyed most of its furnishings, while Louis-Philippe hired ham-handed restorers, who left much of the art a shadow of itself. With contributions from so many monarchs, the château makes an interesting style book. Enter through the **Cour des Adieux**, where Napoleon bid farewell to his Imperial Guard after his abdication on 20 April 1814 and Louis XIII built the magnificent horseshoe staircase.

The tour of the **Grands Appartements** includes the famous Galerie François I (1533–7), with Rosso's repainted frescoes framed in the original stuccoes; the Michelangelo-influenced Chapelle de la Trinité and the extraordinary, sumptuous Salle de Bal, both built under Henri II. It also takes in the Chambre de l'Impératrice, with Marie-Antoinette's elaborate bed, and the Salle du Trône, designed for Napoleon. Other rooms were used by Pius VII during his stay in Paris.

The **Petits Appartements** are less grand than their cousins, but just as interesting.

Also to see in the château is the **Musée Napoléon Ier**, concentrating on the daily life of a self-made emperor.

Gardens

Fontainebleau's gardens, notably the Parterre, were first laid out by François; Henri IV added the water, dubbed the *Tibre*, and Le Nôtre rearranged the whole into geometric gardens, although his urge to create the illusion of infinite perspectives was checked by the plans of his predecessors. In 1812, Napoleon ordered English gardens planted around the Fontaine Belle-Eau.

Where to Stay

There are basically three kinds of hotels in the centre of Paris: big luxury and grand hotels, mainly on the Right Bank; business hotels, scattered everywhere; and small, privately owned hotels, some very fashionable and some dogged dives, mostly on the near Left Bank.

Advance booking is essential in June, September and October, when Paris is awash with conventions. July and August are the low season, and some expensive hotels offer discounts then. As a general rule, you'll be asked to give the first night's charge as a deposit.

The price categories listed below are for a double room. We have tried to put each hotel in a category, but prices are always subject to change. In most places each room has its own price, depending on its view, plumbing, heated towel racks, etc. This is the French way of doing things, and it's also perfectly normal to visit rooms or press the proprietor for details and negotiate. The one hitch is that there are few single rooms.

Optional continental breakfast costs from €4 at the cheapie places to €30 a head at the Ritz. Many proprietors pretend not to know it's optional, but the same cup of coffee and croissant in the bar across the street will be more fun and save you lots of cash.

The annual hotel list for Paris available from the Office du Tourisme (127 Avenue des Champs-Elysées, 75008) indicates all hotels with facilities for the disabled, as well as the most current prices. The Office du Tourisme rates hotels from five stars to none at all. Note that these ratings reflect plumbing and other amenities (lifts, bar, room telephones, etc.) – not intangible qualities such as tranquillity, ambience or good service.

If you turn up without a booking, go to the Bureau d'Accueil in the Office du Tourisme, 127 Av des Champs-Elysées, **t** 01 49 52 53 54, métro Étoile (*open May–Sept daily 9–8, Oct–April Mon–Sat 9–8, Sun and hols 11–6*). The tourist offices at the Gare de Lyon, Gare du Nord and Eiffel Tower also book accommodation. They charge a small commission.

Where we have said a hotel has wheelchair access, there is at least one room modified for wheelchair users.

Price Categories

luxury	over €230
very expensive	€150–230
expensive	€100–150
moderate	€60–100
inexpensive	below €60

The Islands

Islands have a certain magic, even in urban rivers; these are also central but quiet at night.

Luxury

(46) Jeu de Paume**** AA14
54 Rue St-Louis-en-l'Île, 75004,
t 01 43 26 14 18, **f** 01 43 26 14 76,
w www.hoteldujeudepaume.com;
métro Pont-Marie.
Paris' last real-tennis venue is now the most enchanting little inn on the Seine, complete with a sunny garden, gym and sauna. Lift. Cots available.

Very Expensive

(44) Lutèce*** AA14
65 Rue St-Louis-en-l'Île, 75004,
t 01 43 26 23 52, **f** 01 43 29 60 25,
e hotel.lutece@free.fr; **métro** Pont-Marie.
Charming, tasteful and small. Many of the rooms have beams. Lift. Cots available.

Expensive

(45) Des Deux Iles*** AA14
59 Rue St-Louis-en-l'Île, 75004,
t 01 43 26 13 35, **f** 01 43 29 60 25,
e hotel.2.iles@free.fr; **métro** Pont-Marie.
In an 18th-century house (with a lift), smallish rooms but decorated with period pieces and Provençal fabrics. Rooms have TV and air-con.

(43) Saint-Louis*** Z14
75 Rue St-Louis-en-l'Île, 75004,
t 01 46 34 04 80, **f** 01 46 34 02 13,
w www.hotelsaintlouis.com;
métro Pont-Marie; wheelchair access. No Amex.
Fashionable, antique furniture, but smallish rooms. Lift. Cots available.

Moderate

(42) Hospitel, Hôtel-Dieu Y14
1 Place du Parvis-Notre-Dame, 75004, **t** 01 44 32 01 00, **f** 01 44 32 01 16, **e** hospitelhoteldieu@wanadoo.fr; **métro** Hôtel-de-Ville; wheelchair access.
This is an amazing place to stay if you don't mind the surroundings of a working hospital: just 14 small, spotless, quiet rooms with ensuite bathrooms on the 6th floor of the hospital. Breakfast is served in the rooms; room service available until 9pm. Priority is given to people visiting patients. Access until 10pm is through the main entrance; after 10pm through the side entrance on Rue de la Cité. Lift. Cots available.

Inexpensive

(8) Henri IV W13
25 Place Dauphine, 75001, **t** 01 43 54 44 53; **métro** Pont-Neuf or Cité. No reservations by fax; no credit cards.
400 years old, frumpy flowered wallpaper, and toilets and showers down the hall, yet visitors book months in advance to stay in all simplicity in this most serendipitous square.

The Grand Axe

This is the lap of luxury, as far as hotels go; there are few possibilities below the luxury threshold.

Luxury

Crillon***** Q–R9
10 Place de la Concorde, 75008,
t 01 44 71 15 00, **f** 01 44 71 15 02,

reservations@crillon.com,
w www.crillon.com; **métro**
Concorde; wheelchair access.
Behind the classic 18th-century
façade stands the last luxury hotel
in Paris to remain completely in
French hands. Inside are some of
the most exquisite and prestigious suites in town, and rooms,
if not always grand, are done up
choicely with marble baths to
match. There is a brand new
fitness centre here too. Cots
are available.

George V** L9
31 Av George-V, 75008, t 01 49
52 70 00, f 01 49 52 70 10, e par.
reservations@fourseasons.com,
w www.fourseasons.com; **métro**
George-V.
A hotel with a 3-star Michelin
restaurant and a luxury spa for
decadent pampering. Sumptuous
rooms, luxurious bathrooms.

Hôtel Meurice** S10
228 Rue de Rivoli, 75001, t 01 44
58 10 10, f 01 44 58 10 15,
e reservations@meuricehotel.com,
w www.meuricehotel.com; **métro**
Tuileries; wheelchair access.
This old hotel, which reopened in
July 2000 after a two-year, multi-
million makeover, remains one of
Paris' most opulent places to stay.
Even if you can't stretch to a room
here, pop in for tea in the Jardin
d'Hiver, the palm-filled tearoom
beneath its Art Nouveau glass
roof, or have a drink in the
Fontainebleau bar, decked out in
dark wood, leather armchairs and
trompe l'oeil ceiling. If you're in
the money, the Belle Étoile suite
on the top floor has a 360-degree
view of Paris.

Plaza Athénée** M10
25 Av Montaigne, 75008, t 01 53
67 66 65, f 01 53 67 66 66,
e reservation@plaza-athenee-
paris.com, w www.plaza-athenee-
paris.com; **métro** Franklin D.
Roosevelt or Alma-Marceau;
wheelchair access.
Celebrated for its voluptuous
luxury and superb service – there
are twice as many staff as rooms,
and more money spent on fresh

flowers than lights. Mata Hari was
arrested in its bar, but the spies
have since given way to celebrities
and corporate bosses – business
services, stockmarket information,
and ticket agencies are just
some of the services offered.
Renovations have left the top two
floors with an Art Deco look, and
under new chef Alain Ducasse, the
restaurant now has 3 Michelin
stars. Lift. Cots available.

Raphaël** J8
17 Av Kléber, 75016, t 01 53 64 32 00,
f 01 53 64 32 01, e reservation@
raphael-hotel.com, w www.raphael-
hotel.com; **métro** Kléber; wheelchair access.
Built in the 1920s, and like its
namesake in Rome, the Raphaël is
élite, intimate, splendid and artsy.
There's an English bar and garden
terrace with a view over Paris. Lift.
Cots available.

Vernet** K8
25 Rue Vernet, 75008, t 01 44 31 98
00, f 01 44 31 85 69, e hotelvernet@
jetmultimedia.fr, w www.hotel
vernet.com; **métro** George V or
Charles de Gaulle-Étoile.
Just off Place Charles-de-Gaulle,
the Vernet is handsomely
furnished and air-conditioned.
Each room has a marble bath
with a Jacuzzi. Guests have free
access to the Hôtel Royal
Monceau's health centre and
heated pool; and the Vernet's
Belle Époque restaurant, Les
Elysées, has a lovely crystal roof
and two Michelin stars. Lift. Cots
available.

De Vigny** L7
9–11 Rue Balzac, 75008, t 01 42
99 80 80, f 01 42 99 80 40,
e de-vigny@wanadoo.fr,
w www.relaischateaux.fr/vigny;
métro George-V.
The De Vigny was transformed
in 1990 from a town house into
one of Paris' most sumptuous
small hotels, its bar evoking the
Paris of the 1930s salons. With
soundproof bedrooms, marble
bathrooms, a library and cable TV.
Lift. Cots available.

Very Expensive

Lord Byron** L7
5 Rue Chateaubriand, 75008,
t 01 43 59 89 98, f 01 42 89 46 04,
e lord.byron@escapade-paris.com;
métro George-V.
Small, quiet, well-positioned hotel
convenient for the Arc de
Triomphe and the Champs-
Elysées. The quiet courtyard is a
real bonus; in summer breakfast is
served here. Recommended by
BBC journalists. Lift.

Expensive

Étoile Park Hotel** J–K17
10 Av Mac-Mahon, 75017, t 01 42
67 69 63, f 01 43 80 18 99,
e ephot@easynet.fr; **métro** Étoile.
Good location on a leafy avenue in
a 19th-century building that has
always been a hotel. Some rooms
have a view of the Arc de
Triomphe. Downstairs there's a
comfortable sitting area, breakfast
room and bar, with Internet
access. Rooms are a bit impersonal
in comparison, but they're quite
serviceable. Lift. Cots available.

Flaubert** K4
19 Rue Rennequin, 75017; t 01 46 22
44 35, f 01 43 80 32 34, w www.
hotelflaubert.com; **métro** Ternes;
wheelchair access.
A pretty hotel near Parc Monceau,
north of the Étoile, with plants
cascading down the courtyard.
Rooms have modern baths, TV and
mini-bar. Lift. Cots available.

Moderate

**Hôtel des Champs-
Elysées**** N8
2 Rue d'Artois, 75008, t 01 43 59
11 42, f 01 45 61 00 61; **métro**
St-Philippe-du-Roule.
Family-run hotel (3rd generation)
near the Champs-Elysées,
popular with business travellers.
The modern, well-equipped
rooms all have a shower or bath.
The Art Deco sitting room is
delightful. Lift.

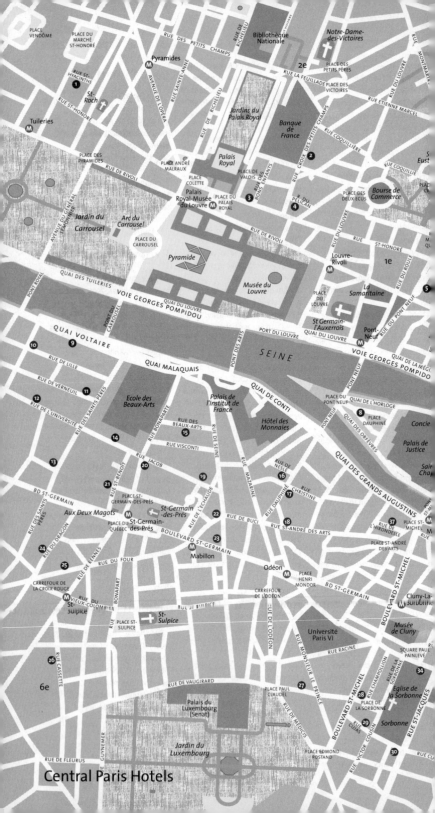

Central Paris Hotels

Map Key

(26) De l'Abbaye
(13) Académie
(54) Andrea
(14) Angleterre
(38) Les Argonautes
(50) Caron de Beaumarchais
(31) Le Central
(21) Crystal
(28) Dacia Luxembourg
(41) Les Degrés de Notre-Dame
(37) Delhy's
(45) Des Deux Iles
(39) Esmeralda
(32) Familia
(47) Le Fauconnier
(6) Grand Hôtel de Champagne
(29) Grand Hôtel St-Michel
(8) Henri IV
(36) Home Latin
(15) L'Hôtel
(10) Hôtel Bersoly's St-Germain
(51) Hôtel de la Bretonnerie
(34) Hôtel Claude Bernard
(33) Hôtel du Collège de France
(57) Hôtel du Cygne
(24) Hôtel du Dragon
(5) Hôtel des Ducs de Bourgogne
(30) Hôtel Excelsior
(48) Hôtel de Fourcy

(3) Hôtel Le Loiret
(4) Hôtel de Lille
(49) Hôtel Maubuisson
(7) Hôtel du Palais
(53) Hôtel Sansonnet
(42) Hospitel, Hôtel-Dieu
(46) Jeu de Paume
(22) La Louisiane
(44) Lutèce
(27) Luxembourg
(35) Marignan
(19) Marronniers
(40) Melia Colbert
(16) Nesle
(9) Quai Voltaire
(17) Relais Christine
(2) De Rouen
(18) St-André des Arts
(25) St-Germain
(43) St-Louis
(55) St-Merry
(1) Tuileries
(12) Université
(56) La Vallée
(58) Victoires Opéra
(52) Vieux Marais
(20) La Villa
(11) Verneuil St-Germain
(23) Welcome

Musée d'Orsay and the Invalides/ Eiffel Tower and Trocadéro

There aren't many places to stay in the immediate vicinity of the Eiffel Tower and Trocadéro, but some of the hotels in the neighbouring Invalides quarter are pretty close, with views of the Eiffel Tower.

Expensive

Bourdonnais* M13–14
111 Av de La-Bourdonnais, 75007,
t *01 47 05 45 42,* **f** *01 45 55 75 54,*
e *otlbourd@clubinternet.fr,*
w *www.hotellabourdonnais.fr;*
métro *Ecole-Militaire.*
An airy, elegant and comfortable hotel, where breakfast is served in a sunlit indoor garden. Lift. Cots available.

Jardins d'Eiffel* N12
8 Rue Amélie, 75007, **t** *01 47 05 46 21,* **f** *01 45 55 28 08,* **e** *paris@hotel jardinseiffel.fr,* **w** *www.hoteljardins eiffel.fr;* **métro** *Latour-Maubourg; wheelchair access.*
Built at the same time as the 1889 Exposition. Rooms are cosy in an old-fashioned way, and there's a sauna; book a room on the top floor for a view of Mr Eiffel's flag-pole. Babysitting service.

Hôtel de Londres Eiffel* I 12
1 Rue Augereau, 75007, **t** *01 45 51 63 02,* **f** *01 47 05 28 96,* **e** *info@ londres-eiffel.com,* **w** *www. londres-eiffel.com;* **métro** *École-Militaire.*
Small, friendly hotel near the Eiffel Tower; some rooms with Tower views. Rooms are comfortable with pretty decoration, while the sitting area downstairs sports stylish furniture. Lift.

Hôtel La Motte Picquet N13
30 Av de la Motte-Picquet, 75007,
t *01 4705 09 57,* **f** *01 47 05 74 36,*

w *www.paris-hotel-mottepicquet. com;* **métro** *École-Militaire.*
A small hotel with flowers in window boxes and 18 rooms over three floors. The bedrooms are simply but pleasantly furnished, with small bathrooms, and there is a small sitting area downstairs. Good location for shopping. Lift. Babysitting available.

Hôtel d'Orsay R12
93 Rue de Lille, 75007, **t** *01 47 05 85 54,* **f** *01 45 55 51 16,* **e** *hotel.orsay@ wanadoo.fr,* **w** *www.hotel-esprit-de-france.com;* **métro** *Solférino; wheelchair access.*
Where once there were two hotels, now there is one, which has been completely renovated to create elegant surroundings with a warm welcome. Splash out on the suite under the eaves (a few steps up from the 5th floor), which has masses of space and its own balcony. Lift to 5th floor.

Hôtel de la Tulipe N12
33 Rue Malar, 75007, **t** *01 45 51 67 21,* **f** *01 47 53 96 37,* **w** *www.hotelde latulipe.com;* **métro** *Latour-Maubourg or Invalides; wheelchair access.*
Former convent, now a charming, small hotel on two floors around a garden courtyard. The rooms have been designed in a country style with warm colours, fresh flowers and wooden beams; no.24 is the most romantic, in what was once the chapel and overlooking the courtyard. No lift. Cots available.

Varenne* P13
44 Rue de Bourgogne, 75007,
t *01 45 51 45 55,* **f** *01 45 51 86 63,*
e *info@hoteldevarenne.com;*
métro *Varenne; wheelchair access.*
An attractive converted town house with an interior courtyard in a peaceful corner of Paris; comfortable rooms, all with bath, TV and air-con. Lift. Cots available.

Moderate

Kensington M13
79 Av de La-Bourdonnais, 75007,
t *01 47 05 74 00,* **f** *01 47 05 25 81,*
e *hk@hotel-kensington.com,*

w www.hotel-kensington.com; *métro* École-Militaire.
Pleasant and friendly, small and tidy. Lift. Cots available.

Grand Hôtel Lévèque M–N13
29 Rue Cler, 75007, **t** 01 47 05 49 15, **f** 01 45 50 49 36, **e** info@hotel leveque.com, **w** www.hotel leveque.com; *métro* École-Militaire.
Another friendly and pleasant place, this one in the middle of Rue Cler market. Lift.

La Serre M13
24 bis Rue Cler, 75007, **t** 01 47 05 52 33, **f** 01 40 62 95 66, **e** laserre@ easynet.fr, **w** eiffeltower-hotel-paris.com; *métro* École-Militaire.
Old-fashioned hotel on Faubourg St-Germain's liveliest market street, and one of the cheapest in the quarter.

Opéra and Palais Royal

Quiet at night – a desert in fact, off the main boulevards – yet in daytime convenient for many sights. The streets around Palais Royal have a discreet charm.

Luxury

Intercontinental S10
3 Rue de Castiglione, 75001, **t** 01 44 77 11 11, **f** 01 44 77 14 60, **e** paris@ interconti.com, **w** www.paris. intercontinental.com; *métro* Tuileries or Concorde.
Built by Garnier nearly as lavishly as his Paris Opéra. Three of the seven grand imperial ballrooms have so much gilt and trimmings that they're listed as national monuments. The hotel takes up a whole city block, encompasses 390 rooms and 62 suites, and has a lift.

The Ritz T9
15 Place Vendôme, 75001, **t** 01 43 16 30 30, **f** 01 43 16 31 78, **e** resa@ritz paris.com, **w** www.ritzparis.com; *métro* Opéra.
One of the most famous hotels in the world. Keeping abreast of the times and the demands of its contemporary clientele, today's

Ritz has not only soundproof but bulletproof glass on the ground floor, a new tiled pool and health centre, free cookery classes that perpetuate the tradition of César Ritz's partner (the legendary chef Escoffier), business services and an exclusive nightclub.

Very Expensive

Brébant W8
30–32 Bd Poissonnière, 75009, **t** 01 47 70 25 55, **f** 01 42 46 65 70, **e** hotel.brebant@wanadoo.fr, **w** www.abpromhotels.com; *métro* Grands Boulevards.
Smart, stylish, crisply run hotel midway between the striped suits in the Bourse and the Folies-Bergère girlie shows. Lift. Cots available.

Le Lavoisier Opéra Q7
21 Rue Lavoisier, 75008, **t** 01 53 30 06 06, **f** 01 53 30 23 00, **e** info@ hotellavoisier.com, **w** www. hotellavoisier.com; *métro* St-Augustin; wheelchair access.
On a quiet street, this recently refurbished, stylish hotel is beautifully furnished with antique and modern furniture. Rooms are fairly spacious and have luxurious bathrooms, there's a cosy bar, and staff are friendly. Lift. Cots available.

Expensive

(3) Hôtel Le Loiret V11
5 Rue des Bons-Enfants, 75001, **t** 01 42 61 47 31, **f** 01 42 61 36 85, **e** reservation@hotelleloiret.com, **w** www.hotelleloiret.com; *métro* Palais Royal-Musée du Louvre.
Friendly hotel run by the same owners for 20 years. Rooms are small but well equipped, with modems on request. Excellent value for the area. Lift only to 4th floor. Cots available.

(1) Des Tuileries T10
10 Rue St-Hyacinthe, 75001, **t** 01 42 61 04 17, **f** 01 49 27 91 56, **e** htuileri@aol.com, **w** www. members.aol.com/htuileri; *métro* Tuileries or Pyramides.

A quiet 18th-century *hôtel particulier* with antiques and a lift.

Moderate

Antin Trinité T7
74 Rue de Provence, 75009, **t** 01 48 74 29 07, **f** 01 42 80 26 68, **e** hotel@hotel-antin-trinite.fr, **w** www.paris-antin-trinite.fr; *métro* Chaussée d'Antin-Lafayette.
Perfect location for shopaholics, just by the *grands magasins* on Boulevard Haussmann. The small rooms are decorated in pretty colours and have all the mod cons. Good value. Lift. Cots available.

Hôtel Baudelaire Opéra U9
61 Rue Ste-Anne, 75002, **t** 01 42 97 50 62, **f** 01 42 86 85 85, **e** hotel@ noos.fr; *métro* Quatre Septembre.
Baudelaire once lived in this mansion, which has recently been turned into a comfortable hotel. Rooms are small but well equipped with colourful décor. Staff are friendly and helpful. Lift. Cots available.

Hôtel Chopin W7–8
46 Passage Jouffroy, 10 Bd Montmartre, 75009, **t** 01 47 70 58 10, **f** 01 42 47 00 70; *métro* Grands Boulevards.
Lovely hotel located at the end of one of Paris' prettiest *passages*. Good area for shopaholics and almost next door to the recently reopened Musée Grévin. The peaceful rooms are simply decorated in bright colours, most with shower or bath. The staff are very friendly and the hotel attracts independent travellers who return time and again. Lift. Cots available.

Favart V8
5 Rue de Marivaux, 75002, **t** 01 42 97 59 83, **f** 01 4015 95 58, **e** favart.hotel@wanadoo.fr; *métro* Richelieu-Drouot; wheelchair access.
The rooms here are traditionally furnished and quite spacious, with decent bathrooms. Downstairs, the sitting area and breakfast room are rather grand, but the service is friendly. Lift. Cots available.

New Orient Hôtel** Q5
*16 Rue de Constantinople, 75008,
t 01 45 22 21 64, f 01 42 93 83 23,
e new.orient.hotel@wanadoo.fr;
métro Villiers.*
Just north of Gare St-Lazare
and near Parc Monceau, this is a
pretty hotel with a warm
welcome and original furnishings.
The rooms are attractively
decorated with an attention to
detail, and the bathrooms are
spotless. Lift. Cots available.

Inexpensive

Cité Rougemont** X8
*4 Cité Rougemont, 75009,
t 01 47 70 25 95, f 01 48 24 14 32,
w www.hotelciterougemont.fr;
métro Grands Boulevards.*
The best economy bet in the
area, located in a traffic-free
street off Rue Bergères. Lift.
Cots available.

(4) Hôtel de Lille** V11
*8 Rue du Pélican, 75001, t 01 42 33
33 42; métro Palais Royal-Musée
du Louvre.*
A rare bargain hotel between the
Louvre and Palais Royal. Old and
plain; some rooms with shower.
Cots available.

(2) De Rouen* V10
*42 Rue Croix-des-Petits-Champs,
75001, t 01 42 61 38 21, f 01 42 61
38 21; métro Palais Royal-Musée
du Louvre.*
Old and comfortable, a good
choice near the Palais Royal. Some
rooms with shower.

Vivienne** W8
*40 Rue Vivienne, 75002, t 01 42 33
13 26, f 01 40 41 98 19, e paris@
hotel-vivienne.com, métro Grands
Boulevards.*
Very basic, near the Bibliothèque
and arcades. Most have ensuite
bathrooms. Lift.

Beaubourg and Les Halles

Your most likely abode on the
Right Bank. Hotels in all categories, near restaurants.

Luxury

(58) Victoires Opéra**** X10
*56 Rue Montorgueil, 75002, t 01
42 36 41 08, f 01 45 08 08 79,
w www.hotelvictoiresopera.com;
métro Châtelet-Les Halles;
wheelchair access.*
This hotel has reopened after a
total makeover; it even has a new
name. It has views over the
Montorgueil market and a lift.
Cots available.

Very Expensive

**(5) Hôtel des Ducs de
Bourgogne***** W–X12
*19 Rue du Pont-Neuf, 75001, t 01 42
33 95 64, f 01 40 39 01 25, e mail@
hotel-paris-bourgogne.com,
w www.hotel-paris-bourgogne.
com; métro Châtelet.*
Characterful hotel with simple
rooms which have excellent facilities and nice bathrooms.
Downstairs, there's a hat rack with
vintage hats and photos of astro-
nauts who stay here when they're
visiting the French Space Centre
on the same street.

(55) St-Merry*** Z12
*78 Rue de la Verrerie, 75004,
t 01 42 78 14 15, f 01 40 29 06 82,
e hotelstmerry@wanadoo.fr
w www.hotelmarais.com; métro
Hôtel-de-Ville.*
A stone's throw from the
Pompidou Centre, this was once
St-Merry's presbytery and later
a bordello. Its latest metamorphosis as a hotel stands out for
the beautiful Gothic rooms.
Cots available

Expensive

**(51) Hôtel de la
Bretonnerie***** AA12
*22 Rue Ste-Croix-de-la-Bretonnerie,
75004, t 01 48 87 77 63, f 01 42 77
26 78, e hotel@bretonnerie.com,
w www.bretonnerie.com;
métro Hôtel-de-Ville.*
A very popular small hotel with
Louis XIII furnishings and televisions in the rooms. Lift.

**(6) Grand Hôtel de
Champagne***** X12
*17 Rue Jean-Lantier, 75001, t 01 42
36 60 00, f 01 45 08 43 33; métro
Châtelet-Les Halles.*
Relatively quiet, near busy Place
du Châtelet; originally decorated
rooms, many with murals, and
a fancy breakfast buffet. Lift.
Cots available.

(52) Vieux Marais** Z12
*8 Rue du Plâtre, 75004, t 01 42 78
47 22, f 01 42 78 34 32; métro Hôtel-
de-Ville.*
Most rooms with TV; all with bath
or shower. Lift. Cots available.

Moderate

(54) Andrea** Y12
*3 Rue St-Bon, 75004, t 01 42 78
43 93, f 01 44 61 28 36, w www.
hotelandrearivoli.com; métro
Hôtel-de-Ville.*
A decent, quiet choice near the
Rue de Rivoli. All the rooms have
bathrooms. Lift, air-con.

(57) Hôtel du Cygne** Y11
*3 Rue du Cygne, 75001, t 01 42 60
14 16, f 01 42 21 37 02, e contact@
hotelducynge.fr, w www.hoteldu
cynge.fr; métro Étienne-Marcel.*
In a 17th-century building on
a pedestrian street just north of
Les Halles. Pretty sitting area
downstairs and comfortable
rooms and bathrooms. Good value
for the location.

(53) Hôtel Sansonnet** Z12
*48 Rue de la Verrerie, 75004,
t 01 48 87 96 14, f 01 48 87 30 46,
e sansonnet@gofornet.fr; métro
Hôtel-de-Ville.*
Small, family-run hotel near the
Pompidou Centre. Rooms are spotless, nicely decorated with good
facilities and not too small, and
most have shower or bath. The
hotel has been run by the same
couple for 25 years and is excellent
value. No lift.

Inexpensive

(7) Hôtel du Palais* X13
*2 Quai de la Mégisserie, 75001,
t 01 42 36 98 25, f 01 42 21 41 67;
métro Châtelet.*

A small hotel on the *quais* near Châtelet, with views of the Seine and Notre-Dame. The facilities could be better – just under half the rooms have their own shower or bath – and it can be noisy, but you won't get a cheaper night's sleep in a better location.

(56) La Vallée* Y11
84–6 Rue St-Denis, 75001, *t* 01 42 36 46 99, *f* 01 42 36 16 66, *e* hvallee@ noos.fr, *w* www.perso.cybercable. fr/hvallee; *métro* Châtelet-Les Halles.
Excellent bargain choice, between Les Halles and Beaubourg. Some of the rooms have showers, all have TV. Cots available.

Marais and Bastille

Expensive

Bastille Speria*** DD14
1 Rue de la Bastille, 75004, *t* 01 42 72 04 01, *f* 01 42 72 56 38, *e* info@ hotel-bastille-speria.com, *w* www. hotel-bastille-speria.com; *métro* Bastille.
Good location near to the Marais and the lively bars and restaurants around Bastille. The hotel has a small garden and is furnished with contemporary pieces and bright colours – including the fish in the large aquarium. Rooms are well-equipped and service is efficient. Lift.

(50) Caron de Beaumarchais*** AA13
12 Rue Vieille-du-Temple, 75004, *t* 01 42 72 34 12, *f* 01 42 72 34 63, *e* hotel@carondebeaumarchais. com, *w* www.carondebeau marchais.com; *métro* Hôtel-de-Ville.
A small, beautifully restored hotel near the Jewish quarter. The lobby sets the tone, with period fireplace and furniture. The small bedrooms and bathrooms are carefully designed for maximum comfort (bathrobes are provided) and some have balconies. A much-loved hotel

with many regular visitors. Lift. Cots available.

Hôtel des Chevaliers*** CC13
30 Rue de Turenne, 75003, *t* 01 42 72 73 47, *f* 01 42 72 54 10, *e* info@hotel deschevaliers.com; *métro* St-Paul; wheelchair access.
Charming hotel in the heart of the Marais, just by the Musée Picasso. Rooms are stylish, comfortable and well equipped (TV, mini-bar), while breakfast is served in the vaulted cellar. Good service. Lift.

Hôtel du Grand Turenne*** CC13
6 Rue de Turenne, 75004, *t* 01 42 78 43 25, *f* 01 42 74 10 72, *w* www. libertel-hotels.com; *métro* St-Paul.
Charming hotel in a great location near the Place des Vosges. Rooms are prettily decorated and the superior rooms are particularly spacious. There are two no-smoking floors. Lift.

St-Louis Marais** CC14
1 Rue Charles-V, 75004, *t* 01 48 87 87 04, *f* 01 48 87 33 26, *e* slmarais@ noos.fr *w* www.saintlouismarais. com; *métro* Sully-Morland, Bastille or St-Paul.
An 18th-century Celestine convent offering romantic if monk-sized rooms. Five floors, but no lift. Cots available.

Moderate

Abotel Villa Sofia FF13–14
29 Rue des Taillandiers, 75011, *t* 01 48 05 30 97, *f* 01 47 00 29 26; *métro* Bastille.
Small, friendly hotel near the lively Bastille area and its restaurants and bars. Rooms are simple but all have a shower or bath. Cots available.

Grand Hôtel Jeanne d'Arc** BB13
3 Rue de Jarente, 75004, *t* 01 48 87 62 11, *f* 01 48 87 37 31, *w* www.paris hotels.com; *métro* St-Paul.
Not so Grand any more, but ancient, cute and well run, close to the Place des Vosges; book far ahead. Lift.

Place des Vosges** CC13–14
12 Rue de Birague, 75004, *t* 01 42 72 60 46, *f* 01 42 72 02 64, *e* hotel. place.des.vosges@gofornet.com; *métro* Bastille.
Well restored, and just a few steps from the Place itself. Lift. Cots available.

Prince Albert Concordia** FF16
38 Bd Diderot, 75012, *t* 01 43 43 54 92, *f* 01 43 47 39 50, *e* aloum@ aol.com, *w* www.hotelprince albert.com.; *métro* Gare de Lyon.
Small hotel near the Promenade Plantée and the Viaduc des Arts. Rooms are small, but all have bath or shower. Lift. Cots available.

Inexpensive

Mary's Hotel* DD10
15 Rue de Malte, 75011, *t* 01 47 00 81 70, *f* 01 47 00 58 06, *e* hotel marys@magic.fr, *w* maryshotel. com/hten; *métro* République.
En suite singles, doubles and triples, all with TV and out-dated wall paper. Reception open 24hrs. Lift. Cot available.

Hôtel Notre-Dame** DD10
51 Rue de Malte, 75011, *t* 01 47 00 78 76, *f* 01 43 55 32 31, *e* hotel notredame@wanadoo.fr; *métro* République.
Family-run hotel near République. A clean, basic choice with no frills. Some rooms have balconies, most have TV, and there's a breakfast/TV room downstairs. Not in a tourist area, but convenient for transport.

Sévigné** BB13
2 Rue Malher, 75004, *t* 01 42 72 76 17, *f* 01 42 78 68 26; *métro* St-Paul.
Nice place right around the corner from the nosher's paradise of Rue des Rosiers. Lift.

Hôtel de Vienne* DD10
43 Rue de Malte, 75011, *t* 01 48 05 44 42; *métro* République.
Only four of the rooms have their own shower, and there are no shared facilities, but this is a reliable, clean hotel near Place de la République that has been attracting budget travellers for 20 years. No lift.

Montmartre and the North

Note that because of the steps in the area, disabled access is very limited.

Luxury

Pavillon de Paris**** S5
7 Rue de Parme, 75009, t 01 55 31 60 00, f 01 55 31 60 01, e mail@ pavillondeparis.com, w www. pavillondeparis.com; métro Liège; wheelchair access.
North of Gare St-Lazare and not far from Place de Clichy, a boutique designer 21st-century hotel which claims to be a home away from home. Rooms are stylish and hi-tech, and designed with feng shui in mind. Breakfast is served in the lovely conservatory. Lift. Cots available. Special rates July and Aug.

Terrass**** U3
12 Rue Joseph-de-Maistre, 75018, t 01 46 06 72 85, f 01 42 52 29 11, e terrass@francenet.fr, w www. terrass-hotel.com; métro Place de Clichy.
Montmartre's most luxurious hotel, overlooking the cemetery and rest of Paris. It has two restaurants, one of them with – surprise, surprise – a terrace (summer only).

Expensive

Timhotel Montmartre** V3
11 Rue Ravignan (Place Emile-Goudeau), 75018, t 01 42 55 74 79, f 01 42 55 71 01, e montmartre@ timhotel.fr, w www.timhotel.fr; métro Abbesses.
Henry Miller knew this when it was called Paradis. It's still one of the most romantic hotels in Paris, overlooking delightful Place Émile-Goudeau; now renovated, with cable TV. Price varies depending on the view. Lift.

Moderate

Hôtel des Arts** U3
5 Rue Tholozé, 75018, t 01 46 06 30 52, f 01 46 06 10 83, e hotel.arts@ wanadoo.fr, w www.arts-hotel-paris.com; métro Blanche.
Excellent value, family-run hotel on a quiet street. Rooms are well furnished in bright colours and there are views of Sacré-Coeur and the Eiffel Tower from the 6th-floor rooms. Lift to the 5th floor. Cots available.

'Hôtel de Charme' Ermitage** X3
24 Rue Lamarck, 75018, t 01 42 64 79 22, f 01 42 64 10 33; métro Lamarck-Caulaincourt. No credit cards.
Charming little white hotel under the gardens around Sacré-Coeur.

Eden** W1
90 Rue Ordener, 75018, t 01 42 64 61 63, f 01 42 64 11 43, e j.delasalle@ free.fr, w www.edenhotel-montmartre.com; métro Jules-Joffrin.
Behind Sacré-Coeur, pleasant, family run, and equipped with satellite TV. Lift.

Régyn's Montmartre** V4
18 Place des Abbesses, 75018, t 01 42 54 45 21, f 01 42 23 76 69, e hotel@ regynsmontmartre.com, w www. regynsmontmartre.com; métro Abbesses.
A simple but good address in the heart of Montmartre, with great views over Paris. Lift.

Inexpensive

Hôtel Bonséjour U3
11 Rue Burq, 75018, t 01 42 54 22 53, f 01 42 54 25 92; métro Abbesses or Blanche.
Simple, cheerful hotel on a quiet street in the heart of Montmartre. Some of the rooms have balconies and one of the rooms on the 5th floor has a view of Sacré-Coeur. Friendly service – they'll listen to the weather forecast on the radio for you. No lift.

Modern Hôtel X1
62 Rue Ramey, 75018, t 01 46 06 29 40, f 01 46 06 48 74; métro Jules-Joffrin.
Just north of Montmartre; the rooms on the top floors have views of Sacré-Coeur.

Prima Lepic** U3
29 Rue Lepic, 75018, t 01 46 06 44 64, f 01 46 06 66 11, e reservation@hotel-prima-lepic.com; métro Abbesses or Blanche.
Pleasant and pretty rooms on the slope of the Butte. Lift and babysitting services.

St-Germain

St-Germain has a high density of smart, charming hotels, but prices tend to smart in another way.

Luxury

Duc de Saint-Simon*** R13
14 Rue de St-Simon, 75007, t 01 44 39 20 20, f 01 45 48 68 25, e duc.de.saint.simon@wanadoo.fr; métro Rue-du-Bac.
In a 17th-century house in a quiet side street off Boulevard St-Germain, one of the most fashionable little hotels on the Left Bank; all antiques, old beams, stone walls and snob appeal, its cellars converted into a string of bars and salons. Lift.

(15) L'Hôtel**** U13
13 Rue des Beaux-Arts, 75006, t 01 44 41 99 00, f 01 43 25 64 81, e reservation@l-hotel.com, w www.l-hotel.com; métro St-Germain-des-Prés.
Besides seeing the last of Oscar Wilde, this is one of the most romantic hotels in Paris; the honeymoon suite is outrageously furnished with a mirrored set which once belonged to Mistinguett, the 1920s and 30s star at the Moulin Rouge and Folies Bergère. Lift. Cots available.

Lutétia**** S15
45 Bd Raspail, 75006, t 01 49 54 46 46, f 01 49 54 46 00, e lutetia-paris@lutetia-paris.com, w www.concorde-hotels.com; métro Sèvres-Babylone.
Renovated early Art Deco palace, a favourite for honeymoons since Pablo and Olga Picasso and Charles and Yvonne de Gaulle canoodled here. When it

was requisitioned by the Nazis, the staff walled up the prize wine cellars, and in spite of German interrogations never gave away the secret. Lift. Cots available.

(17) Relais Christine**** V14
3 Rue Christine, 75006, t 01 40 51 60 80, f 01 40 51 60 81, e relaisch@club-internet.fr, w www.relais-christine.com; *métro* Odéon.
Luxurious, colourful rooms in a 16th-century Augustinian cloister, a quiet oasis. Lift. Cots available.

(20) La Villa**** U13
29 Rue Jacob, 75006, t 01 43 26 60 00, f 01 46 34 63 63, e hotel@villa-saintgermain.com; *métro* St-Germain-des-Prés.
Le dernier cri in St-Germain, with precocious bathrooms of chrome, glass and marble and chi-chi piano bar.

Very Expensive

(26) De l'Abbaye* T15
10 Rue Cassette, 75006, t 01 45 44 38 11, f 01 45 48 07 86, e hotel.abbaye@wanadoo.fr, w www.hotel-abbaye.com; *métro* St-Sulpice.
One of the swankiest small Left-Bank hotels – this one was originally a monastery – and despite the traffic serenely quiet, especially if you get one of the bedrooms over the lovely garden courtyard.

(13) Académie* T13
32 Rue des Sts-Pères, 75007, t 01 45 49 80 00, f 01 45 44 75 24, e academiehotel@aol.com, w www.academiehotel.com; *métro* St-Germain-des-Prés.
A converted 18th-century residence, with Louis XIV, Louis XVI and Directory repros among exposed stone walls and beams that would have shocked the original owners. Lift. Cots available.

(14) Angleterre* T–U13
44 Rue Jacob, 75006, t 01 42 60 34 72, f 01 42 60 16 93, e anglotel@wanadoo.fr; *métro* St-Germain-des-Prés.

A former British embassy, now a hotel with character. Some rooms have vertiginously high ceilings; huge double beds.

(21) Crystal* T–U14
24 Rue St-Benoît, 75006, t 01 45 48 85 14, f 01 45 49 16 45, e hotel.crystal@wanadoo.fr, w www.hotel.crystal.com; *métro* St-Germain-des-Prés.
Just around the corner from the church of St-Germain, a charming, cosy and lovingly cared-for little hotel. Lift.

(27) Luxembourg* V15
4 Rue de Vaugirard, 75006, t 01 43 25 35 90, f 01 43 25 17 18, e luxhotel@luxembourg.mgn.fr, w www.hotel-luxembourg.com; *métro* Odéon.
A small, comfortable hotel by the Luxembourg gardens where Verlaine often stayed at the end of his life, at least when he was flush. No restaurant. Lift.

(19) Marronniers* U13–14
21 Rue Jacob, 75006, t 01 43 25 30 60, f 01 40 46 83 56, w www.hotel-marronniers.com; *métro* St-Germain-des-Prés. Visa and MasterCard only.
An enchanting hotel at the bottom of a courtyard, with a garden at the back, but book well in advance. Lift.

(12) Université* T13
22 Rue de l'Université, 75007, t 01 42 61 09 39, f 01 42 60 40 84, e hoteluniversite@wanadoo.fr, w www.hoteluniversite.com; *métro* Rue-du-Bac or St-Germain-des-Prés.
A refurbished 17th-century house, a few minutes from St-Germain-des-Prés, with 27 stylish, quiet rooms, each with safe, bath and TV.

Expensive

(10) Hôtel Bersoly's St-Germain* T12
28 Rue de Lille, 75007, t 01 42 60 73 79, f 01 49 27 05 55, e hotel bersolys@wanadoo.fr, w www.bersolyshotel.com; *métro* Rue-du-Bac.
An 18th-century mansion converted into a beautiful, small

hotel. Rooms are small and clean with all mod cons, including modem. Each is named after a different artist and features reproductions of their paintings. Lift. Cots and babysitting available. Pets allowed.

(9) Quai Voltaire T12
19 Quai Voltaire, 75007, t 01 42 61 50 91, f 01 42 61 62 26, e info@hotelduquaivoltaire.com, w www.hotelduquaivoltaire.com; *RER* Musée d'Orsay.
A hotel since the 19th century, overlooking the Seine and the Louvre, a favourite of Baudelaire, Sibelius and Richard Wagner. Lift. Cots available.

(25) St-Germain T14
50 Rue du Four, 75006, t 01 45 48 91 64, f 01 45 48 46 22, e hotel.de.st.germain@wanadoo.fr, w www.hotel-saint-germain.fr; *métro* St-Sulpice or Sèvres-Babylone.
With rooms pretty, cosy and homey enough for a hobbit, who would appreciate the mini-bar, if not the French TV.

(11) Verneuil Saint-Germain* T13
8 Rue de Verneuil, 75007, t 01 42 60 82 14, f 01 42 61 40 38, e hotel verneuil@wanadoo.fr, w www.hotelverneuil.com; *métro* St-Germain-des-Prés or Rue-du-Bac.
Small for the price but pleasant rooms by the Musée d'Orsay and the antique dealers. Lift. Cots.

Moderate

(37) Delhy's* W14
22 Rue de l'Hirondelle, 75006, t 01 43 26 58 25, f 01 43 26 51 06; *métro* St-Michel.
Modest choice on a quiet lane tucked near busy Place St-Michel. Some rooms with shower. Cots available.

(24) Hôtel du Dragon T14
36 Rue du Dragon, 75006, t 01 45 48 51 05, f 01 42 22 51 62, e Hotel.Du.Dragon@wanadoo.fr, w www.hoteldudragon.com; *métro* St-Germain-des-Prés or St-Sulpice.
Small, simple budget hotel in a great location and with a warm

welcome. Rooms are simple and clean; most have shower and WC. No lift.

(22) La Louisiane** V14
60 Rue de Seine, 75006, **t** *01 44 32 17 17,* **f** *01 46 34 23 87,* **e** *hotel@ lalouisiane.net;* **métro** *St-Germain-des-Prés.*
Set amid the colourful Rue de Buci market, a celebrated favourite of Left-Bank literati. Most of the rooms are fairly plain and modern, but the friendly, good-humoured atmosphere makes all the difference. Reserve well in advance due to the slow turnaround, as some guests can't bear to leave – Simone de Beauvoir and Sartre stayed long enough to write several books. Lift.

(18) St-André des Arts* V14
66 Rue St-André-des-Arts, 75006, **t** *01 43 26 96 16,* **f** *01 43 29 73 34,* **e** *hsaintand@minitel.net;* **métro** *Odéon.*
A 17th-century musketeers' barracks, lively and often noisy until late.

(23) Welcome** V14
66 Rue de Seine, 75006 **t** *01 46 34 24 80,* **f** *01 40 46 81 59,* **w** *www.welcomehotel-paris.com;* **métro** *Mabillon or Odéon.* Wheelchair access.
Renovated, simple and with soundproofed rooms, it also offers a warm welcome. Lift.

Inexpensive

(16) Nesle* V13
7 Rue de Nesle, 75006, **t** *01 43 54 62 41,* **f** *01 43 54 31 88;* **métro** *Odéon or Pont-Neuf.*
Slightly dilapidated but welcoming hotel of character that hasn't accepted reservations since it was an international be-in in the 1960s. Each room is decorated in a different style: no.9 is Egyptian. Some rooms have shower or bath.

The Latin Quarter

Very convenient, but apt to be noisy at night.

Luxury

(40) Melia Colbert** Y15
7 Rue de l'Hôtel-Colbert, 75005, **t** *01 40 46 79 50,* **f** *01 43 25 80 19,* **e** *melia.colbert@solmelia.com,* **w** *www.solmelia.com;* **métro** *Maubert-Mutualité or St-Michel;* wheelchair access.
Elegant, peaceful hotel with tea room south of Place Maubert. Lift. Cots available.

Very Expensive

Grands Hommes* X16–17
17 Place du Panthéon, 75005, **t** *01 46 34 19 60,* **f** *01 43 26 67 32,* **w** *www.hoteldesgrandshommes. com;* **métro** *Cardinal-Lemoine,* **RER** *Luxembourg.*
The Grands Hommes earned a place in French literary history when resident André Breton defined Surrealism here in the 1920s. The furnishings, however, are more in the spirit of Voltaire and Rousseau. Small garden, cable TV, mini-bar and lift. Cots and babysitting available.

Panthéon* X16–17
19 Place du Panthéon, 75005, **t** *01 43 54 32 95,* **f** *01 43 26 64 65,* **e** *hotel.pantheon@wanadoo.fr;* **métro** *Cardinal-Lemoine,* **RER** *Luxembourg;* wheelchair access.
Small, elegant hotel overlooking the Panthéon. Downstairs there's a bar and lounge, as well as a courtyard garden. Some rooms have balconies. Lift. Cots and babysitting available.

Expensive

(34) Hôtel Claude Bernard* X15
43 Rue des Écoles, 75005, **t** *01 43 26 32 52,* **f** *01 43 26 80 56,* **e** *hotel@ claudebernard.com,* **w** *www. paris-hotel-booking.com;* **métro** *Maubert-Mutualité.*
Recently renovated with nice furnishings and good bathrooms. Beware that rooms overlooking the street can be noisy. Lift. Cots and family rooms available.

(28) Dacia Luxembourg* W15
41 Bd St-Michel, 75005, **t** *01 53 10 27 77,* **f** *01 44 07 10 33,* **e** *info@hotel dacia.com,* **w** *www.hoteldacia. com;* **métro** *Sully-La Sorbonne.*
On brash and bold Boul'Mich, very close to the Sorbonne and Jardin du Luxembourg, but its sound-proofed, prettily decorated rooms offer a quiet haven. Lift.

(29) Grand Hotel St-Michel* W16
19 Rue Cujas, 75005, **t** *01 46 33 33 02,* **f** *01 40 46 96 33,* **e** *grand.hotel. st.michel@wanadoo.fr;* **RER** *Luxembourg;* wheelchair access.
Fully renovated, fairly quiet choice near the Panthéon, with a garden and lift.

Moderate

(38) Les Argonautes** X14
12 Rue de la Huchette, 75005, **t** *01 43 54 09 82,* **f** *01 44 07 18 84;* **métro** *St-Michel.*
Perfect for Latin Quarter night-owls and other urban creatures, on the corner of the narrowest street in Paris. All rooms with bath or shower. Lift. Cots available.

(33) Hôtel du Collège de France** X15
7 Rue Thénard, 75005, **t** *01 43 26 78 36,* **f** *01 46 34 58 29,* **e** *hotel.du. college.de.france@wanadoo.fr,* **w** *www.hotel-collegedefrance. com;* **métro** *Maubert-Mutualité.*
Good-value and very popular small hotel offering spacious, spotless rooms with all mod cons. Some have views of Notre-Dame and some have their own balcony. Lovely dark red salon and breakfast room for the hotel's good breakfasts. Lift. Cots available.

(41) Les Degrés de Notre-Dame Y15
10 Rue des Grands-Degrés, 75005, **t** *01 55 42 88 88,* **f** *01 40 46 95 34;* **métro** *Maubert-Mutualité.*
Ten charming rooms, many with prize views over Quasimodo's favourite perch. A quiet street, and a restaurant downstairs serving classic French and North African

dishes (menus €21 and €23). All rooms have showers and WC.

(39) Esmeralda* X14
4 Rue St-Julien-le-Pauvre, 75005, *t* 01 43 54 19 20, *f* 01 40 51 00 68; *métro* St-Michel.
Endearing, romantic hotel in a 16th-century building with a *classé* stairway and 19th-century furnishings; room price depends on the view.

(30) Hôtel Excelsior* W16
20 Rue Cujas, 75005, *t* 01 46 34 79 50, *f* 01 43 54 87 10, *e* htexcel5@club-internet-fr; *RER* Luxembourg.
No-frills hotel which is excellent value for the location. Downstairs there is a pretty sitting area and a patio for breakfast. Rooms are basic but clean (some can be noisy); most have ensuite bath. Lift serves 3rd floor and above. Better rates available in the low season.

(32) Familia** Y16
11 Rue des Écoles, 75005, *t* 01 43 54 55 27, *f* 01 43 29 61 77, *e* familia. hotel@libertysurf.fr, *w* www. familiahotel.com; *métro* Cardinal-Lemoine.
Comfortable, with frescoes in some rooms and great views of Notre-Dame from the top floors. Lift.

(36) Home Latin** X15
15–17 Rue du Sommerard, 75005, *t* 01 43 26 25 21, *f* 01 43 29 87 04; *métro* Maubert-Mutualité or St-Michel.
Calm, well kept and friendly. Lift.

Inexpensive

(35) Marignan* X15
13 Rue du Sommerard, 75005, *t* 01 43 54 63 81; *métro* Maubert-Mutualité.
Friendly, informal and simple. There are pay showers down the hall, though some rooms have baths. Cots available.

Jardin des Plantes

Pleasant, lively at night and cheaper than St-Germain.

Expensive

Timhotel Jardin des Plantes** Z17
5 Rue Linné, 75005, *t* 01 47 07 06 20, *f* 01 47 07 62 74, *e* jardin-des-plantes@timhotel.fr, *w* www. timhotel.com; *métro* Jussieu.
The best choice in the area, with its sauna, cheerful décor, and sunbathing on 5th-floor terrace overlooking the botanical gardens. Lift.

Moderate

Grandes Écoles*** Y17
75 Rue du Cardinal-Lemoine, 75005, *t* 01 43 26 79 23, *f* 01 43 25 28 15, *e* hotel.grandes.ecoles@wanadoo. fr, *w* www.hotel-grandes-ecoles. com; *métro* Cardinal-Lemoine or Place Monge; wheelchair access.
One of the most amazing settings in Paris, a peaceful cream-coloured villa in a beautiful garden courtyard. Reserve weeks ahead. Lift.

Libertel Maxim Z18
28 Rue Censier, 75005, *t* 01 43 31 16 15, *f* 01 43 31 93 87; *métro* Censier-Daubenton; wheelchair access.
Modest but pretty hotel near the mosque. All rooms have TV, mini-bar and ensuite bathrooms. Lift. Cots available.

Inexpensive

Alliés* X19
20 Rue Berthollet, 75005, *t* 01 43 31 47 52, *f* 01 45 35 13 92; *métro* Censier-Daubenton.
Simple place in a quiet street by the Val de Grâce. Lift.

(31) Le Central* Y16
6 Rue Descartes, 75005, *t* 01 46 33 57 93; *métro* Maubert-Mutualité or Cardinal-Lemoine.
Conveniently located, family-run haven. Most rooms have bath or shower.

Port Royal* Y19
8 Bd Port Royal, 75005, *t* 01 43 31 70 06, *f* 01 43 31 33 67; *métro* Les Gobelins.

Family-run, simple, immaculately clean, with garden and lift.

Montparnasse

Montparnasse has a crop of big-business hotels, modern and low on charm, but there are a few that stand out.

Very Expensive

Villa des Artistes*** T18
9 Rue de la Grande-Chaumière, 75006, *t* 01 43 26 60 86, *f* 01 43 54 73 70, *e* hotel@villa-artistes.com, *w* www.villa-artistes.com; *métro* Vavin.
Where Samuel Beckett stayed; some of Montparnasse's artists had studios across the street. It's had a recent Art Deco facelift. Lift. Cots available.

Expensive

Apollon Montparnasse** R19
91 Rue de l'Ouest, 75014, *t* 01 43 95 62 00, *f* 01 43 95 62 10, *e* apollonm@club-internet.fr, *w* www.apollon-hotel-paris.com; *métro* Pernety.
Small hotel with welcoming entrance in a quiet street just south of Montparnasse. Rooms are a good size and nicely decorated with warm colours, a choice of original prints and nice bathrooms. Breakfast is served in the vaulted cellar. Lift. Cots available. Discounts at weekends.

Lenox Montparnasse*** S–T18
15 Rue Delambre, 75014, *t* 01 43 35 34 50, *f* 01 43 20 46 64, *w* www.hotellenox.com; *métro* Vavin or Edgar-Quinet.
A large, elegant hotel with an Art Deco bar, just off Boulevard Raspail, opposite the seven cinemas. Lift. Cots available.

Orchidée*** Q20
65 Rue de l'Ouest, 75014, *t* 01 43 22 70 50, *f* 01 42 79 97 46; *métro* Gaîté or Pernety; wheelchair access.
Up-to-date, with a Jacuzzi, garden, sauna and lift.

Moderate

Hôtel Daguerre** R20
94 Rue Daguerre, 75014,
t 01 43 22 43 54, f 01 43 20 66 84,
e hoteldaguerre.paris.14@
gofornet.com; métro Gaîté;
wheelchair access.
Just by the Cimetière du
Montparnasse on a partly pedestrianized street (there is access by
car to the hotel). Rooms are
simple, but nicely decorated; some
overlook the small garden, others
have views towards Montmartre
and Sacré-Coeur, or their own
terrace. The sitting and breakfast
rooms downstairs are rather
grander. Lift.

Delambre*** S18
35 Rue Delambre, 75014, t 01 43 20
66 31, f 01 45 38 91 76, e delambre@
club-internet.fr, w www.hotelde
lambre.com; métro Vavin; wheel-
chair access.
André Breton once lived in this
house, now a good-value, attractive hotel. Rooms are decorated in
bright colours, with all mod cons,
including modem connections.
Downstairs is the charming breakfast room. Lift. Cots available.

Innova** O18
32 Bd Pasteur, 75015, t 01 47 34 70
47, f 01 40 56 07 91; métro Pasteur.
Fairly large hotel with cheerful
entrance and public rooms.
Rooms have recently been refurbished with plenty of space and
colourful decoration; most have
shower or bath. Street-facing
rooms can be a little noisy. Lift.
Cots available.

Istria Montparnasse** T19
29 Rue Campagne-Première, 75014,
t 01 43 20 91 82, f 01 43 22 48 45;
métro Raspail.
A charming, kind and cosy hotel
that was a favourite of Man Ray,
Aragon, Marcel Duchamp, Rilke
and Walter Benjamin. Lift.

Parc** R18
6 Rue Jolivet, 75014, t 01 43 20 95
54, f 01 42 79 82 62, e contact@
hotelduparc-paris.com, w www.
hotelduparc-paris.com; métro
Edgar-Quinet or Montparnasse-
Bienvenüe.
Many of the rooms overlook
sunny Square Gaston-Baty; all
have TV, safe and a shower or
bath. Lift. Cots available.

Inexpensive

Des Académies* T18
15 Rue de la Grande-Chaumière,
75006, t 01 43 26 66 44, f 01 43 26
03 72; métro Vavin.
Simple, unpretentious, family
hotel near the Luxembourg
gardens; all rooms have shower.
Cots available. Dogs allowed.

Hôtel de Blois* R22
5 Rue des Plantes, 75014, t 01 45 40
99 48, f 01 45 40 45 62; métro
Mouton-Duvernet.
Cosy hotel good for shopaholics,
near Rue d'Alésia. Nice sitting/
breakfast rooms overlooking the
street. Rooms are decorated with
feminine touches; most are a
good size, and most have bath or
shower. No lift. Cots available.

Stanislas** S17
5 Rue du Montparnasse, 75006,
t 01 45 48 37 05, f 01 45 44 54 43;
métro Notre-Dame-des-Champs.
A well-kept, agreeable hotel in
crêpe alley: TV, WC, shower/bath,
hairdryer and phones in each
room. Cots available.

16e: Passy and Auteuil

Luxury

Villa Maillot**** G–H7
143 Av de Malakoff, 75016, t 01 53
64 52 52, f 01 45 00 60 61, e resa@
lavillamaillot.fr; métro Porte
Maillot; wheelchair access.
Former Art Deco embassy of Sierra
Leone, with vintage furnishings.
Facilities include air-con, mini-bar
and cable TV. Lift. Cots available.

Moderate

Le Hameau de Passy** F12–13
48 Rue de Passy, 75016, t 01 42 88 47
55, f 01 42 30 83 72, e hotel@
hameaudepassy.com, w www.
hameaudepassy.com; métro Passy;
wheelchair access.
Peaceful hotel with a garden near
the shops and bustle of Rue de
Passy. All rooms face the garden,
some have lift access, some have
access from an outside staircase.
Some rooms can be combined
to accommodate a family. Lift.
Cots available.

Nicolo** G12
3 Rue Nicolo, 75016, t 01 42 88 83
40, f 01 42 24 45 41, e hotel.nicolo@
wanadoo.fr; métro Passy.
Small, quiet hotel set back from
the street. Insist on one of the
new rooms that have been indi-
vidually and beautifully
refurbished; the bathrooms have
too, with double sinks and even a
sunken bath in one. Lift to 5th
floor. Cots available.

Inexpensive

Villa d'Auteuil** B16
28 Rue Poussin, 75016, t 01 42 88 30
37, f 01 45 20 74 70, e villaaute@
aol.com, w www.hotel-villa-
dauteuil.com; métro Michel
Ange-Auteuil.
Pleasant tidy rooms; ask for one
over the courtyard. Cots available.

13e: Les Gobelins

Moderate

**Hôtel Résidence
Les Gobelins**** Y20
9 Rue des Gobelins, 75013, t 01 47 07
26 90, f 01 43 31 44 05, e reservation
@hotelgobelins.com, w www.hotel
gobelins.com; métro Les Gobelins.
Friendly hotel at the bottom of
the price range, on a quiet street
just behind the Manufacture
des Gobelins and just a few
minutes' walk from Rue
Mouffetard. The hotel has a lovely
patio with comfortable chairs as
well as a pretty sitting room and
light-filled breakfast room. All
rooms have shower or bath, and
are well equipped and quite
spacious. Lift.

Le Vert Galant*** Y21
43 Rue de Croulebarbe, 75013,
t *01 44 08 83 50,* **f** *01 44 08 83 69;*
métro Les Gobelins; wheelchair access.
Small hotel with just 15 rooms, all of which look on to a small garden filled with vines. Some rooms have kitchens; all are nicely decorated with small modern bathrooms. You'll receive a warm welcome here and at its restaurant next door, L'Auberge Etchegorry, which specializes in Basque dishes and offers hotel guests good deals. The hotel's position, a little out of the way, turns out to be one of its best features.

Inexpensive

Beaux-Arts* AA23
2 Rue Toussaint-Féron, 75013,
t *01 44 24 22 60,* **f** *01 44 24 52 10;*
métro Tolbiac.
Small hotel in the residential neighbourhood west of the Très Grande Bibliothèque. The rooms are decent, with TV and modem. Some look on to the garden, where you can have breakfast. No lift.

Hôtel Tolbiac BB23
122 Rue de Tolbiac, 75013, **t** *01 44 24 25 54,* **f** *01 45 85 43 47,* **e** *htolbiac@club-internet.fr,* **w** *www.hotel-tolbiac.com; métro Tolbiac.*
Friendly hotel in this untouristy, genuine Parisian neighbourhood west of the TGB. There's a courtyard garden where you can have breakfast.

Canal St-Martin

Inexpensive

Hôtel Vicq-d'Azir EE6
21 Rue Vicq-d'Azir, 75010, **t** *01 42 08 06 70,* **f** *01 42 08 06 80; métro Colonel-Fabien.*
Medium-sized hotel between the Canal St-Martin and the Parc des Buttes-Chaumont; its friendly, new owners have given it a bit of a face-lift. Some of the rooms look over the small garden.

Youth Hostels/ Foyers

The three top *foyers* in Paris are superb *hôtels particuliers* in the Marais, all furnished with period pieces and immaculately maintained, where you can stay up to seven days at only €21–26 per person (in a double room), with breakfast. Too good to be true? The hitch is that they are often occupied by groups, they take no individual bookings and you have to be younger than 30; to nab a bed come at 8am (cash only).

They are run by the Maison Internationale de la Jeunesse et des Étudiants (MIJE), **t** 01 42 74 23 45, **f** 01 40 27 81 64.

(47) Le Fauconnier BB14
11 Rue du Fauconnier, 75004; métro St-Paul.

(48) Hôtel de Fourcy BB13
6 Rue de Fourcy, 75004; métro St-Paul.

(49) Hôtel Maubuisson Z13
12 Rue des Barres, 75004; métro Hôtel-de-Ville.

Auberge Internationale des Jeunes GG15
10 Rue Trousseau, 75011, **t** *01 47 00 62 00,* **f** *01 47 00 33 16,* **e** *aij@aijparis.com,* **w** *www.auberge.artinternet.fr; métro Ledru-Rollin.*
Claims to be the cheapest hostel in Paris: Mar–Oct €14 per person per night, including breakfast, Nov–Feb €12.50. Daily lock-out 10am–3pm. Book well in advance.

Other hostel options include:

FIAP Jean Monnet Off maps
30 Rue Cabanis, 75014, **t** *01 43 13 17 17,* **f** *01 45 81 63 91,* **e** *fiapadmi@fiap.asso.fr; métro Glacière.*
Rooms with 2–6 beds for €48 per person per night. Self-service restaurant. No age limit, but mostly a young crowd.

Maison Internationale des Jeunes Off maps
4 Rue Titon, 75011, **t** *01 43 71 99 21,* **f** *01 43 71 78 58; métro Faidherbe-Chaligny; wheelchair access.*
Large hostel with a couple of hundred rooms, 11 of which have

full disabled facilities. A twin room with shower €30.50 per person per night inc. breakfast. Facilities include two restaurants, a bar, Internet access and there's even a garden. Maximum stay 3 months.

Y & H, or Youth's Residence Mouffetard Y17–18
80 Rue Mouffetard, 75005, **t** *01 45 35 09 53,* **f** *01 47 07 22 24,* **e** *smile@youngandhappy.fr,* **w** *www.youngandhappy.fr; métro Place Monge.*
The 'Young and Happy Hostel' on the 'Mouff' has become something of a Paris institution. It has twin, triple and quad rooms and showers; doubles cost €25 per person (inc. breakfast). There's also a kitchen and Internet access. 2am curfew.

Bed and Breakfast

For information about B&Bs in Paris, contact B&B France in the UK or France:

UK: *P.O. Box 55, Bell Street, Henley-on-Thames, Oxon RG9 1XS, UK,* **t** *(01491) 578 803,* **f** *(01491) 410 806,* **e** *bookings@bedbreak.demon.co.uk,* **w** *www.bedbreak.com.* Rooms cost €45–90 and are mostly in small apartments.

France: *B&B France, 6 Rue d'Europe, 95470 Fosses,* **t** *01 34 68 83 15,* **f** *01 34 72 29 31,* **e** *bab@bedbreak.com.*

Campsites

Les Campings du Bois de Boulogne
Allée au Bord-de-l'Eau, **t** *01 45 24 30 00,* **f** *01 42 24 42 95,* **w** *www.mobilehome-paris.com; a bus links it to métro Porte Maillot April–Oct (free July and Aug).*
This campsite in the Bois de Boulogne is the only one in Paris. As a consequence, it is nearly always full. Pitch for a two-person tent from €12.95 per night; lower rates Sept–June. First come, first served.

Short-term Rentals

If you plan to spend a week or more in Paris, a short-term let may save you money, especially if you're travelling with the family, when eating out for every meal including breakfast can be more expensive than a hotel room. Listings per *arrondissement* can be found in the *Pages Jaunes* under *Location d'appartements*.

At Home in Paris M5
16 Rue Médéric, 75017, **t** *01 42 12 40 40,* **f** *01 42 12 40 48.*
Studios to six-bedroom flats. Studios €600–1,000 a month, one-bed flats €900–2,200 a month. English-speaking staff.

Citadines Apart'Hotels
t *08 25 33 33 32,* **w** *www.citadines.com.*
A large and well-run chain of short-term flat operators, with units available in almost all parts of Paris. Prices vary widely from luxury in the 8e to cram-'em-in in the 14e.

Paris Apartments Services W10
69 Rue d'Argout, 75002, **t** *01 40 28 01 28,* **f** *01 40 28 92 01.*
Studios and one-room apartments of character in central Paris.

Paris Séjour Réservation M8
France: 90 Av des Champs-Elysées, **t** *01 53 89 10 50,* **f** *01 53 89 10 59;* *USA: 645 N. Michigan Ave, Chicago, Il,* **t** *(312) 587 7707,* **f** *(312) 587 9887,* **w** *www.psrparis.com.*
Flats to buy or rent. Studios €60–150 per night; one-bed flats €70–250 per night.

Pierre et Vacances Off Maps
11 Rue de Cambrai, 75019, **t** *01 58 21 55 22,* **w** *www.pierre-vacances.fr;* *métro Corentin-Cariou.*
A most reputable agency of long standing with a wide range of units and branches in Bercy, Montmartre and Montparnasse, among other places.

Booking from the UK

Angel Travel
34 High St, Borough Green, Sevenoaks, TN15 8BJ, **t** *(01732) 884109,* **f** *(01732) 883221.*
Flats in Paris. No minimum stay.

The Apartment Service
5–6 Francis Grove, London SW19 4DT, **t** *(020) 8944 1444,* **f** *(020) 8944 6744,* **w** *www.apartmentservice.com.*
Flats available in Paris for short or long stays. Book well ahead.

Booking from the USA

At Home in France
P.O. Box 643, Ashland, OR 97520, **t** *(541) 488 9467,* **f** *(541) 488 9468,* **w** *www.athomeinfrance.com.*
Apartments for rent in Paris, from moderate to deluxe. Minimum stay 7 days.

Doorways Ltd
900 County Line Road, Bryn Mawr, PA 19010, **t** *800 261 4460,* **t** *(610) 520 0806,* **f** *(610) 520 0807,* **e** *info@doorwaysltd.com,* **w** *www.villavacations.com.*
Apartments for rent in Paris.

France By Heart
P.O. Box 614, Mill Valley, CA 94942, **t** *(415) 331 3075,* **f** *(415) 331 3076,* **e** *josette@francebyheart.com,* **w** *www.francebyheart.com.*
Apartments for rent in Paris.

New York Habitat
307 7th Av, Suite 306, New York, NY 10001, **t** *(212) 255 8018,* **f** *(212) 627 1416,* **w** *www.nyhabitat.com.*
Five hundred apartments throughout Paris; minimum stay 4 days. Also offer B & B accommodation; minimum stay 2 nights.

Eating Out

Cooking styles, like everything else in Paris, go in and out of fashion. What some enthusiastic food writers call *haute cuisine* is really what the French call *cuisine bourgeoise*: elaborate dishes concocted as much to impress as to please in the pretentious boulevard restaurants a century ago. Lots of places still cook this way, either for tourists or for nostalgic Parisians.

Nouvelle cuisine (expensive ingredients, new and strange combinations, minute portions artily presented on huge plates at indigestible prices) began as a reaction to bourgeois cooking; you won't see much of it now, but the fad did much to turn the French back to a more natural way of cooking. Although vegetarians will still have a hard time in many restaurants, at home Parisians eat more seafood and vegetables now than ever before, and vegetarian restaurants are becoming more common (*see* 'Vegetarian Restaurants', p.335).

Nearly all the restaurants listed below offer set-price menus, sometimes including wine. Little adventures à la carte are liable to double the price. As anywhere in France, cheap/moderate places usually expect that most of their guests will order one of the menus, especially at lunch, and they do their best to offer a good deal. The easiest way to tell a useless restaurant or a tourist-exploiter without going inside is to look at the menus – any place that offers you *crudités* and a *steak frites* for over €13, for example.

Some expensive restaurants put on an inferior, cheap lunch menu just to get people in the door. On the other hand, some of the most famous places offer excellent bargain lunch menus that even budget-balancers can treat themselves to perhaps once or twice.

For dinner, bookings are essential – weeks in advance (even for lunch) for real gourmet citadels on popular dates (or be prepared

to be flexible). In the moderate/cheap range, you will probably get a table weekday nights without booking, but don't try it on weekends. Brasseries tend to have lots of tables, and spare ones aren't difficult to find except at the most famous.

What restaurants choose to call themselves means little, whether it's an *auberge*, a *relais* or, most fashionable these days, a bistrot. The original bistrots evolved from the old *bougnats bois-et-charbons*, run by rough-edged Auvergnats who sold wine and snacks along with wood and coal. Real ones have a friendly, neighbourhood feel, where you wait for a table over a glass of wine at the bar, and dine on hearty country classics like sausages and *andouillettes*, *bœuf bourguignon* and salt cod. A few examples of the big, working-class restaurants called *bouillons* still survive, such as the famous Chartier.

Brasseries were founded by refugees from Alsace-Lorraine after the war with Prussia in 1871, and specialized in beer and *choucroute* (sauerkraut), along with such Paris classics as *steak frites*, *moules frites*, *plâteau de fruits de mer* and *steak tartare*. Brasseries usually serve meals around the clock until midnight, rather like American diners, and many offer breakfast. Other restaurants open more or less from 12pm with last orders at 2pm and 7 until 10.30 or 11pm. In Paris the trend is towards staying open later and later, though you won't be able to get lunch after 2pm in most places. Remember that many restaurants are closed in August.

For lunch look for the *plat du jour* (the chef's special) or a *formule* (a set-price little-choice menu); nearly any café will make you an omelette, *steak frites*, a hot dog, a horseburger with egg, or ham and melted cheese on toast called *croque-monsieur* or *croque-madame* (a *croque-monsieur* with an egg on top).

Price Categories

The restaurants below are divided into the following price ranges, which are for an average two-course meal for one person:

very expensive over €60
expensive over €30–60
moderate €15–30
cheap under €15

Cafés, *Salons de Thé* and *Glaciers*

Nearly every crossroads in Paris has its café, an institution dating back to the 17th century, where people could shed their social and class distinctions and speak their minds about politics and (eventually) start revolutions. With Haussmann's creation of the Grands Boulevards, cafés became what many remain to this day: passive grandstands of the passing throng, a place to meet friends and be at once private and yet public. A *salon de thé*, on the other hand, tends to be more inward-looking, concentrating on light (and often overpriced) luncheons, but usually good for a cup of coffee or tea and a pastry. *Glaciers* are ice-cream parlours.

The Islands

Restaurants

Very Expensive

(47) Hiramatsu AA14
7 Quai de Bourbon, 4e, t 01 56 81 08 80, w www.hiramatsu.co.jp; *métro* Pont-Marie. *Open* Tues–Sat 12.30–2 and 8–1; closed hols and August. Japanese owned but with entirely French cuisine in a modern, sleek setting. Dishes such as *Crème de grenouille en feuilleté de truffe* or *Bar à la ligne avec sa tapenade* are delicious and lighter than the usual French cooking. Menu €95. See 'Les Halles' map, p.327.

L'Orangerie AA15
28 Rue St-Louis-en-l'Île, 4e, t 01 46 33 93 98; *métro* Pont-Marie. *Open* 8–12; closed Aug; book ahead.

One of the most elegant and romantic dining rooms in Paris, founded by actor Jean-Claude Brialy as an after-theatre rendezvous for his colleagues; refined *cuisine bourgeoise*. Menu at a reasonable €65, wine included.

Expensive

L'Ilot Vache AA15
35 Rue St-Louis-en-l'Île, 4e, t 01 46 33 55 16; *métro Pont-Marie. Open daily 7–11.30pm plus Sun 12–4pm.*
Lovely, old-fashioned and full of flowers, with an honest €23 menu that usually includes lots of seafood.

Moderate

Au Rendez-vous des Camionneurs W13
72 Quai des Orfèvres, Île-de-la-Cité, 1er, t 01 43 54 88 74; *métro Cité. Open daily 12–11.*
Good French-truckers' style cooking. Lunch menu €16, dinner menu €23.

Brasserie de l'Isle Saint-Louis Z14
55 Quai de Bourbon, 4e, t 01 43 54 02 59; *métro Pont-Marie. Open Fri–Tues 12–12.30, Thurs eve. only. No reservations.*
For lovers of old-fashioned *choucroute*. Tables outside.

Caveau du Palais W13
19 Place Dauphine, 4e, t 01 43 26 04 28; *métro Cité or Pont-Neuf. Open Mon–Sat 12–2.30 and 7–10.30 (open Sun May–Sept). No credit cards.*
Excellent quality establishment with a terrace, set in one of the most romantic squares in Paris. Menu €32.

Restaurant Paul W13
15 Place Dauphine and 52 Quai des Orfèvres, 1er, t 01 43 54 21 48; *métro Pont-Neuf. Open Tues–Sun 12–2.30 and 7–10.30.*
White damask tablecloths and red banquettes. A few tables outside overlooking the peaceful square. *Blanquette de veau, salade de lentilles aux petits lardons* and *baba au rhum* (around €30).

Cafés and Salons de Thé

Le Bateau Ivre AA14
19 Rue des Deux-Ponts, Île St-Louis, 7e, t 01 43 26 92 15; *métro Pont-Marie. Open Tues–Sun until 2am.*
Cheap Provencal and Mexican cuisine. Noisy but fun for a late-night drop-in with owners Chris and Gaetan. Menu €10/16.50.

Berthillon AA15
31 Rue St-Louis-en-l'Île, Île St-Louis, 4e, t 01 43 54 31 61; *métro Pont-Marie. Open Wed–Fri 1–8, Sat and Sun 2–8; takeaway Wed–Sun 10–8.*
Paris' best ice creams and sorbets with a list of flavours a mile long; you can also enjoy them sitting down in most of the island's cafés.

Le Flore en l'Île Z14
42 Quai d'Orléans, Île St-Louis, 4e, t 01 43 29 88 27; *métro Pont-Marie. Open daily 8am–2am.*
Great view over Notre-Dame, great tea, great Berthillon ice cream (straight and in exotic cocktails) and a terrace.

The Grand Axe

Restaurants

Very Expensive

Les Ambassadeurs Q–R9
Hôtel de Crillon, 10 Place de la Concorde, 8e, t 01 44 71 16 16; *métro Concorde. Open 12–2 and 7–10.30 (last orders).*
One of Paris' most sumptuous settings and highly-rated cuisine of Byzantine complexity; the €62 lunch menu is a relative bargain. Book well ahead.

Copenhague K7–8
142 Av des Champs-Elysées, 8e, t 01 44 13 86 26; *métro George-V. Open weekdays 12.15–2.30 and 7.15–10.*
Sophisticated Scandinavian cuisine specializing in a wide variety of delicious salmon dishes; or try reindeer *pressé*. Menu €46.50/100.

Maxim's R9
3 Rue Royale, 8e, t 01 42 65 27 94, w www.maxims-de-paris.com; *métro Concorde. Open Tues–Fri 12.30–2 and 7.30–10.*
Still the most beautiful restaurant in the galaxy, with perfectly preserved Belle Époque rooms, and the food isn't bad either; but it is the fate of any place so famous to become more of a tourist attraction than a mere restaurant. Overpriced: be prepared to spend more than €100.

Restaurant Plaza Athénée M10
25, Av Montaigne, 8e, t 01 53 67 66 65, f 01 53 67 66 66 w www. alain-ducasse.com; *métro Franklin-Roosevelt or Alma Marceau. Open Mon–Fri 12–2 and 7.30–10; closed mid-July to mid-Aug, last two weeks in Dec and hols.*
Now under the direction of Alain Ducasse, the only *chef de cuisine* in France to have three Michelin stars in two places at once, here and at the Louis XV in the Hôtel de Paris in Monaco. Book in advance and take out a loan for the experience of a lifetime. Menus €190–250.

Taillevent L7
15 Rue Lamennais, 8e, t 01 44 95 15 01; *métro George-V. Open Mon–Fri 12.30–1.30 and 7.30–10; closed mid-July–mid-Aug. Booking essential.*
Vrinat is still at the top, despite all the young hot-shots, with his brilliantly prepared classic dishes and his care of the customer. In the handsome *hôtel* of the Duc de Morny. The exceptional wine list is reasonably priced. Menus €130–180.

Expensive

L'Avenue M9
41 Av Montaigne, 8e, t 01 40 70 14 91; *métro Franklin D. Roosevelt. Open daily 10am–1am.*
Hip restaurant for the fashionable crowd, where you'll find fish, salads and mobile phones.

La Fermette Marbeuf 1900 L9
5 Rue Marbeuf, 8e, t 01 53 23 08 00; *métro George-V. Open daily 12–3 and 7–11.30.*
Lovingly restored Art Nouveau décor and now part of a chain; almost over the top in its way, but

Couples' City

For a special evening out in the city of lovers try one of the following restaurants, picked for their intimate atmosphere or stylish food and décor:

A Beauvilliers (métro Lamarck-Caulaincourt; see p.329), **Caveau François Villon** (métro Louvre-Rivoli; see p.324), **Caveau du Palais** (métro Cité or Pont-Neuf; see p.317), **Le Grand Colbert** (métro Bourse or Pyramides; see p.322), **Le Grand Véfour** (métro Palais-Royal or Bourse; see p.320), **La Guirlande de Julie** (métro Chemin-Vert or Bastille; see p.328), **L'Ilot Vache** (métro Pont-Marie; see p.317), **Jules Verne** (métro Bir-Hakeim; see p.320), **Lapérouse** (métro St-Michel; see p.331), **L'Orangerie** (métro Pont-Marie; see p.316), **Pavillon Montsouris** (RER Cité-Universitaire; see p.340), **Le Pré Catelan** (métro Porte Dauphine; see p.338), **La Tour d'Argent** (métro Maubert-Mutualité; see p.334).

redeemed by an honest €27/41 lunch/dinner menu.

Flora Danica K7–8
See Copenhague, above, for details, w www.restaurantfloradanica.com. A cheaper alternative downstairs from the Copenhague; tables outside. Menu €30–50.

Le Fouquet's L8
99 Av des Champs-Elysées, 8e, t 01 47 23 50 00; métro George-V. Open daily 8am–2am. See 'Cafés, Salons de Thé and Glaciers', below. Menus for €40.50, €45.75 and €68.50.

Man Ray M9
34 Rue Marbeuf, 8e, t 01 56 88 36 36, w www.manray.info; métro Franklin D. Roosevelt. Open Mon–Fri 12.30–3.30pm, bar 6pm–2am, restaurant 7.30–12am; Sat and Sun bar 6pm–2am, restaurant 7–midnight.
Cavernous, trendy restaurant just off Les Champs owned by a bunch of movie stars. Oriental dishes/sushi and cocktails (its owners also run the Bouddha Bar). Lunch menu €20. In winter there's jazz Mon–Thurs 6pm–8pm.

Nobu M9
15 Rue Marbeuf, 8e, t 01 56 89 53 53; métro Franklin D. Roosevelt. Open Tues–Sat 12–2.15 and 7–11.15, Sat and Sun 7–11.15 only.
Newly opened restaurant and cocktail bar. Part of a glamorous, international group of Japanese restaurants also loved by the fashion crowd.

Renoma Café Gallery L9
32 Av George-V, 8e, t 01 56 89 05 89; métro George-V. Open daily 12.30pm–2am.
Huge gallery-restaurant decked out like a yacht and decorated with black and white photos and film stills. The chic restaurant specializes in fish: Scottish smoked salmon with blinis, turbot grillé et vraie sauce hollandaise, tarte aux tomates, plus delicious desserts. Menu €30/35.

Spoon, Food and Wine M9
14, rue de Marignan, 8e, métro Franklin Roosevelt, t 01 40 76 34 44 f 01 40 76 34 37, w www.spoon. tm.fr. Open Mon–Fri 12–2 and 7–11, closed July 20 to Aug 20.
New concept restaurant by Alain Ducasse. Dishes are categorized under headings such as Cereal, Egg, Fish and you can create your own combinations to suit your taste. Menus €35–37.

Moderate

Café Marly U11
Palais du Louvre, 1er; métro Palais-Royal. Open daily 8am–2am. See 'Cafés, Salons de Thé and Glaciers', below.

Chez La Vieille W12
37 Rue de l'Arbre-Sec, 1er, t 01 42 60 15 78; métro Louvre-Rivoli. Open Mon–Fri lunch, Thurs dinner also. La Vieille may have retired, but the food is still first-rate (e.g. pot-au-feu); a classic French repast. Menu €26.

Chez Savy N9–10
23 Rue Bayard, 8e, t 01 47 23 46 98; métro Franklin D. Roosevelt. Open Mon–Fri 12–2.30 and 7.30–11; closed Aug.
Full-blooded Auvergne cooking. One of our recommendations

à l'ancienne. Surprising for the glitzy area. Lunch menus €19.50/23.50, dinner €26.50.

Findi L9–10
24 Av George-V, 8e t 01 47 20 14 78; métro Alma-Marceau. Open daily 12–3 and 7–midnight.
Trendy Italian restaurant with excellent fresh pasta and Italian wines. Menu €25/30.

Maison de l'Alsace M8
39 Av des Champs-Elysées, 8e, t 01 53 93 97 00, w www.restaurant alsace.com; métro Franklin D. Roosevelt. Open daily 24 hours. Nothing special but always lively and could be useful if you're out late. Menu €24/32.

Montecristo Café M8
68 Av des Champs-Elysées, 8e, t 01 45 62 30 86, w www.monte cristo-cafe.com; métro Franklin D. Roosevelt. Open daily 12pm–dawn. See 'Cafés, Salons de Thé and Glaciers', below.

Cheap

Radis Olive M9
27 rue de Marignan, 8e, metro Franklin Roosevelt, t 01 42 56 55 55. Open daily 12–12.
Fast and easy Lebanese restaurant with lots of vegetarian options. Menu €11.50–16.

Cafés, Salons de Thé and Glaciers

Angelina S10
226 Rue de Rivoli, 1er, t 01 42 60 82 00; métro Tuileries. Open daily 9–7. A Viennese confection, vintage 1903 (when it was called Rumpelmayer), with a special rich African chocolate and the world's best montblanc (chestnut cream, meringue and chantilly).

Aux Délices de Scott N4
39 Av de Villiers, t 01 47 63 71 36; métro Villiers. Open Mon–Fri 9–7, Sat 12–7, closed on Sat in summer. A peaceful salon de thé from the beginning of the 20th century, located near Parc Monceau. A good choice of teas as well as some delicious pastries.

Cador W12

Rue des Prêtres, 1er, **t** *01 45 08 19 18;* **métro** *Louvre-Rivoli or Pont-Neuf.* **Open** *Tues–Sun 8.30am–7pm.*
Traditional *salon de thé* just beyond the Louvre's Cour Carré.

Café Blanc M9

40 Rue François-1er, 8e, **t** *01 53 67 30 13;* **métro** *Franklin D. Roosevelt.* **Open** *Mon–Fri 8.30am–7pm, Sat 11–6.*
Small, sleek café dressed in white, steel and mirrors.

Café Marly U11

In the Louvre courtyard, facing the Pyramid, 1er, **t** *01 49 26 06 60;* **métro** *Palais Royal-Musée du Louvre.* **Open** *daily 8am–2am.*
New, beautifully designed, chic hangout in the old ministries vacated for the Grand Louvre project, serving everything from burgers to caviar. Lunch and dinner cost €30 and up, snacks are cheaper. Especially pretty at night.

Le Fouquet's L8

99 Av des Champs-Elysées, 8e, **t** *01 47 23 50 00,* **w** *www.lucien barriere.com;* **métro** *George-V.* **Open** *daily 8am–2am.*
A wood-panelled, century-old bar, still frequented by the arty-political set; also an expensive restaurant. Tables outside.

Ladurée M8

75 Av des Champs-Elysées, 8e, **t** *01 40 75 08 75* **w** *www.laduree.fr;* **métro** *Franklin D. Roosevelt.* **Open** *daily 8am–midnight.*
Exquisite and precious *salon de thé,* famous for its macaroons. Bring your laciest great-aunt along for tea. It also has a €34.50 menu. The original branch of Ladurée is at 16 Rue Royale (métro Madeleine).

Montecristo Café M8

68 Av des Champs-Elysées, 8e, **t** *01 47 27 81 11,* **w** *www.monte cristo-cafe.com;* **métro** *Franklin D. Roosevelt.* **Open** *daily 12pm–dawn.*
Salsa, lip-smackingly good margaritas and Italian cuisine in a pseudo-hip, pseudo-Havana setting, near capitalist gringo dinosaurs, Planet Hollywood and the Disney shop; Menu €38. Dancers at weekends.

Virgin Café M–N8

52 Av des Champs-Elysées (in the Virgin Megastore), 8e, **t** *01 42 89 46 81;* **métro** *Franklin D. Roosevelt.* **Open** *Mon–Sat 10am–midnight, Sun and hols 12–12.*
No seats outside, but still a trendy favourite, and a big surprise, with innovative cooking at reasonable prices; everything from gazpacho to salmon on toast to hamburgers to *saltimbocca alla romana* (€12–25).

Musée d'Orsay and the Invalides

Restaurants

Very Expensive

L'Arpège P13

84 Rue de Varenne, 7e, **t** *01 47 05 09 06;* **métro** *Varenne.* **Open** *Mon–Fri 12.30–2.30 and 6–10.30.*
Renowned chef Alain Passard now devotes his menu almost exclusively to vegetarian dishes (around €150). Menu dégustation €300.

La Bourdonnais M13

113 Av de La-Bourdonnais, 7e, **t** *01 47 05 47 96;* **métro** *École-Militaire.* **Open** *daily 12–2.30 and 8–11.*
Beautifully prepared dishes from the fragrant Midi: *croustillant de homard risotto safrané, turbot à la crème de citron confit* and delicious raspberry desserts. Great-value menus at €42 (lunch, wine included), dinner €64 and up.

Expensive

Tan Dinh S12

60 Rue de Verneuil, 7e, **t** *01 45 44 04 84;* **métro** *Solférino.* **Open** *Mon–Sat 12–2 and 7.30–11.*
Vietnamese cooking in a way Parisians like it – steamed crab pâté, lobster triangles with ginkgo nuts. Not cheap (€45 à la carte), but excellent.

Moderate

L'Ami Jean M12

27 Rue Malar, 7e, **t** *01 47 05 86 89;* **métro** *Latour-Maubourg.* **Open** *Tues–Sat 12–2 and 7–midnight; closed Aug.*
Owned by a former *pelote* champion, who serves good Basque dishes in a friendly atmosphere.

Il Duomo N14

96 Bd de La-Tour-Maubourg, 7e, **t** *01 44 18 36 37;* **métro** *Latour-Maubourg.* **Open** *Mon–Fri 12–2.45 and 8–11.15, Sat dinner only; closed Aug.*
Small neighbourhood Italian restaurant. Lunch menu €21.

La Fontaine de Mars L–M12

129 Rue St-Dominique, 7e, **t** *01 47 05 46 44;* **métro** *Ecole-Militaire.* **Open** *daily 12–3 and 7.30–midnight; closed mid-July–mid-Aug.*
Traditional *bonne-femme* cooking, with checked tablecloths outside under an arcade in a bijou square near the Eiffel Tower. Lunch menu €14.

Thoumieux N12

79 Rue St-Dominique, 7e, **t** *01 47 05 49 75;* **métro** *Latour-Maubourg.* **Open** *Mon–Sat 12–3 and 6.30–12, Sun 12–12.*
Lively brasserie crowded with civil servants. Cuisine from the south-west: *cassoulet, confit de canard.* Menu €31. Children's menu.

Cheap

Au Pied de Fouet Q15

45 Rue de Babylone, 7e, **t** *01 47 05 12 27;* **métro** *Sèvres-Babylone.* **Open** *Mon–Fri 12–2.30 and 7–9.30, Sat 12–2.30; closed Aug and Christmas.*
Le Corbusier's favourite restaurant, shared table and long queues for its tasty and very affordable meals.

Chez Germaine Q15–16

30 Rue Pierre-Leroux (south of Rue de Babylone, parallel to Rue Vaneau), 7e, **t** *01 42 73 28 34;* **métro** *Vaneau.* **Open** *Mon–Fri 12–2.30 and 7–9.30, Sat 12–2.30; closed hols and Aug. No credit cards or smoking.*

Not to be missed by gourmets on a budget. Arrive early for a delicious lunch for under €10. Dinner menu €12.

Cafés and Salons de Thé

Café in the Musée Rodin Garden P13

Hôtel Biron, 77 Rue de Varenne, 7e, t 01 43 59 17 27; métro Varenne. Open summer 9.30–6.30, winter 9.30–4.30.
There's no better place for a drink or a simple lunch on a lovely day (for €9–14).

Pâtisserie Jean Millet M12

103 Rue St-Dominique, 7e, t 01 45 51 49 80; métro Latour-Maubourg. Open Mon–Sat 9–7, Sun 8–1.
Only a dozen tables, but perfect for a cup of tea, and the cakes are to die for.

Eiffel Tower and Trocadéro

Restaurants

Very Expensive

L'Astrance Off Maps

4 Rue Beethoven, 16e, t 01 40 50 84 40, f 01 40 50 11 45 métro Passy. Open Mon–Fri 12.30–2 (order between 12.30 and 1) and 8–10 (order between 8 and 9).
Lip-smacking food in mouse-sized portions served in austere Bauhaus architecture surroundings. Book well in advance as this restaurant is very popular with the trendies. Menu €35–85 and surprise menu €105.

Jules Verne J12

Eiffel Tower (private lift to 2nd floor), 7e, t 01 45 55 61 44; métro Bir-Hakeim. Open daily 12–2.30 and 7.15–9.30.
Haute cuisine as highly rated as its romantic position, 400ft above Paris. Succulent *poulet de Bresse* with mushrooms and much more; the weekday lunch menu costs €51, but be prepared to spend more than €114. Be sure to reserve, and insist on a window seat.

Expensive

Oum El Banine Off Maps

16 Bis Rue Dufrenoy, 16e, t 01 45 04 91 22, métro Rue de la Pompe. Open Tues–Sat 12–2 and 7–12, Mon 7–12.
Upmarket Moroccan cuisine featuring aromatic lemony tajines, lamb and spicy stews made with bundles of TLC.

Le Totem H-I11

Palais de Chaillot (Musée de l'Homme), 17 Place du Trocadéro, 16e, t 01 47 27 28 29; métro Trocadéro. Open daily 12pm–2am.
Terrace with amazing view of Eiffel Tower. Busy but not cheap. Lunch menu €21.50.

Moderate

Le Scheffer G11

22 Rue Scheffer, 16e, t 01 47 27 81 11; métro Trocadéro. Open Mon–Sat 12–2.30 and 7.30–10.30; closed Sat in July and Aug.
Neighbourhood restaurant serving good *entrecôte bordelaise* and a diet-demolishing dark *mousse au chocolat*.

Cafés and Salons de Thé

Aux Pains Perdus I10

Corner of Rue de Longchamp and Kléber (by the Musée Guimet), 16e, t 01 44 05 12 92; métro Iéna. Open Mon–Fri 8.30–5.
Popular sit-down sandwich bar.

Maison du Japon I13

101 Bis Quai Branly, 15e, t 01 44 37 95 95, w www.mcjp.asso.fr; RER Champ de Mars-Tour Eiffel. Open Tues–Sat 12–7pm; closed Aug.
Salon de thé on 1st floor, with traditional tea-making ceremony every Wed.

Opéra and Palais Royal

Restaurants

Very Expensive

(13) Drouant U9

18 Place Gaillon, 2e, t 01 42 65 15 16; métro Opéra or Quatre Septembre.

Open Mon–Fri 12–3 and 7–midnight.
Since 1914 the seat of the Académie Goncourt, where it bestows France's most sought-after literary prize. Sumptuous Art Deco interior; famous for its elegant sauces, wine cellar and its *grand dessert Drouant*. Lunch menu €44.25. The **Café Drouant** has a €36 menu.

(21) Le Grand Véfour V10

17 Rue de Beaujolais, 1er, t 01 42 96 56 27; métro Palais Royal-Musée du Louvre or Bourse. Open Mon–Fri 12.30–2 and 7.30–10.
More a temple than a crass commercial enterprise, this grandest of grand old restaurants, with one of the loveliest dining rooms in Paris, maintains a tradition in the Palais Royal now 200 years old. Lunch menu €75.

Opéra and Palais Royal
Restaurants and Cafés

(34) Lucas Carton R9
9 Place de la Madeleine, 8e, **t** *01 42 65 22 90, lucas-carton@lucas carton.com;* **métro** *Madeleine.* **Open** *Tues–Fri 12–2.30 and 8–10.30, Sat and Mon 8–10.30; closed first 3 weeks Aug.*
The perfect marriage of tradition, beautiful surroundings and one of the top-rated modern chefs, Alain Senderens. Splurge on the lunch menu of €76; at dinner be prepared to spend up to €200.

Expensive
Brasserie Mollard S7
113 Rue St-Lazare, 8e, across from the métro station, **t** *01 43 87 50 22;* **métro** *St-Lazare.* **Open** *daily 12–12.30.*
Spectacular 1895 decoration: mirrors, terracotta, rare marble and ceiling mosaics of everything that could conceivably be eaten or drunk in a brasserie. Lots of oysters and other seafood. Menus €36–75.

(19) Chez Georges W10
1 Rue du Mail, 2e, t 01 42 60 07 11;
métro Sentier. Open Mon–Sat
12–2.30 and 7.15–9.30.
This fine establishment is at the
very pinnacle of the bistrot range,
with great *frites*. Not cheap, but
the equal of many with much
heftier prices. Be prepared to
spend up to €60.

(33) Goumard S9
9 Rue Duphot, 1er, t 01 42 60 36 07;
métro Madeleine. Open Tues–Sat
12–2.30 and 7.30–10.30; closed
Aug 2–17.
A top-rated seafood restaurant
since the 1890s, recently
completely renovated, though the
original bathrooms are a listed
monument. Menu €40.

(17) Le Grand Colbert V10
Galerie Colbert, Rue des Petits-
Champs, 2e, t 01 42 86 87 88; métro
Bourse or Pyramides. Open 12–1am
and 7–11.30.
Meticulously re-creates the
arcade's 19th-century opulence;
lunch seems dear (€26 and up),
but you may enjoy its incarnation
as a tea room/oyster bar, 4–7pm.

(22) Palais Royal V10
110 Galerie de Valois, under the
arcades, 1er, t 01 40 20 00 27;
métro Palais Royal-Musée du
Louvre. Open Mon–Sat 12–2.30
and 7.15–10.30; closed Sat and Sun
in winter.
Elegant surroundings, and an upmarket menu if you want
next-best to the Grand Véfour.

(27) Le Poquelin U10
17 Rue Molière, 1er, t 01 42 96 22 19;
métro Pyramides. Open Tues–Fri
12–2 and 7–10, Sat and Mon 7–10.
Opposite Molière's birthplace and
popular with actors from the
Comédie-Française, who enjoy
Michel Guillaumin's light, innovative cooking (salmon with cream
of chives sauce and warm *tarte*
aux pommes). Foie gras '*fait*
maison' is a speciality. Menu €33.

(31) Au Petit Théâtre T10
15 Place du Marché-St-Honoré, 1e,
t 01 42 61 00 93; métro Tuileries.
Open Tues–Sat 12–2.30 and
7–10.30.

A restaurant that prides itself on
using all parts of the pig; love for
the animal is even seen in the
décor of pink walls and jovial
ceramic pigs. Non pork-lovers have
other good choices as well. Menu
€18–22.50.

(14) Pierre à la
Fontaine Gaillon U9
Place Gaillon, 2e, t 01 47 42 63 22;
métro Opéra. Open Mon–Fri
12–2.30 and 7–11.15; closed Aug.
Seasonal menus based on seafood
in the mansion of the Duc de
Lorgues; tables out on the terrace
by the Fontaine d'Antin. Menu €32.

Sarladais Q–R6
2 Rue de Vienne, 8e, t 01 45 22
23 62; métro Europe. Open Mon–Fri
12–2 and 7.30–10, winter also Sat
7.30–10.
Here you can have a faultless
upscale Périgord meal with first-
class service; menus range from
€22.10 at lunch time to a pricier
€35 for dinner.

(32) Soufflé S10
36 rue du Mont Thabor, 1e, t 01 42
60 27 19; métro Concorde. Open
Mon–Sat 12–2.30 and 7–10.30,
closed 3 weeks in Aug and 2 weeks
in Feb.
Keep an eye on your dog, the chef
will soufflé anything he gets his
hands on! Examples include
lobster, sole, artichokes, fruit and
even crêpes. Non-souffléd dishes
also feature on the €32 menu. All
soufflé menu €29.

Café Terminus S6–7
108 Rue St-Lazare, 8e, t 01 42 94
22 22; métro St-Lazare. Open daily
12–2.30 and 7–10.
Another trip to the gay 1890s;
excellent cuisine on a bargain
€32 menu.

Moderate

(30) Androuet...sur le Pouce U9
49 Rue St-Roch, 1er, t 01 42 97 57 39;
métro Pyramides; and 23 Rue
Acacias, 17e, t 01 40 68 00 12; métro
Argentine. Open 12–2.30 and
7–9.30.
Cheese-and-wine combinations
recommended. Many wines by the
glass (€4), and huge *tartines*.

(23) Au Bec Fin U10
6 bis Rue Thérèse, 1er, t 01 42 96
29 35; métro Palais Royal-Musée
du Louvre. Open Tues–Sat 12–2.30
and 7–10.
Traditional restaurant: *steak grillé*,
magret de canard etc. Menus €24.
It also has a café-theatre (reservations t 01 42 96 29 35, tickets €12,
reduction if you eat), with children's shows too.

(26) Il Cardinale V10
34 Rue de Richelieu, 1er, t 01 49 27
05 22; métro Pyramides. Open daily
10–3.30 and 6.30–12.
Friendly Italian restaurant with its
own pet budgies, serving fresh
pasta and other dishes. Also sells
Italian products (Illy coffee and
olive oil) if you fancy a change.
Lunch menu €13, dinner €20.

(1) Chartier W8
7 Rue du Faubourg-Montmartre,
9e, t 01 47 70 86 29; métro Grands
Boulevards. Open 11.30–3 and 6–10.
A landmark that hasn't changed
much since 1892. Simple food at
low prices. Menu €16.80.

(6) Café Flo S7
Au Printemps, 64 Bd Haussmann,
9e, t 01 42 82 62 76; métro
Havre-Caumartin. Open Mon–Sat
9.30–7.
Under the dome of Au Printemps,
this is a good place to take a break
from shopping. Wine and cheese
in the late afternoon come particularly recommended.

(3) Le Gavroche W8
19 Rue St-Marc, 2e, t 01 42 96 89 70;
métro Bourse. Open Mon–Sat
7am–2.30am.
The archetypal family-run *bistrot*
a vins of old; authentic without
even trying. Hearty country
cooking from *cassoulet* to *pot-au-*
feu, and very good wines.

(16) Hokkaido V9
14 Rue Chabanais, 2e, t 01 42 60
50 95; métro Pyramides. Open
Thurs–Tues 11.30–10.30.
Just one of the many good
oriental restaurants in the area.

(25) L'Incroyable U–V10
Passage Potier, 26 Rue de Richelieu,
2e, t 01 42 96 24 64; métro

Richelieu-Drouot. **Open** Mon–Sat 12–2.30 and 7–9.30.
Truly incredible cheap bistrot in an alley off the street. Menu €18–25.

(4) Jhelum V8
30 Rue St-Marc, 2e, **t** 01 42 96 99 43; **métro** Richelieu-Drouot. **Open** daily lunch and dinner.
Indian-Pakistani. Menus €12/17.

(36) Lescure X9
7 Rue de Mondovi, 1er, **t** 01 42 60 18 91; **métro** Concorde. **Open** Mon–Fri 12–2.15 and 7–10.30; closed hols, Aug and Christmas.
Run by the same family since 1919, with a classic menu featuring warming stews and game dishes. There are tables outside and a non-smoking section. Menu €21.

(5) Les Noces de Jeannette V8
14 Rue Favart (south of Bd des Italiens), 2e, **t** 01 42 96 36 89; **métro** Richelieu-Drouot. **Open** daily 12–2 and 7–9.30.
A re-minimalized classic with some wonderful dishes, such as the chicken with wild mushrooms, and a good wine list to boot. Menu €15/25.

(8) Le Roi du Pot au Feu S8
34 Rue Vignon, 9e, **t** 01 47 42 37 10; **métro** Madeleine. **Open** Mon–Sat 12–10pm.
Entirely devoted to the most humble and traditional of French dishes, though here they are raised to an art form.

(15) La Souris Verte U9
50 Rue Ste-Anne, 2e, **t** 01 40 20 03 70; **métro** Pyramides. **Open** Mon–Fri 12–2.30 and 7–10.30, Sat 7–10.30.
Good cooking and three courses of it for €11.50; also big salads and a serious €23 dinner menu.

(11) Le Vaudeville V9
29 Rue Vivienne, 2e, **t** 01 40 20 04 62; **métro** Bourse. **Open** daily 12–3.30 and 7pm–2am; closed Christmas eve.
Very good shellfish and foie gras, with a selection of reasonably priced wines by the carafe. Lunch menu €21.50, dinner menu €30.50. Children's menu and terrace. Booking advisable.

Cheap

(18) A Priori Thé V9
35 Galerie Vivienne, 2e, **t** 01 42 97 48 75; **métro** Bourse. **Open** Mon–Fri 9–6, Sat 12–6.30, Sun 12.30–6.30.
See 'Cafés and Salons de Thé'.

(20) Aux Bons Crus V10
7 Rue des Petits-Champs, 1er, **t** 01 42 60 06 45; **métro** Pyramides. **Open** Mon 9–4, Tues–Sat 9am–11pm.
A wine bar with a lunch menu; see p.342.

(12) Chez Danie V9
5 Rue de Louvois, 2e, **t** 01 42 96 64 05; **métro** Richelieu-Drouot. **Open** Mon–Fri 12.2.45; closed hols and 2 weeks in Aug.
A great bargain (menu €8.25/7.70, à la carte €10) with goulash a speciality and home-made desserts. Always packed.

Chez Léon S7
5 Rue de l'Isly, 8e, **t** 01 43 87 42 77; **métro** St-Lazare. **Open** Mon–Sat 11.30am–10pm; closed Aug.
One of the last of the originals complete with chipped Formica table-tops. Genuine truck-stop cooking; plats du jour at €8/10.

(10) Le Domaine de Lintillac V9
10 Rue St-Augustin, 2e, **t** 01 40 20 96 27; **métro** Bourse. **Open** Mon–Fri 12–2.15 and 7–10.15, Sat 7–10.45.
New boutique restaurant with food and wine sourced from the Périgord. Cahors wine, magret de canard, foie gras. There's a toaster on each table for fresh toast to go with your foie gras.

(24) Higuma U10
32 bis Rue Ste-Anne, 1er, **t** 01 47 03 38 52; **métro** Pyramides. **Open** daily 12–10pm.
Classic Japanese noodle bar on the Japanese strip, hot, quick and tasty. There are many similar places to choose from, most with ramen noodles and a wide choice of other dishes for about €10.

Cafés and Salons de Thé

A Priori Thé V9
35–37 Galerie Vivienne, 2e, **t** 01 42 97 48 75; **métro** Bourse. **Open**
Mon–Fri 9–6, Sat 12–6.30, Sun 12.30–6.30.
Take a trip back in time over a cup of English tea and cheesecake under the glass-roofed passage. There's also a simple €22 menu.

(2) L'Arbre à Cannelle W8
57 Passage des Panoramas, 2e, **t** 01 45 08 55 87; **métro** Grands Boulevards. **Open** daily 12–6.
See its sister establishment in 'Jardin des Plantes', p.336.

(9) Café de la Paix T8
12 Bd des Capucines, 9e, **t** 01 40 07 30 20; **métro** Opéra. **Open** daily 12–12.30.
A historic landmark; if you can't afford a ticket to the Opéra, you might just be able to manage the price of a coffee here; architect Garnier's second-best effort in the outlandish style he invented: Napoleon III.

(28) Cafés et Thés Verlet U10
256 Rue St-Honoré, 1er, **t** 01 42 60 05 55; **métro** Pyramides. **Open** Mon–Sat 9.30–7; closed Aug.
Salon de thé with a dark wood interior and a delicious aroma of coffee. It offers a fine selection of teas and coffees, plus light meals and pastries.

(29) La Ferme U9–10
55–57 Rue St Roch, 1er, **t** 01 40 20 12 12; **métro** Pyramides. **Open** Mon–Sat 8–8.
Peaceful salon de thé/sandwich shop where you can sit and read the papers. All fresh produce from farms in the Île-de-France: sandwiches, salads, pastries, cakes, juices, tea and coffee. Look out for more of the same opening elsewhere in Paris.

Le Grand Colbert V10
2e, **t** 01 42 86 87 88; **métro** Bourse or Pyramides. **Open** 12–3 and 7.30–12.30; closed Aug.
See under 'Restaurants', above.

(35) Ladurée R9
16 Rue Royale, 8e, **t** 01 42 60 21 79, **w** www.laduree.fr; **métro** Madeleine. **Open** Mon–Sat 8.30–7, lunch 11.30–3.30, Sun 10–7, brunch 11.30–3.30; closed Christmas and New Year.

Late-night Eats

When it's the small hours of the morning and you're feeling peckish, don't despair. Many places are open till 2am, but the following go right through to morning:

A la Cloche d'Or (métro Blanche; *see* p.330), **Au Pied de Cochon** (métro Les Halles or Louvre-Rivoli; *see* p.324), **Maison de l'Alsace** (métro Franklin D. Roosevelt; *see* p.318), **La Poule au Pot** (métro Les Halles or Louvre; *see* p.325), **La Tour de Montlhéry (Chez Denise)** (métro Les Halles or Louvre-Rivoli; *see* p.324), **L'Alsace aux Halles** (métro Les Halles, see p.324).

Exquisite and precious *salon de thé*, famous for its macaroons. It also does lunch (€10–20) and brunch on Sun for €23 (book ahead for both). There's another branch at 75 Avenue des Champs-Elysées.

Mollard S7
115 Rue St-Lazare, 8e, **t** 01 43 87 50 22; *métro* St-Lazare. **Open** daily 12–12.
Beautiful, well-loved Art Nouveau brasserie.

(7) Paul S7–8
Rue Tronchet, 8e, **t** 01 40 17 99 54, **w** www.paul.fr; *métro* Havre-Caumartin. **Open** Mon–Sat 6am–9pm.
Splendid member of classy chain of *salons de thé/boulangeries/pâtisseries*, with sculpted tortoises and elephants on the façade. Non-smoking *salon de thé* on the first floor, overlooking the hubbub of Boulevard Haussmann. Also on Rue de Buci and in the Carrousel du Louvre.

Beaubourg and Les Halles

Restaurants

Expensive

(24) Benoît Y12
20 Rue St-Martin, 4e, **t** 01 42 72 25 76; *métro* Châtelet. **Open** daily 12–2 and 8–10.

Considered by many the most genuine Parisian bistrot, opened by current owner Michel Petit's grandfather and devoted to the most perfectly prepared dishes of *la grande cuisine bourgeoise française*, with a wondrous *bœuf mode*. Lunch menu €38.

(5) L'Escargot Montorgueil X10
38 Rue Montorgueil, 1er, **t** 01 42 36 83 51; *métro* Les Halles. **Open** Mon–Sat 12.30–2.30 and 7–11; closed 11–21 Aug.
Most of the décor is from the 1830s, and the big snail over the door proclaims the speciality of the house; another favourite is duck *à l'orange*. Twelve snails for €20. Lunch menu €19/32. Reserve in advance.

(8) Pharamond Y11
24 Rue de la Grande-Truanderie, 1er, **t** 01 40 28 45 18; *métro* Étienne-Marcel or Les Halles. **Open** Mon–Sat 12–2.30 and 7.45–10.30; closed first half of Aug.
This has been here since 1832; the Belle Epoque interior is a national monument, and the recipes could be as well, especially the roast rabbit and rich *tripes à la mode de Caen*. Lunch menu €13/18.50/27.

(15) La Tour de Montlhéry (Chez Denise) W11
5 Rue des Prouvaires, 1er, **t** 01 42 36 21 82; *métro* Les Halles or Louvre-Rivoli. **Open** Mon–Fri 24 hours (to 6.30am Sat); closed mid-July to mid-Aug.
An old-fashioned bistrot with character; full of locals not tourists, with hams hanging from the ceiling among the fans. Excellent cooking includes hearty *andouillette*, tripes and *gigot d'agneau*; try the mutton with white beans. There's good wine to boot. Reserve in advance.

Moderate

(13) L'Alsace aux Halles W10–11
16 Rue Coquillère, 1er, **t** 01 42 36 74 24; *métro* Les Halles. **Open** 24 hours.
A brasserie that never closes, with plenty of shellfish to go along with the *choucroute* and Alsatian whites. Menus from €26.

(4) Ambassade d'Auvergne Z11
22 Rue du Grenier-St-Lazare, 3e, **t** or 42 72 31 22, **w** www.ambassade-auvergne.com; *métro* Rambuteau. **Open** daily 12–2 and 7.30–10.30.
Mouthwatering *cuisine de terroir* from the Auvergne (*soupe aux choux et au roquefort, Charlotte aux marrons*), near Beaubourg. Menu €27. Book in advance.

(1) Au Bascou AA10
38 Rue Réaumur, 3e, **t** 01 42 72 69 25; *métro* Arts-et-Métiers. **Open** Tues–Fri 12–2 and 8–11, Mon and Sat 8–11 ; closed hols and Aug.
Nothing to look at from the outside, but wonderful and whacky within, an original with first-class Basque food at reasonable prices. Top it all off with a *marc d'Irouléguy de Brana à St-Jean-Pied-de-Port*.

(3) Auberge Nicolas Flamel Z11
51 Rue de Montmorency, 3e, **t** 01 42 71 77 78; *métro* Rambuteau. **Open** Mon–Fri 12–2.30 and 8–10.45, Sat 8–10.45.
In one of the oldest houses in Paris, refined cooking from *maigrets* cooked with cider to seafood raviolis.

(12) Au Pied de Cochon W–X11
6 Rue Coquillère, 1er, **t** 01 40 13 77 00, **w** www.pieddecochon.com; *métro* Les Halles or Louvre-Rivoli. **Open** 24 hours.
An institution. Famous for its *pied de cochon* as well as its seafood platter.

(17) Caveau François Villon W11
64 Rue de l'Arbre-Sec, 1er, **t** 01 42 36 10 92; *métro* Louvre-Rivoli. **Open** Tues–Fri 12–2.30 and 7.30–midnight, Sat and Mon 7.30–midnight; closed Aug.
A bistrot in a 15th-century cellar, with a strumming guitar in the evening; delicious fresh salmon with orange butter. Menu €24

(9) Chez Vong Y11
10 Rue de la Grande-Truanderie, 1er, **t** 01 40 39 99 89, **w** www.chez-vong.com; *métro* Les Halles. **Open** Mon–Sat 12–2.30 and 7–12.15.
One of the best Chinese restaurants in town. No dingy carp aquarium or Asian pop ear candy,

out instead a dark, atmospheric den superbly decorated to luxurious tastes. Many delicious and unusual dishes such as jellyfish salad or prawns wrapped in lotus leaf, all beautifully presented. Lunch menu €23.

(7) Le Cochon à l'Oreille X10
15 Rue Montmartre, 1er, t 01 42 36 07 56; métro Les Halles. Open Mon–Sat 8am–10.15pm, lunch 12–3; closed hols. No credit cards.
This is the genuine article, but be warned that space is limited. Dine à la carte for around €14.

(25) Le Divin Z12
41 Rue Ste-Croix-la-Bretonnerie, 4e, t 01 42 77 10 20, métro Hôtel-de-Ville. Open dinner only from 7pm.
Provençal cooking as good as it comes north of Orange. Menu from €13.50.

(14) Le Louchebem W–X11
31 Rue Berger, 1er, t 01 42 33 12 99; métro Châtelet-Les Halles. Open Mon–Sat 12–2.30 and 7–11.30.
For hungry meat-eaters only. First-class quality at reasonable prices. A homogenized but acceptable version of the real thing if you find yourself on the south side of the Forum. Menu €13.90. Non-smoking section.

(16) La Poule au Pot W11
9, Rue Vauvilliers, 1er, t 01 42 36 32 96; métro Les Halles or Louvre-Rivoli. Open Tues–Sun 7pm–5am.
Brasserie bustle yet a certain intimacy, coupled with solid *pots-au-feu* and other classics, including the *poule-au-pot* that's worthy of the name. Good service. Menu €28.

Café Ruc V11
159 Rue St-Honoré, 1er, t 01 42 60 97 54; métro Palais Royal-Musée du Louvre. Open 7am–2am.
Moderate chicken curry, burgers and mash. As loved by former tennis star Ilie Nastase.

(23) La Table des Gourmets Y12
14 Rue des Lombards, 4e, t 01 40 27 00 87; métro Châtelet. Open Mon–Sat 12.30–3 and 6–11, closed Aug.
In an old vaulted cellar, light dishes for delicate souls: shrimp

salad, cream of asparagus soup and the like, including lots of vegetarian options. Lunch menu at €15/26/32.

(18) Terrasse de la Samaritaine W12
Quai du Louvre, 1er, t 01 40 41 20 20; métro Pont-Neuf. Open lunch only.
Offers a pleasant lunch on the department store's roof terrace, with €12.50–16 menus and a view over the best of Paris.

(6) Tonneaux des Halles X10
28 Rue Montorgueil, 1er, t 01 42 33 36 19; métro Étienne-Marcel. Open Mon–Sat 8am–midnight, lunch 12–3, dinner 7.30–12.
You'd think that the market porters were still alive and well and about to crowd in through the door. Again, the genuine article: friendly, chaotic and excellent.

Cheap

(21) Le Béarn X12
2 Place Ste-Opportune, 1er, t 01 42 36 93 35; métro Châtelet. Open Mon–Fri 8am–11pm, lunch 12–3.30, Sat 10–9; closed hols. No reservations.
This area's budget champ: cheap *plats du jour* for less than €10 and tables outside. The oyster stall in front is one of the cheapest and best in the area.

(10) Chez Léon de Bruxelles Y11
120 Rue Rambuteau, 3e, t 01 42 36 18 50; métro Les Halles. Open daily 12–11, Sat until 12.
If you are stuck in the area, this is a chain with acceptable Belgian cuisine: mussels, *pommes frites* and good beer. Lunch menu €9.90.

(2) Les Forges Y9
3–5 Rue des Forges, 2e, t 01 42 36 40 83; métro Sentier. Open Mon–Fri 12–3.30pm; closed Aug.
The true Sentier restaurant: owners, models and drivers all eating together. Fresh fish a speciality.

(20) La Tavola Calda X12
39 Rue des Bourdonnais, 1er, t 01 45 08 94 66; métro Châtelet. Open Mon–Sat 12–2.30 and 7–10.30; closed Christmas and Aug.

One of the hardest things to find in Paris is a decent pizza; this is definitely the place. Tiny and crowded.

(19) La Victoire Suprême du Cœur W12
41 Rue des Bourdonnais, 1er, t 01 40 41 93 95; métro Châtelet. Open Mon–Fri 12–2.30 and 6.30–10, Sat 12–3 and 6.30–10.
Vegetarian restaurant: *terrine de champignons et confiture d'oignons, lasagnes aux légumes, crumble aux fruits rouges*. Lunch menu €10.80, dinner menu €19.

Cafés and Salons de Thé

(11) Au Père Tranquille Y11
16 Rue Pierre Lescot, 1er, t 01 45 08 00 34; métro Les Halles. Open daily 9am–midnight.
A large café opposite the Forum des Halles, with seats outside and a range of snacks and cakes.

(22) K.Fé'IN X12
6 Place Ste-Opportune, 1er, t 01 42 21 11 52; métro Châtelet. Open Mon–Fri 10–8 and Sat 10–9.
Trendy bagel house with an enormous choice of both sweet and savoury bagels (even ice-cream filled ones) and other titbits that the French find exotic, such as peanut butter, cheddar and pastrami. Bagels €4–8.

Marais and Bastille

Restaurants

Very Expensive

(34) L'Ambroisie CC13
9 Place des Vosges, 4e, t 01 42 78 51 45; métro Bastille. Open Tues–Sat 12–2 and 8–10.15; closed Aug and Feb school holidays.
Under the supreme fine touch and imagination of master chef Bernard Pacaud, one of the top gastronomic addresses in France, in the elegant Hôtel de Luynes; a short *carte* but every dish a winner from the succulent *feuillantine de langoustines* with sesame to the

Map Key

(13) L'Alsace aux Halles
(4) Ambassade d'Auvergne
(34) L'Ambroisie
(26) Aquarius
(1) Au Bascou
(11) Au Père Tranquille
(12) Au Pied de Cochon
(3) Auberge Nicolas Flamel
(31) La Baracane
(21) Le Béarn
(28) La Belle Horthense
(24) Benoît

(17) Caveau François Villon
(30) Chez Janou
(45) Chez Julien
(10) Chez Léon de Bruxelles
(27) Chez Nénesse
(38) Chez Rami et Hanna
(9) Chez Vong
(7) Le Cochon à l'Oreille
(25) Le Divin
(5) L'Escargot Montorgueil
(2) Les Forges
(32) La Guirlande de Julie
(47) Hiramatsu

(39) Jo Goldenberg
(22) K.Fé'IN
(42) Korcarz
(40) Le Loir dans la Théière
(14) Le Louchebem
(33) Ma Bourgogne
(44) Mariage Frères
(8) Pharamond
(43) Les Philosophes
(41) Piccolo Teatro
(16) La Poule au Pot
(37) Le Ravaillac

Les Halles and the Marais
Restaurants and Cafés

(36) Rouge Gorge
(29) Le Sévigné
(23) La Table des Gourmets
(20) La Tavola Calda
(18) Terrasse de la Samaritaine
(6) Tonneaux des Halles
(15) La Tour de Montlhéry
    (Chez Denise)
(46) Le Trumilou
(19) La Victoire Suprême
    du Cœur
(35) Les Vins des Pyrénées

bitter cocoa tart. You will spend hundreds of euros.

Expensive

Bofinger DD14
*5 Rue de la Bastille, 4e, **t** 01 42 72 87 82; **métro** Bastille. **Open** Mon–Fri 12–3 and 6.30pm–1am, Sat and Sun 12pm–1am.*
One of the prettiest brasseries and an institution for over a century. Wonderful seafood

platters and specialities from Alsace for around €30; daily €30.50 menu (includes wine); wondrous choice of oysters by the dozen or half. Don't be put off by the apparent stiffness – this is a great place. It has a non-smoking section too.

(45) Chez Julien Z13–14
*1 Rue Pont-Louis-Phillipe, 4e, **t** 01 42 78 31 64; **métro** Hôtel-de-Ville.*

Open Tues–Fri 12–2 and 7.30–11, Mon and Sat 7.30–11.
Well-cared-for Belle Époque restaurant. Traditional fare to a high standard. Menus from €25.

(32) La Guirlande de Julie CC13
25 Place des Vosges,3e, **t** 01 48 87 94 07; **métro** Chemin-Vert or Bastille. **Open** daily 12–11.
A memorable lunch and a memorable setting under the arcades; mid- to upper-price.

Moderate

(31) La Baracane DD13
38 Rue des Tournelles, 4e, **t** 01 42 71 43 33; **métro** Chemin Vert. **Open** Mon–Fri 12–2.45 and 7–12, Sat dinner only; closed hols.
This restaurant acts as a magnet for a number of pot-bellied Parisians coming to look for cheap good food in large quantities. Serves the usual Southern staples, such as duck, cassoulet and sausage. Menu €10–37.

La Biche au Bois EE16
45 Av Ledru-Rollin, 12e, **t** 01 43 43 34 38; **métro** Gare de Lyon or Ledru-Rollin. **Open** Tues–Fri 12–2 and 7.30–11, Mon 7.30–11; closed hols and mid-July–mid-Aug.
Example of the best Paris has to offer in moderately priced traditional cuisine. Outdoor terrace. Menu €22–38.

Café Divan EE–FF13
60 Rue de la Roquette, 11e, **t** 01 48 05 72 36; **métro** Bastille. **Open** daily 11am–1am.
Trendy café/restaurant where you can chill out and read the papers. All-day food from moules to Caesar salad to brownies. Weekend brunch €15.25 23.

(30) Chez Janou DD13
2 Rue Roger-Verlomme, 3e, **t** 01 42 72 28 41 (north of Place des Vosges); **métro** Chemin-Vert or Bastille. **Open** Mon–Fri 12–3 and 7.45–midnight, Sat–Sun 12–4 and 7.45–12. No credit cards.
Friendly, tiled bistrot from 1900 with inventive dishes from Provence. A few tables outside. Menu €13.

Chez Paul FF14
13 Rue de Charonne, 11e, **t** 01 47 00 34 57; **métro** Bastille. **Open** daily 12–3 and 7–12.30.
Solid family cooking (rillettes, duckling with prunes) in an old Paris setting straight out of a Doisneau photo, complete with a pretty terrace.

(38) Chez Rami et Hanna BB13
54 Rue des Rosiers, 4e, **t** 01 42 74 74 99; **métro** St-Paul. **Open** daily 12–12.
Falafel, herring, chopped liver, the whole shtick; €13.75 and up for lunch.

La Galoche d'Aurillac EE14
41 Rue de Lappe, 11e, **t** 01 47 00 77 15; **métro** Bastille. **Open** Tues–Sat 11am–11.30pm; charcuterie sold 10am–midnight; closed Aug.
On a street once lined with bal-musette joints (there are still a couple), this surly old Auvergnat bistrot hung with wooden clogs and hams is more popular than ever: try the salade au foie gras de canard and the morels in fresh cream, and on Fridays the potée de Cantal. Menu €24. It's worth booking.

Café Moderne FF14
19 Rue Keller, 11e, **t** 01 47 00 53 62; **métro** Bastille. **Open** Tues–Sun 7.30–11.
Rendezvous for the locals. Blue-and-white checked paper table cloths and classic French dishes (steak frites) as well as couscous and tagines (€23–30.50).

Le Petit Bofinger DD14
6 Rue de la Bastille, 4e, **t** 01 42 72 05 23; **métro** Bastille. **Open** daily 12–3 and 7–midnight.
This cheaper version of Bofinger (see above), across the road, has a Mon–Sat lunch menu for €18, a children's menu and a non-smoking section.

(43) Les Philosophes AA13
28 Rue Vieille-du-Temple, 4e, **t** 01 48 87 49 64; **métro** St-Paul or Hôtel-de-Ville. **Open** daily 9am–2am.
A trendy place with forthright cuisine. Sit amongst the stone walls or outside on the terrace. Menu €17/19/25.

La Plancha FF13
34 Rue Keller, 11e, **t** 01 48 05 20 30; **métro** Ledru-Rollin. **Open** Tues–Sat 6pm–2am; closed 2 weeks in Aug.
A popular little bodega not far from Bastille, featuring tapas and all kinds of other goodies as late-night nibbles.

(37) Le Ravaillac BB13
10 Rue du Roi-de-Sicile, 4e, **t** 01 42 72 85 85; **métro** St-Paul. **Open** Mon–Sat 12–3 and 7–10.30; closed Aug.
Unusual establishment, a Polish restaurant with authentically heavy stuffed cabbage and pirogi. Named after the assassin of Henri IV; a good bargain.

(36) Rouge Gorge BB14
8 Rue St-Paul, **t** 01 48 04 75 89; **métro** St-Paul. **Open** Mon–Sat 12–4 and 7–11; closed last two weeks of Aug.
Instead of wine chosen to accompany the food, the name of the game here is to choose food to go with the wine. Dishes such as civet of venison or fish soup are all prepared to fully appreciate the vast selection of wines from the six corners of France and beyond. Menu €10.

(29) Le Sévigné BB–CC12
15 Rue du Parc Royal, 4e, **t** 01 42 77 00 98; **métro** Chemin-Vert. **Open** daily 9am–8pm.
Here the emphasis is on pies: tarte provençale, quiches, pies with aubergines. Lunch menu €15.25.

Le Souk FF14
1 Rue Keller, 11e, **t** 01 49 29 05 08; **métro** Bastille. **Open** Thurs–Sun 11am–1.30am, Tues and Wed 3pm–1.30am.
Moroccan restaurant/salon de thé. Authentic dishes and décor; and unfortunately authentic music too. A bit touristy but delicious food in generous portions. Good for vegetarians.

(46) Le Trumilou Z–AA14
84 Quai de l'Hôtel-de-Ville, 4e, **t** 01 42 77 63 98; **métro** Hôtel-de-Ville. **Open** daily 8am–1am, lunch 12–3, dinner 7–11; closed Christmas and 2 weeks in Aug.

Another popular old Auvergnat bistrot, on the *quai* although a view of the Seine is blocked by a stone wall; menus €14 (lunch only) and €17, with lamb chops or duck with prunes.

(35) Les Vins des Pyrénées CC14
25 Rue Beautreillis, 4e, t 01 42 72 64
94; *métro* Bastille or St-Paul. **Open**
daily 12–2.30 and 8–11.30; closed
Sat and Sun lunch.
A wine bar serving great food (see
p.343). Lunch menu €12.50.

Cheap

(26) Aquarius AA12
54 Rue St-Croix-de-la-Bretonnerie,
4e, t 01 48 87 48 71; *métro* Hôtel-de-
Ville. **Open** daily 12–1am.
Vegetarian, non-smoking but non-
ideological; it does good salads
and desserts. Menus €11 (lunch
only) and €20. There's also a
produce counter.

Le Bar à Soupes FF14
33 Rue de Charonne, 11e, t 01 43 57
53 79; *métro* Ledru-Rollin. Open
Mon–Fri 12–3 and 6.30–11.
Small soup bar for eat-in or take-
away. Lunch menu €8.80.

Le Caravanserail Off Maps
2 Bis Rue Neuve Popincourt, 11e,
t 01 43 38 64 55, *métro* Parmentier.
Open Tues–Sat 12–3 and 7–11 Sun
dinner only; closed Aug.
Cheap and cheerful, good Turkish
food in a small and airy restaurant
served by friendly staff.

(27) Chez Nénesse BB11
17 Rue de Saintonge, 3e, t 01 42 78
46 49; *métro* Filles-du-Calvaire.
Open Mon–Fri 12–2.30 and
7.45–10.30.
A popular neighbourhood bistrot
run by a husband-and-wife team
with better-than-average cooking;
€12.20 menu for lunch, more
expensive in the evening.

Dame Tartine DD15
59 Rue de Lyon, 12e, t 01 44 68 96
95; *métro* Bastille. **Open** Mon–Fri
11–3 and 7–11, Sat and Sun 11–11.
A snack restaurant that's better
than any chain and handy for the
opera. Hot and cold dishes,
between €2.50 and €6.50.

Le Grand Appétit CC14–15
9 Rue de la Cerisaie, 4e, t 01 40 27
04 95; *métro* Bastille. **Open** Mon–
Thurs 12–7, Fri 12–2.
A rare macrobiotic restaurant in
Paris. Friendly place; good (especially the desserts) and no doubt
good for you; also a macrobiotic
food store.

**(40) Le Loir dans
la Théière** BB13
3 Rue des Rosiers, 4e; *métro* St-Paul.
A café serving light lunches (see
'Cafés and *Salons de Thé*', below).

(41) Piccolo Teatro AA13
6 Rue des Ecouffes, 4e, t 01 42 72 17
79; *métro* St-Paul. **Open** daily 12–3
and 7–11.
Not an Italian restaurant, but
the best vegetarian place in the
area. Imaginative dishes with
pretentious titles. Lunch menu
€8.90/14.70.

Le Temps des Cerises CC14
31 Rue de la Cerisaie, 4e, t 01 42 72
08 63; *métro* Bastille. **Open**
Mon–Fri 7.30am–8pm, lunch
11.30–2.30; closed hols and Aug.
No credit cards.
Small friendly bistrot *à l'ancienne*,
good €12 menu.

Cafés and Salons de Thé

(28) La Belle Horthense BB11
31 Rue Vieille du Temple, t 01 48 04
71 60, 4e; *métro* Filles-du-Calvaire.
Open daily 5pm–2am.
Trendy bookshop/café in the heart
of the Marais.

(39) Jo Goldenberg BB13
7 Rue des Rosiers, 4e, t 01 48 87 20
16; *métro* St-Paul. **Open** daily
9am–1am.
The Marais branch of Paris' most
famous delicatessen. You'll think
you're in New York (the ultimate
compliment for delis). Classic
noshes to eat in or take out; full
lunch at about €30.50.

(42) Korcarz AA13
29 rue des Rosiers, 4e, t 01 42
46 83 33, *métro* St-Paul.
Open Sun–Fri 8–8.
Cosy woodwork café serving an
enormous variety of snacks,

A l'Ancienne

When you tire of swanning
around with the chic set, head for
one of the city's more traditional
bolt-holes: dark, cosy, welcoming
and resolutely un-trendy in the
best possible way:
Allard (métro Odéon; *see* p.331),
Le Buisson Ardent (métro Jussieu;
see p.335), **Chez Claude et Claudine**
(métro Abbesses; *see* p.329), **Chez
Savy** (métro Franklin D. Roosevelt;
see p.318), **Lescure** (métro
Concorde; *see* p.322), **Pharamond**
(métro Étienne-Marcel or Les
Halles; *see* p.324), **Le Volant** (métro
Dupleix; *see* p.340).

---

bagels, pizzas, sandwiches
and pastries.

Le Loir dans la Théière BB13
3 Rue des Rosiers, 4e, t 01 42 72 90
61; *métro* St-Paul. **Open** Mon–Fri
11–7, Sat and Sun 10–7.
Tranquil and popular tea
room/restaurant in the Marais,
with mixed chairs and expectantly
intellectual atmosphere: It also
serves light lunches (tarts and
cheese dishes, *pâtisseries maison*)
for around €10.

(33) Ma Bourgogne CC13
19 Place des Vosges, 4e, t 01 42 78
44 64; *métro* St-Paul. **Open** daily
for breakfast from 8am, then
12pm–12.30am (1am in summer).
Vortex of café life in the Place
des Vosges; also a passable €32
lunch menu.

(44) Mariage Frères AA13
30 Rue du Bourg-Tibourg, 4e, t 01
42 72 28 11, w www.mariagefreres.
com; *métro* St-Paul. **Open** daily
12–6.30. No smoking.
Paris' best-known purveyors of
tea; hundreds of blends to sample
with a pastry.

Montmartre and the North

Restaurants

Expensive

A Beauvilliers W2
52 Rue Lamarck, 18e, t 01 42 54 54
42; *métro* Lamarck-Caulaincourt.

Open Tues–Sat 12.30–2 and 7.30–10.30, Mon 7.30–1030. Montmartre's finest gourmet restaurant and one of the oldest in France (1787) set in a lavish Second-Empire time capsule and very romantic. Good-value lunch with menus for €30 and €45. Be prepared to spend over €100 in the evening.

Charlot Roi des Coquillages S4

12 Place de Clichy, 9e, t 01 53 20 48 00; métro Place de Clichy. Open daily until 1am.

This 1930s brasserie is a true kitsch-palace, renowned for its fish. You would have to head south in the direction of Marseille for better seafood. It has some meat too. Menu €25/30.

Zouave Gobichon V3

8 Rue Durantin des Abbesses, 18e, t 01 42 64 00 08; métro Abbesses. Open Tues–Sat 7.30–11.

Not North African as you might think, but the best of small bistrot cooking and a bit off the tourist route.

Moderate

A la Cloche d'Or U4

3 Rue Mansart, 9e, t 01 48 74 48 88; métro Blanche. Open Mon–Fri 12–2.30 and 7.30pm–4am.

Good for a quick grill and bottle of Beaujolais for breakfast with the journalists. Menu €25.

Al Caratello U7

5 Rue Audran, 18e, t 01 42 62 24 23; métro Abbesses. Open Tues–Sun 12–3 and 7.15–11.30.

Small Italian restaurant tucked away from the loud main streets of Montmartre. Fabulous lasagna and other pastas. Lunch menu €10, dinner menu €16.

Au Rendez-vous des Chauffeurs Y1

11 Rue des Portes-Blanches, 18e, t 01 42 64 04 17; métro Marcadet-Poissonniers. Open Thurs–Mon 12–2.30 and 7.30–11.

Out of the way, perhaps, but good home cooking at reasonable prices. Lunch menu €13 (not Sun).

Au Virage Lepic U3

Rue Lepic, 18e, t 01 42 52 46 79; métro Abbesses. Open Wed–Mon 7pm–11.30pm.

One of Montmartre's last authentic bistrots (dinner only). Menu €18.

Aurelais W2

48 Rue Lamarck, 18e, t 01 46 06 68 32; métro Lamarck-Caulaincourt. Open Mon–Sun 12–2 and 7.30–10; closed Sun evening.

Clean and well-run family brasserie. Lunch menu €21.

Chez Aida Z3

48 Rue Polonceau, 18e, t 01 42 58 26 20; métro Château-Rouge. Open Thurs–Tues 12–12.

Here you are in darkest Africa, but rewards await the intrepid. Authentic Senegalese cooking and a good-value €12 lunch menu. Be sure to try the *mafé* fish with *sauce gombo*.

Chez Claude et Claudine V4

94 Rue des Martyrs, 18e, t 01 46 06 50 73; métro Abbesses. Open Sat and Sun 12–2 and 7–11, Mon and Wed–Fri 7–11.

A cosy neighbourhood place, redoubtable stronghold of onion soup-and-*bourguignon* traditional cooking. Lunch menu €20.

Chez Ginette V2

101 Rue Caulaincourt, near the métro, 18e, t 01 46 06 01 49; métro Lamarck-Caulaincourt. Open Mon–Sat 8am–2am.

Very reasonable, with plenty of fun; a complete night out.

La Crèmaillère W3

15 Place du Tertre, 18e, t 01 46 06 58 59; métro Abbesses or Anvers plus funicular. Open daily 11–12.

Choice of dining either in the pretty Art Nouveau interior or on the outside terrace overlooking the tourist-saturated square. Good duck and seafood. Menus €16/22.

Restaurant Kokolion V4

62 Rue d'Orsel, 18e, t 01 42 58 24 41; métro Anvers. Open Tues–Sat 7.30pm–12.30am.

At the west end of the street. Nothing *à l'ancienne* about it, but

excellent for late-night dining. Menu €17.

Mazurka X3

3 Rue André-del-Sarte, 18e, t 01 42 23 36 45; métro Château-Rouge. Open Thurs–Tues 7pm–midnight; closed Aug.

An experience straight from Gdansk, complete with home-made borscht and blinis. Marek, the owner, sings for you in the evenings. Menu from €18.

Le Montagnard V3

102 Rue Lepic, 18e, t 01 42 58 06 22; métro Abbesses. Open Wed–Mon 12–3 and 6–midnight (or later).

Good-quality traditional country cooking in an old Montmartre grill. Highlights are *fondue pyrénéenne* and other mountain specialities. Impressive attention to detail and excellent value. Menu Club Affaire €18/25.

Le Perroquet Vert S3

7 Rue Cavalotti ,19e, t 01 45 22 49 16, w www.perroquetvert.com; métro Place-de-Clichy. Open Tues–Fri 12–2 and 7–10.30, Mon and Sat dinner only; closed first three weeks Aug.

Named after the novel by Princess Bibesco, who used to come down to the restaurant for inspiration back in the days when it was called Chez Tonton, and popular with French movie stars in the early 1900s. Emphasis on freshness and local produce, including black pudding tart and bitter chocolate cake with almond milk ice-cream. Menu €15/28.50.

La Pomponnette U3

42 Rue Lepic, 18e, t 01 46 06 08 36; métro Blanche. Open daily 11.30–2.30 and 6.30–11 (open until midnight Fri and Sat); closed Aug.

Classic Montmartre bistrot, lively atmosphere and chock-full of posters, watercolours and other souvenirs; delicious mackerel in white wine and home-made desserts. Menu €30.

Le Poulbot Gourmet W2

39 Rue Lamarck; 18e, t 01 46 06 86 00; métro Lamarck-Caulaincourt. Open Mon–Sat 12–2 and 7.30–10, Sun 12–2; closed in Aug.

xcellent and reasonable. Lunch
menu €18.

Village Kabyle X1
Rue Aimé-Lavy, 19e, t 01 42 55 03
14; métro Jules-Joffrin. **Open**
Tues–Sat 12–2 and 7–9.
Good cooking from the more easy-
going part of Algeria, with lots of
vegetarian dishes, stews and even
the likes of stuffed ewe's stomach.
Menu €30.

Cheap

L'Afghani X3
16 Rue Paul-Albert, 18e, t 01 42 51 08
72; métro Château-Rouge. **Open**
Mon–Sat 8–11pm.
Just your average neighbourhood
Afghani restaurant. Delicious
starters and filling main courses:
roast meats, ashak (Afghan raviolis) or vegetarian concoctions for
€15 or less.

Le Poulbot V3
3 Rue Poulbot, 18e, t 01 42 23 32 07;
métro Abbesses. **Open** Mon–Fri
12–2.30 and 6.30–10.30, Sat and
Sun 11.30–11.
One of the less touristy places
around Place du Tertre. Menus
from €15.

Le Restaurant U3
32 Rue Véron, 18e, t 01 42 23 06 22;
métro Abbesses. **Open** Tues–Fri
7.30–11.30, Sat and Sun dinner only.
A typique of high-quality for
Montmartre, with dishes such as
canette rotie au miel. Menu €19.80.

Cafés, *Salons de Thé* and *Glaciers*

Bar Au Rêve V2
89 Rue Caulaincourt, 18e, t 01 46
06 20 87; métro Lamarck-
Caulaincourt. **Open** Tues–Sat
until 2am; closed Aug.
Old-fashioned Montmartre café,
cheap and friendly. Lunch served.

L'Été en Pente Douce X3
23 Rue Muller, 18e, t 01 42 64 02 67;
métro Château-Rouge. **Open** daily
12–12.
Ideal location for tea and pâtisserie on a lovely terrace with a
view, east of Sacré-Cœur; not
worth staying for the full meal.

St-Germain

Restaurants

Very Expensive

(21) Jacques Cagna W14
14 Rue des Grands-Augustins, 6e,
t 01 43 26 49 39; métro Odéon.
Open Tues–Fri 12–2 and 7.30–10,
Sat and Mon 7.30–10; closed
3 weeks Aug.
One of Paris' most gracious
institutions, offering an unforgettable lunch menu (€39) and an
even more unforgettable one for
dinner (€80).

Expensive

(17) Alcazar V14
62 Rue Mazarine, 6e, t 01 53 10
19 99, w www.alcazar.fr; métro
Odéon. **Open** 12–3 and 7pm–2am.
Once home to a famous trans-
vestite cabaret bar, since 1998 a
modern brasserie owned by
English restaurateur, Terence
Conran. Featuring classic English
and French dishes: fish and chips
or plateau de fruits de mer. Sun
brunch €26. The Az Bar, overlooking the restaurant, has
become a pre-clubbing venue
par excellence. With hip music
and hip DJs and often live music
till late; less formal meals, cocktails, etc.

(24) Allard W14
41 Rue St-André-des-Arts, 6e, t 01 43
26 48 23; métro Odéon. **Open**
Mon–Sat 12–2.30 and 7–11.30;
closed Aug.
A bistrot unchanged (except for
the prices) in 40 years; try the
duck with olives and the snails
from Burgundy. Menu €23/30.

(12) Chez Maître Paul V15
12 Rue Monsieur-le-Prince, 6e,
t 01 43 54 74 59; métro Odéon.
Open Sept–June daily 12–2.30 and
7–10.30; July and Aug closed Mon
and Sun; also closed 1 May,
25 Dec–1 Jan.
Ordinary looking but highly
recommended, with dishes from
the Franche-Comté to match –
poulette à la crème gratinée and
delicious apple or walnut desserts,

washed down with wines from
the Jura. Menu €26/30.

(22) Lapérouse W13
51 Quai des Grands-Augustins, 6e,
t 01 43 26 68 04; métro St-Michel.
Open Mon–Fri 12–2.30pm, Sat
7.30–10pm.
Luscious Second Empire décor and
alcoves for romantic rendezvous;
some highly innovative dishes
from the new Basque chef. It's
very romantic, particularly the
private rooms. Lunch menu €30
and €85.

(6) Le Récamier S14
4 Rue Récamier, 7e, t 01 45 48
86 58; métro Sèvres-Babylone.
Open Mon–Sat 12–2.30 and
7.30–10.30pm.
In a quiet cul-de-sac, an Empire
dining room where writers and
publishers dawdle over a perfect
Chateaubriand or bœuf
bourguignon, or linger over a
lobster salad on the delightful
terrace in summer.

(20) La Rôtisserie d'En Face V14
2 Rue Christine, 6e, t 01 43 26 40
98; métro Odéon. **Open** Mon–Fri
12–2.30 and 7–11, Sat 7–11.
Friendly modern brasserie from
the stable of Jacques Cagna
(who's likely to come round
the tables to say hello). Cod aïoli,
carré of lamb, magret de canard,
and good desserts. Menu
€17/24/27/39.

Moderate

(7) Aux Charpentiers U14
10 Rue Mabillon, 6e, t 01 43 26 30
05; métro Mabillon. **Open** 12–3 and
7–11.30.
Located in the former carpenters'
guild hall (with a little museum
about it), serving excellent pot-au-
feu, boudin and other everyday
French basics; economical plats du
jour. Weekday lunch menu €19,
evening menu €25.

(2) Le Bistrot de Paris S–T12
33 Rue de Lille, 7e, t 01 42 61 16 83;
RER Musée d'Orsay. **Open** daily
12–3 and 7–12; closed Mon night
and Sat lunch.
Large, traditional bistrot near
Orsay that comes recommended.

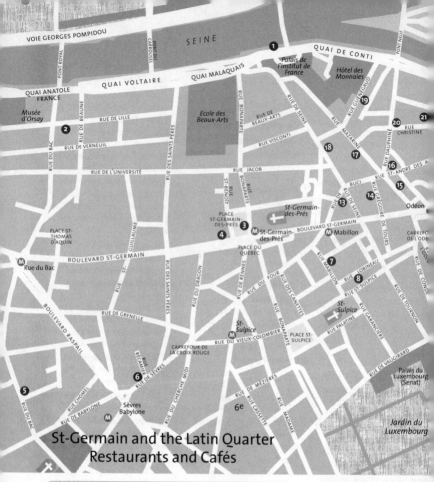

St-Germain and the Latin Quarter
Restaurants and Cafés

Dinner menu €29, lunch menu €14.50 (inc. glass of wine).

(15) Café Procope V14
13 Rue de l'Ancienne-Comédie, 6e,
t 01 40 46 79 00; métro Odéon.
See 'Cafés, *Salons de Thé* and
Glaciers', below.

(9) Indonesia V15
12 Rue de Vaugirard, 6e, t 01 43 25 70
22; métro Odéon. Open Sun–Fri 12–3
and 7–10, Sat 7–10.
A workers' cooperative and Paris'
first Indonesian restaurant. Try lots
of small dishes with the *table de riz*
or *sambel goreng* (seafood in
coconut sauces). Menu €24.50.

(16) La Jacobine V14
59–61 Rue St-André-des-Arts, 6e,
t 01 46 34 15 95; métro Odéon. Open
2–7 for tea and 7–11 for dinner;
closed Mon.
Firm favourite for goat's cheese
salad with honey, frogs' legs

or *filet de bœuf*. Excellent puds from the tea room. There's outside seating in summer. Menu €28.90.

(25) Osteria del Passepartout W14

20 Rue de l'Hirondelle, 6e, t 01 43 54 15 98; métro St-Michel. Open Mon–Fri 12–3 and 7–11, Sat–Sun 7–11 in summer.
Salmon carpaccio, wide choice of pasta and other Italian treats. Lunch menu €13.50/24.

Le Petit St-Benoît U13

4 Rue St-Benoît, 6e, t 01 42 60 27 92; métro St-Germain-des-Prés. Open Mon–Sat 12–2.30 and 7.30–10.30. No credit cards.
Cosy and friendly, basic but tasty French classics for around €18.30. A few pavement tables.

(10) Polidor V–W15

41 Rue Monsieur-le-Prince, 6e, t 01 43 26 95 34; métro Odéon. Open
Mon–Sat 12–2.30 and 7–12.30, Sun until 11pm. No credit cards.
A favourite haunt of Joyce and Verlaine, and one of the few places they could still afford; good brasserie cooking and lots of it. Lunch menu €9.

Cheap

(19) L'Assignat V13

7 Rue Guénégaud, 6e, t 01 43 54 87 68; métro Odeon. Open Mon–Sat 12–3; closed July.
Small and intimate restaurant where mom does the cooking and regular customers keep a tab. Inexpensive, traditional French fare. Menu €11.

(1) Brasserie Six/Huit U–V12

Quai Malaquais, opposite Place de l'Institut, 5e, t 01 46 34 53 05; métro Louvre-Rivoli or Pont-Neuf. Open April–Sept daily 11–3 and 7–11.

Simple decking and wooden chairs and tables on a boat on the Seine; great position. Salads €7.70–10.70 and other dishes under €15.50.

(14) Orestias V14

4 Rue Grégoire-de-Tours, 6e, t 01 43 54 62 01; métro Odéon. Open Mon–Sat 12–2.30 and 6–11.30.
Substantial and excellent Greek starters and main dishes, served with Hellenic bonhomie. Menu €8/14.

(8) Le Petit Vatel U15

5 Rue Lobineau, 6e, t 01 43 54 28 49; métro Mabillon. Open Mon–Sat 12–3 and 7–10.30; closed hols and some of Aug. No smoking.
When they say *petit* they mean minuscule, but out of the kitchen appear good *grand-mère* style meat and vegetable dishes. Lunch menu €11.

Cafés, *Salons de Thés* and *Glaciers*

(5) Le Bac à Glaces R14
*109 Rue du Bac, 7e, t 01 45 48 87 65;
métro Sèvres-Babylone.* **Open**
Mon–Sat 11–7.
Charming, turn-of-the-19th-century tearoom with delectable home-made ice creams and sorbets (€4 for two scoops).

(13) Cacao et Chocolat U–V14
*29 Rue de Buci, 6e, t 01 46 33 77 63;
métro Odéon.* **Open** Tues–Sat
10.30–7.30, Sun 11–1.30 and 2.30–7.
Sit at the counter and sample one of the delicious selection of *pâtisseries*, washed down with the house hot chocolate.

Café Procope V14
*13 Rue de l'Ancienne-Comédie, 6e,
t 01 43 26 99 20; métro Odéon.*
Open daily 11.30am–1am.
Paris' oldest, restored for the Revolution's Bicentennial; also has lunch menus from €24.30.

(3) Les Deux Magots U14
*6 Place St-Germain-des-Prés, 6e,
t 01 45 48 55 25; métro St-Germain-des-Prés.* **Open** daily 7.30am–1am;
closed 1 week in Jan.
A hoot for all its pretensions, and usually full of tourists, but the chocolate and ice cream are compensations. Note, however, if it's crowded, you may be pressured into making a second order or leaving – inexcusable!

(4) Le Flore T14
*172 Bd St-Germain, 6e, t 01 45 48 55
26; métro St-Germain-des-Prés.*
Open daily 7.30–1.30am.
Fabled literary café, everything just so Parisian, but full of tired vampires trying to suck out your soul with their cool, discerning eyes. So popular with tourists that it's opened its own boutique.

(23) Mariage Frères W14
*19 Rue de Savoie, on the corner of Grands-Augustins, 6e, t 01 40 51 82
50, w www.mariagefreres.com;
métro St-Michel.* **Open** daily
12–6.30pm. *No smoking.*
Paris' premier purveyors of fine tea since 1854 (400 varieties) and

a *salon de thé.* It also does a moderately priced brunch.

Marie-Thé Q16
*102 Rue du Cherche-Midi, 6e, t 01 42
22 50 40; métro Vaneau or St-Placide.* **Open** daily 10–7.
Lovely neighbourhood *salon de thé* for English tea – China tea and scones, cake or crumble.

(18) La Palette V13–14
*43 Rue de Seine, 6e, t 01 43 26 68 15;
métro Mabillon.* **Open** Mon–Sat
8pm–2am.
A charming café and terrace, but brace yourself for some of that legendary Parisian snootiness.

(11) Le Pol'Noir V15
*39 Rue Monsieur-le-Prince, 6e;
métro Odéon.* **Open** daily until
3am (4am on Sat).
Next to Polidor, a superb *glacier* serving home-made ice cream.

The Latin Quarter

Restaurants

Very Expensive

La Tour d'Argent Z15
*15 Quai de la Tournelle, 5e, t 01 43
54 23 31; métro Maubert-Mutualité.*
Open Wed–Mon 12–1.30 and
7.30–9, Tues 7.30–9.
Established here in the reign of Henri II in 1582 and recently brought back to splendour by a new chef, who has added his own innovations to the classic *canard au sang* (pressed duck). Add unforgettable, romantic views of Notre-Dame, unique atmosphere and a superlative wine cellar. Lunch menu €65.

Expensive

(34) Atelier de Maître Albert Y15
*1 Rue Maître-Albert, 5e, t 01 46 33 13
78; métro Maubert-Mutualité.*
Open Mon–Wed 6.30–11, Thurs–Sat
6.30–1am; closed Sun.
Stone walls, exposed beams and an open fire create one of Paris' most medieval environments.

(41) Balzar W15
*49 Rue des Écoles, 5e, t 01 43 54 13
67; métro Maubert-Mutualité.*
Open daily 8am–11.45pm.

An institution from the 1930s where stars and Sorbonne *intellectuels* rub shoulders – you might find yourself sitting next to Gwyneth Paltrow! Limited menu, but superb. *See* also 'Moderate'.

(36) Bistrot Côté Mer Z15
*16 Blvd St-Germain, 5e, t 01 43 54 59
10, f 01 43 29 02 08, w www.michel
rostang.com; métro Maubert-Mutualité.* **Open** daily 12–2.30 and
7.30–10.30; closed 2nd week Aug.
Seafood is taken very seriously here; the freshest of the fresh is served daily, even on Mondays (usually a bum day for fish: last Friday's five sardines staring blankly at a wall in a tray of dirty ice is usually all you can get at a fishmonger). Lunch menu €17/22.

(35) Le Vivario Z15
*6 Rue Cochin (south of Quai de la Tournelle), 5e, t 01 43 25 08 19;
métro Maubert-Mutualité.* **Open**
Tues–Fri 12–2.30 and 7–12, Sat and Mon dinner only; closed Sept.
Authentic Corsican-Sicilian cuisine, including pasta dishes and grilled fish, with dense sun-drenched flavours and high-octane wine; reserve a table outside.

Moderate

(31) Al-Dar Y15
*8 Rue Frédéric-Sauton, 5e, t 01 43 25
17 15; métro Maubert-Mutualité.*
Open daily 8–11.30.
Flashy but crowded for its delicious Middle Eastern dishes (menu €14). Also a small café serving snacks and cakes.

Balzar W15
*19 Rue des Écoles, 5e, t 01 43 54 13
67; métro Maubert-Mutualité.*
Open daily 8–11.45pm.
This is the brasserie (bar/restaurant) part of Balzar restaurant (*see* above), a classic in the quarter, with old-fashioned leather seats and lots of mirrors; it's packed with academics and editors at noon. Hearty food from traditional *choucroute* to *raie au beurre noir.* Menu €23–30.50.

(43) Le Berthoud X16
*1 Rue Valette, 5e, t 01 43 54 38 81;
métro Maubert-Mutualité.* **Open**

Mon–Fri 12.30–2.30 and 7–midnight, Sat 7–midnight. Salads, *confit de canard, entrecôte grillée sauce au poivre vert, crème brûlée, île flottante.* Menu €28.

(42) La ChantAirelle X16
5 Rue Laplace, 5e, t 01 46 33 18 59, w www.chantairelle.com; métro Maubert-Mutualité. **Open** *Mon–Fri 12–2 and 7–10.30, Sat 12–2.*
Rustic, hearty food from the Massif Central of the south. Puy lentils, lamb, goat's cheese pie and cured ham all feature on the €18–25 menus. Children's menu, enclosed garden and local produce shop.

(38) Chez Henri Y15
9 Rue de la Montagne-Ste-Geneviève, 5e, t 01 43 29 12 12; métro Maubert-Mutualité. **Open** *daily 12–2.30 and 7–11.*
Friendly restaurant full of locals and tourists. Classic dishes served without fuss: *terrine de légumes, poulet aux champignons sauvages, tarte tatin, plateau de fruits rouges.* Lunch menu €14.

(33) Chieng-Mai Y15
12 Rue Frédéric-Sauton (off Place Maubert), 5e, t 01 43 25 45 45; métro Maubert-Mutualité. **Open** *daily 12–2.30 and 7–11.15.*
Paris' most authentic Thai restaurant; reserve ahead. Menus €11–27.50.

(40) Gaudeamus Y16
47 Rue de la Montagne-Ste-Geneviève, 5e, t 01 40 4693 40; métro Maubert-Mutualité. **Open** *daily 11.30–10.45.*
Good for vegetarians and connoisseurs of teas and coffees.

Le Mauzac W17
7 Rue de l'Abbé-de-l'Espée, 5e, t 01 46 33 75 22; RER Luxembourg. **Open** *Mon–Sat 8.30am–9.30pm.*
Family-run restaurant specializing in wine, with classic cuisine made from the freshest ingredients.

(44) Perraudin W16
157 Rue St-Jacques, 5e, t 01 46 33 15 75; RER Luxembourg. **Open** *daily 12–3 and 7.30–11.30; closed Aug.*
One of the best choices in this part of Paris, a comfortable old-fashioned place with fine food

and few pretensions. Fresh tarts – sweet and savoury – are a speciality; bargain €18 menu.

(28) La Rôtisserie Galande X14–15
57 Rue Galande, 5e, t 01 46 34 70 96; métro Maubert-Mutualité. **Open** *daily 12–2.30 and 7–11; closed Mon lunch.*
Succulent roasts of all kinds. Warm and economical for a winter meal. Lunch menu €8/11.

Cheap

(29) Chez Hamadi X15
12 Rue Boutebrie, 5e, t 01 43 54 03 30; métro St-Michel. **Open** *Mon–Fri 12–3 and 6–midnight, Sat 12pm–1am, Sun 12–12.*
Not much to look at but good North African cuisine with wine. Menu €8.50/12.

(26) Le Grenier de Notre-Dame X14
18 Rue de la Bûcherie, 5e, t 01 43 29 98 29; métro Maubert-Mutualité. **Open** *daily 12–2.30 and 7–11.*
Has simple vegetarian and macrobiotic dishes. Menu €12.50/14.50.

(45) Macchu Pichu W17
9 Rue Royer-Collard, 5e, t 01 43 26 13 13; RER Luxembourg. **Open** *Mon–Fri 12–2 and 7.40–11.*
Good, spicy Peruvian treats like fish marinated with green pepper.

Cafés, *Salons de Thé* and *Glaciers*

(32) Dammann's Glacier Y15
1 Rue des Grands Degrés, 5e, t 01 43 29 15 10; métro Maubert Mutualité.
This parlour's location in a pretty and peaceful square makes this an ideal place to rest and gobble down some delicious home-made ice cream.

(30) La Fourmi Ailée X15
8 Rue du Fouarre, 5e, t 01 43 29 40 99; métro St-Michel or Maubert-Mutualité. **Open** *for lunch Mon–Fri 12–3, Sat and Sun 12–4; for tea 3–7; for dinner 7–midnight.*
A cosy atmosphere in a former glassworks, with a fire in the fireplace, good salads, scones

Vegetarian Restaurants

France has never been in the vanguard of understanding or catering for vegetarians. However, things are beginning to improve (in Paris, at least) and you can be assured of a meat-free feast at the following places:

Aquarius (métro Hôtel-de-Ville; *see* p.329), **L'Arpège** (métro Varenne; *see* p.319), **Au Jardin des Pâtes** (métro Place Monge; *see* p.336), **Le Bar à Soupes** (métro Ledru-Rollin; *see* p.329), **Da Mimmo** (métro Jacques-Bonsergent; *see* p.338), **Gaudeamus** (métro Maubert-Mutualité; *see* p.335), **Le Grenier de Notre-Dame** (métro Maubert-Mutualité; *see* p.335), **La Petite Légume** (métro Cardinal-Lemoine; *see* p.336), **Piccolo Teatro** (métro St-Paul; *see* p.329), **Le Souk** (métro Bastille; *see* p.328), **Tenshin** (métro Père-Lachaise or Voltaire; *see* p.338), **La Victoire Suprême du Cœur** (métro Châtelet; *see* p.325).

and excellent desserts. Weekday lunch menu €12.20, weekend brunch €17.

(27) The Tea Caddy X14
14 Rue St-Julien-le-Pauvre, 5e, t 01 43 54 15 56; métro St-Michel. **Open** *daily 12–7; closed Aug.*
Soft-lit tea room from the 1920s, bestowed by the Rothschilds on a favourite English governess; it's good for lunch, too.

Jardin des Plantes

Restaurants

Expensive

Restaurant de l'Institut du Monde Arabe AA15
Quai St-Bernard, 5e, t 01 53 10 10 20; métro Jussieu or Cardinal-Lemoine. **Open** *Tues–Sat 12–3 and 7.30–9.45.*
French and North African fare served on the terrace overlooking the Seine. Delicious mint tea in the afternoon, but no booze. Menus €26/34.

Moderate

Le Buisson Ardent Z16–AA17
25 Rue Jussieu, 5e, **t** *01 43 54 93 02;*
métro Jussieu. **Open** *Mon–Fri 12–2
and 7.30–11; closed 2 weeks in Aug.*
Much recommended French
classic with quality *à l'ancienne.*
Try *confit de canard, pommes à l'ail*
or *riz de veau à la crème.* Lunch
menu €15, full evening menu €28.

Chez Léna et Mimille Y18
35 Rue Tournefort, 5e, **t** *01 47 07 72
47 (parallel to Rue Mouffetard);*
métro Place Monge. **Open** *Tues–Fri
until 11pm, Mon and Sat dinner;
closed hols.*
A pretty terrace overlooking a
fountain and small park. Solid
cooking. Lunch menu €15.25/21.35
dinner menu €35.

Les Délices d'Aphrodite Y18
*4 Rue de Candolle (opposite the
church of St-Médard), 5e,* **t** *01 43 31
40 39; métro Censier-Daubenton.*
Open *Mon–Sat 12–2.30 and 7–11.30.*
The Mavromatis family serves
some of the best Greek food
in Paris, in one of the most
serendipitous locations. Casual,
lots of tables on the sidewalk.
Menu €16.90.

L'Époque Y17
81 Rue du Cardinal-Lemoine, 5e,
t *01 46 34 15 84; métro Cardinal-
Lemoine.* **Open** *Mon–Fri 12–2.30
and 7–11, Sat 7–11.*
Bistrot worthy of the name (*blanquette de veau, gigot d'agneau* and
other hardy fare) buried among
the touristy ethnics. Menu €12/14.

Moissonnier Z16
28 Rue des Fossés-St-Bernard, 5e,
t *01 43 29 87 65; métro Cardinal-
Lemoine.* **Open** *Tues–Sat 12–2 and
7.30–10; closed hols and Aug.*
Long-established bistrot serving
unadulterated Lyonnais *cuisine de
terroir.* Weekday lunch menu €23.

La Papillote Y17–18
13 Rue du Pot-de-Fer, 5e, **t** *01 43 31 75
66; métro Place Monge.* **Open** *daily
12–2.30 and 7–11.*
Charming restaurant on a pretty
pedestrianized street. The menus
are excellent value (lunch €13.50,

dinner €18/26) and there's a great
selection of wines.

(39) Pema Thang Y16
*13 Rue de la Montagne-Sainte-
Geneviève, 5e,* **t** *01 43 54 34 34;
métro Maubert-Mutualité.* **Open**
*Tues–Sat 12–2.30 and 7–10.30, Mon
7–10.30; closed Sept.*
Tibetan specialities, such as
steamed beef ravioli, sweet and
sour meatballs and noodle soup.
Menu €13–17.

La Petite Légume Z16
36 Rue des Boulangers, 5e, **t** *01 40
46 06 85; métro Cardinal-Lemoine.*
Open *Mon–Sat 10am–10.30pm,
lunch 12–3, dinner 7–10.30.*
Vegetarian organic dishes, plus
produce for sale. Menu €8.25/13.

Le Petit Marguery Y19
9 Bd de Port-Royal, 13e, **t** *01 43 31
58 59; métro Les Gobelins.* **Open**
*Tues–Sat 12–2.15 and 7.30–10.15;
closed Aug.*
Innovative brasserie run by the
Cousin brothers, who perform an
aromatic magic with seasonal
ingredients; black truffles in the
spring, game dishes and wild
mushrooms in the autumn, and a
heavenly *crème cassonade.* Lunch
menu €25; dinner €34 and up.

Cheap

Au Jardin des Pâtes Z17
4 Rue Lacépède, 5e, **t** *01 43 31
50 71; métro Place Monge.* **Open**
Mon–Sat 12–2.30 and 7–11.
Home-made Sicilian pasta dishes
– delicious and 100% organic.
Good for vegetarians.

Crêperie Belliloise Z16–17
11 Rue des Boulangers, 5e, **t** *01 43
25 57 24; métro Jussieu.* **Open**
*Mon–Thurs 12–2 and 7–10,
Fri–Sat 7–11.*
Popular with students from the
nearby Paris VI-VII complex; an
unpretentious place with a wide
selection of crêpes and *galettes*
from Brittany. Excellent value:
daily specials from €7.50.

Le Foyer du Vietnam Z17
80 Rue Monge, 5e, **t** *01 45 35 32 54;
métro Place Monge.* **Open**
Mon–Sat 12–4 and 7–10.

Modest establishment but the
staples – soup, noodles and rice –
are good and filling. Menus
€8.20/12.20.

Cafés, *Salons de Thé* and *Glaciers*

L'Arbre à Cannelle Z17
14 Rue Linné, 5e, **t** *01 43 31 68 31;
métro Jussieu.* **Open** *daily 12–6.*
Warm and cosy tea salon with
good salads and tarts, and delicious desserts.

Café Delmas Y17
24 Place de la Contrescarpe, 5e, **t** *01
43 26 51 26; métro Place Monge.*
Open *Mon–Thurs 8am–2am, Fri
and Sat 8am–4am.*
Comfortable leather armchairs
inside, popular terrace outside.

**Café of the Grande
Mosquée** Z–AA18
39 Rue Geoffroy-St-Hilaire, 5e,
t *01 43 31 38 20; métro Place Monge
or Censier-Daubenton.* **Open** *daily
9am–11.30pm.*
A delightful café where you can
sip mint tea in a garden patio
built in the style of the Alhambra.
No booze.

Gelati d'Alberto Y17
45 Rue Mouffetard, 5e, **t** *01 43 37 88
07; métro Place Monge.* **Open**
Tues–Sun 1–11pm.
For delicious Italian ice cream.

(37) Maison de la Vanille Z16
18 Rue du Cardinal Lemoine, **t** *01 43
25 50 95; métro Cardinal Lemoine.*
Open *Wed–Fri 11.30–6 and Sat, Sun,
hols 2.30–7.*
Quality vanilla from around the
world, brought here as the star
feature in most of the snacks:
hot chocolates, milk-shakes,
crepes, teas.

Montparnasse

Restaurants

Expensive

Aux Iles Marquises R18
15 Rue de la Gaîté, 14e, **t** *01 43 20 93
58; métro Gaîté or Edgar-Quinet.*
Open *Mon–Fri 12–2 and 7–11, Sat
7–11; closed Aug.*

Classy fish restaurant among the also-rans. One of the few to offer wines from Cassis. Full menu €26.

La Bauta T18
*129 Blvd du Montparnasse, 14e, **métro** Vavin, **t** 01 43 22 52 35. **Open** Mon–Fri 12–2 and 7.30–10.45, Sat dinner only.*
A nice change from the usual pizza, pasta and tiramisu genre of Italian restaurants. This one serves strictly traditional Venitian cuisine dating as far back as the 12th century. In an austere décor framed by heavy curtains, Venetian prints and book cases, sample unique delights such as chocolate tagliatelle or spider crab pasta. Menu €38.

La Coupole S18
*102 Bd du Montparnasse, 14e, **t** 01 43 20 14 20; **métro** Vavin. **Open** daily 12–2am.*
The police had to control the crowds when it opened its doors in the 1920s, and it's still a sight to behold in full flight. Wide variety of dishes on the menu, and old-fashioned dancing in the afternoons (Fri and Sat) can be fun. Menus €32–90.

Dominique T17
*19 Rue Bréa, 6e, **t** 01 43 27 08 80; **métro** Vavin. **Open** Tues–Sat 11am–midnight. Restaurant evenings only.*
Restaurant, bar and deli; a favourite of Paris' Russians since the 1920s, with *chachlick caucasien* and *vatrouchka* (Russian cheesecake). Menus €40/55.

Moderate

L'Amuse Bouche R21
*186 Rue du Château, 14e, **t** 01 43 35 31 61; **métro** Mouton-Duvernet. **Open** Tues–Sat 12–2 and 7.30–10.15.*
A minute place run by the former chef of Jacques Cagna, serving lovely ravioli filled with langoustines in a white leek sauce and much more to warm the cockles of your heart. Menus €24–30.

La Comedia Off maps
*51 Rue Boulard, 14e, **t** 01 45 39 38 00; **métro** Mouton-Duvernet. **Open** Mon–Sat 7.30–12; closed mid-Aug.*

Loud eclectic décor but good food – a combination of Italian, Portuguese and Spanish cuisine. Lunch menu €11.

Crêperie Kenavo R18
*20 Rue d'Odessa, 14e, **t** 01 43 20 72 62; **métro** Edgar-Quinet. **Open** Wed–Sun 12–3 and 6–11.30; closed last half Aug.*
Excellent *crêperie* with Breton décor and a delicious choice of sweet and savoury crêpes and *galettes*. Menus €10.50–15.

La Grande Rue Q17
*117 Rue de Vaugirard, 15e, **t** 01 47 34 96 12; **métro** Falguère. **Open** Tues–Sat 12.15–2.30 and 7.30–10.30; closed Aug and 1 week in Feb.*
Grand-sounding dishes at suprisingly low prices; it even boasts an award for best value for money. Mostly seasonal cuisine but favourites such as *risotto cremeux au parmesan et roquette* and *noix de joue de veau braisée avec spatzles maison au beurre* remain regulars. Menu €27.

Le Vin des Rues S20–T21
*21 Rue Boulard, 14e, **t** 01 43 22 19 78; **métro** Mouton-Duvernet. **Open** Mon–Sat 12.30–4 and 7.30–11.30.*
Idiosyncratic traditional bistrot with delicious food *à la Lyonnaise*. Reservation recommended.

Wadja T18
*10 Rue de la Grande-Chaumière, 6e, **t** 01 46 33 02 02; **métro** Vavin. **Open** Tues–Sat 12–2.30 and 7.30–11, Mon dinner only.*
Friendly restaurant serving simple cuisine with Basque specialities. The 7-hour lamb creeps into the moderate category, but it's worth it, or try the breast of duck with prunes. Menu €13.

Cheap

Aux Artistes O18
*63 Rue Falguière, 15e, **t** 01 43 22 05 39; **métro** Pasteur. **Open** Mon–Fri 11–3 and 7–11.30, Sat and Sun dinner; closed Aug.*
Named after Montparnasse's bohemians, and prices are still on the bohemian level with a popular neighbourhood atmosphere thrown in.

Cafés, *Salons de Thé* and *Glaciers*

Calabrese Glacier R18
*15 Rue d'Odessa, 14e, **t** 01 43 20 31 63; **métro** Montparnasse-Bienvenüe. **Open** daily 10am–midnight.*
The Leonardo da Vinci of ice-cream inventions, home of the famous vanilla and cinnamon *soupe anglaise*.

Select S18
*99 Bd du Montparnasse, 6e, **t** 01 45 48 38 24; **métro** Vavin. **Open** daily until 2am.*
The last place to get a feeling for what Montparnasse was all about between the wars. Outside tables.

Café Rhubarbe T18
*118 Bd du Montparnasse, 15e, **t** 01 43 27 22 00; **métro** Montparnasse-Bienvenüe. **Open** daily 10.30–7.*
75 different teas to choose from, accompanied by scones, muffins and delicious cakes.

16e: Passy and Auteuil

Restaurants

Expensive

La Gare D12
*19 Chaussée de la Muette, 16e, **t** 01 42 15 15 31; **métro** La Muette. **Open** daily 12–3 and 7–11.30.*
Lively *rôtisserie* in former station, decorated with station signs, banquettes, luggage racks, etc; popular and young. Outside terrace. Menu €19/25/30.

Moderate

Beaujolais d'Auteuil A16
*99 Bd de Montmorency, 16e, **t** 01 47 43 03 56; **métro** Porte d'Auteuil. **Open** daily 12–3 and 7.30–11.*
Reliable neighbourhood brasserie.

Bon Off maps
*25 Rue de la Pompe, 16e, **t** 01 40 72 70000; **métro** La Muette. **Open** Mon–Fri 12.30–2.30 and 8–12, Sat–Sun dinner only.*
Very fashionable restaurant with excellent dishes you would never imagine preparing at home, such

as aubergine ravioli or octopus with potatoes.

Byblos Café F12
6 Rue Guichard, 16ᵉ, **t** *01 42 30 99 99;* ***métro*** *La Muette.* **Open** *Mon–Sat 12–3 and 7–10.30, Sun 12–3.*
More than just a café, with excellent mezzes and a courtyard where you can dine in the sunshine.

Rosimar B15–16
26 Rue Poussin, 16ᵉ, **t** *01 45 27 74 91;* ***métro*** *Michel Ange-Auteuil.* **Open** *Mon–Fri 12–2 and 6.30–10; closed Aug.*
Spanish restaurant with wonderful paella. Lunch menu €18.30, dinner menu €32.

Cafés and *Glaciers*

Café Mauve,
Chez Franck et Fils E12
80 Rue de Passy, 16ᵉ, **t** *01 44 14 38 00;* ***métro*** *La Muette.* **Open** *Mon–Sat 10–6.*
Stylish in-store café.

Pascal Le Glacier E13
17 Rue Bois-le-Vent, 16ᵉ, **t** *01 45 27 61 84;* ***métro*** *La Muette.* **Open** *Tues–Sat 10.30–7.*
Delicious ice creams and sorbets made from the freshest ingredients (€3.90 for two scoops).

Bois de Boulogne

Restaurants

Expensive

L'Auberge du Bonheur Off maps
Behind La Grande Cascade, 16ᵉ, **t** *01 42 24 10 17;* ***métro*** *Porte d'Auteuil.* **Open** *summer daily 12–3 and 7.30–10.45; winter Sun–Fri lunch only; closed Feb.*
Simple classic dishes. Some tables outside.

La Grande Cascade Off maps
Allée de Longchamp, Bois de Boulogne, **t** *01 45 27 33 51,* **w** *www.lagrandecascade.fr;* ***métro*** *Porte Dauphine.* **Open** *daily 12.15–2.15 and 7.30–10.30; closed mid-Dec–mid-Jan.*

Napoleon III's pavilion in the park, gloriously redecorated and turned into a restaurant for the 1900 World Fair; excruciatingly correct cuisine and service, with one of the biggest wine cellars in town. Overpriced €59–145 menus.

Le Pré Catelan Off maps
Rte de Suresnes, Bois de Boulogne, **t** *01 44 14 41 14;* ***métro*** *Porte Dauphine.* **Open** *Tues–Sat 12–2 and 7.30–10, Sun 12–2; closed Feb and Sun between Nov and May.*
Lovely Belle Époque restaurant immersed in garden far from the hubbub, with food fit for an emperor – pressed pigeon, succulent langoustines, heavenly chocolate desserts. Menu €55.

Salon de Thé

Le Chalet des Iles Off maps
On island in the Lac Inférieur, **t** *01 42 88 04 69;* ***RER*** *Av-Henri-Martin.* **Open** *daily 12–2.30 and 7.45–10.30.*
A *salon de thé* which is only accessible by boat. Not cheap, as *salons de thé* go, but it's a wonderful setting.

La Défense

Restaurants

Moderate

Grande Arche
de la Défense Off maps
35th floor, **t** *01 49 07 27 32;* ***métro/RER*** *Grande Arche de la Défense.* **Open** *daily 12–3.*
Great views. Menu €25.

St-Denis

Restaurants

Moderate

La Table Ronde Off maps
12 Rue de la Boulangerie, **t** *01 48 20 15 75.* **Open** *Mon–Sat 7am–11pm.*
Choucroute, *cassoulet* and the like. Menu €9.50.

Parc de la Villette/Canal St-Martin

Restaurants

Moderate

Chez Michel Z5
10 Rue de Belzunce, 10ᵉ, **t** *01 44 53 06 20;* ***métro*** *Gare-du-Nord.* **Open** *Tues–Sat 12–2 and 7–12; closed Aug.*
Galettes, seafood and other Breton specialities lovingly prepared by a native. Menu €30.

Da Mimmo AA–BB8
39 Bd Magenta, 10ᵉ, **t** *01 42 06 44 47;* ***métro*** *Jacques-Bonsergent.* **Open** *Tues–Sat 12–2.30 and 7–11.30.*
Arguably the best pizza in Paris.

Po Mana BB7
39 Rue des Vinaigriers, 10ᵉ, **t** *01 40 37 19 19;* ***métro*** *Jacques-Bonsergent.* **Open** *Mon–Fri 12.30–2.30 and 7.30–10.30, Sat 7.30–10.30.*
Organic dishes of oriental inspiration. Menu €15.25–22.90.

Cheap

Croq'Cité Off maps
30 Av Corentin-Cariou, 19ᵉ; ***métro*** *Corentin-Cariou or Porte de la Villette.*
Fast-food restaurant with good view of the Géode and Aquarium.

Belleville and Buttes-Chaumont

Restaurants

Moderate

L'Autre Café Off maps
62 Rue Jean-Pierre Timbaud, 11ᵉ, **t** *01 40 21 03 07;* ***métro*** *Parmentier.* **Open** *daily 10am–2am.*
Rub shoulders with Parisian intellectuals as you enjoy a glass of wine, salads, *plats du jour* and excellent desserts.

Mémère au Piano Off Maps
63 Rue Jean Pierre Timbaud, 11ᵉ, **t** *01 43 14 47 28;* ***métro*** *Parmentier.*

Open Tues–Sat 12–2.30 and 7.30–10.30m Sun 7.30–10.30. Serves French classics such as *confit de canard* and *blanquette de veau* intermingled with more unusual dishes such as *filets de rouget flambés au pastis.* Menu €16/22.

Père-Lachaise

Restaurants

Moderate

Tenshin Off maps
8 Rue Rochebrune, 11e, t 01 47 00 62 44; *métro* Père-Lachaise or Voltaire. *Open* Mon–Sat 12–3 and 7–11.
Japanese vegetarian restaurant serving organic dishes. Menus €12–23.

Cheap

Les Lucioles Off maps
102 Bd Ménilmontant, 20e, t 01 40 33 10 24; *métro* Ménilmontant. *Open* daily 8am–2am.
A newcomer that has made itself right at home in the neighbourhood. Mishmash of decorative touches inside. Outside there's a terrace for watching the world go by.

Takichi Off maps
7 Rue du Cher, 20e, t 01 47 97 03 96; *métro* Gambetta. *Open* Mon–Sat 12–2.30 and 7–11.
Japanese restaurant with a good selection of sushi. Lunch specials €6.75–13.

Bois de Vincennes

Restaurants

Moderate

Restaurant Les Magnolias Off maps
Pavillon 23, Parc Floral, t 01 48 08 33 88; *métro* Château-de-Vincennes. *Open* April–Oct daily 10–7.30; Nov–Mar Wed, Sat, Sun and hols from 10–4.30.
Brasserie-type restaurant; menu €15.50/18.

Cheap

Le Chalet de la Porte Jaune Off maps
Av de Nogent, 12e, t 01 43 28 80 11; *RER* Fontenay-sous-Bois. *Open* daily 9–6.
Lunch on an island in summer. Sun brunch 12–5pm. Menu €14.50.

Restaurant Le Bosquet Off maps
Pavillon 11, Parc Floral, t 01 43 98 28 78; *métro* Château-de-Vincennes. *Open* April–Oct daily from 11am; Nov–Mar Wed, Sat, Sun and hols from 10am.
A self-service restaurant with pleasant terrace.

Café

Compagnie des Plantes Off maps
Pavillon 21, Parc Floral, t 01 41 74 92 15; *métro* Château-de-Vincennes. *Open* April–Sept Wed–Sun from 11am; Oct–Mar Wed–Sun from 10am.
Salon de thé, gardening shop and bookshop all in one.

12e: Bercy

Restaurants

Expensive–Moderate

Club Med World II21
39 Cour St-Emilion, 12e, t 0810 810 410; *métro* Cour St-Emilion. *Open* Mon–Fri noon–2am, Sat and Sun 11am–2am.
A choice of Mediterranean restaurant, tapas bar, sushi bar (conveyor-belt food) or café. And you can also book your holiday and buy a bikini.

Le Train Bleu EE17
Gare de Lyon, first floor, 12e, t 01 43 43 09 06; *métro* Gare de Lyon. *Open* daily 11.30am–3pm and 7–11pm.
After Maxim's, perhaps the most spectacular decoration in Paris; frescoes and gilt everywhere in this showpiece, built for the 1900 World Fair. Cuisine not memorable but good enough. Lunch menu €42.

Le Viaduc Café FF16–17
43 Av de Daumesnil, 12e, t 01 44 74 70 70; *métro* Gare de Lyon. *Open* Mon–Sat 9am–4am, Sun 9–2am.
Beneath the Viaduc des Arts, a trendy brasserie serving modern classics. Jazz brunch on Sun. Menu €16.

Cheap

Au Père Tranquille Off maps
75 Av Daumesnil, 12e, t 01 43 43 64 58; *métro* Gare de Lyon. *Open* daily 7.30am–midnight.
A good place to watch the world go by, with salads, *croques* and *tarte au chocolat.*

Café

Tea Mélodie Off maps
72 Bd de Picpus, t 01 44 68 91 77; *métro* Picpus. *Open* Tues–Sat 11.30–6, Mon 11–3.
If you're in the area this *salon de thé* is a lovely place to stop, with its spacious interior and pleasant terrace. Sit and read the papers as you sip a cup of tea or a freshly squeezed juice, and succumb to a Berthillon ice cream or one of the large range of pastries.

13e: Les Gobelins and Around

Restaurants

Expensive

Anacreon AA19
53 Blvd St Marcel, 13e, t 01 43 31 71 18, f 01 43 31 94 91; *métro* Les Gobelins. *Open* Tues–Sat 12–2.30 and 7.30–10.45; closed Wed lunch and Aug.
Typical French gastronomie with a twist; *terrine de lapin au foie gras,* algae ice cream. Very popular with the locals. Lunch menu €20.

L'Auberge Etchegorry Y21
41 Rue Croulebarbe, 13e, t 01 44 08 83 51; *métro* Les Gobelins. *Open* Tues–Sat 12–2.30 and 7.30–10.30.
Excellent Basque restaurant that serves old-fashioned comfort food: a carnivore's delight. Menus €22.50/26.

Moderate

Au Jardin des Pâtes Y20
*33 Bd Arago, 13e, t 01 43 35 93 67;
métro Les Gobelins.* **Open** *Mon–Sat
12–2.30 and 7–10.30.*
Little brother of the one in the 5e
(*see* p.336).

Avant-Goût Off maps
*26 Rue Bobillot, 13e, t 01 53 80 24
00, f 01 53 80 00 77; métro Place
d'Italie.* **Open** *Tues–Sat 12–2 and
7.30–11. Closed 1st week of May, 1st
week Jan and three weeks in Aug.*
Highly seasonal cuisine
depending on what the chef finds
at the market; the menu changes
every two weeks. One of the
dishes that remains constant is
the excellent *pot-au-feu de
cochon*. Lunch menu €11/26.

Chez Paul Y23
*22 Rue de la Butte-aux-Cailles, 13e,
t 01 45 89 22 11; métro Tolbiac.* **Open**
daily 12–2.30 and 7.30–midnight.
Family-run with original daily
specials. Very proud of their
Michelin *fourchette*; menu €26.

Le Jean-Baptiste Clément Y23
*11 Rue de la Butte-aux-Cailles, 13e,
t 01 45 80 27 22; métro Corvisart.*
Open *Mon–Fri 6–12, Sat–Sun 11–3
and 6–12.*
Provincial dishes lovingly done,
a place that is trying hard. Menu
€16.80.

Les Kiosques Flottants GG21
*Quai François Mauriac, 13e, t 01 53
61 23 29; métro Bibliothèque-F.
Mitterand or Nationale.* **Open**
*Tues–Sat 10am–midnight or later,
Sun 10–2.*
Breakfast until noon €7.65, lunch
€15.25, snacks à la carte €23, Sun
brunch until 4pm €21.50.
Scrambled eggs, and the likes.

Le Temps des Cerises Y22–23
*18 Rue de la Butte-aux-Cailles, 13e,
t 01 45 89 69 48; métro Corvisart.*
Open *Mon–Fri 11.45–2.15 and
7.30–11.45, Sat 7.30–11.45.*
This is a worker's co-op restaurant,
but this is Paris: dishes include
avocat sorbet, smoked *magret de
canard*, and rabbit in asparagus
bisque. Lunch menu €12.50.

Cheap

Chez Tang Off maps
*44 Av d'Ivry, 13e, t 01 45 86 88 79;
métro Porte d'Ivry.*
This is the real thing. No atmosphere, no sign over the door (but
easily found under the supermarket of the same name);
grumpy service, but the very
best Chinese food.

Hawaï CC24
*87 Av d'Ivry, 13e, t 01 45 86 91 90;
métro Porte d'Ivry.* **Open** *daily
10.30–3 and 6–11.*
Authentic Vietnamese in the
middle of Chinatown, usually
packed with locals; delicious
soups, barbecued chicken and
grilled shrimp.

Tricotin Off maps
*15 Av de Choisy, 13e, t 01 45 84 74
44; métro Porte de Choisy.* **Open**
daily 9.30am–11.30pm.
Delicious Chinese dishes at excellent prices. Join in the fun at
shared tables.

Salons de Thé and Glaciers

Chamarre X21
*90 Bd Auguste-Blanqui, 13e, t 01
43 31 72 00; métro Glacière.* **Open**
Tues–Sun 8am–7.30pm.
Large *pâtisserie* with a *salon de thé*
and a shady terrace.

La Tropicale AA21
*180 Bd Vincent-Auriol, 13e, t 01 42
16 87 27; métro Place d'Italie.* **Open**
daily 10–8.
A fine ice-cream parlour, if a little
out of the way. Eat in or take
away with a range of flavours
from caramel and ginger to
exotic fruits.

Parc Montsouris/ Cité Universitaire

Restaurants

Expensive

Pavillon Montsouris Off maps
*20 Rue Gazan, 14e, t 01 43 13 29 00;
RER Cité-Universitaire.* **Open** *daily
12.30–2.30 and 8–10.30.*

One of the most delightful and
romantic restaurants in Paris, in a
1900 Belle Époque glass pavilion
with a terrace overlooking pretty
Parc Montsouris. Excellent €49
menu and exhaustive wine list.

Moderate

**Au Rendez-vous des
Camionneurs** Off maps
*34 Rue des Plantes, 14e, t 01 45 40
43 36; métro Alésia.* **Open** *Mon–Fri
11.30–2.30 and 7.30–9.30; closed
Aug. No credit cards.*
Tasty, substantial fare from the
Auvergne (try their *canard confit*);
lots of character and neighbourhood characters. Menu €12; be
sure to book.

15e: Southwest Paris

Restaurants

Moderate

Café du Commerce K16
*51 Rue du Commerce, 15e, t 01 45 75
03 27; métro Av-Emile Zola.* **Open**
daily 12–5 and 7–12.
130 years old, a vast and still
bustling *bouillon* (*see* p.316),
serving some of the cheapest
good meals in Paris – sit in the
gallery if you can, to watch the
pageant unfold below; good
tarragon chicken. Menus €12/23.

Le Clos Morillons Off maps
*50 Rue des Morillons, 15e, t 01 48 28
04 37; métro Convention.* **Open**
*Tues–Fri 12.15–2.15 and 8–10.30, Sat
8–10.30, Mon 12.15–2.15.*
Very personal cuisine with an
exotic southern touch and plenty
of spices.

Le Volant I15
*Rue Beatrix Dussane, 15e, t 01 45
75 27 67; métro Dupleix.* **Open**
*Mon–Sat 10–3 and 6–1am;
closed Aug.*
A bit off the route but a wonderful
treat. Truly *à l'ancienne*, like the
head chef and owner, Monsieur
Houel, who is 88 (but acts like a
28-year-old!). Menu €22.

Nightlife

When the last museums and shops close, the City of Light turns on the switch for a night of fun. There are several main circuits: from the Latin Quarter and across the Seine to Les Halles; Bastille to République; the Butte de Montmartre and Pigalle; St-Germain; Rue Mouffetard; Montparnasse; and the Plaisance-Pernety area in the 14e. In a city as full of fashion slaves as Paris, the most *branché* ('plugged-in', literally) clubs change fairly rapidly.

Major bar hot spots are around the Carrefour de l'Odéon, the Marais, Rue du Trésor, the Butte aux Cailles (behind the Place d'Italie), Rue Oberkampf and Rue St-Maur (behind Bastille and République), and, of course, Place Pigalle. Clubs are concentrated in the same areas and tend to charge admission or an exorbitant price for a first drink, averaging €15. As a general rule, bars remain open until 1 or 2am, whatever the night of the week, but check individual listings for variations.

Wine Bars

Sometimes called *bistrots à vin* or, like the English, *bars à vin*, this once-common city institution is enjoying a revival as Parisians have begun to expand their wine consciousness. There are even chains, such as L'Écluse (w *www. leclusebaravin.com*), that aim to recreate the old *bistrot à vin* environment. It isn't always clear where to draw the line between a wine bar and a restaurant; any old traditional *bistrot à vin* will serve something to go along with the wine: plates of sausages or pâté, onion soup, cheese, sandwiches or even three-course meals.

The Islands

Henri IV W13
13 Place du Pont-Neuf, 1er; métro Pont-Neuf. Open Mon–Fri 12–10pm, Sat 12–4.
Long established; good snacks with a southwest flavour. Beaujolais and Loire wines.

Grand Axe

Le B*fly L8
49 Av Georges-V, 8e, t 01 53 67 84 60; métro Georges-V. Open daily 11am–2am.
A bar-restaurant with plenty of staff to take care of you, serving anything from sushi to pasta. Dark atmosphere with soft lights; large bar and small tables. It was renamed to try to recapture a young, trendy clientele, with mixed success. Music is mainly alternative, drinks are relatively expensive (a beer costs €4.50).

L'Écluse M9
64 Rue François-1er, 8e; métro Alma-Marceau; and 1 Rue d'Armaillé; métro Argentine or Charles de Gaulle-Étoile. Open daily 11.30am–1am.
Well-established and popular chain of wine bars.

Musée d'Orsay and the Invalides

Le Sancerre L12
22 Av Rapp, 7e; métro École-Militaire. Open Mon–Fri 8am–10pm, Sat 3–10pm.
Red, white, rosé: pick your Sancerre and chow down at the oyster bar. Cosy, classy and warm.

Opéra and Palais Royal

A La Cloche des Halles W10
28 Rue Coquillière, 1er, t 01 42 36 93 89,; métro Châtelet. Open Mon–Fri 12–10pm, Sat 12–3.
Wine bar of renown; excellent choices to go with solid country snacks of cheese and charcuterie.

Aux Bons Crus U9
7 Rue des Petits-Champs, 1er; métro Pyramides. Open Mon 9–4, Tues–Sat 9am–11pm.
A gracious, long-established wine bar where you can also get a satisfying lunch for less than €12.

L'Écluse R8
15 Place de la Madeleine, 8e, t 01 42 65 34 69; métro Madeleine. Open daily 11.30–1am.

Well-established and popular chain of wine bars.

L'Entracte V10
47 Rue de Montpensier, 1er, t 01 42 97 57 76; métro Palais Royal-Musée du Louvre. Open Tues–Sun 10am–2am, Mon 10am–9pm.
Specializes in wines from the Loire and plates of tasty charcuterie.

Le Gavroche W8
19 Rue St-Marc, 2e, t 01 42 96 89 70; métro Richelieu-Drouot. Open Mon–Sat 11.30–2am.
A sign on the wall exclaims that wine banishes sadness; excellent food (*côte de bœuf*, etc.) accompanies good Beaujolais.

Juvéniles V10
47 Rue de Richelieu, 1er, t 01 42 97 46 49; métro Palais Royal-Musée du Louvre. Open Mon–Sat 12–11pm.
Casual tapas and sherry bar.

Macéo U9
15 Rue des Petits-Champs, 1er, t 01 42 97 53 85; métro Pyramides. Open Mon–Fri 12–2.30 and 7–3am, Sat 7–10.45.
Same management as Willi's (see below) but dressier. Good vegetarian menu.

Le Rubis T10
10 Rue du Marché-St-Honoré, 1er; métro Pyramides. Open Mon–Fri 8am–10pm, Sat 9am–4pm; closed 3 weeks Aug, 2 weeks Christmas. No credit cards.
One of the oldest and best, with a range of delicious snacks and affordable wines by the glass.

Willi's Wine Bar U9–V10
13 Rue des Petits-Champs, 1er, t 01 42 61 05 09, w www.n2willis.com; métro Pyramides. Open Mon–Sat 11am–11pm.
A well-regarded British wine bar, and one of the few to serve non-French wines, as well as a vast selection of Côtes du Rhône wines by the glass from €3. Book in advance at weekends.

Marais and Bastille

Le Baron Rouge FF15
1 Rue Théophile-Roussel, 12e; métro Ledru-Rollin. Open Tues–Thurs

...oam–2pm and 5–9.30pm, Fri–Sat
...0–9.30, Sun 10am–3pm, Mon
5–9.30.
Fill your bottle from the keg or
savour a glass of wine. Drinks are
accompanied by good food at
reasonable prices.

Clown-Bar DD11
114 Rue Amelot, 11e, **t** 01 43 55 38 20;
métro Filles-du-Calvaire. **Open**
Mon–Sat 12–3pm and 7.30pm–
1am, Sun 7pm–1am; closed one
week in Aug.
An old gathering place for circus
folk near the Cirque d'Hiver.
Fascinating décor of old circus
memorabilia.

L'Écluse EE14
13 Rue de la Roquette, 11e; **métro**
Bastille. **Open** daily 11.30am–1am.
Well-established and popular
chain of wine bars.

La Tartine AA13
24 Rue de Rivoli, 4e; **métro** St-Paul.
Open daily 8–2am.
Unchanged, more or less, for
over 90 years, though newly
fashionable.

Les Vins des Pyrénées CC14
25 Rue Beautreillis, 4e; **métro**
Bastille or St-Paul. **Open** daily
12–2.30 and 8–11.30.
One of the last non-trendy wine
bars à l'ancienne with excellent
regional food; a place of character
and characters.

Montmartre

Au Négociant X2
27 Rue Lambert, 18e, **t** 01 46 06 15
11; **métro** Château-Rouge. **Open**
Tues–Thurs 12–2.30pm and
6–10pm, Mon and Fri 12–2.30pm;
closed Aug.
Very affordable and affable, and a
good bet for lunch.

Chez Grisette V4
14 rue Houdon, 18e, **t** 01 42 62 04 86
métro Abbesses or Pigalle. **Open**
Tues–Sat until 11 pm.
Small and intimate bar that is
always packed, with tables so
close together you're bound to
make new friends. Good selection
of snacks as well.

Le Relais de La Butte V3
12 Rue Ravignan, 18e; **métro**
Abbesses. **Open** daily 12–11pm.
Old-fashioned, friendly and plant-
filled wine bar with plenty of
wines by the glass. Sit at the bar
and while away the afternoon.

St-Germain

L'Écluse W14
15 Quai des Grands-Augustins, 6e;
métro St-Michel. **Open** daily
11.30am–1am.
Popular chain of bars (see above).

Fish-La Boissonnerie V14
69 Rue de Seine, 6e; **métro** Odéon.
Open Tues–Sun 12–2 and 7–10.45,
Mon 7–10.45.
A classic old Paris wine bar with
English owners. The cellar is
extensive, and the welcome warm.

The Latin Quarter

**Café de la Nouvelle
Mairie** W16–17
19 Rue des Fossés-St-Jacques, 5e;
RER Luxembourg. **Open** Mon, Wed
and Fri 9am–9pm, Tues and Thurs
9am–midnight. No credit cards.
A charming wine bar with
banquettes and wooden floors.

Jardin des Plantes

Cave la Bourgogne Y18
144 Rue Mouffetard, 5e; **métro**
Place Monge. **Open** Tues–Sun
7am–2am.
Good wine and everything else to
drink, plus excellent sandwiches.
Fitting termination point to a
walk down the Mouff.

Montparnasse

Fromage Rouge S17
8 Rue Delambre, 14e, **t** 01 42 79 00
40; **métro** Vavin. **Open** Tues–Sat
9–8 Sun 9–11pm.
Endless combinations of wine,
cheese and fancy breads to
make and eat. Formule dégusta-
tion €9.80.

Le Rallye Peret T21
6 Rue Daguerre, 14e, **t** 01 43 22 57
05; **métro** Denfert-Rochereau.
Open Tues–Sat till 8pm; closed Aug.

In the same family for over 80
years, with the biggest variety of
bottles to choose from (especially
Beaujolais) on the Left Bank.

Outside the Centre

Le Baratin Off maps
3 Rue Jouye-Rouve, 20e, **t** 01 43 49
39 70; **métro** Pyrénées. **Open**
Tues–Fri 11am–1am, Sat 6pm–1am.
Popular bistrot à vin, with delicious, hearty snacks.

Café Mélac Off maps
42 Rue Léon Frot, 11e, **t** 01 43 70 59
27; **métro** Charonne. **Open** Tues–Sat
9am–midnight; closed Christmas,
New Year and Aug.
The jovial proprietor ages his
Château Mélac plonk (from his
drainpipe vine) in the fridge, and
has even organized a cooperative
of urban wine-growers, the
Vignerons de Paris; also has a
range of very drinkable wines not
made in Paris, and snacks.

Nicolas HH21
24 Cour St-Emilion, 12e; **métro** Cour
St-Emilion. **Open** daily 12–2.30pm.
Wine bar attached to ubiquitous
wine merchant. Sit on the terrace
and try a plate of cheese or charcuterie with your wine.

Other Bars

Cafés are Parisian, bars are not,
except for the old working-class
watering holes that have all disappeared. Therefore almost all the
bars you will find in this city have
one sort of angle or another:
immigrant bars, gay bars, beer
bars, music bars or whatever (for
those offering entertainment,
see pp.351–3).
Beer is definitely trendy in this
city, and more places devoted to it
are opening up all the time.
In recent years the institution of
the happy hour has hit Paris in a
big way; discounts on drinks can
be spectacular. The biggest
current fad is the 'Irish Pub', with
Guinness, Irish music and often a
genuine Irishman in attendance.
One gets the impression that

what Parisians really want are English pubs, if it weren't for the fact that they are English.

The Grand Axe

Le Bar Fontainebleau S10
Hôtel Meurice, 228 Rue de Rivoli, 1er, t 01 44 58 10 66; métro Tuileries. Open daily until 2am.
Wood-panelled bar with mosaic floor and claret-coloured armchairs. Good cocktails.

Le Fouquet's L8
99 Av des Champs-Elysées, 8e; métro George-V. Open daily 8am–2am.
A Paris institution for the rich and famous.

Le Fumoir W12
6 Rue de l'Amiral-de-Coligny, 1er, t 01 42 92 00 24; métro Louvre-Rivoli. Open daily 11am–2am.
A trendy, spacious bar with a fantastic location and good music.

Trend O8
37 Rue du Colisée, 8e, t 01 42 56 50 75, w www.trendfamily.com; métro St-Philippe-du-Roule. Open Mon–Wed 12–3.30 and 7.30–2am, Thurs–Sat 7.30pm–4am. Closed Aug.
Restaurant and basement bar in the style of a New York club. Beers, cocktails and a live DJ.

Musée d'Orsay and the Invalides

Café Thoumieux N12
4 Rue de la Comète, 7e, t 01 45 51 50 40; métro Invalides. Open daily 12pm–2am.
Plush tapas bar associated with a high-quality restaurant around the corner.

Eiffel Tower and Trocadéro

Le Totem H–I11
Palais de Chaillot (Musée de l'Homme), 17 Place du Trocadéro, 16e, t 01 47 27 28 29; métro Trocadéro. Open bar midnight–2am (restaurant 12–12).
Popular and trendy bar and

restaurant; Le Totem has a terrace with amazing view of the Eiffel Tower.

Opéra and Palais Royal

La Champmeslé V9
4 Rue Chabanais, 2e; métro Bourse or Pyramides. Open Mon–Sat 2–2am.
Very intimate, very feminine and romantic bar.

Costes Bar S9
Hôtel Costes, 239 Rue St-Honoré, 1er; métro Tuileries. Open 24 hours.
A useful address if you need a drink in the middle of the night. Small with very glamorous crowd and expensive drinks.

Footsie T8
10-12 rue Daunou, 2e; métro Opera. Open Mon–Fri 12–3 and 6–2am, Fri–Sat 6–4am.
Unique bar with a jumbo screen showing the changing price of drinks, the whole system being based on the stock exchange. Hence prices vary for beers between €2 and €8. Also serves regular priced food.

Harry's Bar T9
5 Rue Daunou, 2e, t 01 42 61 71 14; métro Opéra. Open daily 10.30am–4am.
Since 1911 the most famous American bar in Paris, home of the Bloody Mary and Side Car, where a big international business clientele gathers to discuss making more do-re-mi over one of 180 different brands of whisky or Pétrifiant: a slightly less lethal version of the Mickey Finn.

Kitty O'Shea's T9
10 Rue des Capucines, 2e, t 01 40 15 00 30; métro Opéra. Open Mon–Thurs 12pm–1.30am, Fri–Sun 12pm–2am.
Popular Irish bar; more of a scrum when Ireland plays France in the Five Nations; Guinness, good Irish coffees and beers.

Le Moloko U5
26 Rue Fontaine, 9e, t 01 48 74 50 26; métro Blanche. Open daily 8–7am.

Once an old haunt of Russian *emigrés*, now a popular bar hosting informal theatre from 8.30–11 and a DJ until dawn.

Waterbar de Colette T10
213 Rue St-Honoré, 1er, t 01 55 35 33 90; métro Tuileries. Open Mon–Sat 10.30–7.30.
Only at Colette (*see* p.362) could you ever find such a bar. In the basement of this lifestyle store, you can try nearly a hundred different types of water. Do you like it fizzy or still, American or European? Light dishes can accompany your choice.

Beaubourg and Les Halles

Bodeguita del Medio Y12
10 Rue des Lombards, 4e, t 01 44 59 66 90; métro Hôtel-de-Ville. Open daily 5pm–2am.
Trendy but authentic Cuban bar-restaurant, similar to its namesake in Havana. Great atmosphere. Ring for details of concerts; the Buena Vista Social Club play here when they're in town.

Café du Pont Neuf W12
27 Rue du Pont Neuf, 1er, t 01 40 26 30 74; métro Pont Neuf. Open daily 7am–2am.
Never a dull moment at this old-fashioned bistrot, which hosts live music, theatre or accordion nights between Sept and May.

Pouchla X10
10 Rue Mandar, 2e; métro Les Halles. Open Tues–Sun 5–1am.
Comfortable bar where you can sip excellent German beers while playing dominoes or chess.

Le Sous Bock W–X11
49 Rue St-Honoré, 1er t 01 40 26 46 61, w www.sous_bock.com; métro Châtelet. Open Mon–Sat 11am–5am, Sun 3pm–5am.
Complicated cocktails and the best imported beers; snacks of mussels and *frites* at all hours. Includes a booze boutique that is a tippler's dream: 45 varieties of whisky and 400 kinds of beer are on offer.

Marais and Bastille

Le Bar Sans Nom EE14
*49 Rue de Lappe, 11e, t 01 48 05 59 36; métro Bastille. **Open** Mon–Sat 6–2am.*
A friendly, easy-going bar that plays edgy international music and doubles up as a restaurant.

La Belle Horthense AA13X
*31 Rue Vieille-du-Temple, 3e, t 01 48 04 71 60; métro St-Paul. **Open** daily 5pm–2am.*
A cross between a bar and a bookshop – browse and imbibe at the same time.

Café de l'Industrie EE13
*16 Rue St-Sabin, 11e, t 01 47 00 13 53; métro Bastille. **Open** daily 10am–2am.*
A Bastille institution. A bistro-style interior, with photos of actors on the walls and corners crammed full of ornaments. A peaceful place in the afternoon, but come evening its fans pile in.

La Chaise au Plafond AA13
*10 Rue du Trésor, 4e, t 01 42 76 03 22; métro St-Paul. **Open** daily 9am–2am.*
Lively, popular bar which is always full. Lovely terrace – if you can find a space.

Les Chimères BB13
*133 Rue de Rivoli, 4e; métro St-Paul. **Open** 24 hours, Happy Hour 7–8.*
Try this small bar if you feel that Paris lacks the essential beach in your holiday. Sandy floors, inflatable dragons and plastic palm trees welcome lively and rowdy crowds every night; the photo collage by the toilets proves it.

China Club EE15
*50 Rue de Charenton, 12e; métro Ledru-Rollin. **Open** Sun–Thurs 7pm–2am, Fri and Sat 7pm–3am. Happy Hour from 7pm.*
One of the most beautiful and romantic bars in Paris, with comfortable leather sofas and high ceilings. Great cocktails, and a piano bar in the basement. Food, served on the first floor, is reasonably priced.

La Galerie EE14
*14 Rue de Lappe, 11e, t 01 47 00 91 09; métro Bastille. **Open** daily 6pm–2am.*
West Indian food and live DJs. A lively place to come for a drink.

Megalo EE14
*6 Rue de Lappe, 11e, t 01 48 05 05 12; métro Bastille. **Open** daily 6pm–2am.*
At the heart of the nightlife around Bastille, a down-to-earth bar with loud rock music and strange murals.

Pause Café FF14
*41 Rue de Charonne, 11e, t 01 48 06 80 33; métro Ledru-Rollin. **Open** Mon–Sat 8am–2am, Sun 8am–8pm.*
Popular café-bar, loved by locals and tourists alike. The service can be unreliable, but there are cheap eats to go with your drink.

La Perla AA13
*26 Rue François-Miron, 4e, t 01 42 77 59 40; métro St-Paul. **Open** 12pm–2am.*
Laid-back Californian-Mexican; good margaritas, Mexican beers, flavoured tequilas and snacks.

Le Trésor EE14
*5–7 Rue du Trésor, 4e, t 01 42 71 35 17; métro St-Paul. **Open** daily 12–1am.*
A quiet place to come for a drink during the day. At night it becomes the place to be seen, particularly on its covered terrace, and to see some of the beautiful people sipping cocktails.

Montmartre

Bar des Deux Moulins U3
*15 Rue Lepic, 18e; métro Abbesses. **Open** daily 7.30–2am.*
Its typical Parisian brasserie look made this bar the ideal setting for the recent cult French film *Le Fabuleux Destin d'Amélie Poulain*. Celebrity status has not made the prices go up either.

Chao Ba Café V4
*22 Bd de Clichy, 18e, t 01 46 06 72 90; métro Pigalle. **Open** Sun–Wed 9am–2am, Thurs–Sat 8.30am–5am.*
Quasi-glamorous Indo-Chinese themed bar overlooking Place Pigalle, with bamboo chairs and Asian food. Not as a trendy as it once was, but a good place to come for a drink, day or night.

Le Dépanneur U4–5
*27 Rue Fontaine, 9e, t 01 40 16 40 20; métro Blanche. **Open** daily 11–7am.*
80s décor in this trendy bar, which will always be there to provide a cocktail when you need one.

La Fourmi V4
*74 Rue des Martyrs, 18e, t 01 42 64 70 35; métro Pigalle. **Open** Mon–Thurs 8am–2am, Fri–Sat 8am–4am, Sun 10–2pm.*
Popular bar just around the corner from Cigale. Jumping at night, particularly if there's a concert, but calmer during the day when you can admire the paintings on the walls.

Le Sancerre U–V3
*35 Rue des Abbesses, 18e, t 01 42 58 08 20; métro Abbesses. **Open** daily 7am–2am.*
No relation to its namesake near the École Militaire, this is a smoky, unpretentious bar where the music is traditional rock or electronic and the atmosphere is jumping.

Un Zèbre à Montmartre U3
*38 Rue Lepic, 18e, t 01 42 23 97 80; métro Abbesses. **Open** daily 10am–2am.*
All-day food, coffee and cocktails.

St-Germain

Bar du Marché V14
*75 Rue de Seine, 6e, t 01 43 26 55 15; métro Mabillon. **Open** daily 7.30am–2am.*
In the thick of the action, a trendy bar where your drinks money will go a little further. Glamorous crowd packed into narrow rows of tables. Particularly busy predinner. Not the place for an intimate tête à tête.

Le Basile S14
*34 Rue de Grenelle, 7e, t 01 42 22 59 46; métro Rue-du-Bac. **Open** Mon–Sat 7am–9.30pm.*

Trendy student bar with noisy, smoky, colourful interior.

Birdland Club U14
8 Rue Guisarde, 6e, t 01 43 26 97 59; métro Mabillon. Open Mon–Sat 7–dawn, Sun 8–dawn.
Popular bar playing current music. Happy Hour 7–9.

Bob Cool V–W14
15 Rue des Grands-Augustins, 6e, t 01 46 33 33 77; métro Odéon. Open Mon–Sat 6–3.
Relaxed, downbeat bar where everything is cool – from the cocktails to the clientele.

The Frog and Princess U14
9 Rue Princesse, 6e, t 01 40 51 77 38; métro Mabillon. Open Mon–Fri 5.30pm–2am, Sat and Sun noon–2am.
If you fancy an English moment. Beers are brewed on the premises, and it's always packed with a young, international crowd. Happy Hour 5.30–8.

Le Lutétia S15
Hotel Lutétia, 45 Bd Raspail, 6e, t 01 49 54 46 46; métro Sèvres-Babylone. Open daily 9am–1am.
The bar in the beautiful Hotel Lutétia is one of the few hotel bars worth recommending. It's not cheap, but it's classy, and you're likely to rub shoulders with stars such as Catherine Deneuve or Paulo Coelho.

Le Mazet V14
61 Rue St-André-des Arts, 6e, t 01 46 33 62 17; métro Odéon. Open Mon–Thurs 10am–2am, Fri and Sat 10am–3.30am.
A serious beer cellar (15 kinds on tap) where you can also get a bowl of onion soup in the wee hours.

La Mezzanine de l'Alcazar V14
62 Rue Mazarine, 6e; w www.conran.co.uk; métro Odéon. Open daily 12–3 and 7–2.
The first-floor bar of Terence Conran's Paris restaurant (see p.331) has become a trendy hangout for the beautiful people (you might see Madonna), and – with its gentle lighting and superb décor – a good spot for a pre-dinner drink or a light meal.

The Moosehead V14
16 Rue de Quatre Vents, 6e, t 01 46 33 77 00; métro Odéon. Open Mon–Wed 4–2, Thurs–Sun 11–2.
Friendly Canadian bar with wide selection of beers, including Moosehead.

Pub Saint-Germain (Parrot's Tavern) V14
17 Rue de l'Ancienne-Comédie, 6e, t 01 43 29 38 70; métro Odéon. Open daily 24hrs; ring the bell if it looks closed.
A popular non-stop Left Bank haven for beer connoisseurs, with over 100 varieties in bottles and some 20 on tap.

The Latin Quarter

Café Oz W16
184 Rue St-Jacques, 5e, t 01 43 54 30 48; RER Luxembourg. Open Mon–Sat 4pm–2am, Sun 5pm–2am; Happy Hour from 6pm.
Paris' first Australian bar, loved by the area's student population, and a good place for beer or wine.

Comptoir du Panthéon W–X16
5 Rue Soufflot, 5e, t 01 43 54 75 36; RER Luxembourg. Open Mon–Sat 7am–2am.
Lively bar-bistrot in the heart of the student quarter, attracting students, professors and tourists alike. Some comfy chairs, and some good, simple dishes to soak up the drink.

Connolly's Corner Y18
12 Rue de Mirbel, t 01 43 31 94 22; métro Censier Daubenton. Open daily 4–2am.
Authentic Irish bar complete with pints of the black stuff and folk music most Wednesdays and Saturdays.

Le Crocodile W17
6 Rue Royer-Collard, 5e, t 01 43 54 32 37; RER Luxembourg. Open Mon–Sat 10.30pm–dawn.
Cosy, intimate night haunt for serious cocktail aficionados, with over 120 varieties – also Irish coffees.

La Gueuze W16
19 Rue Soufflot, 5e, t 01 43 54 63 00; RER Luxembourg. Open Mon–Sat 9pm–2am, Sun 10am–11.30pm.

Extremely popular café with Paris' most impressive *carte des bières* – over 400 kinds of brew from around the world.

Le Piano Vache X16
8 Rue Laplace, 5e, t 01 46 33 75 03; métro Maubert-Mutualité. Open daily 12pm–2am.
Relaxed, noisy and fun student bar, serving up killer cocktails and less lethal beers, wines and snacks.

Polly Magoo X15
11 Rue St-Jacques, 5e; métro St-Michel. Open daily 1pm–4 or 5am.
Once a sleazy, unpretentious haunt, Polly Magoo has been completely re-vamped and is now a very pretty bar/restaurant adorned with shiny mosaics. Hosts small theatre acts on Sunday nights.

Montparnasse

Académie de la Bière W19
88 bis Bd de Port-Royal, 5e, t 01 43 54 66 65; RER Port-Royal. Open Mon–Thurs till 2am, Fri and Sat till 4am.
German beer specialists, with over 50 different varieties, mussels and *frites*.

La Closerie des Lilas U18
171 Bd du Montparnasse, 6e, t 01 40 51 34 50; RER Port-Royal. Open daily 12pm–2am.
Unchanged since Verlaine and Hemingway boozed here; great cocktails but at a price.

Cubana Café T17
47 Rue Vavin, 6e, t 01 40 46 80 81; métro Vavin or Montparnasse-Bienvenue. Open daily 11am–dawn.
Atmospheric bar with busy Cuban décor where laid-back trendies come to listen to salsa while puffing away on cigars.

Tournesol R18
9 Rue de la Gaîté, 14e, t 01 43 27 41 01; métro Edgar-Quinet. Open daily 8am–2am.
A lively bar that is particularly trendy in the evening but more laid back during the day. And very reasonably priced.

Outside the Centre

Bar Belge Off maps
75 Av de St-Ouen, 17e, t 01 46 27 41 01; métro Guy-Môquet. Open Tues–Sun 3.30pm–3am.
Paris' oldest, friendliest, most extensive Belgian beer cellar, with Flemish snacks; *moules* and *frites* too, of course.

Batofar GG21
Opposite 11 Quai François-Mauriac, 13e, t 01 56 29 10 00; métro Bibliothèque-F. Mitterand. Open Tues–Sun 8pm–2am.
One of the trendiest bars in Paris, on the river in the shadow of the TGB. In summer all hands are on deck, and the parties continue well into the night.

Café Charbon Off maps
109 Rue Oberkampf, 11e, t 01 43 57 55 13; métro Parmentier. Open daily 9am–2am.
Fabulous brasserie-style bar loved by allcomers.

Café Mercerie Off maps
98 Rue Oberkampf, 11e, t 01 43 38 81 30; métro Parmentier. Open Mon–Fri 5pm–2am, Sat and Sun 3pm–2am.
North of Bastille, towards Belleville and Père-Lachaise; *the* place for a quiet drink in one of the small intimate rooms, or alternatively a lively drink at the bar or around the large farmhouse table.

Chez Prune Off maps
36 Rue Beaurepaire, 10e, t 01 42 41 30 47; métro République. Open daily 7am–2am.
Trendy bar with young crowd jostling for a seat at a table overlooking the canals. Lovely terrace in summer.

Favela Chic Off maps
18 Rue du Faubourg-du-Temple, 11e, t 01 40 21 38 14; métro République. Open Tues–Sat 7.30pm–2am (till 4am in summer).
Brazilian bar-restaurant near the canal where fashion victims and party animals grab a drink and something to eat, and finish the night dancing on the tables. Loud and popular.

La Folie en Tête Y23
33 Rue de la Butte-aux-Cailles, 13e, t 01 45 80 65 99; métro Place d'Italie. Open Mon–Sat 6pm–2am.
Grungy little bohemian bar in the Butte-aux-Cailles with cheap drinks and 'traditional' toilets, loved by students and locals.

Le Gast Off maps
5 Rue Crespin-du-Gast, 11e, t 01 43 55 53 34; métro Ménilmontant. Open Tues–Sat 6pm–2am.
A cool bar away from the crowds, with beers, cocktails and some food on the side.

Clubs

Unfortunately, most clubs in Paris take themselves seriously and are full of uncool people posing for each other's benefit at the expense of having any real fun. Your appearance tends to be all-important and the bouncers at the door picky if you're not their type; women have an easier time than men and at some of the best Afro-Caribbean clubs the darker your skin colour the better. Other places are so exclusive that getting in is one of the biggest steps a Parisian can make towards social and financial success. As a reaction to all this (very expensive) fuss, many Parisians are taking refuge in music bars (*see* pp.351–3).

Entrance fees to clubs are usually around €15, which includes one drink, and things tend to get going from about 2am. For gay clubs, *see* p.378.

Les Bains Y–Z10
17 Rue du Bourg-L'Abbé, 3e, t 01 48 87 01 80; métro Étienne-Marcel. Open daily 11pm–dawn; restaurant open until 1am; adm €15.25.
Still the ultimate place for beautiful people. You'll have to pass the bouncers' 'look' test.

Le Batofar GG21
11 Quai François Mauriac, 13e, t 01 56 29 10 00, w www.batofar. net; métro Bibliothèque-F. *Mitterand or Quai de la Gare. Open Tues–Sun 8pm–2am; adm €7–12.*
On a boat on the Seine. Specializes in drum'n'bass, jungle, sweet techno, with jazz on Mondays. Its bus will take you home.

Boca Chica FF14
58 Rue de Charonne, 11e, t 01 43 57 93 13, w www.labocachica.com; métro Ledru-Rollin. Open daily 11am–2am; adm free.
Classic Latin bar-restaurant with excellent atmosphere on the dance floor at weekends: for salsa, funk and groove. Young, mixed crowd.

La Casbah GG15
18–20 Rue de la Forge-Royale, 11e, t 01 43 71 71 89; métro Ledru-Rollin. Open Thurs–Sun 8pm–6am; adm €16. Closed Aug.
Recreation of Rick's in Casablanca; Moroccan cuisine in the restaurant (book), funk, house, acid and rock on the dance floor.

Le Club Zed X15
2 Rue des Anglais, 5e, t 01 43 54 93 78; métro Maubert-Mutualité. Open Wed 10.30–3, Thurs–Sat 11–5.30; adm Wed–Fri €8 including one drink, Sat €16.
Perfect if you think you're John Travolta in *Saturday Night Fever*. Friendly club revelling in the classics.

La Coupole S18
102 Bd du Montparnasse, 14e, t 01 43 27 56 00; métro Vavin. Open Tues, Fri and Sat 10pm–4am; adm from €16.
Classic venue for Latin music: tango, salsa, etc. See also p.336.

Elysée Montmartre W4
72 Bd de Rochechouart, 18e, t 01 44 92 45 38, w www.elyseemont martre.com; métro Anvers. Open Fri and Sat 11pm–5am; adm €12–23.
In a hall designed by Eiffel, the place where La Goulue first cancanned now hosts alternative and world-music bands, with one of the best dance floors in Paris. It's also used for big parties organized by radio stations and clubs. Golden oldies, twist, disco, reggae every other Saturday night.

L'Enfer/Red Light R18

34 Rue du Départ, 15e, t 01 42 79 94 53, w www.enfer.fr; métro Montparnasse-Bienvenüe. Open Fri–Sat 11pm–dawn; adm €20.

Has two dance floors, with music ranging from house to techno. Popular after around 5am.

Les Etoiles AA8

61 Rue du Chateau-d'Eau, 10e, t 01 47 70 60 56; métro Chateau-d'Eau. Open 11–dawn Thurs–Sat; adm €10.

Old cinema converted into a Cuban dance club where hot bodies sweat and writhe to the Latino rhythms of a live band.

Le Gibus Off maps

18 Rue du Faubourg-du-Temple, 11e, t 01 47 00 78 88; métro République. Open Wed–Sun 11.30pm–5.30am; adm €5–16.

Huge, multi-level club with a mixed crowd. You'll probably have to queue at weekends.

Ginguette Pirate FF20–21

11 Quai François Mauriac, 13e, t 01 44 24 89 89; métro Bibliothèque-F. Mitterand or Quai de la Gare. Open Tues–Sat 6pm–2am; adm from €8.

Live reggae and funk on a boat on the Seine. Wooden interior; over-crowded at the weekend.

La Java Off maps

105 Rue du Faubourg-du-Temple, 10e, t 01 42 02 20 52; métro Belleville or Goncourt. Open Thurs–Sat 11pm–5am; adm €15.25.

A grand old music hall opened in the 1920s, where Piaf got her first break; Thurs and Fri live salsa, Sat bal musette.

Le Latina Café L8

114 Av des Champs-Elysées, 8e, t 01 42 89 98 89, w www.latina.fr; métro George-V. Open daily 10am–5am; adm Mon–Fri free, Sat and Sun €16.

The dance floor's in the basement – great for trendy salsa-lovers. Live concerts broadcast from here. And if you're a bit rusty, there are salsa classes on Sun nights (€7.70, including a drink).

La Locomotive T4

90 Bd de Clichy, 18e, t 01 53 41 88 88, w www.laloco.com; métro Pigalle or Blanche. Open Fri 11pm–dawn; adm €15.25.

Next to the Moulin Rouge and becoming an institution in itself; glitzy, three-storey nightclub with three dance floors: pop, techno, rap and rock. Very young and fun.

Man Ray M9

34 Rue Marbeuf, 8e, t 01 56 88 36 36; métro Franklin D. Roosevelt. Open Fri–Sun 11.30–4; adm Fri–Sat €20, Sun free.

Once dinner is over (*see p.318*), the tables are cleared and – hey presto – a trendy underground dance-floor appears, surrounded by smiling buddhas. House on Fri, disco on Sat, R&B on Sun.

Péniche Concorde Atlantique R11

23 Quai Anatole-France, Port de Solférino, 7e, t 01 47 05 71 03; métro Concorde. Open daily 10pm–dawn; adm free before midnight, €7.60 after midnight.

Trendy club on a barge near the Place de la Concorde. Two dance floors, house music and top-grade DJs. A bit like a classier Batofar.

Le Queen L8

102 Av Champs-Elysées, 8e, t 01 42 89 31 32; métro George-V. Open Sun–Thurs midnight–7am, Fri and Sat midnight–8am; adm Mon €9, Tues–Thurs and Sun free, Fri and Sat €18.

The hippest and most sophisti-cated gay club draws a fair mix of stylish heteros as well, as long as they look like one of the beautiful people; special Boy Night on Thurs; free gay night on Wed; disco Mon.

Rex Club X8

5 Bd Poissonnière, 2e, t 01 42 36 10 96; métro Grands Boulevards or Bonne-Nouvelle. Open Thurs–Sat 11pm–dawn; adm €8–13.

Hyper-trendy dancing under the cinema, with internationally famous DJs such as Laurent Garnier; jungle music, goa, techno, et al. It gets packed to the gills at weekends.

Le Saint X14

7 Rue St-Séverin, 5e, t 01 43 25 50 04; métro St-Michel. Open daily 11pm–dawn; adm Mon–Fri €7.60, Sat and Sun €13.

Hidden away in vaulted cellars, a club with a busy dancefloor and good mix of music. Unpretentious – you won't have to queue or pose to get in. Young crowd.

Wax EE13–14

15 Rue Daval, 11e, t 01 40 21 16 16; métro Bastille. Open daily 6pm–2am; adm free.

Reborn as a shrine to the 1970s, with psychedelic walls and yellow banquettes. Drinks and dancing – with the trendiest DJs, but elec-tronic rather than true 70s music.

Entertainment

Listings

Besides the plethora of posters that cover the métro stations, cafés and Morriss columns, there are cheap weekly guides which come out on Wednesdays, when the cinemas change their programmes, and are available from all kiosks. Some newspapers also have listings:

Figaro: The Wednesday edition of this newspaper has listings.

Libération: Has good pieces on art and music.

Le Monde: The Wednesday edition has ADEN, a listing of cinemas and exhibitions.

L'Officiel des Spectacles: Similar to *Pariscope* (*see* below).

Pariscope: Lists everything from art exhibitions and museum hours to wife-swapping supper clubs. In summer it includes a short English-language section in collaboration with *Time Out*. You can also call their nightlife hotline (**t** 08 36 68 88 55).

Paris Free Voice: A monthly publication with reviews in English.

Zurban: Newer listings mag with good articles and reviews; **w** *www.zurban.com*.

See also the music listings information below.

Ticket Agents

Billetel (Tourist Office ticket counter) K8
127 Av des Champs-Elysées, 8e; métro Charles de Gaulle-Étoile. Open daily 9–8.
Here you can book tickets for concerts, shows, plays, sporting events, etc., or call **t** 08 92 68 36 22 to buy through an agency they recommend.

FNAC
FNAC Étoile, 26–30 Av des Ternes, 17e, t 01 44 09 18 00; métro Ternes; J6. Open Mon–Sat 10–7.30.
There are other offices too.

Kiosque Théâtre R8
Near 15 Place de la Madeleine, 8e, métro Madeleine; also on the

Parvis de la Gare Montparnasse. Open Tues–Sat 12.30–8 and Sun 12.30–4; closed Sun in July and Aug. Same-day, half-price theatre tickets (plus a commission); expect a queue.

Virgin Megastore N8
52 Av des Champs-Elysées, 8e, t 01 49 53 50 00; métro George-V. Open Mon–Sat 10am–midnight, Sun and hols 12–12.

Music

Classical Music and Opera

Paris has traditionally had an ambivalent attitude towards classical music. It is the only great European capital without a proper symphony auditorium, not to mention a great orchestra to play in it; even the productions in its lavish new opera house only seldom hit a high note of quality. Thanks to the Ministry of Culture and reforms in education that have brought music into the schools, there is more interest in music than before: there are frequent lunchtime concerts in churches, medieval music and choirs at Sainte-Chapelle and chamber music at the Orangerie at La Bagatelle, as well as music festivals throughout the year.

Major Concert Venues

Cité de la Musique Off maps
221 Av Jean-Jaurès, 19e, t 01 44 84 44 84; métro Porte de Pantin.
Two hi-tech concert venues, one home to Pierre Boulez's Ensemble Inter-Contemporain. *See* p.265.

Opéra de Paris Bastille DD14
Place de la Bastille, 12e, t 01 44 73 13 00, w www.opera-de-paris.fr; métro Bastille; wheelchair access.
Opened by Mitterrand in 1990, the slugfest of controversy over its architecture, management and obfuscating productions 'for the masses' has diminished to the occasional slap on the wrist. The

acoustics, however, are great. *See* pp.186–8.

Opéra Comique V8
5 Rue Favart, 2e, t 01 42 44 45 46; métro Richelieu-Drouot.
An older hall used by the Opéra Comique for a repertoire ranging from Lully to Carmen and the occasional operettas.

Salle Pleyel L6
252 Rue du Faubourg-St-Honoré, 8e, t 01 45 61 53 00; métro Ternes.
Chopin last played in public in this hall, although the stories of him coughing blood on the keys are an exaggeration. There are recitals and orchestral performances by the Orchestre Philharmonique de Radio France.

Théâtre des Champs-Elysées M10
15 Av Montaigne, 16e, t 01 49 52 50 50; métro Alma-Marceau.
The Paris equivalent of Carnegie Hall, where Josephine Baker first danced in Paris, and a favourite of big-name classical performers; also some opera.

Théâtre du Châtelet X12–13
Place du Châtelet, 1er, t 01 40 28 28 40, w www.chatelet-theatre.com; métro Châtelet.
A 140-year-old theatre that saw the first season of the Ballet Russe in 1909, and since 1980 very successfully run by the City of Paris, with better opera than the Bastille as well as a vast range of innovative music offerings.

Théâtre de la Ville X–Y13
2 Place du Châtelet, 4e, t 01 42 74 22 77; métro Châtelet.
Excellent city-run theatre; every kind of music, from piano recitals to jazz to African songs.

Other Venues

Many churches and museums in Paris regularly host concerts which are listed in *L'Officiel* and *Pariscope*. Popular venues include:

Centre Georges Pompidou Z11–12
Rue du Renard, 4e, t 01 44 78 48 16; métro Hôtel-de-Ville; wheelchair access.

Église de la Madeleine R8
Place de la Madeleine, 8e; métro Madeleine. Free; no need to book.

Église St-Roch T10
296 Rue St-Honoré, 1er, t 01 45 72 63 26; métro Tuileries.

Église St-Sulpice U15
Place St-Sulpice, 6e, t 01 43 29 61 04; métro St-Sulpice.

Musée National du Moyen-Age (Musée de Cluny) W15
6 Place Paul-Painlevé, 5e, t 01 53 73 78 16; métro Cluny-La Sorbonne.

Musée d'Orsay S12
Quai Anatole-France (postal address 62 Rue de Lille), 7e, t 01 40 49 47 57; métro Solférino, RER Musée d'Orsay; wheelchair access. Tickets for concerts include adm to museum for day of concert.

Radio France (Studio 104) F14
116 Av du Président Kennedy, 16e, t 01 42 30 15 16; RER Av Président Kennedy-Maison de Radio France. Some concerts are free.

Sainte-Chapelle X13
4 Bd du Palais, 1er, t 01 42 77 65 65; métro Cité.

Jazz, Blues, Rock and World Music

In 1925, when La Revue Nègre opened in Paris, it set off a craze for *le jazz hot*, Sidney Bechet, Mezz Mezzrow, the Charleston and Black Bottom so overwhelming that it undermined the old *bal musettes* (*see* p.355). The French had to rewrite the rules, saying that half the members of any band had to be French nationals, a problem the Americans got round by having the French musicians just sit there, holding their instruments. By the next decade France began to catch up by producing its own jazz, led by violinist Stéphane Grappelli and the three-fingered guitarist Django Reinhardt, while continuing to welcome and support black Americans fleeing racial prejudice at home.

Still considered the jazz capital of Europe, Paris since the early 1970s has been in the forefront of another phenomenon: world

music, with its African, North African, Latin, Brazilian and Caribbean *zouk* clubs, where many modern stars found their first audiences. Paris is also the base of Cheb Khaled, the best-known raï singer, whom some people call the Algerian Jim Morrison. Raï, derived from pre-Islamic Bedouin poetry, means 'opinion'; it is similar to rap in content and mostly about alcohol and sex.

For club-style venues, *see* 'Nightlife', pp.347–8.

Finding Out What's On

Check out the smaller independent magazines for their day-by-day listings of all the parties, raves and live gigs in Paris and its 'burbs, along with the price of entrance, drinks, addresses or infolines. Cithea (*see* p.352) has stacks of these, including:

Lylo: A free rag published every three weeks, and generally available in bars, record shops or directly from their office at 55 Rue des Vinaigriers, 10e. It includes a special ravers' page for techno addicts.

Nova Mag: Available in any kiosk. For all events, featuring rap, soul, hip-hop and techno.

It's also worth tuning in to radio stations for day-to-day events:

Radio FG: (Gay Frequency, 98.2 FM) is one of the capital's biggest and hippest radio stations, playing exclusively chemical sounds, house and techno. Radio FG DJs often take part in the events at Queen's and other famous clubs, and between 7.30 and 9pm they broadcast all the essential parties in Paris and checkpoints for underground raves around the city and its periphery.

Nova: (101.5 FM) broadcasts a daily listing of parties.

Major Concert Venues

Le Bataclan DD11
50 Bd Voltaire, 11e, t 01 43 14 35 35; métro Oberkampf.
Not really comfortable as you won't find any place to sit, but surely one of the best spots to listen to roots/reggae music.

Music Festivals

The exact dates of these festivals change annually. For further information contact the tourist office.

Festival de l'Automne Sept–Dec
Festival d'Île-de-France Sept–Oct
Festival des Instruments Anciens March
Festival de St-Denis mid-June– early July
Fête du Marais late June
Fête de la Musique 21 June
La Villette Jazz Festival early July

La Cigale V4
120 Bd de Rochechouart, 18e, t 01 49 25 89 99; métro Pigalle.
Restored vaudeville theatre with the seats removed; plenty of rock.

Elysée Montmartre W4
72 Bd de Rochechouart, 18e, t 01 44 92 45 45; métro Anvers.
One of Paris' most beautiful concert halls. Excellent varied music programme.

Le Grand Rex X8
A cinema also used for concerts (*see* p.354).

Olympia S8
28 Bd des Capucines, 9e, t 01 47 42 25 49; métro Madeleine.
Delightful Art Deco hall, where Piaf and other stars of music hall performed, and still do, with the likes of Tom Waits other days.

Palais Omnisport Bercy GG19
8 Bd de Bercy, 12e, t 08 03 03 00 31; métro Bercy.
The biggest (with 16,000 seats), expensive, and for music obnoxious in almost every possible way, though it puts on more concerts than any other place in this list.

Zénith Off maps
211 Av Jean-Jaurès, 19e, t 01 42 08 60 00; métro Porte de Pantin; wheelchair access.
La Villette's inflatable, pop music hall, decorated with a red aeroplane about to nosedive.

Rock and World Music Bars and Clubs

Baiser Salé Jazz Y12
58 Rue des Lombards, 1er, t 01 42 33 37 71, w www.jazzvalley.com;

métro Châtelet. *Open daily
10pm–6am; adm.*
Afro-fusion, R&B and Latino.

Cithea Off maps
*114 Rue Oberkampf, 11e, t 01 40 21
70 95; métro Ménilmontant. Open
daily 10pm–6am; concert 11pm;
adm Fri, Sat €7.70, otherwise free.*
Live soul, blues, jazz, funk, etc. A
favourite of local musicians, but
unfortunately there's not much
room and it often gets overcrowded. If you can squeeze in,
fun is guaranteed.

La Chapelle des Lombards EE14
*19 Rue de Lappe, 11e, t 01 43 57 24
24; métro Bastille. Open Thurs–Sat
10.30pm–dawn; concerts Thurs
8.30pm; adm €15.25–18.30 (free on
Tues, Wed and Sun).*
Some of the best, newest, affordable Caribbean and African music.

Divan du Monde V4
*75 Rue des Martyrs, 18e, t 01 55 79
09 52; métro Pigalle. Club open
daily 11.30pm–dawn, concerts
Mon–Sat 7.30pm, Sun 2pm; adm
€9.25–18.30.*
Exciting club dedicated to a wide
variety of world music and dance,
mostly from South America.
Cheap drinks.

Le Duplex Z11
*25 Rue Michel-le-Comte, 3e, t 01 42
72 80 86; métro Rambuteau.
Open daily 8pm–2am.*
Friendly, artsy, gay and straight
bar with affordable drink prices.
Music ranges from jazz to indie to
bossa-nova.

L'Escale V15
*15 Rue Monsieur-le-Prince, 6e,
t 01 40 51 80 49; métro Odéon.
Open Tues–Sat 10.30pm–5am; adm
€12.20 (inc. one drink).* Salsa downstairs and Latin American music
on the ground floor.

La Flèche d'Or Off maps
*102 bis Rue de Bagnolet, 20e,
t 01 43 72 04 23, w www.flechedor.
com; métro Porte de Bagnolet.
Open Tues–Sun 6pm–2am.*
You may often hear Parisians
saying the Flèche d'Or is a place
they particularly like: the setting,
in a former train station from a
line that used to go around Paris,

is charming, drinks are cheap
(beer €2) and the music is always
good: roots, rock, reggae and funk,
with many live performers and
jam sessions. During the day, you
can hang around reading the
papers, or playing chess or cards;
there are sometimes exhibitions
of work by local artists. There's
food too (à la carte around €18,
Sun brunch €12). Don't hesitate to
phone to find out what's on.

Folies Pigalle V4
*11 Place Pigalle, 9e, t 01 48 78 55 25;
métro Pigalle. Open Tues–Fri and
Sun midnight–6am, Sat midnight–
noon, show 8–11pm (book on t 01
40 36 71 58); adm €15.25, show €23.*
An old cabaret that hasn't really
changed much. The sound is
mainly house and garage. At 7am
on Saturdays, half of the population will be going to bed, while
others will still be arriving. One
dance floor and a large balcony
(sometimes reserved). On
Saturdays there's a show similar
to the Chippendales.

House of Live N8
*124 Rue la Boëtie, 8e, t 01 42 25 18
06; métro Franklin D. Roosevelt.
Open daily 9am–5am; concerts
daily 6–11; adm free.*
Blues and rock and cheap beer.

Institut du Monde Arabe AA15
*1 Rue des Fossés St-Bernard, 5e,
t 01 40 51 38 14; métro Jussieu.
Open Tues–Sun 10am–6pm;
adm €16 for performances.
No shows in summer.*
One of the best places to hear
Arab music.

Mambo Club W16
*20 Rue Cujas, 5e, t 01 43 54 89 21;
métro St-Michel. Open Thurs–Sat
11pm–dawn; adm €18.*
West Indian music in a rather run-
down club.

**Opus Jazz and Soul
Club** Off maps
*167 Quai de Valmy, 10e, t 01 40 34
70 00, w www.opus-club.com;
métro Louis-Blanc. Open Tues and
Wed 7–2am, Thurs 7–4fham, Fri
7–5am, Sat 7–dawn; adm €10.70.*
Swell bar with a mezzanine where
you can easily sit and have an

affordable drink while listening to
funk rock. Call for the programme.

Le Réservoir GG15
*16 Rue de la Forge-Royale, 11e,
t 01 43 56 39 60; métro Faidherbe-
Chaligny. Open Tues–Thurs
8pm–2am, Fri and Sat 8pm–4am;
adm free.*
Once a textile warehouse, now
the venue for world, trip and
house, among others.

Jazz and Blues Music Bars and Clubs

Au Duc des Lombards Y12
*42 Rue des Lombards, 1er, t 01 42
33 22 88; métro Châtelet. Open
Mon–Sat 8pm–2am, concerts
9pm–1.30am, Aug open Sat only;
adm €16–19.*
One of the best; popular, friendly,
dimly lit lounge, with jazz piano,
trios and crooners ranging from
excellent to competent.

Le Bilboquet U13–14
*13 Rue St-Benoît, 6e, t 01 45 48
81 84; métro St-Germain-des-Prés.
Open daily 8pm–2.30am;
adm €16–21 (inc. one drink).*
St-Germain club, vintage 1947, on
the main drag of cool jazz in the
1950s; popular with tourists
remembering golden days. Pricey;
average French jazz.

Caveau de la Huchette X14
*5 Rue de la Huchette, 5e, t 01 43 26
65 05; métro St-Michel. Open daily
9.30–4am. Concert daily 9.30pm;
adm €10–13.*
Since 1946 the home of traditional
live jazz and bebop in a 14th-
century cellar.

Cithea Off maps
See 'Rock and World Music', above.

Lionel Hampton Off maps
*Meridien Hotel, 81 Bd Gouvion-
St-Cyr, 17e, t 01 40 68 30 42;
métro Porte Maillot. Open daily
10.30pm–2am; adm €11.50 (inc.
one drink).*
Top-of-the-range jazz acts,
including the man himself.

New Morning Z7
*7–9 Rue des Petites-Écuries, 10e,
t 01 45 23 51 41; métro Château-
d'Eau. Concerts daily 9pm; adm
€18.50–20.*

Not very cosy, but it has plenty of room and fine acoustics. The place to find international jazz all-stars and first-rate world music, although it has recently opened its doors to a wider range of musicians.

Le Petit Journal Montparnasse Q19
13 Rue du Commandant-René-Mouchotte, 14e, t 01 43 21 56 70; métro Gaîté. **Open** *Mon–Sat 12–3.30 and 8pm–2am, concerts 10pm; closed 10 July–20 Aug;* **adm** *€18–61 (can include dinner).*
One of the best, with enough space for big bands from France and abroad as well.

Le Réservoir GG15
16 Rue de la Forge-Royale, 11e, t 01 43 56 39 60; métro Faidherbe-Chaligny.
Holds a Sunday jazz brunch from 11.30am.

Slow Club X12
130 Rue de Rivoli, 1er, t 01 42 33 84 30; métro Châtelet-Les Halles or Pont-Neuf. **Open** *Tues–Thurs 10pm–3am, Fri and Sat 10pm–4am, concerts 10pm;* **adm** *€9.15–11.45.*
The late Miles Davis' favourite jazz club in Paris, and a must for lovers of swing, New Orleans and traditional jazz. Occasional R&B nights.

Le Sunset Y12
60 Rue des Lombards, 1er, t 01 40 26 46 60; métro Châtelet. **Open** *Mon–Sat 9pm–2am;* **adm** *€8–25.*
Jazz, fusion and bebop, in the redecorated cellar-cum-tiled métro tunnel. Now includes **Le Sunside** (**t** 01 40 26 21 25) for acoustic jazz.

Chansonniers

Paris' own art form, first popularized by Aristide Bruant, revived in the 1950s and 60s by Jacques Brel, Georges Brassens and Juliette Gréco (who's still alive and kicking) and currently being revived again for both the Parisians and tourists.

Au Lapin Agile V2
22 Rue des Saules, 18e, t 01 46 06 85 87, w www.au-lapin-agile.com;
métro Lamarck-Caulaincourt. **Open** *Tues–Sun 9pm–2am;* **adm** *€24 (inc. drink).*
A valiant attempt at bringing old French traditional song back to life to busloads of Japanese tourists. *See pp.196–7.*

Canotier du Pied de la Butte W4
62 Bd de Rochechouart, 18e, t 01 46 06 02 86; métro Anvers. **Open** *Wed–Mon: 3 shows 9pm–midnight (€38), dancing midnight–dawn (€13.75).*
Sit in romantic gloom and listen to favourite French songs and jokes.

Caveau de la Bolée W14
25 Rue de l'Hirondelle, 6e, t 01 43 54 62 20; métro St-Michel. **Open** *Mon–Sat 6pm–4am.*
A 14th-century prison in a medieval alley, evoking the old Latin Quarter and *les neiges d'antan* with its dinner-cabaret from €40.

Caveau des Oubliettes X12
52 Rue Galande, 5e, t 01 43 29 37 11; métro St-Michel. **Open** *Mon–Sat 9pm–2am.*
French songs from the 12th to 20th centuries and a peek at a medieval dungeon with its torture instruments; JFK as a senator supposedly put his head in the guillotine.

Le Magique P21
42 Rue de Gergovie, 14e, t 01 45 42 26 10; métro Pernety. **Open** *Wed–Sun 8pm–2am, concerts Wed and Thurs 9.30, Fri–Sun 10.30; minimum donation €4.50.*
Cheap meal and politically incorrect *chansons.*

Sentier des Halles X9
50 Rue d'Aboukir, 2e, t 01 42 61 89 96; métro Sentier. Concerts Mon–Sat at 8pm and 10pm; closed Aug; **adm** *€8–17.*
Cellar venue for a variety of *chansons.*

Cabaret and Comedy

Paris rivals Las Vegas for over-the-top kitsch-and-glitter-oozing, tit-and-feather spectaculars, invariably advertised as 'sophisti-cated', for fleecing tourists, provincials and businessmen.

Les Blancs Manteaux AA12
15 Rue des Blancs-Manteaux, 4e, t 01 48 87 15 84, w www.blancs manteaux.claranet.fr; métro Hôtel-de-Ville. Shows from 8pm plus Sat, Sun and Wed afternoons; **adm** *€11–14.*
Stand-up and comedy plus children's shows.

Club des Poètes P–Q12
30 Rue de Bourgogne, 7e, t 01 47 05 06 03; métro Varenne. **Open** *Mon–Sat; dinner and show €22–30.50; just show €9.15.*
A treat for fans of French poetry, with a spectacle featuring the greats from Villon to Boris Vian.

Crazy Horse L10
12 Av George-V, 8e, t 01 47 23 32 32, w www.lecrazyhorseparis.com; métro George-V. Sun–Fri shows at 8.30pm and 11pm, Sat shows at 8pm, 10.15pm and 12.15am; **adm** *€49–90 (inc two drinks), dîner-spectacle €125–65.*
Founded in 1951. High temple of naked Barbie dolls with names like Bettina Uranium and Pussy Duty-Free dressed in leather straps.

Lido L8
116 Av des Champs-Elysées, 8e, t 01 40 76 56 10, w www.lido.fr; métro George-V. Show daily 9.30pm–11.30pm; **adm** *€60–90.*
The best special effects perk up the act of the 60 Bluebell Girls.

Michou V4
80 Rue des Martyrs, 18e, t 01 46 06 16 04, t 01 42 57 20 37; métro Pigalle. Show at 8.30pm daily; dinner and show €90.
Reserve a place at Michou, a funny satirical drag show that draws even the celebrities to see themselves being parodied.

Moulin Rouge T4
82 Bd de Clichy, 18e, t 01 53 09 82 82, w www.moulin-rouge.com; métro Blanche. **Open** *daily from 7pm, show at 9pm and 11pm;* **adm** *from €82, with dinner from €130.*

The most famous and the most Las-Vegasey of the lot, with its guest stars and cancanning Doris Girls. See pp.198–200.

Le Paradis Latin Z16
28 Rue du Cardinal-Lemoine, 5e, t 01 43 25 28 28; métro Cardinal-Lemoine. Dîner-spectacle Wed–Mon at 8pm; from €109.
In an old theatre built by Eiffel, this is the one music-hall-cabaret with Parisian customers.

Le Tartuffe U5
46 Rue Notre-Dame de Lorette, 9e, t 01 45 26 21 37; métro St-Georges. Shows daily from 7pm; adm €15.25–29.
Three one-man shows per night – guaranteed audience participation.

Cinema

The Parisians may well be the biggest film junkies in the world, and chances are that in one of their 320 screens, one will show that obscure flick you've been dying to see for years. Films are a common topic of conversation in the city, often bringing forth some curious and striking cultural differences.

Note that films dubbed in French or which were originally made in several languages and are being shown in French are labelled v.f.; if shown in English, it will say *version anglaise*; if in the original language (including English), with French subtitles, they'll say v.o. (*version originale*). Average admission prices are €6–7; students and senior citizens are often eligible for discounts at weekday matinées. Many cinemas have a showing in the morning, around 11am, for which they usually charge half-price. Some of the cinema chains offer passes to keen film buffs which can work out to be excellent value. In some larger cinemas, the usherette should be tipped.

The three largest cinema chains are Gaumont (not the Gaumont Kinepanorama), MK2 and UGC.

Each offers reductions if you buy multiple tickets.

Accattone W16
20 Rue Cujas, 5e, t 01 46 33 86 86; métro Cluny-La Sorbonne.
Great for lesser-known classics from Russia and Eastern Europe, alternative films from just about everywhere else, and Rossellini films.

Action Z16–Y16
Grand Action: 5 Rue des Ecoles, 5e, t 01 43 29 44 40; métro Cardinal-Lemoine; Z16. Action Écoles: 23 Rue des Écoles, 5e, t 01 43 29 79 89; métro Maubert-Mutualité; Y16.
A small Paris chain of cinemas specializing in retrospectives of great old films; most are on fresh prints drawn from the negatives. Action Ecoles is the smaller of the two.

Cinémathèque
The Cinémathèque is due to move to 51 Rue de Bercy (*see* p.270). At the time of writing it was at two venues: Palais de Chaillot (*see* p.142; I11) and 42 Bd de Bonne Nouvelle, 10e, t 01 56 26 01 01; adm €4.50; Y8 (closed Mon). Vintage films.

Dôme IMAX Off maps
1 Place du Dôme, La Défense, t 08 36 67 06 06; métro Grande-Arche-de-La-Défense.
The 'Largest Wraparound Movie Theatre in the World'.

L'Entrepôt P20–21
7–9 Rue Francis-de-Pressensé, 14e, t 01 45 40 78 38; métro Pernety.
Three cinemas showing some of the best art and third-world fare in Paris; also a bookshop, bar-restaurant, satellite and international cable TV.

L'Escurial Panoramas Y19
11 Bd de Port-Royal, 13e, t 01 47 07 28 04; métro Les Gobelins.
Plush red-velvet movie palace, showing quality films in v.o.

Gaumont Kinopanorama K15
60 Av de La-Motte-Picquet, 15e, t 01 40 30 20 10 (#117); métro La Motte-Picquet; adm €8.50.
Very popular, 180° cinema, 70mm film, equipped for high definition

Showscan (60 images per second) and extraordinary sound.

Gaumont Marignan N9
27 Av des Champs-Elysées, 8e, t 08 92 69 66 96 106; métro Franklin D. Roosevelt.

Gaumont Opéra Premier U8
32 Rue Louis-le-Grand, t 08 92 69 66 96 118; métro Opéra.

Gaumont Parnasse S17
3 Rue d'Odessa, 14e, t 08 92 69 66 96 (#115); métro Montparnasse-Bienvenüe; wheelchair access.

La Géode Off maps
26 Av Corentin-Cariou, 19e, t 01 40 05 12 12; métro Porte de la Villette. Hourly showings Tues–Sun 10–7. Booking strongly suggested for the 7, 8 and 9pm showings, same day only, t 01 42 05 50 50; adm €8.70.
Extraordinary OMNIMAX cinema at the Cité des Sciences shows National-Geographic-type fare with fish-eye-lens cameras that make you feel as if you were in the centre of the action.

Le Grand Rex X8
1 Bd Poissonnière, 2e, t 01 42 36 83 93; métro Bonne-Nouvelle.
Films are all dubbed into French, but the Rex is a must for lovers of old Hollywood Busby Berkeley 1930s extravaganzas, with one of the biggest screens in Europe, 2,750 seats and a great ceiling.

Le Latina Z12
20 Rue du Temple, 4e, t 01 42 78 47 86; métro Hôtel-de-Ville.
Latin American film specialist. Bar with warm Hispanic atmosphere.

Max Linder Panorama X8
24 Bd Poissonnière, 9e, t 08 36 68 50 52, t 01 40 30 30 31; métro Grands Boulevards.
Most sumptuous and plush, state-of-the-art equipment; great for first-run films in v.o.

MK2 Bastille DD14
4 Bd Beaumarchais, 11e, t 08 36 68 14 07, métro Bastille.

MK2 Beaubourg Z11
50 Rue Rambuteau, 3e, t 08 36 68 14 07; métro Rambuteau.

MK2 Hautefeuille W14
7 Rue Hautefeuille, 6e, t 08 36 68 14 07; métro St-Michel.

La Pagode P15
*57 Rue de Babylone, 7e, t 01 45 55 48
48; métro St-François-Xavier.*
Recently reopened after refurbishment, Mme Boucicaut's Japanese folly has been a cinema and tea house since 1931 and, thanks to Marcel Carné, an historical monument since 1982. *See p.133.*

Quartier Latin W15
*9 Rue Champollion, 5e, t 01 43 26
84 65; métro Cluny-La Sorbonne.*
Small alternative cinema.

Salle Garance Z11–12
*Centre Georges Pompidou, 4e,
t 01 42 78 37 29; métro Rambuteau or Chatelet-Les Halles.* **Open**
Wed–Mon; **adm** *€4.*
Shows films from around the world with French subtitles.

Studio 28 U3
*10 Rue Tholozé, 18e, t 01 46 06 36
07; métro Abbesses; closed Mon.*
Founded in 1928, charming, family-run and still going strong. Decorations by Cocteau. Films always in v.o.

Studio Galande X14–15
*42 Rue Galande, 5e, t 01 43 26 94
08; métro St-Michel.*
Brave little cinema, with lots of old Fellini and Terry Gilliam, and *The Rocky Horror Picture Show* Fri and Sat nights, all in v.o.

Les Trois Luxembourgs W16
*67 Rue Monsieur-le-Prince, 6e,
t 01 46 33 97 77; métro Odéon.*
Very basic inside, but worth visiting for its innovative offerings on three screens.

UGC Ciné Cité Les Halles X11
*Place de la Rotonde, Forum des Halles, t 08 92 70 00 00 11;
métro Châtelet-Les Halles.*

UGC Odéon V14
*124 Bd St-Germain, 6e, t 08 92 70
00 00 26; métro Odéon.*

UGC Champs-Elysées M8
*65 Av des Champs-Elysées, 8e, t 08
92 70 00 00 19; métro Franklin D. Roosevelt.*

Vidéothèque de Paris X11
Porte St-Eustache, in the Forum des Halles. 1er, t 01 40 26 34 30; métro Châtelet-Les Halles; wheelchair access. **Open** *Tues–Wed and*

Fri–Sun 2.30–9; adm €4.50 for the day.
Shows films and documentaries on changing themes.

Dance

There's a good range of dance to see in Paris, but little of it is home grown, thanks to the decision of the Culture Ministry to subsidize companies out in the provinces, rather than in Paris. Many of the already-listed theatres and concert halls schedule dance performances, often by visiting companies, and each week's listings seem to bring forth new studios or theatre venues. For places where you can participate, *see* p.368.

Café de la Danse EE14
*5 Passage Louis-Philippe, 11e, t 01 47
00 57 59; métro Bastille.* **Tickets**
€8–35.
The place to see small, innovative, contemporary companies.

Centre Mandapa X23
*6 Rue Wurtz, 13e, t 01 45 89 01 60;
métro Glacière.* **Tickets** *€13.50.*
Traditional international dance – mainly from the East – performances and classes.

Centre Pompidou Z11–12
*Rue Beaubourg, 4e, t 01 44 78 12 33;
métro Rambuteau.* **Tickets** *€10–18.*
Visiting companies.

Opéra Bastille DD14
*120 Rue de Lyon, 12e, t 01 43 87 03
26, w www.opera-de-paris.com;
métro Bastille; wheelchair access.*
Tickets *€7–60.*
Stages some performances of the Ballet de l'Opéra de Paris as well as other companies.

Opéra de Paris-Garnier T8
*Place de l'Opéra, 9e, t 01 43 87 03
26, w www.opera-de-paris.com;
métro Opéra.* **Tickets** *€4.50–33.50.*
Guided tour during the week *(see p.148).*
Home of Ballet de l'Opéra de Paris.

Studio Regard du Cygne Off maps
*210 Rue de Belleville, 20e, t 01 40 38
38 46; métro Place des Fêtes.*
Devoted to innovative international companies.

Théâtre de la Cité Internationale Off maps
*21 Boulevard Jourdan, 14e, t 01 43 13
50 50; RER Cité-Universitaire.*
Tickets €17.
Venue for dance and theatre.

Théâtre National de Chaillot H–I11
*1 Place du Trocadéro, 16e, t 01 53
65 30 00; métro Trocadéro.*
Tickets *€25.*
A variety of top-of-the-range dance alongside the drama.

Théâtre de la Ville X–Y13
*2 Place du Châtelet, 4e, t 01 42
74 22 77; métro Châtelet.* **Tickets**
€15–29.
First-class contemporary dance alongside theatre and concerts.

Bals Musette

These traditional afternoon dances, held in places also called *bals musette* or *guinguettes*, still attract couples dancing to accordion music. If you want to appreciate old-fashioned Parisian entertainment and take a spin with your partner, these are the places for you:

Balajo EE14
*9 Rue de Lappe, 11e, t 01 47 00 07 87,
w www.balajo.fr; métro Bastille.*
Open *Tues and Thurs 8–4.30am, Fri
and Sat 11–5.30am, Wed
9–4.30am, Sun 3–7; adm €15.25.*
A genuine *bal musette* where now you'll find everything from traditional dance to disco.

Guingette de l'Île du Martin-Pêcheur Off maps
*31 Quai Victor Hugo, Champigny-sur-Marne, t 01 49 83 03 02; RER
Champigny.* **Open** *Fri and Sat 10pm–
2am, Sun 4–8pm; adm €5.40.*
Lovely *guingette* by the river.

Le Petit Robinson Off maps
*164 Quai de Polangis, Joinville-le-Pont, t 01 48 89 04 39; RER
Joinville-le-Pont.* **Open** *Fri and Sat
8pm–2am, Sun 3–7pm;* **adm**
€14–16.
This is the place to show off your ballroom-dancing skills to the accompaniment of a live orchestra.

Theatre and Performance Arts

The first theatre in Paris was built by Cardinal Richelieu in the Palais Royal in 1641, and the trickery of the stage machines played as big a role in the performances as the music and dance. Over the last 350 years, Paris has come full circle: the blockbusters in its theatres are multimedia extravaganzas with extraordinary special effects. The only serious contemporary drama is translations from the West End in London. Otherwise, French-speakers can still find plenty of Racine and Molière from the excellent Comédie-Française and frequent revivals of Ionesco, Anouilh, Genet and company, not to mention Paris' perennial bland boulevard comedies, inevitably about extramarital hanky-panky.

The **Festival d'Automne** (mid-Sept–mid-Dec) is a festival of performing arts that attracts participants from around the world.

Les Bouffes du Nord Off maps
37 bis Bd de la Chapelle, 10e, t 01 46 07 34 50; métro La Chapelle.
Former neighbourhood music hall that has become Peter Brook's baby; now a venue for acclaimed experimental productions.

Cartoucherie Théâtre du Soleil Off maps
Rte du Champ-de-Manoeuvre, 12e, t 01 43 74 24 08; métro Château-de-Vincennes, linked with a free theatre shuttle bus.
Ariane Mnouchkine's five-stage complex is home to perhaps the most thought-provoking theatre in Paris, including plays in their

original language. Phone ahead to reserve at the other theatres:
Aquarium: t 01 43 74 99 61
Le Chaudron: t 01 43 28 97 04
L'Epée de Bois: t 01 43 08 39 74
La Tempête: t 01 43 28 36 36

Comédie-Française U11
2 Rue de Richelieu, 1er, t 01 44 58 15 15; métro Palais Royal-Musée du Louvre.
Founded in 1680 and playing in the beautiful Salle Richelieu in the Palais Royal; excellent productions of the old classics by Molière, Beaumarchais, Marivaux and Racine, also foreign classics in translation; seats sold two weeks in advance.

Comédie Italienne R18
17 Rue de la Gaîté, 14e, t 01 43 21 22 22; métro Edgar-Quinet.
The old Comédie Italienne was a rival of the Comédie-Française until Louis XIV banished them for calling Mme de Maintenon a prude and the king Monsieur de Maintenon. In a poky theatre amongst 'live sex' shops, the revived company puts on Goldoni, Commedia dell'Arte and Pirandello in French.

Odéon Théâtre de l'Europe V15
1 Place Paul-Claudel, 6e, t 01 44 41 36 36; métro Odéon.
Shares resources with Comédie-Française, its fellow state theatre. The Grande Salle is often the stage of the Théâtre Populaire National; the Petit Odéon sees alternative theatre and foreign companies' productions in their own language.

Opéra Comique V8
See 'Classical Music and Opera', p.350.

Palais Royal V10
38 Rue de Montpensier, 1er, t 01 42 97 59 81; métro Palais Royal-Musée

du Louvre or Bourse. Tickets €10.70–38.20, dîner-spectacle €58.
The loveliest place to take in a boulevard comedy.

Théâtre de la Bastille FF13
76 Rue de la Roquette, 11e, t 01 43 57 42 14; métro Bastille.
Top-quality modern theatre and dance.

Théâtre de l'Est Parisien Off maps
159 Av Gambetta, 20e, t 01 43 64 80 80; métro St-Fargeau.
Good fringe theatre.

Théâtre de la Huchette X14
23 Rue de la Huchette, 5e, t 01 43 26 38 99; métro St-Michel.
They've been doing Ionesco's *La Cantatrice Chauve* and *La Leçon* for over 40 years.

Théâtre National de Chaillot H–I11
Place du Trocadéro, 16e, t 01 47 27 81 15; métro Trocadéro.
Frequently the stage for lavish productions of Brecht et al.

Théâtre National de la Colline Off maps
15 Rue Malte-Brun, 20e, t 01 44 62 52 52; métro Gambetta; wheelchair access.
Dedicated to contemporary European works.

Théâtre de Nesle V13
8 Rue de Nesle, 6e, t 01 46 34 61 04; métro Odéon.
Often hosts performances of the city's English-language companies.

Théâtre de la Porte St-Martin AA9
16 Bd St-Martin, 10e, t 01 42 08 00 32; métro Strasbourg-St-Denis.
Often sparkling, very Parisian productions and one-man shows.

Shopping

People who think of shopping as an art have long regarded Paris as Europe's masterpiece when it comes to consumption. Throughout its history, the city has enjoyed an enviable reputation for craftsmanship, especially in luxury goods.

Paris also invented the idea of fashion as we know it, upsetting the age-old code of dressing to show one's social status. During the Second Empire, just as Haussmann divided Paris into good and bad addresses, a clever English dressmaker named Worth whetted the desire of wealthy women to set themselves apart from others by the cut of their clothes (and the colour of their clothes – until 1900 working women stuck to black, as it best hid the inevitable, indelible Paris mud).

With the advent of department stores (see Au Bon Marché, pp.213–4), industrial-made imitations of couturier designs became available to a much wider public. The race began for the wealthy to remain a step ahead of the plebeian, crowd-distracting women.

Today you can have a *haute-couture* garment hand-sewn to your measurements for several thousand euros. You can size up the current vogues, or spend a bit less, in the exalted *prêt-à-porter* (ready-to-wear) designer fashion zone in the 8e, specifically along Avenue George-V, Rue du Faubourg-St-Honoré, Rue François-1er and Avenue Montaigne. If the latest designer wear is outside your budget, there are a number of shops that sell last season's or earlier clothes and accessories, or you can tackle Paris' huge department stores.

For shoppers who prefer more intimate safaris, Paris has endless little speciality shops tucked into nearly every *arrondissement*. For the bargain hunter there are mega-flea markets and some interesting second-hand shops.

For shops for kids, see 'Children and Teenagers' Paris', pp.372–3.

As a general rule, shops are open Mon–Sat 10–7; smaller shops may be closed on Mon, for lunch and during August. The big sales (*les soldes*) take place in January and July, when prices on seasonal goods are cut, often by half.

Shopping Tours: Shopping Plus (S15), 99–103 Rue de Sèvres, **t** 01 47 53 91 17, organizes walking tours in various quarters on various themes: high fashion, antiques, gourmet food, home decoration, etc. A half-day tour for two people costs around €2.30 (there are no tours in August).

VAT Refunds: Value-added tax (TVA in France) is around 20% on most goods. Non-EU citizens are entitled to a TVA refund of 12–17% on most goods if they have spent at least €180 in a single trip to one shop and have been in France for less than six months. To get your refund, shop with your passport and ask for a *bordereau de vente à l'exportation* (export sales invoice) at the time of purchase. When you leave France, take the goods and invoice to the customs office at the point of departure and have the invoice stamped. Part of the invoice must then be mailed within 90 days to the shop, which will send you the refund.

Antiques

There are four very pricey strongholds for antique dealers in Paris, where you'll find a Louis XIII chair but never a bargain:

A l Dépôt AA13
3 Rue du Pont-Louis-Philippe; *métro* St-Paul.
Lots of fun Art Deco pieces.

Carrée Rive Gauche T13
Just west of Rue des Saints-Pères; métro Rue-du-Bac.

Louvre des Antiquaires V11
Next to the Louvre; métro Palais Royal-Musée du Louvre. **Open** Tues–Sun 11–7.
The poshest and biggest, and a great place for browsing.

Village St-Paul BB14
Rue St-Paul; métro St-Paul. **Open** Thurs–Mon 11–7.

Village Suisse K15–L14
78 Av de Suffren/54 Av de La Motte-Picquet; métro La Motte-Picquet. **Open** Thurs–Mon 10.30–7.

The keen-eyed arrive early at the **flea markets** (see p.364), which are by far the best place for antiques, or haunt Drouot (see below). Other good places are:

Wyters Chantal Off maps
141 Bd Voltaire; métro Voltaire. **Open** Wed and Sat 10.30–12 and 2–6.
A great place to rummage for treasures from the 1850s–1930s.

Art

It made all the art mags when Colnaghi, the famous dealer in old masters, opened a branch in Rue du Faubourg-St-Honoré in May 1792 (shortly after, the firm was forced by the Revolution to move to London). Apparently old masters are easier to pick up in France than anywhere else (one reason is that most French collectors buy only French painting). This is especially true at the auction house **Drouot**, which sells anything from Impressionists to junk glass lots – all sales are listed in the weekly mags under *Vente aux Enchères*. What Drouot fails to auction off ends up at **Drouot Nord** (64 Rue Doudeauville; *métro* Château-Rouge; Z2).

Commercial galleries are concentrated in certain areas, and unless one of your favourites is showing at a certain address, it's more fun to window-shop (*lèche-vitrines*, 'lick the glass') and pop in when something catches your fancy. From Quai Voltaire to the Institut de France is the place to hunt up an old master; St-Germain, on all sides of the lower Rue de Seine, is nothing but galleries, mostly specializing in artists still living or fairly warm in the grave. The 8e, west of the Palais de l'Elysée, is the area for established artists, while the

Marais, Beaubourg and Bastille are the hot spots for contemporary new artists. *Pariscope* and other entertainment magazines, and the monthly guide *Association des Galeries* (free at the larger galleries) will give you the lowdown on what's showing throughout the city. Also try the Sunday **art market** (10.30–4.30) in Place Ferdinand-Brunot (métro Mouton-Duvernet; S21).

Below are some addresses for art-related items most mortals can afford; other good places to check out are the museum shops: at the Orsay, Louvre and Art Moderne de la Ville de Paris.

L'Art du Papier S17
*48 Rue Vavin; **métro** Vavin.*
If Paris inspires you to take up the brush yourself, this shop has the most reasonably priced paints, easels and canvases.

Art Prestige Off maps
*43 Rue Manin; **métro** Bolívar.*
For frames, posters, lithographs and restoration.

Graphigro S16
*133 Rue de Rennes; **métro** St-Placide.*
Three floors of art supplies.

Lavrut U9
*52 Passage de Choiseul; **métro** Pyramides.*
Large, well-stocked art shop in this lively *passage*.

Books

Paris, especially the Left Bank, is a paradise for book lovers, even if you don't read French.

The *bouquinistes*, who unlock their picturesque green wooden stalls along the Seine on fair-weather afternoons, make good browsing, and the persistent will often be rewarded with second-hand gems.

Abbey Bookshop X14–15
*29 Rue de la Parcheminerie; **métro** St-Michel.*
Genial Canadian-owned book-shop, with a good selection of new and used English and North American titles.

Album X15
*6–8 Rue Dante; **métro** Maubert-Mutualité.*
The best shop for comic-book collectors.

Les Archives de la Presse AA11
*51 Rue des Archives; **métro** Rambuteau.*
Stacks of old French magazines and newspapers, some dating back to the first edition. For a pricey sum, you can buy a forty-year-old *Vogue* and learn how Brigitte Bardot keeps her locks so blond and shiny.

Artcurial O8
*7 Rond-Point des Champs-Elysées; **métro** Franklin D. Roosevelt.*
Glossy art and coffee-table books, in French and English.

Astrolabe U7 and W14
*46 Rue de Provence; **métro** Chaussée d'Antin; 14 Rue Serpente; **métro** Cluny-La Sorbonne.*
Leading travel bookshop.

Atmosphère Y19
*10 Rue Broca; **métro** Censier-Daubenton.*
Has the most extensive collection of books, rare posters and stills; a paradise for all film fetishists.

Brentano's U9
*37 Av de l'Opéra; **métro** Opéra.*
New books and magazines in English, American interests; novels, guides, children's and art sections too.

La Chambre Claire V15
*14 Rue St-Sulpice; **métro** Odéon.*
Grand specialist in photography; posters, manuals, books and more.

Cinédoc W8
*43 Passage Jouffroy; **métro** Grands Boulevards.*
Great for cinema books, posters and memorabilia; also antique sex literature.

Ciné Reflets W14
*14 Rue Serpente; **métro** Cluny-La Sorbonne.*
Films books, posters and a large library of stills.

FNAC
A Paris institution: the city's biggest and fullest book chain (including some titles in English). Key outlets include:
*Forum des Halles, Rue Pierre-Lescot (X11), **métro** Châtelet-Les Halles; 26–30 Av des Ternes (J5–6), **métro** Étoile; 136 Rue de Rennes (S16), **métro** St-Placide; 109 Rue St-Lazare (S7), **métro** St-Lazare.*

Galignani S10
*224 Rue de Rivoli; **métro** Tuileries.*
Cosy place founded in 1802: the oldest English bookshop on the Continent; new titles, children's and glossy art books.

Gilda X12
*36 Rue des Bourdonnais; **métro** Châtelet.*
Huge collection of second-hand books and records in French.

L'Harmattan X15
*16 Rue des Écoles; **métro** Maubert-Mutualité.*
Bookshop devoted to the litera-ture, history, etc. of Africa and other exotic destinations.

Institut Géographique National O7
*107 Rue La Boétie; **métro** Miromesnil.*
Paris' Stanford's, with a superb collection of maps, ordnance surveys, guidebooks and every-thing else you need to venture off the beaten track.

L'Introuvable Off maps
*35 Rue Juliette-Dodu; **métro** Colonel-Fabien.*
As the name suggests, if you haven't been able to find it else-where, you may get it here.

Librairie des Abbesses V4
*30 Rue Yvonne-Le-Tac; **métro** Abbesses. Open Tues–Sat 10–7.30, Sun and Mon 12–7.30.*
Small, but packed with thousands of titles, including an English-language section.

Librairie de l'Ecole Supérieure des Beaux-Arts U13
*17 Quai Malaquais; **métro** St-Germain-des-Prés.*
Architecture books from around the world.

Librairie Théâtrale V8
*3 Rue de Marivaux; **métro** Richelieu-Drouot.*

Vast selection of librettos, plays, scenarios and anything having to do with the performing arts.

Librairie Ulysse AA15
26 Rue St-Louis-en-l'Île; métro Pont-Marie.
The wonderful shop is oldest travel bookstore in the world, with over 20,000 titles.

Parallèles X11–12
47 Rue St-Honoré; métro Châtelet-Les Halles. Open Mon–Sat 10–7.
Media and source centre of alternative Paris, underground publications, books on music, records and more.

San Francisco Book Co V15
17 Rue Monsieur-le-Prince; métro Odéon.
Paris branch of the California-based shop with new and used books in English.

Shakespeare & Co. X14
37 Rue de la Bûcherie; métro St-Michel.
Just what a bookshop should be: a convivial treasure hunt, crammed full of inexpensive second-hand and new books in English (*see* pp.221–2).

Tea & Tattered Pages Q16
24 Rue Mayet; métro Duroc.
A blessing for paupers: this English tearoom with stacks and stacks of old paperbacks at low prices.

Tschann T18
125 Bd du Montparnasse; métro Vavin.
Classic address for French literature and poetry.

The Village Voice U14
6 Rue Princesse; métro Mabillon.
This is where Odile Hellier carries the banner of American literature in Paris, hosting scores of readings by contemporary writers; has anglophone Paris' most discriminating collections of books.

W. H. Smith R10
248 Rue de Rivoli; métro Concorde. Open Mon–Sat 9–7.30, Sun 1–7.30.
Especially good for their English-language magazines; also has reasonable fiction, children's and travel sections.

Clothing

A la Bonne Renommée AA13
26 Rue Vieille-du-Temple; métro St-Paul.
Beautiful, richly coloured satins, silks and velvets with a folkloric touch.

Au Vieux Continent W10
3 Rue d'Argout; métro Sentier.
Minimall for the young and hip; two floors packed full of clothes and accessories from the most fashionable brands.

Chanel S9
29 Rue Cambon; métro Madeleine.
Probably the most famous house in Paris, now under the design wand of Karl Lagerfeld.

Dior S9
384–6 Rue St Honoré; métro Tuileries or Concorde.
New triangular, glass-walled shop full of extravaganzas from one of Paris's fashion mammoths.

Evolutif AA13
13 Rue de Rivoli; métro St-Paul.
Current Yves-St-Laurent and Kenzo styles for men at 20% off.

Gaëlle Barré FF14
17 Rue Keller; métro Bastille. Open Mon 2–8, Tues–Sat 11.30–8.
Boutique atelier run by delightful young designer. Reasonably priced limited editions of colourful clothes with original details. Gaëlle also designs one-off outfits, including unusual wedding dresses.

Hermès R9
24 Rue du Faubourg-St-Honoré; métro Madeleine.
Pay a month's rent for a scarf.

Iglaine Y11
12 Rue de la Grande-Truanderie, t 01 42 36 19 91; métro Étienne-Marcel. Open Mon–Sat 11–7.
Impeccably chic and trendy, with a good range of accessories.

Jean-Paul Gaultier V9 and EE14
6 Rue Vivienne, t 01 42 86 05 05 métro Bourse; 30 Rue du Faubourg-St-Antoine, métro Bastille.
The kilted doctor of Eurotrash's shops are fun for his more extraordinary than usual efforts

to create a mystique around the clothes.

Kiliwatch Y10
64 Rue Tiquetonne, t 01 42 21 17 37, w www.eurekafripe.com; métro Étienne-Marcel. Open Mon 2–7, Tues–Sat 11–7.
Megastore loved by trendy Parisians. New designs rub shoulders with vintage items.

Kokon To Zai X10
48 Rue Tiquetonne, t 01 42 36 92 41, w www.kokontozai.co.uk; métro Étienne-Marcel. Open Mon–Sat 11–7.30.
British-owned store selling funky mix of one-offs and limited editions by young designers such as Antonio Ciutto, Chime and Marjan Pojoski.

Louisor Patricia V4
16 Rue Houdon, t 01 42 62 10 42; métro Abbesses. Open daily 12–8.
Affordable clothes and jewellery from trendy young designers.

Pierre Cardin P8
27 Av de Marigny; métro Miromesnil.
Classic Parisian couture.

Regent Street S10
10 Rue de Castiglione; métro Tuileries.
Tailor-made suits and a great choice of fabrics.

Saint-Laurent Rive Gauche Q9
38 Rue du Faubourg-St-Honoré; métro Concorde.
Flagship of the designer's world-wide chain. Shows in recent years have confirmed YSL as the king of Paris fashion.

Tati X4
2–30 Bd de Rochechouart; métro Barbès-Rochechouart.
While the pampered few swan in the boutiques, the masses of every nationality swarm to the incredible Tati for women's, men's and children's clothes.

Versace Q8–9
62 Rue du Faubourg-St-Honoré; métro Madeleine.
One of first and most opulent 'mega-boutiques' in Paris that must be seen to be believed: Versace's fashion-as-theatre

approach in a glass-domed Roman temple with changing rooms resembling ancient baths or the Paris Opéra. Clothes for men, women and children.

Shoes and Accessories

Accessoire S15
6 Rue du Cherche-Midi; métro Sèvres-Babylone.
Chain of shoeshops with fashionable styles at good prices.

Anthony Peto X10
56 Rue Tiquetonne, t 01 40 26 60 68; métro Étienne-Marcel. Open 11–7.
Superb selection of men's hats from berets to panamas.

Christian Loubotin S14
38 Rue de Grenelle; métro Rue-du-Bac.
Exquisite women's shoes with signature red leather soles (from €220).

Divine S20
39 Rue Daguerre; métro Denfert-Rochereau. Open 10.30–1 and 3–7.30.
Jewellery, masks and hats for men and women, in modern styles and designs from the 1920s.

La Droguerie X11
9 Rue du Jour; métro Les Halles. Open Mon 2–6.45, Tues–Sat 10.30–6.45.
An Aladdin's Cave of buttons, beads, ribbons and feathers.

Franchi Chaussures R7
15 Rue de la Pépinière; métro St-Augustin.
Men's and women's French and Italian shoes at half-price.

Marie Mercié V15
23 Rue St-Sulpice; métro St-Sulpice or Odéon.
For the kind of hat you see in films and have always dreamed of on your own head.

Maud Frizon T14
83 Rue des St-Pères; métro St-Sulpice. Open daily 10.30–1 and 2–7.
The ultimate in chic women's shoes (from €150).

Philippe Model T9–10
33 Place du Marché-St-Honoré; métro Pyramides.
Paris' top glove, hat and shoe designer.

San Marina X11
Forum des Halles, Porte Rambuteau; métro Les Halles.
Enormous shoe store selling good-value shoes for men and women. Styles vary from classic to trendy. Very popular.

Shoe Bizz T14
42 Rue du Dragon; métro St-Germain-des-Prés. Open Mon 2–7.30, Tues–Sat 10.30–7.30.
Fashionable shoes for both men and women.

Sidonis Maroquinerie X–Y3
42 Rue de Clignancourt; métro Château-Rouge.
Vast selection of designer bags, ties, umbrellas and scarves at some of the cheapest prices in Paris.

Stéphane Kélian S14 and W10
13 Bis Rue de Grenelle, métro Sèvres-Babylone; 6 Place des Victoires, métro Sentier.
Perhaps the most extraordinary, and certainly the most expensive, women's shoes in Paris.

Testoni M9 and S9
25 Rue Marbeuf, métro Franklin D. Roosevelt; 267 Rue St-Honoré, métro Concorde.
Beautiful and expensive men's and ladies' shoes and bags from Bologna.

Dépôts-Ventes

Dépôt-Ventes are places where designers dump last season's unsold clothes, where prices are a third to a half off.

Anna Lowe P8
104 Rue du Faubourg-St-Honoré; métro Miromesnil.
One of the oldest high-fashion discount houses in Paris: Chanel, Escada, Lacroix, YSL, etc. at 50% off.

L'Astucerie Off maps
105 Rue de Javel; métro Félix-Faure.
Especially good for accessories by Chanel, Hermès and Vuitton for women and children.

Chercheminippes Q16
109–111 Rue du Cherche-Midi; métro Vaneau.
Last season's fashions and quality second-hand for men, women and their offspring.

Dépôt des Grandes Marques W9
15 Rue de la Banque; métro Bourse.
Big discounts and a good selection of larger sizes by Ungaro, Cerruti, Valentino, etc. for men.

La Marelle V9–10
21–25 Galerie Vivienne; métro Bourse. Open Mon–Fri 10.30–6.30, Sat 12.30–6.30.
One of the nicest *dépôt-ventes*, for women's and children's designer goods.

Le Mouton à Cinq Pattes R15
8, 14, 18 and 48 Rue St-Placide; métro Sèvres-Babylone.
Great deals on French and Italian designs (Gaultier, Vivienne Westwood, Byblos, Ferré). No.8 is for women, 14 for men and women, 18 is for big discounts, and 48 is for men only.

Réciproque F10
92, 103 and 124 Rue de la Pompe; métro Pompe. Open Tues–Sat 11–7.30.
Biggest and best known *dépôt-vente* in Paris, with clothes by Chanel, Lacroix and company, for men and women (including some in larger sizes); also coats, rain-coats, hats, jewellery.

Unishop AA13 and Z12–13
Men: 40 Rue de Rivoli; métro Hôtel-de-Ville. Women: 61 Rue de la Verrerie; métro Hôtel-de-Ville.
High fashions, minimum 20% off the original price.

Second-hand and Antique

In French this is called *la fripe*, whence our word 'frippery'. Retro garments tend to be the kind that have sat unsold in a warehouse for 30 or 40 years.

La Bonne Aventure W8
14 Passage des Panoramas; métro Grands Boulevards.

Antique clothes, accessories and *bijoux* in an arcade.

La Halle aux Fringues
Rétro Off maps
16 Rue de Montreuil; métro Faidherbe-Chaligny.
One of the most interesting, especially for men.

Rag Y12
83 Rue St-Martin; métro Châtelet.
Open Mon–Sat 10–8, Sun 12–8.
Everything from tails to kimonos, for all tastes.

Stéphane Off maps
65–67 Place du Docteur Loligeois; métro Rome.
Excellently restored retro fashions for men and women.

Vertiges Y12
85 Rue St-Martin; métro Rambuteau.
Especially good for the wilder styles of the 1940s–70s.

Department Stores

Au Bon Marché R15
38 Rue de Sèvres; métro Sèvres-Babylone.
The only one on the Left Bank, but the grand-daddy of every department store in the world (*see* pp.213–4) still puts on a pretty good show of desirable stuff: its extraordinary food halls are an unrivalled gourmet cornucopia, and its prices for clothes and other goods tend to be a bit lower than its big-name rivals across the river.

Au Printemps S–T7
64 Bd Haussmann; métro Havre-Caumartin.
Squares off with the Galeries Lafayette like the Hatfields and the McCoys. On the whole Printemps is a wee bit posher, stuffier and nearer the cutting edge of fashion for women's designer clothes and accessories.

Bazar de l'Hôtel de Ville Z13
52 Rue de Rivoli; métro Hôtel-de-Ville.
BHV has been around since 1854 and lacks the pretensions of other department stores. A good bet for

practical items often not easily found in the golden centre: brake fluid, electric outlets and mixing bowls. If you're fixing up a flat, its tool rental is indispensable.

Galeries Lafayette T–U7
40 Bd Haussmann; métro Chaussée d'Antin.
A bit of Art Nouveau splendour has survived the current philistine management. But better than anyone, they know what the Parisiennes like. Every Wednesday morning, the store puts on its own free fashion show, with selections from its various designer boutiques (reserve on **t** 01 42 82 34 56).

La Samaritaine W12
19 Rue de la Monnaie; métro Louvre-Rivoli.
The most beautiful department store in Paris, with its Art Nouveau façade, skylight and balconies (in the old building), though the present management thinks more like Woolworths than Harrods. The café on its 10th-floor terrace (*see* p.325) has one of the most gratifying of all views over Paris, across the Pont Neuf.

Design, Interiors and Lifestyle

Catherine Memmi V15
11 Rue St-Sulpice; métro Odéon.
New lifestyle shop in sleek minimalist style.

Colette T10
213 Rue St-Honoré; métro Tuileries.
The original lifestyle store, with the hippest salespeople. Designer clothes and accessories – the place to spend more than you could possibly imagine on something you never knew you wanted. Downstairs there's a designer water bar (yes, really) and restaurant. Worth a look.

Diptyque Z15
*34 Bd St-Germain, **w** www.diptyque.tm.fr; métro Maubert-Mutualité.*
Where celebrities buy their scented candles. Candles, eau de toilette, bath oils, etc. come in

classic and unusual fragrances: rose, lilac, or perhaps new-mown hay or tea.

Escalier A V16
5 Rue de Médicis; RER Luxembourg.
Recent addition to the lifestyle stable, opposite the Luxembourg Gardens. Zen design and furnishings: furniture, lighting, china, rugs and cushions in neutrals, chocolate, black and white.

Frette Q9
49 Rue du Faubourg St-Honoré; métro Madeleine.
Luxury items for the home. Bed linen, candles, soap, etc., in soft colours, sweet scents and fine materials.

Saponifère U14
59 Rue Bonaparte; métro St-Germain-des-Prés.
Chain of boutiques along the lines of the White Company. Accessories for the home and bathroom: waffle robes and towels, and exclusive toiletries from Trumpers and Penhaligons in the UK.

Food and Wine

Besides the splendid food halls in Au Bon Marché and the markets, you can scatter buckets of euros in the following speciality food shops.

A la Mère de Famille W7
35 Rue du Faubourg-Montmartre; métro Cadet.
Chocolates, home-made sweets, jam in every flavour from rhubarb to eglantine; a charming shop, dating from 1793.

Arietis X15
73 Bd St-Germain; métro Maubert-Mutualité.
Foie gras, *confits* and wines from southwest France.

Barthélemy S14
51 Rue de Grenelle; métro Rue-du-Bac.
The *ne plus ultra* of *fromageries*: only the most refined classic French cheeses.

Bootlegger P20
14 Rue Croce Spinelli; métro Pernety.

Huge selection of beers from around the world.

Brûlerie de l'Odéon V15
*6 Rue Crébillon; **métro** Odéon.*
One of Paris' oldest coffee roasters, still providing fresh roasted coffees and teas for picky java junkies.

La Cave du Moulin Vieux Z22
*4 Rue Butte-aux-Cailles; **métro** Place d'Italie. **Open** Tues–Sat and Sun am.*
One of the last places in Paris where you can buy good loose wine from barrels.

Caves Taillevent L6
*199 Rue du Faubourg-St-Honoré; **métro** Ternes.*
Some 2,500 different perfectly cared for French wines, in all price ranges.

La Cigogne R7
*61 Rue de l'Arcade; **métro** St-Lazare.*
Delicious products and dishes from Alsace, starring tempting *tortes* and tarts and meaty sausages.

Debauve et Gallais T13
*30 Rue des Saints-Pères; **métro** St-Germain-des-Prés.*
Oldest and most beautiful *chocolatier* in Paris; the unusual displays (recently, chocolate passports) are worth a trip in themselves.

Fauchon R8
*26 Place de la Madeleine; **métro** Madeleine.*
The most famous and snobbish grocery in Paris, with the best of everything you can imagine, a huge wine cellar and a self-service to try some of the goodies on the spot. In 1970, Leftists looted the shop to bring caviar to the masses in the *bidonvilles*, or suburban shanty towns.

Fromagerie Cler N13
*31 Rue Cler; **métro** École-Militaire.*
Has 250 to 300 of France's official list of 400 cheeses on offer.

Gosselin V11
*125 Rue St-Honoré; **métro** Louvre-Rivoli.*
Voted best baguette in Paris back in 1996.

Hédiard
*126 Rue du Bac (R15), **métro** Sèvres-Babylone; 118 Rue Monge (Y19), **métro** Censier-Daubenton; 70 Av Paul Doumer (F12), **métro** La Muette; 106 Bd de Courcelles (L6), **métro** Ternes.*
A tiny chain of grocers nearly as extensive and high-falutin as Fauchon.

Izraël AA13
*30 Rue François-Miron; **métro** St-Paul.*
Good for exotic imports from Brazil, China, North Africa and just about everywhere else.

Jean Danflou R9
*36 Rue du Mont-Thabor; **métro** Concorde.*
Great selection of traditional French spirits – Armagnacs, Cognacs and *eaux-de-vie*.

Jo Goldenberg BB13
*7 Rue des Rosiers, **w** www.rest aurantgoldenberg.com; **métro** St-Paul.*
Paris' best Jewish deli, a godsend to any New Yorker living in Paris.

Ladurée R9 and M8
*16 Rue Royale, **métro** Madeleine; 75 Av des Champs-Elysées, **métro** Franklin D. Roosevelt.*
Maker of heavenly chocolates.

Maison du Chocolat
*8 Bd de la Madeleine (S9), **métro** Madeleine; 225 Rue du Faubourg-St-Honoré (L6), **métro** Ternes; 19 Rue de Sèvres (S15–14), **métro** Sèvres-Babylone.*
Sensational variety of chocolates.

Maison de la Truffe R–S8
*19 Place de la Madeleine; **métro** Madeleine.*
Truffles and other costly delicacies from the southwest of France.

Mariage Frères AA13
*30 Rue du Bourg-Tibourg; **métro** St-Paul.*
400 different types of tea and tea-flavoured goodies.

Marie-Anne Cantin M13
*12 Rue du Champ-de-Mars; **métro** Ecole-Militaire.*
A hundred finely ripened cheeses from farms and small producers.

Petrossian N11–12
*18 Bd de La Tour-Maubourg; **métro** Latour-Maubourg.*
Paris' top address for beluga, oscietre and sevruga caviar, vodka, smoked salmon, foie gras, truffles.

Poilâne S15
*8 Rue du Cherche-Midi; **métro** Sèvres-Babylone.*
Tasty sourdough country bread, famous in Paris; used in the best sandwiches across the city.

Point Saumon Off maps
*262 Rue de Charenton; **métro** Dugommier.*
Smoked, marinated and other forms of salmon from Ireland, Scotland and Norway. Also Iranian caviar.

Poujauran N12
*20 Rue Jean-Nicot; **métro** Latour-Maubourg.*
The second most famous bakery in Paris: *pain de campagne* of stone-ground flour, baked in a wood-burning oven; great olive and walnut breads too.

Vins Rares Peter Thustrup Off maps
*11 Rue Pergolèse; **métro** Porte Maillot.*
Old wines, rare wines, collectors' wines, none under €15.

Supermarkets

Monoprix L8 and T14
*52 Av des Champs-Elysées, **métro** Franklin D. Roosevelt; 50 Rue de Rennes, **métro** St-Germain-des-Prés. **Open** Mon-Sat 9am–10pm (most stores), branch on Les Champs open until midnight.*
Useful chain of supermarkets where you can pick up toiletries, make-up, underwear, clothes, shoes and accessories as well as food and freshly baked bread and pastries.

Markets

The C2 organization (**t** 01 47 05 33 22) holds street markets across Paris at weekends. Ring for details. They are often a good place to find reasonably priced antiques.

Food Markets

Open *Tues–Sat and Sun am. Some shops close for lunch off season.*

The permanent street markets listed below are intoxicating to visit, even if you're just picking up the ingredients for a park picnic. Most are lined with shops that spill out into the street: seafood markets where the employees have to wear sailor outfits, white-aproned matrons bustling over their lovely displays of cheeses or pastries, ruddy-cheeked butchers ready to tell you how to prepare the mysterious cut of meat you've just purchased.

For a list of covered markets and the 60 travelling street markets, open one or two days a week, ask at the tourist office.

Buci V14
Métro Mabillon.
One of the liveliest, with a good selection; best on Sun morning.

Montorgueil X10
Métro Étienne-Marcel. **Open** *Mon–Sat and Sun am.*
On the street of the same name, north of Rue Étienne-Marcel, convivial and fun, a whiff of the old atmosphere of nearby Les Halles.

Mouffetard Y18
Métro Censier-Daubenton.
Lower end of Rue Mouffetard, with lots of character – and characters.

Place d'Aligre FF15–GG16
Métro Ledru-Rollin.
Colourful, with a strong North African presence.

Poncelet K8
Begins at Av des Ternes; métro Ternes.
Good for cheese.

Rue Cler M12–N13
Métro École-Militaire.
The market of the aristocratic Faubourg, noted for its high quality.

Rue de Lévis P4
Métro Villiers.
Similar to the above – the *haute bourgeoisie* equivalent of Rue Cler.

Flea Markets

Puces de Montreuil Off maps
Place de la Porte de Montreuil; métro Porte de Montreuil. **Open** *Sat, Sun and Mon.*
Great junky flea market.

Puces de St-Ouen Off maps
Métro Porte de Clignancourt. **Open** *Sat, Sun and Mon.*
The mother of all flea markets; *see* pp.261–2 for a tour.

Puces de Vanves Off maps
Av Georges-Lafenestre; métro Porte de Vanves. **Open** *Sat and Sun 7.30–6.*
The most humble, and potentially most exciting market for the eagle-eyed, with many amateurs.

Special Markets

Marché aux Fleurs
Place de la Madeleine (R8–9); métro Madeleine. **Open** *Mon–Sat 8–7.30. Place des Ternes (K6); métro Ternes.* **Open** *Tues–Sun 8–7. Place Lépine (X13); métro Cité.* **Open** *Mon–Sat 8–7.*
Parisians love flowers and flower markets. The best are listed above.

Marché du Livre Ancien et d'Occasion Off maps
Rue Brancion, Parc Georges-Brassens; métro Porte de Vanves. **Open** *Sat and Sun 8–7.*
Second-hand book market.

Marché aux Timbres P9
North of Théâtre Marigny, near the intersection of Avenues Gabriel and de Marigny; métro Champs-Elysées. **Open** *Thurs, Sat, Sun and hols 9–7.*
The stamp market (the same one that co-starred in *Charade* with Audrey Hepburn and Cary Grant).

Marché aux Vieux Papiers de St-Mandé Off maps
Av de Paris; métro St-Mandé-Tourelle. **Open** *Wed all day.*
One of the more obscure markets – old books, postcards and prints.

Farmers' Markets

The French call these *marchés biologiques* and they are open to farmers in the Île-de-France countryside, who bring in their organic fruits and vegetables, nuts, free-range chickens, home-made breads, cakes, cider, sausages, goat cheeses, etc. The suburban ones have métro or RER connections.

Avenue Jules-Guesde Off maps
Sceaux, Rue des Mouille-Boeuf; RER Robinson (Line B2). **Open** *Sun 8.30–1.*

Boulevard Raspail S16
Métro Rennes. **Open** *Tues, Fri and Sun 9–1.*
Organic produce on Sunday.

Marché Boulogne Off maps
140 Route de la Reine, Boulogne-sur-Seine; métro Boulogne-Porte de St-Cloud. **Open** *1st and 3rd Sat of each month 8am–4pm.*

Marché Joinville-le-Pont Off maps
Place Mozart, Joinville; RER to Joinville and then bus 106 or 108N. **Open** *2nd and 4th Sat of each month 8am–4pm.*
Same market as Marché Boulogne.

Music

La Chaumière à Musique W15
5 Rue de Vaugirard; métro Odéon. **Open** *Mon–Fri 11–8, Sat 10–8, Sun 2–8.*
Huge stock of classical music sold by knowledgeable staff. New and second hand.

Disc King X10
60 Rue Montorgueil; métro Les Halles. **Open** *Mon–Sat 10–8, Sun 9.30–7.30.*
All the latest releases plus archive material at reasonable prices. Browse through the sale racks for the ultimate bargain.

FNAC
See 'Books', p.359.

Jussieu Music Z17
16, 19 and 20 Rue Linné and 5 and 17 Rue Guy-de-la-Brosse; RER Luxembourg. **Open** *Mon–Sat 11–7.30, Sun 2–7.*
Each shop specializes in a particular kind of music: classical, rock, reggae/world music, jazz/blues, rap/funk. New and second hand.

Paris Jazz Corner Z17
*5 Rue de Navarre; **métro** Place
Monge. **Open** Mon–Sat 11.30–8.*
Two floors of jazz records and CDs.

Virgin Megastore L8
*52 Av des Champs-Elysées; **métro**
Franklin D. Roosevelt. **Open**
Mon–Sat 10am–midnight,
Sun 12–12.*
Large Paris branch of the music
superstore. Has its own café on
the top floor.

Souvenirs and Unusual Items

The gift shops in Paris'
museums are often excellent and
full of surprises: marine and meteorological gifts at the **Musée de la
Marine**, books about Paris at the
Carnavalet, copies of the seals of
all the kings of France at the
Archives Nationales, genuine art
prints from original plates at the
Louvre. The **Boutique Paris Musée**
*(29 bis Rue des Francs-Bourgeois;
métro Chemin-Vert)* rounds up
items from all the museum shops
in Paris.

Les Alizés GG19
*12 Rue Henri Desgrange; **métro**
Bercy.*
Ships' models in all sizes, sextants
and other pretty things from or
related to the sea.

A Marie Stuart V10
*3 Galerie Montpensier, Palais
Royal; **métro** Palais Royal-Musée
du Louvre.*
Military trinkets as well as medals
and decorations from around the
world (comes in handy when
you're invited to a diplomatic
reception).

Anna Joliet V10
*95 Jardin du Palais-Royal, **t** 01 42
96 55 13; **métro** Palais Royal-Musée
du Louvre.*

The best shop in the universe for
music boxes, from kid trinkets to
€750 monsters in inlaid wood
cases that play 12 different tunes.

Le Bonheur des Dames EE16
*17 Av Daumesnil (also Passages
Verdeau and Jouffroy); **métro**
Gare de Lyon.*
Airy shop in the arches of the
Viaduc des Arts. A mecca for
stitchers, stuffed with samplers,
tapestries, silks, cottons, etc.

Chronopassion R9
*271 Rue St-Honoré; **métro**
Concorde.*
For Paris' most extraordinary
clocks and watches, astrolabes,
planetary timepieces and golden
cufflinks that tell the time. Also
does repairs.

Citadium S7
*50–56 Rue Caumartin; **métro**
Havre-Caumartin. **Open** Mon–Sat
9.30–7.30, Thurs till 9pm.*
Sports megastore for all the accessories and equipment you could
possibly need. Also restrings
tennis rackets while you wait.

Cuisinophilie AA13
*28 Rue du Bourg-Tibourg; **métro**
Hôtel-de-Ville.*
Kitchen gear from your (or your
mother's) childhood.

Emilio Robba V9–10 and R14
*29–33 Galerie Vivienne; **métro**
Bourse; 63 Rue du Bac; **métro** Rue-
du-Bac. **Open** Mon–Fri 10.30–7,
Sat 11–7.*
Extraordinary boutique crammed
full of fabulous fake flowers.

Entrez Sans Frapper P–Q12
*31 Rue de Bourgogne; **métro**
Varenne.*
Cat-obsessed arts and crafts.

Fiesta AA13
*45 Rue de la Vieille du Temple;
métro Hotel de Ville.*

Colourful Americana art and
kitsch, mostly from the 1950s.

La Galcante W11–12
*52 Rue de l'Arbre-Sec; **métro**
Louvre-Rivoli.*
Old newspapers, books, maga-
zines and posters from as far as
China; pick up the front page of a
French paper from the day of
your birth.

Instants F. Desjours Y14
*17 Quai aux Fleurs; **métro** Cité.*
If you've left your main squeeze at
home while you've painted Paris
red, you can make up with a bust
of yourself, a model of your hand
or an imprint of your smile so he
or she won't feel so lonely next
time you slip off. Made with
lasers; from €450 to €2,300.

Madeleine Gély Y14
*218 Bd St-Germain; **métro** Rue-
du-Bac.*
Since 1834 the most imaginative
cane and umbrella shop in Paris.

La Maison de l'Astronomie Z13
*33 Rue de Rivoli, **w** www.maison-
astronomie.fr; **métro** Hôtel-
de-Ville.*
Everything for the astronomer in
your life; also alarm clocks that
keep track of the position of
the moon.

Paris Magic Off maps
*18 Rue Brillat-Savarin; **métro**
Maison Blanche.*
Where Paris magicians shop for
manuals, videos, and illusions.

Le Prince Jardinier V10
*Jardins du Palais Royal; **métro**
Palais Royal-Musée du Louvre.*
Treasure trove for smart, keen
gardeners: baskets, spades, rakes,
watering cans, books and hats.

Sports and
Green Spaces

Spectator Sports

There are plenty of sports to watch in Paris, though you have to scramble for tickets for the major events in the calendar. The best listings are in Wednesday's *Le Figaro* or the sports-only paper, *L'Équipe*. *Pariscope* also lists the major sporting events taking place each week.

Athletics

Major Events

IAAF Gaz de France Meeting
Stade de France (see 'Football and Rugby', below).
Golden League event. July.

Paris Marathon
t *01 41 33 15 68,*
w *www.parismarathon.com.*
See p.380. April.

Cycling

Major Events

Tour de France
w *www.letour.fr.*
The Last Leg, around the Arc de Triomphe; 3rd week in July.

Football and Rugby

Football is more popular in France since they hosted (and won) the 1998 World Cup, but it still doesn't attract the fanatical support of the English game. Paris' most popular team is Paris St-Germain (PSG), whose home ground is the Parc des Princes.

Rugby is still France's most popular team sport, significantly more popular than football. This peaks with the Six Nations tournament between France, England, Scotland, Ireland, Wales and Italy.

Major Events

Six Nations Rugby Matches
Feb–April.

Coupe de France and Coupe de Ligue Football Finals
Stade de France.
May.

Championnat de France Rugby Final
Stade de France.
June.

Major Venues

Parc des Princes Off maps
24 Rue du Commandant-Guilbaud,
football information **t** *01 10 41 71 71,*
rugby information **t** *01 53 21 15 15;*
métro Porte de St-Cloud.
This large concrete stadium is home to Paris' two soccer teams (PSG and Racing-Paris I), its rugby union team and other rugby events.

Le Stade de France
Off maps
t *01 55 93 00 00,* **w** *www.stade france.fr;* **RER** *Stade-de-France-St-Denis.*
Outside Paris proper, yet the city's latest sporting pride and joy, the sleek new stadium was inaugurated in 1998 as the French team won football's World Cup. Tickets for events are sold through the organizations sponsoring them, or call the number above. Guided tours daily in French at 10, 2, 4; in English at 2.30 in summer (lasts 1hr 30mins); adm €14.

Horse Racing

Off-track betting (even the little old ladies do it) takes place in any bar with the sign PMU. Race courses are closed mid-July–Aug. For information on all courses, call **t** 01 49 10 20 30.

Major Events

Grand Prix de l'Arc de Triomphe
Longchamp.
Flat race; 1st Sun in Oct.

Prix d'Amérique
Hippodrome de Vincennes.
Trotting race; January.

Prix de Diane
Hippodrome de Chantilly.
French equivalent of the Derby; 3rd Sun in June.

Prix du Président de la République
Auteuil.
Steeplechase; April.

Major Venues

Hippodrome d'Auteuil Off maps
Bois de Boulogne, **t** *01 40 71 47 47;*
métro Porte d'Auteuil.
Steeplechase (hurdle) race track.

Hippodrome de Chantilly Off maps
Rue Plaine-des-Aigles, Chantilly,
t *08 21 21 32 13,* **t** *03 44 62 41 00;*
RER/SNCF *Chantilly-Gouvieux and free shuttle bus.*
Prettiest race course in France; site of the prestigious Prix du Jockey Club (2nd Sun in June) and the Prix de Diane (3rd Sun in June).

Hippodrome de Longchamp Off maps
Bois de Boulogne, **t** *01 44 30 75 00;*
métro Porte d'Auteuil, no.244 bus.
Flat races.

Hippodrome de Vincennes Off maps
2 Route de la Ferme, Bois de Vincennes, 12e, **t** *01 49 77 17 17;*
métro Château-de-Vincennes,
RER *Joinville-le-Pont.*
Trotting (harness racing).

Tennis

Major Events

French Open
Roland Garros, **w** *www.french open.org.*
Grand-slam championship; end May–early June.

Open Gaz de France
Stade Pierre de Coubertin, 82 Av Georges-Lafont, **t** *01 44 31 44 31,*
t *08 03 80 40 00,* **w** *www.gazde france.fr/open;* *métro Porte de St-Cloud.*
International women's tournament; February.

Paris Open
Palais Omnisport de Bercy.
International men's tournament; November.

Major Venues

Palais Omnisport Paris-Bercy FF19
8 Bd de Bercy, **t** *01 43 46 12 21;*
métro Gare de Lyon.
A distinctive stadium with slanted walls that require the attention of

a lawnmower; designed to host 21 other sports along with tennis, from hockey to motorcross.

Roland Garros Off maps
2 Av Gordon-Bennett, **t** *01 47 43 48 00;* **métro** *Porte d'Auteuil.*
Site of the prestigious French Open. Reserve by Feb in writing to: FFT, Service Réservation, BP 333-16, 75767 Paris Cédex 16. Guided tours daily 2.30 and 4.30 in French and English; **adm** €10.

Activities

Bowling (12 Pin)

AMF Bowling de Paris Off maps
Av Mahatma Gandhi, Jardin d'Acclimatation, Bois de Boulogne, **t** *01 53 64 93 00;* **métro** *Sablons.* **Open** *Mon–Fri 10am–2am, Sat and Sun 9am–5am;* **adm** *from €2 (plus shoe hire and adm to Jardin), special deals available.*
This bowling alley also has a restaurant, bar, billiards and games room.

Bowling de Montparnasse Q19
25 Rue du Cdt-René-Mouchotte, **t** *01 43 21 61 32;* **métro** *Montparnasse-Bienvenüe.* **Open** *Sun–Thurs 10am–2am, Fri–Sat 10am–4am;* **adm** *€6.*
Also has a bar, billiards and games room.

Cycling

Citibike (Roue Libre) X11
95 bis Rue Rambuteau, **t** *01 53 46 43 77;* **métro** *Les Halles.*
Free guided tours of Paris on the last Sat of the month. Bike hire €6 for weekdays, €12 for weekends.

Paris à vélo, c'est sympa! DD14
37 Bd Bourdon, **t** *01 48 87 60 01;* **métro** *Bastille.*
Various guided tours of Paris, as well as bike and tandem hire.

Dance

Le Centre du Marais Z12
41 Rue de Temple, **t** *01 42 72 15 42,* **w** *www.parisdanse.com;* **métro** *Hôtel-de-Ville.* **Open** *Mon–Fri*

9am–10pm, Sat 9–8, Sun 9–6. Classes from €15.
Trendiest dance classes in Paris: ballet, jazz, flamenco, tap, tango are taught along with yoga, piano, singing, etc.

Latina Café L8
114 Av des Champs-Elysées, **t** *01 42 89 98 89;* **métro** *George-V;* **adm** *€7.*
Sun drink with salsa classes thrown in, 8–10.30pm.

Swing Tap FF14
21 Rue Keller, **t** *01 48 06 38 18;* **métro** *Bastille.* **Open** *Tues–Sat 2–7pm.*
Well-respected tap classes, plus all the gear for sale.

Diving

Surplouf X15
25 ter Rue du Sommerard, **t** *06 75 03 51 00;* **métro** *St-Michel. Courses from €250 (some classes take place in other pools).*
Ideal if you want to get your diving certificate in advance of jetting off to somewhere more exotic.

Gyms

Club Quartier Latin
See Piscine Pontoise, under 'Swimming', below.

Espace Vit'Halles Z11
Place Beaubourg, 48 Rue Rambuteau, **t** *01 42 77 21 71;* **métro** *Rambuteau.* **Open** *Mon–Fri 8am–10.30pm;* **adm** *day pass €20.*
Well-equipped gym, plus dance classes and sauna.

Real Tennis (Jeu de Puume)

Jeu de Paume de Paris I9
74 ter Rue Lauriston, **t** *01 47 27 46 86;* **métro** *Boissière.* **Open** *daily 9am–10pm; adm €600/year membership.*
More like a gentleman's club than a sports club, and the only place in Paris where you can play real tennis (it replaced the famous court in the Tuileries). It also has squash courts.

Rollerskating

'Friday Night Fever' Off maps
Pari Roller, 62 Rue Dulong, **t** *01 43 36 89 81,* **w** *www.pari-roller.com.*
On Fri evenings at 10pm thousands of skaters gather at Place d'Italie (Z–AA21) to follow a 3-hour, several-mile route through the streets of the city. Only for experienced skaters, and only in good weather.

Squash

See Club Quartier Latin ('Swimming'), Jeu de Paume de Paris ('Real Tennis') and Aquaboulevard ('Waterpark').

Swimming

Piscine de la Butte-aux-Cailles Z23
5 Place Paul-Verlaine, **t** *01 45 89 60 05;* **métro** *Place d'Italie.* **Open** *Tues–Sat 7am–7 or 7.45pm, Sun 8–5.30;* **adm** *€2.40.*
Swim in warm spring water in a beautiful listed building.

Piscine Hébert Off maps
2 Rue des Fillettes, **t** *01 46 07 60 01;* **métro** *Marx-Dormoy.* **Open** *hours vary, call for information;* **adm** *€2.50.*
Roof opens in fine weather. Separate kids' pool.

**Piscine Pontoise/
Club Quartier Latin** Y–Z15
19 Rue de Pontoise, **t** *01 55 42 77 88,* **w** *www.clubquartierlatin.com;* **métro** *Maubert-Mutualité.* **Open:** *pool Mon–Fri 7am–midnight, Sat, Sun and hols 10am–8.45pm; club Mon–Fri 8am–midnight, Sat and Sun 9.30–7;* **adm** *pool €4.25, club €15.*
Popular, attractive pool with *the* fitness club attached, for squash, sauna, etc.

Piscine Roger-le-Gall Off maps
34 Bd Carnot, **t** *01 44 73 81 12;* **métro** *Porte de Vincennes.* **Open** *hours vary, call for information;* **adm** *€4–5.50.*
Open-air pool with separate kids' pool, sauna and sun beds. Covered in winter.

Tennis

Jardin de Luxembourg U16
RER Luxembourg.
The courts in the Luxembourg gardens are a great place to have a game of tennis. Entry is on a first-come first-served basis (busy on Wed, Sat and Sun). 30mins costs from €1.60.

Tennis Sporting Club N16
160 Av de Suffren, t 01 43 06 12 14; métro Ségur.
Coaching year-round for adults and kids.

Waterpark

Aquaboulevard Off maps
4 Rue Louis Armand, t 01 40 60 10 00; métro Balard or Porte de Versailles. Open Mon–Thurs 9am–11pm, Fri 9am–midnight, Sat 8am–midnight, Sun 8am–11pm; adm from €10.
Europe's biggest waterpark, plus tennis, squash, mini-golf, shops, restaurants, etc.

Yoga

Centre Sivananda de Yoga Vedanta Z9
123 Bd de Sébastopol, 2e, t 01 40 26 77 49, w www.sivananda.org; métro Réaumur-Sébastopol. Open daily 11–9.30.
Free trial class Tues 8pm.

Green Spaces

All parks are open dawn–dusk.
Arènes de Lutèce Z17
See p.237.

Bois de Boulogne Off maps
See p.257.

Bois de Vincennes Off maps
See p.267.

Carreau du Temple BB10
See p.181.

Garden of the Musée Rodin P13–14
See p.129.

Jardin de l'Ecole Polytechnique Y16
11–19 Rue Descartes; métro Cardinal-Lemoine.
Large garden open to the public.

Jardin du Luxembourg U15–V18
See p.211.

Jardin Naturel Off maps
Entrances from Rue de la Réunion, Rue de Lesseps; métro Alexandre-Dumas.
A recently established garden adjacent to Père-Lachaise cemetery. Trees and plants are left to grow wild, making it feel like a corner of the countryside in the city.

Jardin des Plantes AA–CC17
See p.234.

Jardin du Palais Royal V10
See p.154.

Jardin du Ranelagh C11–D13
Métro La Muette.
Pretty garden just east of the Bois de Boulogne. The Musée Marmottan (see p.255) perches at its edge.

Jardin des Tuileries R10–U12
See p.110.

Parc André-Citroën E18
Entrances Rue Balard, Rue St-Charles, Quai Citroën; métro Javel or Balard.
The most modern-looking of the city's parks, with six colour-coded flower gardens, angular glass houses filled with tropical plants, and a computer-controlled water garden. Bring your swimsuits – kids love dodging the jets which erupt according to a random pattern.

Parc des Buttes-Chaumont Off maps
See p.266.

Parc du Champ de Mars J13–M14
See p.139.

Parc Georges-Brassens Off maps
Main entrance Rue des Morillons; métro Convention or Porte de Vanves.
On the site of an old abattoir, a pleasant park with puppet shows and carrousels for the kids, and an aromatic garden designed particularly for the visually impaired.
See p.364 for second-hand book market.

Parc de Monceau M5–O6
See p.118.

Parc Montsouris Off maps
See p.272.

Parc de St-Cloud Off maps
St-Cloud, 11km west of Paris; métro Pont de Sèvres.
A park where the grass is not out of bounds. Still quite formal, with fountains and shady avenues.

Parc de la Villette Off maps
See p.263.

Place des Vosges CC13
See p.183.

Promenade Plantée EE15–GG17
See p.188.

Square Georges-Cain CC12
Entrances from Rue Payenne, Rue du Parc-Royal, Rue de Sévigné; métro St-Paul.
A peaceful square in the heart of the Marais, near the Musée Picasso.

Square du Vert-Galant V13
See p.92.

Children and
Teenagers' Paris

Children

Paris is a great city for children. All but the most exclusive places welcome them with open arms and many of the attractions in the guide will appeal to kids of all ages. There are also loads of things to do and see that have been designed with kids in mind; the following is a selection of the best.

Reductions are available for almost all museums and sights as well as on all public transport. More and more restaurants provide children's menus (see 'Eating Out', below).

For emergency medical treatment, French pharmacists are highly trained and very helpful, and can prescribe a wide range of drugs. For 24hr pharmacies and to contact an emergency doctor, see p.72.

Also see the 'Sports and Green Spaces' chapter, pp.366–9.

Babysitting

In the 'Where to Stay' chapter, we list hotels that offer babysitting services. Otherwise, try one of the following English-speaking agencies:

Allô Assistance Babychou
t 01 43 13 33 23.
Qualified babysitters recognised by the Préfecture. €10 initial fee (valid 6 months) plus €5.70 per hour or €52 per day (10 hours).

Babysitting Services
t 01 46 21 33 16.
Qualified babysitters recognised by the Préfecture. €10.90 initial fee plus €6.30 an hour.

Le CROUS
t 01 40 51 37 52.
Student organization that organizes babysitting (among other things). €7.50 an hour; €0.75 more after 10pm.

Kid Services
t 08 20 00 02 30.
Qualified nurses will look after newborns (less than 3 months) or older babies. Initial fee €11. Newborns €7.70 an hour, €58 a

night; older babies €5.50 an hour, €30.50 a night.

Other options are listed under 'gardes d'enfants' in L'Officiel.

Eating Out

In our 'Eating Out' chapter (pp.315–40) we indicate where a restaurant has a children's menu. Two child-friendly chains to look out for are **Bistro Romain** and **Hippopotamus**. Both serve burgers, chips, etc., and the Hippo chain will provide games and puzzles. Other good places include the following:

Altitude 95 J–K12
First Level, Eiffel Tower, Champ de Mars; métro Bir-Hakeim. Open daily 12–2 and 7–9. Children's menu €9.50.
Perhaps the best location in Paris, with spectacular views. There's a children's menu and they are very welcoming to families.

Berthillon AA15
31 Rue St-Louis-en-l'Île, Île St-Louis. Open Wed–Sun 10–8.
The best ice creams and sorbets in town, and always popular. Be prepared to queue.

Bistro Romain N9 and Off maps
26 Av des Champs-Elysées, métro Franklin D. Roosevelt; 6 Place Victor Hugo, métro Victor-Hugo. Open daily 11.30am–1am.
Children's menu €7.

Hippopotamus N9 and DD14
42 Av des Champs-Elysées, métro Franklin D. Roosevelt; 1 Bd Beaumarchais, métro Bastille. Open daily 11.30am–5am.
Children's menu €7.25.

Home Sweet Môme U3
61 Rue Lepic, t 01 42 57 88 93; métro Abbesses. Open Tues-Sun 11-7.30
Non-smoking, child-devoted restaurant and shop serving mainly salads and pasta. Not only is there a fun-filled kid corner, but you can also play games or read comic books while you eat.

Terrasse de la Samaritaine W12
Quai du Louvre; métro Pont-Neuf or Châtelet. Open daily 9.30–7, Thurs till 10pm.

Decent café on the roof of the department store. Good for a drink, a snack or a reasonably priced meal. And the views aren't bad either.

Le Totem H–I11
Musée de l'Homme, 17 Place du Trocadéro; métro Trocadéro. Open daily noon–2.30am.
A good place for families to come during the day, when it serves snacks and drinks. The interior reflects the exhibits in the museum, and there's a breath-taking view of the Eiffel Tower.

Views

Eiffel Tower J–K12
See p.138.
An excursion up to the top may be corny, but they'll always remember it.

Montmartre V2–X4
See p.192.
Take the funicular up to Sacré-Cœur (métro tickets valid) for an effortless and fun alternative to climbing all those steps. The views from the top stretch all the way across Paris.

Towers of Notre-Dame Y14
See p.86.
More great views, with the added bonus that it's been immortalized by Disney.

Museums and Attractions

Aquaboulevard Off maps
See p.369.
If you've brought swimming gear, the tropical pool complex should keep kids of all ages happy.

Cité des Sciences et de l'Industrie Off maps
See p.264.
An all-but-obligatory day out, with its fabulous Inventorium for kids from 3–6 and 6–12, its various Folies with more kid activities and workshops, and the Géode cinema, which even the most hardened teenagers enjoy. The Cité de la Musique holds concerts for children (t 01 44 84 44 84).

Les Égouts L11
See p.134.
If your kids are still at that scatological stage, a trip down the city's stinky sewers might be intriguing.

Galerie de Paléontologie BB–CC17
See p.235.
Not for the squeamish. As well as skeletons of rhinos, hippos, elephants, etc., there's a collection of 19th-century medical and scientific exhibits, e.g. a pickled one-eyed cat and skeletons of Siamese twins.

Grande Galerie de l'Evolution AA18
See p.234.
Interactive exhibits tell the story of life on earth. There are also plenty of traditional stuffed creatures and a huge blue whale skeleton suspended from the ceiling. The displays promote an environmental message, and there's a Discovery Room for the under-12s.

Jardin d'Acclimatation Off maps
See p.257.
Another sure winner for younger kids, in the Bois de Boulogne, with lots of participatory activities.

Jardin des Enfants aux Halles X11
105 Rue Rambuteau, t 01 45 08 07 18; métro Châtelet-Les Halles. **Open** *Tues, Wed, Thurs and Sat 10–7, Fri 2–7, Sun 1–7; adm €0.50 for 1hr.*
If the weather's good, you can park your 7–11-year-olds for a couple of hours in this delightful fantasy playground, especially in the Labyrinth. This is the only redeeming feature of the Jardin des Halles. The rest of the park is rather seedy.

Musée de la Curiosité et de la Magie BB14
See p.185.
Performance-based museum with skilled magicians on hand to perform tricks and illusions. Audience participation is encouraged, and they hold magic courses for children during the school holidays.

Musée Grévin W8
See p.150.
Even young children enjoy the hoaked-up wax people at Paris' answer to Mme Tussaud's.

Musée de la Marine H11–I11
See p.142.
Ships, sea battles and historical reconstructions in the Palais de Chaillot.

Palais de la Découverte O10
See p.114.
Another sure-fire kid-pleaser, with tons of gadgetry.

Entertainment

Cirque d'Hiver DD11
110 Rue Amelot, t 01 47 00 12 25; métro Filles-du-Calvaire. Shows Oct–Jan; times vary, call in advance; adm €15–35.
Hosts a variety of visiting troupes. Still popular after 150 years.

Cirque de Paris Off maps
115 Bd Charles-de-Gaulle, Villeneuve-la-Garenne, t 01 47 99 40 40; métro Porte de Clignancourt, then bus 137. Shows Nov–June: in term-time on Wed and Sun; during school holidays daily; July–Oct the circus is on the road; adm child €29–34.50, adult €26.50–€41; performance only: child €7–14.50, adult €11–24. Reservation (weeks in advance) essential.
An extra-extra-extra special all-day treat for kids of any age. The performers put children through the fundamentals of their art as they rehearse, have lunch with them and from 3 to 5pm the children attend the circus itself.

La Géode Off maps
See p.265.
Films in a giant ball.

MK2 Sur Seine Off maps
14 Quai de la Seine, 19e, t 08 36 68 48 07; métro Stalingrad.
Part of the large cinema chain that has special children's programmes on Wed and weekend mornings.

Puppet Shows

As well as the shows in the Bois de Boulogne and Jardin du Luxembourg listed below, there are puppet shows in other of the city's parks, including Montsouris and the Buttes-Chaumont.

Guignol du Jardin d'Acclimatation Off maps
Bois de Boulogne, t 01 45 01 53 52; métro Les Sablons or Petit Train from Porte Maillot. Shows Wed, Sat and Sun 3pm and 4pm.

Marionnettes du Luxembourg U16
Jardin du Luxembourg, t 01 43 26 46 47; métro Vavin or Notre-Dame-des-Champs. Shows Wed, Sat and Sun from 11am.

Théâtre Astral Off maps
Parc Floral, Route de la Pyramide, Bois de Vincennes, t 01 43 71 31 10; métro Château-de-Vincennes. Shows Wed 3pm, Sun and hols 4.30pm; adm €6.
Fairy and morality tales dramatized in French.

Théâtre du Nesle V13
8 Rue de Nesle, t 01 46 34 61 04; métro St-Michel or Odéon. Adm adults €7.65, children €6.10.
Often stages English-language productions of classics and modern works.

Festivals

The following festivals might particularly appeal to children (for further details *see* the 'Festivals' chapter, pp.379–81):**La Grande Parade de Paris** (1 Jan), **La Fête des Rois** (6 Jan), **Chinese New Year** (late Jan/early Feb), **April Fool's Day** (1 April), **Les Grandes Eaux Musicales**, Versailles (mid-April–mid-Oct; *see* p.287), **Foire du Trône** (late April) **St John's Eve** (late June), **Technoparade** (3rd Sat in Sept), **Hallowe'en** (31 Oct).

Shops

Unless stated otherwise, shops are open Mon–Sat 10–7. *See also* 'Souvenirs and Unusual Items' on p.365.

Books

Album W16 and X15
60 Rue Monsieur-le-Prince, métro Odéon; 6–8 Rue Dante, métro

Maubert-Mutualité. **Open** Tues–Sat
10–8.
Comic books.

Chantelivre S14

13 Rue de Sèvres; **métro** Sèvres-
Babylone. **Open** Mon 1–7, Tues–Sat
10–7.
Bookshop just for kids, with a
large English-language section.

FNAC Junior T17 and Off maps

19 Rue Vavin, **métro** Vavin; 148 Av
Victor Hugo, **métro** Victor-Hugo.
Open Mon–Sat 10–7.30.
Books, videos, CDs and CD-Roms
for the under-12s, plus storytelling
on Wed and Sat (call for details).

Librairie d'Images U14

84 Bd St-Germain; **métro** Cluny-La
Sorbonne or Maubert-Mutualité.
Open Mon–Sat 10–8, Sun 12–7.
Comic books, T-shirts, posters, etc.

W. H. Smith –
The English Bookshop R10

248 Rue de Rivoli; **métro** Concorde.
Open Mon–Sat 9–7.30, Sun 1–7.30.
Large Parisian branch of the
English bookshop, with books,
magazines and newspapers, and
a good children's section.

Clothes

Bonpoint T10 and U14

320 Rue St-Honoré, **métro** Tuileries;
229 Bd St-Germain, **métro** Rue-
du-Bac; and other branches
throughout Paris.
The most exclusive and expensive
children's clothes in Paris –
adorable frills and bows and
sumptuous materials.

Du Pareil au Même T14 and S7

168 Bd St-Germain, **métro** St-
Germain-des-Prés; 15 Rue des
Mathurins, **métro** Havre-
Caumartin; and other branches
throughout Paris.
Bargain-priced clothes for chil-
dren: dungarees, coats and
T-shirts, etc. in bright colours and
sturdy materials.

Kerstin Adolphson T14

157 Bd St-Germain; **métro** St-
Germain-des-Prés.
Welcoming and somewhat
chaotic shop full of brightly
coloured clothes.

Petit Petons R15 and FF15

20 Rue St-Placide, **métro** St-Placide;
135 Rue Faubourg-St-Antoine,
métro Ledru-Rollin.
Good range of children's shoes at
reasonable prices.

Gifts and Hobbies

La Maison du Cerf-Volant FF15

7 Rue de Prague, **métro** Ledru-
Rollin. **Open** Tues–Sat 10–2 and 3–7.
For all types of kites, from serious
racing and stunt kites to novelty
kites in the shape of dragons or
butterflies.

Nature et Découvertes
U–V11 and X11

Carrousel du Louvre, **métro** Palais
Royal-Musée du Louvre; Forum des
Halles, **métro** Châtelet-Les Halles;
other branches throughout Paris.
Open daily 10–8.
A large selection of gifts themed
loosely on nature. Products from
all over the world, including
turquoise jewellery from South
America and paper made from
coffee beans, as well as wooden
toys and dinosaur model kits.

Pylones W4 and Z14

57 Rue Tardieu, **métro** Abbesses; 57
Rue St-Louis-en-l'Île, **métro** Pont-
Marie; other branches throughout
Paris. **Open** daily 10.30–7.30.
Gadgets and toys for adults and
children: shark staplers, designer
toasters, etc.

Toys

Au Nain Bleu R9

406–10 Rue St-Honoré; **métro**
Concorde or Madeleine. **Open**
Mon–Sat 9.45–6.30.
A toy department store since 1836,
with toy cars, dolls houses, board
games, etc.

Le Ciel est à Tout le
Monde U–V11 and W17

Carrousel du Louvre, **métro** Palais
Royal-Musée du Louvre; 10 Rue
Gay-Lussac, **RER** Luxembourg.
Traditional toys: puppets, dolls
houses, rocking horses and kites.

L'Oiseau de Paradis W15

211 Bd St-Germain; **métro** Rue-
du-Bac.
Down-to-earth toy shop selling
plastic animals, dolls, boats, etc.

Parks

Kids used to running around like
banshees and kicking a ball
around a field won't have it quite
all their own way in Paris. Grass is
still a sacred herb in the more
formal parks, although access is
being liberalized. **Parc des Buttes-
Chaumont** (see p.266), **Parc
Georges-Brassens** (see p.274) and
Parc de la Villette (see p.263) offer
the most activities for squirmy
youth. But do not despair: almost
every little green space shown on
the Michelin map 11 has a playground ranging from the
rudimentary to sandpits, climbing
bars and slides. The larger parks
will offer seasonal pony rides, a
carousel, puppet shows and roller-
skating rinks. There are **zoos** at the
Jardin des Plantes (see p.234) and
the Bois de Vincennes (see p.268).

See also 'Sports and Green
Spaces', pp.366–9.

Outside Paris

Disneyland

See p.295.
Indulging the little rascals in (or
talking them out of) a visit here
is the first major hurdle for
most parents.

La Mer de Sable

See p.295.
Take the rug rats to one of the
biggest sandboxes in Europe, in
the beautiful forest near Chantilly.

Parc Astérix

In Plailly, 38km north of Paris off
the A1, **t** 08 36 68 30 10,
w www.parcasterix.com. **Getting
there**: take RER B to Charles-de-
Gaulle 1. Shuttle buses (Courriers
Île-de-France) provide a link to and
from the park every 30 mins. **Open**
April–June and Sept–mid-Oct daily
10–6, July and Aug daily 9.30–7.
Adm adults €31, children €23.
It may not have as many rides and
attractions as Disneyland, but Parc
Astérix is, at least, genuinely
French. Astérix, the Roman-
bashing Gaul, has long been
France's most popular cartoon
character and his adventures are

one of its most successful literary exports – translated into over 40 languages. The theme park has, unsurprisingly, proved a big hit with both locals and tourists. It is divided into themed areas, including a Gaulish village, a Roman city and Ancient Greece, each inhabited by rubber-suited cartoon characters. There are also lots of hair-raising rides, including the 'Tonnerre de Zeus', one of the most terrifying rollercoasters in Europe, capable of travelling at over 80kmh.

Teenagers

The sights and sounds of Paris have plenty to offer a visiting teenager. The Marais is a great neighbourhood for a wander, with beautiful old buildings, as well as plenty of boutiques for browsing and cafés for watching the world go by. Take bus no. 29 for some of the way and they are sure to enjoy standing on the open-air platform at the back.

For shopaholic teens, St-Germain has plenty of potential, and if they want to see some *haute couture* a stroll down the Rue du Faubourg-St-Honoré never fails to impress. Les Halles is something of a teen hangout, with plenty of clothes shops, cafés and a cinema, although it doesn't really offer a true taste of Paris life. FNAC (*see* p.359), the books and music store, has an endless

selection of music, videos, electronic equipment and books (including an English-language section), and there's always the Virgin Megastore (*see* p.365) on the Champs-Elysées, which has a good café on the top floor.

To pick up a bargain, teenagers might like one of Paris' many markets, particularly Les Puces at St-Ouen (*see* p.261), an entertaining place to pass a few hours.

Of the major sights, those with a taste for the grisly might head for the Conciergerie (*see* p.89) or the Catacombs (*see* p.249), while more artistic teens will certainly enjoy a visit to the Musée Picasso (*see* p.179) or the Musée Rodin (*see* p.129) – as well as the Pompidou Centre and Stravinksy fountain (*see* pp.162–4) and the Louvre (*see* p.98). To see the sights of Paris without much effort, a ride on a *bateau-mouche* is a good recommendation (*see* p.67), and, of course, no self-respecting teenager would be happy to visit Paris without climbing to the top of its most famous landmark, the Eiffel Tower (*see* p.138).

Other potential teen hangouts include:

Bowling de Montparnasse Q19
See p.368.
12-pin bowling.

Centre Sega V8
*5 Bd des Italiens, Passage des Princes; **métro** Richelieu-Drouot. **Open** 10am–midnight.*

Here, incurable video-game heads will find the means to blow all their pocket money.

Étoiles du Rex X–Y8
*1 Bd Poissonnière, **t** 08 36 68 05 96, **w** www.legrandrex.com; **métro** Bonne-Nouvelle. Tours Wed–Sun 10–7 every 5mins; **adm** €7.*
Behind-the-scenes tour (50mins) of a famous old cinema (*see* p.354)

'Friday Night Fever' Off maps
See p.368.
Rollerblading through Paris on fine Friday evenings.

Palais de la Découverte O10
See p.115.
A science museum offering activities that will keep even teenagers amused.

Stade de France Off maps
*w www.stadefrance.fr; RER Stade-de-France-St-Denis; wheelchair access for Introductory tour only. **Open** daily 10–6 for tours, except event days; **adm** Introductory tour €5.80, Behind the Scenes €13.75.*
The city's big new sports stadium (*see* p.367) offers two tours: Introductory (about 30mins) and Behind the Scenes (about 1½hrs; tour in English at 2.30pm).

La Tête dans les Nuages L10
*4 Av Marceau, **t** 01 42 44 19 19; **métro** Alma-Marceau. **Open** Mon–Fri 11–11, Sat–Sun 11–midnight.*
A video game mecca with more traditional games (such as pool) as well. There's a McDonald's for sustenance.

Gay and Lesbian Paris

The Gay Scene

Historically Paris has always been one of the most tolerant cities anywhere, especially in sexual matters; so tolerant, in fact, that the gay community has become a fairly integral part of Parisian society. Paris even has an openly gay mayor, Bertrand Delanoë.

AIDS (SIDA) has hit Paris hard (the city has some 60% of the nation's victims), and this has made the homophobes more vocal, but to a much milder degree than in Britain or the United States. Most Parisians are only aware of their gay fellow citizens during the Bastille Ball, tradition-ally the biggest annual event in the gay calendar, with dancing and fun until dawn. Or, on a more sombre note, when there have been large demonstrations, usually motivated by ACT UP, to inform the public about AIDS and lobby for a greater commitment from the government to research funds – resulting in schemes like the 1F condom (préservatif).

Many of Paris' gay-owned restaurants, bars and businesses (see listings, below) tend to be centred around métro St-Paul in the Marais district, although there are gay-friendly establishments throughout the city. A rainbow sticker is a universally recognized indication that a place welcomes gay and lesbian customers.

Organizations and Information

Organizations

ACT UP Paris Off maps
45 Rue Sedaine, **t** 01 48 06 13 89, **w** www.actupp.org; **métro** Voltaire.
Branch of ACT UP, which was founded in New York in 1987. It aims to maintain awareness of AIDS and its effect on society – gay and straight, but is less mili-tant than it used to be. Regular meetings take place on Tuesdays

at 7pm in the École Nationale des Beaux-Arts, Rue Bonaparte (U12–T13) (contact them for venues during school holidays).

Centre Gai et Lesbien FF14
3 Rue Keller, **t** 01 43 57 21 47, **w** www.cglparis.org; **métro** Bastille. **Open** Mon–Sat 4–8.
A full programme of meetings, discussions and social events.

Gay Association of Paris Professionals Y11
c/o La Traverse Bar, 62 Rue Quincampoix, 75004, **w** www.latraverse.fr; **métro** Rambuteau. **Open** 7–2am.
Created by Americans in Paris to welcome gay visitors to the city and facilitate business relations. Monthly newsletter and meeting on 3rd Thursday of each month. To receive the newsletter or other information write to the above address.

Lesbian and Gay Pride Île-de-France FF14
3 Rue Keller, **t** 01 53 01 47 01, **w** www.lgp.idf.org; **métro** Ledru-Rollin.
Organizes the annual march, and works to defend gay rights and fight discrimination.

Maison des Femmes Off maps
163 Rue de Charenton, **t** 01 43 79 61 91; **métro** Reuilly-Diderot.
For women (gay and straight), this is an address worth knowing (see p.78).

Listings

Illico
t 01 48 04 92 95.
Free fortnightly newspaper avail-able in bars and clubs. Good listings and info on what's happening in Paris.

Lesbia Magazine
t 01 43 48 89 54.
The only magazine aimed solely at lesbians. Articles, listings, small ads, etc. €3.80.

Helplines

Ligne Azur
t 0801 20 30 40. **Open** Mon–Sat 5–9.

Anonymous and confidential helpline for young people coming to terms with their sexuality. Also for their families.

Ligne Info Traitement
t 01 43 67 00 00. **Open** Mon–Fri 3–6.
Advice and info on treating HIV.

SIDA Info Service
t 0800 84 08 00. **Open** 24 hours.
Calls are anonymous and free. Information on HIV and its prevention.

Web Sites

w www.gaytravel.co.uk.
Includes travel information as well as listings of gay-friendly hotels, restaurants, bars, etc. in Paris.
w www.rainbownetwork.com.
Includes Paris listings.

Books and Magazines

Le Kiosque des Amis S8
1 Bd des Capucines, **t** 01 42 65 00 94, **w** www.kiosquedesamis.com; **métro** Opéra or Richelieu-Drouot. **Open** Mon–Sat 10am–9.30pm, Sun 11–9.30; stays open later in summer if it's busy.
Near the old gay quarter of Rue Ste-Anne. The best choice of gay newspapers and magazines from around the world. Also stocks the free weekly and monthly maga-zines which are available in gay bars and clubs in the Marais.

Les Mots à la Bouche AA12
6 Rue Ste-Croix-de-la-Bretonnerie, **t** 01 42 78 88 30, **w** www.motala houche.com; **métro** Hôtel de Ville. **Open** Mon–Sat 11–11, Sun 2–8.
The best place to find gay and lesbian literature, with a large collection of gay and lesbian books and magazines, meeting rooms and exhibitions.

Hotels

Moderate

Hôtel Américain** CC10
72 Rue Charlot, 75003, **t** 01 48 87 58 92; **métro** Filles-du-Calvaire.

Gay-friendly hotel on the edge of the Marais, with a warm welcome. All rooms have ensuite bathrooms and TV.

Hôtel Central AA13

33 Rue Vieille-du-Temple, 75003, t 01 48 87 56 08; métro Hôtel-de-Ville or St-Paul.

The only purely gay hotel in Paris in a 17th-century Marais six-storey building. The rooms (seven doubles) have their own character and are quiet. Only the apartment (sleeps four) has ensuite bathroom. There's a communal sitting area on the 1st floor where you are welcome to bring guests not staying in the hotel. Bar Central downstairs has separate entrance. No TV.

Inexpensive

Hôtel de Nevers* DD10

53 Rue de Malte, 75011, t 01 47 00 56 18, w www.hoteldenevers.com; métro République or Oberkampf. Inexpensive.

Charming hotel in Art Deco style, with English-speaking staff (and lots of cats). Doubles with en suite bathrooms; extra beds available.

Restaurants

A Deux Pas du Dos BB12

101 Rue Vieille-du-Temple, 3e, t 01 42 77 10 52; métro Hôtel-de-Ville. Open Tues–Fri 12–2.30 and 8–11, Sat and Sun 8–11.30.

Mixed restaurant popular with gays, businesspeople and locals. Paintings exhibited on 1st floor are for sale. €12 lunch menu; evening menus €20.50 and €25. There's always a vegetarian choice. Short wine list.

Au Tibourg AA13

29 Rue du Bourg-Tibourg, 4e, t 01 42 74 45 25, w www.autibourg. com; métro Hôtel-de-Ville. Open Mon–Sat 7–12, Sun 12–11.

Excellent traditional French cuisine with modern touches. Menus €19 and €25. Wide à la carte choice. Short but good-value wine list. Mixed clientele with a gay majority from the *quartier.* Non-smoking area.

Le Bûcheron AA13

9 Rue du Roi-de-Sicile, 4e, t 01 48 87 71 31; métro St-Paul. Open Mon–Sat 8am–12am, Sun 9am–7.30pm.

Discreetly gay and lesbian during the day, this restaurant becomes more clearly so in the evening. The place to come for a coffee, a snack (eat in or take away) or a full meal: crêpes, pasta, salads. The food tends towards the Italian but the wine list is French. Meals €15–22.80. It's worth booking at lunch or dinner. No-smoking area.

Le Gai Moulin Z12

4 Rue St-Merri, 4e, t 01 48 87 47 59, w www.le-gai-moulin.com; métro Hôtel-de-Ville or Rambuteau. Open daily 7pm–midnight.

Small, friendly, almost exclusively gay restaurant with tables close together (all the better for making friends). €17 menu changes daily. Good, simple food and efficient service.

Un Saumon à Paris FF14

34 Rue de Charonne, 11e, t 01 49 29 07 15; métro Bastille. Open Mon–Fri 12–3 and 7pm–2am, Sat dinner only.

Fish restaurant which looks like an *épicerie,* and the range on the shelves – vodka, whisky, acacia honey, virgin olive oil etc. – can be taken away. Wide choice of dishes in the restaurant, including vegetarian options.

Le Temps au Temps Off maps

13 Rue Paul-Bert, 11e, t 01 43 79 63 40; métro Faidherbe-Chaligny. Open Mon–Sat 7.30–11pm.

The walls are decorated with clocks and watches. Menu €17. Traditional French dishes – *magret de canard, charlotte aux pommes* – accompanied by South American music. Good no-fuss cooking and relaxed atmosphere. Regular student and gay clientele.

Bars

Amnesia Café AA–BB12

42 Rue Vieille-du-Temple, 4e, t 01 42 72 02 59; métro Hôtel-de-Ville. Open daily 10am–2am.

Comfortable armchairs, very popular at night, and not style-obsessed. Mostly, but not exclusively gay crowd. Good for brunch at the weekend.

Banana Café X12

13 Rue de la Ferronnerie, 1er, t 01 42 33 35 31; métro Châtelet-Les Halles. Open daily 6pm–7am; Happy Hour 6–9.

No longer as trendy as it once was, but still the place to come at the end of the night.

Le Bear's Den Y12

6 Rue des Lombards, 4e, t 01 42 71 08 20, w www.bearsden.fr; métro Hôtel-de-Ville or Châtelet. Open daily 4pm–2am; Happy Hour 5–8.

Where beards and moustaches are all the rage. Tea dances on Sunday afternoons, square dances on Wednesday evenings and Nordic aperitifs on Tuesday afternoons. Beer €2.30.

Café Moustache BB7

138 Rue du Faubourg-St-Martin, 10e, t 01 46 07 72 20; métro Gare de l'Est. Open daily 5pm–2am; Happy Hour 7–9.

Relaxed gay bar popular with the older international set.

Le Central AA13

33 Rue Vieille-du-Temple, 4e, t 01 48 87 99 33; métro Hôtel-de-Ville. Open Sun–Thurs 4pm–2am, Fri and Sat 2pm–2am.

The oldest hotel-bar in the Marais, with customers nostalgic for the 1980s. Dancing on the tables not unlikely by the end of the night. (See also 'Hotels', above.)

La Champmeslé V9

4 Rue Chabanais, 2e, t 01 42 96 85 20; métro Pyramides. Open Mon–Sat 2pm–2am.

Welcoming and friendly lesbian bar; risqué décor, cheap drinks, a cabaret every Thurs night and fortune-telling on Friday nights. Food served 12pm–2am: quiches, salads, etc.

Le Coeur Couronné X12

6 Rue de la Ferronnerie, 1er, t 01 45 08 11 15; métro Châtelet. Open daily 7am–11pm.

The place to meet in Les Halles. Bar-brasserie with two terraces. Gays and lesbians prefer the terrace overlooking Rue de la

Ferronnerie. Dishes €4.50–9.15. Beers €2.30.

Le Cox Z12
15 Rue des Archives, 4e, t 01 42 72 08 00; métro Hôtel-de-Ville. Open daily 12pm–2am.
Packed and chaotic. Spills over on to terrace. Beer €2.90.

Le Dépôt Z11
10 Rue aux Ours, 3e, t 01 44 54 96 96; métro Rambuteau. Open daily 2pm–8am; adm €6.90 (Mon–Thurs), €8.40 (Fri–Sun).
Hard concrete walls, army camouflage and cheap vodka. Hot basement with many dark corners. Good music. Men only.

Le Duplex Z11
25 Rue Michel-le-Comte, 3e, t 01 42 72 80 86; métro Rambuteau. Open daily 8pm–2am.
Friendly, artsy, gay and straight bar with affordable drink prices. Music ranges from jazz and indie to bossa-nova.

Open Café Z–AA12
17 Rue des Archives, 4e, t 01 48 87 80 25; métro Hôtel-de-Ville. Open daily 11am–2am; Happy Hour for beer 6–9.
You'll have difficulty getting a table, especially on the terrace – this is at the crossroads of the gay quarter. Drinks €2.15–6.90, snacks and salads €2.75–7.35 (12pm–6pm only).

Le Quetzal Z13
10 Rue de la Verrerie, 4e, t 01 48 87 99 07, w www.quetzalbar.com; métro Hôtel-de-Ville. Open daily 5pm–4am; Happy Hour 5–9pm and 11–midnight.
Historic Marais bar which was in vogue in the 80s and is still an important part of the gay scene.

Les Pietons Y12
8 Rue des Lombards, 4e, t 01 48 87 82 87, w www.lespietons.com, métro Chatelet. Open daily 12-2am.

Friendly tapas bar with sunny frescoes and loud flamenco music. Food served between 12–6, tapas for around €3.50.

Le Thermik Z13
7 Rue de la Verrerie, 4e, t 01 44 78 08 18; métro Hôtel-de-Ville. Open daily 4pm–2am.
For karaoke-lovers. Drift between here and Le Quetzal, opposite (*see* above).

Le Unity Bar Z11
176–8 Rue St-Martin, 3e, t 01 42 72 70 59; métro Rambuteau or Etienne-Marcel. Open daily 4pm–2am; Happy Hour Mon–Fri 4–8.
The largest lesbian bar in Paris. Men allowed but preferably not alone. Billiards and dodgy 1950s décor.

Discos and Clubs

L'Insolite U9
33 Rue des Petits-Champs, 1e, t 01 40 20 98 59; métro Pyramides. Open Sun–Thurs 11pm–5am Fri–Sat 11–6am.
Small club playing mainly disco music apart from Fiesta Night on Sunday. Popular with the over 30s.

L'Enfer/Red Light R18
34 Rue du Départ, 15e, t 01 42 79 94 53; métro Montparnasse-Bienvenüe. Open Thurs–Sun 11pm–dawn; adm €8.40.
Boy George has DJ-ed here. Mixed young crowd. Techno and house.

Le Pulp X8
25 Bd Poissonnière, 2e, t 01 40 26 01 93; métro Grands Boulevards. Open Thurs–Sat midnight–6am; Thurs strictly women only; adm €7.70 with one drink.
One of the best. House and techno.

Le Queen L8
102 Av des Champs-Elysées, 8e, t 01 53 89 08 89, w www.queen.fr;

métro George-V. Open daily 11.30pm–7am; adm €18 (Fri and Sat; one drink inc), €9 (Mon; one drink inc.).
The hippest and most sophisticated gay disco draws a fair mix of stylish heteros as well, as long as they look like one of the beautiful people; special Boy Night on Thurs; disco Mon.

Les Scandaleuses AA13
8 Rue des Ecouffes, 4e, t 01 48 87 39 26; métro St-Paul. Open daily 6pm–2am; Happy Hour 6–8.
A lesbian club with a chilly ambience. Techno and house. Theme nights. Drinks €3.50–7.

Le Scorp X8
25 Bd Poissonnière, 2e, t 01 40 26 28 30; métro Grands Boulevards. Open daily 12pm–dawn; adm Fri and Sat €7.60.
Each night a different theme: Sun, Mon and Tues cabaret and gogo dancers, Fri and Sat house.

Events and Festivals

Bastille Day Gay Ball
13–14 July.
A rollicking all-night gay party, which takes place on Quai de la Tournelle from around 10pm till dawn. All welcome. Contact the Centre Gai et Lesbien (*see* above) for more details.

Gay Pride
w www.gaypride.fr; June.
March of thousands between Porte Dorée and République.

Paris Gay and Lesbian Film Festival
December.
A well-respected film festival founded in 1994 in order to increase the realistic portrayal of gays and lesbians in the cinema. See the press for details.

Festivals

Dates for nearly all the events listed below change every year. The central tourist office at 127 Avenue des Champs-Elysées provides precise dates in their annual publication *Saisons de Paris* and their monthly *Paris Sélection*.

Tourist offices (*see* p.77) will also be able to provide further information.

January

La Grande Parade de Paris
1 January
A New Year's Day parade from Porte St-Martin to the Madeleine via the Grands Boulevards, with floats, bands, clowns, etc.

La Fête des Rois
6 January
Boulangeries and *pâtisseries* sell *galettes des Rois* – delicious almond pastries – and the child who is given the slice with the charm in it is crowned king or queen.

Chinese New Year
Late January/early February
Chinatown (around Avenue d'Ivry and Avenue de Choisy) celebrates with firecrackers, lanterns and dragons.

February

Salon de l'Agriculture
Vast exhibition of animals, tools and regional produce in the Parc des Expositions.

March

Festival des Instruments Anciens
Medieval, Renaissance and Baroque music, mostly in the city's churches.

International Festival of Women's Films at Créteil Maison des Arts
Late March

Orchid show
Late March
At Bois de Vincennes.

Festival du Chien
Late March
Dog show at Bercy.

April

April Fool's Day
1 April
Celebrated with *Poissons d'Avril* jokes and hoaxes, the most popular of which involves sticking a paper fish to someone's back without them noticing.

Paris Marathon
42km race from Place de la Concorde to the Hippodrome de Vincennes.

Les Grandes Eaux Musicales, Versailles (Musical Fountains)
Mid-April–mid-October
See p.287.

Foire du Trône
Late April
Ancient traditional funfair, Porte Dorée, Bois de Vincennes.

May

Trade Unions March
1 May
People buy sprigs of *muguet* (lily of the valley) for good luck while the National Front rallies around the statue of Joan of Arc in Place des Pyramides.

Foire de Paris at the Porte de Versailles
1st week
The closest equivalent of the old St-Germain fair (*see* p.208), with all kinds of new-fangled gadgets, food, wine and more.

Salon de Montrouge
One of Paris' more intriguing annual art shows.

Five-day Antiquarian Fair
Mid-May
In the Carré Rive Gauche, west of Rue des Saints-Pères.

La Course au Ralenti
30 May
Vintage car race up the Butte, between Rue Lepic and Place du Tertre.

Late May–June

French Open Tennis Championships
See p.367.

Pentecost
Dual pilgrimages by modern Catholics and traditionalist Lefèbvrites from Chartres to Sacré-Cœur.

Foire St-Germain in St-Germain des Prés
Early June–early July
Antiques fair with accompanying entertainment.

International Fireworks Contest
Mid-June
In Chantilly.

Festival de St-Denis
Mid-June–early July
Classical music concerts.

Fête de la Musique
21 June
Free concerts across town.

St John's Eve
Late June
Fireworks show at Sacré-Cœur.

Fête du Marais
Late June
Jazz and classical music and drama.

Course des Garçons et Serveuses de Café
End June
Hundreds of waiters and waitresses race over a 5-mile course to and from the Hôtel de Ville.

July

La Villette Jazz Festival
2-week long, big-name jazz fest at Parc de la Villette.

Firemen's Feasts and Balls in the Neighbourhoods
13 July

Bastille Day
14 July
Military parade on the Champs-Elysées; fireworks at Trocadéro; Bastille Ball, a rollicking all-night gay party.

End of the Tour de France in the Champs-Elysées
A few days later

September

Fête de l'Humanité
Lively national Communist festival, in suburban La Courneuve.

Festival de l'Automne
Music, dance and drama lasting until December.

FIAC (Foire Internationale de l'Art Contemporain)

Choice selections from contemporary galleries around the world.

Technoparade
3rd Sat

Giant parade of floats featuring every kind of modern electronic music.

September–October

Festival d'Île-de-France

Concerts in little-known venues.

October

Wine Harvest in Montmartre
1st Sat

Lots of good clean fun at the Vineyard (*see* p.196).

20km de Paris Race
Mid-October

Open to all and sundry; entries in past years have numbered over 20,000.

Salon du Chocolat
End October

Festival of chocolate at Espace Eiffel Branly (23 Quai Branly).

Hallowe'en
31 October

No trick-or-treating, but people do take the opportunity to dress up in silly costumes.

November

Salon d'Automne

Major art salon in the Grand Palais.

Coiffer la Ste-Catherine
25 November

Les Catherinettes, women in the fashion trade who are 26 that year and single, don outrageous hats made by co-workers.

December

Midnight Réveillon feast
Christmas Eve

Parisians eat out and gorge like geese. Billions of oysters meet their maker.

St-Sylvestre
New Year's Eve

Occasion for another ultra-rich midnight feast; in a week, Paris downs 2,000 tons of foie gras.

Language

Everywhere in France the same level of politeness is expected: use *monsieur, madame* or *mademoiselle* when speaking to everyone (and never *garçon* in restaurants!), from your first *bonjour* to your last *au revoir*.

Pronunciation

Vowels

a, à, â between *a* in 'bat' and 'part'
é, er, ez at end of word as *a* in 'plate' but a bit shorter
e, è, ê as *e* in 'bet'
e at end of word not pronounced
e at end of syllable or in one-syllable word pronounced weakly, like *er* in 'mother'
i as *ee* in 'bee'
o as *o* in 'pot'
ô as *o* in 'go'
u, û between *oo* in 'boot' and *ee* in 'bee'

Vowel Combinations

ai as *a* in 'plate'
aî as *e* in 'bet'
ail as *i* in 'kite'
au, eau as *o* in 'go'
ei as *e* in 'bet'
eu, œu as *er* in 'mother'
oi between *wa* in 'swam' and *wu* in 'swum'
oy as 'why'
ui as *wee* in 'twee'

Nasal Vowels

Vowels followed by an **n** or **m** have a nasal sound.
an, en as *o* in 'pot' + nasal sound
ain, ein, in as *a* in 'bat' + nasal sound
on as *aw* in 'paw' + nasal sound
un as *u* in 'nut' + nasal sound

Consonants

Many French consonants are pronounced as in English, but there are some exceptions:
c followed by **e, i** or **y**, and **ç** as *s* in 'sit'
c followed by **a, o, u** as *c* in 'cat'
g followed by **e, i** or **y** as *s* in 'pleasure'
g followed by **a, o, u** as *g* in 'good'
gn as *ni* in 'opinion'
j as *s* in 'pleasure'
ll as *y* in 'yes'
qu as *k* in 'kite'

s between vowels as *z* in 'zebra'
s otherwise as *s* in 'sit'
w except in English words as *v* in 'vest'
x at end of word as *s* in 'sit'
x otherwise as *x* in 'six'

Stress

The stress usually falls on the last syllable except when the word ends with an unaccented **e**.

Basic Vocabulary

General

hello *bonjour*
good evening *bonsoir*
good night *bonne nuit*
goodbye *au revoir*
please *s'il vous plaît*
thank you (very much) *merci (beaucoup)*
yes *oui*
no *non*
good *bon (bonne)*
bad *mauvais*
excuse me *pardon, excusez-moi*
My name is... *Je m'appelle...*
How are you? *Comment allez-vous?*
Fine *Ça va bien*
I don't understand *Je ne comprend pas*
Help! *Au secours!*
WC *les toilettes*
men *hommes*
ladies *dames* or *femmes*
doctor *le médecin*
hospital *un hôpital*
emergency room *la salle des urgences*
police station *le commissariat de police*
tourist information office *l'office de tourisme*
No Smoking *Défense de fumer*

Shopping and Sightseeing

Do you have...? *Est-ce que vous avez...?*
I would like... *J'aimerais...*
Where is/are...? *Où est/sont...*
How much is it? *C'est combien?*
entrance *l'entrée*
exit *la sortie*
open *ouvert*
closed *fermé*
push *poussez*

pull *tirez*
bank *une banque*
money *l'argent*
traveller's cheque *un chèque de voyage*
post office *la poste*
stamp *un timbre*
phone card *la télécarte*
postcard *une carte postale*
shop *un magasin*
tobacconist *un tabac*
pharmacy *la pharmacie*
aspirin *l'aspirine*
condoms *les préservatifs*

Accommodation

Do you have a room? *Avez-vous une chambre?*
Can I look at the room? *Puis-je voir la chambre?*
How much is the room per day/week? *La chambre coûte combien par jour/semaine?*
single room *une chambre pour une personne*
twin room *une chambre à deux lits*
double room *une chambre pour deux personnes*
...with a shower/bath *...avec douche/salle de bains*
...for one night/one week *...pour une nuit/une semaine*
cot (child's bed) *un lit d'enfant*

Directions

Where is...? *Où se trouve...?*
left *à gauche*
right *à droite*
straight on *tout droit*
here *ici*
there *là*
close *proche* or *près*
far *loin*
corner *le coin*
square *la place*
street *la rue*

Transport

I want to go to... *Je voudrais aller à...*
Do you stop at...? *Passez-vous par...?*
How long does the trip take? *Combien de temps dure le voyage?*
A (single/return) ticket to... *un aller* or *aller simple/aller et retour) pour...*

aeroplane *l'avion*
airport *l'aéroport*
bicycle *la bicyclette/le vélo*
bus *l'autobus*
bus stop *l'arrêt d'autobus*
car *la voiture*
left-luggage locker *la consigne automatique*
on foot *à pied*
platform *le quai*
railway station *la gare*
ship *le bateau*
subway *le métro*
taxi *le taxi*
ticket *le billet*
ticket office *le guichet*
timetable *l'horaire*
train *le train*

Months

January *janvier*
February *février*
March *mars*
April *avril*
May *mai*
June *juin*
July *juillet*
August *août*
September *septembre*
October *octobre*
November *novembre*
December *décembre*

Days

Monday *lundi*
Tuesday *mardi*
Wednesday *mercredi*
Thursday *jeudi*
Friday *vendredi*
Saturday *samedi*
Sunday *dimanche*

Numbers

quarter *un quart*
half *une moitié* or *un demi*
one *un*
two *deux*
three *trois*
four *quatre*
five *cinq*
six *six*
seven *sept*
eight *huit*
nine *neuf*
ten *dix*
eleven *onze*
twelve *douze*
thirteen *treize*
fourteen *quatorze*

fifteen *quinze*
sixteen *seize*
seventeen *dix-sept*
eighteen *dix-huit*
nineteen *dix-neuf*
twenty *vingt*
twenty-one *vingt et un*
twenty-two *vingt-deux*
thirty *trente*
forty *quarante*
fifty *cinquante*
sixty *soixante*
seventy *soixante-dix*
seventy-one *soixante et onze*
eighty *quatre-vingts*
eighty-one *quatre-vingt-un*
ninety *quatre-vingt-dix*
one hundred *cent*
two hundred *deux cents*
one thousand *mille*

Time

What time is it? *Quelle heure est-il?*
It's 2 o'clock (am/pm) *Il est deux heures (du matin/de l'après-midi)*
... half past 2 *...deux heures et demie*
... a quarter past 2 *...deux heures et quart*
... a quarter to 3 *...trois heures moins le quart*
month *un mois*
fortnight *une quinzaine*
week *une semaine*
day *un jour/une journée*
morning *le matin*
afternoon *l'après-midi*
evening *le soir*
night *la nuit*
today *aujourd'hui*
yesterday *hier*
tomorrow *demain*

Eating Out

Restaurant Vocabulary

menu *carte*
set meal *menu/formule*
waiter/waitress *garçon*
Do you have a table? *Avez-vouz de la place?*
...for one/two? *pour une personne/pour deux?*
Can I see the menu, please? *Puis-je avoir la carte, s'il vous plaît?*
Can I have the bill (check), please? *L'addition, s'il vous plaît.*

Can I pay by credit card? *Puis-je payer avec carte de crédit?*
Where are the toilets/restrooms? *Où sont les toilettes, s'il vous plaît?*

Fish and Shellfish (*Poissons* et *Coquillages*)

anchois *anchovies*
anguille *eel*
bar *sea bass*
barbue *brill*
beurre blanc *sauce of shallots and wine vinegar whisked with butter*
bigorneau *winkle*
blanchailles *whitebait*
brème *bream*
brochet *pike*
bulot *whelk*
cabillaud *cod*
calmar *squid*
carrelet *plaice*
colin *hake*
congre *conger eel*
coque *cockle*
coquillages *shellfish*
coquille St-Jacques *scallop*
crabe *crab*
crevette grise *shrimp*
crevette rose *prawn*
cuisses de grenouilles *frogs' legs*
daurade *sea bream*
écrevisse *freshwater crayfish*
escabèche *fish fried, marinated and served cold*
espadon *swordfish*
flétan *halibut*
friture *deep-fried fish*
fruits de mer *seafood*
gambas *giant prawn*
hareng *herring*
homard *Atlantic (Norway) lobster*
huître *oyster*
langouste *spiny Mediterranean lobster*
langoustines *Norway lobster (often called Dublin Bay prawns or scampi)*
limande *lemon sole*
lotte *monkfish*
loup (de mer) *sea bass*
maquereau *mackerel*
merlan *whiting*
morue *salt cod*
moules *mussels*
oursin *sea urchin*

bagel *sea bream*
palourde *clam*
poulpe *octopus*
raie *skate*
rouget *red mullet*
St-Pierre *John Dory*
saumon *salmon*
sole (meunière) *sole (with butter, lemon and parsley)*
thon *tuna*
truite *trout*
truite saumonée *salmon trout*

Meat and Poultry (*Viandes* et *Volailles*)

agneau *lamb*
andouillette *chitterling (tripe) sausage*
biftek *beefsteak*
blanc *breast or white meat*
blanquette *stew of white meat, thickened with egg yolk*
bœuf *beef*
boudin blanc *sausage of white meat*
boudin noir *black pudding*
brochette *meat (or fish) on a skewer*
caille *quail*
canard, caneton *duck, duckling*
cassoulet *haricot bean stew with sausage, duck, goose, etc.*
chateaubriand *porterhouse steak*
cheval *horsemeat*
chevreau *kid*
chevreuil *venison*
confit *meat cooked and preserved in its own fat*
contre-filet *sirloin steak*
côte, côtelette *chop, cutlet*
cuisse *thigh or leg*
dinde, dindon *turkey*
entrecôte *ribsteak*
epaule *shoulder*
escargot *snail*
estouffade *a meat stew marinated, fried and then braised*
faisan *pheasant*
faux-filet *sirloin*
foie *liver*
foie gras *goose liver*
fricadelle *meatball*
gigot *leg of lamb*
graisse, gras *fat*
grillade *grilled meat, often a mixed grill*
jambon *ham*
jarret *knuckle*

langue *tongue*
lapin *rabbit*
lard (lardons) *bacon (diced bacon)*
maigret/magret (de canard) *breast (of duck)*
merguez *spicy red sausage*
mouton *mutton*
navarin *lamb stew with root vegetables*
noix de veau (agneau) *topside of veal (lamb)*
oie *goose*
os *bone*
perdreau, perdrix *partridge*
pieds *trotters*
pintade *guinea fowl*
plat-de-côtes *short ribs or rib chops*
porc *pork*
pot-au-feu *meat and vegetables cooked in stock*
poulet *chicken*
poussin *baby chicken*
queue de bœuf *oxtail*
ris (de veau) *sweetbreads (veal)*
rognon *kidney*
rosbif *roast beef*
rôti *roast*
sanglier *wild boar*
saucisse *sausage*
saucisson *salami-like sausage*
selle (d'agneau) *saddle (of lamb)*
steak tartare *raw minced beef, often topped with a raw egg yolk*
suprême de volaille *fillet of chicken breast and wing*
tournedos *thick round slices of beef fillet*
travers de porc *spare ribs*
tripes *tripe*
veau *veal*
venaison *venison*

Vegetables, Herbs, etc. (*Légumes, Herbes*, etc.)

ail *garlic*
aneth *dill*
anis *anis*
artichaut *artichoke*
asperge *asparagus*
aubergine *aubergine (eggplant)*
avocat *avocado*
basilic *basil*
céleri (-rave) *celery (celeriac)*
cèpe *ceps, wild boletus mushroom*
champignon *mushroom*
chou *cabbage*

chou-fleur *cauliflower*
choucroute *sauerkraut*
choux de bruxelles *Brussels sprouts*
ciboulette *chives*
concombre *cucumber*
cornichon *gherkin*
courgette *courgette (zucchini)*
cresson *watercress*
échalote *shallot*
endive *chicory (endive)*
épinards *spinach*
estragon *tarragon*
fenouil *fennel*
fève *broad (fava) bean*
flageolet *white bean*
frites *chips (French fries)*
haricot *bean (rouge, blanc) (kidney, white)*
haricot vert *green (French) bean*
jardinière *mixed vegetables*
laitue *lettuce*
lentilles *lentils*
macédoine *diced vegetables*
maïs (épis de) *sweetcorn (on the cob)*
menthe *mint*
mesclun *salad of various leaves*
morille *morel mushroom*
navet *turnip*
oignon *onion*
panais *parsnip*
persil *parsley*
petits pois *small peas*
piment *pimento*
poireau *leek*
pois chiche *chickpeas*
pois mange-tout *sugar pea, mangetout*
poivron *sweet pepper (capsicum)*
pomme de terre *potato*
primeurs *young vegetables*
radis *radish*
riz *rice*
romarin *rosemary*
roquette *rocket*
safran *saffron*
salade verte *green salad*
thym *thyme*
truffe *truffle*

Fruit and Nuts (*Fruits et Noix*)

abricot *apricot*
amande *almond*
ananas *pineapple*
banane *banana*
brugnon *nectarine*

cacahouète *peanut*
cassis *blackcurrant*
cerise *cherry*
citron *lemon*
citron vert *lime*
coco (noix de) *coconut*
dattes *dates*
figue (de Barbarie) *fig (prickly pear)*
fraise *strawberry*
framboise *raspberry*
fruit de la passion *passion fruit*
grenade *pomegranate*
griotte *morello cherry*
mandarine *tangerine*
mangue *mango*
marron *chestnut*
merise *black cherry*
noisette *hazelnut*
noix *walnut*
noix de cajou *cashew*
pamplemousse *grapefruit*
pastèque *watermelon*
pêche (blanche) *peach (white)*
pignon *pine nut*
pistache *pistachio*
poire *pear*
pomme *apple*
prune *plum*
pruneau *prune*
raisin (sec) *grape (raisin)*
reine-claude *greengage plum*

Desserts

bombe *ice-cream dessert in a round mould*
brioche *light sweet yeast bread*
charlotte *sponge fingers and custard cream dessert*
chausson *turnover*
compote *stewed fruit*
corbeille de fruits *basket of fruit*
coulis *thick fruit sauce*
coupe *ice cream: a scoop or in cup*
crème anglaise *egg custard*
crème caramel *vanilla custard with caramel sauce*
crème Chantilly *sweet whipped cream*
crème fraîche *slightly sour cream*
crème pâtissière *thick pastry cream filling made with eggs*
gâteau *cake*
gaufre *waffle*
glace *ice cream*
macaron *macaroon*
madeleine *small sponge cake*
miel *honey*

mignardise *same as petits fours*
œufs à la neige *floating island/ meringue on a bed of custard*
parfait *frozen mousse*
petits fours *sweetmeats; tiny cakes and pastries*
profiteroles *choux pastry balls, often filled with crème pâtissière or ice cream, and covered with chocolate*
savarin *a filled cake, shaped like a ring*
tarte, tartelette *tart, little tart*
truffe *chocolate truffle*
yaourt *yoghurt*

Cheese (*Fromage*)

brebis (fromage de) *ewe's milk cheese*
chèvre *goat's cheese*
doux *mild*
fromage (plateau de) *cheese (board)*
fromage blanc *yoghurty cream cheese*
fromage frais *a bit like sour cream*
fromage sec *general name for solid cheeses*
fort *strong*

Cooking Terms

à point *medium steak*
à l'anglaise *boiled*
au four *baked*
bien cuit *well-done steak*
bleu *very rare steak*
broche *roasted on a spit*
chaud *hot*
cru *raw*
cuit *cooked*
en croûte *cooked in a pastry crust*
en papillote *baked in buttered paper*
flambé *set aflame with alcohol*
frit *fried*
froid *cold*
fumé *smoked*
garni *with vegetables*
(au) gratin *topped with melted cheese and breadcrumbs*
grillé *grilled*
haché *minced*
médaillon *round piece*
piquant *spicy hot*
poché *poached*
sanglant *rare steak*
sucré *sweet*

vapeur *steamed*

Miscellaneous

baguette *long loaf of bread*
beurre *butter*
confiture *jam*
couteau *knife*
crème *cream*
cuillère *spoon*
fourchette *fork*
huile (d'olive) *oil (olive)*
lait *milk*
moutarde *mustard*
œuf *egg*
pain *bread*
poivre *pepper*
sel *salt*
service compris/non compris *service included/not included*
sucre *sugar*
vinaigre *vinegar*
vinaigrette *oil and vinegar dressing*

Drinks (*Boissons*)

bière (pression) *beer (draught)*
bouteille (demi) *bottle (half)*
brut *very dry*
café *coffee*
café au lait *white coffee*
café express *espresso coffee*
café filtre *filter coffee*
chocolat chaud *hot chocolate*
citron pressé *fresh lemon juice*
demi *a third of a litre*
doux *sweet (wine)*
eau *water*
   gazeuse *sparkling*
   minérale *mineral*
   plate *still*
eau-de-vie *brandy*
eau potable *drinking water*
glaçon *ice cube*
infusion/tisane *herbal tea*
jus *juice*
lait *milk*
moelleux *semi-dry*
orange pressée *fresh orange juice*
pichet *pitcher*
pression *draught*
sec *dry*
thé *tea*
verre *glass*
vin *wine*
   blanc *white*
   mousseaux *sparkling*
   rosé *rosé*
   rouge *red*

Index

Numbers in **bold** indicate main references. Numbers in *italic* indicate maps.

Paris Street Maps

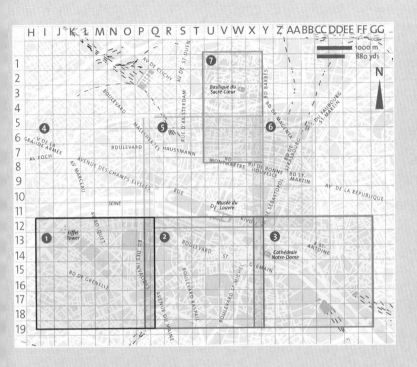

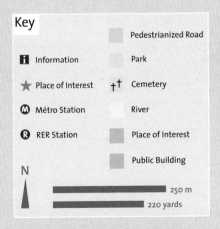

Key

		Pedestrianized Road
i	Information	Park
★	Place of Interest	†† Cemetery
Ⓜ	Métro Station	River
Ⓡ	RER Station	Place of Interest
		Public Building

N

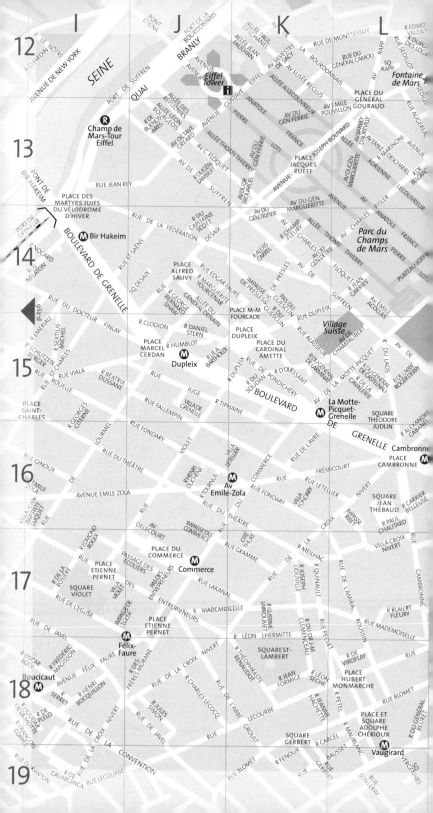

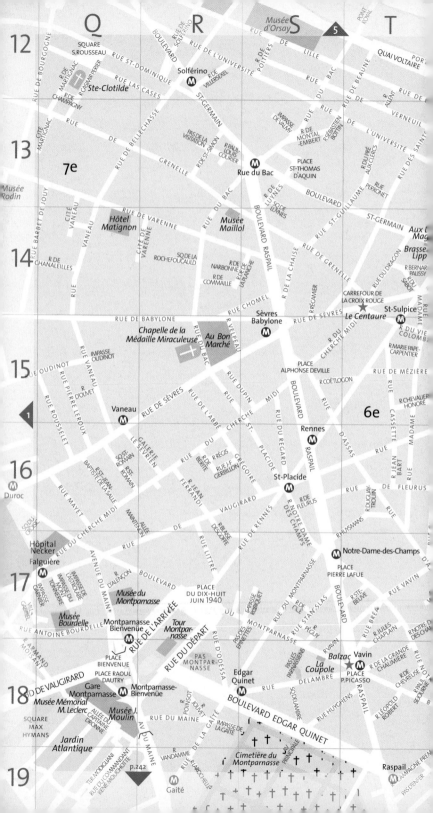

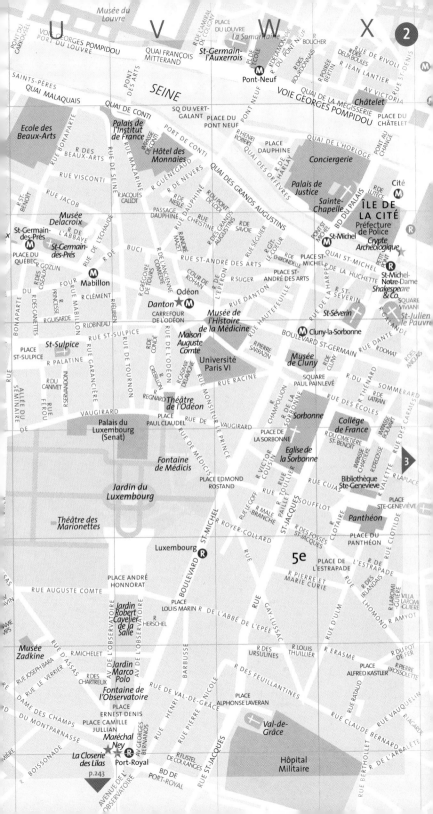

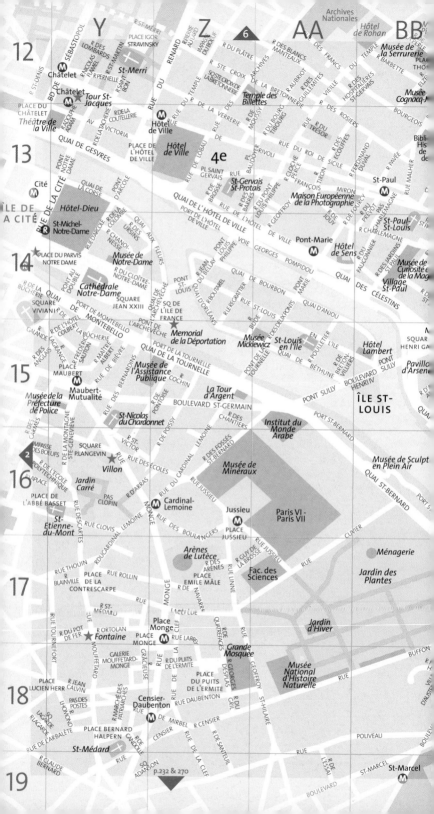

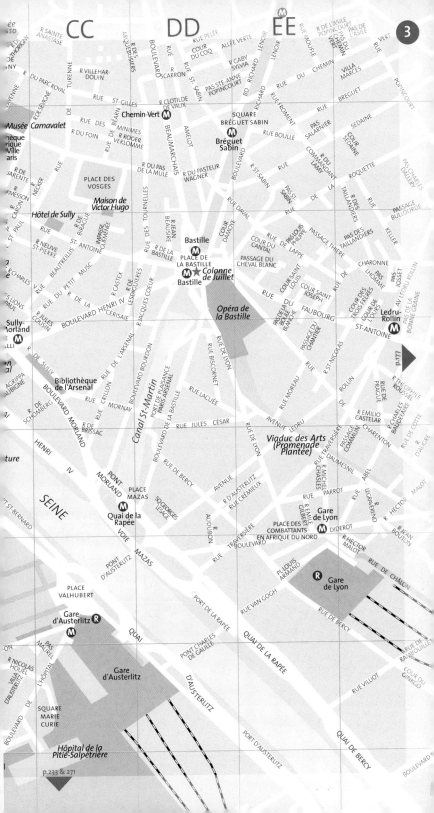

5
BD PÉREIRE NORD
PÉREIRE SUD
RUE GUERSANT
RUE LABIE
PLACE SAINT FERDINAND
AVENUE
RUE PIERRE DEMOURS
R PIERRE RENAULT
R MARCEL RENAULT
RUE VILLEBOIS MAREUIL
RUE BAYEN
P.96
J
RUE NIEL
RUE FOURCROY
R SAUSSIER LEROY
K
PONCELET
PAS PONCELET
RUE LAUGIER
AV DE WAGRAM
RUE DES RENAUDES
RUE THÉODULE RIBOT
L
R MARGUERITE
R DE COURCELL
RUE
R PIERRE LE GRAND
R DE LA NEVA
BOULEVARD

PLACE TRISTAN BERNARD
PAS DOISY
DES
TERNES
Ternes
PLACE DES TERNES
VILLA WAGRAM ST-HONORÉ
SQ DU ROULE
RUE PONCELET

6
RUE ST-FERDINAND
RUE BRUNEL
CITÉ FEREMBACH
R DES COLONELS RENARD
R D'ARMAILLE
RUE GUYOT
RUE DES ACACIAS
R DE L'ARC DE TRIOMPHE
AVENUE MAC-MAHON
RUE DE MONTENOTTE
RUE DE L'ÉTOILE
RUE BREY
AVENUE DE WAGRAM
VILLA NOUVELLE
RUE DU FAUBOURG
Cathédral
Alexandre-Nevsky
R DE BEAUCOUR

PLACE YVON ET CLAIRE MORANDAT
Argentine
VILLA DE LA GRANDE ARMÉE
R VILLARET DE JOYEUSE
SQ VILLARET DE JOYEUSE
RUE BRUNEL
RUE POISSON
R ANATOLE DE LA FORGE
R DU GÉNÉRAL LANREZAC
RUE TROYON
HOCHE
AVENUE
RUE
BEAUJON
AV BERTHIE ALBRECHT
Centre National Photogra

7
R LE P
R CHALGRIN
R D'ARGENTINE
R DE SAIGON
AVENUE DE LA GRANDE ARMÉE
DE
Charles de Gaulle Etoile
PLACE CHARLES DE GAULLE
Arc de Triomphe
RUE DE TILSITT
AVENUE
RUE ARSÈNE
HOUSSAYE
DE
BALZAC
R DE CHÂTEAUBRIAND
RUE LORD BYRON

AVENUE FOCH
AVENUE FOCH
R DE PRESBOURG
AVENUE
AVENUE
RUE
AVENUE
George V

8
VILLA DUVAL
RUE PAUL VALÉRY
AVENUE VICTOR HUGO
R DE TRAKTIR
R DE HUGO
RUE DU DÔME
Kléber
AV DES PORTUGAIS
RUE LA PÉROUSE
R NEWTON
R AUGUSTE VACQUERIE
RUE GALILÉE
MARCEAU
RUE EULER
RUE VERNET
AV GEORGES V
R QUENTIN BAUCHART
Musée Dapper
R GEORGES VILLE
LAURISTON
KLÉBER
AVENUE
LA DUMONT D'URVILLE
RUE GALILÉE
BASSANO
RUE MAGELLAN
PLACE JEAN HENRI DUNANT

9
VILLA COPERNIC
RUE
RUE COPERNIC
R CIMAROSA
R DE BELLOY
KLÉBER
RUE
RUE GALILÉE
PLACE DE L'URUGUAY
RUE JEAN GIRAUDOUX
R CHRISTOPHE COLOMB
R QUENTIN BAUCHART
American Cathedral
AVENUE GEORGES V
R DE CERIS
R DE
SQUARE DE L'UNION
RUE LÉO DELIBES
Boissière
RUE HAMELIN
R DE L'AMIRAL D'ESTAING
PLACE DES ETATS-UNIS
PLACE DE L'AMIRAL DE GRASSE
RUE GEORGES BIZET
AVENUE
RUE PIERRE 1ER DE SERBIE
PLACE
R DE LA
RUE DU

10
RUE ST-DIDIER
VILLADE LONGCHAMP
R DU BOUQUET DE LONGCHAMP
VILLA BOSSIÈRE
BOISSIÈRE
AVENUE
DE
LONGCHAMP
Musée Guimet
Iéna
PLACE D'IÉNA
RUE DE LUBECK
D'IÉNA
RUE
RUE GOETHE
R FREYCINET
R LÉONCE REYNAUD
MARCEAU
DE LA
GALÉRA
Musée de la Mode et du Costume Palais Galliera
PLACE PIERRE BRISSON
Palais de Tokyo
Musée d'Art Moderne
PLACE DE L'ALMA
Alma Marceau
R DE LA
RUE DES FRÈRES PÉRIER
R DE MAGDEBOURG
DE
RUE
WILSON
AV DU PRÉSIDENT WILSON
RIBOULDE
RCASSIMIR ST-NEL
DEBROUSSE
VOIE

11
Trocadéro
AVENUE DU PRÉSIDENT
AVENUE
Musée Nationales Monuments Français
AVENUE ALBERT DE MUN
RUE FRESNEL
Palais de Chaillot
P.137
Jardins du Trocadéro
AVENUE DES NATIONS UNIES
AVENUE
POMPIDOU
AVENUE
DE LA MANUTENTION
FOUCAULT
RUE
DE
NEW
YORK
PORT DEBILLY
PASSERELLE DEBILLY
Liberty Flame
Pont de l'Alma
PLACE DE LA RÉSISTANCE
PONT DE L'ALMA
BRANLY

12
RUE LAURE
AV DES NATIONS UNIES
AVENUE ALBERT 1ER DE MONACO
PLACE DE VARSOVIE
VOIE GEORGES
PONT D'IÉNA
PORT
QUAI
ALLÉE DES
ALLÉE PAUL PAULMAN
ALLÉE JEAN DESCHANEL
AV DE LA BOURDONNAIS
BOURDONNAIS
QUAI
Musée du Quai Branly
DE
AV FRANCO-RUSSE
RUE
L'UNIVERSITÉ
RUE DE MONTTESSUY
RAPP
AVENUE
CITÉ DE L'ALMA
R EDMOND VALENTIN
R DUPONT DES LOGES
SÉDILLOT
Eiffel

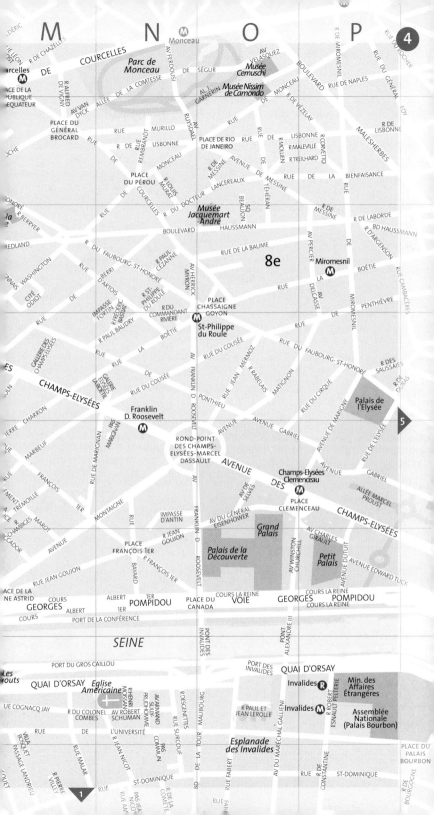

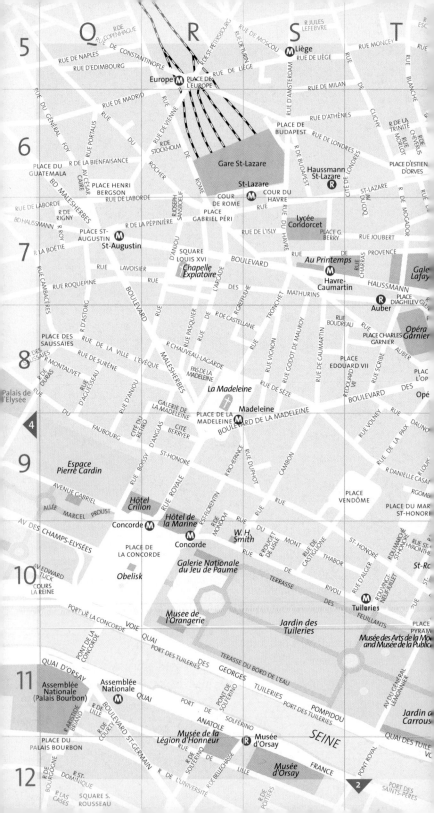

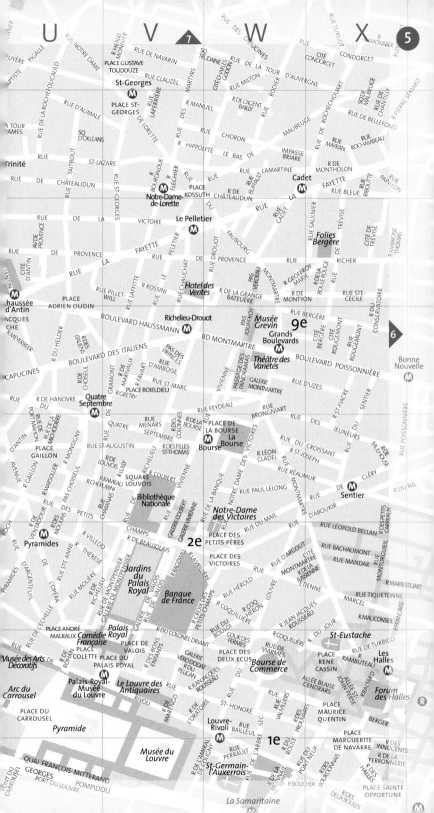

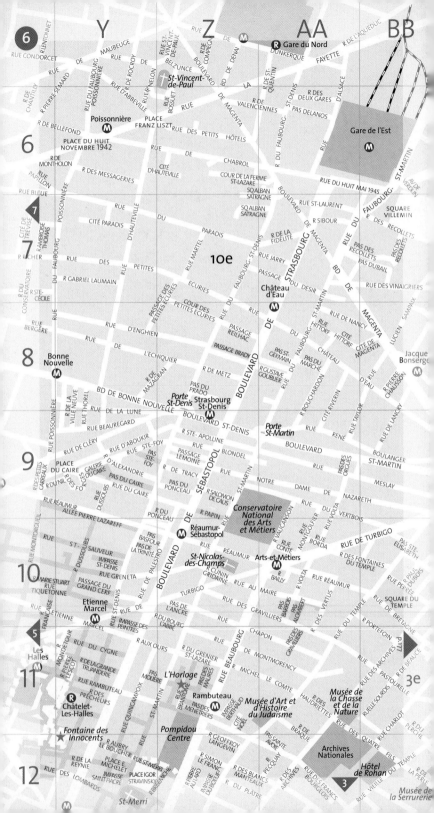

No more excuses – *just go!*

Flying Visits make
travel simple

CADOGANguides
well travelled **well read**